THE ROUTLEDGE INT. HANDBOOK OF JUNGIAN FILM STUDIES

The Routledge International Handbook of Jungian Film Studies weaves together the various strands of Jungian film theory, revealing a coherent theoretical position underpinning this exciting recent area of research, while also exploring and suggesting new directions for further study.

The book maps the current state of debates within Jungian orientated film studies and sets them within a more expansive academic landscape. Taken as a whole, the collection shows how different Jungian approaches can inform and interact with a broad range of disciplines, including literature, digital media studies, clinical debates and concerns. The book also explores the life of film outside cinema – what is sometimes termed 'post-cinema' – offering a series of articles exploring Jungian approaches to cinema and social media, computer games, mobile screens, and online communities.

The book represents an essential resource for students and researchers interested in Jungian approaches to film. It will also appeal to those interested in film theory more widely, and in the application of Jung's ideas to contemporary and popular culture.

Luke Hockley is Research Professor of Media Analysis at the University of Bedfordshire, UK. He is a practising psychotherapist and is registered with the United Kingdom Council for Psychotherapy (UKCP).

THE ROUTLEDGE INTERNATIONAL HANDBOOK SERIES

THE ROUTLEDGE INTERNATIONAL HANDBOOK OF JUNGIAN FILM STUDIES

Edited by Luke Hockley

Routledge
Taylor & Francis Grou
LONDON AND NEW YORK

First published 2018
by Routledge

2 Park Square, Milton Park, Abingdon, Oxfordshire OX14 4RN
52 Vanderbilt Avenue, New York, NY 10017

Routledge is an imprint of the Taylor & Francis Group, an informa business

First issued in paperback 2019

British Library Cataloguing-in-Publication Data
A catalogue record for this book is available from the British Library

Library of Congress Cataloging-in-Publication Data
A catalog record for this book has been requested

ISBN: 978-1-138-66696-2 (hbk)
ISBN: 978-0-367-33979-1 (pbk)

Typeset in Bembo
by Wearset Ltd, Boldon, Tyne and Wear

Cover photograph by Mathieu Degrotte: 'Son of the Sun'.

The eye, O priests, is on fire;
forms are on fire;
eye-consciousness is on fire;
impressions received by the eye are on fire;
and whatever sensation, pleasant, unpleasant,
or indifferent,
originates in dependence on impressions received by the eye,
that also is on fire.

Mahâ-Vagga (i21)

The Fire Sermon,

Buddha

CONTENTS

CONTRIBUTORS

Amalya Layla Ashman (PhD) completed her doctoral studies where she looked at the intersection between post-Jungian cultural complexes and trauma. She is currently Assistant Professor at Daegu University. Her upcoming monograph with Routledge, *Han as Embodied Trauma in New Korean Cinema: A Post-Jungian Cultural Complex* considers gendered experiences of historical trauma in contemporary South Korean film. Here she argues that past injustices are felt psychically and somatically through the Korean emotion of *han*. Taking on wider issues of gender and sexuality in South Korean society, she also writes on sexism in online communities and how the Japanese Occupation is re-imagined as queer Gothic on film.

Aaron Balick (PhD) is a psychotherapist and Honorary Senior Lecturer at the Centre for Psychoanalytic Studies, University of Essex. Outside the clinical arena his main research interest lies in applying ideas from depth psychology to contemporary cultural artefacts, most notably technology. He is a speaker, media consultant and contributor, and author of *The Psychodynamics of Social Networking: Connected-up Instantaneous Culture and the Self* (Karnac, 2014). He is also the director of Stillpoint Spaces London, where psychology is explored, in depth, both inside and outside the consulting room.

John Beebe (Jungian analyst) is the author of *Integrity in Depth* and of *Energies and Patterns in Psychological Type* (Routledge, 2017). He is co-author, with Virginia Apperson, of *The Presence of the Feminine in Film* (Cambridge Scholars Publishing, 2008). He has written and lectured around the world about works by such filmmakers as Woody Allen, Stephen Frears, Alfred Hitchcock, Mira Nair, Max Ophuls and Steven Spielberg.

Helena Bassil-Morozow (PhD) is a cultural philosopher, media and film scholar, and academic writer whose many publications include *Tim Burton: The Monster and the Crowd* (Routledge, 2010), *The Trickster in Contemporary Film* (Routledge, 2011), *The Trickster and the System: Identity and Agency in Contemporary Society* (Routledge, 2014) and *Jungian Film Studies: The Essential Guide* (Routledge, 2016; co-authored with Luke Hockley). She is a lecturer in Media and Journalism at Glasgow Caledonian University. www.hbassilmorozow.com/.

xi

Alec Charles (PhD) is Professor and Dean of Arts at the University of Winchester. He has worked as a print and broadcast journalist and has taught at universities in Falmouth, Kumamoto, Tallinn, Luton, Chester and Hull. He is the author of *Interactivity* (2012), *Interactivity 2* (2014), *Out of Time* (2015) and *Political Animals* (2016), the co-editor of *The End of Journalism* (2011), and the editor of *Media in the Enlarged Europe* (2009), *Media/Democracy* (2013) and *The End of Journalism* (2014).

Angela Connolly (PhD) is an analyst of CIPA with training and supervisory functions. She lived and worked in Russia from 1996 to 2001 and has continued to teach, lecture and supervise internationally. She was deputy editor of the *Journal of Analytical Psychology* and is currently on the advisory board. She was the Honorary Secretary of the IAAP from 2010 to 2013 and the Vice-President from 2013 to 2016. She has published widely in English and Italian and her articles have been translated into Russian and German. Her most recent works include, 'Bridging the reductive and the synthetic: some reflections on the clinical significance of synchronicity' published in the *Journal of Analytical Psychology*, 'Masochismus: ein jungianischer Ansatz' published in *Analytische Psychologie*, 'The delivery of training: personal experiences as a trainer in other cultures', in *From Tradition to Innovation*, edited by Catherine Crowther and Jan Wiener and 'Broken time: disturbances of temporality in analysis' in *Time and the Psyche: Jungian Perspectives*, edited by Angeliki Yiassemides.

Steven Conway (PhD) is Senior Lecturer and Course Director of Games and Interactivity at Swinburne University of Technology. He has presented on many aspects of game philosophy, aesthetics and culture, and has had a variety of articles published on these subjects in journals such as *Eludamos*, *Game Studies*, *Journal of Gaming and Virtual Worlds*, *Westminster Papers in Communication and Culture*, *Sport, Ethics and Philosophy*, *Analog Game Studies* and *ToDiGRA: Transactions of the Digital Games Research Association*. He is the co-editor of the first book on the relationship between video games and policy, *Video Games Policy: Production, Distribution and Consumption*.

Judith R. Cooper (PhD) is a clinical psychologist and diplomate Jungian Analyst in private practice in Chicago. A graduate and member of the C. G. Jung Institute of Chicago, she teaches in the Institute's Analyst Training Program, Jungian Psychotherapy and Studies Program, and lectures widely on the *anima/animus* and utilizing film in clinical treatment. She most recently taught a year-long class in the Institute's Analyst Training Program on Eros in Analysis. She was formerly adjunct faculty at Argosy University, teaching projective testing and served as a clinical supervisor and director of training at an APA-accredited psychology doctoral internship program at a community mental health center. She recently presented at the Art and Psyche Conference in Sicily, Italy on Jung and Barthes ('When Art Wounds').

August J. Cwik (PsyD) is a clinical psychologist, hypnotherapist and Jungian analyst in private practice in the Chicago area. He is a member of the Chicago Society of Jungian Analysts and the Interregional Society of Jungian Analysts. He is also an Assistant Editor of the *Journal of Analytical Psychology*. He was Co-Director of Training of the Analyst Training Program and Co-Director of the Clinical Training Program in Analytical Psychotherapy at the C. G. Jung Institute of Chicago. He has published articles on the structure of analysis, alchemy, supervision, dreams, active imagination and numerous reviews.

Joanna Dovalis is a marriage, family therapist in Laguna Hills, CA. She is currently training as a Jungian Analyst at the Marie Von Franz and Carl Jung Research and Training Center for Depth

Psychology in Zurich. She writes the psychological interpretations of film with her co-author John Izod. Their book *Cinema as Therapy: Grief and Transformational Film* was published in 2015.

Nadi Fadina (PhD) is a London-based media entrepreneur, writer, performer and scholar. With her academic hat on she is the co-editor of *The Happiness Illusion: How the Media Sold us a Fairytale* and the author of *The Second Loss of Androgyny: The Fairytale of Dualism* (both published by Routledge, 2015). She is currently working on her upcoming monograph *Fairytale Women in the Lands of Socialist Realism* based on her ground-breaking research into the unknown worlds of ancient fairy tales and gender representations of totalitarian regimes. She teaches film and psychoanalysis at Goldsmiths College, University of London and the University of Bedfordshire. She has been involved in a variety of arts and media related projects, working in front and behind the camera on locations around the world. Her most recent show *Dr. Fadina & her Puppets* was premiered in 2017 at The Players (New York). www.nadi-fadina.com.

Stephen Anthony Farah (MA) is the head of research and learning at the Centre for Applied Jungian Studies and an executive member of the International Association of Jungian studies. His interests include film theory, consciousness, Futures studies and the Simulation Hypothesis.

Kelli Fuery (PhD) is Assistant Professor of Film Studies at Dodge College of Film and Media Arts, Chapman University, CA. She is the author of *New Media: Culture and Image* (Palgrave, 2009) and *Visual Culture and Critical Theory* (co-author, 2003). Her research interests include philosophical and psychoanalytic approaches to questions of emotion, politics and aesthetics within visual culture. Her forthcoming book *Being Embedded: Wilfred Bion, Thinking and Emotional Experience in Moving Images* explores the affect of embeddedness within moving image experience.

Leslie Gardner (PhD) is a Fellow at the Centre Psychoanalytic Studies at the University of Essex with a PhD in rhetoric. Her book *Rhetorical Investigations: G. B. Vico and C. G. Jung* was published in 2010; she has contributed to various books in Jungian studies and most recently co-edited *Feminist Views from Somewhere* with Frances Gray in which her chapter on the poetics of the feminine pronoun appears. An early participant in International Association of Jungian Studies, she also heads up Artellus Limited, a literary agency in London.

Michael Glock (PhD) is a director, digital architect and author. He gained his doctorate in philosophy from Pacifica Graduate Institute, CA, in 2007. He has developed concepts and methodologies such as Cultural and Film Futuristics, Way Forward Engineering and has designed personal future forecasting tools for personal transformation. From 2013 to 2017 he was the co-chair of the IAJS (International Association for Jungian Studies). He was the co-editor of *Jungian Perspectives on Rebirth & Renewal* with Elizabeth Brodersen (2017) and the author of *Raisin Bread Toast and Other Collected Stories of Fantastica* (2004) and *DestinyOS* (2017).

Phil Goss (PhD) is Director of Counselling and Psychotherapy programmes in the Centre for Lifelong Learning at the University of Warwick, where he oversees the BACP accredited Person Centred Counselling and Psychotherapy Foundation Degree and BA (Hons). He is a Humanistic counsellor and UKCP registered Jungian psychotherapist who has extensive therapeutic experience with adults, as well as children and young people. His academic publications reflect his research interests in gender, learning difficulties and spirituality in counselling and psychotherapy. He has published two books: *Men, Women and Relationships, A Post-Jungian Approach* (Routledge, 2010) and *Jung: A Complete Introduction* (Hodder and Stoughton, 2015).

Eric Greene (PhD) is a psychologist in Los Angeles, CA. He has worked in the mental health field since 2004. He has published on critical theory, social justice and psychology. He chairs the mental health division of the Popular Culture Association of America.

Christopher Hauke is a Jungian analyst in private practice, and a Senior Lecturer at Goldsmiths, University of London interested in the applications of depth psychology to a wide range of social and cultural phenomena. His books include *Jung and the Postmodern: The Interpretation of Realities* (2000) and *Human being Human: Culture and the Soul* (2005). He has co-edited *Contemporary Jungian Analysis* (1998), *Jung & Film: Post-Jungian takes on the Moving Image* (2001) and a second collection of Jungian film writing, co-edited with Luke Hockley *Jung & Film II: The Return*. His short films, documentaries *One Colour Red* and *Green Ray*, and the psychological drama *Again*, premiered in London venues and at congresses in Barcelona, Zurich and Montreal. His latest book is *Visible Mind: Movies, Modernity and the Unconscious* (2013). www.christopherhauke.com.

Luke Hockley (PhD), SFHEA, FRSA, UKCP is Research Professor of Media Analysis at the University of Bedfordshire, UK. He is a practising psychotherapist and is registered with the United Kingdom Council for Psychotherapy (UKCP). He is joint Editor in Chief of the *International Journal of Jungian Studies* (IJJS) and Series Editor for *Jung the Essential Guides* published by Routledge. His recent publications include: *Jungian Film Studies: The Essential Guide* (Routledge, 2016; co-authored with Helena Bassil-Morozow) and *Somatic Cinema: The Relationship between Body and Screen, a Jungian Perspective*. www.lukehockley.com.

John Izod (PhD) is Emeritus Professor of Screen Analysis in Communications, Media and Culture at the University of Stirling. He also counsels clients as a shamanic practitioner. His and Joanna Dovalis's *Cinema as Therapy: Grief and Transformational Film* was published in 2015.

Donald E. Kalsched is a Jungian psychoanalyst with a private practice in Santa Fe, New Mexico. He has published widely in the area of early childhood trauma and lectures nationally and internationally on this subject. His two major books, *The Inner World of Trauma* (Routledge, 1996) and *Trauma and the Soul* (Routledge, 2013) have been widely acclaimed, and explore the interface between contemporary psychoanalytic approaches and Jungian thought on the subject of trauma and its treatment.

Shara D. Knight (PhD) is a professional writer and independent scholar. Her focus is on communication in relationship to image and it is enhanced by interests in film and the visual arts. Her research interests involve working with established filmmakers to understand the role that psyche plays in the creative process.

Kevin Lu (PhD) is Director of Graduate Studies and Director of the MA Jungian and Post-Jungian Studies in the Centre Psychoanalytic Studies, University of Essex. His publications include articles and chapters on Jung's relationship to the discipline of history, Arnold J. Toynbee's use of analytical psychology, sibling relationships in the Chinese/Vietnamese Diaspora and critical assessments of the theory of *cultural complexes*.

Andrew McWhirter (PhD) is a lecturer at Glasgow Caledonian University. He is currently Film Reviews editor for the *International Journal of Jungian Studies*, and has published with *Screen Journal, Journalism Practice* and I. B. Tauris with his monograph, *Film Criticism and Digital Cultures* in 2016. He is currently working on his second book *Learning Teaching and Social Media* to be published by Routledge in 2019. His other research activities include social media research ethics, propaganda and social media, audiovisual pedagogies, and sustainability in the creative and screen industries.

Leigh Melander (PhD) has a doctorate in cultural mythology and psychology and wrote her dissertation on frivolity as an entry into imagination. She has been published in academic and popular media, and edits a popular blog series for the Joseph Campbell Foundation, for which she is also currently serving as Vice President. She has appeared on various media outlets, including the History Channel, as a mythology expert. She hosts a weekly NPR affiliate radio show, *Myth America*, on how myth shapes our sense of identity, and is the founder of Spillian, a creative retreat centre in the Catskills in New York.

Catriona Miller (PhD) is a Senior Lecturer in Media at Glasgow Caledonian University. She publishes in the field of film and television studies, with a particular interest in Horror, Cult TV and Science Fiction genres from a Jungian perspective. She is writing a joint book *The Heroine's Journey: Female Individuation on Screen* for Routledge and *Cult TV Heroines* for I. B. Tauris.

Steve Myers is a former business consultant who is now an independent researcher and writer. He holds a Masters in Jungian and Post-Jungian Studies, and a PhD based on Jung's use of mythology. He used Jungian concepts and film in his commercial work, and has published several articles that examine film and its cultural implications from a Jungian point of view.

Benjamin Nagari (PhD) is a composer of various genres, including pop, rock, musical (both stage and film), concert music (solo chamber, choral and symphony) and film music. He is a Jungian scholar with an MA degree from the University of Essex (Colchester, UK) and PhD from the University of Westminster (London, UK). His book *Music as Image: Analytical Psychology and Music in Film* was published in 2016 (Routledge). This research based book postulates music and sound to act and react within the psyche in proximity and similarity to the visual image. Hence the two work within film as two sets of images, complementing and/or contradicting each other. This research is now being followed up to explore the possible connection between music/sound and the cooperation between the music image and the visual image in the psyche of Autistic people.

Elizabeth Nelson (PhD) is a core faculty member and Dissertation Policy Director at Pacifica Graduate Institute. She teaches a broad range of courses in research process, methodology and dissertation development along with classes in dream, literature and cultural studies. Her books include *Psyche's Knife: Archetypal Explorations of Love and Power* (Chiron, 2012) and *The Art of Inquiry: A Depth Psychological Perspective* (Spring Publications, 2017), co-authored with Joseph Coppin, which is now in its third edition.

Toby Reynolds is an early career film researcher and award winning teacher with research interests in post-Jungian cinema theory, gender and masculinities, auteur theory and film history. He enjoys teaching, reading, *t'ai chi chu'an* and the outdoors.

Susan Rowland (PhD) is Chair of MA Engaged Humanities and the Creative Life at Pacifica Graduate Institute, and teaches on the doctoral program in Jungian psychology and Archetypal Studies. Author of *The Sleuth and the Goddess in Women's Detective Fiction* (2015), she has also written books on literary theory, gender and Jung including *Jung as a Writer* (2005), *Jung: A*

Feminist Revision (2002), *C. G. Jung in the Humanities* (2010) and *The Ecocritical Psyche: Literature, Evolutionary Complexity and Jung* (2012). Her new book is *Remembering Dionysus: Revisioning Psychology and Literature in C. G. Jung and James Hillman* (2017).

Greg Singh (PhD) SFHEA, FRSA, is an Associate Professor in Media and Communications and programme Director for Digital Media at the University of Stirling. He is author of *Film after Jung: Post-Jungian Approaches to Film Theory, Feeling Film* and the forthcoming *Death of Web 2.0* (all published by Routledge Mental Health). He has published widely on media and cultural studies topics, including CGI, cinephilia, gaming, science fiction television and cinema, celebrity, and psychosocial approaches to Web culture. Current research interests include data civics and connectivity ethics, human-centred data networks, and technological affordances and constraints in media ecosystems. He is currently working on a mini-monograph, on Charlie Brooker's *Black Mirror* for the Routledge In Focus series, and is Co-Director of the RSE 'Life in Data' Research Network.

Glen Slater (PhD) has taught for over twenty years at Pacifica Graduate Institute in Santa Barbara, CA, where he is currently the Associate Chair of the Jungian and Archetypal Studies Program. He has written for a number of Jungian publications and edited the third volume of James Hillman's Uniform Edition, *Senex and Puer*, as well as the essay collection, *Varieties of Mythic Experience*. The relationship between cinematic expression and patterns of the human psyche has been a long-standing element of his teaching and writing.

Terrie Waddell (PhD) is a Reader/Associate Professor of Screen Studies and Head of the Department of Creative Arts and English at La Trobe University, Australia. Her work focuses on the relationship between screen media, literature, gender, popular culture and psychology. As well as chapter and journal contributions, she has authored and edited *Eavesdropping: The Psychotherapist in Film and Television* (co-editor 2015), *Wild/Lives: Trickster, Place and Liminality on Screen* (2010), *Mis/takes: Archetype, Myth and Identity in Screen Fiction* (2006), *Lounge Critic: The Couch Theorist's Companion* (co-editor, 2004) and *Cultural Expressions of Evil and Wickedness: Wrath, Sex, Crime* (editor, 2003).

Megumi Yama (PhD) is a Professor in the Faculty of Humanities at Kyoto Gakuen University in Japan, where she teaches clinical psychology and depth psychology. She also engages in clinical work as a psychotherapist, mainly based on Jungian thought. She was educated in clinical psychology at Kyoto University under Professor Hayao Kawai. She has also been active as a Visiting Scholar at Harvard University (September to October 2015) and a Visiting Fellow at University of Essex (April 2008 to March 2009). She is interested in images and words; what takes place in the invisible silence, seemingly 'nothingness'. She deals with the theme by exploring clinical materials, art, myth, literature and Japanese culture. Her recent interests focus on Haruki Murakami's process of creative work. She has written many articles and books including translations both in English and Japanese and has lectured in the USA, UK, China and Taiwan.

ACKNOWLEDGEMENTS

Many thanks to all the members of the research network, *Psychology and the Moving Image International* (PAMII) who have supported the production of this book. www.pamii.org.

Every epic production sports a cast of thousands and the crew on this book is no exception. Thank you first to Susannah Frearson who with the spirit and insight of a brilliant Executive Producer came up with the original idea, found the money (!) and helped to assembled the core team. To our copy-editor, Sally Quinn, we extend our deep thanks and gratitude.

A special thank you must go to another one of the stars of this book. Not only a contributor, Nadi Fadina was also the Chief Editorial Consultant, catching many clumsy stylistic turns of phrase, lapses in punctuation and errors in formatting. Like a film editor, her role was essential and as with all superbly edited movies her work, craft and contribution remains largely invisible having been carried out with consummate skill and attention to detail. I am deeply indebted to her. Any remaining errors are, of course, entirely my own responsibility.

Luke Hockley

INTRODUCTION

It might surprise some readers to discover the Jungian study of film is not an entirely new field. In fact it was as far back as 1979 that Don Fredericksen's article 'Jung/Sign/Symbol' appeared in the *Quarterly Review of Film and Video* with part two of that same article being published the following year. That was probably the first time Jungian thinking had made its way on to the pages of a journal of academic film theory. Interestingly, filmmakers had discovered Jung much earlier. That Fellini, Bergman, Argento and the documentary filmmaker Basil Wright were all familiar with the work of C. G. Jung and influenced by his ideas is well known. More recently, while not without its problems, Christopher Vogler has also successfully popularized a combination of Jung and Joseph Campbell's Hero's Journey in mainstream Hollywood. Campbell himself famously visited George Lucas' Skywalker Ranch as Lucas had drawn heavily on Campbell's writing in the original trilogy of the *Star Wars* films. Yet, in terms of film theory, it was not until the years following 1991 that the field really developed. There is now a well-established cannon of work – not large to be sure – but viable and growing, with over forty books of film theory, criticism and appreciation, and several special issues of academic journals devoted to the subject.

This *International Handbook* sets out to capture the current state of Jungian film theory. It does not seek to be definitive. Rather it provides an overview of the diversity of approaches that the subject includes. Students of film, media and television studies will find it offers a ready way into the latest Jungian thinking in their subject. Those with more clinical interests will see just how effective Jungian theory can be when it is used outside the consulting room. This book is peppered with clinical insights, offered by therapists and film theorists alike. Indeed, in the realm of Jungian film theory the distinction between the clinical and theoretical approaches is particularly fluid and fertile.

The book also points out the direction of travel for Jungian film and related theories, namely to head out of the cinema and into the digital world of everyday life. (In the following section I will refer to film and cinema; however, most of the observations hold good for the study of television, the Internet and other audio-visual media.) While many scholars want to engage in textual analysis, others are seeing how a Jungian view of 'Image' can help to understand both the impact of technology on society and the lives of individuals alike. Fresh theoretical developments include the shift of meaning away from the text and towards viewers' broader relationships with films, television programmes, computer games and so forth. Taking its cue from phenomenological film theory, such writing sets out to decentre the text, and to deploy a hermeneutic of negotiation and relationship as a means to establish a matrix of meaning, in which meaning itself is wonderfully unstable – as in Hockley's concept of the Third Image.

Jungian theory is laden with jargon. We've just had an example! To the reader who is new to this approach it might not be immediately apparent that all the contributors to this volume have tried to keep specialist vocabulary to a minimum. However, in a technical subject such as Analytical Psychology (this is Jung's name for his approach, and it distinguishes it from Freud's Psychoanalysis) specialist terms are inevitable. When such terms are used, a very brief working definition of them is offered. The interested reader who wants to acquire more than a working understanding of the terminology would be well advised to consult the excellent *A Critical Dictionary of Jungian Analysis* by Andrew Samuels *et al.* (1986). Of course, since it was written the theoretical debates have moved on, yet that book remains an essential reference point.

Notwithstanding the preceding preamble it is perfectly reasonable to claim there is no such thing as Jungian film studies! Let me explain. Jungian Analysts sometimes claim there is no technique in Jungian analytic work. What they are actually driving at is that there is a multiplicity of techniques and that each analyst works in their individual way (probably something that is true for most therapists and therapies nowadays). In a similar manner there are very few orthodoxies in Jungian film theory but there are some. What follows are some of its central concerns. There are others, but these serve to give a flavour of what is distinctive about the Jungian approach to audio-visual media.

First, the image is centre stage. In a way, the Eye is on Fire – as in the epigraph that starts this book. Such fire does not necessarily imply an ocular centric approach, of which more in a moment. That said, Jungian film theory is highly sensitive towards the visual subtleties of images. Yet, in keeping with the quotation itself, a Jungian view of image encompasses not just actual images, or even dream images. Instead it draws on Jung's idea of image which rather than referring to physical images is much closer in its conception to what can be thought of as an embodied felt-sense. This means it is forms, perceptions and sense impressions that are 'seen' and on fire, as it were. In this way, Jungian psychology is a corporal psychology, an idea that is echoed in Greg Singh's (2014) formulation of cinematic encounter as 'psychologically warm'.

The folding of the ocular with the felt is helpful as it provides a way to articulate those otherwise hard to explain reactions we have when watching films, television programmes, computer games and so forth. It is when we unexpectedly feel something, when we have emotional reactions that seem disproportionally intense given the content of the narrative, that we experience this very Jungian understanding of image. This is crucial for Jungian film studies as for Jung the psyche is built in and from these images; images are a pathway to the unconscious and also provide a means to understand our emotional life. Consequently, while the psychological meaning of a film might be the same as its narrative, equally it might not. Jungian theory helps to understand this disjuncture and it provides a framework within which to make sense of what can be the striking dissonances between narrative and meaning.

Second, the unconscious is seen as progressive, developmental and teleological – life is lived looking forward. By extension, the meaning of films and other audio-visual media tends towards the future. Of course, we carry our past with us, both in terms of our personal history and also as our cultural heritage. Similarly, films have historically specific important cultural meanings, yet they also have an unfolding life in the present. A Jungian interpretation tends to favour the latter. While it sees psychological meanings developmentally as intrinsic parts of cultural trajectories, it also locates such texts as part of a personal narrative, the life long love affair that so many of us have with the cinema and with other visual entertainments. Of course, both the historical and the psychological are important. Even so, the general contention of Jungian orientated film theory is that as a subject area film studies has neglected the individual emotional relationships viewers have with films in favour of historical analysis and acts of cultural deconstruction.

Third, viewers while individual subjects are located as constructed within broader social and cultural frameworks. It will become evident in this volume how questions of the 'cultural complex' are articulated in Jungian thinking. The hypothesis is that just as we have personal complexes so too we experience cultural complexes. Here Jungian thinking is helpful particularly because its understanding of a complex is different from the way in which it is understood by psychoanalysis. In Analytical Psychology, a complex is the frustration of the innate teleological drive of the unconscious. In other words, a complex tells us where something has been blocked and unblocking it helps us to gain fresh insights into our culture and ourselves. Films, then, provide ways to identify such complexes. This is potentially helpful in historical work but it is also useful in revealing how the interpretation of films shifts over time, as seen through the lens of different cultural complexes.

Fourth, in a move away from the Lacanian emphasis on the Father, Jungian psychology is every bit as interested in Mothers, both physical and archetypal (an archetype is psychological cultural pattern). For a subject area that has been so influenced by Freud and Lacan it is curious that scholars of film studies have not written much about fathers or mothers. Jungian film theory is intensely interested in both, and indeed in some cases, in the image of the child too.

Fifth, questions of gender and contrasexuality are at the core of Jungian theory. Jung's insight that gender and biological sex were separate but interrelated aspects of human sexuality was in its day groundbreaking. His writing explored how all of us contain masculine and feminine elements and the ways in which we are both attracted to and wary of this interplay. To be fair, Jung did not really explore the implications of this in any depth. That work is ongoing. However, for film theory, a Jungian understanding of human sexuality opens up what are potentially productive ways to articulate the issues that surround spectatorship; it offers a new framework through which to understand visual pleasure, and for that matter visual dis-pleasure, in the cinema.

Finally, some of the chapters interweave mythological material into their analyses and also into their theoretical approaches. To anyone familiar with the cannon of film studies, this might well seem curious, at times a little odd, and perhaps frankly even rather bizarre. However, in Jungian praxis in order to reveal the psychological meaning of an image it is necessary to 'amplify' it by finding mythological parallels to accompany the image. This process entails finding occurrences of the same, or similar images, in unrelated contexts and using these to reframe the initial image. This might seem counter intuitive and perhaps even anti-intellectual: after all surely everyone knows that what matters are the actual social and cultural contexts and how they influence meaning – we don't need some mythological coincidence. Indeed, traditionally film theory has emphasized the context of production as a determining factor in a film's meaning.

However, Jungian theory resists the idea of a fixed or inscribed textual meaning. Instead it asserts we have an understandable resistance to the psychological meaning of images, for once understood such meanings shine a light on those corners of our psyche we would much rather remain unknown. Seen from this perspective, our conscious selves are somewhat ambivalent about our relationship with the unconscious. On the one hand we want to fully understand ourselves, yet on the other we tell ourselves it is best to just keep things as they are. (This is another way of understanding what psychologists term 'confirmation bias' – engaging in behaviour that confirms we have understood events correctly, even if we have actually misunderstood them.) From the Jungian point of view, if we want to discover the meaning of those 'images' we see and experience in our lives it is necessary to develop techniques that circumvent the defensive manoeuvres of our conscious mind. Amplification is one such tactic.

Given the diversity of what constitutes Jungian film theory, it is inevitable that there will be an overlap between the different parts of this book. Indeed, some chapters could have been positioned perfectly comfortably in several chapters. However, in order to impose some structure on this somewhat unruly landscape it became clear it was going to be necessary to erect some fences and to create some separate areas of thought and investigation. As a result, the book is organized into five theoretical approaches, although the gaps between these conceptual dividing lines are plentiful and productive.

This *International Handbook* opens with a series of chapters that are concerned with *Theoretical Approaches*; while focused on conceptual issues, such issues are also often applied directly in film analysis. Part II on *Applied Approaches* emphasizes textual concerns, while again the debates are often theoretically informed. *Transnational Approaches* looks at cinema outside Anglophone regions – there is one exception that explores the hero in the USA as a transnational phenomenon. Here Jungian insights are helpful in locating viewers' affective responses in culturally specific ways that are also replete with overtones that ring loud and clear across international borders.

Another distinctive element of Jungian film studies is the number of practising psychotherapists and Jungian Analysts who write about film. Some of them are included in this volume but significantly not all are in Part IV, *Clinical Approaches*. That part explores the interrelationship between clinical theory and practice and its use in both the textual analysis of films and also as a means to understand the psychological impact of watching films. This is fertile territory for Jungian work and it demonstrates the utility of Analytical Psychology as a powerful tool for understanding the complex and complicated relationship viewers have with visual material. In an age where images are becoming ever more central to our lives this is important work.

Finally, the baton is passed to the *Post-Cinema* authors. This is an emerging area in Jungian film theory. It examines the life of the image on screens other than in the cinema. Here computer games, fan fiction, mobile screens and non-immersive image environments are all helpfully seen from a broadly Jungian point of view. The authors in this part open up exciting new ways in which to deploy Jungian theory to understand how the contemporary media world can be understood in depth psychological terms.

Jungian film studies provide a different view of familiar issues. Accompanying the current book is Hockley and Bassil-Morozow's *Jungian Film Studies: The Essential Guide* (2017). It too offers a good vantage point from which to see the media landscape, and indeed our various cultural contexts, from a Jungian perspective. The spirit of the subject like Jung's psychology itself is forward looking. The chapters included here stand on their own right yet, as there are new monographs being published all the time, they are also an invitation to engage with each author's work in more depth. My hope is that having seen the trailer, you will find the prospect of the feature film irresistible.

Luke Hockley
Professor of Media Analysis, Research Centre for Media, Art and Performance (RIMAP),
University of Bedfordshire, UK

References

Bassil-Morozow, H. and Hockley, L. (2017) *Jungian film studies: the essential guide*. Abingdon: Routledge.

Samuels, A., Shorter, B. and Plaut, F. (1986) *A critical dictionary of Jungian analysis*. London: Routledge & Kegan Paul.

Singh, G. (2014) *Feeling film: affect and authenticity in popular cinema*. London: Routledge.

Vogler, C. (2007) *The writer's journey: mythic structure for writers*, 3rd edn. Studio City, CA: Michael Wiese Productions.

PART I

Theoretical approaches

Edited by
Catriona Miller

1

A JUNGIAN TEXTUAL *TERROIR*

Catriona Miller

Introduction

Andrew Samuels begins his consideration of the Jungian and post-Jungian field by pointing out how the inheritance of Jung's work no longer rests solely upon his legacy of the twenty volumes of the *Collected Works*. It has, he suggested, 'become a many stranded skein of thought, which has inspired, influenced, challenged, and, in some cases infuriated those who followed' (Samuels, 1985/1994, p. 1). Within the more specific area of screen studies, Hockley has spoken of the 'deep rhizomatic structures in Jungian screen theory', a 'deep mycological transmission of psychological ideas and concepts in ways that permeate the work at an almost chemical and subterranean manner' (Hockley, 2015, p. 57). The metaphor that I would like to employ, however, is that of the *terroir*, from the French *terre* meaning 'land' or 'soil', and is normally used to describe the complete environment within which a vineyard sits and which contributes to and influences the flavour of the wine, including the geography, the soil and the climate for example, but in addition to such 'natural' characteristics, *terroir* can also take account of human intervention such as cultivation and farming techniques. All these elements affect the wine's final aroma and taste.

In this chapter I will tease out some of the elements of the Jungian textual *terroir* to make more explicit some of the tensions within the subterranean ideas and perspectives that infuse the field, and which can make it challenging for non-Jungians to engage with. The investigation of the *terroir*, will begin by exploring the purpose and process of textual analysis as more routinely practised within the humanities in order to consider what the post-Jungians might be doing differently in their approach to film texts, or, indeed, where they might sit within a more familiar post-structuralist milieu, before considering a possible methodology for a post-Jungian approach to the text.

What is a text? The ground

The first issue to tackle is the ground of the *terroir* itself, the question of the 'text'. In the generally understood notion of the 'text', film followed in the same territory as literary theory, where, alongside analysis of various elements of aesthetics and style, initially a close consideration of authorial (or directorial) intention formed the core of textual analysis.

Towards the middle of the twentieth century however a fresh way of examining the workings of the text itself began to develop, but this trend of analysis which emerged through the French literary journal *Tel Quel* (meaning 'such as it is') then began to change the understanding of the object under analysis, the text itself. Between 1960 and 1982, *Tel Quel* published a mixture of theory, creative writing and radical critique, and its list of contributing authors was an impressive 'who's who' of influential critical theorists including Lacan, Derrida and Kristeva, amongst others. There was an aspiration for the 'theory of literature to attain some of the logical hardness and rigour of mathematics' (ffrench, 2015, p. 108), beginning with semiotics.

Roland Barthes cogently summed up much of the discussion in a short essay *From Work to Text* published in 1971 (in Heath (ed.), 1978) followed up shortly afterwards with *Theory of the Text* in 1973 (in Young (ed.), 1990). In the first essay Barthes pointed out how the journal had engaged with a series of 'initiatory discourses' (semiotics, psychoanalysis and Marxism) that seemed to give rise to an epistemological break (or slide as he put it) leading away from a consideration of 'the work' towards a consideration of 'the text'. The work, he wrote, 'is a fragment of substance, occupying a part of the space of books (in a library for example), the Text is a methodological field' (Barthes in Heath, 1978, p. 156) – one is displayed and the other demonstrated; one is an object and the other a process. Barthes went on to offer several propositions that he suggested sat at the intersection of the Text. For example, that a Text is not confined to any particular genre; that it did not rely upon the author to guarantee meaning (which Barthes called 'filiation') but instead the reader must collaborate with the Text to create meaning, as a musician collaborates with a score to create music.

This approach, developed through *Tel Quel*, came to predominate within the general discipline of cultural studies, including film and media of course, as the idea of the Text was gradually extended to include more than language per se till in contemporary academia it has come to mean anything that we can make meaning from. In fact 'a text is anything that generates meaning through signifying practices. That is, a text is a metaphor that invokes the constitution of meaning through the organisation of signs into representations' (Barker, 2004, p. 199). Any organised system of signs (signifiers with a generally understood signified) can be read as a Text. This extended the idea of a Text far beyond the realm of language to music, cooking, fashion, the body itself and, of course, film and media.

So far, this is a fairly straightforward version of what might be intended by Text, drawing heavily on Saussure's basic concept that the 'signifer + signified = a sign'; where influenced by this crucial period of largely literary focused theory, 'text' moves from being a work/object with a relatively stable meaning whose secrets and symbols can be uncovered with the right hermeneutic approach, towards being a 'methodological field'. So looking at texts (such as film) is a study in a text's sense making practice.

However, by opening up the idea of the 'methodological field' as Text, the question of how it comes to mean was already becoming more complex. By 1971, the supposedly stable relationship between signifier and signified posited by structuralism was already under significant scrutiny. Barthes himself pointed out that the:

> logic regulating the Text is not comprehensive (define 'what the work means') but metonymic; the activity of associations, contiguities, carryings-over coincides with a liberation of symbolic energy; ... the work ... is *moderately* symbolic (its symbolic runs out, comes to a halt); the Text is *radically* symbolic; *a work conceived, perceived and received in its integrally symbolic nature is a text.*
>
> *(Barthes in Heath, 1978, pp. 158–9, italics as original)*

With this he emphasised the plurality of meaning offered within the Text. A work, he said, has meaning that might be uncovered through hermeneutics and interpretation. From a semiotic point of view, a work is a sign with a relatively stable relationship between signifier and signified, but the Text had an 'irreducible ... plurality' (Barthes in Heath, 1978, p. 159) which practised the infinite deferment of the signified, it was a network, reaching out to other texts. 'The plural of the Text depends', he pointed out, 'not on the ambiguity of its contents but on what might be called the *stereographic plurality* of its weave of signifiers (etymologically, the text is a tissue, a woven fabric)' (Barthes in Heath, 1978, p. 159). In fact, Derrida (largely responsible for unsettling the relationship between signifier and signified), writing in 1979 made this point even more robustly:

> A 'text' is henceforth no longer a finished corpus of writing, some content enclosed in a book or its margins, but a differential network, a fabric of traces referring endlessly to something other than itself, to other differential traces. Thus the text overruns all the limits assigned to it so far (not submerging or drowning them in an undifferentiated homogeneity, but rather making them more complex, dividing and multiplying strokes and lines).
>
> *(Derrida in Bloom, 2004, p. 69)*

We will return to Derrida later, while noting there that this post-structuralist perspective began to throw some interesting issues into the spotlight as the quest for 'meaning' moved beyond the stability of the signifier/signified relationship. In refusing to close down the possibilities of play, and insisting upon the 'radical symbolism' of the text, the *Tel Quel* approach began to reach towards another kind of 'meaning making' or quality being expressed within the Text. There was something more or perhaps something *else* happening within texts that the structuralist perspective could not adequately account for. As Barthes put it, 'As soon as the text is conceived as a polysemic space where the paths of several possible meanings intersect, it is necessary to cast off the monological, legal status of signification, and to pluralise it' (Barthes in Young, 1990, p. 37).

In fact, this 'other logic' raised the question of subjectivity: *who* is making sense of the Text? To tackle this question, Barthes drew upon the work of Kristeva, a member of *Tel Quel*'s editorial board, and used the term 'signifiance' in distinction with 'signification'. He commented:

> When the text is read (or written) as a mobile play of signifiers, with no possible reference to one or several fixed signifieds, it becomes necessary to distinguish very carefully between signification, which belongs to the level of the product, of the statement, of communication, and the signifying work, which belongs to the level of production, enunciation, symbolisation: it is this work that we call 'signifiance'.
>
> *(Barthes* in *Young, 1990, pp. 37–8)*

Kristeva had been engaging with Lacan's radical reworking of Freud. Lacan's importance to the development of textual analysis was central because he offered an account of how the subject came to be constituted. The subject, from this point of view, was not a pre-existing essence per se, but was in fact constituted by language, or at least, until there was language there was no way to represent whatever might have 'gone before'. Lacan's theory tied the creation of subjectivity, (the conscious ego) to the acquisition of language itself, where experience is mediated by language, as Kugler puts it by 'creating a self representation in language through the use of the first person pronoun "I"' (Kugler in Barnaby and D'Acierno (eds), 1990, p. 311). This had the effect of dividing the personality into an experiential self and a represented self, and because the experiential self is excluded from the realm of representation (i.e. no language, no representation) it leads to the appearance of the unconscious order of experience (*ibid.*, 1990, p. 311).

Thus language was seen to be the mechanism by which consciousness is initiated and the question of the Text, and of textuality, becomes intimately connected with questions around the formation of consciousness itself. When Derrida said *il n'y a pas de hors-texte* – 'there is no outside text' (Derrida, 1976, p. 158) – it meant there is no way of understanding consciousness without language, without Text, and we come to the notion instead of the 'dissolved' or 'constructed' subject, whereby what we think of as the individual is really a product of social and linguistic forces that is, not an essence at all, merely a 'tissue of textualities' (Barry, 1995/2009, p. 65). This is a view of subjectivity that is inseparable from language or from indeed from Text. In this landscape, it is easy to wander away from the Text itself to consideration of how the subject is constituted, as we have just done. It is a common slippage in textual analysis because it is difficult to consider how meaning is created from the weave and texture of signs, without starting to wonder who is doing the 'meaning making'.

Lacan devised a tripartite scheme that revolved around language; the Real, the Imaginary and the Symbolic orders – the Real is the place before language, and thus before subjectivity. Kristeva however chose to name that place without language the semiotic *chora* (a term taken from Plato). It is 'a non-expressive (i.e. non verbal) totality underlying language, a non spatial, non temporal receptacle of energy and drives which she calls the chora' (Smith, 1998, p. 121). The subject is expelled from the *chora* in a series of pulsations into the symbolic realm.

To return to *signifiance*, the term Barthes used to describe a different kind of meaning within the text, Kristeva described it as an excess of meaning created by the co-presence of the semiotic and the symbolic. Some confusion can arise in this instance, as Kristeva chose to reinterpret 'semiotic' here to refer to 'a sort of corporeal memory, a reminiscence of the play of energy and drives experienced in the body with great intensity before the separation from the mother and the foundation of consciousness, entry into the symbolic' (Smith, 1998, p. 16). Thus the Lacanian Real is replaced by the Kristevan semiotic *chora* as 'the space of the articulation of the drives and the arrangement of instincts' (Grossberg, 1997, p. 77).

The concept of *signifiance* moved beyond the Text (in any sense of a material trace) to a methodological field where language is a structuring force, in an attempt to offer an account of the relationship between the subject and the text. Kristeva postulated the idea of the 'subject in process' where:

> *signifiance* is an alternative signifying process that is the result of the heterogenous workings of language which articulates both symbolic and semiotic dispositions. This double articulation of language allows a text or artwork to signify what the communicative or representational function of the work cannot say.
>
> *(Kristeva, 1980, p. 18)*

Much of Kristeva's work in textual analysis was centred around tracing *signifiance* within poetry. What is intriguing, is that despite the desire of *Tel Quel* to have the 'theory of literature … attain some of the logical hardness and rigour of mathematics' (ffrench, 2015, p. 108), they found themselves chasing a different kind of meaning and reaching into the unknowable depths of the psyche where/when consciousness is just potential, calling it the *Real* or the *semiotic chora*, pre-language and full of drives and positing the subject as a co-creation of the semiotic and the symbolic, an unstable subject, constantly in motion and in production.

Jung too sought to understand the unknowable depths of the psyche, full of drives and before consciousness but named it the collective unconscious, and saw the ego as a (more or less) unstable coalescence of the totality of psyche. Although Jung did not look to language per se as the catalyst for consciousness, but rather to patterning forces he called archetypal. The archetype is, he said 'a condensation of the living process' (1921: §749). As Rowland puts it, '[t]he unconscious is structured through archetypes as the potentials for images and psychic signifying. Archetypes are not inherited images but the inherited possibilities for certain sorts of meaning' (Rowland, 1999, p. 191). The archetypes *an sich* cannot be directly apprehended (also true for the Real and Imaginary orders and the semiotic *chora*). However the archetypal images arising from the archetypes *can* and most Jungian textual analysis has been concerned with exploring archetypal imagery within culture.

So textual analysis as it began to emerge as a practice, recognised that there were different kinds of meaning in texts, and that whilst there were structures and organising forces at work within a text, there was also its opposite: slips ups, cracks in the facade of meaning, *aporia* where meaning seemed to become more than the sum of its parts. The cinematic text seems to be a category of text particularly prone to this excess of complex signification. It consists of web within web of signification: complex and interlocking systems, as meaning that ties narrative (if it exists) to the visual complexities of *mise-en-scène*, to sound textures, to the speed and rhythm of camera work and editing. It is a multiplicious kaleidoscope of signification and yet meaning emerges and audiences have become adept at decoding them.

The cinematic text, like literature, is variegated, ranging from mainstream narratives to *avant garde* audio visual 'happenings' but even the most experimental texts are still organised. In fact film has developed well-established norms of grammar that are particularly obvious within continuity editing style and standard framing strategies, for example, but often times manifest in production design and sound as well. For example, the voice and dialogue track will almost always be privileged in the sound mix.

This mixture of complexity and organisation however makes the audio-visual text particularly prone to slippages. The term 'cinematic excess' (Thompson in Rosen, 1986) has been used to denote this tendency to exceed the bounds of what is necessary to the narrative. 'The concept of cinematic excess emerged amid a shift in film theory from critical readings of a film's unifying narrative towards analyses of the conflicting forces in a film conceived as a heterogeneous textual system' (Thompson, 1986, p. 130). The textual system was seen to be unable to contain and unify all the conflicting forces, and what remained outside was called cinematic excess (Branigan and Buckland, 2013, p. 178). Even the dominant style of the classical Hollywood film which has the most strict formal organisation subordinated to the narrative, will still contain moments of excess meaning. This is because the cinematic text is really a 'braid of codes' (Lindeman in Rosen, 1986, p. 143) which has been burnished to disguise its 'segmentary modality and make it appear natural, endowed with mimetic truth and narrative fluency' (Lindeman in Rosen, 1986, p. 142) but a braid it remains which can be undone.

In thinking about the Text as a 'methodological field', however excessive and unruly, the question of method is already raised: what might a (post) Jungian textual analysis look like?

The prevailing weather

Before suggesting a way forward with a method, however, it is important to look at the prevailing weather that has shaped the landscape and make three points about the wider Jungian *terroir* which go some way to explaining why the question of a Jungian textual analysis is still so diffuse.

First, and now well documented, was the rift between Freud and Jung. Jung had been a colleague and friend of Freud's but in 1913 there came an irretrievable break between the two men. Writing in 2001, Eisold pointed out:

> For analytical psychology, psychoanalysis has been both powerfully influential and inimical; it represents both an established and competitive tradition of psychological treatment and an injurious source of disparagement and neglect. The effects of this on analytical psychology have been pervasive and deep, though not always easy to discern and, certainly, experienced very differently in different sectors of the Jungian community.... From the perspective of psychoanalysis, on the other hand, analytical psychology is a deviant and marginal presence; as such, it is not without influence or power ... but it is not generally included within its discussions and debates.
>
> *(p. 336)*

Thus on the surface what was perhaps a personal matter has had a lasting impact within the field, with an effort to discredit Jung and Jungian ideas in general. This might have remained within the clinical world (see Glover, 1950, for example), but through *Tel Quel*'s championing of Freud and Lacan, the suspicion around Jung subsequently extended to the wider Academy. The journal itself took a dim view of Jung and in so far as he was mentioned at all, it was negatively. A 1979 article, for example, states that Jung's reading of Joyce was a Nazi one (Houdebine, 1979, p. 65). More usually Jung has been painted as a mystic lacking in that 'logical hardness and rigour of mathematics' sought by the journal's authors, and which formed the basis of the approach to film analysis in the 1970s and 1980s.

This accusation about lack of rigour found its target partly because of Jung's own ambivalent attitude to theory, an ambivalence that led to other tensions within the Jungian field itself between clinicians and academics. The general attitude to theory was cautious if not suspicious with Jung himself saying in the 1938 Foreword to *The Development of the Personality*:

> [t]heories in psychology are the very devil. It is true that we need certain points of view for their orienting and heuristic value: but they should always be regarded as mere auxiliary concepts that can be laid aside at any time.
>
> *(1938, p. 7)*

The attitude to theory within the Jungian field reveals a suspicion of logic that Samuels very usefully sums up in the opening chapter of *Jung and the Post-Jungians* (1985/1994). He pointed out that Jung's own approach to theory was a circular one: human material – theory – illustration – application to human behaviour. Research might introduce, illustrate or amplify theory but it does not *prove* it. There was a concern that theory could be deployed defensively: pure logic, over intellectualising could block the analytical process, which needed to remain flexible, responsive and contingent. Reification was also a danger – 'to render as concrete, literal and actual that which is shifting, fluid and experiential, for example the unconscious. Reification not only tempts one to apply a predetermined theory but it bypasses the role of the psyche in psychology' (Samuels, 1985/1994, p. 6). Finally, Jung had made a distinction between directed and non-directed thinking, but Jung thought that a complementarity was possible in which 'the more rational and logical parts of the mental apparatus go to work on imaginal raw material' (Samuels, 1985/1994, p. 6). Ego-consciousness, after all, was only one style of consciousness (Samuels in Casement, 1998, p. 22), albeit the one most concerned with theory, and thus could not be left to have it all its own way.

The concern with theory is at the centre of the unease that exists between therapists and academics, usefully laid out in Samuels's foreword to 2004's *Post-Jungian Criticism: Theory and Practice* (pp. viiff.). So whilst analysts distrust a too intellectual only application of Jung's ideas, academics distrust a lack of theoretical rigour. The issue perhaps from a Jungian point of view is that '[a]nything derived merely from rationality risks being profoundly inauthentic unless it also bears witness to the destabilising presence of unconsciousness' (Rowland, 2005, p. 23) which is inherently unknowable.

Finally, in terms of the prevailing weather, the field itself has continued to develop, leading to what has been called a *post*-Jungian perspective. In 1985, Samuels first described three schools of thought (four by 1998) and it is worth mentioning here because within the field of Jungian film studies, the varying emphases are often more implicit than explicit.

Samuels called his nomenclature a creative fiction which should not be taken as definitive, with Kirsch noting in 2000 that 'most analysts did not like being labelled in this way' (p. 53). However, it can be useful in understanding how the field has developed. The Classical School focused on the self and individuation, consciously working in Jung's footsteps, with a focus very much on therapeutic work. The Developmental School put a focus on the importance of infancy in the evolution of the adult personality and an 'equally stringent emphasis on the analysis of transference–countertransference dynamics in clinical work' (Samuels in Casement, 1998, p. 20). Finally the Archetypal School in which psychic images were investigated as the primary activity of consciousness. This was less clinical in its emphasis and Samuels later thought it had been integrated into the other two schools that had then themselves been subdivided. However, with its emphasis on imagery, Hillman's Archetypal School has continued to exert an influence on the analysis of culture in general, including film.

Film scholars borrow from all three and the issue here is not the borrowing per se, but the fact that the characterisation of the three schools are largely based around the practice of Jungian clinical analysis. Clinicians are analysing people, academics are analysing texts, and whilst the previous section pointed out the frequent slippage between the two via the question of subject-ivity (and notwithstanding the influential work proffered by clinicians who are also film theor-ists) it remains an open question as to how much of the approach should be transposed from a clinical setting to an academic one. In fact, given the general suspicion towards making a too powerful theoretical model, one might wonder if the perspectives are in fact diametrically opposed, but the on-going link between the clinic and the academy facilitated through organi-sations such as the International Association of Jungian Studies and the Jungian Society for Scholarly Studies, though sometimes tense, is one of the unique elements of the Jungian *terroir*, 'a rhizome of interconnectedness' as Hockley puts it (2015, p. 57).

These are some of the tensions that form the prevailing weather affecting the Jungian *terroir* sometimes in obvious ways, sometimes in more subtle ways.

Cultivation: what are Jungians doing with the film text?

It has often been considered difficult to speak of a post-structuralist method because '[a]ll they offer is an orientation towards a characteristic central issue and a body of work which constitutes a repertoire of examples' (Barry, 1995/2009, p. 70). A point that has also been made about Jungian film theory where discussion often begins with the suggestion that the Jungian approach is one that centres on a shared attitude rather than a theoretical toolkit. However, whilst that might be broadly true, it *is* possible to discern certain streams within the field, and in this section I will try to tease out some of those shared attitudes and perspectives before moving on to offer some specific suggestions for a (post) Jungian textual analysis methodology.

The shared attitude can be said to include a number of Jungian concepts such as archetypes, a Jungian understanding of symbols and the role of affect, ideas which overlap with one another. Archetypes are a much discussed aspect of Jungian theory, but for the purposes of this chapter it is easiest to consider them as 'an inherited organisation of psychic energy' (1921: §754) which can never be apprehended by the conscious mind directly. Jung warned that we must 'constantly bear in mind that what we mean by "archetype" is in itself irrepresentable' (1954: §417) which is 'never conscious and never will be' (1940: §266). The archetype *an sich* belongs to the unrepresentable collective unconscious, but its 'effects … make visualisations of it possible, namely the archetypal images' (1954: §417). Lacan and Kristeva too certainly thought that vestiges of the Imaginary and the semiotic could be found within the symbolic. There has long been debate around the characteristics of archetypal images and their symbolic nature, although in 2004 Samuels suggested that the way to identify an archetypal image is through the 'intensity of affective response' (Samuels in Baumlin *et al.*, 2004, p. xiv).

To introduce another Jungian idea, the affective response may indicate that the 'transcendent function' has been activated, of which Jung said 'tendencies of the conscious and the unconscious are the two factors that together make up the transcendent function. It is called "transcendent" because it makes the transition from one attitude to another organically possible, without loss of the unconscious' (1957: §145). This highlights the fact that the Jungian model of the psyche certainly sees the conscious and the unconscious as connected but *also* to some extent in communication. Jungians are looking for counter-balancing images that might come from the unconscious as compensation to the conscious attitude, where the clinician is dealing with images from clients and the academic is dealing with images from culture, but both attend to affect and compensation with a view to understanding where the symptoms might be leading. Understanding the unconscious as an active agent in this self-balancing model of the psyche *is* different from Lacan and Kristeva's view.

One way of investigating such affect laden archetypal images is through a process that Jung called 'amplification' where cultural and historical instances of the image are sought in order to give a wider context in which to consider its meaning. Clinicians, for example, might choose to amplify certain elements of a client's dreams in order to help understand its significance, because the psyche in Jung's model is seen, as noted, as self balancing (a homeostatic biological system) and symptoms are therefore teleological. This is an important element within the Jungian model, where theorist and clinician alike are intensely interested not only in a kind of forensic archaeology but also in the direction of travel. Therefore a Jungian vantage point on any text is likely to include a sense of teleological purpose within the images under investigation. This means there is always a therapeutic angle to an examination of archetypal images, driven in part by Jung himself, and in part by the, not always straightforward but nonetheless continuing, dialogue between therapists and academics in the post-Jungian field. So there is in the Jungian orientation a sense of teleology offered in part by Jung's idea of individuation (the process of becoming an individual) and his view of the psyche as self-balancing, with the understanding that these are processes in motion rather than a 'once and for all' destination.

One Jungian oriented approach to the text derives from the distinction made by Jung between the sign and the symbol, where the sign stands for a known thing – a straightforward semiotic understanding of 'signifer + signified = sign'. The symbol on the other hand is the 'best possible formulation of a relatively unknown thing' (1921: §815). So following in the footsteps of a literary approach, there is the possibility of examining symbols within the text. As Rowland put it 'traditional Jungian literary critics follow the master's lead in seeking transhistorical archetypes in literary texts. These critics seek in literature a powerful psychic image (often related to myth), which can be identified in more than one literary work' (Rowland, 1999, p. 3). And so it is with film.

Fredericksen's 'Jung/sign/symbol/film' originally published in 1979 (see Hauke and Hockley (eds), 2012) makes this approach very clear with regard to film, particularly those that do not fit in the classical Hollywood style. However, although films are certainly conscious creations (unlike dreams for example), they are the conscious creations of large groups of people who are themselves responding to the even larger group of 'the public' often in very intuitive ways, as most mainstream filmmaking is attempting to capture the public imagination with an eye to potential profits, of course. So in this sense, films also have a collective flavour that can encourage an approach not dissimilar to the work of the Zurich School and Marie Louise von Franz's examination of fairy tales. This approach has also included consideration of mythological motifs in contemporary culture as examples of archetypal images, using amplification as a technique. Perhaps one of the most widespread versions of this is Campbell's 'hero's journey' (1949/2008) popularised for screenwriters through the work of Christopher Vogler (2007).

However this has not been without its critics, at least as it was being practised within a clinical setting. James Hillman, one time Director of Studies at the Zurich School repeatedly pointed out the dangers of seeking out symbols, only to explain them. To paraphrase Hillman (1977, p. 67ff.) if we use amplification to come to a generally accepted meaning then we have turned the symbol into a sign. The practice with symbols no longer accords with the theory of them – they are no longer 'relatively unknown' – quite the contrary, we know all about them. Jungians therefore have not been immune to the temptation to fix meaning, to 'reduce' unconscious phenomena via amplification and dictionaries, to a known thing. Hillman's approach was to insist upon resisting the temptation to *explain* the images of the unconscious and to settle on their meaning – an approach that will be discussed in more detail below. Although such a method is not without its attractions, as Hillman made clear, it can be quite straightforwardly structuralist. The signifier of the mythological trope meets the signified of the archetypal image, and its meaning is explained and known.

However in 2004, Jensen wrote that Jung was '[e]ssentialist but surprisingly poststructuralist' (Jensen in Baumlin *et al.*, 2004, p. 20) which appears rather a paradoxical statement, but its point was well made. Jung certainly can be read from a structuralist point of view, but he can *also* be read from a post-structuralist one. A big challenge to depth psychology in the humanities was the post-structuralist move towards deconstruction where neither authorial intention nor indeed the stability of the text's own structure could be taken for granted as places to find meaning, and although Jung's writing seems rife with essentialism and dependent upon various originary myths about the psyche, with the Self as the ultimate transcendental signifier, from the late 1980s there was a growing move to view his ideas from a post-structuralist perspective.

It is a small but significant strand within post-Jungian publications, beginning with an essay by Vannoy-Adams in a collection on deconstruction in 1989, along with an essay by David Miller on postmodern meaning published the same year in *Spring* (in Papadopoulos, 1992). They were followed by others such as a trio of chapters in *C. G. Jung and the Humanities: Toward a Hermeneutics of Culture* (Kugler, 1990), where Kugler, Casey and Miller made the case for reconsidering Jungian theory within a postmodern framework, whilst Rowland and Hauke made a more concerted effort in 1999 and 2000 respectively. Rowland (1999) in a detailed argument sought to 'deconstruct Jungian theory as authority and reinstate it as textuality' (p. 6). She aligned Jungian ideas first with structuralism, then with deconstruction, postmodernism and crucial aspects of feminist theory. Subsequent publications (2002, 2005 and 2017) have continued to explore Jung's writing as text, after all, the post-structural approach does not allow much room for the author's intentions. Hauke's book was another extended attempt to place

Jung into the wider context of the humanities at the start of the twenty-first century, with the core suggestion that Jung's project was one of deconstructing modern consciousness. Hauke laid out in some detail the ways in which Jung's work critiqued the enlightenment world view and questioned the modernist agenda, opening up space for plurality in the discussion of meaning, offering complexity, ambiguity and contradiction that are the hallmarks of the postmodern.

Such explorations demonstrated that Jung's writing did not dissolve when confronted with the possibility of deconstruction and that in fact Jung's own writing contained doubt. For example Miller (1992) discussed Jung's use of the image of the alchemical Philosopher's Stone taking it to mean that Jung was aware of a slipperiness of meaning in such ideas, a sliding and even deferral, that meant despite the apparent Aristotelian meanings in his writing, there is also alongside it *at the same time* a sense in which meaning cannot be fixed and paradoxical meanings co-exist, hence 'essentialist, but surprisingly post-structuralist'. Rowland's *Jung as a Writer* (2005) offered a more extended deconstruction of Jung's writing.

However, taking things even further was the point of view that whilst Jung's writing certainly could be deconstructed with interesting results, there was also the possibility put forward by Rowland that Jung's ideas could also be used *to* deconstruct. For instance, rather than seeing individuation as a constant search for unity within the psyche, Jung's model also opened up the possibility of a polycentric psyche, where 'mental existence was a continual dialogue with archetypal forces in the unconscious; that subjectivity was the result of unconscious processes shaping the ego' (Rowland, 1999, p. 11) and thus 'individuation is a deconstructive process, privileging the ungraspable unconscious over the limitations of the ego as it continually reshapes identity and perceptions of reality' (Rowland, 1999, p. 11). The conscious ego, which Jung himself described as only 'a relatively constant personification of the unconscious itself' (1955–6: §128) and which Berry calls simply 'a sense of continuity' (1974, p. 69) is therefore in constant process and subjectivity is only a temporary stabilisation, reminiscent of Kristeva's 'subject in process'.

In this scenario, a post-Jungian textual analysis must be alert to the 'intensity of affective response' (Samuels in Baumlin *et al.*, 2004, p. xiv) to any given image as a pointer to activation of the transcendent function within the text, rather than immediately extracting symbols only to explain them. Instead, post-Jungians might trace the presence of the unconscious in a similar way (though using a different vocabulary) to Kristeva's interest in *significance* as vestiges of the semiotic seeping through the warp and weft of the text (that is, the subject itself), because the unconscious forms part of the total psyche and affects our 'sense making practices'. In fact doubly so in Jung's model, because the unconscious is not a passive receptacle but an active agent in the ecosystem of the psyche such that the collective unconscious might even be said to be the foundation of all 'sense making'. The unconscious contains the archetypes which are the 'organisation of psychic energy' (1921: §754) which allow patterns of perception to emerge in the first place. So looking to amplify and explain symbols plucked out of the text is to remove them from the ecosystem, the processes, within which they sit, and perhaps kill them stone dead.

Although sometimes discussed as if they are, archetypal images do not have fixed content and a search for meaning through textual analysis yields more contingent, shifting and even contradictory results, more in keeping with a post-structuralist perspective than might at first be supposed. The idea that the unconscious is an active agent means that meaning *cannot* be fixed because the workings of archetypal energies within the text are dependent upon a variety of contexts, for example the culture and moment of production, how that affects the structure of the text itself and the reception of the text by the audiences. Some of the lack of clarity around a methodology of Jungian textual analysis, undoubtedly comes from the fact that writers within the field might flit back and forth between what one might loosely call a structuralist and a post-structuralist perspective, and those utilising post/Jungian theory to understand cultural phenomena have done either and both.

Those inclining towards a structuralist approach within the Jungian framework might tend towards using the collective unconscious and archetypes as the underlying structure common to all where meaning is created by pointing out the correspondences between the phenomenon present in the text and an archetype. An approach that is not without its uses, but it does tend to lead back to the position that with the right tools, the secrets of the 'text' can be unlocked through filiation with Jung the author. It is a form of textual analysis that, as Barthes suggested, might be said to investigate 'the work' rather than the Text.

The post-structuralist perspective recognises the inherent instability of meaning, with post-Jungians understanding 'symbols' as the best possible formulation of an otherwise unknown thing, and the collective unconscious as that active agent which creates the 'sense of continuity', the subject, in coming to consciousness. This viewpoint encourages a more radical investigation of the text, with a deconstructive aim of opening up texts to focus on the traces of the unconscious workings of the psyche. In fact, 'trace' in the Derridean sense is an interesting idea here and worth a little more examination, because it seems unexpectedly to take us in the same direction as Lacan's Real, Kristeva's semiotic chora and perhaps Jung's collective unconscious.

Taken from the French meaning 'footprint', trace refers to something no longer present and as such it incorporates both elements of Derrida's *différance* – difference and deferral. The structuralist semiotic model regarded the difference between binary opposites as the source of meaning. Derrida agreed that signs depend upon other signs for meaning and therefore each sign contained traces of all others. As Bradley puts it:

> If every sign in the system obtains its identity through its difference from all the other signs, then this means every sign is intrinsically marked by what it is not. Every sign must retain the traces of the other signs against which it is to be defined … in order to have any meaning at all.
>
> *(2008, pp. 69–70)*

But more than this, for Derrida meaning is deferred because the signifier (language/signs) is always standing between us and meaning itself. Language works 'through a process of infinite supplementation where the job of completing or fulfilling meaning is always devolved onto the *next* sign along in space and time: a fully present meaning is thus perpetually out of reach' (Bradley, 2008, p. 71). So Derrida introduced the term *différance* to mark this twin difference/deferral of meaning, saying that '*The (pure) trace is différance*' (Derrida, 1976, p. 62). In fact, '[r]ather than imagining language as a discrete set of signifiers, Derrida's concept of the trace indicates something like a boundless sea of shifting, fundamentally interrelated references' (Reynolds and Roffe, 2004, p. 105) set against a field of the 'originary trace'.

What exactly Derrida meant by 'originary trace' is not entirely straightforward and often appears paradoxical: it does not exist, it is both present and absent; 'the originary trace can never be 'there' because it is 'always-already-there [*toujours deja-la*]: it both recedes into an infinite past and projects itself into an infinite future' (Bradley, 2008, p. 74); it is anterior (that is, 'coming before') 'all that one calls sign (signified/signifier, content/expression, etc.), concept or operation, motor or sensory' (Derrida, 1976, p. 62); it is the 'absolute other', the concept of the originary trace, where 'the absolutely other [*le tout autre*] is announced as such – without any simplicity, any identity, any resemblance or continuity – within what is not it' articulates its possibility 'in the entire field of being [*étant*], which metaphysics has defined as the being-present [*étant-present*]' (Bradley, 2008 quoting Derrida, 1976, p. 47 but translation modified:

p. 73); '[the] *trace is in fact the absolute origin of sense in general*' (Derrida, 1976, p. 65) and yet '[w]e cannot think it … because, … the difference between ideas or concepts cannot strictly speaking *itself* be a concept' (Bradley, 2008, p. 73). As Derrida says 'it permits the articulation of signs among themselves' (Derrida, 1976, p. 62). It is the gap *between*, where '[m]eaning arises magically and spontaneously from that blank space' (Gaston and Maclachlan, 2011, p. 50).

Once again, it seems we reach the limits of what can be known. Derrida calls it the trace; Kristeva the 'semiotic chora'; Lacan 'the Real' and Jung the 'collective unconscious'. All seem to be trying to express 'what lies before', before there is consciousness or subjectivity, or it might be more accurate to say 'before that which gives rise to consciousness', the complex biological systems from which consciousness arises as a property of those systems.

From this perspective, Jung's contribution of seeing the unconscious as an 'active agent' in the psyche as a whole may be helpful in edging towards a fresh perspective on the unrepresentable unconscious as he emphasises its inclusion within his model of the psyche. He says: '[w]e must … accustom ourselves to the thought that conscious and unconscious have no clear demarcations, the one beginning where the other leaves off. It is rather the case that the psyche is a conscious–unconscious whole' (1954: §397). It is tempting to suggest that the total psyche is the ultimate Derridean 'undecideable', 'something that cannot conform to either polarity of a dichotomy (such as present/absent, cure/poison, and inside/outside' (Reynolds and Roffe, 2004, p. 46) or indeed 'conscious/unconscious').

Thus it might also be helpful to resist the conscious/unconscious binary opposite in favour of 'both/and' or 'more or less' statements. Consciousness does not appear to be either on or off, but a gradient. Jung notes of the dream for example, which bears all the characteristics of *abaissement du niveau mental* (a term he borrows from Pierre Janet, literally meaning 'reduction of mental level') as showing:

> low energy-tension: logical discontinuity, fragmentary character, analogy formations, superficial associations of the verbal, clang [association of words based on their sound rather than their meaning – from the German *klang* meaning 'sound'], or visual type, condensations, irrational expressions, confusion etc. With an increase of energy-tension the dreams acquire a more ordered character; they become dramatically composed and reveal clear sense-connections, and the valency of the associations increases.
>
> *(1957: §152)*

The effect of more or less consciousness is more or less organisation. For Jung, a lowered mental state is useful in allowing contents from the unconscious to manifest, whether through dreams or through a technique he termed active imagination.

But, just as a structuralist textual analysis moved towards a trying to understand subjectivity in order to get at 'meaning', so post-structuralism leads towards phenomenology in order to consider the subject, as indeed, does post-Jungian theory (see in particular Brooke [1991] and Singh [2014]). However, to confine ourselves more specifically to textual analysis, the goal of a post-Jungian approach is not to close down or fix meaning, but rather to open up, to be attentive to those moments of undecidability within the text which are inevitably there:

> [betraying] stable meaning that an author might seek to impose upon his or her text. The process of writing always reveals that which has been suppressed, covers over that which has been disclosed, and breaches the very oppositions that are thought to sustain it.
>
> *(Reynolds and Roffe, 2004, p. 47)*

The trace, the Imaginary Order, the *semiotic chora* and the collective unconscious all seem to leave traces that the subject, the fragmented, contingent, in-process 'ego' is irresistibly drawn to as it seeps into the conscious world, as 'other'.

Such traces of 'before consciousness' but still part of the total psyche can be detected within the film text, but it does raise the question of how to acknowledge its unrepresentable nature, to resist closure and definition, and avoid the temptation to assign a fixed meaning. A post-Jungian consideration of the filmic text must pay careful attention to the hints, whispers and 'just out of the corner of one's eye' moments where the presence of affect is a clue to this 'other' nature and 'other meaning'.

Jungian textual analysis: some gadgets

This section offers some ways of approaching a text from a post-Jungian point of view and avoiding a reductionist methodology, where 'long things are penises for Freudians, dark things are shadows for Jungians' (Hillman, 1976, p. 8) and resist the desire to explain. As Terence Dawson has pointed out, 'it has to do more than stick Jungian labels on otherwise standard readings of a text' (in Young-Eisendrath, 2008, p. 292). I will propose some 'gadgets' as Hillman (1978, p. 152) puts it, that might help things along.

It seems inevitable however to begin with a word of caution. It is vital to keep in mind the '*as if*' nature of Jung's model and avoid reification. Or to put it another way, Jungian concepts ought to be written about 'under erasure' to use a term from Derrida, where a term may be used, but what it commits one to is denied or placed *sous rature*. As Norris points out '[t]o use "*sous rapture*" means to acknowledge the inadequacy of the terms employed – their highly provisional status – and the fact that thinking simply cannot manage without them in the work of deconstruction' (2003, p. 68). It is beguilingly easy to begin to speak of archetypes as if they had concrete status, to speak about the unconscious as something that can be easily known, whereas of course by its very nature, the unconscious is not conscious and therefore cannot be known. What can be discerned within the text is merely an echo or a trace. Having said that, I would propose perhaps three 'gadgets' that might help in approaching a text in a post-Jungian fashion, so drawing on Berry (1974) we might suggest three stages to a post-Jungian textual analysis: attend to the image, implication and supposition.

Beginning with an appeal to 'attend to the image' drawn from the work of the Archetypal School and, particularly, Berry and Hillman, this approach was originally intended to help the analyst consider the dream in a therapeutic context but as a way forward for textual analysis for the film it has the advantage of encouraging attention being paid to what is actually, in all its specificity, there and not leaping immediately to archetypes. 'Our basic premise', said Berry, 'is that the dream is something in and of itself. It is an imaginal product in its own right. Despite what we do or don't do with it – it is an image' (1974, p. 61), while Hillman suggested that the dreamer should stick to the image, adhere to the 'precisely qualifying context' (1977, p. 67) of the image. This is worth emphasising because Jungian film theorists, drawing connections to the therapeutic practice of paying attention to a client's dreams as a starting point for discussion and the co-creation of understanding (see Hockley, 2011, p. 133 for more) can sometimes lose the emphasis on the text itself and attention quickly shifts elsewhere to the general movement of narrative and character, or to the audience and wider culture.

So the first stage of a textual analysis might be close attention to the apparatus of the text, perhaps in terms of what is there and how it is organised. As discussed earlier, the film text is a complex amalgam of its multimodal elements that create important contextualisation cues for the audience. As noted above, there is no such thing as a 'simple' cinematic image. It is a 'braid of codes' some of which might be subordinated to the structures of the narrative, but which will always provide an overabundance of detail. The *mise-en-scène* sets mood and emotional tone by contextualising where and who; camera framing and angle height and distance sets vantage point; editing conveys cadence as well as ordering; sound can deepen diegetic engagement, but also introduce non-diegetic commentary. However it is, of course, not enough to consider each of these in turn, because the multimodality of the film text should encourage the analyst to consider the way each of these systems interact with each other, sometimes to create the appearance of a polished seamless whole (as in the Hollywood style), sometimes to introduce ambiguity and doubt. These multimodal systems are the textural warp and weft of the cinematic text.

The choice to start here is of course in sync with more traditional forms of textual analysis in film and media. In *Visual Methodologies*, for example, Rose would call this the 'compositional modality' of the text, taking account of the material qualities of the image, its formal strategies such as colour and spatial organisation (2016, p. 25). Barker's (2009) 'textural' analysis with its emphasis on body, asking how the film 'touches' the spectator within categories of haptics, kinetics and rhythm, is also a useful way of beginning to delineate what is there on screen. It also does not preclude a semiotic parsing of paradigmatic/syntagmatic elements, for example, or any particular technical vocabulary for being clear about what is there on the screen. It would thus seem to sit comfortably within what Hockley (2011) refers to as the 'first image', the image on the screen. As he points out, it is the 'base from which the chains of meaning emerge' (Hockley, 2011, p. 137). The first image is 'denotative and mimetic', but as Hillman points out everything necessary is here: 'All images … adhere, cohere, inhere – this inhesion is fundamental to the image' (Hillman, 1977, p. 69).

The stage of attending closely to what is on the screen is worth emphasising because textual analysis (of the non-Jungian and Jungian variety) has not always focused on an examination of what is there on the screen, preferring to consider narrative and character, although Izod and Dovalis (2015) offer some beautifully detailed work on films exploring the subject of grief.

For ways to explore around the image, Berry's (1974) lead on approaching dreams (which Hillman draws heavily upon in his 1977 article), whilst remaining aware of sensate qualities of the image offers some useful signposts. She points out (as Barthes did):

> [the] word 'text' is related to weave. So to be faithful to a text is to feel and follow its weave … the dream is sensate, has texture, is woven with patterns offering a finished and full context…. Image in itself has texture.
>
> *(Berry, 1974, p. 63)*

In addition to texture, she suggests attention to the sensuality of the image is important, a perspective that might work well with Barker's approach to the filmic body/text. Next, *emotional tone* which may not be portrayed verbally, but through music, or lighting. For example, the overly saturated colour palette and high fashion aesthetic of *Neon Demon* (dir. Winding-Refn, 2016) immediately raises the possibility of hysteria. By way of comparison his 2009 film *Valhalla Rising* is so de-saturated that it appears at times almost black and white, reflecting and emphasising the emotionless nature of the central character.

Berry then encourages consideration of the interconnectedness of the image which she calls 'intra-relations' where all parts of the image have an equal right to be heard, and which ought to encourage the analyst once again not to concentrate solely upon the protagonist, but all elements of the film's stylistic system and how they work together. She then considers 'value' as a reminder that while some images might seem more potent than others, the mundane is as important as the unusual. Small details in the cinematic text can offer a different contextualisation cue for the audience and work to undermine what is presented. The lengthy opening scenes of *I Am Love* (dir. Guadagnino, 2009) are full of small details about the family but which in fact tell the viewer all they need to know about the characters and their milieu. Berry concludes with a plea that form and content should not be considered separately. (The one element to her dream analysis which is less useful for consideration of the film text, is 'simultaneity' which is intended as a reminder not to impose narrative or progression upon a dream image, as this can detract from what is present and is likely to be an overlay of conscious activity on the image. Most film texts generally already have a narrative structure of some kind, though for more *avant garde* film texts this might prove an interesting perspective.)

Moving on from a strict consideration of the overt structures within the film text, a *post*-Jungian, post-structuralist point of view must then encourage a sensitivity to the 'excess' of the image (and sound) discussed earlier. Attention to what Rowland describes as 'the fleeting momentary presence of something that forever mutates and reaches beyond the ego's inadequate understanding' (Rowland, 2005, p. 3) that might include Kristeva's *signifiance*. To read in this way suggests a '[d]econstructive Jung challeng[ing] the founding dualism of ego and unconscious by reversing hierarchies and subjecting the ego to the multiple predations of the unconscious in individuation' (Rowland, 1999, p. 23). We must 'keep the ego out of it'. That 'sense of continuity' which seeks for structures and stability must be held to one side in order to allow the whispers, the movement out of the corner of one's eye, the fault lines in the filmic system, a still moment to come into focus; to look and listen for the presence in the filmic text 'of countertextual, interruptive locutions that may be embedded in the heterogenous quotations, phrases, formulas, already written discourse which each text as it were rewrites' (Linderman in Rosen, 1986, p. 144). Allowing that 'sense of continuity' to remain unchallenged is to fall back on a structuralist reading and leave the sense-making ego at the centre of any analysis. The opposing tendencies can be thought of as 'order and disorder' or perhaps 'arrangement' and 'derangement'.

From a post-Jungian point of view this must also be extended to any consideration of the archetypes. As Rowland so cogently points out:

> Jungian psychic images can fairly be called a 'kind of writing' after Derrida because they do work on a principle of 'difference' and 'deferral' or *différance*. Archetypal images are distinguished by their difference from each other and crucially defer infinitely a full and sufficient signified which would allow closure. The archetypal image can never comprehend the protean multiplicity of the archetype: its signified in the unconscious is deferred.
>
> *(Rowland, 1999, pp. 189–90)*

Since the post-Jungian model of the psyche understands it as always in motion, where the ego is but a temporary stabilisation of meaning, not a fixed eternal subject, any meaning associated with traces of the unconscious and the archetype must also remain contingent and temporary or the risk of reification and the closing down of meaning is all too present.

In *practical* terms this might mean attention to any unresolved details of the narrative, any *aporia*, any moment of non-coherence or moments of undecidability. It might also require consideration of what is 'not there' as a de-sedimenting of the text in a deconstructive mode requires alertness to the sides of the binary opposites not mentioned. It might also mean further attention to the excessiveness of the cinematic text, with its braids of codes. This might seem a relatively easy task with a film such as *The Piano Tuner of Earthquakes* (dir. Quay Brothers, 2005) which is replete with complex, evocative and troubling images within a drifting, hazy narrative; fragmentary texts such as *Don't Look Now* (dir. Roeg, 1973) or more recently the work of director Shane Carruth in *Primer* (2004) and *Upstream Color* (2013) where questions of identity and meaning abound in visually and aurally complex work. However, even the most classical Hollywood style of Hollywood classics such as *Casablanca* (dir. Curtiz, 1942) or *The Lady From Shanghai* (dir. Welles, 1948) have their famous moments of memory and fragmentation respectively.

Having examined the composition of the image, the next phase of elaboration is to make these elements of 'arrangement' and 'derangement' 'louder and larger' (Berry, 1974, p. 71) while still resisting closure of meaning. Berry calls this phase 'Implication' meaning one can draw implication from the image, though this is at a price. By moving away from image and into implication she says we forego the depths of the image – its limitless ambiguities, which can only partly be grasped as implications. 'So to expand upon the dream [text] is also to narrow it – a further reason we wish never to stray too far from the source' (Berry, 1974, p. 68). The purpose of this phase is to expand upon the image (not reduce) through techniques of such as amplification, restatement and analogy. This phase corresponds to Hockley's 'second image' where the text's meaning is explored 'as it arises from the necessarily distorting lens of interpretation' (Hockley, 2011, p. 140).

Berry's favoured method is amplification through cultural analogues, a well-established Jungian technique where as noted above 'mythic, historical and cultural parallels to clarify and make ample the metaphorical content of dream symbolism' (Samuels *et al.*, 1986, p. 16). As an approach it can, and has been, used within film analysis. Hillman, however, was suspicious of amplification as a technique as he felt it risked generality at the cost of precision and turning a symbol into a sign. He said 'we amplify an image by means of myth in order not to find its archetypal meaning, but in order to feed it with further images that increase its volume and depth and release its fecundity' (Hillman, 1990, p. 59). Instead of amplification, Hillman favoured a term borrowed from Berry, 'restatement' as a way of elaborating on and 'making ample' the image. She says 'By restatement I mean a metaphorical nuance, echoing or reflecting the text beyond its literal statement' (Berry, 1974, p. 73) which might be done in two ways – by replacing the actual words with synonyms and equivalents; second by restating in the same words but emphasising the metaphorical quality within the words themselves.

Hillman proposed a more radical 'rewriting' or analogy approach, which he describes at some length in *An Inquiry into Image*. Analogy, he suggests, asks the question 'what is this like?', where the answers are multiple not singular and are connected with each other but not identical, and are a way to keep the image fresh. Of course, any kind of analysis is a form of rewriting of the text, but more recently the practice of the 'video essay' has gained traction as a form of criticism (see McWhirter [2015] for more). Cinemetrics and other forms of data visualisation also constitute a more radical form of analogy that could develop in interesting directions as technology makes it more accessible.

Whilst this phase encourages elaboration and rewriting of the cinematic it is intended to emphasise the opening up of the text and resist closing down meaning. Instead the aim is to 'hold opposites in tension'; to 'sit with'; to ponder analogies; to make ample, to explore, to peer between the cracks, examine instabilities and contradictions, in order to glimpse the workings of a psyche which includes an active unconscious, a realm of the psyche as important as the more focused ego, an unconscious in the Jungian model that might whisper of compensation, a fresh perspective, of balance. This leads to the final phase which Berry titles, 'Supposition'.

Under 'supposition', suggests Berry, we might place any 'statement of causality, any if–then, because of this–that, interpretive move; likewise any generalisation made on the basis of the dream, any evaluation, prognosis, any use of past or future tense' (Berry, 1974, p. 74).

The Jungian perspective might thus offer a point of view that is both teleological and potentially therapeutic. As Dawson points out, Jung

> always tried to peer into its [the text's] underbelly, to reach beneath its surface structure of *literal concerns* to uncover unexpected tensions *and dynamics*. The primary characteristic of Jung's own criticism is that its conclusions are *radically* unexpected. By extension *Jungian criticism should never be predictable.*
>
> *(in Young-Eisendrath and Dawson, 2008, p. 292)*

This offers more than the traditional textual analysis by looking to where images of compensation can lead. Popularity of certain genres at certain times often correlate to cultural concerns and as discussed elsewhere (Miller, 2011b) a discourse analysis approach can be helpful in exploring collections of films in relation to the cultural unconscious.

Contemporary literary practice (such as feminism and post-colonialism) has aimed to employ deconstruction for ethical purposes and post-Jungian theory follows where it 'challenges the supremacy of the heroic ego, founded upon the binary suppression of the Other. Individuation means developing a narrative of becoming not I. The Other must be wooed as Other not possessed or suppressed' (Rowland, 1999, p. 23). Therefore the goal might be, along with other deconstructive practices to 'undo the mastering codes that subordinate the Other' (Rowland, 1999, p. 23). The challenge here may be to read against the grain and decentre the protagonist to hear the fainter voices of the supporting characters (see Miller, 2011a).

The teleological nature of the Jungian perspective is perhaps the hardest element to consider within the frame of a textual analysis per se, because it seems to demand a move away from the text. We have to turn to the audience and its relationship with the text. One might even suggest that there is a prevailing wind within Jungian theory that seems to encourage analysis away from the text itself, to incorporate a range of paratexts and transmediatised phenomenon, that stretches the concept of 'text' to breaking point. The teleological nature of the Jungian perspective coupled with the ongoing relationship with practising therapists within the field, mean that the question of the audience is always arising – a real, embodied, emotional, individual audience member. The role of the audience in meaning making *with* the film text within the wider cultural (collective) context is often where the post-Jungian textual analyst is drawn – as in Hockley's formulation of The Third Image.

This chapter has explored the text as a 'methodological field' examining some of the theoretical moves that took us from 'work' to 'text' along with some of the historical context of that theory, recognising that the study of film has situated itself within the same framework. Subjectivity proved an area of particular importance, with the formation of the subject seen as depending upon language and by extension textuality as a way of accounting for consciousness. I suggested that the ways of understanding the realm of 'before conscious' (the Real, semiotic *chora*, trace and collective unconscious) are metonymically related, but that Jung's view of this realm as a continuing integral part of the total psyche and an *active* agent in maintaining balance, is of additional use in textual analysis.

The *terroir* of Jungian textual analysis might be seen to partake of both structuralist and post-structuralist climates depending upon where one might be standing upon the slopes of the academy. Just as Kristeva sought to follow the traces of *signifiance* through the Text, or Derrida paid attention to the 'trace', a post-Jungian textual analysis is a way of attending to the image, sitting with that 'fleeting momentary presence' (to borrow from Rowland) of something beyond conscious knowledge that seems to elude us and yet which often times draws us back with its affect laden images. The *terroir* of Jungian textual analysis is a complex one, not ignorant of the effectiveness of structuralist and post-structuralist foundations, it is none the less developing its own distinctive flavours.

References

Barker, C. (2004) *The SAGE dictionary of cultural studies*. London: SAGE Publications Ltd.

Barker, J. (2009) *The tactile eye: touch and the cinematic experience*. Berkeley, CA: University of California Press.

Barry, P. (1995/2009) *Beginning theory: an introduction to literary and cultural theory*. Manchester: Manchester University Press.

Barthes, R. (1978) 'From work to text', in S. Heath (ed.), *Image – music – text*. New York: Farrar, Straus & Giroux. pp. 155–64.

Barthes, R. (1990) 'Theory of the text', in R. Young (ed.), *Untying the text: a post structuralist reader*. London: Routledge. pp. 31–47.

Baumlin, J. S., Baumlin, T. F. and Jensen, G. H. (eds) (2004) *Post-Jungian criticism: theory and practice*. Albany, NY: State University of New York Press.

Berry, P. (1974) 'An approach to the dream', *Spring: A Journal of Archetype and Culture*. New Orleans: Spring Journal and Books. pp. 58–79.

Bradley, A. (2008) *Derrida's of grammatology*. Edinburgh: Edinburgh University Press.

Branigan, E. and Buckland, W. (2013) *The Routledge encyclopedia of film theory*. London: Routledge.

Brooke, R. (1991) *Jung and phenomenology*. Routledge: London.

Campbell, J. (2008) *The hero with a thousand faces*. Novato, CA: New World Library.

Dawson, T. (2008) 'Literary criticism and analytical psychology', in P. Young-Eisendrath and T. Dawson (eds), *The Cambridge companion to Jung*. Cambridge: Cambridge University Press. pp. 269–98.

Derrida, J. (1976) *Of grammatology*. Baltimore, MD: Johns Hopkins University Press.

Derrida, J. (2004) 'Living on', in H. Bloom (ed.), *Deconstruction and criticism*. London and New York: Continuum Publishing Company. pp. 62–142.

Eisold, K. (2001) 'Institutional conflicts in Jungian analysis', *Journal of Analytical Psychology*, 46(2), pp. 335–53.

ffrench, P. (2015) 'Tel Quel: theory and practice', in M. Grishakova and S. Salupere (eds), *Theoretical schools and circles in the twentieth-century humanities*. London: Routledge. pp. 99–114.

Gaston, S. and Maclachlan, I. (2011) *Reading Derrida's of grammatology*. London: Continuum.

Glover, E. (1950) *Freud or Jung*. London: George Allan & Unwin.

Grossberg, L. (1997) *Bringing it all back home: essays on cultural studies*. Durham, NC: Duke University Press.

Hauke, C. (2000) *Jung and the postmodern: the interpretation of realities*. London: Routledge.

Hauke, C. and Hockley, L. (2011) *Jung & film II: the return*. Hove: Routledge.

Hillman, J. (1976) *Re-visioning psychology*. New York: Harper & Row.

Hillman, J. (1977) 'An inquiry into image', *Spring: A Journal of Archetype and Culture*. New Orleans: Spring Journal and Books. pp. 62–88.

Hillman, J. (1978) 'Further notes on images', *Spring: A Journal of Archetype and Culture*. New Orleans: Spring Journal and Books. pp. 152–82.

Hillman, J. (1990) *The essential James Hillman: a blue fire*, ed. T. Moore. London: Routledge.

Hockley, L. (2011) 'The third image: depth psychology and the cinematic experience', in C. Hauke and L. Hockley (eds), *Jung and film II: the return*. Hove: Routledge. pp. 32–147.

Hockley, L. (2015) 'Jungian screen studies – "Everything is awesome …?"' *International Journal of Jungian Studies*, 7(1), pp. 55–66.

Houdebine, J. (1979) 'Jung et Joyce', *Tel Quel*, 81(Autumn), pp. 63–5.

Izod, J. and Dovalis, J. (2015) *Cinema as therapy: grief and transformational film*. Hove: Routledge.

Jung, C. G. (1921) 'Definitions', in *The collected works of C. G. Jung*, Vol. 6, *Psychological types*, 3rd edn. London: Routledge & Kegan Paul, 1971.

Jung, C. G. (1938) 'Foreword to the third edition of the development of the personality', in *The collected works of C. G. Jung*, Vol. 17, *The development of the personality*, 3rd edn. London: Routledge, 1954.

Jung, C. G. (1940) 'The psychology of the child archetype', in *The collected works of C. G. Jung*, Vol. 9i, *The archetypes and the collective unconscious*, 2nd edn. London: Routledge, 1968.

Jung, C. G. (1954) 'On the nature of the psyche', in *The collected works of C. G. Jung*, Vol. 8, *The structure and dynamics of the psyche*, 2nd edn. London: Routledge & Kegan Paul, 1960.

Jung, C. G. (1955–6) 'The personification of the opposites', in *The collected works of C. G. Jung*, Vol. 14, *Mysterium coniunctionis*, 2nd edn. London: Routledge, 1955–6.

Jung, C. G. (1957) 'The transcendent function', in *The collected works of C. G. Jung*, Vol. 8, *The structure and dynamics of the psyche*, 2nd edn. London: Routledge & Kegan Paul Ltd, 1960.

Kirsch, T. (2000) *The Jungians: a comparative and historical perspective.* London: Routledge.

Kristeva, J. (1980) *Desire in language: a semiotic approach to literature and art.* Columbia, NY: Columbia University Press.

Kugler, P. (1990) 'The unconscious in a postmodern depth psychology', in K. Barnaby and P. D'Acierno (eds), *C. G. Jung and the humanities: toward a hermeneutics of culture.* London: Routledge. pp. 307–17.

Linderman, D. (1986) 'Uncoded images in the heterogenous text', in P. Rosen (ed.), *Narrative, apparatus, ideology: a film theory reader.* Columbia, NY: Columbia University Press. pp. 143–5.

McWhirter, A. (2015) 'Film criticism, film scholarship and the video essay', *Screen*, 56(3), pp. 369–77.

Miller, C. (2011a) 'I feel like a failure: in-house feminism', in L. Hockley and L. Gardner (eds), *House: the wounded healer on television: Jungian and post-Jungian reflections.* Hove: Routledge. pp. 188–203.

Miller, C. (2011b) 'Twilight: discourse theory and Jung', in C. Hauke and L. Hockley (eds), *Jung & film II: the return.* Hove: Routledge. pp. 185–205.

Miller, D. L. (1992) 'The "stone" which is not a stone: C. G. Jung and the postmodern meaning of "meaning"', in R. K. Papadopoulos (ed.), *Carl Gustav Jung: critical assessments.* London: Routledge. pp. 268–78.

Norris, C. (2003) *Deconstruction: theory and practice.* London: Routledge.

Reynolds, J. and Roffe, J. (2004) *Understanding Derrida.* London: Continuum.

Rose, G. (2016) *Visual methodologies: an introduction to researching with visual materials*, 4th edn. London: SAGE Publications.

Rowland, S. (1999) *C. G. Jung and literary theory: the challenge from fiction.* Basingstoke and London: Macmillan Press.

Rowland, S. (2002) *Jung: a feminist revision.* Cambridge, Polity Press.

Rowland, S. (2005) *Jung as a writer.* London: Routledge.

Rowland, S. (2017) *Remembering Dionysus.* Hove: Routledge.

Samuels, A. (1985/1994) *Jung and the post-Jungians.* London: Routledge.

Samuels, A. (1998) 'Will the post-Jungians survive?' in A. Casement (ed.), *Post-Jungians today: key papers in contemporary analytical psychology.* London: Routledge. pp. 15–32.

Samuels, A., Shorter, B. and Plaut, F. (1991) *A critical dictionary of Jungian analysis.* London: Routledge.

Singh, G. (2014) *Feeling film: affect and authenticity in popular cinema.* Hove: Routledge.

Smith, A. (1998) *Julia Kristeva: speaking the unspeakable.* London: Pluto Press.

Thompson, K. (1986) 'The concept of cinematic excess', in P. Rosen (ed.), *Narrative, apparatus, ideology: a film theory reader.* Columbia, NY: Columbia University Press. pp. 130–42.

Vannoy, A. M. (1989) 'Deconstructive philosophy and imaginal psychology: comparative perspectives on Jacques Derrida and James Hillman', in Rajnath (ed.), *Deconstruction: a critique.* Basingstoke: Macmillan Press. pp. 138–57.

Vogler, C. (2007) *The writer's journey: mythic structure for writers.* San Francisco, CA: Michael Wiese Productions.

Filmography

Casablanca. (1942) [film] Directed by Michael Curtiz. USA.

Don't look now. (1973) [film] Directed by Nicolas Roeg. UK.

I am love. (2009) [film] Directed by Luca Guadagino. Italy.

Lady from Shanghai, The. (1948) [film] Directed by Orson Welles. USA.

Neon demon. (2016) [film] Directed by Nicholas Winding-Refn. Denmark.

Piano tuner of earthquakes, The. (2005) [film] Directed by Quay Brothers. Germany.

Primer. (2004) [film] Directed by Shane Carruth. USA.

Upstream color. (2013) [film] Directed by Shane Carruth. USA.

Valhalla rising. (2009) [film] Directed by Nicholas Winding-Refn. Denmark.

2

DIONYSUS AND TEXTUALITY

Hockley's somatic cinema for a transdisciplinary film studies

Susan Rowland

Introduction

There is a problem in applying the psychology of C. G. Jung to the textual analysis of films. It is a problem for all such psychological processes and is apparent in the word 'apply'. How can what has been devised for one reality, the human psyche, be a means of making knowledge about another reality, the film as text? After all, unlike the dreams that the psychologies of the unconscious, like Jung's, consider their base material, films have a substantial existence outside human subjectivity. They are constructed by highly specialized professions, using increasingly esoteric technology and are addressed to a mass audience in the case of mainstream 'Hollywood' movies. Surely to 'apply' a psychology is to violate something in the very nature of film itself as a *cultural* rather than psychological artefact?

This chapter will argue that Dionysus should be admitted to the study of making meaning from texts – the practice known as hermeneutics. There are more gods in film texts than tricky Hermes for which hermeneutics is named. By exploring and contextualizing Luke Hockley's groundbreaking research in his *Somatic Cinema* (2014), I will show how his exploration of the somatic or bodily image in cinema experience can be regarded as heralding a new, Dionysian and transdisciplinary paradigm for Film Studies.

Hockley's somatic image will be characterized as a Dionysian textuality that is simultaneously validated by Basarab Nicolescu's transdisciplinarity (Rowland, 2017). In the world of competing and multiple academic disciplines, transdisciplinarity is predicated on multiple realities and the logic of the included middle between them (more on this later). Such a revisioned somatic textuality is Jungian because it is activated through his understanding of the archetypal and Dionysian nature of the psyche. Characterized by transgressing boundaries, Dionysus is a god designed to overcome disciplinary borders. Far from destroying them, his capacity to re-member provides a new disciplinary framework leading to a rejuvenation of consciousness. In Dionysian textuality, knowing renews being.

In this way analysis of films is no longer limited to treating them as texts in the sense of privileged objects, or determined *only* by collective historical forces. I will end by showing how Jung anticipates such a dismembering move in his radically experimental *Red Book* (Jung, 2009). Jungian film studies shows how the embodied image is potentially a Dionysian re-membering of who we can be – through movies. We begin with the 'third image'.

Hockley's somatic 'third image'

Hockley's third image could be regarded as divorcing itself from the analysis of the film as text.

> Meaning comes from the intermingling of our individual psychology with the film, its narrative, images and sounds, in order to create a new meaning. This new meaning does not come directly from the screen, nor does it come from the intellectual investigations of consciousness. To repeat, this is the third image and it takes the form of an unexpected, powerful emotional response, almost as though we have lost our mind and have been taken over by something else. We are losing the plot, yet as the narrative of the film fades into the background, so the narrative of our life comes to the fore.
>
> *(Hockley, 2014, p. 135)*

What is so exciting about this somatic 'third image' is that it overcomes the epistemological and ontological objections to 'applying' Jungian psychology as yet another intellectual frame to those already organizing our understanding of films. It does so by allowing the dynamic experience of the cinema to populate the psychological drama that makes up an individual. This chapter will show just how Dionysian, rejuvenating and transdisciplinary such a move can be.

As Hockley positions his innovation, his 'first image' is that painted by technology upon the screen itself; the film as we witness it. The second image is the intellectually constructed meaning beloved of Film Studies as an academic discipline of the film, as having its own discrete being in the world. After all, a film possesses material substance and is often constructed as a text.

> The object of understanding is the film and the approach is one of conscious hermeneutic activity … I call this the second image as it is the image that we create in our mind of what the film is about, of what the film is trying to explore and how we understand it.
>
> *(ibid., p. 134)*

Key words here are 'object' and 'conscious'. This is hermeneutics of the film as discrete object, privileging the conscious mind (not body) and its intellectual capacities. This rational preference in film analysis might push aside a psychology that includes the unconscious as a vital, even vitalizing part of its reach. Hence the need for a 'third image' as Hockley shows, not just for the desire to include the body as an organ of knowing in cinema experience, but because conventional textual approaches to film either omit, or cannot account for, the personal investment and idiosyncratic reactions we have when going to the movies. Since the unconscious is invoked in the cinema *and as a result of cinema*, it is a worthy component of a hermeneutics that regards the film text as an active and unpredictable contributor to psychological meaning and being.

Crucially, the notion of the third image expands the dynamic of film beyond the film as separate object. It mingles the experience of film with the experiencing psyche which is also an embodied psyche. Hence the third image requires what Hockley defines as the 'cinematic frame' (ibid., pp. 82–7). Unlike the film frame of movies as text and object, the cinematic frame encompasses the entire ritual of attending a cinema, the embodied psychological experience and reactions to the movie, and how we unconsciously, unknowingly, produce a meaningful reaction to the film afterwards.

Hockley explores his cinematic frame in order to look at the somatic expression of unconscious affects that develop as we encounter a film in the ritual space of the cinema (ibid., pp. 33–4). He draws attention to the way cinema going evokes an aspect of ancient religious practices such as the paying of money to enter another world (like paying the ferryman to cross the river Styx), entering a darkened space at a set time and place, and the way we like to discuss films afterwards in an uprush of emotion, often negotiating meanings with other people as part of a rite of intimacy (ibid., p. 37).

Somatic Cinema's exploration of film as ritual in a Jungian context suggests that the drive we have towards meaning, however personal and idiosyncratic, is what Jung called 'archetypal', drawing upon collective psychic energies housed in the body that tend to incarnate images and meaning that are culturally influenced yet not culturally determined. Some Jungians, notably James Hillman, prefer to call theses energies gods for their powerful, often overwhelming influence upon being (Hillman, 1972).

Taking Hockley's third image as a hermeneutical practice, as I do here, points to even more gods than tricky Hermes in the negotiation of texts. Above all, regarding the text in the *cinematic* frame of embodiment, collective communal ritual and as producing ecstatic results that entirely erode the distinction between human observing subject and film as textual object; such an immersion in fluid epistemological potency belongs to Dionysus. To show how such a framing of the frame has radical disciplinary consequences brings us to questions of how textuality came to be so dismembered in the first place. Why should hermeneutics be restricted to one god, meaning one orientation to psychic being?

Film texts and literary studies in the subject/object split

Film Studies derives much of its emphasis on the text as discrete object of narrative analysis from the relatively recent academic traditions of literary studies, itself established not long after the formation of psychology as a discipline (Eagleton, 1983). Psychology and literature as academic fields emerged from social, educational and cultural revolutions in the nineteenth century. Indeed, prior to the expansion of education especially the United States and Britain, power over knowing in Western universities polarized between the natural sciences and philology, the study of language in written forms. Philology was then a combination of its successor areas of literature, history and linguistics. It concentrated upon examining the reliability of historical sources, language variations and their interpretation (Wilson, 2002).

During the later nineteenth century, a progressive movement developed that demanded education be extended beyond the upper classes, and that learning should be oriented to what was socially useful. An immediate result was the rejection of philology's stress on historical documents, in favour of adopting the empirical methods of the natural sciences for the same intellectual pursuits. The Social Sciences were born of this triumph of empiricism, the notion that all knowledge is derived from actual experience, and positivism, the standpoint that reality is intrinsically independent of consciousness (Saban, 2014, p. 35). If reality is ontologically separate from the psyche, 'out there', rather than caught up with our perceptions, then it can be studied objectively as quite apart from human desires, feelings and motivations, whether known or unknown. Here is born the notion that even the proper study of what produces strong emotion, such as the arts and cinema, should be studied with detachment, as an object.

Literary studies, a discipline devoted to imaginative works in the vernacular, began with a complex relationship to the rise of progressive Social Sciences. On the one hand, it proclaimed a progressive emphasis on the communication of human experience, rather than abstract ideas deemed less socially useful. On the other hand, it was devised as a discipline to replace Classics as the vehicle for moulding aesthetic taste, promulgating great 'truths', and communicating imaginative realities (Wilson, 2002, p. 67).

In an academy dominated by empiricism, given that English, as literary studies is commonly known, had taken on the socially coded justification as the guardian of aesthetics and values, it badly needed a way to fend off charges that it lacked such validation for the knowledge it produced. Literature as a discipline was driven by the need for a theory that could justify its own existence by showing that it was open to an objective and concrete grasp of reality. The result was what came to be known as New Criticism, which enshrined a form of hermeneutics that proved influential for the emergence of textual analysis in Film Studies.

The New Criticism: as a progenitor of film analysis

New Criticism began in America and Britain with a partial endorsement of positivism and empiricism in objectivity, and a determined attempt to carve out an independent ontology or 'being' for literature. Literary works would be examined as wholly independent artefacts. Knowledge of them would be severed from the circumstances of their production (authors) and reception (readers). Inevitably, this attitude would wall off new social science disciplines devoted to other fragments of reality in this torn apart empiricist paradigm, such as psychology.

Literature was endowed with its own Being, which can be understood entirely 'objectively'. Literary texts (and later films) were to be objects explored with as little reference to human subjects as possible. The author has no say in the critical meaning of her work, nor should anything personal from the critic be a factor (Wimsatt, 1954; Brooks, 1956). A literary text, and later a film, is an object with its own meaning.

A new discipline, however in debt to scientific positivism, needs a new epistemology and methodology to exhibit its unique perspective on being and knowing. Named by Richards as 'practical criticism', and later known as 'close reading', this newly focused hermeneutics enforced the most careful scrutiny of words on the page, while stripping out any possible context that might daringly claim to be a co-text capable of affecting interpretation (Richards, 1929).

Forbidden contexts include emotions, feelings, personal associations, anything known of the author or time of writing and word etymologies. The poem, play, novel (and later film) etc. is an organic, autonomous entity (Eagleton, 1983, p. 29). Existing in an independent reality, it is capable of a wholeness and balance not to be disturbed by human inadequacy, historical contingency or cultural differences.

Nothing can be more dismissive of psychology than such textual criticism's ideology of empirical objectivity: the words of *this* text are empirical data wholly severed from contaminating consciousness. It is here that Jung's work is a counter-tendency to the splitting of learning into ever more scholarly disciplines, as he too advocates hermeneutics, the study of making meaning from texts.

Jung's way of knowing or epistemology, is primarily through the image, which means the manifestation of psyche that is ultimately oriented towards meaning-making. Images can be found in dreams, sounds, bodily symptoms, visual manifestations and words. When images are suffused with psyche as not fully knowable, they become what Jung called symbols for they evoke being beyond the full possibility of conscious knowing or expressing (1921: §819). The symbol to Jung is rooted in the body and shaped by its archetypal energies. Hockley's third image, somatic, non-rational and with an emphasis on the mysterious, is a Jungian symbol.

Hence the symbol and third image are, in Jungian terms, materialized imagination. Such entities are hermeneutic *and* creative of psychological being. The third image is textual in the sense that it creates body, psyche and cinematic frame into a textual mesh with the body that is radically transgressive of boundaries of being. Moreover, Jung explicitly recognizes that hermeneutics (as the art of interpreting texts) is a way of knowing the world by provoking exploration and discovery. Such work unites individual subjectivity with objective collectivity, whether the collective is of the unknown psyche or of human disciplinary knowledge. As Jung notes:

> The essential character of hermeneutics, a science which was widely practiced in former times, consists in making successive additions of other analogies to the analogy given in the symbol: in the first place of subjective analogies found by the analyst in the course of erudite research … in which certain 'lines' of psychological development stand out as possibilities that are at once individual and collective. There is no science on earth by which these lines could be proved 'right'. Their validity is proved by their intense value for life.
>
> *(1916: §495)*

In espousing 'intense value for life', Jung is talking the language of a hermeneutics reaching beyond Hermes to a more somatically rejuvenating deity. It is time to recognize the presence of Dionysus animating Hockley's cinematic frame.

Dionysus and dismembering/remembering for Jung and film

We come to Dionysus in film by way of psychologist James Hillman's ground changing perception that this boundary transgressing god signifies a radical deconstruction of being to Jung. In 'Dionysus in Jung's Writings', Hillman points out that Jung stresses 'dismemberment' as his key narrative in the many stories of Dionysus (1972/2007). In Jung's version, Hillman sees a possibility of psychic rejuvenation in the corporeal dismembering of an ageing god. The god ripe for dismemberment is for Hillman an Apollonian version of monotheism. 'He' is ageing because his Apollonian distancing devices such as empiricism have become arid because they are too long taken the dominant way of knowing. In his loneliness, 'he' condemns us to an over-emphasis of rational knowing and separateness taken to excess. The result is a repression of bodily and instinctual life with tragic results for psychic wellbeing.

Born from an illicit union of mortal, Semele, and god, Zeus, baby Dionysus is ripped apart by the titans, instigated by Hera, Zeus's jealous wife. Rhea, daughter of Earth goddess, Gaia and sky god Uranus re-members the divine child. Subsequently, of course, Dionysus inspires what he has suffered: for refusing to worship this dangerous deity, Pentheus is torn to pieces by maenads, women maddened by Dionysian rites. Those who do not make a place for Dionysian excesses in being are at risk of being dismembered by the savagery they have defied.

According to Hillman, Jung sees a two stage dismembering process: first comes a division into opposites, such as the very notion of the Apollonian and Dionysian itself. Less prominent in Jung's writing is the second stage of Dionysian dismemberment, the god is scattered into pieces. Therefore Hillman's understanding of Jung's Dionysus shows a dualistic opposition transfigured into multiplicity. The god is dismembered, seeding the divine in matter. To both Jung and Hillman inspired matter is archetypal, the multiplicity of psychic archetypes. As Jung comments: 'Dionysus is the abyss of impassioned dissolution, where all human distinctions are merged in the animal divinity of the primordial psyche – a blissful and terrible experience' (1944: §118).

Dionysus re-forms, is re-membered, in order to renew consciousness. Instead of a distant divinity that has lost contact with the human psyche, a god of frenzy or of the shady woods (like a darkened cinema) is torn apart to re-member the divine in nature, including human nature. Dionysus dismembered can find his way from the wild woods to the somatic cinematic frame as I will show. He does so in the material presence of symbols rooted in the body and inspired, in-spirited, by movies.

For Hillman we enter a new cosmos with the dispersed fragments of the body of the god (1983/2007, p. 26). Distance from the divine is replaced, re-placed, by interiority and animistic multiplicity within the domain of the god. We are *inside* his instinctual being that also has a home *within* us. 'The movement between the first and second view of dismemberment compares with crossing a psychic border between seeing the god from outside or from within his cosmos' (ibid., p. 26).

Do we not similarly experience film as a confounding of inside and outside? Cinema promotes a sense of entry into the magical space of film, which we then take away as renewed interiority. Symptomatically, Hillman notes that *zoe*, the life force of the body in *Eros*, is roused by this process of divine dismemberment (ibid., p. 29). This new consciousness, or *zoe*, is an intimation of wholeness that does not remove differences. New enlivening *zoe* is animistic in a particular awareness of its own *partial* consciousness, e.g. aware of itself as *parts*. Hillman comments:

> Rather the crucial experience would be the awareness of the parts *as parts* distinct from each other, dismembered, each with its own light, a state in which the body becomes conscious of itself as a composite of differences. The scintillae and fishes eyes of which Jung speaks … may be experienced as embedded in physical expressions. The distribution of Dionysus through matter may be compared with the distribution of consciousness through members, organs, and zones.
>
> *(ibid., p. 28)*

Renewed consciousness returns in Jung's work as dismembered Dionysus, the fragmented divine body seeding the universe with its archetypes, and so too film in the 'third image' activates bodily and instinctual life. But this is not all, since the Greek pantheon itself is by nature polytheistic. One god alone makes no sense, is nonsense. It is no accident that these gods are involved with each other, incestuous, quarrelsome and unable to leave humans alone. They *must* be mated or related.

Dionysus brings with his energies a relation to human vulnerability. He rescues a forlorn woman, Ariadne, who was abandoned by her lover, Theseus. She becomes his wife and is deified. Here too is a suggestion that Dionysian renewal is a taste of the sacred; that cinema is a path to rejuvenation because its symbolic properties transcend human limitations, just as a film can outlive us.

Archetypalist Karl Kerenyi puts it this way, 'Just as Dionysos is the archetypal reality of *zoe*, so Ariadne is the archetypal reality of the bestowal of soul, of what makes a living creature an individual' (1976, p. 124). He describes *zoe* as instinctual life experienced without limits, just as cinema takes us beyond our creaturely incarnation to other worlds (ibid., p. xxxvi). To Kerenyi, Ariadne wedding Dionysus is the marriage of instinctual differentiated life force with soul focus and the compassion of a human animal with its creaturely limits. Ariadne ensouls Dionysian *zoe*, gives it humanity just as Hockley describes happening in the consulting room. There patients possessed by Dionysian film symbols need to make a marriage with their actual pains, histories and lives.

Ariadne, or the feminine, makes Dionysian limitlessness creaturely, bearable, experienceable. I will propose that the marriage of Ariadne and Dionysus makes the rejuvenation by *zoe knowable*. In this way Hockley's third image becomes a Dionysian hermeneutics. It is a way of knowing film texts by being dismembered by them, and re-membered in the consulting room or wherever and however we find ways to humanize those beyond-human properties of cinema. To provide an academic context for film's Dionysian hermeneutics, I will introduce transdisciplinarity. First approach to transdisciplinarity is by a closer look at the third image as Jungian symbols.

Holding symbols as Ariadne marriage to Dionysus

Whether a thing is a symbol or not depends chiefly on the attitude of the observing consciousness; for instance, on whether it regards a given fact not merely as such but also as an expression for something unknown.

(Jung, 1921: §818)

I suggest that Dionysian dismemberment as Jung and Hillman together see it is a fundamental condition of fragmented modern consciousness that is directly addressed by the cinematic frame and larger contexts. For not only does dismemberment haunt the fragile modern Western ego, but it also pervades knowledge itself through its splintering into academic disciplines. So let us consider the psychology of both Jung and Hillman as offering the opportunity of *zoe* as rejuvenated consciousness, by remembering the Dionysian body *as parts*.

Such remembering occurs individually in patients in psychotherapy, and, I have suggested, collectively in the cinema. Could this psychic rejuvenation also happen collectively in academia by re-modelling disciplines as *parts* of a never entirely knowable (and so divine), body? It would mean that the urge to know would be infused with the desire to be alive, just as cinema provides such a Dionysian initiation.

Three aspects this mythical perspective on knowing could contribute to re-membering disciplines as parts, which would, at the very least, re-member film studies in relation to its adjacent forms of knowing. They are the role of symbols in wedding immanent and transcendent modes of being, Ariadne as symbol of feminine ensoulment of *zoe*, and, third, transdisciplinarity, which will be considered below.

First of all, on the symbol: Jung saw its most defining quality as its capacity to express something unknown that wants to come into being. His symbols are dynamic and alive. They provide what Hillman calls *zoe*, an experience of instinctual life, in their rebirthing of consciousness. As Jung comments: 'A symbol really lives only when it is the best and highest expression for something divined but not yet known to the observer. It then compels his unconscious participation and has a life-giving and life-enhancing effect' *(ibid.: §819)*.

Jung's reference here to the 'best and highest' is a clue to the symbol's ability to unite transcendence and immanence. For a symbol's route to the unknown invokes the archetypal qualities of psyche, those capacities possess roots in the instinctual body, while also extending to the realm of spirit and rational knowing. In this context, even academic disciplinary concepts are symbols when they do *not* forget their connection to the 'living mystery'. As Jung puts it: 'We have to break down life and events, which are self-contained processes, into meanings, images, concepts, well knowing that in doing so we are getting further away from the living mystery' (1922: §121).

Dionysus is the mythical embodiment of such 'living mystery' (ibid.). It follows that if knowledge can break down life and events into parts that retain awareness of the living mystery, then that knowledge, written in symbols is Dionysian re-membering. Such a renewed vision of the array of different disciplines to be found in universities would return *zoe* to learning itself.

Such a reanimation of disciplinary relations as would see them as *parts* joined by immersion in living mystery, in the body of knowledge as dismembering, remembering Dionysus, rather than distant, dead Apollo. Such knowledge in *zoe* will be written in symbols. 'Since every scientific theory contains an hypothesis … it is a symbol' (1921: §817). On the other hand, Dionysus is a dangerous god to approach too closely, or to offend. Limitless instinctual life as consciousness sounds like a prelude to a maenad condition of inhuman frenzy. *Zoe* must be ensouled, so that Dionysus enters the human world through compassionate love, rather than mindless sacrifice, or sacrifice of the mind. Here Ariadne returns as the mistreated, undervalued and abandoned feminine of our age. Stranded far from home, she has been divorced from her divine earthly roots and denied the hero's embrace and queenly status. She is lost, and she has been lost to us just as our academic disciplines have renounced feeling as *Eros*.

Filmgoers intuitively experience knowledge enacted in symbols (the third image) are fragments of the living mystery, or ecstatic god, made soul-full by psyche as Ariadne. It is time to look at how transdisciplinary practice also plots to re-story being through knowing.

Transdisciplinarity and Dionysus for Dionysian cinema

A psychologically promising form of transdisciplinarity is that proposed by Basarab Nicolescu as a vision of an open system of knowing (Nicolescu, 2005). For this transdisciplinary paradigm, no knowledge can ever be considered complete (ibid.). Nicolescu gave an overview in his talk at the Congress of Transdisciplinarity in Brazil in 2005, later published as 'Transdisciplinarity – Past, Present and Future' (ibid.). G. C. Tympas is probably the first to make extensive use of transdisciplinarity in Jungian research in his fine *Carl Jung and Maximus the Confessor on Psychic Development* (2014).

Nicolescu refuses the totalizing project inherent in some definitions of transdisciplinarity by rejecting any possibility of a hyperdiscipline, one capable of subsuming all human knowing into a system of perfect knowledge, or ultimate truth. Rather, his structuring emphasizes what he calls 'beyond disciplines' in his transdisciplinarity, which means beyond the claims of any one epistemological construct to encompass all meaning. In this sense, a single god-like vision for total knowledge gives way to a polyvalent polytheism of knowing. Dionysus gets into the picture.

Bound up in Nicolescu's rejection of a hyperdiscipline is his dismissal of the traditional unified human subject of Western modernity, or, to put another way, of rational consciousness as a sufficient and only basis for knowledge. After the discoveries of quantum physics, he posits a new human subject for *all* research. No longer should research assume the primacy of the criteria of objectivity, e.g. absolute separation between the observer and the observed, because the quantum scientist discovered that the way phenomena are measured radically changes the results. Empiricism as the dominant mode of making knowledge is over.

While on the one hand transdisciplinarity does aim for a hypothesized unity in knowing, Nicolescu's radically 'open' unity means accepting that humans live on many levels of reality simultaneously. It will never be possible to rationally know all psycho-physical realities, not least because some are neither measurable nor stable. In transdisciplinarity, these realities cannot be eroded or simplified (ibid., p. 4). Knowledge therefore will always be in a state of dismemberment despite, or maybe because of, our legacy of a culture of only one divine body (of truth).

Nicolescu recognizes that different disciplines are necessary to respond to these irreconcilable plural realities of being. Here we start to see a role for Hockley's third image and Dionysian textuality. While much Film Studies analyses of texts concentrate on the second image of rational argument, Hockley's somatic cinema image is a momentary union of body, psyche and text largely invisible to rationalization. It occurs where Film Studies's concern with screen texts meets the Jungian understanding of the embodied psyche. Somatic cinema re-members in Dionysian ecstatic imaging, imagining, a dismembered body of multiple realities.

Returning briefly to transdisciplinarity, Nicolescu offers three axioms of transdisciplinarity to replace those of traditional science that go back to Galileo. Hitherto, many scientific disciplines adhered to the following axioms or fundamental assumptions (extracted from Nicolescu, 2005, p. 5):

1   The universe is governed by mathematical laws.
2   These laws can be discovered by scientific experiment.
3   Such experiments, if valid, can be perfectly replicated.

Such a privileging of objectivity founds the historical human subject as a creature of purely rational consciousness. All other unfortunate or messy human qualities need to be screened out so that the unvarnished empirical facts of the universe may be received without interference or prejudice. Of course, as Nicolescu emphasizes, such an approach to knowledge has the effect of turning the human subject into an object by removing feeling and values (ibid.). Fortunately those qualities are poised to return in the somatic third image.

Transdisciplinarity addresses head on the problem lies in the positing of *one* level of reality as foundational to all others. This single way of structuring knowing (hyperdiscipline) then subsumes realities like society or the psyche to its objectivizing paradigm. In such a framework, the rational *objective* study of film texts is to be preferred above the joyful, instinctual, bodily reaction to them. By contrast, Nicolescu's transdisciplinarity does away with privileging objectivity based on separation because of the human subject's complexity, which exists in both simple and theoretical senses as we will see. Nicolescu's fundamental principles (ibid., p. 6), or three axioms for knowing in transdisciplinarity, are as follows:

1   The ontological axiom: *there are, in Nature and in our knowledge of Nature, different levels of Reality and, correspondingly, different levels of perception.*
2   The logical axiom: *the passage from one level of Reality to another is insured by the logic of the included middle.*
3   The complexity axiom: *the Structure of the totality of levels of Reality or perception is a complex structure: every level is what it is because all levels exist at the same time.*

This approach to what we know and how we know it amounts to a paradigm shift from the competition of disciplines insisting on their separate perspectives to one that treats the universe as multi-dimensional. Reality is now complex. So are human beings. Nicolescu insists that no one level of reality, such as sight perception, for example, can constitute a dominant position for knowing. No sense organ or academic discipline is capable of understanding all the other levels of reality. Whatever the knowledge claims, it will be incomplete or open (ibid., p. 7). The single god of our historic privileging of rational objectivity is in pieces. 'He' cannot be put together to make a perfect being. Knowing can no longer be carved to imitate an ego divorced from the other.

Here transdisciplinarity joins Jung and the third image in showing that the boundaries of subjectivity are as fluid as those of knowing. We are not imprisoned in our bodies; rather 'inside' and 'outside' are revealed as cultural constructs, not inevitable and fixed states. 'Knowledge is neither exterior nor interior: it is simultaneously exterior and interior. The studies of the universe and of the human being sustain one another' (ibid., p. 8).

Or, put another way, the text of the film does not end with the frame of the screen but embraces the somatic psyche of the viewer. As Nicolescu reiterates, his transdisciplinarity vitally undoes the classical subject/object division in favour of the ternary: subject, object, hidden third that is both subject and object (ibid.). Here a film is the material prompt for the 'hidden third' that is Hockley's third image.

In fact Hockley's third image is a superb example of the 'included middle' that Nicolescu says is characteristic of transdisciplinarity. Logic governing the old scientific paradigm dictated that A cannot also be B. The included middle says otherwise. A can also be non-A. The somatic image is both viewer and screen, the included middle between two hitherto considered separate entities.

'Complexity', too, needs a context for its inclusion in Nicolescu's transdisciplinarity. Arguably, the development of Complexity Theory, or 'emergence' as an evolutionary paradigm towards the end of the twentieth century was a necessary prerequisite for Nicolescu's project. Complexity Theory, or emergence, suggests that evolutionary change occurred *and still occurs*, not by species competing for resources, but rather by the interpenetration of complex life systems. For Dionysian textuality the irreducible complexity of the human embodied psyche meets the material, cultural and historical complexity of a movie and what happens when complex systems meet is that the result is unpredictable, new, the third image.

This hypothesis of complexity has been extended to Jungian psychology by scholars such as Helene Shulman and Joe Cambray (Shulman, 1997; Cambray, 2012). They look at how Jung's synchronicity and archetypes could connect with this new evolutionary perspective. For archetypes can be seen as organs of complexity evolution in which complex adaptive systems like the human psyche and body interact with incredibly complex environmental systems to produce something unpredictable by the old scientific paradigm. Transdisciplinarity provides a loose, fragmented and continually changing not-limited-to-human disciplinary body for complexity evolution. It is, I suggest, a Dionysian body of dismembering and remembering.

For transdisciplinarity explicitly returns feeling, *Eros* and values to disciplinary mating and severing. Nicolescu sees his three axioms as inherently values generating. The included middle, emphasizes interdependence. Given that humans and the universe are regarded as mutually sustaining, we either have values or chaos. It follows that education as the cultivation of disciplines needs a rethinking that moves them towards plurality. Transdisciplinarity requires at least three types of intelligence, including the conventional understanding of it as rational and analytical. Yet, added to what Jung would describe as *Logos* consciousness, are also intelligences close to Dionysian knowing: the intelligences of feeling and of the body (Nicolescu, 2005, p. 17).

For far from acknowledging dismembered Dionysus, traditional academic disciplines in sciences and the arts are all too used to rejecting any consciousness of each other as viable, yet different levels of reality. Typically in the modern university disciplines are mutually indifferent, or even antagonistic. They have no consciousness of themselves as dismembered parts. Here even Film Studies possesses no *zoe*, no dynamic life-force in their separate unacknowledged incompleteness.

I suggest that human consciousness plays out unconscious needs and desires within collective disciplinary structure. Disciplines too may long for rejuvenation from Dionysian *zoe* while also being vulnerable to its inhuman, undifferentiated divinity. Kerenyi insists that by marrying Dionysus and being elevated to the stars, Ariadne traces the path of the soul reborn. In the way of knowing of Hockley's somatic image, we become Ariadne united with Dionysus in the embodied symbol made by cinema going. The cinematic experience of going beyond boundaries, to touch other worlds and ways of being is translated into *zoe* in this ecstatic textuality. It is a way of knowing that becomes a way of being.

Transdisciplinarity has story, a history in Dionysian dismemberment and remembering. It celebrates the marriage of Ariadne and Dionysus in embodying, incarnating knowing in symbols. Disciplines in Nicolescu's transdisciplinarity are written in Jungian symbols because all their languages have to remain open to the 'living mystery'. Disciplinary language becomes symbolic language, because to follow any discipline in a transdisciplinary (and Dionysian way) requires a symbolic attitude.

To retain that vital 'openness', even so-called facts become symbols. As Jung puts it, and extending on previous quotation:

> Whether a thing is a symbol or not depends chiefly on the attitude of the observing consciousness; for instance, on whether it regards a given fact not merely as such but also as an expression for something unknown. Hence it is quite possible for a man to

establish a fact which does not appear in the least symbolic to himself, but is profoundly so to another consciousness.

(1921: §818)

One can be 'disciplined' as in our traditional warring disciplines and reject a symbolic attitude.
An alternative is to be transdisciplinary and re-member Dionysus to evoke symbols in the language of knowing.

Dionysian textuality in Film Studies and Jung's *Red Book*

This chapter has come a long way in suggesting that the somatic image in film can be considered
as a variety of hermeneutics; one owing allegiance to a dangerously ecstatic and dismembering
god. In fact, the powerful example of Hockley's 'third' image becomes an instance in a revolution in knowing, named transdisciplinarity by its most lucid theorist, Basarab Nicolescu.

Adding Jungian principles of the importance of non-rational states of psyche reveals their
capacity to augment and underpin transdisciplinarity's philosophy. Taking Hillman's diagnosis
of Jung's use of Dionysus as the psychic necessity of dismembering and re-membering, provides
understanding of the importance of seeing a revolution in knowing as inseparable from a transformation in being.

For Dionysian textuality re-members more than the body as indissolubly wed to the psyche.
It enacts the marriage of Ariadne and Dionysus in a hermeneutics of film that re-members the
joyful, terrifying, nightmarish and dazzling qualities of cinema (to name just a few ego-
transgressing experiences). Too often, film textual criticism concentrates on 'making sense' of
films to the detriment of recognizing how they inhabit and act out that which evades rational
theory. Such film criticism is confined to what Jung called 'signs', rational meanings and missing
the symbolic register of cinematic experience (1922: §100).

By contrast, transdisciplinarity teaches us to value the Jungian symbol as the included middle. As
in Hockley's third image it breaks down the separation of subject versus object as the only basis for
knowing. It is psyche activated by words in touch with the body, feeling, imagination, spirit. Hence
the third image is a Dionysian hermeneutic of re-membering, re-embodying the psyche.

I end by offering Jung's own vision of the cinematic experience in his twenty-first century publication, *The Red Book* (2009). Not surprisingly, he also remembers the sacred in the dismembering
of film. In this work, the Jung figure meets a man who tells him that he enjoys town life because of
the availability of cinematic experience. 'There was a man who ran up houses. Another carried his
head under his arm. Another even stood in the middle of a fire and wasn't burnt' (ibid., p. 233). At
first Jung is inclined to scoff at the man's unintellectual pleasures in these unnatural feats of the
human body. Then he recalls that these proclivities are also to be found in the dismemberment of
Saints. In this irreligious era the images of the dismembered and superhuman body are created by
technology rather than God. Yet where some might see a fundamental split between a religious
sensibility and a secular society, Jung perceives a vital, *and vitalizing* continuum in the man's acceptance of cinematic visions as wonders beyond his understanding. 'I regard my companion with
feeling – he lives the history of the world – and I?' (ibid., p. 234).

We glimpse Hockley's somatic, unintellectual image in Jung's companion. Significantly,
Jung regards the man as possessing something he does not: a pathway to an historical and religious consciousness gone from modernity. Cinema, not in its apparent technology (Hockley's
first image), nor in its capacity to be analysed as a discrete text (second image), but rather in its
ability to evoke somatic and non-rational depths (third image), is a gateway to re-membering
what has been lost in a more rational, scientific and secular age.

36

Jung perceives his lowly man is enjoying in cinema what Nicolescu calls several types of reality, now re-membered. Another perspective would be that Jung regards the man's cinematic images of standing in fire or carrying one's head as a symbol, as the included middle between present and past consciousness. In Jung's treatment of the humble film fan is the perception of what the whole of *The Red Book* enacts, the necessity to re-member the dismembered consciousness of modernity. Such renewal will be *Dionysian*, of the body in somatic images.

The lowly man in *The Red Book* is an Ariadne who has found his Dionysian *zoe* in the cinema. With help from Hockley's third image within Dionysian hermeneutics, so can we.

References

Brooks, C. (1956) *The well wrought urn: studies in the structure of poetry*. New York: Mariner Books.

Cambray, J. (2012) *Synchronicity: nature and psyche in an interconnected universe*. College Station: Texas A & M Press.

Eagleton, T. (1983/2008) *Literary theory: an introduction*. Oxford: Blackwell Publishing; Minneapolis, MN: University of Minnesota Press.

Hillman, J. (1972) 'Dionysus in Jung's writings', *Spring: A Journal of Archetype and Culture*, in *Mythic figures: uniform edition of the writings of James Hillman, volume 6.1*. Putnam, CT: Spring Publications Inc., 2007. pp. 15–30.

Hockley, L. (2014) *Somatic cinema: the relationship between body and screen – a Jungian perspective*. Hove and New York: Routledge.

Jung, C. G. (1916) 'The structure of the unconscious', in *The collected works of C. G. Jung*, Vol. 7, *Two essays on analytical psychology*, 2nd edn. London: Routledge, 1966.

Jung, C. G. (1921) 'Definitions', in *The collected works of C. G. Jung*, Vol. 6, *Psychological types*, 3rd edn. London: Routledge & Kegan Paul, 1971.

Jung, C. G. (1922) 'On the relation of analytical psychology to poetry', in *The collected works of C. G. Jung*, Vol. 15, *The spirit in man, art, and literature*. London: Routledge, 1966.

Jung, C. G. (1944) 'Individual dream symbolism in relation to alchemy: the initial dreams', in *The collected works of C. G. Jung*, Vol. 12, *Psychology and alchemy*, 2nd edn. London: Routledge, 1968.

Jung, C. G. (2009) *The red book: liber novus*, ed. S. Shamdasani, trans. M. Kyburz, J. Peck and S. Shamdasani. New York: W. W. Norton & Co.

Kerenyi, K. (1976) *Dionysos: archetypal image of indestructible life*. Princeton, NJ: Princeton University Press.

Richards, I. A. (1929) *Practical criticism: a study of literary judgement*. London: Kegan, Paul, Trench, Tubner.

Rowland, S. (2017) *Remembering Dionysus: revisioning psychology and literature*, in *C. G. Jung and James Hillman*. Hove and New York: Routledge.

Saban, M. (2014) 'Science friction: Jung, Goethe and scientific objectivity', in R. A. Jones (ed.), *Jung and the question of science*. London and New York: Routledge, pp. 30–49.

Shulman, H. (1997) *Living at the edge of chaos: complex systems in culture and psyche*. Zurich: Daimon Verlag.

Tympas, G. C. (2014) *Carl Jung and Maximus the Confessor: the dynamics between the 'psychological' and the 'spiritual'*. London and New York: Routledge.

Wilson, E. A. (2002) 'A short history of a border war: social science, school reform, and the study of literature', in D. R. Shuway and C. Dionne (eds), *Disciplining English: alternative histories, critical perspectives*. Albany, NY: State University of New York Press, pp. 59–81.

Wimsatt, W. K. (1954) *The verbal icon: studies in the meaning of poetry*, Lexington, KY: University of Kentucky Press.

Online source

Nicolescu, B. (2005) 'Transdisciplinarity – past, present and future', Palestra apresentada no II Congresso Mundial de Transdisciplinaridade. 06 a 12 de setembro de 2005, Vila Velha/Vitória – SC – Brasil, *CETRANS – Centro de Educação Transdisciplinar*, pp. 1–24 [online]. Available at: www.cetrans.com.br [Accessed 20 May 2015].

3

STICK TO THE IMAGE?

No thanks!

Eric Greene

Introduction

This chapter is informed by two systems of thought that define antithetical ontologies of subjectivity: the critical theory of Karl Marx and the analytical psychology of C. G. Jung. Critical theory claims that the 'ensemble of social relations' structures everything, including the psyche, and that 'human essence is no abstraction inherent in each single individual' (Marx and Engels, 1978, p. 145). Running contrary to this position is Jung's analytical psychology that claims that the psyche is essential to each individual, and is itself a source of knowledge. Despite the apparent incompatibility, this chapter deploys both systems of thought towards a single goal which is inherent in each: namely, to resist mass psychological thinking. Put another way, both systems of thought are demystifying critical theories of consciousness.

One location where such a critique can occur is in the cinema where one confronts ideological images on the screen. (Homologous to this are the images which emerge in our minds.) However, a problem of interpreting these images can be the affectivity, which emerges in the viewer while watching a film, which itself might be a kind of false consciousness. From this perspective it is the dimensions of the commodity form (e.g. the film) that are 'mystical' or 'transcendent' (Marx, 1978, p. 320) and which might be generating the numinous experience. The same argument can be made for the images that emerge in one's mind.

In order to resist this particular configuration of subjectivity, that is, to gain mental clarity so to better evaluate the verity of the images and the affective response to them, the singular form or archetype of capitalism which defines them needs to be subject to a critique – one very Jungian way to do that is to critique its numinosity.

Today, as the features of neoliberalism dominate political and economic systems globally, so too they colonize and define consciousness and psyche. Now so more than ever everything, including the images in the mind and in the cinema, perverts or violently shapes persons into the mass psychology of the capitalist way of life. In other words, the numinosity of the capitalist image is everywhere. This is why we need Jung's work more than ever, so that humans once having found their souls do not moan in torture and sell them because their worth is no different from that of a mass manufactured automaton.

To begin, this chapter draws a brief connection between mind and cinema in order to present the homology of their functioning. Then it will proceed by comparing and deploying critical theory and analytical psychology in the task of critiquing the image. The chapter will proceed with a discussion of Jung's interpretation of images. Then it will use *The Fast and The Furious: Furious 7* (dir. Wan, 2015) as an example of one of Jung's warnings regarding narcissistic interpretations of images. Then it will proceed with a final warning by James Hillman, and critique of that warning. Finally it will illustrate the ways in which the film *Titanic* (dir. Cameron, 1997) is an example of ideology, and then the chapter will end with concluding remarks.

Jung and Marx

Since the time of the Ancient Greeks, comparisons have been at least prefigured and drawn between the mind and phantasmic moving images. Famously, Plato in book seven of the Republic (514a–520a), prefigured the idea of the cinema in his well known allegory of the cave in which the mind is likened to moving images which are projected from behind viewers onto a front facing wall; the viewers, who are chained to the floor, confuse these moving images with the true nature of things (Bloom, 1968). The movement of these images on the wall, is homologous to the mythopoetical function of the psyche in the ways it produces and animates images in the mind (Ellenberger, 1981, p. 314). That is, images are a necessary feature of our consciousness (c.f. Jonas, 1966, pp. 157ff.; Hillman, 1970; Bachelard, 1971). The complexity of the relationship between cinema and mind is made in Pat Berry's observation that, 'Film began at the same time as depth psychology, at the end of the 19th century' (2001, p. 70). Additional comparisons to cinema have been made. For example, McGinn (2007) compares the activity in church to the activity in the cinema – a comparison of religion. Hockley (2013) draws comparisons between therapy and cinema – a comparison of psychotherapy.

All of this suggests the basic homology of envisioning mental images and watching images move across a cinema screen should include a discussion of Jung's practice of active imagination – 'a sequence of fantasies produced by deliberate concentration' (1936: §101). In both activities, one is attempting to bear witness to the movement of images, which have the potential to be extremely psycho-activating, and, additionally, both provide primary material for mental or ethical acquisition. Put succinctly:

> Cinema has the possibility of becoming an imaginal space – a temenos – and by engaging with films a version of active imagination is stimulated which can then engage the unconscious – potentially in as successful a fashion as our conscious attention to dream imagery and other fantasies.
>
> *(Hauke and Alister, 2001 p. 2)*

But, these very images that are stimulated via active imagination or by watching a film, and how one interprets them, can also be ideologically configured, that is to say, they offer a source of false knowledge, as opposed to a source of true knowledge of oneself or the world. The psyche as a dimension of experience that one assumes to be the groundwork of one's life, can be the manufactured experience which comes from being a part of the material conditions of the mass psychological or social world. This is to argue that the configuration of subjectivity within 'the ensemble of social relations' (i.e. capitalism) prescribes or determines specific intrapsychic as well as extrapsychic experiences. As Marx writes:

> Hitherto men have constantly made up for themselves false conceptions about themselves, about what they are and what they ought to be. They have arranged their

relationships according to their ideas of God, of normal man, etc. The phantoms of their brains have got out of their hands.

(Marx and Engels, 1978, p. 146)

One possible critique of Jungian interpretative procedures of images is that the belief that all intrapsychic experience including the affect or somatization generated from contact with the numinous is necessarily true, is quite possibly false. That is, the sum total of one's experience could be nothing more than a phantom that has gotten out of one's hands.

What structures these phantoms? According to critical theory, it is ideology. As Marx puts it:

If in all ideology men and their circumstances appear upside-down as in a camera obscura, this phenomenon arises just as much from their historical life-process as the inversion of objects on the retina does from their physical life-process.

(ibid., p. 154)

(That he compares ideology to a camera is a noteworthy synchronicity.) Ideology emerges from one's historical life-process, that is, from the material conditions which define life today. He continues: 'The phantoms formed in the human brain are also, necessarily, sublimates of their material life-process … [Ideology has] no history, no development…. Life is not determined by consciousness, but consciousness by life' (ibid., pp. 154–155).

What forms the consciousness of the mass-psychology human is the global domination of neoliberalism, and, one could add, its corresponding image. The simplification of Marx's work to the abovementioned phrase that 'consciousness [is determined] by life' aligns well with Jung's notion of the collective unconscious and his oft repeated quip that we are in psyche, and not the other way around. That is to say, Marx and Jung share a concern about the forces of collective and social life which shape and influence the nature of subjectivity and psychology.

Jung's comments on the problems of mass psychology align well with Marx's critique of ideology. But while Marx focuses his attention on labor and alienation, Jung focuses his on the mass psychological human, or the problems of the mass psyche. For example, Jung writes:

Thanks to industrialization, large portions of the population were up-rooted and were herded together in large centres. This new form of existence – with its mass psychology and social dependence on the fluctuation of the markets and wages – produced an individual who was unstable, insecure, and suggestible.

(1946: §453)

Jung characterizes the modern mass psychological human as unstable, insecure, and suggestible, and in doing so what he offers is akin to Marx's description of the worker or subject under capitalism as 'alienated' and characterized by a 'loss of self' and 'animal' (Marx and Engels, 1978, p. 74). This is noteworthy because it means that mass culture fractures a person's psychological strength, creates misery, soullessness and dependence on the system. The importance of this characterization for this chapter will come further down, but it is sufficient for now to suggest the dynamic of a miserable person desiring ideological life, is reproduced in the cinema.

Jung continues:

The dangerous slope leading down to mass psychology begins with this plausible thinking in large numbers, in terms of powerful organizations where the individual dwindles to a mere cipher. Everything that exceeds a certain human size evokes equally inhuman powers in man's unconscious.

(ibid.: §457)

These words apply to the world now more than ever. As a singular, dominant ideology colonizes our globe and our psyches, the threat of being reduced to a mere cypher applies to everyone. This definition of subjectivity as an empty or zero-person, has the potential to be reproduced within the dynamic of the cinema. Even further, film images hold the potential to shape or pervert us by telling and teaching us how to behave and what to believe, as Slavoj Zizek points out in *The Pervert's Guide to Ideology* (dir. Fiennes, 2012).

This theme of the image of mass psychological human within analytical psychology, combined with the ways in which false consciousness today shapes us to think we have self-knowledge when really that knowledge is false (as shown by critical theory) will be the focus of investigation for the next portion of the chapter. The chapter will proceed with a discussion of Jung's interpretation of images.

Jung's interpretations and warnings of images

Jung was largely concerned with the phenomenological investigation of the instinct of images. Also, he claimed that the main interest of his life's work was 'with the approach to the numinous' (Jaffe, 1989, p. 16). One might add, 'by means of the image'. He offers a method by which one could interpret an object of art or an intrapsychic image.

Jung identified two categories of creative processes that were effective in analyzing and or interpreting images, as one would interpret the images of art. He terms one the 'Psychological' and the other the 'Visionary' (1930/50: §139). This fork in the interpretive road between these two different perspectives takes us down diverging hermeneutical paths into somewhat distinct universes of discourse. The first path leads us into a reductionist medical universe of discourse and a psychologizing of the subject in which creative work is thought to be a symptom of psychopathology or a disease of the artist (ibid.: §107). It is not unlike the scene in the film *Gremlins* (dir. Dante, 1984) where when water is poured on the adorable Mogwai a nasty little gremlin emerges out of his back. According to this procedure, interpreting the images of art beyond the manifest content reveals the so-called truth, naturally, hidden in the artist. Along these lines, we would interpret the figure of Superman as Jerry Siegel's attempt to resolve his Oedipal complex through the fantasy of asserting dominance in the world, to impress his mother and destroy his father, with leaps and bounds, movement faster than a speeding bullet, and all the rest.

Among other things, this reductionism excludes the dimensions of the collective unconscious. In addition, of this deconstructive, restrictive, psychologizing interpretative procedure, Jung comments:

The reduction of the vision to a personal experience makes it something unreal and unauthentic – mere substitute, as we have said. The vision thus loses its primordial quality and becomes nothing but a symptom; the teeming chaos shrinks to the proportions of a psychic disturbance.... We should do well, I think, to bear clearly in mind the full consequences of this reduction of art to personal factors, and see where it leads. The truth is that it deflects our attention from the psychology of the work of art and focuses it on the psychology of the artist.

(ibid.: §146–147)

41

In short, reducing a work of art, such as a film, to be a product of the artist's pathology or psychonarrative, misses the value and meaning of the object of art itself and fails to provide value for the collective world.

The second path of artistic interpretation identified by Jung leads into a visionary and compelling universe of discourse. Jung explains:

> In dealing with the psychological mode of creation we need never ask ourselves what the material consists of or what it means. But this question forces itself upon us when we turn to the visionary mode. We are astonished, confused, bewildered, put on our guard, even repelled; we demand commentaries and explanations. We are reminded of nothing in everyday life, but rather of dreams, night-time fears, and the dark, uncanny recesses of the human mind.
>
> *(ibid.: §143)*

The states of experience from the visionary are astonishing and are at times confusing, bewildering and terrifying. All of this can be reduced to a single criterion for the definition of the visionary category, which is also one of Jung's most oft-used words: numinous. With its root 'numen' and its variation 'numinosity', the word occurs on average of about once every 13–14 pages from the beginning to the end of the 4963 pages of his *Collected Works*. Specifically, the *Collected Works* contains the word 'numinous' about 190 times, while its root 'numen' occurs roughly 67 times and its variation 'numinosity' around 89 times. The feeling of astonishment, confusion, etc., is the magical feeling of numinosity, as the archetypes are the numinous and structural elements of the psyche. According to Jung's argument the visionary contains the 'imagery of the collective unconscious' (ibid.: §152).

However, modern scholars and analytic therapists have struggled to define exactly what Jung meant by 'numinous'. According to Huskinson (2006, p. 201), the numinous is difficult to define because it is non-rational. Thus, one dimension of the word is that it is a mystery, i.e. beyond ego comprehension. Further, Huskinson shows that Jung borrowed the term from Rudolf Otto who used it in the context of its etymology 'spirit', that is, within the discourse of religion, specifically Christianity. Thus, another dimension of the word is a Christian one. However, according to Huskinson, Jung 'facilitates its mistranslation into his psychological theory' (ibid., p. 202). That is, most of Jung's allusions to the numinous are 'concerned with the emotional affective experience of the unconscious' (ibid.). In short, Jung, for better or worse, took the word from a religious discourse, and within the discourse of his psychology refocused its meaning on the affectivity of confronting the mysterious. What one struggles with today is upon what criteria is it possible to agree that a given moment, in the cinema or elsewhere, is truly numinous and not something else, such as traumatizing, or amazing. In other words, if one accepts critical theory's argument that 'life determines consciousness' how would one evaluate if a numinous moment is or is not ideological?

The failure to answer this question adequately has been problematic to the Jungian community generally, and a source of naive wholesale introjection by mainstream culture. That is, the redefinition of the word, i.e. sanitizing its religious dimension and focusing on the affective experience of the confrontation with the mysterious, became easy fodder specifically for the feel-good nature of the New Age Movement, and its tendency to incorporate so-called mystery moments into one's psycho-narrative, or, one's so-called 'journey'. A good report of this can be found in the article in the *New York Times* that came out during the publication of the *Red Book*, entitled, 'The Holy Grail of the Unconscious', by Sara Corbett (2009):

Whether or not he would have wanted it this way, Jung – who regarded himself as a scientist – is today remembered more as a countercultural icon, a proponent of spirituality outside religion and the ultimate champion of dreamers and seekers everywhere, which has earned him both posthumous respect and posthumous ridicule.... His central tenets – the existence of a collective unconscious and the power of archetypes – have seeped into the larger domain of New Age thinking while remaining more at the fringes of mainstream psychology.

The subject in these instances of New Ageism and of Jungianism is very susceptible to ideology. (The coupling of religion with business would need to be the subject of another paper, but sufficient for now is to suggest that the marketing of numinous experiences tends to be an incredibly attractive sales pitch and highly lucrative (cf. Weber, 1920/2011)). All affective moments from the numinous, all moments in which something has appeared to have emerged from someplace mysterious or secret, all moments in which one exchanges and cheapens a critical consciousness for a feel-good experience, have the potential to send one to some destructive psychological place where one is completely lost and furthest from one's self, all the while thinking that one is closest to one's self. As Tacey (2001) reminds us, Jung's writing in *Symbols and Transformation* was largely concerned with this problem. He approaches the same issue from a different angle when he writes:

> In archetypal terms, we have to do with a fatal erotic attraction, where the ego longs to 'marry' the archetypal mother in death. To educate us beyond this fatal attraction, the ego has to be shown how to serve the sacred reality in this life, and not to hanker after another life to consummate the erotic union. This opaque, dull, or inert world has to be made translucent, has to become the legitimate home of the sacred reality, so that in our longing for the sacred we do not always betray this world and flee to another world in ecstatic death or egoic dissolution. Jung ... was hugely concerned with this problem, and with the way in which an otherworldly divine image can 'poison humanity' and bring about psychic destruction in individuals. In Symbols [and Transformation], Jung described a case study in which an incestuous longing for fusion with the matrix subverts a human life, brings on fragmentation of the mind, and engenders the illusion of creativity and power in the face of evident self-destruction.
>
> *(p. 52)*

Today, perhaps these images are necessarily 'incestuous' because images of mind and of world are configured by the same ideology, which reinforces one's gaze to be constructed narcissistically. This makes the intrapsychic experience prescribed within a determined dynamic. Specific to this chapter, it is possible that the interpretation of the affectivity elicited in the viewer in the cinema runs the risk of being confused with a so-called authentic experience of self.

The complexity of the issue of the numinous is caught up too in the desire for the experience, such as when Holowitz writes in Hauke and Alister (2001): '[c]ertainly Iago can be seen as shadow, or Circe as an anima figure ... [b]ut our *experience* of Othello or Homer is not much enriched as a result' (p. 84, italics added). This desire to feel something so that one could become more authentic by integrating the god-like (i.e. the Self) material on one's path toward individuation, that is to be transformed, obscures the fact that these experiences may not be transformative at all (cf. Cushman, 1990). And, one runs the risk of commoditizing, stockpiling and fetishizing the moment into only that – an experience. This very reduction of the work of art to its experience might be the precise interpretive procedure or desire that needs to be resisted in order to understand more accurately the purpose of the film. The trap set by the jargon of authenticity is that the experience, which one tends to elevate to a superior moral status, could be nothing more than a cheapened manufacturing or reproduction of affectivity.

Jung was aware of further complications inherent in encountering numinous images, and he warns the reader of the traps along the way. Curiously, one will not find the warnings in relation to literature, but one will find them in his method of active imagination that is a sequence of fantasies produced by deliberate concentration on an image. Even so these warnings are pertinent to the creative arts. Jung provides three warnings to the person who undergoes active imagination. The first warning is similar to the first mode of interpretation with one major exception: the so-called artist, in this sense, is the subject. That is, one may get stuck in a cycle of Freudian free interpretation such that one becomes 'caught in the sterile circle of his own complexes, from which he is in any case unable to escape' (1916/57: Prefatory note before §131). In short: resist the urge to psychologize one's self.

This warning deserves further elaboration and cannot be overstated enough because of its central importance today to the destructiveness of consciousness and imagination (Bloom, 1987), contributing to the 'culture of incapacity' (Zaslavsky, 2015, personal correspondence) and to the implicit acceptance and reinforcement of domination. In other words, the dominant hermeneutic of works of art today including literature, paintings and film, is to make the work personalized within the viewer. While all works of art, in fact any object, may stir some personal meaning or reflect our invisible worlds, the central focus of the viewer on personal meaning is as a socially constructed interpretive or ideologically constructed procedure (Foucault, 1995). Jung's injunction here is that such a personal psychologization leads to an inescapable and sterile circle of one's own complexes. In short, one loses the object of art altogether while retreating into a world of interiority. This precise warning aligns with social theory's notion of the commoditization of the self, which necessarily forces subjects to focus their attention inwardly thus foreclosing knowledge of the effects of the social world (Fisher, 2009; Parker, 2007). That the viewer accepts the ontological experience of their subjectivity as absolute truth potentially could not be more dangerous, more perverted, more ideological, that is, it could not be further from the truth. In short, we run the risk of becoming anesthetized by the ideology of subjectivism, when we interpret our external experiences within the discourse of psychogenic narratives.

The second warning states that one might get 'stuck in an all-enveloping phantasmagoria' (1916/57: Prefatory note before §131). This too needs further elaboration. Some images fail to be integrated into the personality because their meaning and moral demands are missed. The images become too personalized. This fetishization of the image turns one's viewing into a narcissistic gaze that collapses the depth and value of the image into the cheap two-dimensionality of its façade. One gets the spirit of the times without the depths. Being stuck in this kind of what could be called an aesthetic trance is not unlike the far out encounter with the phantasmagoria produced by a mescaline trip. In his letter to Betty Grover Eisener, Jung (1957/84) writes unhappily:

> Experiments along the line of mescaline and related drugs are certainly most interesting, since such drugs lay bare a level of the unconscious that is otherwise accessible only under peculiar psychic conditions [perhaps, during active imagination?]. It is a fact that you get certain perceptions and experiences of things appearing either in mystical states or in the analysis of unconscious phenomena, just like the primitives in their orgiastic or intoxicated conditions. I don't feel happy about these things, since you merely fall into such experience without being able to integrate them. The result is not a moral and mental acquisition. It is the eternally primitive man having experience of his ghost-hand, but it is not an achievement of your cultural development.

(p. 159)

In Jung's critique, the encounter with drug induced psychic visions does not become integrated. In the parlance of those times, one cannot handle it. One experiences the images without any 'moral or mental acquisition'.

This failure to integrate aligns with the popular critique today of blockbuster films: all show, no substance; all visual, no content. One leaves the theater as if one gained absolutely nothing, except for diminished hearing and a wowing from the aesthetics of cinematic transmogrification. This experience is codified in social dynamics so that one may forget about the pain of everyday life.

Consider the seventh iteration of *The Fast and The Furious: Furious 7* (dir. Wan, 2015) (the eighth came out in 2017, and there is talk of making up to ten), a completely vacuous movie with symbols that should be as dead as dust. Why, then, should this film reach such heights of success? The series was Universal's biggest franchise of all time, perhaps because it races into the American psyche and injects a tank full of nitrous into the collective symbolism of driving on the open road of freedom. Today in mundane life, that archetypal content has been psychically congested, like being caught in 50 lanes of traffic (literally) on the G4 Beijing–Hong Kong–Macau Expressway, or in Heathrow airport Christmas eve, or in any Walmart on Black Friday, or Times Square on New Year's Eve, or at the checkout line at the supermarket pretty much any day, any time. One's 'day in day out' life is completely miserable and frustrating, and a cinematic experience makes one forget that. In addition, the steroidal images of driving absurdly fast, over, past, through, around, or under any traffic jam, or any jam, with fire-breathing engines and roaringly loud music, is a fantasy, evidently, everyone can identify with. The film in this sense is totally meaningless except after the mystification of its visual trip dissipates, one is left with the sober, painful reality of one's daily commute, that it dramatizes our collective impotence of our 'day-to-day' lives. The inverse is supported and can be read meaningfully, too: one's daily, mundane life is socially constructed, and the film allows one to release imaginally one's so-called authentic self from within with a blast of raw psychic energy through which to complete a 'whole' vision of the current times. In short, this boring film is configured to either supplement or complement our lives. The warning then is clear: analyze the mind-numbing effects of the narcissistic aesthetics to create analytic space, because most likely, what one will be left with, otherwise, is nothing in mind or pocket.

Jung puts his last warning as follows:

> Finally, a third danger – and this may in certain circumstances be a very serious matter – is that the subliminal contents already possess such a high energy charge that, when afforded an outlet by active imagination, they may overpower the conscious mind and take possession of the personality. This gives rise to a condition which – temporarily, at least – cannot easily be distinguished from schizophrenia, and may even lead to a genuine 'psychotic interval.' The method of active imagination, therefore, is not a plaything for children.
>
> *(1916/57: Prefatory note before §131)*

Jung attributed to schizophrenia the quality of the numinous and, therefore, this psychotic interval is not easily distinguished from symptoms of schizophrenia. He opines:

> [W]e might conclude that the schizophrenic state of mind, so far as it yields archaic material, has all the characteristics of a 'big dream' – in other words, that it is an important event, exhibiting the same 'numinous' quality which in primitive cultures is attributed to a magic ritual.
>
> *(1939: §528)*

This third and final warning from Jung is serious and the most complicated of all the concerns that he enumerates as the unconscious content emerging from active imagination can possess an energy charge that is intense enough to cause a psychotic interval albeit a numinous one. The danger is that the ego becomes consumed by the contents of the unconscious. By extension it follows that it might well be possible for a film image to have a similar effect. If that were to happen then the ego would be subsumed and temporarily lost. In other words, the sensuous dimensions of the cinematic experience, to use the language of one of Jung's oft-cited fore-thinkers, Pierre Janet, causes an *abaissement du niveau mental*. This lowering or weakening of mental functioning dissipates the *fonction du reel* like a mist into the background while unconscious image and film image merge. The result is that '[w]e are astonished, confused, bewildered, put on our guard, even repelled' (1930/50: §143).

The visionary mode of interpretation in film, when we are caught by archetypal content, functions much like a temporary 'psychotic interval' and should not be explored from the automatic assumption or belief that the experience is purely 'magical', 'religious', 'mystical' or 'spiritual'. Jung writes:

> It is abundantly clear that such an *abaissement du niveau mental*, i.e., the overpowering of the ego by unconscious contents and the consequent identification with preconscious wholes, possesses a prodigious psychic virulence, or power of contagion, and is capable of the most disastrous results.
>
> *(1947/54: §430)*

Put another way, during the psychotic break, the tension of the ego becomes slackened, like a limp rope, and then drops into the dark abyss of interiority while the collision or union of over-image and under-image, or inner-image and outer-image, generates a 'feeling-toned' charge. The danger is that this precise category of experience becomes fetishized as some mystical, magical or spiritual experience, when it could be nothing at all except a socially constructed affect or the desire to forget the boring events of day-to-day life, or the felt experience of the loss of ego akin to intoxication or psychosis, or even nothing at all. An empathic interpretation would suggest that the desire for this so-called numinous experience is the way for the ego to take a trip away from our painfully boring reality which we encounter daily, a kind of reverse order of, or inverting values of the transcendent function. Additionally, perhaps at this very moment when inner and outer merge, the ego jumps ship into the abyss because it cannot bear the pain of the experience. In this reading, that so-called numinous moment is traumatizing. In short, feeling-toned, so-called numinous experiences are not always what they seem to be, and should be approached with rigorous analytical distance.

In summation: the first warning is to resist making the images something personal about you-the-viewer; the second is to resist only enjoying the pure aesthetics of the film; the third is to re-evaluate the criteria upon which the category of the numinous experience is defined and to resist the urge to misinterpret non-numinous experiences as numinous, and to have, stockpile, fetishize or eroticize, experiences.

If a characterization of individuation, a goal of analytic psychology, is to be able to face reality, and to be individuated is to be one's own authority, to face the world and to use one's abilities to do so, then the perpetual deflection or displacement of one's faculties for the enjoyment of a potentially so-called numinous experience soothes or numbs someone away from reality and, therefore, runs counter to the entire process of individuation.

An additional warning: stick to the image? No thanks!

James Hillman (1970) was aware of the problem of subjectively interpreting images, and this led to his well known dictum 'Stick to the image'. The upside of this means that sticking to the image stops the amplification of the image straying too far away from the original image. For example if one dreams about snakes, and then amplifies that image to find a meaning in it of divine wisdom, or the uroborous, or the penis, one fails to stick to the image. If one continues by discussing the images of divine wisdom etc., then one has effectively depotentiated the numinous quality of the dream image. For Hillman, the power of the image is in sticking to the description of its quality and movement and in doing so it becomes possible to know and experience its numinous qualities.

The second reading of 'Stick to the Image' exposes the dictum to a critique which has not yet been discussed in Jungian or Post-Jungian literature: Stick to the image, can be read as 'stick the image to yourself', or 'stick yourself to the image', such that there is no differentiation. Here the double reading reveals the mantra's hidden narcissistic and psychotic meaning. If we are too close to the image, it subsumes us, and we lose all reflective or descriptive capacity. If there is no space between ego and image, if one sticks to it, without the further step to critique through it, or distance oneself from it, then one is no different from it, one is but a slave that is chained down in a dark cave, who has confused one's own mind for the images of the world.

An additional step is needed which would result in the dictum's re-formulation: Stay Close to the Image, then Critique It. That is, it is only by staying close to the image and then critiquing it can one retroactively know its numinosity by means of the critical distance attained, by the language applied afterwards. This is an important step to facing and then displacing the dominant image of capitalism that has defined our ontology and colonized the consciousness of our collective psyche. The central image of our times is one of capitalism, and sticking to it without a critique would inevitably lead to the subsuming of and identification with one's manufactured and tortured psyche, including affect, somatization and thoughts. By sticking to the numinous content and critiquing it one is able to put language to the very things collectively that turns one into a zombie, that is, that which puts one under a spell, charms or poisons one. Furthermore, one is better able to know the films one watches on the film's own terms.

Titanic: an example

The following example will demonstrate two responses to the film *Titanic* (dir. Cameron, 1997), one positive and one negative. The purpose will be to show the predetermination of mass-psychology human's response to the film. Thus, the affectivity which viewers may claim is their own, i.e. personalized or capitalized, is nothing more than manufactured ideology. Further, the chapter will position Hockley's (2014) critique with critical theory's to demystify this manufactured affect. This strips the film bare of its so-called numinosity revealing its concealed characteristic, that is, the film is flat and empty. Furthermore, this chapter will offer two readings of *Titanic*, one Jungian and one Marxist.

Titanic is the second highest grossing film of all time at $2.1 billion, just behind *Avatar* (dir. Cameron, 2009) at $2.7 billion. The film captured the attention and imagination of so many, perhaps, at least for the Americans, because of its historical significance (the ship was on its way to New York), its expression as a stereotypically American desire (i.e. *Titanic* was the biggest of its day), its enormous budget totaled about $200 million which included a re-creation of a near perfect and only slightly smaller model of the original ship, and its location in the American collective psyche as a story about the American Dream and the fetishization of love.

The vast amount of money spent, its cutting edge cinematography techniques, the amount of labor needed to produce the film, combined with a methodized storyline, all contribute to the 'mystical character of [this particular] commodity' (Marx and Engels, 1978, p. 320). In short, before the film was shown, the mass psychological human was primed to enjoy its presentation as if it were 'something transcendent' (ibid., p. 320). This purely capitalistic logic generates numinosity.

The pure image of capitalism and its ineffable relationality has become so effective and pervasive that viewers, and even the most esteemed critics, become unconscious of it perverting them to desire ideology. Roger Ebert (2017) writes of the *Titanic*: 'James Cameron's 194-minute, $200 million film of the tragic voyage is in the tradition of the great Hollywood epics. It is flawlessly crafted, intelligently constructed, strongly acted and spellbinding.'

It is clear that Ebert's response reflects an affective experience from a numinous encounter. That he felt the film was 'spellbinding' demonstrates the depth of capitalistic logic that defines psychological life today. The response from the general public was fairly similar. Rotten Tomatoes gave it a tomatometer of 88 percent and the audience gave it a rating of 69 percent. IMDB gave it 7.7/10 and Google users gave it a 93 percent. In general, the film was hailed as a great blockbuster success.

However, some scholars and viewers have critiqued the film on the grounds that it was psychologically or affectively flat, that is to say, boring, despite Cameron's intention to deal with 'archetypes' in the film (Hockley, 2014, p. 22). That the film elicited such extreme and contrary reactions is not unusual, however, perhaps trying to understand the responses proves more complicated. This chapter suggests that the film is pure ideology and therefore had the potential to generate two different registers of experience: one ideological and one critical.

Hockley's (2014) lamentations about *Titanic* suggest that the film is psychologically flat because the process of working with unconscious material in a conscious manner robs it of its affect. Hockley (2014) writes, 'When unconscious material is used in a calculating and conscious manner it is unable to speak with the voice of the unconscious' (p. 24). This is a characteristically Jungian critique.

Jung resisted creating a method for his psychology because he was concerned that people would mindlessly apply it to unconscious content, therein destroying potential meaning or affect. The method, in short, would ruin any meaningful relationship to the psychic content. Jung provided an answer to this problem with his practice of active imagination, enabling one to encounter unconscious material in a way which respects the material on its own terms, allowing the image to play out, so to speak, on its own without conscious interference. However, as shown by Hockley (2014), for *Titanic*, director James Cameron used Christopher Vogler's work with the intention to create a modern myth which spans all cultures (p. 22). Vogler's work methodizes Campbell's hero's journey. This very methodizing (i.e. formalizing) runs the risk of denying access to affectivity. *Titanic* is psychologically flat, Hockley (2014) argues, because the conscious application of this methodized storyline robs the material of its natural affectivity. That is, by applying a frame to organic content, much of the content is cut-off and lost. But how was it such a success?

Hockley recognizes the apparent contradiction but does not further develop the point. He suggests that despite the fact that the film left him (and many others) feeling 'cold', that perhaps the film's success could be the result of its marketing (2014, p. 25). This apparent contradiction is recognizable. On the one hand, the film is boring and cold; on the other, the film is a cultural myth that is lauded as a spellbinding success. The spellbinding-ness is generated from the cultural myth of capitalism and its ideology. The ideology says that one's desire is for a fantastical notion of love, for the catastrophe of a great, capitalist ship, for an easily digestible (i.e. methodized) storyline which does nothing to generate friction in the viewer (i.e. the meeting of two images, here, are identical, that is, narcissistic, leaving the viewer not changed, but rather reinforced), and, as mentioned, for the amount of money spent to make the film.

Two readings of the film serve to critique its capitalistic functioning and reveal its rather trite and perhaps even offensive storyline. On the one hand, it is Rose's boredom with the austerity of bourgeois life which propels her to descend down into the belly of the ship to rejuvenate her spirit with a poor proletariat boy, Jack, where bodily movement, sensual pleasures and sex are permitted. Once she has her fill, much like a 'vampire' (Marx, 1867 [2008], p. 149) that feeds off of labor, she ascends the ship and continues to live out her normal life. Meaning, the bourgeois sap the life energy of the proletariat for their own vitality.

The second reading is a Jungian one: the ship, which represents the self, is under intense pressure from a tension of the opposites. The tension is horizontal and mythic. Above is the Apollonian discipline that characterizes bourgeois culture and below is Dionysian chaos that characterizes proletarian culture. God, as so often is done when one does not pay attention to one's self, throws a stumbling block in the ship's way because the opposing forces have not been integrated. Then the ship collides with the iceberg, tearing it apart. What emerges, albeit for a brief moment, is the heart of the story, the great symbol of affect, and of the ocean: the blue diamond in the shape of a heart, which of course symbolizes eternal strength and love. Blue of course, containing so many meanings, represents the sea, depth, sadness, power, strength and much more (cf. Hillman, 2015). And the diamond signifies indestructible love or a union. Shortly thereafter, the ultimate symbol of love descends back into the dark icy waters of the unconscious ocean. Jack freezes to death and dies, while Rose floats to safety on her wooden raft. Perhaps Rose has integrated some of her opposite and has transformed on account of it. This cheapened and immature version of an alchemical or psychological union of opposites fails to account for so much of the harrowing and mundane difficulties that characterizes both realistic life and true growth. That is, the film romanticizes and perverts the image for a quick buck.

These critiques of the film are reductive readings, but where they succeed is in revealing the film's paltry narrative, basic motifs and immoral messages. What the marketing and ideology of the film did was commoditize and romanticize class-conflict stories and mythic dimensions of social life, cheapen them, and sell them to the public who gobbled them up like children eating drug-inducing candy. The two registers, one of the numinosity of capitalism, and the other, of the critiques, perhaps helps to explain the film's polarized reception.

Rolling credits

Nowhere else can one find the research supporting the collective unconscious and the function of man as an image making mortal, than in the work of Jung. This is why one needs Jung's work more than ever. Jung writes, '[p]sychological treatment, taken in its widest sense, seeks the values that satisfy the psychic needs of contemporary man [*sic*], so that he [*sic*] shall not fall victim to the destructive influence of mass psychology' (1946: §903). The problems we face are not the same as the *fin de siècle* hysterics, whose symptoms could be located in their personal history of some traumatic mommy–daddy–me dynamic, which was the basis to Freud's work. Nor are they filled with the psychotic rants or visions of the lunatic asylum at the Burgholzli, as is the basis of Jung's work.

Today the unconscious is not a personal one, not at all. It is both totally collective, and totally objective, that is, it is everyone's and it is not-ours. Today the last psychology has colonized our imaginations, and it is incredibly torturous. Erich Fromm (1994) claimed that today we suffer from symptoms of the schizoid personality and that we are too isolated and self-involved. Noam Chomsky (1998) characterizes us as 'atoms of consumption'. Zizek (1989) explains that we are cynical subjects. Sloterdijk (1988) argues that we are melancholics who can bear the tension of reality just enough to get through our day. Marcuse (1964) claimed that we are constructed to be one-dimensional functionaries. Marx and Engels (1978) claimed that we are alienated from ourselves, and Durkheim (1893/1984) that we have become anomies. According to Wolfe (1976) today is defined as the 'Me' period, where alchemy is used to transform the self. In short, man searched for his soul, found it and sold it for a cheap penny. And this idea of our humanness is torturing everyone collectively, yet one still interprets and treats pain as if it were experienced only personally. This notion is constructed by completely capitalistic logic – so anyone can possess the pain and make it personally theirs. The deflection or obscuring of the truth – that everyone is becoming more un-free and cynical – is due to the effects of the fragmentation and isolation of persons in modern times. Our psyches have been constructed to be completely isolated, mass manufactured and tortured. Interpretations which reinforce that isolation necessarily convert outer experiences into inner journeys. The image of capitalism defines humans to behave in this way by means of its numinosity. And, the images in the movie theater have the potential to reinforce this ideology.

The movie theater is a precise location of the battleground to work through new interpretive procedures, or to take up old ones in new ways, so that one can come to know and explain the images before one's eyes and to resist their numinous affect to pervert one. Sticking to the image runs the risk of subsuming one; critiquing it may help to expand one's psychological horizons. This critique hopefully offers to people a chance against the monolithic presence that dominates the globe, oppresses one and colonizes one's imagination turning one into miserable and tortured persons.

References

Bachelard, G. (1971) *The poetics of reverie*. New York: Beacon Press.

Bloom, A. (1968) *The republic of Plato*. New York: Basic Books.

Bloom, A. (1987) *The closing of the American mind*. New York: Simon & Schuster.

Chomsky, N. (1998) *Class war: the attack on working people*. Oakland, CA: AK Press.

Cushman, P. (1990) 'Why the Self is empty: toward a historically situated psychology', *American Psychologist*, 45(5), pp. 599–611.

Durkheim, E. (1893/1984) *The division of labour in society*. New York: Simon & Schuster.

Ellenberger, H. F. (1981) *The discovery of the unconscious: the history and evolution of dynamic psychiatry*. New York: Basic Books.

Fisher, M. (2009) *Capitalist realism: is there no alternative?* Winchester, UK: Zero Books.

Foucault, M. (1995) *Discipline and punish: the birth of the prison*. New York: Vintage Books.

Fromm, E. (1994) *The art of listening*. New York: Continuum.

Hauke, C. and Alister, I. (eds) (2001) *Jung & film: post-Jungian takes on the moving image*. New York: Routledge.

Hillman, J. (1970) *Re-visioning psychology*. New York: Harper & Row.

Hillman, J. (2015) *Uniform edition of James Hillman: volume 5 'alchemical psychology'*. New Orleans, IL: Spring Publications.

Hockley, L. (2013) *Somatic cinema: the relationship between body and screen – a Jungian perspective*. New York: Routledge.

Hockley, L. (2014) *Somatic cinema: the relationship between body and screen – a Jungian perspective*. Abingdon: Routledge.

Huskinson, L. (2006) 'Holy, holy, holy: the misappropriation of the numinous in Jung', in A. Casement and D. Tacey (eds), *The idea of the numinous: contemporary Jungian and psychoanalytic perspectives*. New York: Routledge. pp. 200–12.

Jaffe, A. (1989) *Was C. G. Jung a mystic? and other essays*. Einsiedeln, Switzerland: Daimon Verlag.

Jonas, H. (1966) 'Image-making and the freedom of man', in H. Jonas (ed.), *The phenomenon of life: toward a philosophical biology*. Chicago, IL: Northwestern University Press. pp. 157–82.

Jung, C. G. (1916/57) 'The transcendent function', in *The collected works of C. G. Jung*, Vol. 8, *The structure and dynamics of the psyche*, 2nd edn. New York: Bollingen Foundation, 1969.

Jung, C. G. (1930/50) 'Psychology and literature', in *The collected works of C. G. Jung*, Vol. 15, *The spirit in man, art and literature*. New York: Bollingen Foundation, 1966.

Jung, C. G. (1936) 'The concept of the collective unconscious', in *The collected works of C. G. Jung*, Vol. 9i, *The archetypes of the collective unconscious*, 2nd edn. New York: Bollingen Foundation, 1968.

Jung, C. G. (1939) 'The psychogenesis of schizophrenia', in *The collected works of C. G. Jung*, Vol. 3, *The psychogenesis of mental disease*. New York: Bollingen Foundation, 1972.

Jung, C. G. (1946) 'Introduction to Wolff's studies', in *The collected works of C. G. Jung*, Vol. 10, *Civilisation in transition*, 2nd edn. New York: Bollingen Foundation, 1970.

Jung, C. G. (1947/54.) 'On the nature of the psyche', in *The collected works of C. G. Jung*, Vol. 8, *The structure and dynamics of the psyche*, 2nd edn. New York: Bollingen Foundation, 1969.

Jung, C. G. (1957/84) *The selected letters of C. G. Jung, 1909–1961*, trans. R. F. C. Hull, eds G. Adler and A. Jaffe. Princeton, NJ: Princeton University Press.

McGinn, C. (2007) *The power of movies: how screen and mind interact*. New York: Vintage Books.

Marcuse, H. (1964) *One-dimensional man: studies in the ideology of advanced industrial society*. Boston, MA: Beacon Press.

Marx, K. (1867/2008). *Capital*. Oxford: World's Classics Paperback.

Marx, K. and Engels, F. (1978) *The Marx-Engels reader*, ed. Robert Tucker. New York: W. W. Norton.

Parker, I. (2007) *Revolution in psychology: alienation to emancipation*. London: Pluto Press.

Sloterdijk, P. (1988) *The critique of cynical reason*. Minneapolis, MN: University of Minnesota Press.

Tacey, D. (2001) *Jung and the new age*. New York: Routledge.

Weber, M. (1920/2011) *The Protestant ethic and the spirit of capitalism*. New York: Oxford University Press.

Wolfe, T. (1976) 'The me decade and the third great awakening', *New York Magazine*, 8(1976), pp. 1–13.

Zaslavsky, R. (2015) Professor of the humanities (personal communication).

Zizek, S. (1989) *The sublime object of ideology*. New York: Verso.

Online sources

Corbett, S. (2009) 'The holy grail of the unconscious', *New York Times* [online]. Available at: www.nytimes.com/2009/09/20/magazine/20jung-t.html?_r=0 [Accessed 10 May 2017].

Ebert, R. (2017) 'Titanic' [online]. Available at: www.rogerebert.com/reviews/titanic-1997 [Accessed 8 June 2017].

Filmography

Avatar. (2009) [film] Directed by James Cameron. USA.

Fast and the furious 7, The. (2015) [film] Directed by James Wan. USA.

Gremlins. (1984) [film] Directed by Joe Dante. USA.

Pervert's guide to ideology, The. (2012) [film] Directed by Sophie Fiennes. USA.

Titanic. (1997) [film] Directed by James Cameron. USA.

4

ARCHETYPAL POSSIBILITIES

Meta-representations, a critique of von Franz's interpretation of fairy tale genre focusing on Jean Cocteau's retelling of *Beauty and the Beast*

Leslie Gardner

Introduction

A colleague of Jung's, Marie Louise von Franz (1915–1998) was a widely acclaimed comment-ator on the fairy tale form that she said was an instance of 'pure' archetype. In this chapter, I want to examine this claim and other facets of her interpretations of fairy tales by using poet, artist, film and theatre director Jean Cocteau's film of the ancient tale of *Beauty and the Beast* (La Belle et la Bête, 1946) as a focal point.

It was Cocteau's second film, and one of his most accessible, fashioning a plausible psycho-logical performance of the traditional story of true love winning out. Its success was assured also by the presence of a leading actor of the time, one of the first celebrities of French cinema, and Cocteau's current boyfriend, Jean Marais (1913–1998).

Von Franz and fairy tale interpretation

Marie-Louise von Franz proposed an approach to the fairy tale that offered analytical tools for a psychological reading that demonstrated the presence of a collective unconscious. As a close associate of Jung's, she sought to set out his theories in a variety of ways. Trained as a physicist she was imbued with a scientific approach and she sought evidence, as proof for discoveries before acknowledging them as 'fact'. In this case she applied that principle to fairy tales, collect-ing evidence from past theories and from stories across time and place.

Von Franz's claim is derived from Jung's theories, namely that fairy tales were the 'naïve, spontaneous' and 'purest representations of archetypes'; they presented eternal and ubiquitous motifs, emanations from the collective unconscious, familiar and unmediated, being outside time and place. They are recognised by that traditional opening phrase, 'once upon a time in a far off place ...'.

In the series of lectures that comprise *The interpretation of fairy tales* (1996) Von Franz sets out as preparation before specific analysis of a story – in summary form – a history of commentary on fairy tales, ranging from Plato to German idealists, anthropologists and romantics. Her conclusion is that just as Jung described rumours in his essay on flying saucers (*Flying Saucers:*

A Modern Myth of Things Seen in the Sky, 1959), fairy tales are understood best as psychic events, contagious and essentialist in their spread through history and across the globe. Scientists reporting the appearance of UFOs on their screens spread the rumour that perhaps they were true, due to their monitors registering a presence. Yet scientifically speaking we know this is not possible. A doubt enters the collective psyche comprising receptive people, vulnerable due to the insecurities of the times to project their anxieties into any trace of an anomaly such as a flying saucer and to believe in it. This 'radial projection' forms an autonomous and dynamic cultural form in Jung's earlier essay.

The psychological tenets of appearance and reality and their 'blurring' – the truth 'behind' the mask – are deep-seated irrational propositions radiating from human psyches that are weakened in times of general anxiety. The tale of *Beauty and the Beast* derives specific energies from the irrationality of love in this thematic scenario. Von Franz, and European literary philologists at the time, such as philologist and mythologist Karol Kerenyi (1897–1973) and collector of international myths Franz Boas (1858–1942), including Creuzer whose studies of mythology both she and Jung also studied, explore this split philosophically, aesthetically and psychologically.

Common elements of fairy tales, von Franz proposes, can be extracted with an eye to the psychology of the collective unconscious. Psychological analyses reveal the archetype of the Self for her, playing out in ways that Jungian psychology defines best. The 'Self' is a collective motif comprising ego (usually the 'hero' of the tale, the agent/actor who will work towards resolution), and collective unconscious 'contributions' to the performance and presence of the individual. Individuation is a process by which each person with his or her own personality and attributes, moves towards a balanced and harmonious 'Self'. In turn, a story has its own unconscious collective trajectory, and the figures in the story comply in the movement towards resolution.

In another parallel recounting of this collective phenomenon as set out in contemporary genre studies, film theorist and philosopher Robert Pippin (2011) points out in his essay on *The Lady from Shanghai* (dir. Welles, 1947) that the Rita Hayworth character responds to the 'noir' genre, playing out the logic of the formula rather than feeling or thinking an individualised psychological logic.

To restate it in von Franz's terms: the collective underlying dimension of the genre plays out through the 'femme fatale' character Hayworth plays – who does not contemplate or know why she acts as she does. The audience is satisfied however as she plays out the instinctive trajectory of the genre. In the fairy tale of *Beauty and the Beast*, true love will win out whatever the psychological dimension we perceive in the shallow figure of Beauty as she is standardly portrayed. Below, I will also refer to Jameson's discussion of Brecht's use of folk parables, which he posits targets those same universal motifs and in so doing add to the philosophical dimension in assessing the German tradition.

In von Franz's theories, the elements of the personality manifest themselves in the characters of the fairy tale. For example 'puer' the adolescent self-regarding impulses are embodied in Cocteau's film in Beauty's brother and her suitor, Avenant. The 'anima' with its transforming or bridging quality as the meaning-making drive (a contested post-Jungian definition of what was originally deemed the feminine theme) probably finds expression in Beauty/Josette, the actor. The 'shadow' projection on to others of dark motives and traits belonging to oneself can putatively be seen in the Beast in Cocteau's film. While the 'trickster' and its havoc-causing irresponsible drive becomes the narrator's voice in the film, for one. As impulses struggling with each other, an overall 'Self' emerges, striving towards harmony and balance. This is 'individuation' and to reiterate, in the fairy tale, it is the move towards resolution.

For the Jungian analytical psychologist of stories or of individuals, such as von Franz who was a practising analyst, these elements all play out in ways that show specific 'scientifically' designated and precise psychological drives – revealing imbalances or deep flaws as the knowing analyst can uncover, using techniques of amplification (hypothesising intentions and significance broadly from actions) and wide knowledge of fairy stories and myths of all time. Having trained as a physicist, Von Franz talks in these terms to underscore the scientific nature of what may appear to be an enquiry into irrational, unconscious psychological elements (deemed 'unscientific'), just as Cocteau asserted paradoxically in a similar impulse that unreality requires great realistic precision to be effective.

In fact, there is a defensive tension in von Franz's work in those early days of Jungian psychology as the early theorists battled with positivist psychological theories of that time. Plausible theory in psychology ought to refer to the higher status that adheres to scientific endeavour. This is reflected in the underlying narrative of the intention in her discussion. She seeks by use of verifiable examples to prove her point that archetypal collective drives are operating in the fairy tale genre.

There were other factors too that inform her enquiry. Naturally von Franz responded to German antecedents and to the Grimm brothers first of all, for example, who collected old tales by scouring the country obtaining evidence from local storytellers. As French and German theorists particularly were, she too was also influenced by the Russian theorist, formalist Vladimir Propp (1895–1970) who she refers to in her summary as a provider of clear articulation, making it easier to parse out the tales. She was particularly drawn to his 'paradigmatic' analysis, aimed at revealing the underlying pattern of a piece of folklore's text – even if the sequence was broken up, the elements are decipherable and constant.

Cocteau's film aesthetic in his time

Although von Franz and Cocteau overlapped in time, their careers and orientations were vastly different: hers as a scientist, and his wholly in the artistic field; he does not refer to science except for his technical proficiency finding aesthetic solutions to representations on film, demonstrated in the jump scene at the end of the film, where Marais and Josette, the actor playing Beauty in the film, found a way to leap up on camera at the end by repeatedly climbing and then dropping, Cocteau reversing the film afterwards; of course Cocteau's mastery of effects and camera placement as symbolic and poetic comment are essential to his artistry and renown.

In the 1920s, Cocteau had flirted with the Surrealists whose abstracted notion of narrative was contrary and polemical. They derived many ideas from Freud's *Interpretation of Dreams* whose work had opened up the unconscious to them as a resource. Working alongside the *Ballet Russe*, with Picasso and Stravinsky, Cocteau fashioned the ballet *Parade* which drew on those surrealist ideas but he soon drifted away (see Steegmuller, 1970 for a gossipy yet thoroughly researched biography).

After publication of many romantic and symbolically fluent books of poetry, and at least one other libretto, Cocteau began working in film. His first, *The Blood of a Poet* (*Le sang, d'un poète*, 1932) used psychological 'quotations' from fixed symbolic meanings he found in Freud – an interest that the surrealists shared. In a progressive effort, Cocteau responded by using film to reveal underlying forms and wishes in more materialist/symbolic fashion and his symbols were poetic emblems performing their meanings. He used innovative film techniques of time delays, cut shots, close ups and over-lays to effect his meanings in creating the precise poetry of *Beauty and the Beast*.

In the traditional tale, the actress playing the young woman is the 'Beauty' of the fairy tale – the daughter of a failed merchant, traded for his freedom to live in the castle of an ugly beast.

We expect it will play out well and that she will release the Beast from his personal incarceration, and love will prevail. However, it is clear that the real 'Beauty' in Jean Cocteau's film of 1939 is the actor, Jean Marais: he plays all the sexy, pivotal and most fully characterised roles in the film – the Beast and the Prince and also the thuggish suitor Avenant: a part added by Cocteau to the de Beaumont version of the story which is the basis of his film; the suitor does not appear in the other major French eighteenth century retellings of the tale either – notably the Villeneuve written version (1740).

As ever in Cocteau's work, his personal life and psychological solutions worked out in his plays, poetry and film. His relationships with the men and women in his life appeared onstage and on film: for example, a tragic early boyfriend, the adolescent poet and novelist Raymond Radiguet influenced Cocteau's novel on incestuous love between brother and sister (*Les Enfants Terribles* [1950] – heavily censored theatrical piece and later film): the camera's intimate gaze as the spectator viewed the incestuous relationship was commented on by Andre Bazin, the film critic, as an innovative camera approach performing the psychological relationship, implicating us. In the scenario, the binary close-sexual partners were playing out his intimate older-sibling-relationship with the younger writer Radiguet where the image of the sister/female's eyes and the male/brother's mouth enunciating their closeness was a filmic technical achievement not used before. Cocteau's closeness to his mother played out in his books of poetry revealing a penchant for unconditional love and the merging of lover and object of desire. And *Beauty and the Beast* was no different in acting out psychological coordinates operating in his personal life. We have the additional resource of his diary of the making of the film to trace the course of his relationship with Marais at least during filming.

An underlying filter is in place as Cocteau focuses on the primary love object and naturally it impacts on the stylistics of the film – it is the 'secret' psychological attitude behind the creation of the film and constitutes the film's core thread. The secret is that the Beast is Beauty. Clearly this is very particular, and founds itself on a collective tale of resolution in love but in a unique way. I would argue with von Franz that 'individuation' is always particular even if perhaps the archetypal 'Self' and its constitution are a motif playing out: it is always played out in particular ways.

It is the inevitable 'twisting' of the proverbial dimension of the original tale (tales are always mediated in their presentations) that questions the 'archetypal' claim for the fairy tale form altogether. There is always a storyteller in a specific time and place, telling the tale for her reason.

Fredric Jameson reminds us, in his discussion of Brecht's method (Jameson, 2011) that the playwright, contemporary to both von Franz and Cocteau, claimed his work was based on scenarios extrapolated from ancient tales and used as 'proverbial foundational narrative' specifically effective on stage. But the trajectory is driven by intentional use of those commonplace 'known' narratives. It is the variables emerging from the use of the proverbial underlying narrative that allows any meaning at all to emerge. *Beauty and the Beast* will have different significance depending on how the artist presents the elements, for there is no such thing as 'pure' archetype as von Franz claims there is.

As mentioned above, Von Franz borrows her sense of the structural certainties of the Russian formalists who analysed the elements of tales in such terms as 'agent', 'action' and secondary structures in clear and provable, scientific ways which appealed to her. By abstracting the hero figure as agent, for example, and tracing the commonplace formulae of action, she derives proof of archetypal formulae – a kind of anthropology based on cultural evidence from reading tales from the past. In fact, many handbooks used by screenwriters and novelists rely on Jungian-orientated lists of essential story formula, famously often deriving from Joseph Campbell's books on myth. The impulse to look there was galvanised by speculations in Jungian circles. But they do not hold. Interpretations utterly rejig the collective motifs. Propp's work has been foundational but is refuted by later structural experts on fairy tales who looked to meanings rather than designated roles (such as I. A. Richards, and Zipes who I will refer to below, not to speak of Marina Warner and many others).

Von Franz certainly brought innovative ideas to bear by focusing on the psychological aspect in her interpretations: in fact her reason overall in talking about fairy tales is to pinpoint archetype as collective unconscious – proof there are universal archetypal motifs. But there are real problems.

The tale itself

First, a summary of the de Beaumont version of the story which Cocteau used with additions: the family of a widowed merchant down on his luck, living in the country in some penury, gets news that a ship has come in that will pay off all his debts. He asks his daughters and son what he should bring back with him as he sets off to reclaim his wealth. They all ask for clothing or horses, except Beauty, his youngest daughter, who asks for a rose. However, he soon discovers when he arrives, that there is nothing left of the monies due, and he is left in the same state if not worse than before.

He makes his way sadly home. A storm drives him towards a castle that is buried deep in a forest: the doors magically open and he finds a meal prepared for him inside; his horse is tended to, and he sleeps quietly. As he leaves next morning, he plucks a rose for Beauty – at least he can bring that back for his loveliest daughter (the older ones are snobs and his son is feckless, a gambler whose friend, Avenant, aggressively importunes Beauty to marry him).

But this 'theft' of a rose enrages the castle's owner who has been hidden from him: the Beast. Growling and fearsome, he insists that either the merchant stay with him or that he trade his daughter in marriage to him – the merchant sorrowfully goes home. They are all upset about their losses and their continued country life, but Beauty insists she will take her father's place as requested by the Beast. They return together, and Beauty prepares to stay – she is horrified too when she sees the Beast's visage and despite his asking her nightly over a magical meal, and dressed in clothes that have appeared magically making her into a Princess – she refuses his request to marry. She witnesses a dire scene of him ravaging an animal and devouring it in his forest.

One night in a magic mirror that allows her to see her home, she notes that her father is ill and she misses him very much – the Beast allows her to return for a limited time period – and sends her off with riches that should assuage her family's poverty. The bracelet she brings with her can call the horse to transport her back, flying over the terrain between country and forest domains; and she still has the mirror that allows her to see back to the castle. If she does not return on time, he says, he will die.

Her sisters and brother and suitor/friend enjoy the riches she's brought with her, but hope to keep it for themselves – they make her forget the timetable. But she recalls her promise especially when she sees in the magical mirror that he is near dying. Meanwhile Avenant discovers the key to the horse himself, and goes ahead of Beauty to the castle with her brother to steal the riches there. Beauty joins up with the Beast and saves him at the ultimate moment telling him she loves him. He is transformed into a Prince, explaining that he'd been bewitched by an evil sorceress who condemned him to this form until a woman could see through it and love him all the same. At the same time, Avenant lets loose an arrow at the stone guardian of the Beast's riches, and is transformed himself into a Beast – entrapped now in the castle grounds – meanwhile Beauty and the newly morphed Prince fly up into the air, the voice over pronouncing that they lived happily ever after and had many children.

Backdrop to story

There were other contemporary versions of this story, as renowned fairy-tale collector and sociologist/anthropologist Jack Zipes points out – at least two were more important than others. The Villeneuve version which was the most competitive to de Beaumont's included night time dreams – the Prince appears in Beauty's night life telling her to look beyond the appearance (a US–Israeli production starring Jon Savage and Rebecca de Mornay contrasted her dreams and his beseeching her in her dreams to look beyond the superficial, and was very successful in its day (dir. Marner, 1987). In that version, it never occurs to her until the very end that the Prince of her dreams is the Beast in disguise. Strangely by using this dream device the film is rendered less magical, and reduced to explanation and diminishes Beauty by demonstrating her lack of imagination. Conventional stylists were in place – the night time dream world very similar to the forest the Beast roams in during the day; the blurring camera indicates a dream is coming as it plays on Mornay's face. But it plays out straightforwardly – no magic.

Other even earlier versions too demonstrated that this is all about testing Beauty – further, in such versions, she is an aristocrat herself, marrying across classes was hardly tolerated and certainly incidental to the archetypal form of the fairy tale that she marry 'outside'. The Beaumont version Cocteau uses accommodates her lower class, while designating she is 'different' from the rest of her rather vulgar family. Importantly, as mentioned, in Cocteau's revision of the de Beaumont tale a suitor is added (which the first Disney animated version picks up for very different reasons in 1991). In the Disney version it is a battle for the unusual Beauty, bookish and virtuous between her countrified arrogant knucklehead suitor, and the sympathetic and intelligent, refined Beast. No dreams, just her essential instinctive goodness figures it out. (A live-action Disney remake was released in 2017, which the time of writing I have not seen.)

Rhetorical issues of the tale: Cocteau/von Franz

Cocteau's poetic approach to the monochrome-filmed fairy tale is mediated by a fully appropriate film language of metamorphosis and irony, deploying what Williams calls Cocteau's 'gay aesthetic' that problematises further von Franz's claims about fairy tales. Eyes in the candelabra regard Beauty and her father as they swish through the castle, drawn on by opening doors. We are complicit with those watching eyes – Beauty and her father do not see them. Those eyes comment on us looking, sharing with neutral gaze the unfolding tale. Tears turn into jewels, floating hands pour wine, and fill dishes; dresses swoop over her shoulders – a technical virtuosity that created an 'appearance' made of detailed hyper-reality. The 'oppositional' binary of appearance/reality is interrogated thoroughly. It is deployed but not questioned.

In the tale of *The Three Feathers* that von Franz uses as her example, there are three sons and an old king – their dilemma is the loss of a crucial powerful instrument to assure the heir is safe on his throne. In psychological terms, the missing element is the 'anima' figure – the mother; von Franz points out that there is no mention of her, and this reveals a lack of cohesiveness (or 'bridging') that in turn has had an impact upon the line of inheritance. Trouble in the land; and the ego figure, the hero saves them all. In fact, he is not the likeliest heir but he is the third son, dull and stupid, whose empathy and persistence and link to a princess saves the kingdom. The 'anima' had been missing. So a psychological technical element drives the story; there is no mention of the mother except through her absence.

Von Franz felt that fairy tales were unmediated cultural forms in a way that myths and legends were not. It must have been that she determined the act of transmission in oral form was more authentic. Yet she does not distinguish oral from verbal storytelling. In other words somehow she missed the mediation that was being questioned around her in philosophical and literary discussion. Theoretical comment on the oral tradition of fairy tales had evolved even as she was setting down her ideas. Derrida (1930–2004) insisted on the unattributable reality of written work – once it has left its author's hands, it becomes a kind of flotsam, and writing about oral literature, Walter Ong (1912–2003) highlights the deeper embedding of the fairy tale in oral tradition but insists the story is to the occasion of its enunciation. The storyteller is implicated. In fact, Zipes points out that fairy tales were specifically written forms, for one thing, and, for another, the storyteller herself, whether transmitting her tale verbally or in writing, has a purpose and this purpose was mostly pedagogic. Zipes points out that although *Beauty and the Beast* had legendary ancient antecedents, the tale achieved its renown in the literary salons of Paris after the Revolution as pedagogic, class-based writer forms. While he admits that there are many scholars who point to the *Psyche and Amor* story of the testing of Psyche before she makes sufficient reparation – he does not utterly concur that it has direct association. Beauty is hardly tested, after all, and she has not broken faith in the de Beaumont version.

In classic rhetorical theory, as Perelman and other rhetoricians point out, fairy tales serve to teach, celebrate and confirm the mores of the land, as epideictic form; they set out tales of praise or blame, and operate by the criteria of a culture's style to underscore the ethos of a community, drawing on cultural memes, certainly, or unspoken patterns in the culture. To reiterate: contexts of time, place and expediency (the occasion on which it is told) mark a tale and, indeed, also the personality of the teller has impact but von Franz does not address this except to say that it is possible. Instead, Von Franz usefully attempts to isolate the eternal motifs of tales by tracing postures of psychological essence; but I'd argue, with others, that there are crucial particular shadings. Those tracings may indicate formal attitudes or determinants of personality but they do not indicate an essence.

What is of great value, however, is her proposal that by having precepts of Jungian psychology in mind, there is a convincing way to argue that the mapping out of psychological play in a tale can suggest varied forms of individuation, the aim of archetypal analysis. The psychological solutions to dilemmas of the individual in the culture can be successfully and helpfully characterised. However, there are gaps. As well as the missing sense of the particular, and the lack of a sense of the importance of exigency, she also rests her analysis on a binary formula which she thinks is ubiquitous – more of that later. Further she mistakes the impact of the framing of the tale at its beginning and its end: how does the tale invite us in and how does it break the spell?

In order to demonstrate how she misses this last element, I will first look at her rhetorical analysis of a story's structure, and highlight where she might have added a feature to address this gap. In doing so, the binary inadequacy is flagged up.

Rhetorical structures

In her discussion of the structure of a fairy tale, von Franz utilises rhetorical terms that are classical but used in a distinct way that is similar to Jung's (1950: §561–4) use of those terms in his discussion of Cicero's definition of libido in which they use this analysis to separate the parts of a tale for hermeneutic purpose. Von Franz insists first of all the tale speaks for itself and the archetypes are autonomous drives, and it is the rhetorical/psychological terms which fit those drives. (It is as if the rhetorical devices are themselves symbols. In fact as I commented in an earlier work, Jung's discussion of the Ciceronian 'long period' – the layering and spinning-out of associations [verbosity] which is meant to replicate inner thought, was a ploy to demonstrate psychological authenticity, among other things, in order to persuade.)

In her recommendations about how to analyse a tale, von Franz suggests that the first step is to note number of characters; this is part of the *exposition*. The theorist/analyst must also look to include as part of the opening examination attention to the place the fairy tale sets out. Following on, then, is the *peripeteia*: the incidents of the story. Often times 'primitives' end their stories at this point she proposes. But a sophisticated storyteller moves on to the *lysis* or 'catastrophe' – some 'turn' which jolts the sequence of events irretrievably in the story, leading to a solution. And then in the fairy tale, the storyteller moves on to the final step, what I will call a *meta-lysis* of sorts which is designed to help the listener or reader to climb out of the world of make believe by an ironising comment or normative twist at the end.

The standard line is 'they lived happily after'. In the case of *Beauty and the Beast*, a voice calls out (it is Cocteau's): 'and they lived happily ever after' and the voice adds a phrase that we read also as ironic, and not simply a straightforward return to reality. The phrase is 'and they had many children'. Knowing Cocteau's ideas about what a soul-destroying life that would be – a fact which we note is reflected in Beauty's hesitancy and the Prince's over-ripe face and body – it makes comment on the purported resolution of the ending. Apart also from the fact we know that the Prince's specific alter ego, Avenant (with the same face and the same love) has been transformed into the Beast – there is still a Beast in the world awaiting the chance to entrap another woman to help free himself ... at the expense of her own incarceration for life.

However, at this 'meta-lysis' stage, von Franz suggests a kind of harmony has been achieved. She goes on to suggest analysis of the steps of individuation as the figures evoked from the overall collective pattern of the Self from here. The hero has overcome odds against his own worse nature and the difficulties of the environment. The hero, the ego and the shadow, warring with each other verbally (dialectically) or in physical combat, prevails having incorporated shadow elements to reach the dynamic stasis of individuation. But, as I have suggested in Cocteau's film, this notion is thrown over by the trickster-ish notion invited by that final 'assist' to the reader/listener in getting back to reality. It is ironic and not wholly a resolution. A lack of resolution in this case also leads on to an examination of the foundational belief in the presence of the binaries that underlies von Franz's theories.

The trope of heterosexuality

Feminists like Betty Hearne, Angela Carter, S. Bryant and Teresa de Lauretis focus on the straightforward abuse of a female in the tale: her subservience and acceptance of the monster-turned-Prince as her husband, saving him in terms of an archetypal analysis, at least, from loss in his animality and masculinity. In their reimagined tales, Carter and Hearne counter what they see as an Oedipal story gone anti-feminist. They critique Cocteau's retelling too as buying into the anti-feminist attitude of the tale. But I think another archetype has intruded that undermines the very foundation of the tale: the trickster voice in the meta-lysis which unsettles archetypal analysis. And while von Franz helps us in an analysis, it is a step beyond an archetypal critique where we might find an interpretation that is closer to what Cocteau was about: must the boy get the girl? Is that where *Eros* leads for a satisfactory ending? Is true love about joining 'opposites' in this way? Cocteau often admonished his young lovers who went on to marry women and have a family that they were choosing a reprehensible way of life. It offended him. The nature of the love with a person of the opposite sex is finally unsatisfactory as relations with 'another' altogether is not ever a resolution.

A film scholar, specialising in Cocteau's work, John Williams sets out that the nature of the utterly romantic love Cocteau sought involved identification with the love object, and thereafter an aim at merging and incorporation. Boundaries between a loved one and the self were bound into a larger collective Self: self-less but joined harmoniously. Heterosexuality was a bad idea. It was a failing. Not only personal taste but also a recognition of the economic binds of matrimony were involved (that would not be a factor today). Heterosexuality proves to be a trope, and if von Franz were to examine the ways it operates in Cocteau's presentation of the fairy tale, I suppose she would point at the way the 'anima' and, as she does in *Three Feathers* analysis, the lack of a mother figure plays into the scenario.

In Cocteau's film, Beauty figures among a quaternity of men in the film. Her sisters are cartoonish figures, representing snobbery and maliciousness (they neglect to tell her the month is up she promised the Beast she would return). While suitor and brother play tricks on them they fit into the parable of the petty lives of country folk and they simply act out, and flesh out, the social ethos of the tale's deep construct.

The powerful ironic posture of those last moments in the film, frames the exigency of the fairy tale as Cocteau conceives it. Thinking back over it there are several ironic commentaries that emerge to jeopardise an archetypal 'pure' psychological reading. There are several parts to this: one is a sense of the dullness of a woman's subservient life as a housewife, which Beauty has taken on and her sisters long for (what role do we imagine their long-gone mother had?) and an assumption that raising children is hard, other-oriented work. Is that what Beauty looks forward to as the ending proposes? This is how many feminists have read the tale. Trading her incarceration and drudgery in her father's house for incarceration in a castle, yet required forever to be obliged to adore the metamorphosed Beast − her hesitation at his change in those last moments of the film reveal a sinking heart; and then they float up into another unreality. The underlying ethos of the original de Beaumont story is hit on here: a tale told to young women aspiring to marry rich, ugly old men − maintain your decorum, maintain your social standing − and here's how to do it for a good life.

Cocteau subverts underlying meanings, and twists away from what may seem core significance. There is no happy and resolved ending. Has the Self been sketched out? Archetypes speak to the 'collective unconscious', von Franz claims; yet, she says, contexts are important too. What I have called the *meta-lysis* blurs that boundary. In effect, this twist refutes her concept: if archetypes manifest in divergent ways, the notion is altogether negated of core meaning.

This problem is not recognised by von Franz. In fact she extends her claims about fairy tales' purity to say that individual countries have their own biases and fairy tales, and can colour a nation's cultural output. She cites Rousseau's views and in her own country, Herder's, to suggest there are national distinctions. She lauds the authenticity of the Grimm Brothers' collection without noting that their transcriptions of tales were not always genuine. She says the brothers had no agenda (and so they are genuine recollections of tales) yet she dismisses their nationalistic and pedagogic purposes. It seems it is her view too that by their nature archetypes are binary and oppositional propositions and they are deployed in the fairy tale to constitute their dialectical nature, the heart of the tension of the plot, the 'catastrophe'. Proper interpretation and discovery of archetypes aim instinctively at compensation and balance. That is 'individuation' and in *Beauty and the Beast* the dominant tropes seem to be appearance/reality and *Eros*: specifically the male/female axis unless we examine Cocteau's intentions more closely.

But, as I contend, these very binary and oppositional necessities are made problematic in Cocteau's film and add dimensions that conflict with her ideas of the archetypal nature of fairy tales.

Psychological dimensions: love me even if I am repulsive

Finally, Von Franz brings up another element in her talk of varied interpretations of the feeling or sensational type or the intuitive and thinking type. The storyteller herself flags up unique significance. De Beaumont focused on a fallen aristocrat, entitled to marry into that class; she sets out to admonish young girls to aim at older, rich men for their own future security (and their family's).

Discussion of de Beaumont's tale as a primer to train yourself to accommodate a man you may find repulsive is set out in Marina Warner's (2014) important work on fairy tales. A generation later, she recounts, Villeneuve suggested a different route to the same goal in which Beauty sees a mysterious handsome Prince in her dreams telling her to look beyond what appears. So the man before you is not what he seems. Earlier tales that seem to feed into the same theme involve terrible tasks for Beauty to test her worthiness, and suggest that she become as abusive as her testing prince.

In his diary of making the film, Cocteau recounts suffering bouts of skin rashes and time spent in hospital during the filming; all the time pointing out that Marais suffered illness throughout too, sometimes mirroring Cocteau's skin disease. The terrible agonies we witness when the Beast longs for Beauty's love, and is caught bloody and spent after a kill play off the real life sufferings offstage. A recurring theme in Cocteau's oeuvre is that the suffering of the artist for his work is essential – the *Blood of the Poet* not only was the name of one of his films, but is the cost he believed his work required for creativity. That film shows the poet inflicting cuts to himself, and suffering arrows. Faithful artistic work and suffering counted greatly for him, and Marais seemed to be competing with Cocteau to demonstrate this fealty.

Physical stamina and presence are core virtues we gather from Cocteau's diaries and they are a theme in the film. There is physicality in the film: Avenant corners Beauty against a wall, pressing his love on her; it is only when they hear her father stumbling below that he moves away fearful of taking on a fierce protective male. Later, nimbly scaling a wall, he lets loose an arrow aimed at the stone/guardian of the Beast's treasure in the Palace grounds and falls, transforming into the Beast himself in his greed: he has failed to secure love and the treasure. The Beast is covered in gore when he kills another animal for sustenance, but Beauty finds him depleted, fallen against a rock when she belatedly returns.

As a Beast, repulsive and physically inappropriate Avenant now will hope to find release unsatisfactorily in heterosexual love. In reading Cocteau's accompanying diary, these themes of interaction with Marais and with their approach to creativity, are reflected in the psychological performance of the figures in the film. The psychological make up of the teller of the tale has impact too.

Exigencies

My purposes in this chapter were varied but set out to demonstrate that the fairy tale creates its own exigency and comprises contexts, including the intention of the storyteller, and that it helps its audience of either listener or reader to return to un-fairy tale domain. Isn't this a trickster-ish manipulation, undermining the notion of the archetypal aspect of the fairy tale? We can conclude that an archetype is never a pure emblem without contexts or representations – it resides in just those elements or it is nothing at all. It is in the meta-representation that significance emerges. Cocteau's intention is to undermine those archetypal drives that seemed to drive the story.

Cocteau particularly used the language of film for making poetry that 'spoke' its significance in a particular way. He traduces borders artistically between human and anything other by partaking of the ubiquitous drive to create meaning. Individuation is characterised in Cocteau's product as an incorporation of ego projections on to others and absorbing those projections that engage him as an artist into his personal vision and stylistic.

Opposition dissolves, and the 'other' merges with you. You and the other are on a continuum as the dialectic dissolves. The heterosexual gender-implied opposition and, indeed, appearance and reality oppositions are both similarly on a continuum rather than in opposition. Before I conclude I want also to examine more closely that binary of appearance and reality mentioned at the start.

Cocteau's stylistic and archetype

Another ancient formula that many commentators on *Beauty and the Beast* mention is the classic motif of the 'animal lover'; he seems human but he is animal. Due to long sessions of application of makeup, Marais could be the Beast and transform and fly up because of filmic portrayal. He became that gross animal/lover suffering mightily in the transition. (Watching the film with him, Marlene Dietrich, Steegmuller reports, sighed deeply to Cocteau, upset when the sexy beast disappeared to become the pretty-boy cleaned up Prince. She was not the only one.)

In the end, they fly up, technically masterful – Beauty's hesitancy over she is dazzled and the Prince is beaming, but that voice-over expresses bored rote comment – neither joyful nor bedazzled.

Underlying the ambivalence of legal/commercial bindings of marriage are the questions: am I beautiful or ardent enough for her or for him; will he or she stay with me? Am I loved? The style and themes of the film pivot on shiny dresses and courtly servitude as proper relations with a heterosexual woman as it is both part of the fairy-tale scenario and an attribute of male–female marriage. This is the universal and also the personal drive we attend to in the audience.

But I argue here that it was not only for reasons of his own sexual inclinations, but also for reasons of cultural/societal insight that had to do with the notion of individuation (no matter what name he gave it) which made heterosexuality a problem. Would Cocteau's opinion of the treachery of marriage have been assuaged had he been able to marry his partner, Jean Marais, the actor playing the Beast/Prince in the film? I do not think so; I propose that there was something broader going on. Therefore I come again to the technique of 'meta-representation' (to use narratology scholar Linda Zunshine's word) which Cocteau's rendering of the fairy story-as-film an ironic shift making the reality dimension equally implausible. We are asked to recast what we have thought or seen of the story of *Beauty and the Beast*.

Exploring the appearance/reality theme is a central strategy in how Cocteau picks up the tale just as it is central to the story of *Beauty and the Beast*. Indeed, the very way it is implemented shows it as distinctly Cocteau's themes as poet and stylist.

Their struggles to bring the film to screen hampered by bad lighting, bad weather, lack of funding, illness all combined to make it on a dogmatic level of his own devising, a valid artful product. The struggles of working within the trope of appearance/reality are apparent in the ironies and pragmatic solutions of *mise-en-scène*, actors' physical presence, social and financial difficulties. This underlying tension suggests that such tropes are constitutive in a way that I do not think von Franz accommodates. Von Franz writes that the appearance/reality trope is an unfailingly powerful one throughout history. It is tantamount to an archetype.

However, the specific elements of the film such as costume and hair and atmosphere/scenario are vital to the integrated presence of the story. Unspoken visual prompts, as Zipes and other commentators suggest, contrasting country/farm settings where Beauty's sisters flounce around in their inappropriate garb, constantly impeding them in operating in the household. These contrast with Beauty's simpler, peasant clothing and develops the theme of social aspiration which correlates to the sisters' nastiness. Are those scenes 'reality' in this domain? They are fanciful and tainted with the social longings of the characters. A distinctly cartoonish money-lender oversees a card-playing session with Avenant and Beauty's brother – straight out of a book of clichéd tropes, surely? Avenant, the suitor, friend of her brother, is similarly garbed in country wear. In the setting of the Beast's lair, the castle, the Beast's regal costume and elaborate table setting and jewels don't impede life – they assume a splendour and beings move easily in the surrounding as doors open for them and Beauty glides along the long corridors, enabled by a superb cameraman.

The lifestyle implicates a magical authority, outside the bumps and smells and aspirational longings of the people living in the country. Appearance and reality speak to each other when the suitor and brother break the rules and use the horse to steal the beast's wealth; the ineptitude and bumpy landings of the country are brought to the palace and vanquished. Their horses stumble and bump into fences. In the castle, as I have mentioned, eyes watch us and independent limbs feed her father and Beauty yet in what respect is all not as it seems as after all this is a magical domain. It is 'reality'.

'Reality' for the Beast is blurred with 'appearance': he moves in his house and across country transported effortlessly by a magic mirror. He is graceful and charismatic, his movements efficacious as he turns a tear into a jewel. His unsettling 'other' animal-nature emerges in the hunt for smaller prey. His garb is covered in blood and torn in those transformations. Is that a representation of reality in the midst of the magical castle? Yet it accommodates and insists on his bestial nature. It talks to that secret anxiety of us all, trumpeted large in the Beast that questions 'am I too ugly to be loved?' and echoes in the audience's psyche.

This is also about the weakness of self-esteem: in the meta-life of this film, as mentioned, Cocteau was deeply engaged with the actor, a handsome, young, and very masculine, Jean Marais who enjoyed tremendous popularity due to his appearance in some of Cocteau's earlier films. Putting Marais to the test in a disfiguring mask must have given Cocteau a kind of frisson, not least as he was much older than Marais who was beset in his life by women as well as by other men: a celebrity sex symbol. Cocteau contended with that in life outside the film. As an instance of individuation, here is an opportunity for Cocteau to play out a projection of anxiety. It is my contention that this sensibility enters into the film as an artistic feature. Does personalised psychological exploration of the underpinnings of a cultural product undermine its collective potency? I think not and, as Foucault has said, we are all nominalists. Archetypes are not pure and they are mediated in retellings of a fairy tale each and every time.

References

Cocteau, J. (1986) *Beauty and the beast: diary of a film*. New York: Dover Publications.

Derrida, J. (1974) *Of grammatology*. Baltimore, MD: Johns Hopkins University Press.

Hutcheon, L. (1994) *Irony's edge*. London: Routledge.

Jameson, F. (2011) *Brecht and method*. London and New York: Verso.

Jung, C. G. (1950) 'A study in the process of individuation.' in *The collected works of C. G. Jung*, Vol. 9i, *The archetypes and the collective unconscious*. London: Routledge & Kegan Paul, 1968.

Jung, C. G. (1959/1977) *Flying saucers: a modern myth of things seen in the skies*. London: Routledge & Kegan Paul.

Ong, W. (1982) *Orality and literacy: the technologizing of the word*. London: Methuen.

Pippin, R. (2011) 'Agency and fate in Orson Welles's "The lady from Shanghai"', *Critical Inquiry*, 37(Winter), pp. 214–44.

Propp, V. (1968) *Morphology of the folktale*. Austin, TX: University of Texas Press.

Steegmuller, F. (1970) *Cocteau: a biography*. London: Macmillan.

Villeneuve, G.-S. B. de (1740) 'La Belle et la Bête' (Beauty and the beast), in *La Jeune Américaine et les contes marins* (The young American and marine tales).

Von Franz, M.-L. (1996) *The interpretation of fairy tales*. Boston, MA: Shambhala Publications.

Von Franz, M.-L. (1997) *Archetypal patterns in fairy tales (studies in Jungian psychology by Jungian analysts)*. Toronto: Inner City Books.

Warner, M. (2014) *Once upon a time: a short history of the fairy tale*. Oxford: Oxford University Press.

Williams, J. S. (2008) *Jean Cocteau (critical lives)*. London: Reaktion Books.

Zipes, J. (2011) *Fairy tales and the art of subversion*. London: Routledge.

Zunshine, L. (2006) *Why we read fiction: theory of mind and the novel*. Columbus, OH: Ohio State University Press.

Filmography

Beauty and the beast. (1987) [film] Directed by Eugene Marner. USA, Israel.

Beauty and the beast. (1991) [film – animation] Directed by Gary Trousdale and Kirk Wise. USA.

Beauty and the beast. (2017) [film] Directed by Bill Condon. USA.

Belle et la bête, La. (Beauty and the beast) (1946) [film] Directed by Jean Cocteau and René Clément. France.

Enfants terrible, Les. (1950) [film] Directed by Jean Cocteau. France.

Lady from Shanghai, The. (1947) [film] Directed by Orson Welles. USA.

Sang, d'un poète, le. (Blood of a poet, The). (1932) [film] Directed by Jean Cocteau. France.

5

HUMAN BEANS AND THE FLIGHT FROM OTHERNESS

Jungian constructions of gender in film

Phil Goss

Gender, film and the unreal

'It's a winksquiffler...!'
(Dahl, 2015, p. 62)

'remember the gendered'
(Jung, 2009, p. 264)

According to the Big Friendly Giant (Dahl, 2015, p. 77) 'Human Beans' do not accept the reality of something unless it presents itself before their noses (or 'schnozzles' as he calls them), including different types of dreams (of which a 'winksquiffler' is one). So, what is *real* and what is *unreal*? Beyond that, in thinking of the territory explored in this chapter, what does *masculine* mean and what does *feminine* mean? Further to these questions, can we (and, if so, then how), distinguish between 'real' and 'unreal', and between 'masculine' and 'feminine'?

Simple questions; simplistic even. But, the power and beauty of human imagination, and its capacity to reveal, to shock, to inspire and entertain – not least in the powerful narratives, characterisation and cinematography of the world of the moving image – allows for such simple questions to be rendered as vividly complex. Here, the distinctions they refer to are at times utterly over-run, inundating our phenomenological field with experiences which contradict the binary notions of real versus unreal, feminine versus masculine. At other times, however, these binaries get thrown into stark relief within the filmic portrayal of story, personified experience and reactions, and relational and spatial dynamics.

In this chapter I want to demonstrate how a Jungian/post-Jungian take on the ways in which gendered polarities expressed in archetypal (masculine or feminine) terms, and experienced in embodied and socialised manifestations of gender difference (male or female – or *and*, with respect to transgender), get revealed in films. In this respect I concur with Beebe's (2001) focus on seeing characters in films as representative of complexes undergoing change, especially where contra-sexual influences are concerned (i.e. the inner feminine or masculine). However, I go further than this in my emphasis on the fundamental centrality of the multi-coloured, shaded and textured palette of *gender* (from which films can paint all sorts of pictures) in terms of how

65

gender pervades our sense of self, our relationships and our engagement with the cultural, polit-ical, social and ecological dynamics of the world(s) we inhabit. I will draw strongly on my own post-Jungian approach to this (Goss, 2010) which emphasises the power of subtle contra-sexual psychic influences on our development, relationships and lived experience.

Film, I argue, provides the tools to help us paint the pictures suggested by this palette of influences, real and unreal, so we can see where these may overlap or stand apart, correspond or clash. By illuminating the symbolism of gender in film, a Jungian/post-Jungian approach stands apart from more reductionist and deconstructionist approaches to film image and narrative, in how it strives to reveal profound experiential and archetypal meanings attached to gendered representation. Within my exploration of how a bridged Jungian and post-Jungian perspective can illuminate the rigidities and fluidities of gendered experiencing, I will juxtapose the question of what is *real* and what is *unreal* about gender.

'Gender' in this respect is partly seen as beholden to the subjectivity and individuality of lived experience. Here 'gendered experiencing' is key. This advocates the holding of the notion of 'gender' lightly, as a moment-by-moment, fluid, lived phenomenon. However, this also includes managing as well as one can, the balancing between this stance, and one of respect for more traditional narratives which imply there might be some *real* points of distinction between the experience of being a man and being a woman. Here I argue there is an archetypal polarity to hold in our attitude towards gender 'difference': between the seeing of this as *real* on the one hand, and on the other position which holds such notions are *unreal*, a mirage of dated social construction, and the importance of avoiding over-simplification (Connell, 2002) let alone the dangers of stereotyping and the spectre of sexism.

The approach advocated which I strive to hold to – not without difficulty I might add – tries not to be definitive about what makes for gender, or for gendered difference and similarity, par-ticularly between *female* and *male* as this is a complex mix of environmental and constitutional factors. At the same time, in recognising what might be socially and relationally constructed on the one hand (and in this sense *unreal*), it also recognises what can be more bodily based, neuro-biologically rooted and instinctual on the other (where the possibility of *real* difference arises). All this feeds into how 'gendered experiencing' reflects the phenomenology of what it feels (and senses, thinks and intuits) like to be a woman or a man (Samuels, 1989), as well as what it may be like to have a transgendered sense of self and identity.

Here Jung's insights into the presence of contra-sexual influences in the human psyche (Jung, 1968) offers a valuable, if in places inevitably dated, frame of reference for looking at the hermeneutics of gender captured in films. His notion of *anima* as an archetypally constellated, and collectively influenced, presence of the feminine in the psyches of men, and *animus* as a corresponding masculine presence in the psyches of women may appear to us now as too defini-tive a binary of the play of opposites in human experiencing. However, this and Jung's some-what awkward ascription of characteristics which tend to accompany their presence (e.g. *anima* can bring out the feeling capacity of the man as well as the touchy and over-sentimental, while *animus* enables women to think clearly and/or to become irrationally judgemental) is not by any means the whole story. Instead, by creating a range of possibilities for the interplay of inner contra-sexual influences with outer experiences and relationships, a more fluid and individual living out, 'performance' of these dynamics can be described and played with.

In my own 'play' with these possibilities (Goss, 2010) I have posited a differently nuanced emphasis in the use of *anima/animus*. Instead of their influence bringing out contra-sexual 'positive' or 'negative' characteristics in a man or woman, I find it more helpful to see this influ-ence as *energic* in quality. In other words the 'tone' of how a person can experience particular situations, or life in general, is subtly influenced by the presence of *anima* (men) or *animus* (women). In this respect I combine Freud's notions of the life instinct (*Eros*) as drawing us more into engagement with life and love, juxtaposed with the death instinct (*Thanatos*) which pulls us into more depressed and destructive patterns of relating and being (Freud, 2001), with Jung's contra-sexual model. So, where the masculine in the psyche of a woman interacts with the life or death instinct I term this as the constellation of *erosimus* (*Eros + animus*) or *thanimus* (*Thanatos + animus*) and where the feminine in the psyche of a man interacts with the life or death instinct I term this as the constellation of *erosima* (*Eros + anima*) or *thanima* (*Thanatos + anima*). I will apply these terms to examples from the films explored in this chapter, as a tool for bringing into view the nature and activity of gendered dynamics within and between human beings where, to use the language of the BFG, human *beans* gets cooked in archetypal energy.

Gender, as a theme or presence in films and other arts forms, as well as something which hallmarks all our journeys through life, can be a highly charged area – such as, for example, in how we talk about and ascribe gendered roles and characteristics, or where gender performs a key role in life dramas which may invoke more sexualised, confrontational or even violent manifestations of human 'being'. This makes it a natural and ubiquitous narrative and visual ingredient in most, if not all, films. It is hard to think of a well-received (or less so!) film where gender relations and identity do not feature in a notable way. Even where animals or machines are the main players – whether in animated or 'real-life' form – female or male ascriptions of identity usually get deployed to properly anthropomorphise the action in ways which bring a feel of familiarity and heighten the potential for identification to our viewing. Gender as an actor will never be short of work in the film industry.

This chapter is exploring, through a Jungian lens, how gender plays out this far-reaching influence on us, and why approaching film through this lens, complemented by insights from various other theoretical and clinical standpoints, can shed light on the depth and living presence of archetypal feminine and masculine influences (and all points between). This will be done through first using the adaptation of Roald Dahl's children's story *The Big Friendly Giant* (dir. Spielberg, 2016) from a human sized book to the giant scale of the big screen, to demonstrate how a classical contra-sexual reading of film narrative and visual symbols can help us understand how these influences operate on a daily basis in our gendered experiencing. Second, a blend of Jungian and post-Jungian insights will be deployed to examine how the dyads of feminine/masculine (archetypal), male/female (relational) and concrete/imaginal (experiential) intersect, divide and combine, in films which focus in on the struggles to live out, broaden, change or dissolve gendered identity and aspects of experience. This will include a consideration of the following films: *Force Majeure* (dir. Oslund, 2014), *The Piano Teacher* [*La Pianista*] (dir. Haneke, 2001), *American Beauty* (dir. Mendes, 1999), *Tomboy* (dir. Sciamma, 2011) and *Biutiful* (dir. Iñárritu, 2010).

Big friendly *animus* and little vulnerable *anima*

The transfer of the telling of Roald Dahl's vivid tale of enchantment *The Big Friendly Giant*, or *BFG*, from illustrated storybook (Dahl, illustrated by Blake, 1982), to full coloured illustrated colour edition (2015) and then blockbuster family film (Spielberg, 2016) reflects the visual wonder of its imagery in it as much as its narrative power. In this film, Spielberg's cinematic eye for the capacity of image to memorably capture the symbolic significance of ideas and characters, plays to the full to provide us with a wonderful portrayal of classical *anima/animus* dynamics.

As the story unfolds, from the girl Sophie's (Ruby Barnhill) unexpected visitation in the night by a male Giant (Mark Rylance) – or her exaggerated *animus*, we might say – the relationship between them powerfully portrays an unfolding narrative centred around their relationship.

He provides fearful but eventually redeeming and freeing – or *individuating* – adventures for the girl, and she seems to represent a need for him to encounter and (literally) 'carry' a vulnerable but brave and perceptive version of *anima* to help him free himself from the apparently all-male hoard of brutal giants who are fixated on eating as many 'human beans' as they can…. There are other portrayals of the giant's *anima* and the girl's *animus* in the story which provide a kind of powerful imagistic evidence for the evolving and pluralistic nature of contra-sexual life within us. *Anima* and *animus*, in line with Jung's development of Freud's monistic (psychosexual) application of the nature of libido into something more pluralistic (where forms of libidinal energy can include relational, vocational, creative and spiritual manifestations), as well as Jung's interest in variations in responses to lived experience at different life stages, *evolve* and *diversify*.

At the opening of the film, we find Sophie lying in her bed in the 'norphanage' (as the BFG terms it). She is awake in the middle of the night and restless and apparently not just because she cannot get to sleep in the normal way. She goes to the window, as if looking for something 'out there', maybe her mother and father who she never really knew (though she was a baby when they died, so there is a hint of them both being 'in her somewhere …').

As she stares out of the window she sees a huge hand reach across to pick up a bin which has been noisily knocked over. We also see images of a moving giant shadow going past at the end of the street – apparently a huge human form walking between the houses. This striking image carries both *shadow*, and something parental and therefore either *contra-sexual* ('father') or, in this author's best attempt to name the opposite of this *para-sexual* ('mother'). As an audience we are almost certain to know that this is the BFG so therefore '*contra-*', but we cannot be sure, especially as the girl does not know what she is encountering. From a Jungian perspective, this observation carries symbolic and phenomenological weight, as the very nature of *shadow*, according to Jung, is that it obscures parts of ourselves we do not know, blocks out aspects of our personality, desires and behaviours we refuse to recognise, but also houses potentials in us which we cannot yet see and will only do so if we face the more difficult, uncomfortable and unknown dimensions of who we are. Sophie spotting the BFG's shadow within the night time townscape – as he searches the streets for a child to be his friend, his soul mate, his *anima* (holding in mind the classical Jungian equation of *soul* and *anima* (Jung, 1968), and otherwise expertly hiding from human view – suggests to us she is awake to her *shadow* at some level and ready to plunge into it, in order to try to resolve contra-sexual questions left hanging within her by the rupture to her psychic development which the death of both her parents will have generated. This of course includes the Oedipal question, and for Sophie the disturbance to the psycho-sexual layer of her experiencing caused by this earth shattering double-loss is implied in the contrasting imagery of her white nightie and the dark figure of the approaching giant, whose cloaked head also speaks to the presence of death which has indeed overshadowed the beginnings of her journey through life from an enormous height.

This problem, and the capacity of psyche to wake us up to the need to face such things (portrayed by the shaft of silver moonlight which flashes into her bedroom), reflects how parents or other primary carers fill up a giant-sized space in us, as they lumber, and carry or push us, around the confined world we live in as infants, as well as creating an equally giant-sized hole if we lose them to death or separation in childhood (or if they were never there in the first place) (Goss, 2010). Their faces and hands loom towards us as we lie in our cots or prams to coo at us or lift us up high into the outer space of the big scary or friendly world. This feeling is evoked in the film by the sudden reaching in of the giant's huge, gangly, hand through the bedroom window where it scrabbles around in the bed where she is hiding (again evocative of psycho-sexual, Oedipal, threat) and on finding the terrified girl, scoops her up and carries her away to the land of the giants.

Giants, film and contra-sexual evocation

A word here about giants and films. The place of giants in written narratives and oral storytelling over the centuries is well established, from ancient mythology (e.g. the Greek 'Titans', nicely rendered in animation in *Hercules* (dirs, Clements and Musker, 1997)) and the biblical *Nephilim* (Van Ruiten, 2000) through medieval stories such as *Jack and the Beanstalk* and *Jack the Giant Killer* the latter of which in particular has transferred well on to the big screen (dir. Juran, 1962). Jung himself writes of a powerful encounter with a giant, *Izdubar*, in *Liber Secundus* (Jung, 2009) as he nearly destroys its power simply through the deadly power (his *thanima*, in the sense of an absence of feeling, of soul) of an over-rational state of mind. In all these cases it is the power of the image which is conjured up and facilitates the constellation of the presence of giants in our psyches; a numinous presence. The challenge for film directors and *anima*tors (animation as access to soul, to the numinous …) has been to capture this numinous presence for cinema audiences, so they can feel fear and awe which story giants evoke. Where this works, I propose, contra-sexual forces are present. Ray Harryhausen's remarkable special effects in *Giant Killer* for example evoke fearful fascination towards a mesmerising range of masculine *animus* giants that are eventually defeated by an adolescent *animus* figure (projected perhaps from unresolved feminine expressions of oppressed medieval female experiencing?). Likewise, the sight of the giant glamorous feminine in *Attack of the 50ft. Woman* (dir. Juran, 1958) manages to grip us, however preposterous (and maybe because it is) I suggest, because of the equally awesome presence of destructive and the erotic *anima* qualities presented in such an exaggerated form.

So, equally in *BFG*, when the giant removes his hooded cloak once they are in his cavernously large kitchen, and we finally see who this is – it is *animus*, giant *animus*. We feel the power of the constellation of the contra-sexual on this hugely enlarged scale, like crawling into the living room as a young child, and looking up to see Mum or Dad staring at us. In this case the BFG is a version of the girl's *animus*, which in turn has been seeking his lost *anima* partner. He is ridiculously big, and much older than her, but from the way he talks he does not come across as the most sophisticated of men, and he uses peculiar words when he talks.

However, we see from his warm, friendly face we know quickly that this is largely speaking a version of *erosimus*, a life-giving, caring version of *animus*, and we realise that though very tall, he is much smaller than the brutal band of marauding giants who threaten his safety as much hers (in that respect he stands between the archetypal and the personal). We watch as the girl's attempts to escape are gradually replaced by an acceptance and gradual appreciation of his presence and of their relationship.

His age and size also imply a compensatory role for her *erosimus*, which is revealed as old but apparently simple in approach to life, while also being deceptively wise. The expert portrayal of his giant-ness as he at times clumsily, and others daintily, attends to his domestic duties, or his huge face looms towards Sophie, presents us with an image of something which is clearly out of scale in her, and therefore he represents her chance to get more of an appropriate to-scale *animus* installed in her, in the absence of a real father presence to help her do this.

He, in turn, clearly prizes what he has managed to capture – the illusive child *anima* he has lost, or never really had. We can see this in his face – the sparkly eyes, the warming, smiling mouth and the gaze of tenderness etched into his forehead, bringing out the adoring potential *paterfamilias* in him. Again compensation in the Jungian sense of balancing the psyche is key here. The girl is a child (maybe eight or nine?) with all that implies about her innocence and readiness for fresh encounter with life. This is the *erosima* version the BFG has been seeking to fill the space opened up by his rough and lonely existence as a friendly giant surrounded by the violent mob mentality of his compatriots. We are impacted by the difference in size between the two main protagonists as she is carried around and protected by his huge hand, and this imagery conveys vividly the sense of him seeking out of a life more to-scale; more ordinary.

Finally, Sophie's pre-pubescent youthfulness, conveyed vividly as she jumps, squeezes or falls in trying to escape the clutches of the marauding Bloodbottler (Bill Hader), tells us how young the BFG's *anima* is, and of his need to grow up. First though he needs a play mate to get him to the point where he is ready to do just this, and as they both drink *frobscottle* and produce *whizzpoppers* from there, they are able to move him into and through the adolescence he has not properly negotiated yet in himself. With her help, he goes on to find his way to a properly adult experience of taking responsibility for a vulnerable other, and help her solve her *animus* problem at the same time.

Filmic imagery and contra-sexual recognition in the *BFG*

This consideration of the portrayal of contra-sexual imagery, themes and characterisation con-cludes with a snapshot of how *anima* and *animus* evolve and diversify across the *BFG* film. Sophie's relationship with *animus* influences, develops largely through her frightened but deter-mined struggle with the giants who threaten to consume not just her but all the children of England. The narrative locates these giants as threats and obstacles to her integration of poten-tially deadly and more life giving masculine energies (*erosimus* and *thanimus*) and this is portrayed lucidly in the scene where the giants are all sleeping and the BFG sneaks up to the most fearsome – *Fleshlumpeater* (Jermaine Clement) and releases a nightmare from his dreamcatcher collection up the huge creature's nose, and the fifty-four-foot tall giant writhes and shrieks in terror. Here, the screen is filled with the drama of *thanimus* undermined – the tyrannical and rapacious masculine, all instinct and brutality thrown into fear and timidity, shaking the foundations of the world or giants. The clear analogy of dream country as source of this undermining power offers, through its imagery of the pool which turns things on their head, a vision of the unconscious source of compensatory contra-sexual energies and images.

In turn, as the film unfolds further, the contrast between the crude, destructive *thanimus* energy of the collective of 'bad' giants (a distant echo of Jung's contestable but interesting asser-tion that a woman's *animus* will often constellate as a collective of male figures (Jung, 1966), and the shy but determinedly caring BFG is perfectly captured by Spielberg. He has the giant stand-ing hidden in the trees outside Buckingham Palace. For a moment all we see are his two giant eyes staring out from between the branches: softly, fearfully … sadly even? Sophie's *erosimus* is getting nearer to the royal palace where the gathering together of masculine influences in her to healthy effect is happening. The image of the eyes in the trees which can see from the hidden depths, tell us the more uncertain, shy but kinder version of *animus* holds the key to this.

Alongside this imagery we become aware of the visual contrast between the out of propor-tion masculinity of the giant, and the down to earth but regal presence of the queen. Here the BFG's *erosima* is portrayed as possessing the power to provide collective leadership and resources to help him defeat the destructive *thanima* energies in his psyche, as represented by the giants. She is even portrayed drinking *frobscottle* and farting (regally of course), as if his playful, messy *anima* has been integrated into the most authoritative versions of *erosima*. This contributes to the panorama of imagery which portrays the alchemy of contra-sexual opposites, as the *erosimus* influences in Sophie meet the *erosima* ones in the BFG to defeat the giants.

The movie ends differently from the book, with its heart-warming description of the queen getting the story published. Instead, just before the closing images of Sophie and the BFG, there is a scene where we pan back from the image of *Fleshlumpeater* stranded on top of the highest point of the tiny remote island where he and his fellow giants have been left as punishment; a final farewell to the girl's fearsome *thanimus* complex which has finally faded into the distant recesses of her psyche, though it might well have not been utterly dissolved. Here is an image which captures the unreal power of a contra-sexual complex to disrupt and threaten psychic health, and the potential to marginalise its influence through our real capacity to team up with our inner, healthy, unreal partner in pursuit of this.

Gender, film and realism

Now, to turn the camera around the other way, and instead of looking at *anima* and *animus* and their reality as symbolised graphically in the 'unreal' imaginal, we will now look at portrayals of their presence in the 'real' lives of contemporary on-screen protagonists. The ways in which contra-sexual energies may influence gender relations and in particular the interplay of erotic features of these will be explored. The focus will be predominantly on presentations of hetero-sexual relations but with one or two references to same-sex and transgendered relations. This emphasis is deliberate, and with no intention to marginalise the latter. My main theoretical, clinical and cultural interest is in the dynamics between men and women, believing there is still so much we do not understand about what gets constellated between them at personal-relational, socio-cultural and archetypal-collective levels, in intimate partnerships as well as in wider familial and social contexts. Film offers just such a way in, with its capacity to reflect back to us what we know (impacting on us with a range of familiar reactions from ecstatic to horrified …) as well as what we have not seen in ourselves, or our relationships before.

A force of nature: an avalanche of *anima* and *animus*

Force Majeure (dir. Ostlund, 2015) is a film with a very specific focus – what happens when the very foundations of a husband and father's place in the family are swept away in a moment – not by the (moderate) avalanche which sweeps into their hotel restaurant terrace as they have their lunch, but by his reaction to it. Frightened, he is seemingly unable to contain this fear enough to remain attendant to the vulnerability of his family whatever the potentially mortal risk to himself. He leaves his wife and two children to fend for themselves as the wall of snow approaches, removing himself from the scene, post-haste. This moment acts as the hook for a tortuous but ultimately growthful journey for the family at the centre of this perfect relational snowstorm.

What seems to rescue this situation changing from an illusionary natural disaster (an ava-lanche which has a bark worse than its bite) to a relational one is the way Tomas – the man who is caught bang to rights for deserting his wife and family in their hour of need – accepts his human and his masculine weaknesses and then how Ebba, his partner, comes to see the only way forward is to accept these. This only happens after his failed attempts to contradict his partner's version of events as he argues that he did not run away at all, but he is caught out when Ebba points out he has himself videoed the scene. As they watch this, he has to admit he walked away in front of her, his friend Mats and the latter's younger girlfriend, Fanni.

We then see Tomas collapse into a state of wreckage, lying on the floor, shirtless and sobbing, as his children try to comfort their Daddy, demanding to know why their mother, alienated and shocked, is not doing the same thing. This image of the patriarch, so completely failing to live up to the expectation on him as the protective knight who will protect his wife and children irrespective of any danger to himself, brought down to this humiliating state, is powerful. Here is western, civilised (?), man stripped bare and revealed as broken, uncertain of his identity and alone with his confusion about how to be a father and husband. Him and the rest. But this nadir

71

of selfhood, revealed in front of his children who may have previously idealised him as the professionally and personally successful father, acts as the turning point for them to accept that while he can be a coward, he can also be the hero when the moment is right. This opportunity arises when Ebba has a fall on the ski slope. The air is thick with snowy fragments, which echoes the earlier scene following the avalanche where visibility is negligible, as a cloud of snowy fog clears and Ebba comforts her children ahead of Tomas returning from his position of refuge.

Tomas leaves his two young children alone on the snow blind mountain landscape and he disappears into the white before returning with his wife and her (hurt?) leg, carrying her back over the threshold into the space where there may be some possibility for their marriage to live again. We are left questioning whether this has been a real 'accident' or one she has contrived in order to provide an opportunity for him to show he is able to 'be the man' for her and his children. In watching this, and as a father and husband myself, I noticed a mix of feeling: on the one hand touched by Ebba's apparent gesture towards her partner, an act of grace towards her 'cowardly' husband; and on the other a more aggravated response, I think because the sense of having to 'perform' the role of protective husband and father could easily get exposed in me (and in any man who finds himself in this classic heterosexual male position). Though, I also need to recognise the benefit which can accrue from being seen as 'the protector'.

For Tomas, this benefit is blown wide open and his weaknesses become an undeniably *abject* presence in the film's narrative. I use this term in respect to Kristeva's (1982) use of abject to describe psychologically that which we cannot stand, and I want to play with this in relation to the discussion about the Jungian presence of contra-sexual energies in narratives presented in film. Her writings deploy this term to situate something which in Jungian terms is somehow *beyond shadow* – in other words it is beyond being capable of integration in the psyche because it is so thoroughly unacceptable; the only option is to reject it and banish it from conscious awareness.

My interest here is in whether there are (in a generalised manner) ways in which women and men might deal with the *abject*, or the intolerable, in each other within the sometimes claustrophobic, or even *claustrum*-dominated (Meltzer, 2008), confines of a close partnership. The imagery and narrative in this film strongly suggests that the abject in us needs to be revealed in our closest relationships in order for those relationships to survive, let alone move on. Without this happening they remain a hidden threat with the potential to wreck and destroy randomly. In contra-sexual terms, the ultimately deadly and destructive aspects of ourselves as in this case the *thanima* in Tomas, and the abject *thanimus* possibly projected by Ebba need to be exposed and recognised to avert disaster.

Here, the place of nature in the film becomes important. Prior to the avalanche seeming to threaten the safety of the family (whereas it is actually a bit of a mirage apparently designed to threaten its emotional integrity) we see, and hear, controlled explosions in the distant mountains, like hints of something threatening us from the depths of the unconscious. The irony here, it turns out, is that it is probably one of these controlled explosions that has caused the avalanche which creates such apparent mortal danger, which is really *relational, contra-sexual* danger. By this I mean that a crucial bridge has opened up between the relational – that is, the loving partnership between Tomas and Ebba – and the influence of contra-sexual energies that threaten to destroy their marriage.

The conscious ('real') realisation by Ebba that her partner walked away from her and the children at a moment of apparent mortal danger, compounded by his refusal to admit this is what he did, constellates a dangerous dyadic contra-sexual complex, whereby he can only defend himself via a *thanima* infused – destructive, deadening – denial of the truth, and she can only see him via a *thanimus* charged spirit of angry rejection. This gets defused through Tomas's willingness to admit his actions (he could hardly do otherwise as his retreat from danger was caught on camera, subverting his corresponding retreat into a rigid ego defence). Here a contra-sexual *enantiodromia* occurs (where one archetypal position eventually turns into its opposite), a notion Jung derived from the thinking of Heraclitus (Kahn, 1979), as he breaks down completely in front of his children, recognises his utterly *abject* state in the eyes of his partner, and the space for *erosima* to come into play begins to open up. The interplay between human heterosexual gender relations, and the archetypal/contra-sexual (male–feminine and female–masculine) here reveals in front of us how socially constructed and instinctually influenced 'maleness' and 'femaleness' can get driven into a corner which generates potentially explosive consequences, once destructive contra-sexual influences are activated.

As it moves towards its conclusion, we come to see a central message from the film: what we perceive as fate in the form of a force of nature can at least sometimes actually be something we have brought upon ourselves. The film narrative and characterisation also reiterates however that this reading of meaning is not entirely pejorative and self-critical. In other words, we also find ourselves choosing what makes us vulnerable in close relationships because something in us recognises the need to take this risk, as it is potentially growthful and can cauterise relational wounds. This is reiterated in the closing scenes as their coach leaves the ski resort for home. The driver does not seem to have safe control and now it is the turn of Ebba to panic – or at least become frightened. She demands the driver lets them off the bus rather than risk plunging over the edge of the precipice next to the mountain road. Her taking the traditional 'male' role in leading her family and all on the bus to safety (though how real is the danger?) means they all have to walk some distance down the winding, exposed road, including Tomas, who does not question this move.

Not only does this provide a vision of the collective vulnerability of humanity in the face of nature but it symbolises the way we need to 'come down' from the heights of uncontained contra-sexual influences within our closest relationships to inhabit our gendered identity, even when this involves a cost to the image we may have of that identity. Here, healthy relational integration of contra-sexual influences relies on not identifying too much with where powerful, unreal, contra-sexual energies may take us. This tends to become *Thanatos* driven, so better to allow *Eros* to gently open up relational connection via the breathing of soul into our human frailties.

Gendered realities: *Eros* and film

If the conclusion reached above appears too straightforward, then of course that is because in some ways it *is*. It begs the question of what happens when *Eros* energies come to over-dominate gender relations and tip relationships and behaviours into chaos and danger? This concluding section considers this question through a series of brief examples from films where this happens. First, from Michael Haneke's (2001) *The Piano Teacher*, where the repressed protagonist, brilliantly played by Isabelle Huppert, eventually gives in to the sexual demands of one of her pupils only to frustrate those desires, attack a girl she sees as a rival, and then eventually get what she wanted (for him to beat and assault her, which he does outside her mother's bedroom). It seems her capacity to express desire, let alone relational love, can only be expressed in these ways as she fights her sexual urges (by censoring men looking at porno-graphic magazines while also voyeuristically watching a couple have sex at a drive-in movie). A distorted *erosimus* dominates her sexuality in these ways, invoking a *thanimus* destructive-ness in her relationships. We cannot but be touched by the sadness of her failed attempt to seriously injure herself at the end of the film, while also wondering if only stabbing herself in the shoulder rather than somewhere a whole lot more life threatening means healthy contra-sexual energies are at work in her somewhere.

There is something of a comparable dynamic at work in the character of the Colonel in *American Beauty* (dir. Mendes, 1999). He refuses to allow his gay sexuality to breathe comfortably and uses his military dominated worldview to contain this the best he can, punishing his son for daring to be part of a more flexible, alternative, culture as befits his age. When he sees Lester, his neighbour, body building in the garage, he asks to be let in from the teeming rain and kisses him. The tragic look in the Colonel's eyes when Lester spurns his advances, betokens his acute vulnerability in this moment of long denied expression of his authentic desire for sexual and relational intimacy with another man. Long hidden and frightened *erosima* has been rejected and the traumatic wound to his contra-sexual other tips this man into his all too easily activated *thanima* destructiveness. Although we cannot be sure it is him who shoots Lester dead he has surely killed his hoped for lover in his mind at the very least. Like Erika, it proves impossible to reach a kind of relational 'depressive position' (Klein, 1946), which can accept the affection–rejection archetypal dyad as parts of love which do not have to define one's overall experience of it. However, he has activated *erosima* genuinely in a relational gesture, and this surely counts for something.

In contrast Lester's death comes after he resolves his *anima* problem. In a loveless marriage, his infatuation with sixteen-year-old Anjela, betrays the 'age' of his contra-sexual other, which needs to 'grow up'. He achieves this by pulling back from sexual intimacy with her and does this with respect and care, therefore affirming her budding womanhood and his own maturation as a middle-aged man who accepts the frustrations of his life. He therefore crosses the threshold from life to death having accepted *erosima*'s gift.

The portrayal of transgendered identity and experience in film provides a way to highlight the way contra-sexual energies are ultimately fluid and have a life of their own, while also being within our scope to interact with, moderate and channel into forms which work for us, irrespective of social norms and prejudices. In the film *Tomboy* (dir. Sciamma, 2011), we follow the efforts of Laure to find acceptance as a boy (Mikael) amongst peers who gradually become curious about who he really is and eventually biologically 'real'(?) identity as a girl comes to light. But, instead of the caricature of transgendered presentation as glaringly obvious, say through (Phillips, 2006) the tendency of comedies to portray it in terms of cross-dressing (for example in the British *Carry On* film series (dir. Thomas, 1958–74) this film keeps it subtle, with little moments of possible revelation, such as when Mikael checks how noticeable his nipples are through a t-shirt. His/her relationship with Lisa is beautifully portrayed and despite uncomfortable moments for Laure/Mikael, *eros-ima/mus* is allowed to find expression and breathe naturally as puberty looms.

Finally, I want to end with a couple of snapshots from Iñárritu's memorable *Biutiful* (2010), which portrays the struggles of Uxbal, as he contends with Barcelona's criminal underbelly (which he is a part of). More than this he is struggling with the seemingly ubiquitous presence of death, including the deaths of twenty-five immigrant workers who are inadvertently gassed in the large room they sleep in, which he feels responsible for. He, too, is dying and as the film narrative unfolds, the presence of *thanatos* hangs heavy in the air. But within Uxbal's encounter with the imminence of his own death, *erosima* finds its voice. First in a scene where he asks to see his father's embalmed body for the first time, after it was entombed since his death before Uxbal was born. Uxbal touches his long deceased father's face with love. Then, at the close of the film, Uxbal's *thanima* influences lead him seemingly in partnership with *erosima*, away from his deathbed, where his final act is to pass to Ana, his daughter, the diamond ring his father gave to his mother. Ana asks 'is it real …?' We then find out what is 'real' in the unreal world beyond death, as Uxbal meets his father in a snowy forest rather than at the bottom of the sea, which Uxbal feared from childhood was the place he would end up. The end of the film suggests a kind of *syzygy*, a yoking of the feminine and masculine, in whatever form is resonant for a person awaiting the end of mortal life, in this case the meeting of both men's *animas* with the masculine of their father or son.

This and numerous other scenes confirm the capacity of cinema to reveal the unreal presence of the contra-sexual, and its real influence on each of us. Gender, as portrayed on the big screen, transforms into a vehicle for accessing contra-sexual energies – erotic, deathly and all points between. As film imagery, narrative and character embodiment shows, these subtly but powerfully haunt our sense of self; and liberates possibilities for deeper relationships and self-revelation.

References

Beebe, J. (2001) 'The anima in film', in C. Hauke and I. Alister (eds), *Jung & film: post-Jungian takes on the moving image*. Hove: Routledge. pp. 208–25.

Connell, R. (2002) *Gender*. Cambridge: Polity.

Dahl, R. (1982) *The big friendly giant*. London: Jonathan Cape. Full colour version: (2015) London: Penguin.

Freud, S. (2001) 'Beyond the pleasure principle', in *Complete psychological works of Sigmund Freud*. London: Vintage.

Goss, P. (2010) *Men, women and relationships, a post-Jungian approach: gender electrics and magic beans*. Hove: Routledge.

Jung, C. G. (1966) 'The relations between the ego and the unconscious: anima and animus', in *The collected works of C. G. Jung*, Vol. 7, *Two essays on analytical psychology*, 2nd edn. London: Routledge & Kegan Paul Ltd, 1966.

Jung, C. G. (1968) 'The syzygy: anima and animus', in *The collected works of C. G. Jung*, Vol. 9ii, *Aion*, 2nd edn. London: Routledge & Kegan Paul Ltd, 1968.

Jung, C. G. (2009) 'Liber secundus', in *The red book: liber novus*, ed. S. Shamdasani. New York: W. W. Norton & Co.

Kahn, C. (1979) *The art and thought of Heraclitus*. Cambridge: Cambridge University Press.

Klein, M. (1946) 'Notes on some schizoid mechanisms', in *The writings of Melanie Klein, vol. 3*. New York: Free Press. pp. 1–24.

Kristeva, J. (1982) *Powers of horror: an essay on abjection*. New York: Columbia University Press.

Meltzer, D. (2008) *The claustrum: an investigation of claustrophobic phenomena*. London: Karnac.

Phillips, J. (2006) *Transgender on screen*. London: Palgrave Macmillan.

Samuels, A. (1989) *The plural psyche*. London and New York: Routledge.

Van Ruiten, J. (2000) *Primaeval history interpreted: the rewriting of Genesis I–II in the book of jubilees*. Leiden: Brill.

Filmography

American beauty. (1999) [film] Directed by Sam Mendes. USA.

Attack of the 50ft. woman. (1958) [film] Directed by Nathan Juran. USA.

Big friendly giant, The. (2016) [film] Directed by Steven Spielberg. USA.

Biutiful. (2010) [film] Directed by Alejandro Iñárritu. Mexico.

Carry On films (original series). (1958–1974) G. Thomas. Rank. UK.

Force majeure. (2014) [film] Directed by Ruben Ostlund. Sweden.

Hercules. (1997) [film – animation] Directed by Ron Clements and John Musker. USA.

Jack the giant killer. (1962) [film] Directed by Nathan Juran. USA.

Pianista, La (Piano teacher, The). (2001) [film] Directed by Michael Heneke. Austria.

Tomboy. (2011) [film] Directed by Céline Sciamma. France.

6

IT'S ALIVE

The evolving archetypal image and
Mary Shelley's *Frankenstein*

Elizabeth Nelson

Introduction

Mary Shelley's 1818 novel *Frankenstein; or, The Modern Prometheus*, is one of the great enduring works of literature that has been retold endlessly and rarely faithfully. The creature at the heart of the novel exemplifies David Skal's point that 'monsters are the shape-changing entities that move in the modern imagination like dream-carvings on a dark carousel. With each revolution they mutate and evolve, the better to hold our attention' (2001, p. 19). Briefly, the central story describes a brilliant young scientist, Victor Frankenstein, who assembles cadaver parts into an eight-foot tall creature and imbues it with life. Horrified when the creature awakens, Victor abandons him, hoping the wretch will perish. Instead, he survives, painfully educates himself, and learns his birth story and the identity of his so-called father, whom the creature tracks, relentlessly, through the rest of the tale. Though Victor Frankenstein is a memorable character—the prototype of morally reckless scientific ambition—it is the psychologically complex creature who fascinates. Within only a few short years of its publication, the first of many adaptations commenced. In the nineteenth century, it was dramatized on the stage beginning with *Presumption; or the Fate of Frankenstein*, produced in 1823 (Skal, 2001, p. 101). In the twentieth century, multiple cinematic renditions were produced, beginning with the 1910 *Frankenstein* (dir. Dawley) a 16-minute short, produced by the Thomas A. Edison Company. One scholar (Wolfe, 2015, n.p.) estimates that there have been more than 50 versions of the story produced in the last 100 years. The 1910 short was quickly eclipsed in cultural memory by the heavy symbolic footprint of the 1931 film directed by James Whale which starred Boris Karloff as the creature.

Shelley, an 18-year-old with an impeccable intellectual pedigree but no claim to literary fame at the time she began writing the novel, invented an entire genre of literature, science fiction (Aldiss, 1973). She also generated one of the genre's key tropes: what happens when a creation exceeds the control of the creator and turns on him or her, which Aldiss pithily describes as 'hubris clobbered by nemesis' (ibid., p. 26). There is abundant evidence Mary Shelley's literary creation exceeded her control, to wit, the numerous adaptations mentioned above and the odd fact that these adaptations by and large fueled an entirely different genre from the one she is credited with inventing: horror. Shelley probably had little idea that her novel would introduce the world to a fascinating literary monstrosity whose allure would persist for 200 years.

Indeed, as we approach the bicentennial of *Frankenstein; or, The Modern Prometheus*, Shelley's creature is alive, as is her tale, and shows little signs of decrepitude. Thus it offers a rich case study for the aim of this chapter, which is to present a fresh, surprising, and (appropriately) animated approach to analyzing films as texts.

Shelley's novel also helps organize the central questions I propose. First, how can an archetypal approach to images in film deepen critical discourse about, and analysis of, a cinematic work? Second, how does the evolution of an archetypal image in film reveal the shifting cultural landscape that text and audience occupy in any given moment? The idea that a meaningful relationship can be found between public images, such as those found in film, and the collective psyche is a cornerstone of Jungian film theory and its fresh approach to textual analysis. 'In an era dominated by materialism, where our unconscious processes, our images and our dreams are still only poorly attended to,' say Hauke and Alister, 'cinema offers both a means and a space to witness the psyche—almost literally in projection' (2001, pp. 1–2). As a 'psychological art' films allow viewers to 'engage at a feeling level and release our own associative train of fantasies' much like dream material (ibid., p. 12). Jungian analyst John Beebe concurs: films 'enable the audience to hold complex states of mind in a creative way—a state that's not unlike our dreams' (Beebe and Peay, 2011, n.p.).

The idea that film is a psychological medium, and can be approached as one would a dream, is not a uniquely Jungian insight. Speaking of the early years in film a century ago, Skal says, 'never before had it been possible for human beings to create, reproduce, and share such an evocative simulacrum of the dream state' (2001, p. 31). 'A film is like an involuntary imitation of a dream,' says director Luis Buñuel; 'on the screen, as within the human being, the nocturnal voyage into the unconscious begins' (quoted in Fredericksen, 2001, p. 32). Film scholar Noel Carroll argues that filmmakers have historically functioned as 'informal psychologists' through constructing an accessible symbol system that 'addresses elements of our common humanity' (2003, p. 55). The power of film includes the ways that its symbols, which exceed linguistic comprehension also exceed conscious understanding. This is a key assertion of Fredericksen's essay, *Jung/Sign/Symbol/Film*, which proposes an alternative viewpoint from the standard semiotic and psycho-analytic approach to film texts. Fredericksen explains how the Jungian technique of dream amplification can be fruitfully applied to cinematic images (see Hauke and Alister, 2001, pp. 17ff.). The result can be a rich, deep, and meaningful sense of the image that eschews the hubris of claiming to be the last word. Thus, a symbolic as opposed to a reductive semiotic reading places a film in an evolving, creative discourse with the culture that produced it. In fact, 'films often reveal unconscious attitudes, values, and viewpoints that an entire culture needs to bring to consciousness and to integrate' (Leonard, 1997, p. xii).

Hauke and Alister compare the movie theater to 'an imaginal space—a *temenos*' (2001, p. 2). In this *temenos*, 'a version of active imagination is stimulated' to engage the unconscious similar to 'our conscious attention to dream imagery and other fantasies' (ibid., p. 2). The possibility of active imagination with cinematic images will be especially germane to the following discussion. In addition to the central premise I propose in this chapter—film images, when viewed in all their particularity, reflect contemporary concerns dwelling within the collective psyche—I propose an uncommon approach. That is, I will follow Jung's surprising, bold, and irrational moves in his own work with dream figures, not his (or anyone else's) theory about what he did, but the actual moves he described in the chapter entitled 'Confrontation with the Unconscious' from his semi-autobiography *Memories, Dreams, Reflections* (1961/1989). In that account, Jung took seriously his dream figures as autonomous and animated, with their own mind and will, as if they were actual living people. Moreover, he approached them in much the same way one might get to know a new and fascinating friend. Since we would not ask a new friend 'what do you mean?' but rather 'who are you?' kindly curiosity, not analysis, is the guiding ethic in working with dream figures. Jungians are well acquainted with *Memories, Dreams, Reflections*, but I sometimes wonder whether even they take seriously the full implications of 'walking up and down the garden with [Philemon]' (p. 183), the potent figure who emerged, for Jung, like a guide or ally in his work with dreams and visionary experiences.

For this chapter, I intend to treat Victor's creature as a fully autonomous image, with a mind and will of his own, who invites us to befriend him *as he presents himself* and learn what he has to say about his moment in film history. I am omitting from this analysis the filmmakers' intentions, both conscious and unconscious, in shaping the creature, and his personal associations to the image. That is, I will be working at what Fredericksen refers to as the transpersonal level, revealing the creature's 'links to a psychic base broader than the individual [ego] personality of the director' (2001, p. 38).

To host Victor and his creature in something like the way Jung hosted Philemon, the ensuing discussion uses a theoretical framework provided by a trio of essays on image written by James Hillman and published in 1977, 1978, and 1979. Although Hillman's essays ostensibly address how to think about, and work with, images from dream and waking vision, they are an equally rich resource for attending to cinematic images. Thus, this chapter is my contribution to developing a 'new attitude to our engagement with the [film] images' that Hauke and Alister advocated (2001, p. 13). The theoretical framework, described below, is used to examine four adaptations of *Frankenstein; or, The Modern Prometheus*. They include: the James Whale 1931 film, starring Boris Karloff (dir. Whale); the 1973 televised film *Frankenstein: The True Story* (which it was not) (dir. Smight); Kenneth Branagh's 1994 film, *Mary Shelley's Frankenstein*, considered by critics and audience to be the most faithful adaptation of the novel; and the 2014 film *I, Frankenstein* (dir. Beatie), a mild exercise in masochism for the hapless viewer but a fascinating image of the monstrous nonetheless.

An archetypal approach to images

To lay the theoretical groundwork for this chapter, let me begin by asserting that Hillman's approach to working with dream images is a radical extension of Jungian theory but a faithful application of Jung's personal dream practice as described in his *Memories, Dreams, Reflections* (1989). It is less like dream interpretation or dream analysis and more like translation in the hermeneutic sense: the means by which the dreamer begins to understand something that is foreign or alien because, 'like the god Hermes, the translator mediates between one world and another' (Palmer, 1969, p. 27). The 'something' is an image or figure; the world can be a dream or a film. Yet even 'translation' falls short of describing what it is like to have a living relationship with dream images, such as Jung's relationship with Philemon mentioned earlier. 'Interpretation' and 'analysis' remove one even further from the felt sense of this idea. What Jung actually did was *dwell* with Philemon and other dream figures, a lovely little word that implies slow time, patience, interested attention, and acceptance. One dwells with things and people, creatures and activities—such as dear friends, a good novel, a garden, a child—which offer pleasure or learning or both.

Hillman develops his imagistic approach to dreams in three key essays published in *Spring* journal in 1977, 1978, and 1979. It is his response to the way in which symbols have, through long use, become signs. Their unknowability is no longer ontological, as Jung maintained it was, but merely practical, resolved as soon as one lays hands on a symbol dictionary. Hillman speaks as a third generation Jungian who was striving 'to get back to the unknown ... by exploring the image' (1977, p. 68). This begs the question what is distinctive about the image?

First, images are precise, 'particularized by a specific context, mood, and scene' (1977, p. 62). There are no general or typical images; not even a special subclass of 'archetypal images,' a point I return to below. Hillman warns, however, against taking precision literally, as in 'the more and sharper the better' (p. 69). Rather, 'precision means whatever is actually presented. Simply: the actual qualities of the image. Vagueness, dullness, indifference—and imprecision too—are also qualities' (p. 69). Second, 'an image is complete just as it presents itself,' whole, full, with nothing missing (p. 68). Part of this completeness is the assumption that 'everything there is necessary, which further suggests that everything necessary is there' (p. 68). Third, images are not 'flat, two-dimensional mental things that I look at' nor are they 'mainly visual, hence optical and intellectually distant, hence gutless' (1978, p. 159). Instead, they are full-bodied, a felt presence, with the power to affect someone's thought, mood, or behavior. Anyone who has awakened from a powerful dream or exited a theater after viewing a powerful film and felt the lingering effect for hours afterwards can understand this. 'Images hold us; we can be in the grip of an image' (p. 159). Fourth, precise, particular images within a dream (and, I contend, in a film), are interconnected with other images, hence it is crucial to stay close and watch what the image is actually doing. Asking 'what?' not 'why?' discloses the network of relationships among the images (1977, pp. 80, 68). Finally (though much more could be said), the image retains its unknowability no matter how long one dwells with it, because 'the depth of the image, like that of psyche, is endless' (1978, p. 158).

In other texts (1975, 1985) Hillman describes bringing 'anima consciousness' which is 'an animating consciousness' to our work with images (1985, p. x). Hillman does not discuss the animated quality of images in the three key essays described above (1977, 1978, and 1979), nor does he speak of animation as a 'gadget' for working with dreams. However, he had already pointed out the significance of animation in the 1975 book *Revisioning Psychology*, where he rejects the narrow identification of psyche with ego. We assume, wrongly, that the aliveness of dream figures is a result of the dreamer's aliveness, as though 'their animation derived from my breath' (p. 2). Hillman argues that we do not animate them; the images are already animated. Hillman develops this idea much further in his 1982 essay on the *anima mundi* and the 1985 book *Anima: Anatomy of a Personified Notion*. Since images are alive, expressive, mutable, and surprising our work with them must be equally lively. Hillman sums up his approach in this memorable statement:

> If, as Jung says, 'image is psyche', then why not go on to say, 'images are souls', and our job with them is to meet them on that soul level. … We watch its behavior—how the image behaves within itself. And we watch its ecology—how it interconnects, by analogies, in the fields of my life. This is indeed different from interpretation. *No friend or animal wants to be interpreted, even though it may cry for understanding.*
>
> *(1977, p. 80, emphasis added)*

The last few words should remind us of the pathos of Frankenstein's creature and support an imagistic approach to the four films under consideration. What is it like to meet the creature as a soul? Certainly it should bring viewers closer to Mary Shelley's 1818 novel, no matter how narratively erratic the film and television adaptations may be. In fact, watching the creature as actually presented—that is, 'particularized by a specific context, mood, and scene' (the first guideline, above)—distinguishes the adaptations from one another. It is as though in a dream-like manner we, the audience, get the creature we need or deserve: the 1931 creature, the 1973 creature, the 1994 creature, the 2014 creature, as well as many, many others, each as particular as the next. Frankenstein's 'monster,' a term the creature uses to describe himself, is a mirror held up to humanity.

Archetypes and archetypal images

In order to assert that Frankenstein's creature is a 200-year-old mirror that functions to expose the more monstrous aspects of our humanity, it is important to say something about archetypal images as well as answer the question, what makes Frankenstein's creature archetypal? Jung's notion of the archetypes has troubled our discipline, and the reception of Jungians in inter-disciplinary discourse, especially as it has been conducted within the anti-essentialist milieu of post-modernism. Scholars have noted that Jung defines archetypes in different ways, and it is the inconsistency of his definition that creates trouble. This is hardly surprising considering that Jung's professional writing is so extensive—18 thick volumes of the collected works alone—and that his thinking evolved over a highly creative lifetime. It is also unsurprising 'seeing that a kind of fluid interpenetration belongs to the very nature of all archetypes' which 'change their shape continually' (1951/1969: §301). That is, the difficulty of definition is given with the very phenomenon Jung is attempting to define.

Appropriately for the emphasis of this chapter, Jung achieves the greatest precision when he speaks in images. The archetypes, he writes, are,

> only determined as regards their form and then only to a very limited degree ... [their] form ... might perhaps be compared to the axial stem of a crystal, which, as it were, preforms the crystalline structure in the mother liquid, although it has no material existence of its own. This first appears according to the specific ways in which the ions and molecules aggregate.
>
> *(1954/1969: §155)*

Among the many explanations of the archetype throughout the collected works, this has added forcefulness because it is the one Emma Jung and Marie-Louise von Franz select for their work on the Grail legend. Archetypes, they argue, 'first take on a specific form when they merge into consciousness in the shape of images; it is therefore necessary to differentiate between the unap-prehendable archetype, the unconscious, pre-existent disposition, and *the archetypal images*' (1970, pp. 36–37, emphasis added).

How does one apply this definition to the subject of the monstrous? Monsters, which have been key characters in literature from around the world for thousands of years, are an arche-type—an invisible structure, pattern, or form that is filled out (or filled in) by specific archetypal images of what a people of a particular time and place find horrifying, threatening, or both. Examples include the chimaera, Medusa, Grendel, and Mary Shelley's creature. It would be more difficult, but not impossible, to argue that Shelley's creature is also an archetype—not just an archetypal image of the monstrous—or that it has become one in the last 200 years. The evidence for this claim is the great variety of images that have poured forth from the 1818 novel, all of them retaining some semblance of the original, either through a more-or-less faithful ren-dering of the text or on adaptations based on the text. In fact, the adaptations offer a surprisingly wide array of creatures. For instance, Michael Sarrazin's luminous beauty in the 1973 *Franken-stein* is a far cry from the mottled, cadaverous skin and rough stitching of Robert De Niro's patchwork face in the 1994 film, and neither is even remotely like the 1931 Boris Karloff. *I, Frankenstein* offers us a creature with a six-pack, as though he has spent hours in the gym, prob-ably wearing a hoodie to hide his seamed face.

The variety of creatures sprung from Shelley's original conception can more easily support Hillman's use of the word 'archetypal' as an adjective. He explains: 'Rather than pointing at something, "archetypal" points to something, and this is value. By attaching "archetypal" to an image, we ennoble or empower the image with the widest, richest, and deepest possible significance' (1977, p. 83). For an individual person, an archetypal image draws that person into relationship. The image is something one dwells with, puzzles over, and perhaps returns to again and again. An archetypal image, because of its personal value, may re-arise in the imagination decades after the original dream or waking vision. If it has no personal value, Hillman tells us, it is not archetypal. For an entire culture, a similar guide can be used. When cultural products, including novels, film, and television, return to an image again and again, then it earns the adjective 'archetypal,' even though some people within the culture will find it uninteresting or of little importance. Mary Shelley's *Frankenstein; or, The Modern Prometheus*, is clearly archetypal, having been rendered innumerable times in many formats. It may be more accurate to say that we return to Mary Shelley's *creature* again and again because who, in their wildest dream, could have imagined her novel would one day inspire a breakfast cereal?

To summarize: monsters, a feature of world literature for millennia, can be called archetypes and also archetypal. They have held their value. Mary Shelley's creature *might* be a new archetype. Setting that issue aside, the creature is an archetypal image as I mentioned above, rendered in a fascinating variety of forms. The remainder of this chapter uses Hillman's imagistic approach to befriend four creatures at a key moment in the narrative, the creature's first moment of life. I will observe the context, mood, and scene, assuming that the image is whole and complete, that everything necessary is there and everything there is necessary (Hillman, 1977, 1978). Dwelling with each creature for a time enables me to observe closely what he does with his expressive body and notice how he faces the world into which he is new born. That is, I follow Hillman and treat these cinematic images as souls.

The soulfulness of the creature

First-time readers of *Frankenstein; or, The Modern Prometheus*, whose knowledge of the creature derives from popular culture, are frequently surprised by his soulfulness. Unlike the humans in the story (other than 'Father,' the blind patriarch of the DeLacy family), readers are amenable to the creature's poetry, easily looking past the horror of his appearance. Thus it easier, perhaps, to think of this image as a soul than, say, the cottonwood tree or bottle cap from last night's dream. Cinematic images may be viewed as souls more easily because they are already presented to the viewer as animated, with a will and desires, emotions, preferences, and moods already given with the image. Mary Shelley's creature, already animated in the culture's imagination and in the cinematic adaptations the culture produces, is alive.

I would also argue that the creature is speaking to us, not merely to his creator. Or perhaps it might be more provocative to say that the creature is speaking to all of us as Victor Frankenstein, challenging us with the ethical questions at the heart of the novel. Has our moral education kept pace with our scientific-technical education? If so, what face do we turn to our creatures in their moment of awakening?

Frankenstein, 1931

There might be no rendition of the creature more powerful and enduring than Boris Karloff's performance in the 1931 film directed by James Whale. The story, based on Peggy Webling's script, which Skal (2001, p. 97) describes as a 'stilted, fussy, preachy piece of theater,' was the loosest possible adaptation of the 1818 novel. Partly due to my allegiance to Shelley's story, I consider it nearly unrecognizable as *Frankenstein*. Or, considering that 'Frankenstein' has become a convenient label for 'a monstrous creation, especially a work or agency that ruins its originator' according to the Merriam-Webster dictionary, the film, powerful and critically acclaimed though it is, may be 'a Frankenstein' and not *Frankenstein*. Jameson writes 'there is a sense in which this milestone of the horror genre and indelible fixture in Western culture uncannily took on a life of its own—perhaps even, to an extent, created itself' beginning with a 'misapprehension' and notes:

> Almost immediately, audiences (and people who had only heard about the movie) started applying the name to the creature—superhuman in size and strength, effectively unkillable, and murderously insane. This was reinforced by 'Frankenstein' becoming all but interchangeable with 'Boris Karloff,' the harsh, foreign-sounding, slightly ersatz name of the actor who had played the Monster.
>
> *(2002, n.p.)*

The film, now preserved in the U.S. National Film Registry as 'culturally, historically, or aesthetically significant,' solidifies its worth as a cultural artifact. Nevertheless, the greatest monstrosity in the film is the erasure of the creature's poetic, impassioned speech. Yes, the cadence and word choice in the novel are Miltonic, which sounds odd to contemporary ears, but there is little question that the acquisition of language is the creature's greatest triumph and his only possible passage into human community. Boris Karloff's creature is expressive, his face poignant, but rendering him silent is an indefensible creative choice. If one agrees with Aldiss (1973, p. 14), and I do, this is the image of the monstrous the 1930s deserved.

David Skal makes several cogent points about this particular monster, beginning with the fact that Whale's shooting script had 'a deep note of pathos throughout' (2001, p. 129). Although the creature did not have articulate speech, the script specified that 'its first off-screen sound was to be haunting, piteous ... like that of a lost animal' (p. 130). This is an interesting observation since two of the three most common domesticated animals, cats and horses, do not have the facial muscles that permit a wide repertoire of expressions. (The most facially expressive animals are dogs.) People who love cats, horses, as well as dog, have to learn their language and, once they do, they focus on whole-body expressiveness. The creature's face, too, is relatively immobile, particularly in the narrative moments this chapter focuses on, the first interaction between creature and creator, almost as though members of two species are encountering one another for the first time. The power differential between the creator and his creature is evident in the way Dr. Frankenstein (named Henry in this film, not Victor) directs the creature's actions, as though he were a preverbal child or, more accurately, a puppy. Thus, the fact that his moans are meant to resemble a lost animal is significant.

Though the creature might sound like a lost animal, something else shaped his appearance in the film. By 1931 'the stylized machine-age aesthetic' says Skal, 'had become a dominant force in applied arts' (2001, p. 130). The creature's square head 'powerfully evokes the plight of an old consciousness forced to occupy a new paradigm ... a machine-tooled skull' (ibid., p. 132). The most notable features of this creature's face are flat skull that meets the forehead nearly at a 90-degree angle, gaunt, sunken cheeks, and the protruding bolts at either side of his neck. Otherwise, his skin is more or less free of scarring, in stark contrast to the other three archetypal images under consideration. There is something ominous about this blankness, which the following assessment hints at:

> Untold millions had been left with the feeling that modern life—and death—was nothing but an anonymous, crushing assembly line. Whale's film depicted a monster

> squarely in the grip of this confusion, a pathetic figure caught, as it were, on the barbed
> wire between humanism and mechanism.
>
> *(ibid., p. 135)*

Perhaps the animal moans of the 1931 creature—the absence even of the capacity for speech—expresses the incoherent pathos of human beings in an inhumane historical, economic, and cultural moment. Of interest, 1931 was the deepest year of the great Depression in America, whose effects had already spread to Europe.

The creature's silence also expresses the master–slave theme prominent in the novel, dramatized in the shifting and unstable power relations between creature and creator who are paired for life. As the creature first experiences language, this 'godlike science' belongs to his master, and 'is thus explicitly a cultural compensation for the deficient nature' of the slave (Brooks, 1993, p. 374). Until he overcomes slave mentality, by what right has the creature to speak? And if he did, who would listen? Perhaps the pathos of this creature is that so much felt horror has no expressive outlet—until it explodes.

The enduring power of the 1931 creature—flat skull, sunken cheeks, and thick bolts protruding from either side of the neck—is freshly apparent in a 2016 Christmas holiday advertisement for the Apple iPhone 7. (The central message, 'open your heart everyone,' is timely and necessary in light of the abhorrent racism, sexism, and xenophobia unleashed by Donald Trump's election as President of the USA in 2017.) The creature is not entirely silent, but his attempt to sing a holiday song in the village square, where a group has gathered to celebrate around a lighted tree, is piteously close to an animal moan. Though villagers recoil at first, in the end they enfold the creature in the community and help him find his voice.

Frankenstein: The True Story, 1973

This 1973 televised film billed itself as 'the true story,' which might lead the unwary to assume it is a faithful retelling of Mary Shelley's 1818 novel. It is not. However, it was critically acclaimed in part because of the lush production values, the eminence of the international cast, and the bold homoeroticism of a screenplay intended for mainstream audiences. The script was co-authored by Don Bachardy and Christopher Isherwood; at the time, Isherwood was one of the very few openly gay writers in Hollywood. The homoeroticism appears principally in two key relationships and one startling and culturally ominous narrative choice. The first homoerotic relationship pairs Henry Clerval and Victor Frankenstein, who in this version of the story are dear friends, medical doctors, and allies in scientific experimentation, wholly devoted to one another and the cause that unites them. The second relationship pairs Victor and his creature who, to intensify the homoerotic bond, has the brain of Clerval because Clerval died of apoplexy shortly before Victor brings the creature to life. The moment of narrative choice occurs when the creature first awakens; his fresh, exquisite beauty is a source of delight for himself and his creator. Played by Michael Sarrazin, he has large, liquid eyes, perfect skin, and 'lips that would make Vogue model weep with envy' (GFT, 2007, n.p.). His body—clothed at first in strategically placed gauze that leaves a great deal of flesh exposed—also is perfect, exhibiting none of the scars one would expect from a creature stitched together from bits of cadaver. Victor Frankenstein, played by Leonard Whiting who is best known for his role as Romeo in the 1968 Zeffirelli, *Romeo and Juliet,* is clearly enchanted.

The creature and his creator unmask each other in their first moment together, a slow, graceful encounter that has been aptly compared to a strip-tease. The creature lifts the heavy iron and leather mask Victor used to protect his eyes from the intense light produced by his experimental apparatus. Victor lifts the white gauze that partly obscures the face of the creature. Gazing at one another, Victor is truly stunned by what he has wrought and pronounces the first word the creature will ever hear: 'beautiful.' The creature responds in kind. 'Beautiful,' he tells Victor. The irony, or perhaps the tragedy, of this initial exchange soon becomes apparent. Although the creature is exquisite at birth, he begins a slow, irreversible deterioration.

It seems implausible that this beautiful creature is an image of the monstrous. At 'birth' Michael Sarrazin's facial expression is open, curious, and trusting, which makes his physical deterioration—also focused on the face—more dramatic and disturbing. As an image of unblemished youth, he may be a living fulfillment of Victor's hunger for the *puer aeternus*, the archetype of the eternal youth. He is enchanted with the creature's lithe purity and loathes the transformation. The creature, who does not understand, is most expressively poignant when bewildered by a rejection he did not cause and cannot control; the way Victor recoils, followed by others. Perhaps this creature confronts us with the bewildering experience of being judged by appearance, shape, or form when each of us knows that deterioration is inevitable.

It is fascinating that *Frankenstein: The True Story* was aired in the same year, 1973, that Ernest Becker published his Pulitzer prize-winning book *The Denial of Death*. In it he describes the 'terrifying dilemma' that confronts human beings as a result of our dual nature. We have 'literally the status of a small god' and yet, at the same time, 'man is a worm and food for worms' (1973, p. 26).

> He is … housed in a heart-pumping, breath-gasping body that once belonged to a fish and still carries the gill-marks to prove it. His body is a material fleshy casing that is alien to him in many ways—the strangest and most repugnant way being that it aches and bleeds and will decay and die. Man is literally split in two: he has an awareness of his own splendid uniqueness in that he sticks out of nature with a towering majesty, and yet he goes back into the ground a few feet in order blindly and dumbly to rot and disappear forever.
>
> *(ibid., p. 26)*

Frankenstein: The True Story offers viewers a fantasy of creation that is entirely cleansed of its slimy, bloody, and fleshy aspects. The perfect eroticized body of the creature allows Victor, his creator, a moment of god-like towering majesty. What is monstrous is the attempt to escape death and live only one-half of the paradox. Becker could be speaking to the Victor in all of us when he says 'whatever man does on this planet has to be done in the lived truth of the terror of creation, of the grotesque, of the rumble of panic underneath everything. Otherwise it is false' (1973, p. 283). In this respect, it is Victor's dream that is false, not his creature.

With the acute vision of hindsight, it is also meaningful that a homoerotic adaptation of *Frankenstein* was televised just a few short years before the AIDS epidemic attracted serious social, political, and cultural attention. It is as though Sarrazin's creature foreshadowed the death of thousands of beautiful young men (and other victims) who would begin to physically deteriorate in ways that are eerily similar to his transformation. AIDS had not yet been addressed by epidemiologists in 1973, and would not for another few years (Brier, 2004, p. 27). Yet the urge to discover its origin led to speculation about a so-called 'Patient Zero' who may have been invisibly spreading the virus in the early 1970s. In the highly lauded cultural history of AIDS *And the Band Played On* (1987), author Randy Shilts interviewed members of the urban gay communities of New York, San Francisco, and Los Angeles who pinpointed 1976 as the last year in which they were confident their friends were healthy. Shilts names 1980 as the turning point, when carefree, casual sex became potentially dangerous (1987, p. 12). However, the results of new genetic research published in the esteemed scientific journal *Nature* (Worobey et al., 2016) offers persuasive evidence that the virus traveled from Zaire around 1967 and arrived in New York City around 1971 (McNeil, 2016, n.p.). Although the scriptwriters could not have consciously been aware of the virus, its appearance matches the time frame of script writing and production to an uncanny degree. Tragically, the creature's visible deterioration in *Frankenstein: The True Story* soon would be replicated in life.

Mary Shelley's Frankenstein, 1994

One might anticipate from the title of this film and from the classical theatrical training of its director Kenneth Branagh that *Mary Shelley's Frankenstein* would stick closely to the original text. It does, for the most part, but it also elevates some of the Gothic aspects in the novel. For instance, Victor's mother Caroline dies in bloody childbirth, not from scarlet fever. When Victor's father stumbles out of the birth chamber, shocked at his failure to save his wife, he descends an elongated, Escher-like marble staircase far too large for even the grandest of grand houses. The high camera angle and desaturated color call attention to the bright red blood that coats his naked torso, arms, and hands. When Victor races up the stairs and enters the birth room shortly thereafter, his dead mother is still drenched in her own blood. If we agree with Aldiss that Shelley's story is the first science fiction novel, the Gothic elements in the film are nonetheless apt since science fiction is a 'sub-species of the Gothic' (1973, p. 17) concerned with 'problems of power, either literal or metaphorical' (p. 14). Though Branagh's rendition of Caroline Frankenstein's death is unlike Shelley's novel, it is akin to Shelley's own life. More to the point, it illustrates the failure of male power—his father's and his own—to save the woman they both (differently) cherish, thereby motivating Victor's dream of becoming like god.

The sequence in which Victor animates the creature in his laboratory is a detailed homage to many different scientific disciplines, including biology, physiology, anatomy, biochemistry, as well as electrical and mechanical engineering. It is rapid and dynamic, showing Victor, stripped to the waist, sweaty, setting everything in motion with verve, passion, and confidence. The first moment he and his creature come face-to-face occurs when he climbs onto the lid of the large copper tub of amniotic fluid that holds the creature. Victor aggressively gazes through a tiny window built into the lid, repeatedly pounds his fist on the thick metal, and commands the creature to 'Live!' The moment the creature opens his eyes, Victor jumps to the floor and rapidly disconnects the conduits that electrified the chemical bath. The pace of the creation sequence does not lapse until Victor peers through a small side window of the tub. To his horror, the creature's eyes are closed, the body still. He walks away, dejected. Then a sharp sound draws him back. 'It's alive,' he says. 'It's alive.' The camera cuts to an interior view of the copper tub, the creature writhing, fighting for its life. Cut to an exterior view, the tub, which had been rocking side to side as the creature writhed, is once again still. Victor approaches slowly and peers over the edge. A beat. Silence. Then the creature rears up, reaching for Victor, overpowering him. The tub topples over, drenching both figures while viscous fluid floods the laboratory.

The next sequence in the film is beautiful, horrible, and evocative. In something like a slow dance, Victor ostensibly is helping the ungainly creature to stand upright for the first time. However, the slippery floor and the slippery bodies—which begin to look more alike as Victor, too, becomes saturated with amniotic fluid—give it the appearance of a wrestling match. Are they helping each other stand or are they pulling each other down? This is a question that can be explored on many levels, Branagh undoubtedly drawing on the theme of doubling so evident in the 1818 novel. The sequence ends when clever Victor uses some nearby garlands of chain to prop the creature upright. This ends in abject failure through a mechanical accident that leaves the creature suspended high above Victor, motionless, resembling a crucifixion. The symbolic weight of this tableau is emphasized through extreme camera angles that call attention to the vertical distance between the two. As the camera moves down, closing in on Victor's horrified face, he finally says, 'What have I done?' Victor makes his final journal entry: 'The resulting reanimate is malfunctional, pitiful, vile, and dead' before retreating into sleep. But it is not dead. When the creature appears by his bed, a horrified Victor runs away, then returns with an axe in his hand to destroy what he has wrought. The creature is gone.

Though there are clear Gothic elements in *Mary Shelley's Frankenstein*, part of the power of this film derives from the intentional use of realistic elements. This is particularly true of the scenes in which Victor sews the creature together, with the camera offering close-up views of the result: a painfully scarred, disfigured face, including a long sagittal scar over his shorn scalp, circular stitching around his right eye, an arc of stitches along the cheeks, and thick suturing of his upper and lower lip that perpetually distorts his mouth into a grimace and makes the acquisition of spoken language difficult. *This* creature is visibly horrifying; his scars a continual reminder of his terrible origins; a visceral felt sense of what it is like to live in his body even before his painful rejection by society.

How does this particular archetypal image express the monstrous in 1994? It may reflect the increasing realism of film and television more generally which, some have argued, actually anesthetizes viewers to real-life horror or, contrarily, indicates we are better able to face that horror. I conjecture that the realism of De Niro's creature exposes the ways in which any individual, community, or nation is composed of pieces and parts, sutured together—and the frightening possibility that it will all come apart at the seams. For instance, the film was released only five short years after the Soviet Union dissolved, revealing the long-repressed ethnic tensions in Eastern Europe. Those tensions have not disappeared. With 'Brexit,'—the decision by the United Kingdom to leave the European Union—the possibility of the dissolution of the union spreading to other countries, and the ugly conflict at the heart of the 2016 American presidential election which has only deepened since Trump's win, the visibly disfigured, enraged creature is still alive, still mirroring tensions that have followed us into the twenty-first century and show little sign of resolution.

Yet there is another answer to the question and it is one that is less full of despair. As horrible as this creature's appearance is, the combination of brilliant makeup and De Niro's brilliant performance make viewers feel into the experience of monstrosity. As he attempts to form words through distorted lips, as he picks the black sutures from his inflamed scars, as he weeps from loneliness, viewers witness the suffering of the abject for whom loneliness is just one small part of a wretched existence. Is this not the starting point for genuine empathy? Kristeva, speaking of the foreigner, would answer yes. She could be describing the creature when she says:

> Strangely, the foreigner lives within us: he is the hidden face of our identity, the space that wrecks our abode, the time in which understanding and affinity founder. By recognizing him within ourselves, we are spared detesting him in himself.... The foreigner comes in when the consciousness of my difference arises, and he disappears when we all acknowledge ourselves as foreigners, unamenable to bonds and communities.
>
> *(2002, p. 264)*

Of the four films under consideration, *Mary Shelley's Frankenstein* offers the most viscerally detestable creature who is, paradoxically, the most empathetic. Thus Kristeva's challenge: can we recognize 'him' in ourselves rather than detest 'him' in himself? I hope the answer is yes. If not, the turning point in the creature's dramatic arc is a tragedy for him and for us. After he is rejected by the cottagers, the film cuts to the creature, huddled at the base of a tree in the snow, sobbing and rocking forward and back, forward and back. He pauses, finds a small red flower in the fold of his cuff (once again, the red bright against the desaturated film), and runs back to the cottagers as though their shared appreciation of beauty might bridge the gap between them. He stands on the threshold of the empty rooms, trying to comprehend its emptiness. They have abandoned it, and him. This final rejection dramatizes the tenacity of hope in the face of pain, offering us a deeply human monster and, if we are willing, a glimpse into our shared human vulnerability.

I, Frankenstein, 2014

To appreciate *I, Frankenstein*, the viewer should know that the entire arc of Shelley's 1818 novel is swiftly summarized in the first two minutes of the film. Thus, it does not show the creature at his moment of awakening. Rather, there is a quick collage of close-up images, like shards of a mirror that reflect and represent moments in Victor Frankenstein's creative process. If a script is like a dream, one might say that Kevin Grevioux and Stewart Beattie followed Jung's injunction to dream the story onward and give it a modern dress (1951/1969: §271). A modern dress it certainly has, not only literally in terms of makeup and costume, but also in terms of setting. The central conceit of the story is that the creature, due to his superhuman strength, has survived for 200 years following the death of his creator, and now haunts the most dangerous corners of a decrepit urban landscape inhabited by people who are similarly scarred, either visibly or invisibly. In that time, his scars have faded though not disappeared. His rage, alienation, and loneliness are undiminished. The creature is unwittingly drawn into war between demons and gargoyles that endured for centuries, a pawn in a game that hapless humans know nothing of. Though being a coveted ally is unusual for one who is accustomed to rejection, he is not eager to join despite his loneliness. He trusts no one.

I, Frankenstein includes no scene in which the Victor witnesses his creature come to life. Their relationship is expressed by Victor's attempt to destroy him by rolling the wrapped and bound corpse off of a high bridge, the camera following its steep plunge to the river below. One might say that Victor refuses to face his creature, literally or metaphorically. He discards it as he would a bundle of trash, thinking to be rid of it once and for all. The creature, demonstrating his aptitude for life, crawls out of the mud and onto the riverbank; a second birth, replicating one stage of human evolution.

Despite the absence of the customary 'birth' scene in *I, Frankenstein* however, there is a moment with the feeling-tone of birth worth mentioning. The creature is captured by the gargoyles, which are frankly curious as to why he is the valuable prey of their enemy, the demons. When the creature is presented to the gargoyle queen Leonore, she corrects her lieutenant who calls the creature 'it' and refers to 'it' as a thing. '*Him*, not *it*,' she insists. Then she approaches the creature tenderly, without fear, brushing aside a lock of hair to see his face more clearly. The creature flinches, by turns suspicious, afraid, and confused. Leonore is not threatening, but he does not know this. The creature's confusion, in this moment, bespeaks his complete unfamiliarity with love, simple kindness, or the touch of someone's gaze. The camera moves in for an extreme close-up, inviting the empathy of the viewer: what it is like to be so unfamiliar with tenderness that one recoils, the body on high alert, rather than relaxes? To support the idea that the queen enacts a parental role, she gives the creature a gift. 'I understand that Victor Frankenstein never offered you a name,' she says. 'I would like to call you "Adam."' '

The remainder of the film shows, with some degree of subtlety, the power in a name and the sometimes tricky path of growing into it. The image of the creature that has captured the popular imagination occurs later in the film, after he has been injured and 'rescued the girl' Dr. Terra Wade, who is, it must be admitted, useful to him for her expertise in evolutionary bio-chemistry and surgical skill. They escape to a dismal garret furnished with a single iron bed and a washbasin, where the creature proceeds to strip off his shirt so that she can stitch up the still-bleeding gash in his upper back. Before this, he had been covered from head to toe in scruffy urban attire, which included a long canvas trench coat the costumers chose because the swing looks good during fight sequences (2014, *'Frankenstein's Creatures' Featurette*, n.p.). This is the audience's first glimpse of the creature's lean, well-muscled body with the 'six-pack' of gleaming abdominal muscles. Without the scars that betray his patchwork origin, he could easily be a fitness model. In fact, this is the image that adorned the cover of the February 2014 issue of *Muscle & Fitness* magazine in the U.S., along with an article on how the actor, Aaron Eckhart, achieved his look.

My first response to the intentionally sculpted body of the creature was disbelief: *this* is our idea of the monstrous? Laughable. Yet, after dwelling with the image and watching this particular scene in the garret with psychological attention, other thoughts emerged. At this moment in the narrative, the creature—who is still troubled by the name Adam and rejects being called Frankenstein, his rightful surname if Victor is his father—expresses his profound discomfort at being seen. When Dr. Wade gazes directly at the creature with pity not horror, he flinches, turns away partially, then turns his back on her completely (ostensibly, one might argue, to permit her to stitch the wound). The creature remains stoic when she sews shut the deep, still-bleeding gash without anesthesia, but his hunched posture, particularly the pronated shoulders, curved neck, and dropped chin, tell another, more troubling story: he is the abject, the abomination without another of his own kind, the monster.

How does this particular archetypal image express the monstrous in the twenty-first century? There is some resemblance between the creature's heavy scarring and the fresh effects of cosmetic surgery. There is a striking resemblance between his physique and one contemporary standard of male beauty, a standard that is achieved only through enormous effort. I conjecture that this monster calls attention to our monstrous relationship to the body as an aesthetic object in a scientific age. Rather than the lived body, the body at ease in its own animal power, a body that one inhabits naturally, this body is viewed at a cool, objective distance, judged and found wanting. It must be perfected through surgery, punishing training, and extreme diet. As though to remind viewers of the body as object, the camera first reveals Eckhart's creature-cum-fitness-model in reflection, not directly. This is a subtle reminder of the cold, mirrored surfaces in indoor fitness gyms as well as dance studios, modern temples to the perfect body. *I, Frankenstein* is calling attention to a monstrous form of worship.

Conclusion

It is worth revisiting the idea that *Frankenstein; or, The Modern Prometheus*, for all its Gothic and realistic attributes, is an early work of science fiction. Moreover, it is well worth revisiting the key theme in the novel for its contemporary relevance in a scientific-technological age: the consequences of Promethean ambition. 'Are scientists ready for what they might create or uncover?' asks Montillo (2013, p. 287). More to the point, are *we* ready? In partial answer, I offer Jung's reflection on our relationship to new gadgets, all the more frightening because it was written 40 years before the advent of the mobile digital technology that infuses modern life:

Reforms by advances, that is, by new methods or gadgets, are of course impressive at first, but in the long run they are dubious and in any case dearly paid for. They by no means increase the contentment or the happiness of people on the whole. Mostly, they are deceptive sweetenings of existence, like speedier communications which unpleasantly accelerate the tempo of life and leave us with less time than ever before. *Omnis festinatio ex parte diaboli est*—all haste is of the devil, as the old master used to say.

(1961/1989, p. 236)

Jung's *Memories, Dreams, Reflections* was published a few short years before Marshall McLuhan's landmark 1964 text, *Understanding Media: The Extensions of Man*. McLuhan offers a more comprehensive view of technology than Jung's word 'gadgets' can disguise. Technology is an active, shaping process that alters our physical and social environment. The science fiction genre, including Mary Shelley's novel and its cinematic adaptations, prominently feature technology, and it is clear that it actively shapes Victor's character and fate. The filmmakers as examined in this chapter—lovingly render the laboratory in which Victor assembles his creature—which is the setting for the first meeting between the two people. In fact, the laboratory is Victor's first creation; the creature his second.

Where are our laboratories today? For most of us the answer is: in a back pocket, a handbag, a briefcase, or under our fingertips. The thin, glowing screen 'bulldozes our doubts with its bounties and conveniences. It is so much our servant that it would seem churlish to notice that it is also our master' (Carr, 2011, p. 4).

I wonder what Mary Shelley might say to that!

References

Aldiss, B. (1973) *Trillion year spree: the true history of science fiction.* New York: Atheneum.

Becker, E. (1973) *The denial of death.* New York: The Free Press.

Berry, P. (2001) 'Image in motion', in C. Hauke and I. Alister (eds), *Jung & film: post-Jungian takes on the moving image.* London: Brunner-Routledge. pp. 70–9.

Brier, J. (2004) 'AIDS and people with AIDS', in M. Stein (ed.), *Encyclopedia of lesbian, gay, bisexual and transgendered history in America,* Vol. 1. Detroit, MI: Charles Scribner's Sons. pp. 27–34.

Brooks, P. (1993) 'What is a monster? (according to *Frankenstein*)', in *Body work: objects of desire in modern narrative.* Cambridge, MA: Harvard University Press. pp. 199–220.

Carr, A. (2011) *Positive psychology: the science of happiness and human strengths.* Hove: Routledge.

Carroll, N. (2003) *Engaging the moving image.* New Haven, CT: Yale University Press.

Fredericksen, D. (2001) 'Jung/sign/symbol/film', in C. Hauke and I. Alister (eds), *Jung & film: post-Jungian takes on the moving image.* London: Brunner-Routledge. pp. 17–55.

Hauke, C. and Alister, I. (2001) *Jung & film: post-Jungian takes on the moving image.* London: Brunner-Routledge.

Hillman, J. (1975) *Re-visioning psychology.* New York: Harper & Row.

Hillman, J. (1977) 'An inquiry into image', *Spring,* pp. 62–88.

Hillman, J. (1978) 'Further notes on image', *Spring,* pp. 152–82.

Hillman, J. (1979) 'Image sense', *Spring,* pp. 130–43.

Hillman, J. (1985) *Anima: anatomy of a personified notion.* Dallas, TX: Spring Publications.

Jung, C. G. (1951/1969) 'The psychology of the child archetype', in *The collected works of C. G. Jung,* Vol. 9i, *The archetypes and the collective unconscious,* 2nd edn. Princeton, NJ: Princeton University Press, 1968.

Jung, C. G. (1954/1969) 'Psychological aspects of the mother archetype', in *The collected works of C. G. Jung,* Vol. 9i, *The archetypes and the collective unconscious,* 2nd edn. Princeton, NJ: Princeton University Press, 1968.

Jung, C. G. (1989 [1961]) *Memories, dreams, reflections.* New York: Vintage Books.

Jung, E. and von Franz, M.-L. (1970) *The grail legend,* 2nd edn, ed. A. Dykes. Princeton, NJ: Princeton University Press.

Kristeva, J. (2002) *The portable Kristeva*, updated edn, ed. K. Oliver. New York: Columbia University Press.

Leonard, L. (1997) 'Foreword', in D. Sandner and S. Wong (eds). *The sacred heritage: the influence of shamanism on analytical psychology*. London: Routledge. pp. xi–xvi.

McLuhan, M. (1964) *Understanding media: the extensions of man*. New York: McGraw-Hill.

Montillo, R. (2013) *The lady and her monsters: a tale of dissections, real-life Dr. Frankensteins, and the creation of Mary Shelley's masterpiece*. New York: HarperCollins.

Palmer, R. (1969) *Hermeneutics: interpretation theory in Schleiermacher, Dilthey, Heidegger, and Gadamer*. ss, IL: Northwestern University Press.

Shilts, R. (1987) *And the band played on*. New York: St. Martin's Press.

Skal, D. (2001) *The monster show: a cultural history of horror, revised edition*. New York: Faber & Faber.

Wolf, G. (2015) [audio recording] *How great science fiction works*, Season 1. Chantilly, VA: The Teaching Company.

Worobey, M., Watts, T. D., McKay, R. A., Suchard, M. A., Granade, T., Teuwen, D. E., Koblin, B. A., Heneine, W., Lemey, P., and Jaffe, H. W. (2016) '1970s and "Patient 0" HIV-1 genomes illuminate early HIV/AIDS history in North America', *Nature*, 539, pp. 98–101.

Online sources

Beebe, J. and Peay, P. (2011) 'Academy Awards 2011: which myth will America choose?' [online]. Available at: www.huffingtonpost.com/pythia-peay/academy-awards_b_826464.html [Accessed 2 March 2011].

GFTBILOXI. (2007, June 11) 'Psycho-sexual, homo-erotic, and unexpectedly subversive for it's era' [online]. Available at: www.imdb.com/title/tt0070074/reviews?ref_=tt_urv [Accessed 2 March 2011].

Jameson, R. (2002) 'Frankenstein and the bride of Frankenstein', *The A list: the National Society of Film Critics 100 essential films* [online]. Available at: www.loc.gov/programs/static/national-film-preservation-board/documents/bride_frank.pdf [Accessed 2 March 2011].

McNeil, D. (2016) 'H.I.V. arrived in the U.S. long before "Patient Zero,"' *New York Times*, 26 October [online]. Available at: www.nytimes.com/2016/10/27/health/hiv-patient-zero-genetic-analysis.html?_r=0 [Accessed 2 March 2011].

U.S. Library of Congress National Film Preservation Board. 'Brief descriptions and expanded essays of National Film Registry titles' [online]. Available at: www.loc.gov/programs/national-film-preservation-board/film-registry/descriptions-and-essays/ [Accessed 18 October 2016].

Filmography

Frankenstein. (1910) [film] Directed by J. Searle Dawley. USA.

Frankenstein. (1931) [film] Directed by James Whale. USA.

Frankenstein: the true story. (1973) [film] Directed by Jack Smight. USA.

I, Frankenstein. (2014) [film] Directed by Stuart Beatie. USA.

Mary Shelley's Frankenstein. (1994) [film] Directed by Kenneth Branagh. USA.

Romeo and Juliet. (1968) [film] Directed by Franco Zeffirelli. UK/Italy.

7

MUSIC IN FILM

Its functions as image

Benjamin Nagari

Introduction

Jung's ideas and understanding of image developed and changed through time. Starting with the notion of image as a pure concept it evolved into being an expression of unconscious contents, but not the whole of those contents, only those that are momentarily constellated. He observed how such a constellation is:

> the result of the spontaneous activity of the unconscious on the one hand and of the momentary conscious situation on the other.... The interpretation of its meaning, therefore, can start neither from the conscious alone nor from the unconscious alone, but only from their reciprocal relationship.
>
> *(1921: §745)*

Following this postulate, it is clear that the image is a *container* of opposites. As such it exists, 'in contradistinction to the symbol which is a *mediator* of opposites, it does not adhere to any one position but elements of it can be found in either' (see Samuels *et al.*, 1986, p. 72). This position suggests that what works well for a visual image also seems to work similarly with music, hence my formulation of the music-image which encapsulates its psychological aspects. The fact that music is a form of 'organised sound' adds to the systemic patterns of its archetypal nature and flow, by 'containing' opposites and mediating them symbolically.

Music functions as image both when standing alone and/or when collaborating with other types of image. In the case of film, music can be present in different functions within the film as a whole; it can complement or contradict and it can also build up or intervene with what otherwise a film would try to present without music. Based on my book *Music as Image: Analytical Psychology and Music in Film* (Nagari, 2015) and research into Jung's concept of image, as well as that of post-Jungians and non-Jungians alike, this chapter will present both theoretical and practical considerations. It will also explore different ways of implementing the music-image within a film, thus taking its experience into the realm of 'film-as-a-whole'. Taking in account the collective, individual and cultural elements of image, the chapter will emphasise the psychic-process and potential of the music-image that exists beyond the scope of 'picture-decorating-through-sound' and as such constitute itself as an entity that is independently and cooperatively active in the broader construction of image in film.

Music in film: contribution or problem

In a master class in front of a full house of musicians and film professionals, a famous film-music composer once defined and described the 'types of film directors' according to how they used music in their films. He observed following his many years of personal experience the 'types' would be of one or more of the following persuasions:

- Those who'll tell their composer how the music in each placement in the film should sound (style, melody, rhythm, etc.). These types, so our lecturer believed, wish they would be the composer him/herself, if they only could.
- Those who cannot be happy with any music style they are not compliant with.
- Those who expect the music to 'cover' for flaws in the script or the acting.
- Those who will cleverly choose the 'right' composer, sit together with him/her to decide where and where not music is required, explain the spirit of things then let the composer create and supply the music.

Whether or not the above definitions and observations are apposite, or just a part of the lecturer's witty sense of humour, there is no doubt that many still believe music in film to be a mere decoration that is attached to the image. Some might try to explain it by the historical need to cover the noise of the projector or to compensate for the 'discomfort of silence' in film, while others might believe that music is the best background for events in the film. Yet, incidental music is not necessarily accidental, and music has a unique character and immediate significance that is quite complementary to the visual moving images on screen. Having its own soul and mind music can cooperate, complement, contradict or compete with the other image types. The above lecturing composer had inevitably experienced the frustrations of a visual-image maestro (e.g. director, sound designer) and a musician (e.g. composer, orchestrator, editor) which one is likely to encounter when combining visual to sound.

In 1908, French classical composer Camille Saint-Saëns especially composed the first film-score for the silent film *The Assassination of the Duke de Guise* (dirs Charles Le Bargy and André Calmettes, 1908 – for more see Davis, 1999, p. 17). Until then film music would have been made and performed by bands or single musicians who played for the screen. Even though not yet embedded in the celluloid, this was still the first 'official' appearance of *music as image* in which it adopted a cooperative character with the film in its own right.

In addition to acting, directing and producing, Charlie Chaplin also composed the music for a great number of his films, among which we find *Shoulder Arms* (1918), *The Kid* (1921), *The Gold Rush* (1925), *City Lights* (1931), *Modern Times* (1936), *The Great Dictator* (1940) and *Monsieur Verdoux* (1947) among many others. One can wonder whether that was our lecturer's reasoning for his first point's assumption. These two points in the history of both film and music clearly express the need, development and even the confusion over the ways music and picture have come together alongside film history; both these marvellous developments and confusions have been, and still are, milestones in understanding the many facets, shapes and variations of image in general and the music-image in particular.

When film met music

Unless music is the *subject* of a film (e.g. a musical, an opera, a story of a specific music or musician) it merges with the visual scenery, possessing a narrative quality-potential of a similar quality to that of the visual image, whether in direct conjunction with an immediately present one or indirectly, connecting with the imagery capacity of the viewer's psyche. Such conjunctions tend to address feeling-toned psychological elements such as time-and-space, motion (action) and mood. Music-image when embedded in a narrative can assume the capacity of a 'super-ego' to the adjacent visual image, that is, if we wish to use the ego/super-ego metaphor in reference to the visual-image/music-image relation within the concept of film-as-a-whole.

The term 'film-as-a-whole' refers to an understanding of the cinematic experience in its entirety – picture, sound, music, picture-size, screening and viewing conditions etc., thus permeating psychological responses to the total on-screen presentation through both the collective and individual orientation of the viewer's psyche. While an image as such (visual or otherwise) bears no inherent or mandatory meaning when it is isolated on its own, it 'acquires' and becomes pregnant with meaning once the recipient (viewer) attaches it through a psychic process stemming from his/her individual and/or collective experience. (The term *psychic* refers to the pure grammatical form, denoting 'of the psyche' and not to any mystical experience.) While film frames, like music or speech, do not usually represent themselves in a frozen, 'still' manner but rather through motional connectivity over a time axis, so the psychic 'meaning attachment' faculty is being 'helped' or directed towards some 'narrowing' of the abstract choices of attachment. Imagine a film projecting just still frames over a time sequence; the longer the time-gap between the frames the more diverse will be the 'packages' of meaning attached by every viewer – meanings that might vary considerably between each interpreting individual. This 'narrowing' process does not indicate (as the very word can) a reductive process but rather a process of location and placement; such a process is collectively inherit in the human psyche, yet it also works personally within each individual. Jung postulated that the essential basis of our personality consists of affectivity:

> The essential basis of our personality is affectivity. Thought and action are, as it were, only symptoms of affectivity. The elements of psychic life, sensations, ideas and feelings, are given to consciousness in the form of certain units, which can perhaps be compared – if one may risk a chemical analogy – to molecules.
>
> *(1907: §78)*

Elaborating on this analogy Jung adds that:

> In this unit, or 'molecule,' we can distinguish three components, or 'radicals': sense-perception, intellectual components (ideas, memory-images, judgments, etc.), and feeling-tone. These three components are firmly united, so that if the memory-image of X rises to the surface all the elements belonging to it usually come with it, too. (Sense-perception is represented by a simultaneous, centrifugal excitation of the sensory spheres concerned.) I am therefore justified in speaking of a functional unit.
>
> *(ibid.: §78)*

Sadly, unfortunately, and

> considering his life-long interest in the great cultural movements, in the sciences and in the humanities, one finds it rather puzzling that the art of music hardly attracted the attention of Jung's enquiring mind. There are less than twenty references to music in the general index to his Collected Works.
>
> *(Pulvermacher in Papadopoulos and Saayman, 1991, p. 256)*

This might well not be the appropriate place to attempt to understand Jung's lack of interest in this great art's immense power to signal or symbolise, express or manipulate, direct or derail emotions and feelings. Notwithstanding, we shall consider Jung's Analytical Psychology as providing a solid ground from which to understand the image-power that exists and which is active in music; in this case it will be music when it coincides with visual moving images.

Symbols, writes Pulvermacher, can stand for the most varied contents ranging from natural events to internal psychological processes, namely the contents that can never be fully expressed rationally. There is no doubt that owing to Jung's metaphysical outlook, symbols played an important part in his psychological enquiries, because they come out of that 'between-world of subtle reality which can be adequately expressed through the symbol alone' (ibid., p. 256; quoting Jung in Jolande, 1942, p. 91). In attempting to understand and hopefully explain Jung's fascination with the visual while almost ignoring the audial (especially music), Pulvermacher notes that:

> Generally speaking, it is true that the psychological study of the visual arts has been accepted far more readily and widely than that of music. This seems to be a paradox, because music is an important part of every culture on earth, especially in the form of song – that is in its combination with language – while the visual arts are not universally present in every cultural setting of man.
>
> *(in Papadopoulos and Saayman, 1991, p. 257)*

Moreover, Pulvermacher adds:

> The psychologist cannot ignore the fact that music is especially receptive of symbols, because it uses the most abstract material: sound, which is invisible, non-tangible and transitory.... Music expresses in sounds what fantasies and visions express in visual images ... music represents the movement, development, and transformation of motifs of the Collective Unconscious.
>
> *(ibid., p. 257)*

Music, meaning, space and placement

It was the composer Igor Stravinsky who quite shockingly commented:

> Music is, by its very nature, powerless to express anything at all, whether a feeling, an attitude of mind, a psychological mood, a phenomenon of nature. If, as is nearly always the case, music appears to express something, this is only an illusion and not a reality.
>
> *(1936, p. 91)*

While illusion and reality are far from being coherent terms in Stravinsky's perception of music, we can easily accept the idea that music is by no means a 'language' that is here to represent, or describe or precisely point to a defined feeling, attitudes of mind, psychological moods or phenomena of nature. The very same music, whether independent or alongside other types of image can affect different people in different, even opposite ways. Hence music is *not* semiotic, bearing fixed meaning, if any; it is *not* a language. However, it does run through as blocks of a flexibly open communication between the conscious and unconscious, where symbols are the *mediators* between the two – described by Samuels *et al.* as 'the best possible expression of still unconscious facts' (1986, p. 49). This understanding stands parallel to Jung's understanding of dreams, as opposed to Freud's perception of them as a stream of mainly fixed meanings.

In his 1956 *Sound and Symbol in Music and the External World*, Victor Zuckerkandl expressed his belief that:

> Whereas the representational and descriptive peculiarities of symbols found in the visual arts bear a kinship to those found in literature, the symbols of music belong to a different, more abstract category, because they are usually not readily amenable to precise defini- tion. Could it be that this fundamental aspect of musical symbolism was a contributing factor for Jung's exclusion of music in his symbolic analyses of the arts?
>
> *(ch. XX)*

He also argues (1969) that music has a 'special kind of reality'. On one hand he believes it is outside us, located in the external world, yet it is neither a physical phenomenon nor a projec- tion of psychic states. According to Zuckerkandl, what we hear is not traceable to the properties of sound waves, nor can we define hearing as a 'hallucination' in which psychological responses become objectified. This notion is invaluable to any musical and psychological research into Jung's multiple realities. It suggests how music possesses a potentially 'independent' reality that has the capacity to connect with the 'linear' here-and-now reality.

These multiple realities are presented in the core dynamics of change and development. Once upon a time people would gather around a bonfire telling mythological, magic legends and fairy tales. Now people go to cinema and/or watch television, media that are capable of containing and combining the 'old' elements and narratives with new technological features no one ever dreamt of before, yet which have now become a reality.

A hundred years after Kant's 'liberation of image' started the call for new movements in art and philosophy, Freud began to:

> explore the recesses of the human mind through an analysis of psychic images. Dreams, fantasies, and associations were carefully examined in an attempt to understand how psychic images are involved in personality development, psychopathology, and our experience of the past, present and future.
>
> *(Kugler, 2002, p. 78)*

Kant proclaimed the process of imaging (*Einbildungskraft*) to be:

> the indispensable precondition of all knowledge. In the first edition of his Critique of Pure Reason, he demonstrated that both reason and sensation, the two primary terms in most theories of knowledge up to this point, were produced, not reproduced, by imaging.
>
> *(ibid., pp. 78–79)*

Following this line of thought, image may now depart from being a reflection of physical objects and assume its role as a unit or collection of its own entities, whether related to 'real' objects or abstract ideas. Jung's delicate distinction between *sign* and *symbol* can exhibit in music the similarity, difference and dichotomy between what is collective or personal and what is conscious and unconscious. Cultural and personal influences of both past and present can create different musical experiences in different people and groups, to the extent that one person's romantic music is another's tragic song. Yet, it is also true that due to 'migration' (through geo- graphical watching/hearing, co-producing etc.) musical elements can meet and 'adopt' under- standings and interpretations despite the physical distances between the 'sources' and the influence of cultures. Such adoptions easily pass through the sign–symbol confusion, thus imposing at times some unintelligible ideas such as brass instruments' stabs and/or dissonant chords as thriller scene music while violins play romantic music. Through intensive viewing such 'understandings' migrated quickly into global filmmaking and music conventions.

While poetically expressed in fairy tales as 'once upon a time' now the expressions of *space* and *time* fill in what the narrated story could not easily create, which is image (especially visual), alongside sound, music and placement. Space has now been overridden, skipped or ignored with the capacity of editing to bring 'now', 'then' and 'someday' into an easy coexistence; real sounds, sound effects and 'organised sound' make the abstract or unattainable voice-mimic real, or they can add far reaching artistic and imaginary dimensions to the here-and-now narrative.

The decisions about where in the film, for how long, what type of musically expected effect, the physical volume and presence of music along with the technical capacity to alter the 'direction' music can come at the viewer from (through sound panning, speakers' position etc.) are now under the control of the director, composer, sound editor or sound designer. They can add aspects of great power and influence over the entire film's narrative.

Claudia Gorbman (1980, 1988) and Michel Chion (1994, 1999, 2009) expanded this idea of placement into what was to become known as *diegetic* and the *nondiegetic* sound and music in film. This concept deals with the physical sound and music *within* the film, whether made in real time and sources as opposed to coming from unseen sources. This complex theory suggests if a person or any object produces sound while the visual is seen to also be producing it makes the connection differently from when it comes from a non-seen connection. Thus, music that is played live (by a person, on stage, by a seen transmitter such as radio, record player etc.) carries different meanings and/or values to the viewer from those that come from unseen sources. Gorbman defines 'diegesis' as 'being the narratively implied spatiotemporal world of the actions and characters' (1980, p. 21), suggesting that diegetic and non-diegetic relate directly to the placement of sound and/or music within the narrative.

Chion, being more elaborate, creates more subtle subdivisions than the previously suggested pair by coining terms and categories such as *acousmatic sound*, being the opposite of visualised sound; *empathetic sound*, sound or music whose mood matches the corresponding visual images (possibly matching by participating in the visual action, rhythm or tone) and its opposite, *anempathetic sound*, being a sound or music that

> seems to exhibit conspicuous indifference to what is going on in the film's plot, creating a strong sense of the tragic (e.g., a radio continues to play a happy tune even as the character that first turned it on has died).
>
> *(Chion, 1994, pp. 8–9)*

From the conflation of two terms – synchronism and synthesis – Chion creates a yet new term – *Synchresis*. This term reflects a mental fusion between a sound image and a visual image when these occur at exactly the same time. As a sound technique, synchresis may vary from combining visual with very accurate audio, to the extreme of using sound completely 'estranged' from the visual image. For example, a person tiptoes barefoot on screen, while the sound heard is of woman's high heels clicking. From some similarity to *synaesthesia* (though not operating in a similar way), Chion also believes that *transsensoriality* means that hearing might not take place solely through the ears and that seeing may not take place solely with the eyes (ibid., p. 137). Both senses – the auditory and the visual, Chion argues – create a complementary psychic process of vision of a new kind, born of the transcendence created by the encounter of the two images – visual and sound/music.

While in the here-and-now reality sight, motion and dialogue can easily conjoin, the involvement of music with these is somewhat trickier, as music is not attached, nor accompanies the everyday movement. Rather, music in film is a 'value added reality' that wishes to add to, enhance or suggest the possible meanings of the 'whole picture'. Yet, as music reality is more complexly abstract than the holy trinity of sight-motion-dialogue, there is no wonder that we – the viewers, composers, directors and production companies – resort to create collectively agreed meanings and semiotics as they offer a means to decipher and understand that kind of image.

The possible functions of music in film

It is my experience as a Jungian and a composer, through studying and through composing for a wide range of musical media (including film music) that music in film tries to address and cover three major aspects. Acting as images, these three stand-alone yet all encompassing, independent if inseparable functions are:

1   incidental
2   transitional
3   conditional.

These can be referred to as modes, modus operandi, major components, radicals or molecules in any order and/or preference. These functions, or modes, do not correspond respectively with *sense-perception*, *intellectual* and *feeling-tone* as in Jung's reference, but can rather be thought of as 'atoms' in them exclusively or in an overlapping flow.

The incidental mode

This mode of music is presented alongside, in and around an event in the narrative to become a part of an action or a focused event. It can also be used *before* the start of an actual happening in an anticipatory and alerting manner. In its extreme use, this type of music can resemble the characteristics of programme music composed in a meticulously timing-based manner to 'fit' the events in the scene; at the other end it may carry atmospheric affect only, to match the 'spirit' of the given action without any timing precision. In any case this mode attempts to invoke affect intensity in relation to the visual action. As in all the other modes, there are no 'prescribed' music styles or genres to adhere to; iconic patterns, popularly named 'suspense music', 'action music', 'love-scene music' and the like are just markers of cultural conditioning (mainly referring to Hollywood-type films) and are prone to everlasting cultural changes. What defines this mode is rather its relatedness to the action scene and its capacity to increase and/or 'choice-narrow' the viewer's affect in relation to a specific narrative of action.

As an affect-based 'radical' this molecule in its entirety or just parts of its 'atoms' might well merge into and/or overlap with the other two. This merging/overlapping effect runs simultaneously on two reality levels – the film creators' reality and the spectators' reality – a notion that works in line with Jung's idea of plurality of psychic reality, thus using 'realities' rather than 'reality'. The former can deliberately create merging points to boost the viewers' 'choice-narrowing' process by various deliberations, e.g. music duration, tempo and tempo changes, connecting to a previously heard music and so on. Yet the spectator, even while absorbing the creators' 'dictate' can take into wider affect, as set in his/her own psychological setup, thus merging with additional and even different image-making associations.

The transitional mode

Usually attached to the visual imaging of time/space transition (flashbacks, editorial cuts to another place or time etc.) this mode stands for the completion and 'sense-making' of the otherwise non-linear flow in a cinematic scene. While the conscious mind apprehends realities linearly and sequentially, a leap in space or time amidst a sequence can interfere with the conscious process of 'sense-making'; the more abstract quality of music can then be called to bridge between this consciousness limitation and the unconscious capacity of apprehending time/space differently, thus 'making up' for the loss.

We may borrow from music the notion of *harmony* capturing tones in a 'stand-still' outlook, treating the appearance of simultaneous tone in a given freeze-time (theoretical or practical), as opposed to *counterpoint* that follows the relations between tones *in motion*. Under this metaphor we will have to agree that the cinematic experience is counterpointal. Being as such, the counterpointal flow sets the viewers' (and/or listeners') anticipation to await a time frame that is as consciously followed typically linear. When cutting the time line, the less interrupted the cut the more psychic 'making-up' is available, whereas the more abrupt the fewer connection points are available to the conscious mind.

Transitional music can then create in a viewer's psyche an 'added' reality (or realities) not explicitly described and/or experienced through the visual images. It is worth noting that in silent movies that lack diegetic sound (dialogue as well as environmental sound), music – external or embedded – would undertake the time-frame capacity to replace the time/space sequential progress being potentially incomplete due to the lack of the 'natural' sound. On the other hand, in a sound film music replaces a transition by filling in the deliberately 'missed' narrative sequence.

The conditional mode

The words 'condition' and 'conditional' are not used here in the sense of behavioural psychological mental processes, but rather in the plain grammatical/definitive meaning of 'subject to one or more conditions being met' or 'expressing a condition'. In the film-music instance it refers to the *intentional* capacity of music-in-film to 'direct' and so condition the viewer into possibly triggered 'moods'; the word mood will best be used under the plain definition of a state of mind or feeling, the atmosphere or pervading tone of something or as *modifier* – in other words, the road to affect.

Whether under, above or instead of a dialogue, 'music-as-mood' type seems to be the most obviously 'busy' mode used. It comes in a vast variety both in content and in location within a film; it can 'tackle' any affective functionality the film creators (director and composer in this instance) wish and believe to condition the viewer's psyche through music. Its presence and consequently its affect-creating power can present itself subliminally – e.g. when it is low volume and under dialogue – or explicitly as when it accompanies a text-less scene. In the first instance it might only attempt to reinforce an affect that is already being expressed through vision and text, as if to ensure the recipient's 'right' state of mind. When brought to the fore to convey a non-verbally expressed feeling this music may 'become' the character him/herself or the very situation. It may be directly attached to the counterpointal continuity of a scene (or scenes) when interwoven in them, or externally and more aloof, like, for instance, in the case of a theme-song or theme melody appearing at the beginning of a film, attempting to 'draw' both the viewer's attention and 'channel' his/her affect direction. Similar effects may be achieved when using music on end-titles, attempting to allow some of the viewer's film experience and mood to slowly dissolve into the transition between one's reality experiences (the cinematic experience) to another, the individual's own.

In the conditional mode (as well as in the others) diegetic music may work with more precision and rigour, due to being an integral part of a scene or a visual occurrence; it can affect the 'choice-narrowing' process more vigorously since 'by nature' of being an unquestionable part of the whole scene it brings forth a possibly immediate, 'prescribed', 'biased' and explicitly suggestive reference, less open to a wider scope of associations. At the same time, non-diegetic musical conditioning – notwithstanding the intention of the creators – can achieve a wider, more individual meaning-producing interpretation of the creators' desired notions, such as, love, sadness, drama and suspense, to mention only few. Due to extensive usage of this music mode in films many repeating musical patterns, styles and specific colouration are iconic, such as the use of strings (more referred to 'violins') in love scenes, syncopated music for edginess dissonant intervals for suspense etc. It is interesting that a lot of tips, advice and prescriptions for the 'how to' can be found as early as 1925 in Erno Rapee's *The Encyclopedia of Music for Pictures*. This kind of general conditioning should be seen through cultural dynamic changes and cannot be taken as 'proven' rules or dictates.

The overlapping of the modes

In the definitions of the above three modes and through examining them in many films their overlapping quality and attributes become apparent, especially when observing the film-as-a-whole. This is because emotions triggered by music are naturally intertwined in the meaning-making, image-creating processes of the psyche. Only if we take apart the cinematic experience can we single out and isolate specific modes accurately. Within the reality of film-as-a-whole, these modes enable psychological image-making and exactly as the visual images do they become images capable of meaning. As such they are a part of the narrative, be it diegetic or non-diegetic in source.

In the early days of the silent movie there was a heavy burden on music which had to carry all the above qualities, since it had to stand for and fill in the gaps opened up by the lack of speech and diegetic sound. Music also had to be more present quantitatively, meaning that at times the music-image would have even more presence than the visual characters (images) themselves. The subsequent need to deploy the music modes to convey images more implicitly has contributed to the creation of acceptable music patterns, unique sub-genres and colouration. With the advent of video and audio developments these elements have become ever more sophisticated participants in the narrative of the film-as-a-whole.

Music image: to use, or how to use

Incorporating the music-image in film loosely corresponds to classical programme music, which is a type of musical composition that is intended to evoke images or remind the listener of events. Only that in the case of film the music-image will try to connect and attach itself to the visual image(s) on the screen instead of to the psychically imagined images of a story. This statement can be mistakenly attributed to the incidental function of music only; yet, and as with the case of the two other functions, the incidental music can be repeated to enhance a filmic situation (conditional) or be used as a 'start point' to space and time changes (transitional). An incidental music sequence can use a repeated motif (or leitmotif) to draw the listener/viewer's attention, even though this is already in the domain of the conditional.

Can a film (narrative, documentary or any other) do without the music-image? Apparently so, yet does that mean it is necessary to give up on the subject of having really participating (diegetic) music-image inside the plot, when it is played and exhibited as an integral part of the narrative. Can anyone imagine the final concert scene in Hitchcock's *The Man who Knew too Much* (1956) without Arthur Benjamin's *Storm Clouds Cantata* being performed as the viewers wait for the cymbal's loud clash to cue the gun shot? While film remains an expressive form, without music and giving up on the music-image would undoubtedly be a great loss to the art of film. Did our ancestors sing or hum around the bonfire while telling or listening to fairy tales? We cannot tell, but if they did it would be in anticipation for the music-image to join them...

Intentionally or not, our master class lecture raised the issue of *creating* the triggering music-image, a process that is psychologically complicated. At least two minds are involved in this creation process, namely the director and the composer (unless they are the same person). There are two personalities that hear and see music individually, yet both are trying to give birth to an amicably accepted expression, bearing in mind at the same time, that the different viewers absorb the music-images differently and in unexpected ways.

The director's choice of composer and/or the type of music he/she believes will deliver the music-image in the best way, including taking decisions such as using existing music or having an original music composed – is his/her artistic, technical and commercial decision about how to get to the 'understanding ears' of the viewers. Unlike visual images, sound and especially music-images are open to many more interpretations because of the higher abstraction that is embedded in them. Yet, within the scope of the three modes, these added images are capable of participating in and enhancing the experience of film-as-a-whole by being as vivid as its characters and its visual images alike.

References

Chion, M. (1994) *Audio-vision, sound on screen*. New York: Columbia University Press.

Chion, M. (1999) *The voice in cinema*. New York: Columbia University Press.

Chion, M. (2009) *Film, a sound art*. New York: Columbia University Press.

Davis, R. (1999) *Complete guide to films scoring*. Boston, MA: Berklee Press.

Gorbman, C. (1980) *Narrative film music* (in Yale French Studies, No. 60). New Haven, CT: Yale University Press.

Gorbman, C. (1988) *Unheard melodies: narrative film music*. London: British Film Institute.

Jolande, J. (1942) *The psychology of C. G. Jung*. London: Routledge & Kegan Paul.

Jung, C. G. (1907) 'The psychology of Dementia Praecox', in *The collected works of C. G. Jung*, Vol. 3, *The psychogenesis of mental disease*, 2nd edn. London, Routledge, 1972.

Jung, C. G. (1921) 'Definitions', in *The collected works of C. G. Jung*, Vol. 6, *Psychological types*, 3rd edn. Princeton, NJ: Princeton University Press, 1971.

Kugler, P. (2002) *The alchemy of discourse: image, sound and psyche*. Einsiedeln, Switzerland: Daimon.

Nagari, B. (2015) *Music as image: analytical psychology and music in film*. London and New York: Routledge.

Papadopoulos, R. K. and Saayman, G. S. (eds) (1991) *Jung in modern perspective*. Bridport, UK: Prism Press.

Rapee, E. (1925) *The encyclopedia of music for pictures*. New York: Belwin, Inc.

Samuels, A., Shorter, B. and Plaut, F. (1986) *A critical dictionary of Jungian analysis*. London: Routledge & Kegan Paul.

Stravinsky, I. (1936) *Chronicle of my life*. London: Gollancz.

Zuckerkandl, V. (1956) *Sound and symbol in music and the external world*. London: Routledge & Kegan Paul.

Zuckerkandl, V. (1967) *The sense of music*. Princeton, NJ: Princeton University Press.

Zuckerkandl, V. (1969) *Sound and symbol, volume 1: music and the external world*. In Bollingen Series (General). Princeton, NJ: Princeton University Press.

Filmography

Assassination of the Duke de Guise, The. (1908) [film] Directed by Charles Le Bargy and André Calmettes. France.

City lights. (1931) [film] Directed by Charles Chaplin. USA.

Gold rush, The. (1925) [film] Directed by Charles Chaplin. USA.

Great dictator, The. (1940) [film] Directed by Charles Chaplin. USA.

Kid, The. (1921) [film] Directed by Charles Chaplin. USA.

Man who knew too much, The. (1956) [film] Directed by Alfred Hitchcock. USA.

Modern times. (1936) [film] Directed by Charles Chaplin. USA.

Monsieur Verdoux. (1947) [film] Directed by Charles Chaplin. USA.

Shoulder arms. (1918) [film] Directed by Charles Chaplin. USA.

8

PSYCHOLOGICAL IMAGES AND MULTIMODALITY IN *BOYHOOD* AND *BIRDMAN*

Shara D. Knight

Introduction

This chapter explores an experimental leap into the unknown: the relevant potential of a Jungian theoretical lens conjoined with filmmakers in the constant discovery of their technical abilities. Central to the discussion is the simultaneous inevitability and impossibility of change, in which cinematography is expanded to its limits to reveal human emotions and psychological images across time – the analysis of film images – or is considered in the context of multimodal elements and psychological perspectives, the attention to a film's narrative notwithstanding. Psychological meaning results from the perception of a set of signs encountered through innovative modalities in filmmaking. As signs are objects of perception, their modalities will determine at least part of their essence. The cinematic technique of the extended camera shot which will be at the heart of this discussion is one modality that enables Jungian thought and film studies to connect in an interdisciplinary manner.

Reflections of reality

Two films that push the limits of cinematography and the idea of the 'long take' as something that is psychological are *Boyhood* (dir. Linklater, 2014) and *Birdman* (dir. Iñárritu, 2014). *Boyhood*'s imagery reflects a twelve-year human life, all be it one that is compressed into three hours of nuanced sequential editing. Hints at the passage of time can be recognized through the music selections on the film soundtrack, physical growth and the aging of characters, their changes in hairstyles, along with other audiovisual clues. A camera tracking shot in *Birdman* that appears singular and continuous throughout the film is accomplished through precisely designed long scenes edited together with computer graphics – a good example of which is offered in the night-to-day segue. The modality or representational format of the extended camera shot, creatively holds information as a film image that is both a medium and text for cinematic language.

A brief review on the cinematic technique of an extended camera shot is helpful at this point. Critic and film theorist André Bazin (1967), co-founder of the influential French film magazine *Cahiers du Cinema*, argued the 'long shot,' 'long take,' or unedited gaze of the camera lens mediated an awareness of being in the world, an uninterrupted sense of space and time. Bazin saw a long, uncut camera shot as expanding the world to the viewer for interpretation. Bazin insisted that the long shot respects the spatial unity of an event, locates it in reality, and emphasizes continuity of dramatic space, its duration, and continuous, unbroken action. Bazin's viewpoint enabled analysis of the dramatic field in time and it did so as a challenge to Eisenstein's earlier montage theory. Eisenstein's approach regarded film as an unfolding story in a series of montage image set-ups, e.g., shot-reverse-shot in a dialogue scene with the camera following the order of the script and alternating the character shown with each speech. Such montage technique employs a separation and creative re-assemblage of discrete segments of film imagery in a manner that Bazin considered interpretive, non-objective because their function was to intensify emotional impact.

Camera shots in depth of field also enable deep emotional impressions and were introduced, according to Bazin, by film directors including Orson Welles and William Wyler. The two modalities of depth in field and long shot enabled those filmmakers to cover whole scenes in one take with long duration sequences and unobtrusive edits. It follows that the actors working within a fixed visual framework of a relatively static camera primarily created the dramatic effects in their films. Historically, film composition in depth of field accomplished a partial replacement of images previously crafted in the montage style of Eisenstein. Bazin posited that within an extended camera shot, objects and characters are related in such a way that it is impossible for the viewer to miss the significance or meaning of the scene – as will become clear in the analyses below.

In addition to affecting the structure of film language, depth of field also imparted a sense of the ambiguity of reality, which psychologically signifies the uncertainty and opacity of life. Image based representations of psychic reality, including reflections of prevailing belief systems or cultural milieu, enable the viewing audience to recognize itself, at least symbolically, in the film text. Further, how the camera 'looks' at images might well rest with the cinematographer's skill, the creative, inner vision of the director, and relationships to the unconscious.

Cinematographic long takes as modalities serve to elevate the genre of realism and place a particular emphasis on the 'real world.' In the two films considered in this chapter, realism takes an account of inner, psychological life as well as external reality and the films show the social and physical world as a dynamic rather than a merely passive and determining environment. One version of the long shot modality enhanced the jarring realism depicted in *Boyhood*, and as a film it intentionally excluded cinematic devices such as segmented scenes, flashback images, and the use of editing just for the sake of dramatic effects. In contrast the film *Birdman* constitutes a magical realism that encompasses unreal elements as natural parts in an otherwise realistic or mundane environment. This genre is especially suited to the world of theater (the subject of the film) with its onstage depiction of the irrational and non-comprehensible forces of emotion.

Images and the symbolic

The extended camera shot expands a Jungian symbolic reading of cinema films. Extraordinary films and filmmakers seem to be instinctively connected to this visual possibility as a means to represent the inner, emotional dynamics of psychological life. Further, Jungian analytical psychology with its sensitivities opens up different and potentially deeper interdisciplinary conversations to Freudian oriented psychoanalysis, particularly in areas that are connected to creative expression.

A key Jungian concept (the archetype) hypothesizes there are universal patterns that lend form and structure to the basic themes in human life. Such conceptual archetypal representations reflect primordial images as elements of the collective unconscious and they function as precursors to ideation. As ancient patterns that exist in human consciousness, archetype representations are essentially neutral concepts with both productive and, conversely, unproductive polarities. Therefore these images theoretically hold a *potential* for one thing or another with a diverse range of possible expressions, and their collective qualities and patterns link with unconscious processes. For Jung, individuals experience the different stages of life via these collective species-wide structures in psychological thought and physiology in such events as birth, initiation, maturation, mating, and death. Such archetypal images express themselves as symbols in culture through literature, art, religion, mythology, and films.

Jung's work led him to consider that the unconscious itself is structured with symbolic representations as the reflecting units of meaning. Seen from this point of view, the unconscious is arranged as an elaborate system with specific associations that make themselves known as metaphors. The existence of this network of metaphoric associations is recognizable through analysis of unconscious products such as psychological complexes, dreams, and cultural artifacts including films. Cinema developed concurrently on the cultural stage with the discipline of psychoanalysis and as John Beebe has noted both 'share a drive to explore and realize the psyche' (2009, p. 17). The cinematic modality of realism or 'continuous reality' that lends itself to aesthetics additionally offers a creative field that allows for the exploration of inner images and the insights of analytical psychology. A better understanding of meaning-making in psychic life as well as filmmaking can be glimpsed in Jungian-informed approaches to the intricate interactions that are fundamental to both psychological and filmmaking processes.

Archetypal representations and their associated symbolic patterns constitute what Jung called the collective unconscious and provide the 'gradient' in which instinctual libido finds energetic representation in psychic images and ideas (1956: §337). He claimed that ignoring rather than participating with diverse parts of the psyche introduced psychological conflict and patterns of anxiety. This idea of psychological participation enfolds self-introspection and engagement with a larger sense of self; progress is consciously or unconsciously in relation to others, including the diverse expressions of psychic life. While the human quest for rooted connections to self and others is traditionally reflected in historical and artistic traditions it can also be found in contemporary film. As such the Jungian sense of working toward a psychological essence, unity, or wholeness is articulated conceptually as the 'self' archetype coupled with the expansive cinematic modality of the long take – this insight has the effect of widening the form of both *Boyhood* and *Birdman* and it also shapes their textual meanings in cultural and psychological ways.

Jung held that archetypal representations and patterning are timeless and are one way to express, apprehend, and understand the fluid nature of psychic activity. For example, the child archetype as a motif or primordial image can coalesce with *components* of myth rather than a definite, solitary, formulation of a mythology (1940: §260). Jung detailed the difference between archetypal representation and the bias to literally identify the child motif with the concrete experience, *child*, as though the real child were the cause and pre-condition of the child motif – the archetypal quality conceptually represents something psychologically that existed both in the past and now: 'It [the child archetype] is not just a vestige but a system functioning in the present whose purpose is to compensate or correct, in a meaningful manner, the inevitable one-sidedness or extravagances of the conscious mind' (1940: §276).

Jung's idea of a self-correcting psychic system is in relation to the individual's ego state or will and therein is the trajectory of his work in analytical psychology. Cognizance and integration of these unfamiliar psychic components (often obscured by ego) afford the possibility of psychological balance and improved quality of life.

Multimodality in film

As a mass media for communicating ideas, cinematic images visually represent a full range of human emotions, but how might technological advances in cinematography and editing help to coalesce psychological significance in the image texts? Onscreen visuals potentially bridge inner psychic realities for reciprocity in expression, as signifiers that evoke different levels of psychological relatedness. Inherent in the ways cinematic language is punctuated is the concept of time, its ineffable quality, and the psychological dimensions of what it means to be human moving through time. Human perception of the concept of time might involve real time, extended time, and dream-time while cinematic lenses have the ability to adjust duration and transitions for onscreen images that represent these intervals. Further ways in which Jungian thought might advance a fresh approach will be shown in the context of two contemporary films, *Boyhood* (2014) and *Birdman* (2014). In these films, the directors, cinematographers, and film editors either were the same person or assumed shared roles and worked in ensemble (multimodal), yet with the directorial vision in place. These two remarkable films were released in the same year, focus on the nature of time itself as a subject, are multimodal, and are powerful psychological dramas. Specifically, contemporary cinematography and the modality of the extended camera shot widens the form of both films and it also shapes the films' textual meanings in cultural and psychological ways.

Boyhood (2014)

As observed by cultural critic Raymond Williams (1991), realism in drama is inextricable from new social forces and new versions of social relationships. In an original and unconventional style Linklater filmed *Boyhood* over a twelve-year span, a dramatic film that glides in time across the life of its protagonist, Mason (Ellar Coltrane), and his family: an older sister (Lorelei Linklater, the director's daughter) and separated parents (Patricia Arquette and Ethan Hawke). From the age of six years old to eighteen years old, the audience witnesses and accompanies Mason on his journey. Ellar Coltrane, the child actor, also grew up in 'real time' on camera as the character of Mason across the years. Viewers watch Mason navigate childhood and leave home to go to university. At the close of the film, audiences have not only witnessed Mason's transformation but shared it through realistic images of his personality development. The director and crew who worked on the film project also aged and changed in different ways across its extended production cycle.

Director Richard Linklater's storytelling and filmmaking are intuitive and the realism in *Boyhood* is clearly an important aspect of this film as it reflects the ineffable passage of time and the humanity of psychological life. Linklater employed his usual eye-level, medium-to-wide shot frame and conveys a sense of realistic proximity to the characters during the nearly three-hour film. There were no on-screen texts in *Boyhood* that articulated each year of Mason's life or montage or flashbacks as designations of time periods. The story of Mason and his relationships with others and life does not occur in a 'fictional' or substitute world. Linklater did not avoid looking at the realities of social and human experience in life and realistically filmed it in motion without theatricality. The dramatic action is contemporary and worked through in solely human terms so that none of the characters escape – the realism is consistent across the images as film text.

Two cinematographers, Shane F. Kelly and Lee Daniel (responsible for the first two-thirds of the film), brought the director's vision to the photography in *Boyhood*. Filming took place every one or two years and each shooting session lasted three or four days. Technical innovations and changes occurred during the length of the shoot and digital production began to replace the use of film stock in the industry. Kelly shared his attitude toward quality, variations in camera lenses, and the evolution of digital intermediate (DI) which allowed changes and adjustments to be made in the postproduction phase of the film:

> We had to use several different film stocks, but thankfully the film stocks got better and faster.... Rick likes to do a lot of takes, so there was a helluva lot of footage.... I aimed for color consistency in the DI, which helped immensely to bring those disparate years together. That was something we couldn't have done until a few years ago.
>
> *(Egan, 2015, §6–7)*

Advances in film technologies were concurrently introduced into the filmmakers' creative work processes and also presented challenges on that front. Cinematic meaning-making in the film expanded across years as unrelated moments were visually 'held' for all of the characters, eventually to accumulate in future phases of their lives. In this respect, Bazin's idea of the technical apparatus and its methodology is present, although not entirely. The consistency of visual points (use of the same actors throughout the years) and the linear, albeit compressed, illusion of time passing in sequence gives the film its singular uniqueness.

Technological changes also occurred during the span of editing *Boyhood* (2014) over the twelve years it was filmed, including: a switch between nonlinear editing systems (from Final Cut to Avid Media Composer), changes in frame rate between storage formats for the footage, and coping with film labs during a transitional period for the medium (Lucca, 2015, §1). Film editor Sandra Adair, ACE, led the way as one of Linklater's collaborators for over two decades with a special sense for realistic performances and capturing the emotional core of each scene.

There were subtle differences between the intuitive and planned strategies in the photography and editing processes of the film and also in the transitions between the different years of the character Mason's life. Adair has discussed how each segment often concludes with an image of Mason gazing at something off-screen:

> I think that came about pretty naturally. It wasn't a spoken rule where we said, 'We're going to end every year on Mason.' It just felt like the most natural way to stay connected to his experience, having that last look at him at that period of time. I was very conscious of selecting shots to [let the audience] stay as connected to him and his experience as possible, even as everybody else in his family was changing. The last time I went back through the film, I was really looking to see if there were more little moments – just little looks, little pieces of Mason I could pepper in throughout the film, making him more active and more present in as many scenes as I could. I think I found three or four of those moments that I added in the last year.
>
> *(Alter, 2014, §16)*

The image of Mason's gaze at something off screen seems akin to Jung's idea of imaginative reverie (Figure 8.1); his dream-like gaze at certain points in the film's timeline evokes a sense of uncertainty or the unknown. The film text here hints at something symbolic, in the Jungian sense, of the best possible expression of an otherwise unknown thing. Perhaps the character is mentally processing, adapting to his environment or its social conditioning. Viewed through the lens of Jungian thought, one of the essential features of the child archetype representation is its futurity (Jung, 1940: §278), that is to say the child is the potential future. After twelve years editing *Boyhood*, Adair openly considered the genesis of the character's transformation with her yet-to-come sensibility as a film editor:

Figure 8.1 Ethan Hawke and Ellar Coltrane in character as father and son discuss elves, symbolic understanding.

Source: © 2014 Boyhood Inc./IFC Productions I, L.L.C.

> As Mason matures and starts to have ideas he can talk about and express verbally, the film goes there with the character and allows him to talk about who he is and what he thinks and what his philosophy is. A little kid isn't going to do that; they are kind of more experiencing things moment-by-moment and experience-by-experience. So I think that's what changed – I don't think the style of the movie-making changed.
>
> *(Alter, 2014, §20)*

The character of Mason struggles with psychological integration of his feelings throughout the film's narrative. As if by instinctual cue, the cinematographers and editor on *Boyhood* (2014) stepped back in order not to influence the unfolding emotional responses, psychologically they withdrew their projections. A psychological projection is a type of unconscious identification with the object which may be personal and collective. The reality of unconscious projections and fantasies might be situated in the cultural milieu through examples in the arts, myth, and religion as platforms for deeper comprehension of human experience. The cinematic long take or observation, uninterrupted by interpretation can have psychological parallels in the forms of analytic process and praxis such as active listening to analysands, the dynamics of therapeutic interactions, and counter-projections.

Cinematographer Shane Kelly and film editor Sandra Adair both discussed the importance of simple observation in their craft. Photographer Lee Daniel began the project and then became unavailable – at that point Shane Kelly took over as director of photography: 'I was there almost from the start so I knew what Lee created, and I wasn't going to force my style on the movie,' noted Kelly (Egan, 2015, §4) and he further shared his inner dialogue on the set at the time:

> It was a very hands-off approach. This is life happening, so don't get in the way and just record it. I love doing fancy things, but it's also very freeing to say no, this is too beautiful. It has to be real and the actors have to feel that it's real too. Rick didn't want anything to get between him and the actors. So, as a DP, I stepped back. You light the space and you allow the actors to move within that space.
>
> *(Egan, 2015, §5)*

Kelly used psychological, creative instincts as well as cinematography technique in allowing time for the sequence of images to emerge on their own. The stability of the visual space on the screen is important to the short-term coding of cinematic language and how the film narrative impacts the viewer. Linklater is known for framing the 'two-shot' and he uses this relational dyad to sift through the many variables that can disrupt valuable spatial information and then simply shows how the characters are naturally relating to environment. The significance of these cinematic modalities is they connect with the instinctual vitality carried by both the inner, psychic images of the filmmaker and the resulting onscreen visual images. For the filmmaker, this approach creates the natural flow and the illusion of what time might look like as it happens to humans and vice versa. Instead of reliance on fixed, chronological markers and edited segments, the images in *Boyhood* convey the richness of the filmmaker's inner visions in a type of stream of consciousness. The filmmaking choices selected for *Boyhood* are a weave of phenomenological units, however they have been sequenced and paced for the film's denouement and that suggests a bigger, synchronistic overview of existence.

Viewed from a Jungian perspective, the structure used by the director has a timeless feeling and archetypal sensibility in its representations. Jungian insight might hold that the psyche pre-existent to consciousness, e.g., in the child Mason, participates in his mother's psyche in one phase of life, while reaching across to the grown-son psyche of college-bound Mason. Jung felt that the conscious experience of these ties were connected with an uncertainty regarding time and that they produced a feeling 'that life is spread out over generations – the first step towards the immediate experience and conviction of being outside of time, which brings with it a feeling of immortality' (Jung, 1941: §316). The visual images also point to an expansion of Mason's conscious personality along with his physiological growth across the film text.

The phenomenon of a cinematic initiative that spanned over a decade was not static and nor did it occur in a vacuum. The filmmakers involved undoubtedly changed during filming and also after the wrap of the movie. The progression of the film can be thought of as an exercise in psychological integration of a main character in narrative terms but also for the entire cast, crew, and director. *Boyhood* stands as a relevant example of filmmakers who aligned their inner, creative vision with a unique cinematic technique and translated those moments into onscreen visuals. The ensemble worked their way forward in the enormous sweep of the project across time and human experience. The film's theme, as viewed through the child motif, might provide a depth of understanding of the level of creativity at work on unconscious levels of the filmmakers. 'The "child" paves the way for a future change of personality' (Jung, 1940: §278) and it refers to a quality that synthesizes conscious and unconscious elements and numerous transformations. In the film story, as Mason's father toasts to the future at a high school graduation party, an uncertain future looms for Mason. While away at college, Mason comes into relation with the unknown elements of his personal puzzle and a symbolic recognition appears to dawn on both cinematic and psychological horizons. *Boyhood* offers a long take on psychological life in the form of a twelve-year time capsule while *Birdman* extends its camera shot in a more conventional manner but with an unorthodox twist.

Birdman (2014)

The enigmatic satire *Birdman or (The Unexpected Virtue of Ignorance)* circles around Riggan Thomson (Michael Keaton), a has-been actor whose celebrity is a result of superhero movies in which he portrayed a masked crime-fighter with a menacing wingspread. To revive his career and propel himself into the league of 'serious' actors, Riggan adapts, directs, and stars in a Broadway play based on the Raymond Carver short story *What We Talk About When We Talk About Love*. As opening night approaches and personal and professional pressures mount, Riggan experiences a psychological crisis that moves toward resolution in unexpected ways. The story is laden with emotional and psychological currents: personal relationships, parenthood, ego and success, and the dynamics of one's relationship to a chosen art and craft. Screen images of the overlapping complexities of different consciousnesses would seem difficult enough for any filmmaker, however these intricacies appear to benefit from the choice of extended long shot photography as evidenced in the film texts.

Director of photography Emannuel Lubezki, ASC, AMC in collaboration with director Alejandro G. Iñárritu created the illusion of one long, unbroken take in the dark comedy. The visual syntax of film had already shifted with the advent of new technology, however this progress did not resolve all of the creative challenges and possibly increased already heightened levels of precision. Lubezki has shared his puzzlement at the director's technical and aesthetic vision publicly, noting, 'Cuts are very important in comedy … the rhythm in comedy [comes from] great comedians but also great editing, to not have any cuts was one of the craziest ideas I had ever heard' (Oppenheimer, 2014, p. 55). Use of the long take modality is an unusual choice of style for comedy genre. Visual images as discrete segments are traditionally reassembled in cinematic montage to build or set-up the comparison/contrast for a comedic base. However, the long shot also has the ability to capture comedy bits derived from spatial unity and the relation of individuals to others, things, and the surrounding world. Lubezki's early incredulity resonates with Bazin's observation that comedy was customarily dependent on the logic of strict line-by-line progression, the rhythmic resources of classical editing, and approaches such as Eisenstein's montage for successful results.

The debate surrounding the long take is also relevant when understanding the extraordinary complexity of the director's overall vision and the cinematographer's initial skepticism. The conventional long visual take deeply grounds *Birdman* in the psychological realism of the characters and yet conversely opens up the narrative with ambiguous visuals that subvert logic and introduce magical elements, such as Riggan's extraordinary levitation and telekinesis. From a directorial standpoint, Iñárritu explained that he wanted to engage audiences in Riggan's world so they would feel what the character is going through as his life unravels, 'I thought [connecting all the spaces] would serve the dramatic tension and put the audience in this guy's shoes in a radical way' (Oppenheimer, 2014, p. 55).

Riggan's life experience is alternately funny and harrowing and a study in human complexity. Psychological conflict gnaws at Riggan who equates the play's success with his very existence. A quotation in the film's opening titles sums up Riggan's goal: 'To feel myself beloved on the earth.' Later in his play, in character, Riggan the actor uses his personal emotional distress to convey not being in that treasured picture: 'I am not here. I don't exist.' The anxiety, friction, or conflict drives the narrative forward from both a theatrical and psychological point of view. Metaphoric associations here align with Jungian thought and symbolic analysis of film texts, e.g., theater as life or spectacle, inception of something new, gestating creativity, hallways as transitional paths, and the dimly lit depths of unconscious contents.

A psychological perspective toward film finds its value in a primary concern with inner, creative representations, or psychic images, e.g., a director's initial, creative vision for a film. These internal, symbolic patterns can also be further translated to onscreen film visuals through the skill of cinematographers; and have similarities with theatrical productions that work to show and decipher the human condition. To briefly analyze *Birdman* from a Jungian standpoint entails gathering universal or mythic elements from the film image texts and connecting with deeper narratives consistent with archetypal representations in forms, figures, and patterning. Use of amplification also as a psychological technique entails using allegorical or metaphorical elements to create a meaningful context around a symbol requiring examination and assimilation. Riggan's story (in his film character life and in his stage character in the film) could be considered in this way through the mythic themes surrounding Dionysus, god of the vine and patron god of theater, and Euripides' play *The Bacchae*. The universal motifs in this ancient Greek play illuminate, or amplify, the archetypal symbols present in the contemporary cinematic production of *Birdman*. From a cinematic standpoint, not once during the first sixty years of the twentieth century did Euripides' play *The Bacchae* and its Dionysian dynamics appear on the American commercial stage (Hartigan, 1995, p. 81). The compelling power of *The Bacchae* has since rectified the play's absence in cinematic productions of *Suddenly Last Summer* (1960), *The Fugitive Kind* (1960), and *Orpheus Descending* (1990) to name a few.

These universal themes are recognizable in *Birdman* (2014) and provoke symbolic consideration especially in the current socio-political times. The audience is tipped during the opening soundscape of *Birdman* that something big is about to happen. An archetypal representation from the text of the Greek play looms large throughout the film in the form of an incessant drum rift that marks time audibly and later displays in surreal visuals. This element in the soundtrack mimics the *dhithiramvos*, or dithyramb percussion, that heralds Dionysian presence in the Greek staging of the myth, and is also reminiscent of Cocteau's majestic, underworld scene that closes *Le Testament d'Orphée* (1960). In Iñárritu's film vision for *Birdman*, Riggan's progressive unraveling is imaginatively shadowed by the appearance of a drummer in a suit and tie with full drum kit, first on a New York sidewalk and later in the theater coffee nook. As if in rhythmic countdown after Riggan's suicide attempt, the director and cinematographer also create dream images of a marching drum corps that seems to signal the breathtaking vitality and creativity of Dionysus and also a type of underworld death dirge simultaneously.

In the context of this imagined perspective of psyche and Jungian sensitivities, the cinematic sequence preceding Riggan's trip to the underworld offers clues to his psychological breaking point. In a masterful extended two-shot, Lubezki filmed a scene showing a confrontation between a theater critic and the playwright, actor, and director Riggan. The topic is Riggan's play. It is not hard to imagine the film critic character Tabitha Dickinson as a type of Cerberus hound; the guardian of the gate who bars the way to Riggan's creative depths. Psychologically, Cerberus is a symbolic representation of the unconscious and, in the film, this critical character is the self-appointed sentinel at the threshold of theater (life, or Riggan's version of it). Riggan runs into Tabitha at a bar in the theater district before his play's opening night and the critic establishes her idea of theatrical tradition with a withering promise:

> You don't get to come in here and pretend you can write, direct, and act in your own propaganda piece without coming through me first. You're no actor, you're a celebrity. Let's be clear on that. I'm gonna kill your play.

Iñárritu's work in this film invites comparison with the metaphor of an unrecognized god who comes to town to break through the conformity: a coming to terms with self and others through relationships based on truth. After years of derivative super hero movies, Riggan's main psychological challenge is ripping away the mask of Birdman (here a goading persona of celebrity) in order to achieve a degree of self-actualization with his new creative life. Post-Jungian James Hillman noted that a feel for scenes reverts dream work to myths of Dionysus and the underworld, 'to the sense of life as an enactment of masks, and dreams as these masks. Theater creates that dissociative illusion of being in and out at the same moment' (1979, p. 191). A visual, dream-like scene in motion is something that cinema, alone of all the arts, is capable of representing in onscreen image. No other medium can recreate the flow of a dream in quite the same way.

In the 'play' within the film, the heightened climax is a Dionysian *sparagmos*, or tearing apart, symbolized by Riggan shooting his nose off; or rather an attempt to kill off what he knows to be creatively true. The psychological trajectory of *Birdman* suggests what it looks like when individuals overlook the eternally human nature of psychological problems. Riggan had already ignored psyche before and 'sacrificed' himself emotionally to corporate and cultural rending and splitting with each of the three Birdman film productions. The scene deeply reflects on a universal level what it means to struggle psychologically and also illustrates an intersection within interdisciplinary studies that connects psychology and cinema in a dynamic way.

It can be said that the best cinematography is simple or at least appears to be. The seamless result of onscreen visuals in *Birdman* belies the painstakingly crafted precision behind the final result. The film was shot digital capture, with Arri Alexa M, Alexa XT, Leica Summilux-C, Arri/Zeiss Master Prime, and framed for 1:85:1 release. A few visual resolves were required, specifically transitions that indicated the passage of time between night and day (symbolically, between consciousness and unconsciousness). According to Lubezki, the most complex task was blocking scenes in a way that both supported the concept of a single, continuous take and reflected Riggan's gradual emotional disintegration.

Riggan's daughter Sam is representative of a generation enamored with new media and technology, and she delightfully pulls Riggan into this very real world of new social forces and relationships. There is an example of contemporary realism. However, the ambiguous ending of *Birdman* leaves space for imaginative expansion alongside its experimental vision in magical realism and cinematography. The closing scene of the film finds its power in what is absent from the onscreen image and recalls Bazin's observation that what was imaginary onscreen must have the spatial density of something real. Iñárritu's vision here and the image texts seem to remind us that a little magic is also included in life's goodies alongside love and creativity. No spoiler intended, the film closes with a camera shot of Sam gazing upward out of a window in Riggan's empty hospital room. Similar to Mason's off screen gaze in the final scene in *Boyhood*, it remains for viewers to arrive at their own conclusion in *Birdman*, their own notion of who is now onstage, where is it taking place, and what is 'real' in the course of time and their own being.

Both directors and their films were nominated for 2014 Academy Awards with Alejandro Iñárritu awarded the Oscar for Best Director and *Birdman* the Oscar for Best Motion Picture. Richard Linklater won the 2014 Golden Globe for Best Director and *Boyhood* the Golden Globe for Best Motion Picture. These films are a reminder of the importance of keeping multimodal elements of the film in mind as they carry important energetic information for emotional quotient in filmmaking, connections to symbolic realms, and potential to facilitate psychological awareness. Creative, inner images translated to onscreen visuals by filmmakers open up new modalities for discussion in analytic, therapeutic, and teaching environments. One such modality is the cinematography technique of the long take and the opportunities it presents for symbolic or Jungian readings of film texts.

As literalism in both psychology and cinema has the effect of stasis, fresh ways of looking at internal and external images are useful to expand both disciplines. Films that are amenable to symbolic readings suggest image metaphors that resonate with the concept of archetypal representations, the symbolic forms and figures of psychological life. This approach to audiovisual texts has the ability to expand psychological discussion and move past outworn structures of pathologizing the complexity of human experience. Bazin reflected on film image:

The truth is that the vast majority of images on the screen conform to the psychology of the theater or to the novel of classical analysis. They proceed from the common-sense supposition that a necessary and unambiguous causal relationship exists between feelings and their outward manifestations. They postulate that all is in the conscious-ness and that this consciousness can be known.

(1967, p. 61)

The extended, continuous camera take is a modality that once more enabled scenes to unfold in new ways for *Boyhood* and *Birdman*, pushing the limits of contemporary cinematography. The effect may also be recognized as a phenomenal experience, in-the-moment, with creative, inner images carrying the energy for emotional impact as they translate to onscreen visuals.

References

Bazin, A. (1967) *What is cinema?* trans. H. Gray. Berkeley, CA: University of California Press.

Beebe, J. (2009) 'Jungian illumination of film', in V. Apperson and J. Beebe (eds), *The presence of the feminine in film*. Newcastle: Cambridge Scholars Publishing. pp. 17–25.

Eisenstein, S. (1987) *Nonindifferent nature*. Cambridge: Cambridge University Press.

Hartigan, K. (1995) *Greek tragedy on the American stage: ancient drama in the commercial theater, 1881–1994*. Westport, CT: Greenwood Press.

Hillman, J. (1979) *The dream and the underworld*. New York: Harper Perennial.

Jung, C. G. (1940) 'The psychology of the child archetype', in *The collected works of C. G. Jung*, Vol. 9i, *The archetypes and the collective unconscious*, 2nd edn. Princeton, NJ: Princeton University Press, 1968.

Jung, C. G. (1941) 'The psychological aspects of the Kore', in *The collected works of C. G. Jung*, Vol. 9i, *The archetypes and the collective unconscious*, 2nd edn. Princeton, NJ: Princeton University Press, 1968.

Jung, C. G. (1956) 'Symbols of the mother and of rebirth', in *The collected works of C. G. Jung*, Vol. 5, *Symbols of transformation*, 2nd edn. Princeton, NJ: Princeton University Press, 1956.

Oppenheimer, J. (2014) 'Backstage drama', *American Cinematographer: The International Journal of Motion Imaging*, 95(12), pp. 54–67.

Williams, R. (1991) 'Realism, naturalism, and their alternatives', in R. Burnett (ed.), *Explorations in film theory: selected essays from Ciné-Tracts*. Indianapolis, IN: Indiana University Press. pp. 121–154.

Online sources

Alter, E. (2014) 'How "Boyhood" editor Sandra Adair helped shape the film's 12-year evolution', *Indiewire* [online]. Available at: www.indiewire.com/2014/07/how-boyhood-editor-sandra-adair-helped-shape-the-films-12-year-evolution-24211/ [Accessed 4 May 2015].

Egan, J. (2015) 'Contenders: cinematographers Shane Kelly and Lee Daniel, *Boyhood*', *Below the line: voice of the crew* [online]. Available at: www.btlnews.com/awards/contenders-cinematographers-shane-kelly-and-lee-daniel [Accessed 16 September 2016].

Lucca, V. (2015) 'Interview: Sandra Adair', *Film comment* [online]. Available at: www.filmcomment.com/entry/interview-sandra-adair-boyhood [Accessed 4 May 2015].

Filmography

Boyhood. (2014) [film] Directed by Richard Linklater. USA.

Birdman or (the unexpected virtue of ignorance). (2014) [film] Directed by Alejandro Iñárritu. USA.

Fugitive kind, The. (1960) [film] Directed by Sidney Lumet, USA.

Orpheus descending. (1990) [film] Directed by George Zervoulakos, Greece.

Suddenly last summer. (1959) [film] Directed by Joseph Mankiewicz, USA.

Testament d'Orphée, La (Testament of Orpheus). (1960) [film] Directed by Jean Cocteau. France.

PART II

Applied approaches

Edited by
Helena Bassil-Morozow

9

FEMINIST FILM CRITICISM

Towards a Jungian approach

Helena Bassil-Morozow

Introduction

For the past forty years we have been told that postmodern culture excludes originality, and that it has become impossible to come up with original ideas. Everything has been written, composed and painted, and the only creative thing left to contemporary artists is to produce patchworks of pre-existent ideas. Most of the postmodern theorists, however, are male. It is easy to see why they think that every creative possibility has been exhausted. *In their world* it has, indeed, been exhausted. There is nothing new left to say about the male protagonist out in search for life's meaning (not least because in postmodern culture the very concept of meaning has been cancelled). Yet, the new breed of female authors, TV writers, directors and producers – the creators of *Orange is the New Black* (Netflix, 2013–), *Fleabag* (BBC, 2016–) and *I Love Dick* (Amazon, 2017–) – are now producing shockingly fresh perspectives on the female protagonist; perspectives that are free from traditional presumptions of what it means and how it feels to be a woman, or what constitutes a female journey.

Recently there has been a significant increase in the number of female protagonists in moving image narratives, both in film and TV. These new heroines – the titular protagonist of BBC's sitcom *Fleabag* (played by Chloe Waller-Bridge), Rey (Daisy Ridley in *Star Wars: The Force Awakens* (dir. Abrams, 2015), Jyn Erso (Felicity Jones) in *Rogue One* (dir. Edwards, 2016), Jessica Jones (Krysten Ritter) from the Marvel spinoff of the same name (2015–); Imperator Furiosa (Charlize Theron) in *Mad Max: Fury Road* (dir. Miller, 2015,), the female characters in *Game of Thrones* (2011–), the Nordic Noir detectives from *Forbrydelsen* (2007–2012) and *The Bridge* (2011–) and Alice (Mia Wasikowska) in Tim Burton's *Alice in Wonderland* (2010) to name but a few. Once ground-breaking and rare, Ridley Scott's strong female characters such as Ripley from the *Alien* films (Sigourney Weaver) (dir. Scott, 1979; dir. Cameron, 1986), Jordan O'Neill from *G.I. Jane* (dir. Scott, 1997) and Thelma and Louise (*Thelma and Louise*, dir. Scott, 1991) are now in good company. Meanwhile, the comic book industry has been trialling female superheroes since the 1960s – much earlier than mainstream cinema and television.

Feminist film criticism has been traditionally dominated by Freudian and Lacanian analyses both of women on screen and of female spectatorship. Occasional (most of them recent) attempts to introduce Jungian ideas into film criticism (Susan Rowland, Terrie Waddell, Catriona Miller, Helena Bassil-Morozow and Luke Hockley) have not been substantial enough to challenge the dominance of Lacanian thought in feminist analyses of screen media. This chapter aims to redress this imbalance, and to produce a framework for discussing the representation of female characters on screen in general, and the narrative path of female protagonists in particular. Now more than ever television and film criticism needs a Jungian view on the heroine. It is a good time to start divorcing ourselves from Freudian and Lacanian ideas, which concentrate on what woman does not have and is now allowed to do rather than what she is capable of achieving.

This chapter will argue that Jungian feminism is able to offer a true insight into the issues encountered by female characters (and particularly protagonists) in contemporary screen narratives. The proactive, desiring woman, often stereotyped as a 'goddess' in Jungian psychology, is labelled (and often self-labelled) as a monster in Freudian thinking. 'Goddess' is, of course, a dubious tag, but 'monster' presupposes a total impossibility for the woman to be an agent and to feel good about herself. In this sense, the Oedipus complex is a trap which for years has been mistaken by film feminists for a philosophy of liberation.

The new dynamic heroine cannot be reduced to a 'monster' (although some of them feel like this, which is itself proof of the longevity of Freudian ideas). Jungian concepts, and particularly the individuation process, are invaluable for creating a theoretical framework that is women-friendly; a framework that does not pathologize the heroine as deficient in anything, but shows instead how she deals with the obstacles she is facing on her journey.

What is wrong with the Freudian framework?

The 'new heroine' is an attempt to overthrow binary gender expectations, and to explore the issues encountered by women as independent questors (the quest, of course, being a metaphor for autonomous existence). The old theoretical framework, represented by Lacanian feminists, is no longer suitable for the discussion of female protagonists, mainly because it is preoccupied with the absence of agency (and the absence of the real and figurative penis) rather than with the issues and problems that come with this kind of responsibility. To give it its due, the framework did a lot of important work in the 1970s and 1980s, dismantling the underlying patriarchal structure, uncovering the elements that keep the woman in her place and prevent her from activating her agency. However, its main tools are not female-friendly, and its language almost completely lacks terms to explore the dimensions of female agency, including motivation (the impulse to go on a journey), the types of issues encountered by contemporary women in everyday life and the various ways in which they can be dealt with. Freudian language is good at exposing and critiquing the female passivity enforced by patriarchal structures, but its resources quite simply do not stretch to dealing with female agency.

This new heroine gradually emerged in response to the changing perception of women's place in society. The woman was gradually becoming 'an individual', expected to have her own journey. In his book *Neoliberal Culture* (2016) Jim McGuigan argues that the liberation of women from societal perceptions has been part of a more general tendency which has been prevalent in the West since the middle of the twentieth century – the neoliberalization of society. The current prevalent world order and the latest form of capitalism, neoliberalism presupposes that everyone should take personal responsibility for their life choices, and not rely on a support network, community or the state. Neoliberalism thus defies tradition which stifles individual expression, freeing people from the pressure to conform to a particular ideology or behavioural framework. Yet, by removing and dismantling support frameworks, it also makes people vulnerable to economic exploitation, emotionally disconnected from each other, drowning in (most often than not illusory) choice and, ultimately, left on their own to make difficult decisions in uncertain times. McGuigan explains that neoliberalism can be:

both immensely liberating and quite possibly terrifying. Those who were previously denied choice now have much greater room for manoeuvre along life's way. In this respect, life situations have changed and improved markedly for many women. Assumptions about women's prescribed social role have been called definitely into question, and there is much greater formal equality between the sexes, particularly in affluent segments of the world's population. There is a downside, though, because women's improved opportunities for employment and self-realization – the prospect for 'having it all' – actually make life harder for many who must, in consequence, juggle a set of very contradictory role obligations at work and in the home.

(2016, p. 42)

Whereas Freudian–Lacanian theory does not take into account the complexities of the neoliberal (or postmodern) existence, the Jungian theoretical framework transforms the difficult 'juggling' of 'contradictory role obligations' into an individuation path complete with archetypal images and situations. No longer as passive as she was before, the new heroine is nevertheless a suffering and struggling protagonist whose path is never smooth or perfect.

For the new breed of sword-wielding combat-trained adrenaline junkies, Laura Mulvey's analysis of the passive female in 'Visual pleasure and narrative cinema' (1975), or Mary Ann Doane's discussion of the limited identification options offered by male directors to the female spectator ('Film and masquerade: theorising the female spectator', 1982), will not be of much use. Mulvey, Doane, Barbara Creed and Kaja Silverman all employed the Lacanian theoretical framework in their discussion of women as characters and spectators. When used in feminist film analysis, Lacanian theory, which presents women as 'the other' and identifies masculine symbols as the seat of power, turns against itself, creating theoretical gaps. Lacanian theory, so preoccupied with phalluses as social and political symbols, and equating the female with the unknowable, the motherly, and the 'lacking' is almost incompatible with feminism. The Freudian–Lacanian psychoanalysis was only used by feminists because little else was on offer. It could not offer any freedom to the female heroine, pinned to the wall by the male gaze or trapped in the narrow confines of a male projection.

Mulvey's analysis of the traditional Hollywood approach to depicting females on screen, although out of date, is still influential in feminist film criticism. Writing about the classical Hollywood cinema in the 1940–50s in her article 'Visual pleasure and narrative cinema', she famously outlined the ways in which the silent female is manipulated and commodified by the industry. In her view, cinema is only a reflection of the general social attitude towards women as the bearers of meaning, not the makers of meaning, condemned to be silent, both on and off screen:

The function of woman in forming the patriarchal unconscious is two-fold, she first symbolises the castration threat by her real absence of a penis and second thereby raises her child into the symbolic. Once this has been achieved, her meaning in the process is at an end, it does not last into the world of law and language except as a memory which oscillates between memory of maternal plenitude and memory of lack. Both are posited on nature (or on anatomy in Freud's famous phrase). Woman's desire is subjected to her image as bearer of the bleeding wound, she can exist only in relation to castration and cannot transcend it. She turns her child into the signifier of her own desire to possess a penis (the condition, she imagines, of entry into the symbolic).

(1975, p. 6)

Mulvey sums it up by describing cinema as generating an illusion of reality created by the symbolic order for the purpose of enjoyment of objects without responsibility or obligation – rather like a strip-club. Women are mere props for male fetishism, unwilling participants in male scopophilia:

> During its history, the cinema seems to have evolved a particular illusion of reality in which this contradiction between libido and ego has found a beautifully complementary phantasy world. In reality the phantasy world of the screen is subject to the law which produces it. Sexual instincts and identification processes have a meaning within the symbolic order which articulates desire. Desire, born with language, allows the possibility of transcending the instinctual and the imaginary, but its point of reference continually returns to the traumatic moment of its birth: the castration complex. Hence the look, pleasurable in form, can be threatening in content, and it is woman as representation/image that crystallises this paradox.
>
> *(Mulvey, 1975, p. 10)*

Feminist film criticism focused on the issue of proximity and availability of the object via the concepts of the gaze ('looking'), the voice ('speaking') and curiosity ('looking', 'investigating'). All these are linked to the woman's Oedipal position in society. If she speaks or looks, she will cease to be a mirror, she will be misrecognized, will become 'the other' – a potentially traumatic experience for the man.

Kaja Silverman writes that, as a castrated object, women are not allowed to speak because they represent 'an alien and unwanted quality' (1988, p. 17). They are desired, but from a distance, in a fetishist way so as to prevent the fearful male subject from getting affected by 'castration'. A castrated object who speaks is a male nightmare personified. It is important that women remain silent, which proves to be difficult in real life. The screen therefore provides an ideal safe distance for such consumption of the silent object, for it is a fantasy life in which the male can look but not be looked at; in which he can consume females without having to deal with the actual woman; and in which the woman is guaranteed to be silenced without any chance of her being out of control. The woman is absent from the process of signification as she represents lack. Lack, loss and castration, film feminists have argued, are at the base of both the production and consumption processes of the film industry.

Silverman notes in *The Acoustic Mirror* (1988) how the female voice is manipulated by the industry to match the fetishized screen image, while the authentic woman is never heard. Silverman evokes the silent cinema star Lina Lamont (Jean Hagen) in *Singin' in the Rain* (dir. Kelly and Dolen, 1952), who is not allowed to give interviews by the studio for which she works, Monumental Pictures, for she has a shrilly annoying voice. Lamont was perfect for the silent cinema, but in the wake of the sound era she suddenly became a liability, and the discrepancy between her silly voice and polished appearance needed to be concealed (p. 45). Voice, Silverman notes, significantly changes the meaning of the image as it makes it all too real, it destroys the beautiful illusion (and the illusion of control over the object): 'When the voice is identified … with presence, it is given the imaginary power to place not only sounds but meaning in the here and now' (p. 43).

The silent woman is not just the woman who does not speak – she also does not look. In other words, she does not act. Throughout her texts, Mulvey keeps exploring the link between proactive behaviour (traditionally criticized in females) and the act of looking which reflects the desire to penetrate, to investigate, to set something free, to uncover the hidden. One investigates first, and then voices one's opinion – and women are not expected to do any of these. An active female is the woman who directs her look at the objects; she is a detective, acting out of stubborn curiosity. By so doing, she defies male orders and wards off male attempts to direct the gaze *at her*. She does not accept the fact that she is 'castrated' – that (as the patriarchal order would have it) she has nothing to penetrate the mystery with.

Mulvey explains this exclusion of the female from the cinematic space using the allegory of Pandora's box. In the myth, Pandora opens the box containing all the evils of the world out of curiosity. Her drive to discover and to investigate 'is directed at a culture in which woman has not, traditionally, been the possessor of knowledge and which has, traditionally, tended to consider femininity as an enigma' (Pietropaolo and Testaferri, 1995, p. 4). Pandora's compulsive desire to look and to explore instead of passively mirroring the male gaze is a serious threat to male dominance and, thus, is presented as 'the end of the world'. This mythological character, Mulvey argues, represents feminist defiance of objectified passivity expected of women in male-dominated cultures:

> While curiosity is a compulsive desire to see and to know, to investigate which is secret and to reveal the contents of a concealed space, fetishism is born out of a refusal to see, a refusal to know, and a refusal to accept the difference that the female body symbolises. Out of this series of turnings away, of covering over, not the eyes but understanding, of looking fixedly at any object that holds the gaze, female sexuality is bound to remain a mystery, condemned to return as a symbol of anxiety while over-valued and idealised in imaginary. Hollywood cinema has built its appeal and promoted its fascination by emphasising the erotic nature of the female star concentrated in a highly stylised and artificial presentation of femininity.... The myth of Pandora and the box are similarly imbricated with the structure of fetishism. But Pandora opens the box containing everything that fetishism disavows. The box is, in this sense, a fetish that fails.
>
> *(1995, p. 18)*

Curiosity, Mulvey notes, sets up a 'configuration of space through its association with investigation' (ibid., p. 9). The box lures Pandora, and prompts her to act and to discover, thus breaking down the 'regime of fetishism' (1995, p. 18). Transgressing the rules of the regime, exposing it to unsafe objects, forcing it to look at the horror of castration without the distance, is seen by the patriarchy not just as a mere act of defiance as it creates an association between the feminine and fear of evil (ibid., p. 18).

Like Pandora, other women in traditional narratives are either politely asked to comply with the rules of the male world or, failing that, threatened into submission. Such narratives are full of warnings about the dangers of curiosity expressed by women:

> Although Eve's story highlights the knowledge theme, the epistomophelia, as it were, inherent in the drive of curiosity, the myth associates female curiosity with forbidden fruit rather than with forbidden space. The motif of space and curiosity can be found again symptomatically in the fairy story *Bluebeard*. The story is about his last wife, a young girl who is given the free run of his vast palace with the exception of one room which her husband forbids her to enter. Its little key begins to excite her curiosity until she ignores the luxury all around her and thinks of nothing else. Then, one day, when she thinks her husband is away, she opens the door and finds the bodies of all his former wives still bleeding magically from terrible wounds and tortures.
>
> *(ibid., p. 9)*

In her essay 'Woman's stake: filming the female body' Mary Ann Doane writes that 'to those who still ask, "What do women want?" (a paraphrase of Freud's famous line), the cinema seems to provide no answer' (1988, p. 216). She also equates 'the simple gesture of directing a camera toward a woman' with 'a terrorist act' because 'cinematic images of woman have been … consistently oppressive and repressive' (p. 216). This state of affairs, which is:

> the result of a history which inscribes woman as subordinate – is not simply to be overturned by a contemporary practice that is more aware, more self-conscious. The impasse confronting feminist filmmakers today is linked to the force of a certain theoretical discourse which denies the neutrality of the cinematic apparatus itself. A machine for the production of images and sounds, the cinema generates and guarantees pleasure by a corroboration of the spectator's identity. Because that identity is bound up with that of the voyeur and the fetishist, because it requires for its support the attributes of the 'noncastrated', the potential for illusory mastery of the signifier, it is not accessible for the female spectator, who, in buying her ticket, must deny her sex. There are no images either *for* her or *of* her.
>
> *(p. 216)*

Similarly, Joan Copjec notes that women are

> the external, who are repeatedly excluded by the homeostatic system – the constant reproduction of the male by the patriarchal mechanisms of film, language … the point of view and the structures of voyeurism, exhibition, identification which follow from it are always, repeatedly, male. Women, therefore, cannot look, cannot be represented – as women.
>
> *(1988, p. 233)*

Freudian and Lacanian film feminists emphasize that women are banned from participating in male activities – i.e. activities that involve investigating and discovering, speaking one's mind, killing and conquering, and pursuing the grail awaiting at the end of the journey. Their discussion of women's position both on screen and in society is also deeply politicized, and their psychological analysis of the situation is linked to social and political issues.

Some 'new heroine' narratives (the more conceptual ones) have clearly been created with the 'Oedipus complex' and the 'female monster' in mind. Both BBC's *Fleabag* and Amazon's *I Love Dick* have been adapted from feminist texts, and both tell the story of a self-loathing, bumbling woman on a search for meaning and identity. Both see themselves as monsters for not complying with the Oedipal framework in which the feminine is equated with a combination of taboo and passivity. An escape from this rigid definition is, indeed, like opening Pandora's box: an active woman is a woman who breaks the taboo; she is a dirty creature and a transgressor. In order to stay 'clean', she must remain static, and eschew attempts to achieve self-development not overshadowed by her husband and family. What else would a woman want beside a husband and babies?

The evolution of the heroine

More often than not, however, women in myths and fairy tales are mere props in the male hero's journey: princesses and hags, mothers and daughters, dragons and water spirits, sirens and beautiful sorceresses. They were various incarnations of two archetypes – the *anima* and the

Great Mother. Perhaps not surprisingly, up until the end of the 1970s, cinema and television have mostly been depicting female development as tied to the male as well as connected with the family.

A product of modernity, cinema was nevertheless very slow in recognizing a woman as an individual separate from a man, as someone who deserves to be the hero of her own story. Meanwhile, cinema has kept the traditional hero structure for narratives with male protagonists in that the hero had to prove himself worthy of being called a man by overcoming difficulties, discovering new things, attaining a new status and capable of achieving success (think Frank Capra's *It's a Wonderful Life* (1946), Michael Curtiz's *Casablanca* (1942) or Alfred Hitchcock's *Rear Window* (1954). The male protagonists only reflected what society expected of its men, namely responsibility, perseverance and success.

Meanwhile the few female protagonists in the first six or so decades of cinema's existence were very limited in their choice of life paths and options. Marylin Monroe's leading heroines are always on the search for 'the right man' (and by the right man they meant a millionaire, of course). Clearly, the female protagonists of Hollywood's Golden Era wanted to get married. At best, they wanted a rich, famous, adventurous and interesting man. In the very least, their partner has to be safe and dependable. Lorelei Li (*Gentlemen Prefer Blondes*, dir. Hawks, 1953) and Pola Debevoise (*How to Marry a Millionaire*, dir. Negulesco, 1953) are the pinnacle of this mediated self-realization – an individuation by proxy – an individuation via the man. Monroe was one of the very few actresses actually allowed to play protagonists – and only the ones who were obsessed with male power and influence. Their whole individuation was based around 'finding' the right man, be it true love or millions of dollars.

Similarly, Rita Hayworth's Gilda (*Gilda*, dir. Vidor, 1946) relies on her seduction skills and 'female patience' to capture and tame Johnny (who she obviously regards as being worthy of all this attention and effort). The heroine of Powel and Pressburger's *The Red Shoes* (1948), a talented ballerina, is not allowed to be an independent individual as she is torn between her agent and her composer boyfriend both of whom expect her to be totally compliant, and a blank canvass on to which they would project their grand projects.

Rarely protagonists and often in the background, women were cast by male authors and directors in the roles of cunning seductresses or beautiful angels, but almost never shown as agents capable of making decisions divorced from 'the world of men'. The edgier directors such as Alfred Hitchcock often made the boundary between the woman's freedom and her immersion into the male world more elastic, but they also showed the consequences of female disobedience. Dr Constance Petersen (Ingrid Bergman) in *Spellbound* (dir. Hitchcock, 1945) is surrounded by sniggering male colleagues who consider her to be 'cold' and 'lifeless', just because she refuses to accept their fantasy projections on to her. Meanwhile, herself a brilliant psychoanalyst, she still looks up to, and is dependent on, the research of her male colleagues. Even the dazzling and successful Lisa (Grace Kelly) from Hitchcock's *Rear Window* (1954) still needs Jeff – a loose and rather self-obsessed photographer, and hopes that she would eventually be able to 'tame' him.

Female characters who dared to cross this boundary, like Marion Crane (Janet Leigh) in *Psycho* (dir. Hitchcock, 1960) were punished for attempting to escape the world of male power, male interests and male control. In this sense, for sixty years or so female supporting characters and protagonists in screen narratives had limited agency and their actions were mainly determined by the order around them. Those who tried to break free and become agents (rebellious agents or intentional agents), were stopped in their tracks.

These heroines' choices are side-lined to make room for the creativity and decisions of the men who they accompany. In this sense, despite technically being protagonists, these female characters nevertheless cannot be seen as 'going on a journey' as the society in which they live does not deem it necessary for a woman to look for her own path in life. The old-style female protagonist, polished and beautiful as she is, does not have either agency or decision-making power independently from her male puppet-master.

The new heroine's journey differs from that of the 'traditional' passive female. She refuses to be the victim of projections, and she fights for the freedom of self-identification, for instance, by refusing to marry the man chosen for her by the mother (Alice from Tim Burton's *Alice in Wonderland*, 2010), by refusing to be 'feminine' and electing to be a fighter (Arya Stark and Brienne of Tarth in *Game of Thrones*), by risking her life to save slave women from their ugly owner (Imperator Furiosa in *Mad Max: Fury Road*) and by refusing to be nice, clean and perfect altogether (the female prison population in *Orange is the New Black* (2013); Amazon's *I Love Dick*, 2017–). It might sound perverse, but it is refreshing to see the heroine of *Rogue One* die without having an opportunity to start a family with the man with whom she has recently fallen in love.

It is also important that both Netflix and Amazon, the two big contenders in the media streaming market, are taking on traditional Hollywood by introducing fresh new angles on gender and sexuality with shows such as *Jessica Jones*, *Orange is the New Black* and *I love Dick*. BBC's *Fleabag* is also inspired by this trend, and makes the best of it by presenting a heroine who is neither nice nor particularly feminine, but is struggling (and in ways that are not at all pretty) to find her own meaning in life.

What can Jungians offer to the new heroine?

The New Heroine is on a journey of self-discovery. The idea behind the individuation process is to strike a certain balance between personal interests and the interests of his or her family, community, society. Human beings cannot develop in isolation, without any external influences: they form themselves in relation to, and in conflict with, their environment. Only by interacting with others does the individual see the difference between self and environment, and only by building oneself into the social structure does one become fully human. As Jung also writes in *Psychological Types*:

> In general, [individuation] is the process by which individual beings are formed and differentiated; in particular, it is the development of the psychological *individual* as a being distinct from the general, collective psychology. Individuation, therefore, is a process of *differentiation*, having for its goal the development of the individual personality.
>
> *(1921: §757, emphasis as original)*

The process includes many psychological tasks to be solved, metaphorically presented as archetypal figures.

Individuation thus is half integration into society and half a process by which change happens. Yet, classic narratives have traditionally been preoccupied with male individuation, and the difficulties a male hero encounters on his way towards his goal (often metaphorized as a some kind of treasure). Neither female change nor female societal integration, apparently, were regarded as phenomena worthy of creative attention. Moreover, fairy tales with female protagonists tended to be either cautionary tales about the dangers of women wanting to be free (*Little Red Riding Hood*, *The Beauty and the Beast*, the Russian *Morozko*), or narratives of status acquisition via a far more socially advanced male (*Cinderella*, *The Beauty and the Beast*).

Jungian discussion of women as actresses and spectators differs significantly from the one employed by the Freudian and post-Freudian theorists. First, Jungian feminist analysis is not as politicized as its Freudian counterpart. Andrew Samuels rightly notes that Jungian discourse on the feminine is 'directed away from political and social action' (2015, p. 102). This is also generally true of Jung's writings, for he was more interested in the spiritual than in the socio-political applications of psychological phenomena – though he was also concerned with the relationship of the individual to society at large. As in all Jung-influenced analyses, a Jungian feminist approach to women on screen is bound to be mildly spiritualized and discussed in terms of the woman's transcendental journey instead of being a closely focused examination of the social and political conditions that oppress her.

This, however, does not mean that Jungian concepts are completely apolitical or could not be used to discuss social issues such as the position of women in society or gender fluidity. Jung's concepts of the *anima*, the *animus* and the mother are certainly useful in the discussion of cinematic representation of women as well as female spectatorship. Moreover, with Jung's emphasis on the feminine, his psychology may even be more relevant for the study of women on screen. Unlike Freud's psychology, which is explicitly patriarchal and father-centred, Samuels argues, Jung provided 'a mother-based psychology in which influence is often traced back much earlier, even to pre-natal events' (2015, p. 213).

Moreover, Jungian thought has never stressed gender differences the way its Freudian counterpart did. Lacan's theory is built on gender difference, just like Freud's. In his writings, Lacan also projects all kinds of male perceptions and fantasies on to women, such as the myth of female 'silent mystery': 'women do not know what they are saying, which is all the difference between them and me' (Lacan, SXX: 68, in Merck, 1990, p. 50). Importantly, Lacan, as Stephen Heath rightly points out, reads the symbolic and the metaphorical through the physical; he 'instates the visible as the condition of symbolic functioning, with the phallus the standard of the visibility required' which, ultimately, means that those who 'lack' a penis and those who 'possess' are so fundamentally different that their psychological and social experiences are inherently incomparable (Merck, 1990, p. 50). Automatically in this cage of the social order, the woman becomes 'the hysteric', fighting the very definition of identity through the physical possession of a penis (pp. 50–2). The woman, Lacan insists, is 'not-all, there is always something with her which eludes discourse' (Lacan, SXX: 34, in ibid.). So shockingly sexist is Lacan's essentialism that Western feminists' insistence on using his theory as a valid critical framework is all the more surprising.

Conversely, rather than emphasizing the 'lack', sexed or sexless, Jung writes about both the genders lacking something on their own, without each other. Hence his extensive use of the gnostic idea of syzygy – the divine unity, the double-gendered nature of God. Psychological wholeness is a matter of equality and enlightenment, not a retrospective exercise in eliminating difference or an immature search for similarity and perfect mirroring.

A Freudian interpretation of narratives is limited to a single structure – the Oedipus complex; effectively a structural prison. Laura Mulvey notes in her essay 'Changes: thoughts on myth, narrative and historical experience' that, as a journey, the Oedipus complex has very limited options for a woman on a journey, and in all cases this journey ends with a realization that a female body is a trap and some kind of inescapable destiny which prevents women from achieving:

> In this scheme, any attempt at exploring the maternal relationship and its fantasies must appear as a retreat into the body, as a rejection of the symbolic and the Word, into a Utopian quest for a natural femininity, outside the 'tragic and beneficial' experience of castration.
>
> *(1987, p. 172)*

This defining presence of the concept of castration in the Freudian/Lacanian theoretical framework effectively limits the range of paths a heroine could undertake as well as the number of possible interpretations of her journey.

For Jung, myth is not limited to a single narrative scheme. Susan Rowland writes that:

> where a Freudian interpretation reduces visual pleasure to a sexuality organised around the phallus as the significant organ of pleasure and meaning, Jung regarded psychic energy as essentially neutral and hence not privileging one gender. Where Freud (and Lacan after him) considers the Oedipus myth to possess an originating role in the structuring of the psyche, Jung makes room for many potential myths of being. Some of them can even emphasise the feminine!
>
> *(2011, pp. 148–9)*

Where the post-Freudians (including Lacanian feminists) stress the importance of the all-encompassing Oedipal metaphor claiming that the whole of society is built on it, the principal focus of Jungian thought is the journey of self-discovery and change – the so-called individuation process. However, individuation is not only a personal process, it is also very much about society. This Jungian interpretation of what it means to be an actualised, proactive, decision-making human being will hopefully take us through the neoliberal crisis or meaning, which inevitably comes with the cancellation of tradition and weakening of the role of community in industrialized and post-industrial societies. The female protagonist is finally allowed to see her life *as a journey* instead of as *tableau vivant* – a beautiful but static life of an object.

It does not even matter if the journey is unglorious and even banal. Hollywood's (mostly white and male) producers tend, while trying to be progressive, to think that female individuation is a carbon copy of the hero's adventures but made with a sexualized 'hero woman' – and *Kill Bill* (dir. Tarantino, 2003), *Mad Max: The Fury Road* and *Wonder Woman* (dir. Jenkins, 2017) are good examples of this attitude. Meanwhile, texts written or produced by women show a different protagonist – bumbling, rude, often uncouth and a loser. The population of the female prison from *OITNB*, Fleabag (who goes by her nickname) and Chris from *I Love Dick* represent this swearing, rough new heroine who refuses to be clean and nice even though this is the key societal expectation for a woman. Freed from the Oedipus complex which reduces her to the status of a castrated body, the 'dirty' woman in Analytical Psychology is still a goddess who insists on her right of choosing her path even if this path is full of bumps, rejections, pain and wrong turns.

There is also a significant difference in the way women perceive themselves within Jungian psychology. Within the theoretical framework that is the Oedipus complex, the proactive woman is inevitably seen as a monster. Conversely, archetypes (both male and female) are neither good nor bad, but possess moral and ethical dynamics. Each has a good side and a bad side, and neither is judged or criticised. For instance, unlike in Freudian psychology, Jung did not see the mother as something silent, innocuous or dominated by the masculine. In Jungian psychology this archetype is regarded as a real force, as a metaphor for power. Moreover, Jung is not prescriptive in his assessment of the mother, either real or metaphorical. She is not only the one who cares but also the one who destroys. Although the terminology he uses is still rather sexist, Jung does not downplay the influence of the feminine. He writes in 'Psychological aspects of the mother archetype':

> The qualities associated with [the mother archetype] are maternal solicitude and sympathy; the magic authority of the female; the wisdom and spiritual exaltation that

transcend reason; any helpful instinct or impulse; all that is benign, all that cherishes and sustains, even fosters growth and fertility. The place of magic transformation and rebirth, together with the underworld and its inhabitants, are presided over by the mother. On the negative side the mother archetype may connote anything secret, hidden, dark, the abyss, the world of the dead, anything that devours, seduces, and poisons, that is terrifying and inescapable like fate.

(1938/54: §158)

Thus, the mother is both 'loving' and 'terrible', and the two aspects of this archetype are often inseparable. The mother is 'unsafe', and it's fine for her to be unsafe. Like the unconscious, the feminine is something that should be reckoned with; something untameable and potent.

It would be unfair not to mention here some of the Jungian narrative theorists with fairly rigid (and often muddled) views on female individuation. For instance, Joseph Campbell allegedly maintained that female characters do not need to go on a journey because 'in the whole mythological tradition the woman is *there*', already perfect and content. All she has to do is 'to realize that she is in the place where people are trying to get to' (Murdock, 1990, p. 7). Similarly, Christopher Vogler, who was heavily inspired by both Jung and Campbell, makes clumsy attempts to describe what constitutes the path of the female protagonist, and ends up theorizing that, unlike a male 'straightforward' way, the female journey is a 'spiral' or even 'a series of concentric rings' (Vogler, 1999, pp. xxi–xxii). Clearly, a Jungian framework can also be misused and employed to confine women to a particular image (passive; incapable of acting straightforwardly, going round in circles) instead of admitting that the female protagonist – just like the male protagonist – can end up with any trajectory which only depends on their unique circumstances.

Thus, to individuate, means to be a special kind of human agent – the kind that completes his mission, equating this completion of a task with self-fulfilment. There are many reasons why the heroine leaves the house to 'seek her fortune': some want to go on a journey of self-discovery, others enjoy a good chase, or are out on a revenge spree, or try to be a superhero. The obstacles and problems on their way are also varied: a neglectful parent (mothers in *OITNB*, the father in *Fleabag*), a difficult or unattainable love object, male or female (*I Love Dick*, *Thelma and Louise*), an oppressive patriarch (*Mad Max: The Fury Road*, the *Star Wars* franchise), a child demanding attention (the original *Killing*), an enemy or rival (Arya Stark from *Game of Thrones*, the original *Millennium* franchise, *Kill Bill*) and even sexist assumptions about female fragility which the protagonists set out to disprove (Tim Burton's *Alice in Wonderland*, *Game of Thrones'* Brienne of Tarth, Ridley Scott's *G.I. Jane*). Some of the heroines travel for miles to achieve their goal; others do not physically go anywhere, and the journey is all internal.

The figures they encounter on their individuation journey can be seen as archetypes: the *animus*, the old wise man, the old wise woman, the child, the shadow, the self. The protagonist's relationship with these archetypes, however, differs dramatically from how it used to be in the past: the love object can be either an *animus* and *anima*, women are finally allowed to have a shadow and explore their imperfection and darkness, and the Self is shown to be as unattainable for a woman as it is for a man. Female love objects are introduced for the first time not for the pleasure of the male viewer, but to show the development of the female protagonist. Ultimately, the New Heroines want the same things as their male counterparts – to explore choices and options, to individuate, to achieve new status and to find meaning in life. It is shocking to think that this has been denied to them for decades.

References

Copjec, J. (1988) '*India Song/Son Nom de Venise dans Calcutta Desert*: the compulsion to repeat', in C. Penley (ed.), *Feminism and film theory*, London: BFI and Routledge. pp. 229–43.

Doane, M. (1982) 'Film and masquerade: theorising the female spectator', *Screen*, 23(3/4), pp. 74–88.

Doane, M. A. (1988) 'Woman's stake: filming the female body', in C. Penley (ed.), *Feminism and film theory*. New York: Routledge. pp. 216–28.

Jung, C. G. (1921) 'Definitions', in *The collected works of C. G. Jung*, Vol. 6, *Psychological types*, 3rd edn. London: Routledge & Kegan Paul, 1971.

Jung, C. G. (1938/54) 'Psychological aspects of the mother archetype', in *The collected works of C. G. Jung*, Vol. 9i, *The archetypes and the collective unconscious*, 2nd edn. London: Routledge & Kegan Paul, 1968.

Lacan, J. (1977) *Écrits: a selection*, trans. A. Sheridan. London: Routledge.

Lacan, J. (1999) *The seminar of Jacques Lacan: Bk. 20: on feminine sexuality, the limits of love and knowledge*. New York: W. W. Norton & Company.

McGuigan, J. (2016) *Neoliberal culture*. London: Palgrave Macmillan.

Merck, M. (ed.) (1990/2013) *The sexual subject: screen reader in sexuality*. London: Routledge.

Mulvey, L. (1975) 'Visual pleasure and narrative cinema', *Screen*, (16)3, pp. 6–18.

Mulvey, L. (1987) 'Changes: thoughts on myth, narrative and historical experience', *History Workshop Journal*, 23(1), pp. 3–19.

Mulvey, L. (1995) 'The myth of Pandora: a psychoanalytic approach', in L. Pietropaolo and A. Testaferri (eds), *Feminisms in the cinema*. Bloomington and Indianapolis, IN: Indiana University Press. pp. 3–19.

Murdock, M. (1990) *The heroine's journey: a woman's quest for wholeness*. Boston, MA: Shambhala.

Penley, C. (ed.) (1988) *Feminism and film theory*. New York: Routledge.

Pietropaolo, L. and Testaferri, A. (eds) (1995) *Feminisms in the cinema*. Indianapolis: IN: Indiana University Press.

Rowland, S. (2011) 'The nature of adaptation: myth and sthe feminine gaze in Ang Lee's *Sense and Sensibility*', in C. Hauke and L. Hockley (eds), *Jung & film II: the return*. London: Routledge. pp. 148–62.

Samuels, A. (2015) *A new therapy for politics*. London: Karnac.

Silverman, K. (1988) *The acoustic mirror: the female voice in psychoanalysis and cinema*. Bloomington, IN: Indiana University Press.

Vogler, C. (1999) *The writer's journey: mythic structure for writers*. London: Pan.

Filmography and television programmes

Alice in Wonderland. (2010) [film] Directed by Tim Burton. USA.

Alien. (1979) [film] Directed by Ridley Scott. USA.

Aliens. (1986) [film] Directed by James Cameron. USA.

Bridge, The. (2011–) [television series] Filmlance International AB, Nimbus Film Productions, Sveriges. Television. Sweden, Denmark.

Casablanca. (1942) [film] Directed by Michael Curtiz. USA.

Fleabag. (2016–) [television series] BBC. UK.

Forbrydelsen. (2007–2012) [television series]. Danmarks Radio (DR), Norsk Rikskringkasting (NRK), Denmark.

Game of thrones. (2011–) [television series] HBO. USA.

Gentlemen prefer blondes. (1953) [film] Directed by Howard Hawks. USA.

G. I. Jane. (1997) [film] Directed by Ridley Scott. USA.

Gilda. (1946) [film] Directed by Charles Vidor. USA.

How to marry a millionaire. (1953) [film] Directed by Jean Negulesco. USA.

I love Dick. (2017–) [television series] Amazon. USA.

It's a wonderful life. (1946) [film] Directed by Frank Capra. USA.

Jessica Jones. (2015–) [television series]. ABC Studios. USA.

Kill Bill: vol. 1. (2003) [film] Directed by Quentin Tarantino. USA.

Mad Max: Fury road. (2015) [film] Directed by George Miller. USA.

Orange is the new black. (2013–) [television series] Netflix.

Psycho. (1960) [film] Directed by Alfred Hitchcock. USA.

Rear window. (1954) [film] Directed by Alfred Hitchcock. USA.

Red shoes, The. (1948) [film] Directed by Michael Powell and Emeric Pressburger. UK.

Rogue one. (2016) [film] Directed by Gareth Edwards. USA.

Singin' in the rain. (1952) [film] Directed by Stanley Dolen and Gene Kelly. USA.

Spellbound. (1945) [film] Directed by Alfred Hitchcock. USA.

Star wars: the force awakens. (2015) [film] Directed by J. J. Abrams. USA.

Wonder Woman. (2017) [film] Directed by Patty Jenkins. USA.

10

TEACHING JUNG IN THE ACADEMY

The representation of comic book heroes on the big screen

Kevin Lu

Introduction

The debate as to whether it is possible to teach C. G. Jung's analytical psychology in the academy and the challenges of attempting to do so are not new (c.f. Tacey, 1997a, 1997b; Brook, 1997; Papadopoulos, 1997; Belford, 1997). It is a question that continues to be discussed and it is one that is particularly relevant for the Department of Psychoanalytic and Psychosocial Studies at the University of Essex, UK, in light of the launch of its new BA Psychoanalytic Studies in 2016. The challenges of teaching depth psychological ideas (both psychoanalytic and those from analytical psychology) to undergraduates are legion as the students come with little knowledge of either Freud or Jung. How do we motivate students and convey both the importance and relevance of depth psychological ideas in a way that is simultaneously approachable and critical?

In conjunction with a former colleague, Dr Aaron Balick, we designed two modules that made psychoanalysis (broadly defined) accessible to a younger audience. One way of doing so was to explore the extent to which depth psychology could speak to contemporary interests and concerns and how, in turn, contemporary uses of the psychoanalytic could define and redefine the field. In essence, we were hoping to excite our students through applied psychoanalysis and Jungian applications (Samuels, 1996). One of the modules created was 'Popular Film, Literature and Television: A Psychoanalytic Approach (Freud and Jung)', which continues to attract students from various disciplines across the university.

Two key Jungian concepts that are taught, and which are of particular interest, are *individuation* and the driving force behind it, the *Self*. I suspect these concepts resonate with the majority of students as they help frame and give meaning to a key life transition and point of maturation many are experiencing at this time. The vehicle through which I have taught these concepts is through comics, graphic novels and the adaptation of its characters to film (Gordon *et al.*, 2007; Kaveney, 2008). Steve Edgell has described the difference between a comic and graphic novel as follows:

> The most useful distinction in comics is to be drawn between periodical and book-style publication. A periodical is comprised of issues, one of which always replaces the previous one. The title is continuous, but one issue always differs from another. A book is a publication in which the title and issue are the same. A new printing does

not require abandoning the contents in favour of a new set. A graphic novel is a unified comic art form that exploits the relationship between the two: book and periodical.

(Edgell quoted in *Reynolds, 1992, p. 121)*

Given the rising popularity of the superhero genre in cinema (a genre towards which many students gravitate), it serves as a timely example of the complex ways in which psychological knowledge is constituted and represented, both consciously and unconsciously, in popular culture. In this chapter, I argue that Ang Lee's *Hulk* (2003), while in many ways a commercial disappointment in comparison to other films in the Marvel Cinematic Universe, is a deeply psychological text that aptly conveys, and allows one to explore, Jung's concepts of individuation and the Self. I examine the ways in which Bruce Banner's transformation into the Hulk may be considered a step in his path of individuation, a reading which is supported by Bruce's struggle to manage his emotions in the face of uncovering childhood trauma (a Freudian psychoanalytic interpretation that, ironically enough, supports a Jungian one) and the recurring themes of rebirth throughout the film. I suggest that Banner's monstrous alter ego may also be treated as a representation of the Self, in both its positive and negative aspects. Specifically, I argue that the imperfections of the Hulk's digital body which vexed critics, diehard and casual fans alike is central to understanding the dual nature of the Self specifically and the bipolarity of archetypes more generally. The imperfections of this dialectical, digital body encapsulate several tensions running throughout the film that seek resolution (Gilmore, 2014; Reynolds, 1992; Yockey, 2014). These include Banner's struggle between the human and monstrous sides of his personality (reason vs emotion [Yockey, 2014]), the tension between science and nature (Gilmore, 2014), science and the military (ibid.), nature and the digital (ibid., p. 23), and the attempt to balance storytelling and character development with the allure and spectacle of CGI (Computer-Generated Images). The digital body is, and further becomes, the site of transformation at multiple levels, including the psychological. Reactions to, and resistance against, accepting the 'reality' of the Hulk's digital body is a springboard to understanding our own psychological tensions that may be activated when viewing the film.

Arguing comics

Before exploring Lee's adaptation of the Hulk for the big screen, it is necessary to reflect on the study of comics or sequential art within an academic setting (Smith and Duncan, 2012). I have also found McCloud's definition of comics most instructive: 'Juxtaposed pictorial and other images in deliberate sequence, intended to convey information and/or to produce an aesthetic response in the viewer' (1993, p. 9). Even so, in many ways, the medium remains largely unrecognised as a genuine field of study; it seems every serious book written about comics begins with a defence of the genre. As Saunders aptly notes, superhero comics allow readers an avenue through which their fantasies and desires may be vicariously lived out; an instance of wish fulfilment par excellence. 'It's all just too crudely', he writes, 'painfully obvious, and marks the genre as infantile and immature – something to be outgrown at best' (2013, p. 4). Yet this limitation can also be seen as a strength and potential source of knowledge. Our fantasies and the objects on to which we project them betray a divide between what *is* and what *ought to be*. This yearning for something better, to be more than who we are and transcend the limitations of our current situation, is a tension that is fundamental to many disciplines, including theology, philosophy and literature. Quoting the philosopher Susan Neiman, Saunders points out that,

> [t]he fact that the world [apparently] contains neither justice nor meaning threatens our ability to act in the world and to understand it. The demand that the world be intelligible is [therefore] a demand of practical and theoretical reason, the ground of thought that philosophy is called to provide.
>
> *(Neiman quoted in Saunders, 2013, p. 5)*

Saunders argues that this tension between what *is* and what *ought to be* is at the heart of many superhero comics. Read in this light, sequential art, which is at times synonymous with fantasy, is not 'the opposite of reality, but is another way of making sense of reality' (ibid., p. 5).

Some of the best academic work has focused on the history of comics (Duncan and Smith, 2009) and its use as a springboard to exploring the development of mainly American culture (Babic, 2014; Costello, 2009; DiPaolo, 2011; Pustz, 2012; Romagnoli and Pagnucci, 2013). In particular, Wright's (2001) definitive text investigates the extent to which the real and the realm of fantasy have found common ground and the ways in which comics can be used to reflect upon national events and attitudes, from Captain America's war against Nazi Germany and Communism to Spiderman's appearance at Ground Zero in the aftermath of 9/11. Other studies have contemplated the points of convergence between comics, religion, theology and spirituality, but with mixed results (Garrett, 2008; Knowles, 2007; Saunders, 2013). Knowles (2007) argues that the origin of many superheroes can be found in mysticism and the occult. While the study does shed some light on the interests of early writers and illustrators, its depth of engagement could be deepened by a more detailed investigation of the many lines of inquiry covered throughout the text. Reynolds (1992) argues that comics are mythological texts, but not in the Jungian sense as new manifestations of archetypal themes (i.e. contemporary society's attempt to 'dream the myth onwards' [Huskinson, 2008]). As tempting as it is to read his recognition of recurring motifs, patterns and narrative arcs (Reynolds, 1992, pp. 12–16) in the superhero story as an expression of an archetypically structured psyche, bringing to mind Campbell's (1968) work on the hero's journey, Reynolds suggests that superhero comics create their own mythology through an emphasis on narrative continuity. Interestingly, he also contends that the villain and not the hero is the main protagonist of any given superhero text. The former represents change; the latter maintains the status quo through 'an almost archaic code of personal honour' (ibid., p. 83). This notion is more fully elaborated in Hassler-Forest's *Capitalist Superheroes*, where he proposes that superhero movies sustain a 'stable mythology' that express the values of neoliberal capitalism noting, 'the many contradictions, fantasies, and anxieties that inform this age of neoliberal policies alongside neoconservative values' (2012, p. 3). These films reaffirm the mythical status of superheroes by focusing on their origins, which in turn 'are commonly organized around father figures, Oedipal trajectories, and patriarchal genealogies' (ibid., p. 24). What is ultimately endorsed is the rule of the father; superheroes do not transgress boundaries, but '[retain] loyalty to the "Name of the Father"' (ibid., p. 105).

Other contributions to the field have shown a keen reflexivity, concentrating on the medium itself and its ability to convey information, emotion, interiority and meaning in ways no other form of communication can (Eisner, 2008; McCloud, 1993). Sequential art 'offers range and versatility with all the potential imagery of film and painting plus the intimacy of the written word' (McCloud, 1993, p. 212). The textual 'alchemy' of comics is to be found not only in the unique ways it combines word and image (Bateman, 2014) as a 'single unified language' (McCloud, 1993, p. 47), but its interactivity and the ways in which readers are implicated in the creation of meaning. Such meaning can be found and analysed *within* panels in the use of colours and lines, the efficacy of the storytelling, its pacing, etc. and also *between* them (known as the 'gutter' [ibid., p. 66]) and both are of vital importance. Through a process known as *closure*, the reader must complete the action that occurs between panels, utilising their imagination to connect two separate images into one idea. It is 'a silent dance between the seen and unseen', conscious and unconscious. This makes sequential art a 'medium where the audience is a willing and conscious collaborator' (ibid., p. 65). Such perspectives may be usefully applied to explore an example of sequential art with which the Jungian field may be more familiar, mainly, Jung's *Red Book*.

With countless academic books being published on the subject and journals dedicated to its study, the development of Comic Studies is an emerging field to which analytical psychology can contribute. Topics such as the function of panels as vehicles for containment, the applicability of Jung's theories on art and creativity to understand the collaboration between writer and illustrator, the social and psychological significance of comics for culture and society and comics as a medium that is particularly well-suited to the expression of emotions and, in particular, the unconscious, are highly relevant lines of inquiry meriting further exploration. Specifically, an analysis of the adaptation of comic book superheroes and their stories to film seems especially timely, given the growing influence the medium and the impact of Jungian perspectives on film studies (Anslow, 2012; Bassil-Morozow, 2010, 2011; Hauke and Alister, 2001; Hauke and Hockley, 2011; Hockley, 2001, 2007, 2013; Izod, 2001; Singh, 2009).

From comics to the big screen

Hassler-Forest points out that *Hulk* is a particularly rich psychological character, 'is perhaps the strongest example of the way in which psychological complexity was added into the established formula of cartoonish action heroes engaging in spectacular battles with supervillains' (2012, p. 87). Part of the Marvel universe and created by Stan Lee (writer) and Jack Kirby (illustrator), The Incredible Hulk made his first appearance in comics in May 1962. The literary precursors to the Hulk are not hard to ascertain. We see the symbiotic relationship between the scientist and his monstrous creation in Mary Shelley's *Frankenstein; or, The Modern Prometheus* (1818/2003), and the transformation of Dr Jekyll into Mr Hyde in Robert Louis Stevenson's novella (1886/2002). Bruce Banner is a physicist who creates the gamma bomb that would transform him into the Hulk. In the original narrative, Banner is exposed during a bomb test while trying to save the life of Rick Jones. As with many Marvel storylines during this period, Banner's origin story is a cultural artefact through which American fantasies, desires and fears may be deduced. His transformation at the hands of a nuclear bomb accident evokes America's anxieties about the bomb in the early 1960s (Costello, 2009). Banner's fate in gaining immeasurable strength at the cost of becoming an unthinking, monstrous Other (the opposite of Banner's scientist facade) expresses the 'ambiguity about the ethical value of the bomb, technology, power and responsibility' (ibid., p. 74).

The Cold War milieu, moreover, in which many of Marvel's most popular heroes were created suggests that their significance for American culture cannot be divorced from the anti-communist sentiment they embodied. The Hulk's earliest adventures alternated between fighting communists seeking to obtain American nuclear secrets and combating alien threats, all the while avoiding capture by the US military. As Costello points out, this narrative combination constituted one-quarter of the Hulk stories between 1962 and 1966 (ibid., p. 63). Yet the Hulk's invincibility in the face of which human opposition seemed rather implausible and meant that the series moved away quickly from anti-communist themes.

During the 1970s, the Hulk's portrayal shifted from that of victim of nuclear testing to a misunderstood creature alienated from society and desperately seeking a sense of belonging. It was also during this period that the 'psychologising' of the Hulk began. It started with the addition of Doc Samson, a psychiatrist working with Banner, who was also exposed to gamma radiation. In the early 1980s, many stories focused on the domestic lives of Banner and those affected by him. The narratives became personalised, and were a far cry from the alien invasions against which Hulk was fighting in the 1960s. By 1986, Hulk's transformation is not the result of technology gone wrong, but due to mental illness. There was something already innate to Banner, a 'split personality', which led to the Hulk's emergence. The explanation for Banner's transformation ceases to be an external event, but one that stems from an internal inadequacy. The psychologising of the Hulk is complete by the early 1990s. Banner's metamorphosis is the result of his dysfunctional upbringing and abusive family. His father, in addition to abusing him, killed his mother. This familial trauma and betrayal becomes the source of his rage, the trigger that sets off his transformation. It is this psychological strand of the Hulk story that Ang Lee emphasises and effectively depicts in his film.

While Lee's adaptation remains faithful to the cast of characters introduced in the 1962 comic, it alters the manner of Banner's transformation, thereby stripping away a more contextually nuanced understanding of the character's Cold War origins. Bruce Banner (Eric Bana) is a genetic scientist working alongside Betty Ross (Jennifer Connelly) hoping to improve the regenerative capacities of the human body. Lee then follows the development of Hulk's character in the 1990s, exploring the relationship between Bruce and his father, David (Nick Nolte and Paul Kersey [as young Banner]). Indeed, the proverbial apple does not fall far from the tree; David was also conducting genetic experiments for the military and used Bruce as a test subject. When David's refusal to follow military protocols is discovered by General Thaddeus 'Thunderbolt' Ross (Sam Elliot and Todd Tesen [as young Ross]), David's work is terminated, but not before he kills his wife Edith (Cara Buono), who intervenes to save Bruce from his father's murderous rage. It is Bruce's exposure to gamma radiation during the lab accident in conjunction with his father's earlier experiments that creates the Hulk. More importantly, it is the lingering presence of his repressed memories of the death of his mother at the hands of his father that propels Bruce's transformation.

A Freudian interpretation

The possibility of a Freudian reading is undeniable. At a very basic level, Bruce's transition from scientist to green monster is particular effective in conveying the difference between conscious and unconscious, or the *id*. In his 'angry man' state, he is pure instinct, bursting forth with uncontrollable emotion. Bruce is described as 'bottled up' and his 'repressed memories' are referenced on several occasions (*Hulk*, 2003). Specifically, Bruce is encouraged by Betty to recover the original childhood trauma he suffered. This is skilfully depicted in a scene shortly after Betty has betrayed Bruce, and both are brought back to the military base where they grew up. Betty spurs him to open a room door in his old house, and to see what is on the other side. The music builds the suspense as Bruce moves quickly to open the door after Betty attempts to do so. The music comes to a sudden halt as the door swings open to expose a barren room. Bruce observes, 'See, there's nothing. It's empty' (*Hulk*, 2003). His observation of the obvious is simultaneously a reflection of his current psychological state, mainly, his resistance that prevents that which is unconscious from being made conscious. Dreams also play a prominent role in the film. Bruce's nightmares are used to present flashbacks of his past, which allows the viewer to reconstruct the nature of his childhood trauma. Betty's dream points to the absence of her father and the Hulk's transformation and is described as being akin to a dream state. The somewhat casual use of depth psychological ideas in *Hulk* displays the extent to which the discipline has penetrated the mainstream. That is not to say, however, that the film fails to comprehensively explore and express more complex psychological themes.

Hulk is essentially a psychological drama that scrutinises a son's relationship to his father (Bruce's relationship to David) and, to a lesser degree, a daughter's relationship to her father (Betty's relationship to Thaddeus Ross). In many ways, the *Oedipus complex* finds symbolic expression throughout the film. David is not afraid of conducting genetic experiments on his son, disregarding the damage this may cause him. When the army discovers David's use of human subjects, he attempts to kill his son. The lack of paternal recognition that is so crucial in the nurturance and development of individuals (Benjamin, 1988, 1998) is palpable during their dramatic dialogue on the military base. David makes a distinction between the merely weak, human shell that is Bruce and his real son (the green monster). Bruce (as the Hulk) eventually kills his father, who has transformed into an entity able to absorb energy. It is his inability to contain the energy imbibed from the Hulk that leads to his demise. Whereas the father fails to kill the son in his first attempt, the son succeeds. David's wish to exterminate Bruce is unambiguous. During the dramatic exchange between father and son at the military base, David says to Bruce, 'I should have killed you' (*Hulk*, 2003). The father's fear of the son stems from his own castration complex; it is he who dreads the son's potential to overtake him. Both David and Bruce are scientists working on genetic research, but whereas David's experiments are ultimately unsuccessful, Bruce's succeed. His mutation, moreover, is stable, as he is able to contain the energy produced through the transformation. David cannot, and coaxes his son's metamorphosis in order to absorb the Hulk's ability to stabilise the genetic mutation (which ultimately fails). The killing of the father, read symbolically, is the proverbial 'cutting of the apron strings', or Banner's ultimate release from the tyranny of both his father's presence and absence from his life.

Oedipal themes are also present in Lee's respective representations of Bruce's mother and love interest, Betty. Both are brunettes with long hair, being played by actresses who are roughly the same height (Cara Buono is 5 foot 5 inches and Jennifer Connelly is 5 foot 6½ inches). Whether intentional or not, these similarities suggest that the unresolved internal attachment is played out in Bruce's future relationship with Betty. Indeed, a sexual tension and dynamic between mother and son is apparent. Bruce's only description of his mother is laden with romantic undercurrents:

> I saw her last night, saw her face. Brown hair, brown eyes. She smiled at me. She reached out and kissed my cheek. I can almost remember her smell. It was like desert flowers.... It's my mother, and I don't even know her name.
>
> *(Hulk, 2003)*

The sketch resembles a memory of a long lost love affair, one that is affectionately and idealistically recollected. Bruce's subsequent detachment in his love relationships can be understood as a repetition of unresolved Oedipal issues from his past. Both mother and girlfriend look the same and, ultimately, the result is the same: Bruce is left abandoned by the women in his life. While a Freudian reading of the film's themes is highly suggestive, a Jungian reading is equally compelling as the focus shifts from a recollection of the past to the potential, future personality represented by digitised Hulk.

A Jungian interpretation

At first glance, the Jungian concept most useful to explore the themes of *Hulk* is *shadow*. The shadow embodies the dark side of the personality; those inferior traits intrinsic to our own character that we would rather disown and project on to others (1951: §14–15). Jung is adamant, however, that shadow is not entirely negative (ibid.: §423). Anything that has yet to reach consciousness, which includes our fullest potential, lies in shadow. David Banner's under-standing of the symbiotic relationship between his son and the Hulk skilfully illuminates the nature of one's connection to the shadow. The green monster his son would rather disown is actually a part of who he is. That is why Bruce cannot isolate and treat it. It is a part of him, and to exterminate it would be an attempt to kill a part of himself. A shadow relationship also exists at the societal level, between Hulk and the military. The latter acts, presumably, in the interest of public safety. As the Hulk's rampage reaches downtown San Francisco, the need for contain-ment grows ever more pressing. The Hulk is perceived as the threat and personification of viol-ence. Yet in pursuing him, the army causes an equal amount of damage and havoc, which brings to mind Jung's description of shadow projection (ibid.: §16). The Hulk can be seen as a personi-fication of society's and, in particular, the army's shadow as that is what it does not wish to know about itself, but that which in fact it is: an ugly, green killing machine.

Ultimately, the military is responsible for the Hulk, as it funds the science that leads to its creation. The green behemoth is a product of society's scientific ethos, its thirst for knowledge and its wish to conquer and control nature. The opposition between science and nature is com-petently depicted, where scenes of scientific experimentation are juxtaposed with images of nature: flora and fauna (on which experiments are conducted) and, notably, the desert. An encounter with shadow, however, is only one step in the larger examination of Bruce's person-ality development. The concept of individuation may be usefully mobilised to frame the psycho-logical transformation that parallels Bruce's physical one.

Individuation is defined as a process through which one becomes wholly oneself and that which one was born to be and realising one's own innate potential (Jung, 1928: §266–267). The call to individuation may manifest as a deep sense of vocation, which the protagonist or hero must consciously choose to answer (ibid.: §295). To deny it would not only mean doing viol-ence to oneself, but robbing society of the individual's larger contribution. For Jung, individu-ation is not *individualism*. The latter denotes an egocentricity that would grant an indulgence in one's own self-centredness. Rather, individuation cultivates the collective aspects of the person-ality. Jung writes:

> Individualism means deliberately stressing and giving prominence to some supposed peculiarity rather than to collective considerations and obligations. But individuation means precisely the better and more complete fulfilment of the collective qualities of the human being, since adequate consideration of the peculiarity of the individual is more conducive to a better social performance than when the peculiarity is neglected or suppressed.
>
> *(ibid.: §267)*

Moments of introspection and withdrawal from society are certainly necessary, but, ultimately, there must be a conscious return to it, enriching it with the insights one has gained through one's sojourn into the unconscious. Individuation can also be described as the process through which one '[divests] the self of the false wrappings of the persona on the one hand, and of the suggestive power of primordial images on the other' (ibid: §269). If one becomes more con-scious of the ways in which archetypal imperatives can inform our behaviour, one places oneself in a better position to minimise its potentially deleterious effects. The integration of uncon-scious material, in the process of making that which is unconscious, conscious, leads to a widen-ing of consciousness. 'This widened consciousness', Jung writes, 'is no longer imprisoned in that touchy, egotistical bundle of personal wishes, fears, hopes and ambitions which always has to be compensated or corrected by unconscious counter-tendencies' (ibid.: §275). Rather, it becomes a 'function of relationship to the world of objects, bringing the individual into absolute, binding and indissoluble communion with the world at large' (ibid.: §275).

The archetypal *Self* is the *telos* driving the individuation process. It is a representation of the total personality and encompasses both the conscious and unconscious psyche (ibid.: §274). It is an image of one's fullest potential and represents a unity of the personality, which must not be confused with perfection. As an image of one's wholeness would be incomplete without an integration of shadow, it would be problematic to regard the Self as the mere accumulation of all the good within an individual. Like all archetypes, the Self cannot be known in its entirety (1951: §7). One can integrate aspects of the Self into one's conscious personality, but a full realisation of its nature is impossible. Hence, a part of the Self will always remain beyond human cognition. When describing the Self, Jung notes its connection to the God-image (ibid.: §42). Rightly or wrongly, the two become interchangeable terms in Jung's writing. By extension, Jung's interest in the dark side of God is equally a concern for the dark side of the Self (1952: §553–758). Like all archetypes, the Self is bipolar in nature, and to presume that all encounters with it are benevolent would be naive. One can be, for example, overwhelmed by its numinosity, which can lead to archetypal possession and a loosening of one's grip on reality.

The theme of individuation is enacted in several ways in *Hulk*, amongst them, the focus on rebirth. Every time Bruce changes into the Hulk, he is undergoing a psychological shift. While it could be argued that his altered state is defined by its destructive capacity, it is also the only state in which he feels anything. This is preferable to the cold and emotionally distant Bruce who seems incapable of love (as manifested in his relationship with Betty). Equally, Bruce as the Hulk also possesses the capacity for compassion and vulnerability. After Hulk's confrontation with Talbot, he escapes to see Betty. Once she realises who he is, he gently picks her up, places her on a car and looks at her with great affection before saving her from the genetically mutated dogs sent by Bruce's father. The rebirth motif is also expressed when Talbot attempts to extract Bruce's genes 'subconsciously' (*Hulk*, 2003). As Banner will not willingly give a blood sample, Talbot places him in an underwater chamber, where he attempts to extract the enzymes during Bruce's nightmare. Transforming into Hulk, he eventually breaks free from his watery prison and the compound at which he is being held. What sets this particular transformation apart from others is the way in which Lee has weaved David's confession to Betty with Bruce's re-emergence from the symbolic womb. It suggests that during the nightmare itself, Bruce has either confronted or come to some realisation of the trauma which lies at the heart of his transformation (Yockey, 2014, p. 37).

Bruce is reborn from this symbolic amniotic fluid as the Hulk, which begs the question as to whether the green monster might be a representation of the Self. As alluded to previously, such an interpretation is not far-fetched, as the creature certainly conveys the Janus-faced nature of this archetypal imperative: it can be both destructive and nurturing. Whether the Hulk manifests as an explosion of unmediated unconscious energy or is able to display his compassionate nature hinges on Bruce's ability to consciously control the transformation. This speaks, psychologically, to the important role of consciousness when engaging unconscious contents. Sufficient ego-strength and a foot firmly planted in reality are necessary pre-conditions protecting the ego from being overwhelmed by archetypal material, as Jung seeks to demonstrate in relation to his own confrontation with the unconscious (Jung, 1963/1989). Although no continuity exists between *Hulk* and the 2008 reboot, *The Incredible Hulk*, one of Bruce's major goals throughout both films is to consciously control his metamorphosis, which he seems to attain in the first *Avengers* film (*Avengers Assemble*, 2012). What is being depicted in *Hulk* (2003) is one step in Bruce's journey in developing a strong container that will allow him to harness Hulk's potential. Through his emotional ordeal in uncovering his past and engaging with the more instinctual side of his personality, he has learned to *feel*, a counterpoint, in typological terms, to his overdeveloped *thinking* (depicted by Bruce's commitment to rationality and science). He is now able to assign greater value to those concerns that are most crucial to his life: Betty, and coming to grips with the Hulk as an aspect of himself. In one telling scene, only Betty is able to calm Hulk's rage as he transforms back into Bruce (*Hulk*, 2003):

BRUCE: You found me.
BETTY: You weren't hard to find.
BRUCE: Yes I was.

Bruce recognises both his emotional unavailability and how his own ego is being swallowed by the Hulk with each uncontrolled transformation. Although the film certainly depicts a progression in the development of his personality, it is not to say that he achieves individuation by the film's end.

Bruce's transformation is once again triggered when he is unable to contain his anger. The ending usefully portrays Jung's contention that individuation is rarely attained within one's lifetime, and includes experiencing suffering, acknowledging one's limitations and accepting the mistakes one makes along the way. 'But when one follows the path of individuation', Jung reflects:

> When one lives one's own life, one must take mistakes into the bargain; life would not be complete without them. There is no guarantee – not for a single moment – that we will not fall into error or stumble into deadly peril. We may think there is a sure road. But that would be the road of death…. Anyone who takes the sure road is as good as dead.
>
> *(1963/1989, p. 297)*

While it is not a 'fairy tale' ending, it is certainly a realistic one, given how psychologically unaware both Bruce and Hulk are prone to be.

The dual nature of the Self specifically and the bipolarity of archetypes more generally are difficult concepts to convey to undergraduates, but I have found the image of the Hulk in Lee's adaptation most appropriate as a heuristic tool. Throughout the film, the green monster is described as Bruce's true self; his conscious personality is but a mere shell hiding his true nature. As we have noted, Hulk's capacity for both aggression and compassion speaks to the bipolarity of archetypal imperatives. Archetypes possess both positive and negative poles and have the potential to overwhelm an ego not yet ready to engage with it. I would suggest that the Hulk is an image of the Self but in a very raw, undeveloped form. Yet upon closer examination, it might be the best representation of the Self (perhaps unintentionally) to be found among the multitude of superhero films inundating the market today. Arguing along the lines of Yockey (2014), the imperfections of the digital image itself, and the effects it seeks to produce, encapsulate the tension between the optimal image one can hold and the extent to which its realisation may only fulfil a small part of one's original idealisation. Similarly, while the aim is to come ever closer to realising our fullest potential and to actualise our unique image of the Self in fact this turns out ultimately to be impossible. Yet the fact we are guided and driven by the achievement of an ideal compels us to continue on our quest for an image that comes closer to that very quintessence.

Gilmore and Stork (2014) rightly point out that the superhero genre and its subsequent success has been made possible because of its use of digital technologies, the ultimate goal of which is to achieve photorealism: 'The superhero genre', they contend, is constantly expanding through technology, finding new ways to speak to its ideas, to represent them, through a continued consideration of what technology makes possible on the level of the spectacular, the affective, the intellectual, and any other number of emotional or cognitive registers.

(2014, p. 4)

This is particularly true in the case of the Hulk in his digital manifestations (*Hulk*, 2003; *The Incredible Hulk*, 2008; *Avengers Assemble*, 2012; *Avengers: Age of Ultron*, 2015).

Lee's 2003 digital representation of the Hulk was particular disappointing, with many fans and critics alike panning the CGI. John Kenneth Muir writes that the 'CGI work was totally inadequate in dramatizing the green behemoth. One … shot showed the Hulk tossing a tank across the desert, looking like a blown-up cartoon, with no detail, depth, or sense of reality' (quoted in Yockey, 2014, p. 30). Yet the creators certainly endeavoured to design the most photorealistic representation of the Hulk possible, given the technology at the time. Gilmore cites the extra features on the special edition DVD, where we discover that '12,996 different controllable components, known as texture maps, went into the look of the Hulk's CG skin to create layers of veins, pores, wrinkles, blemishes, hair and dirt' (2014, p. 15). In addition, 'the ILM [Industrial Light & Magic] crew was comprised of 69 technical artists, 41 animators, 35 compositors [and] 10 muscle animators' (ibid.).

While the substandard CG effects contributed to the film's poor box office and critical reception, I argue along the lines of Yockey that the digital Hulk is perfectly imperfect, but for different reasons and with distinct implications. Yockey rightly suggests that 'the very artificiality of this digital Hulk is the source of his significance' (2014, p. 30), pointing to Lee's auteur sensibilities in challenging and violating a viewer's original image of the Hulk. Yockey explains:

> Just as each transformation into the Hulk by Bruce is a kind of rebirth, each new textual iteration re-presents the character to audiences already familiar with him. Each new version evokes those past representations, even as it exceeds them in its difference. Consequently the viewers change in some way themselves because their relationship to the character has been altered [...] Lee's expressive use of digital effects in *Hulk* confirms the underlying attraction of the digital: its capacity for difference.
>
> *(pp. 29–30)*

The imperfections of the digital Hulk, then, is meant to challenge the identity of viewers and that with which they have identified. While I do not disagree with Yockey's argument, I wonder to what extent the analysis places a disproportionate emphasis on the role of the director/artist and his/her ability to consciously mould, shape and translate what he/she originally envisioned. McCloud reflects: 'Ask any writer or filmmaker or painter just how much of a given project truly represents what he/she envisioned it to be. You'll hear twenty percent … ten … five … Few will claim more than thirty' (1993, p. 196). In this regard, Jung's distinction between *psychological* and *visionary art* is effective in redressing an over-emphasis on the psychology of the artist at the expense of the psychology of art (1933/2001). While it is extremely relevant and, I suggest, possible to recover authorial intention (Skinner, 2002), it is equally essential to note the varying subjectivities each individual brings to his/her reading of a text, and the 'meaning' of some works to transcend an artist's original motives.

In the drive to perfect photorealism, the inevitable imperfections of the digital Hulk give way to a more authentic representation of the Self's duality, expressing the ultimate inability to become fully individuated within a lifetime. The Self constitutes one's ideal image of wholeness, but not perfection. We may constantly strive to come closer to realising this image (or goal of photorealism), but the end result will never attain the image we see or about which we fantasise. Yet that in itself should not be a source of disappointment if we take seriously the more humanistic aspects of Jung's psychology. Similarly, strong emotional reactions to the film may be a springboard to assessing the psychology of the reception itself. It can show us what potentially lurks in the unconscious. The uneasiness of reactions to the digital Hulk, and outright criticisms of it, may be read as our own anxiety about the inability to ever realise our fullest potential, no matter how ideal the outer conditions are or, by extension, how advanced the technology is. The message is not that we should 'get used to disappointment', but that we should embrace this very imperfection as part of the human condition. After all, the digital Hulk was, in the final analysis, created by human ingenuity and made possible by software and hardware created by humans. In this regard, the digital body of the Hulk is only an extension of ourselves and our ability to create, imagine and project such an image on to the big screen. Crucially it illustrates our capacity to dream and strive for something better. We project our own insecurities on to the Hulk's digital body because it serves as a suitable scapegoat. By withdrawing them, we are reminded of a more sober and realistic understanding of the Self that does not demand the realisation of an unattainable ideal, but encourages a striving for something better with each subsequent attempt.

Conclusion

I have argued along the lines of Yockey that the affect with which viewers responded to the digital Hulk in Ang Lee's adaptation is psychologically significant. The image's efficacy lies not in its achievement of photorealism, but in its failure to do so, which has psychological implications. It fosters a more realistic understanding and appreciation of Jung's concepts, in particular, that of individuation and the Self. The digital Hulk's appearance constantly reminds the audience of the dual nature of the Self and the imperfections and difficulties that plague the individuation process. The realisation of our fullest potential is an impossibility, just as it is equally inconceivable to create a digital Hulk that reflects the idealised image of him/it we may see in our fantasies. Yet the striving to actualise and perfect this image i.e. the Self's role in propelling the individuation process, is still decisive, so long as we can forgive ourselves for falling slightly short of our expectations with each subsequent undertaking. The adaptation of comic book superheroes and their stories into Hollywood blockbusters is a transformation that parallels Hulk's own, and which has proven to be a fruitful avenue through which depth psychological concepts and particularly Jungian ones have been made accessible to, and (hopefully) enjoyable for, undergraduate students. The joy of learning, I trust, becomes intricately intertwined with the *jouissance* experienced at witnessing the Hulk's transformations and the individuation process to which they speak.

References

Anslow, J. (2012) 'Archetypes assemble: how superhero teams save the world from the apocalypse and lead the way to individuation. Marvel's *The Avengers*', Spring, 88, pp. 233–46.

Babic, A. A. (ed.) (2014) *Comics as history, comics as literature: roles of the comic book in scholarship, society and entertainment*. Madison, NJ: Fairleigh Dickinson University Press.

Bassil-Morozow, H. (2010) *Tim Burton: the monster and the crowd*. London and New York: Routledge.

Bassil-Morozow, H. (2011) *The trickster in contemporary film*. Hove: Routledge.

Bateman, J. A. (2014) *Text and image: a critical introduction to the visual/verbal divide*. London and New York: Routledge.

Belford, A. U. (1997) 'Teaching Jung in a theological seminary and a graduate school of religion: a response to David Tacey', *Journal of Analytical Psychology*, 42(2), pp. 303–11.

Benjamin, J. (1988) *The bonds of love: psychoanalysis, feminism and the problems of domination*. New York: Pantheon Books.

Benjamin, J. (1998) *Shadow of the other: intersubjectivity and gender in psychoanalysis*. New York and London: Routledge.

Brook, R. (1997) 'Jung in the academy: a response to David Tacey', *Journal of Analytical Psychology*, 42(2), pp. 285–96.

Campbell, J. (1968) *The hero with a thousand faces*, 2nd edn. Princeton, NJ: Princeton University Press.

Costello, M. J. (2009) *Secret identity crisis: comic books and the unmasking of Cold War America*. New York: Continuum.

DiPaolo, M. (2011) *War, politics and superheroes: ethics and propaganda in comics and films*. Jefferson, NC: McFarland & Company.

Duncan, R. and Smith, M. J. (2009) *The power of comics: history, form and culture*. New York: Continuum.

Eisner, W. (2008) *Comics and sequential art*, revd edn. New York: W. W. Norton.

Garrett, G. (2008) *Holy superheroes! Exploring the sacred in comics, graphic novels and film*, revd edn. Louisville, KY: Westminster John Knox Press.

Gilmore, J. N. (2014) 'Will you like me when I'm angry? Discourses of the digital in *Hulk* and *The Incredible Hulk*', in J. N. Gilmore and M. Stork (eds), *Superhero synergies: comic book characters go digital*. Lanham, MD: Rowman & Littlefield. pp. 11–26.

Gilmore, J. N. and Stork, M. (2014) 'Introduction: heroes, converge!' in J. N. Gilmore and M. Stork (eds), *Superhero synergies: comic book characters go digital*. Lanham, MD: Rowman & Littlefield. pp. 1–10.

Gordon, I., Jancovich, M. and McAllister, M. P. (eds) (2007) *Film and comic books*. Jackson, MI: University Press of Mississippi.

Hassler-Forest, D. (2012) *Capitalist superheroes: caped crusader in the neoliberal age*. Winchester, UK: Zero Books.

Hauke, C. and Alister, I. (eds) (2001) *Jung & film: post-Jungian takes on the moving image*. Philadelphia, PA: Brunner-Routledge.

Hauke, C. and Hockley, L. (eds) (2011) *Jung & film II: the return*. London: Routledge.

Hockley, L. (2001) *Cinematic projections: the analytical psychology of C. G. Jung and film theory*. Luton, UK: University of Luton Press.

Hockley, L. (2007) *Frames of mind: a post-Jungian look at film, television and technology*. Chicago, IL: Intellect.

Hockley, L. (2013) *Somatic cinema: the relationship between body and screen – a Jungian perspective*. London and New York: Routledge.

Huskinson, L. (ed.) (2008) *Dreaming the myth onwards: new directions in Jungian therapy and thought*. London: Routledge.

Izod, J. (2001) *Myth, mind and the screen: understanding the heroes of our times*. Cambridge: Cambridge University Press.

Jung, C. G. (1928) 'The relations between the ego and the unconscious', in *The collected works of C. G. Jung*, Vol. 7, *Two essays on analytical psychology*, 2nd edn. London: Routledge, 1966.

Jung, C. G. (1933/2001) *Modern man in search of a soul*. New York: Routledge.

Jung, C. G. (1951) 'The shadow', in *The collected works of C. G. Jung*, Vol. 9ii, *Aion: researches into the phenomenology of the self*, 2nd edn. London: Routledge, 1968.

Jung, C. G. (1952) 'Answer to Job', in *The collected works of C. G. Jung*, Vol. 11, *Psychology and religion: west and east*, 2nd edn. London: Routledge, 1969.

Jung, C. G. (1963/1989) *Memories, dreams, reflections*. New York: Vintage Books.

Jung, C. G. (2009) *The red book: liber novus*. New York and London: W. W. Norton & Company.

Kaveney, R. (2008) *Superheroes! Capes and crusaders in comics and films*. London: I. B. Tauris.

Knowles, C. (2007) *Our gods wear spandex: the secret history of comic book heroes*. San Francisco, CA: Weiser Books.

McCloud, S. (1993) *Understanding comics: the invisible art*. New York: HarperPerennial.

Papadopoulos, R. (1997) 'Is teaching Jung within university possible? A response to David Tacey', *Journal of Analytical Psychology*, 42(2), pp. 297–301.

Pustz, M. (2012) *Comic books and American cultural history: an anthology*. New York: Continuum.

Reynolds, R. (1992) *Superheroes: a modern mythology*. London: B. T. Batsford Ltd.

Romagnoli, A. S. and Pagnucci, G. S. (2013) *Enter the superheroes: American values, culture, and the canon of superhero literature*. Lanham, MD: Scarecrow Press.

Samuels, A. (1996) 'The future of Jungian studies: a personal agenda', in M. Stanton and D. Reason (eds), *Teaching transference: on the foundations of psychoanalytic studies*. London: Rebus. pp. 15–26.

Saunders, B. (2013) *Do the gods wear capes? Spirituality, fantasy, and superheroes*. London: Bloomsbury.

Shelley, M. J. (1818/2003) *Frankenstein; or, the modern Prometheus*, revd edn. London: Penguin Books.

Singh, G. (2009) *Film after Jung*. London and New York: Routledge.

Skinner, Q. (2002) *Vision of politics, vol. 1: regarding method*. Cambridge: Cambridge University Press.

Smith, M. J. and Duncan, R. (eds) (2012) *Critical approaches to comics: theories and methods*. New York and London: Routledge.

Stevenson, R. L. (1886/2002) *The strange case of Dr. Jekyll and Mr. Hyde and other tales of terror*. London: Penguin Books.

Tacey, D. (1997a) 'Jung in the academy: devotions and resistances', *Journal of Analytical Psychology*, 42(2), pp. 269–83.

Tacey, D. (1997b) 'Reply to responses', *Journal of Analytical Psychology*, 42(2), pp. 313–16.

Wright, B. W. (2001) *Comic book nation: the transformation of youth culture in America*. Baltimore, MD: Johns Hopkins University Press.

Yockey, M. (2014) 'Secret origins: melodrama and the digital, in Ang Lee's *Hulk*', in J. N. Gilmore and M. Stork (eds), *Superhero synergies: comic book characters go digital*. Lanham, MD: Rowman & Littlefield. pp. 27–39.

Filmography

Avengers: Age of Ultron. (2015) [film] Directed by Joss Whedon. USA.

Avengers assemble. (2012) [film] Directed by Joss Whedon. USA.

Hulk. (2003) [film] Directed by Ang Lee. USA.

Incredible Hulk, The. (2008) [film] Directed by Louis Leterrier. USA.

11

HORROR AND THE SUBLIME

Psychology, transcendence and the role of terror

Christopher Hauke

The sublime and the limits of the rational

I am not a particular fan of the horror genre in film or literature but I have always been fascinated to know why horror attracts people as it does. Coming across the modern horror writer Thomas Ligotti, his reading of Lovecraft and the general distrust of human consciousness and pessimism regarding the human place in the world, I associated this with Jung's critique of dominant conscious rationality and his Nietzschean scepticism about the achievements of rationality since the Enlightenment. For Jung,

> reason and the will that is grounded in reason are valid only up to a point. The further we go in the direction selected by reason, the surer we may be that we are excluding the irrational possibilities of life which have just as much right to be lived.
>
> *(1943: §72)*

In this way the attraction and use of horror as a genre of entertainment and interest came together with a postmodern Jungian distrust in the achievements and place of human consciousness in nature. This then led to the idea that what was being sought was a transcendence of the limits of rational consciousness in an experience of the *sublime*. At its core, the horror genre sees our humanness and consciousness not as an enhancement or culmination of nature but an aberration. A mistake. In horror we may be seeking a route past such limitations. Otherwise we are left like the renegade Kurtz in Joseph Conrad's *Heart of Darkness* who, when confronted by the numinosity of life far beyond civilisation and human values, overwhelmed with awe merely whispers, 'The horror! The horror!'

The popular growth of Gothic horror, Freud and the psychoanalytic perspective

It is no coincidence that Gothic horror literature began just as a dominant style of consciousness described as Enlightenment rationality became established in the late eighteenth century. After Walpole's seminal *The Castle of Otranto* (1764) Gothic horror confirmed its popularity in the 1790s with Mrs Ann Radcliffe (1764–1823) 'whose famous novels made terror and suspense a fashion, and who set new and higher standards in the domain of macabre and fear-inspiring atmosphere'

(Lovecraft, 1927) in the novels *A Sicilian Romance* (1790), *Udolpho* (1794) and others. After this period we enter an era of horror fiction more familiar to modern times, largely due to the way cinema has repeatedly turned to such narratives for popular films. Mary Shelley's *Frankenstein; or The Modern Prometheus* (1818) uttered in a new era while her friend Dr John Polidori composed his story *The Vampyre* shortly after. Edgar Allen Poe (1809–49) took the genre to further heights in the nineteenth century followed by Sir Walter Scott, Capt. Marryat (*The Werewolf*, 1839), Conan Doyle, H. G. Wells and then Robert Louis Stevenson with his seminal *The Strange Case of Dr. Jekyll & Mr. Hyde* (1886). All these lead up to the stories of H. P. Lovecraft himself (1890–1937) who, convinced of the pre-human, archetypal roots of supernatural horror wrote:

> No amount of rationalisation, reform, or Freudian analysis can quite annul the thrill of the chimney-corner whisper or the lonely wood ... there is an actual physiological fixation of the old instincts in our nervous tissue which would make them obscurely operative even were the conscious mind to be purged of all sources of wonder.
>
> *(1927, p. 2)*

From a psychoanalytic point of view Day has observed that,

> The Gothic arises out of the immediate needs of the reading public to escape from conventional life and articulate and define the turbulence of their psychic existence. We may see Freud as the intellectual counterpart of this process.... The Gothic ... acclimatised the culture to the types of ideas Freud was to present as truth by presenting them as fiction.
>
> *(1985, p. 179)*

Steven Jay Schneider in his introduction to *Horror Film and Psychoanalysis*, follows this with:

> If Day is right, then one of the key tasks performed by the psychoanalytic literary critic is *neither* revelation of the Gothic novel's 'real (hidden) meaning' *nor* mere description of its surface characteristics. Rather, it is the in-between one of *translation*, of writing and rewriting the Gothic novel's 'thematized, narrativized, and embodied' ideas and constructs in terms that are more explicitly Freudian, Jungian, Kleinian, Lacanian, etc.
>
> *(2004, pp. 11–12)*

Another, very different, example is Julian Hoxter's look at how, in the Italian *giallo* horror films of Dario Argento, the 'complex, shifting connection between individuals and ... the world of objects which they inhabit' (1998, p. 99) exemplifies certain key principles of Kleinian object-relations theory. But a direct psychoanalytic approach may be the wrong way to go, as Crane suggests:

> In irrevocably linking horror to the unconscious we dismiss, all too hastily, the possibility that horror films have something to say about popular epistemology, about the status of contemporary community, or about the fearsome power of modern technology.
>
> *(1994, p. 29)*

This chapter takes up this challenge by examining our fascination with horror through the Jungian critique of rational consciousness. The idea is that through a confrontation with the primordial, the irrational and the Sublime, the tension between the rational and the irrational is transcended by a Sublime third. As Jung observes:

Through our senses we experience the known, but our intuitions point to things that are unknown and hidden, that by their very nature are secret. If they ever become conscious, they are intentionally kept secret and concealed, for which reason they have been regarded from earliest times as mysterious, uncanny, and deceptive. They are hidden from man, and he hides himself from them out of religious awe, protecting himself with the shield of science and reason.

(1930/50: §148)

Jung's psychological writing poses a challenge and a response to modernity and to modern consciousness. Jung makes it quite clear that the material and technological benefits brought about by scientific rationality over the last 500 years have come at great cost to the human psyche itself. In objectifying our orientation towards nature so as better to examine and exploit the world we have cut ourselves off from that world. As Edelglass *et al.*, put it, 'If we systematically think of a world in which human beings do not exist (except as the detached observer), we should not be surprised to find ourselves creating a world in which they can't exist' (1992, p. 19). Just as we have cut ourselves off from the outer world of nature, so we have also cut ourselves off from our inner nature – the unconscious psyche. The danger of this, as Jung realised, is that, unattended and unintegrated into consciousness, the unconscious contents get projected on to the world so that, unknown to consciousness, human beings gradually inhabit a world of shadows, projections that fall far short of the 'objective' and 'rational' which Enlightenment thinking believed it had achieved (1943: §72–75). Further, Jung comments, 'The ordered cosmos he believes in by day is meant to protect him from the fear of chaos that bests him by night – his enlightenment is born of night-fears!' (1930/50: §148).

Common both to Jung's critique of modernity – the oppression of the psyche developed in psychological terms – and to the postmodern critique of Enlightenment rationality along political lines is the concept of the *Sublime*. Edmund Burke in 1757 first makes the critical connection between the sublime and terror, 'whatever is in any source terrible, ... or operates in a manner analogous to terror, is a source of the *sublime*, that is, it is productive of the strongest emotion which the mind is capable of feeling' (1958, p. 39). It is significant that in our own times Adorno maintains, in *Aesthetic Theory* (1984), that the experience of the Sublime is needed for us to experience the terror of the times – it is through the experience of the Sublime that we recognise we are historically insignificant. Indeed, the depth psychology of Jung can be seen as very much in harmony with the criticism of the Enlightenment project to be found in the political-historical sphere of analysis – the critical theory of Adorno and Horkheimer in *Dialectic of Enlightenment* (1944). As Thomas Docherty puts it, 'The Enlightenment aimed at human emancipation from myth, superstition and enthralled enchantment to mysterious powers and forces of nature through the progressive operations of critical reason.... Enlightenment set out to think the natural world in an abstract form' (1993, p. 5).

However, encountering the non-rational gives rise to terror. As Nietzsche wrote in *Beyond Good and Evil*, 'He who fights with monsters might take care lest he thereby become a monster. And when you gaze long into an abyss the abyss also gazes into you' (2003, aphorism 146), and at greater length:

There is a great ladder of religious cruelty, and, of its many rungs, three are the most important. People used to make human sacrifices to their god, perhaps even sacrificing those they loved best.... Then, during the moral epoch of humanity, people sacrificed the strongest instincts they had, their 'nature,' to their god; the joy of this particular festival shines in the cruel eyes of the ascetic, that enthusiastic piece of 'anti-nature.' Finally: what was left to be sacrificed? In the end, didn't people have to sacrifice all comfort and hope, everything holy or healing, any faith in hidden harmony or a future filled with justice and bliss? Didn't people have to sacrifice God himself and worship rocks, stupidity, gravity, fate, or nothingness out of sheer cruelty to themselves? To sacrifice God for nothingness – that paradoxical mystery of the final cruelty has been reserved for the race that is now approaching: by now we all know something about this.

(Aphorism 55)

Even in the origins of the Sublime in the writings of Longinus (200 BCE) we find its meaning goes beyond the beautiful and soulful in literature as the Sublime manifests itself 'also in what is sufficiently distressing to cause *bewilderment, wonder* and even *fear*' (Longinus, 2015). Jung predicts, 'It may justly be maintained that the acquisition of reason is the greatest achievement of humanity; but that is not to say that things must or will always continue in that direction' (1943: §72). Interestingly postmodern criticism and Jung's critique of rationality seem to come together in Lyotard's treatment of the Kantian sublime. 'For Kant, the sublime is that which exceeds all our powers of representation.... The sublime figures for Kant as a means of expressing (by analogy) what would otherwise be strictly inexpressible' (Sarup, 1993, p. 151). For Lyotard, the sublime reminds us of the gap – the 'differend' – between the irresolvable discourses. Importantly,

> the sublime brings us up against that limit point of thought where judgement has to recognize its own lack of resources, or the absence of agreed-upon criteria, for dealing with cases that exceed all the bounds of rule-governed, 'rational' adjudication.
>
> *(ibid., p. 152)*

Here we arrive at acknowledging not only the limits of rationality but of consciousness itself – making it for some the worst mistake nature made. Consciousness creates an 'ego tunnel' (Metzinger, 2009) through which our brains convince us that the world is as it appears to us, including our 'self' as unique entities (Ligotti, 2012, p. 25). Writers of horror literature from H. P. Lovecraft to Thomas Ligotti (influenced by Norwegian pessimistic philosopher Peter Wessel Zapffe and his monograph *The Last Messiah*) have long emphasised that we live with a barely concealed awareness of the insignificance of human life in a meaningless universe. It is this sense of ourselves that is stirred up and confirmed in the horror story. As Ligotti states, 'Because of consciousness, parent of all horrors, we became susceptible to thoughts that were startling and dreadful to us, thoughts that have never been equitably balanced by those that are collected and reassuring' (2012, p. 27).

A margin of horror: why we volunteer to be terrified

Moving away from the rational is full of dangers. As Ligotti comments:

> Consciousness has forced us into the paradoxical position of striving to be unselfconscious of what we are, hunks of spoiling flesh on disintegrating bones ... we need some fabulous illusions ... life is a confidence trick we must run on ourselves, hoping we do not ... [find ourselves] stripped of our defence mechanisms and standing stark naked before the silent staring void.
>
> *(2012, pp. 28–29)*

In the void experience Jungian analyst Peter Hodson explains, 'what has been lost is a sense of self, of the external world or of a meaningful relationship between self and world' (2004, p. 1). This is the unconscious *elsewhere*, the Other of non-ordinary reality, which creates a chasm between our sense of self and its sheer otherness. There will be fear and terror in this – the fear of death and the terror of going mad. We often find in the horror literature of Edgar Allen Poe and H. P. Lovecraft how entering death or madness may seem an attractive way to resolve the gap between everyday consciousness and non-ordinary realities. A fear of death or madness may function more as an emotional metaphor in this case, to help the subject keep a psychological grasp on the *otherness* which is experienced as so alien to 'normal' consciousness. As Jung himself puts it:

> It is true indeed that those whom the gods wish to destroy they first make mad. However dark and unconscious this night-world may be, it is not wholly unfamiliar. Man has known it from time immemorial, and for primitives it is a self-evident part of their cosmos. It is only we who have repudiated it because of our fear of superstition and metaphysics, building up in its place an apparently safer and more manageable world of consciousness in which natural law operates like human law in a society.
>
> *(1930/50: §149)*

I think this is a further way of thinking about the role of horror, and our willingness to experience horror through film, games or literature, that goes beyond current understandings in psychology and film cognition. Why would people voluntarily enter a cinema, open a book, fire up a game or DVD to experience terror? Is it perhaps an effort to engage with transcendent experience – achieved in other traditions through ritual, epiphany, prayer or meditation? Apart from being side-lined in modernity, these are long-haul activities requiring practice, faith and a belief in the authority of the institutions that support them. Plugging into horror gives an experience that transcends assured realities in its own way. Like the instinct for religion, maybe we need to know that our conscious experience is not all there is to reality, and the horror film delivers this with impact – but without real danger. Jung recognised that the spirit of the times shows itself, amongst other ways, through the cinema which:

> like the detective story, enables us to experience without danger to ourselves all the excitements, passions and fantasies which have to be repressed in a humanistic age. It is not difficult to see how these symptoms link up with our psychological situation.
>
> *(1931: §195)*

Jung is on record as admiring *The Student of Prague* (dir. Galeen, 1926) for its accurate depiction of the archetypal Shadow. In this film a penniless student makes a Faustian pact that results in him losing his soul; the horror of his condition is brought home when he finds he has no reflection in the mirror and his doppelganger appears showing how his identity has been taken over completely.

Media psychologist Ed Tan notes how films and games evoke emotions that would otherwise be avoided in real life. Audiences enhance enjoyment by moving in and out of belief in the film – distancing themselves from the reality of the fiction – adapting their identifying and projective experience of the characters' situations and the terror it evokes. Watching horror in the cinema our emotions are contagious; terror gets maximised as it is experienced by the audience around us. A certain de-individuation and relaxing of social norms is created by the darkness and closeness of others in the cinema audience. It has been found that here viewers are more subject to collective behaviour, conformity of feelings, an increasing compulsiveness and lowered self-control (Zimbardo, 1969, in Tan, 2011, p. 79).

The difference between real life events and the film or video game horror is that there is no chance – and no *need* – to take action. This is because, significantly, we are not experiencing the emotions on our own behalf; our source concern is for the welfare of *others* – characters, victims and protagonists who we identify with imaginatively. The viewer may feel terror through such identification *even when the character themselves is not experiencing it* – (not yet at any rate!). Because we cannot take action to save them, that emotional impulse stays with us and is driven into the body so the arousal is not discharged – not until a new scene and a new emotional response helps any such discharge – again through the imagination only.

Films or games evoke and regulate emotion in the way the narrative steers it. 'Fear, once *evoked*, is made *specific* by the rest of the scene … the close of an episode rounds off the evoked emotion' (Tan, 2011, pp. 78–80). Given the prospect of resolution, the more intense an emotion the better. In real life, situations are coded by us so as to minimise unpleasant, negative emotions but when watching a film or game negative emotions (especially fear and sadness) are *not* kept to a minimum. We have struck a bargain with our fear when we choose to watch (ibid., p. 81).

What the experience of horror is offering is another take on the distrust of cognitive rationality and the assumption that human life is a secure and familiar reality that is predictable and ultimately reliable and consistent. A challenge to the idea that human conscious minds are some sort of guarantee of reality. The ultimate arrogance being that such a reality – even Nature itself – is not only fairly benign but is also ultimately cooperative towards human aims and goals. Horror literature and media want to implode such assumptions by showing us things that break down natural laws and reveal the chaos lurking beneath. As H. P. Lovecraft writes in his essay 'Supernatural Horror in Literature':

> A certain atmosphere of breathless and unexplainable dread of outer, unknown forces must be present; and there must be a hint … of that most terrible conception of the human brain – a malign and particular suspension or defeat of those fixed laws of Nature which are our only safeguard against the assaults of chaos and the daemons of unplumbed space.
>
> *(1927, p. 144)*

Quite apart from the sublime imagery of horror literature and the terrible disturbances of the world it depicts, for the last eighty years it has been through the medium of film that horror has grabbed and disturbed our imaginations. Nietzsche noted that modernity gave rise to an ever increasing need for stimulation and later,

> Walter Benjamin observed that modernity was characterized by the experience of shock. Looking back over the century, we can see that the history of modernity – played out by the horror film – has been that of exposing the audience to images which are more shocking than those of the previous decade.
>
> *(Creed, 2004, p. 196)*

As Creed goes on to argue:

> The horror film has always demanded an emotional gut response rather than the 'detached' approach (the assumption that detachment is possible is itself questionable) stemming from the logical categories and precise formulations of positivism and

formalism. A theoretical approach to the horror film based on theories of the uncon-scious (a murky realm), repression (never successful), abjection (the crossing of borders), and screen memories (a covering over of past anxieties) offers a way into the horror film which best suits its macabre intention and form.

(p. 197)

Some theorists use Freud's theories on anxiety to understand horror film, but the theory itself may be fatally flawed as Schneider writes:

If so, then neither the terror nor the pleasure generated by horror film monsters can truly be said to stem from their returning certain repressed fears or desires to con-sciousness. But this wouldn't mean that such beings still do not represent or stand for something very much like a return of the ideologically or instinctually repressed.

(2004, p. 9)

Even so Creed argues: 'Like Freud's dreams and case histories, the horror film was quick to explore the nature of perversity. Themes of castration, bestiality, masochism, sexual abuse, and animal phobias all made early appearances' (2004, p. 189). Further a widely adopted approach to horror is in terms of *unheimlich* – German meaning literally 'unhomelike' but usually trans-lated as the *uncanny*. The far-from-home-ness induced by tales of terror in the horror literature and films has a similar anti-human opposition in its qualities that we see in the otherness of the sublime and which propels the witness to a need for transcendence. As Barbara Creed writes, 'The horror genre is also radical in that it explores the formation of human subjectivity, the conditions under which subjectivity disintegrates, and the subject's fascination for and dread of ... death' (2004, p. 192). The divided and displaced self is often a theme for horror movies – many (such as *Invasion of the Body Snatchers* (dir. Segal, 1956) and *The Thing* (dir. Carpenter, 1982) depict the breakdown of identity; others the breakdown of difference between the living and the dead as in the vampire films, *Let the Right One In* (dir. Alfredson, 2008), and zombie films like *Night of the Living Dead* (dir. Romero, 1968). Such splits in reality and in the integrity of human identity can be found in Freud's case history titles such as *The Wolf Man* and *The Rat Man* while, equally, Jung writes of *The girl who lived on the moon* and the *Seven Sermons to the Dead*. In *Alien* (dir. Scott, 1979) and *Aliens* (dir. Cameron, 1986) the struggle and suffering of the female protagonist Ripley (Sigourney Weaver) – in 'space, where no one can hear you scream' – compare to Jung's patient 'on the Moon' suffering in her own psychic, alien environment.

Jung noted how elements of myth appear in movies,

but clothed in modern dress; instead of the eagle of Zeus, or the great roc, there is an aeroplane; the fight with the dragon is a railway smash ... the Pluto who abducts Persephone is a reckless chauffeur, and so on.

(1930/50: §152)

But beyond this rather comfortable understanding of the ancient roots of modern storytelling, Jung was well aware of glimpses into the 'abyss of prehuman ages' (1930: §141). Note also Dominique Paini's observation, delivered in her analysis of Hitchcock's use of rear projection, 'The screen could be seen as a page on which images are inscribed. In this context, cinema is like an imprint of reality, a flat mould, a bottomless abyss, as Jacques Derrida has said' (Paini, 2001 in Schneider, 2004, p. 69). In a similar vein Jung found that visionary literature:

is a primordial experience which surpasses man's understanding and to which in his weakness he may easily succumb … sublime, pregnant with meaning, yet chilling the blood with its strangeness, it arises from timeless depths; glamorous, daemonic, and grotesque, it bursts asunder our human standards of value and aesthetic form, a terrifying tangle of eternal chaos.… We are reminded of nothing in everyday life, but rather of dreams, night-time fears, and the dark uncanny recesses of the human mind.

(1930/50: §141–143)

Jung cites the vision of Dante, the second part of *Faust*, Blake's visions but also Rider Hagard's *She* and E. T. A. Hoffman's *The Golden Pot* (1814). Implied in this must be the paintings of Hieronymus Bosch which achieve a nadir of dehumanising imagery that still disturbs and horrifies long after its own era.

Conclusion: 'The horror! The horror!'

Joseph Conrad found a particular kind of horror in his novella *The Heart of Darkness* (1902). As his protagonist Charles Marlow journeys further up river and away from the known and the civilised, he moves further from what guarantees rationality and safety in human conscious life.

> Going up that river was like travelling back to the earliest beginnings of the world, when vegetation rioted on the earth … you lost your way on that river … till you thought yourself bewitched and cut off forever from everything you had known once – somewhere – far away – in another existence perhaps.
>
> *(Conrad, 1902)*

Marlow's final meeting with Kurtz is not simply an encounter with the embodiment of wickedness in the man. Kurtz's last words 'The horror! The horror!' signify a far broader evil. Conrad once wrote:

> What makes mankind tragic is not that they are the victims of *nature*, it is that they are conscious of it. To be part of the *animal kingdom* under the conditions of this earth is very well – but as soon as you know of your slavery, the pain, the anger, the strife – the tragedy begins. We can't return to nature, since we can't change our place in it. Our refuge is in stupidity.… There is no morality, no knowledge and no hope; there is only *the consciousness of ourselves* which drives us about in a world that … is always but a vain floating appearance.
>
> *(Conrad, 1898, emphasis in original, quoted in Ligotti, 2012, p. 209)*

Horror media and stories achieve their terrorising effect best when they are set within the comfortable and familiar at the start. Many are happy to think that a life lived rationally – with only just enough 'irrationality' in the form of 'human' emotion (not too much to upset the apple cart of sanity) – might confirm that being alive as a conscious being is 'all right'. But not for Jung:

> What if there were a living agency beyond our everyday human world – something even more purposeful than electrons? Do we delude ourselves in thinking we possess our own psyches, and is what science calls the 'psyche' not just a question-mark arbitrarily confined within the skull, but rather a door that opens upon the human world

from a world beyond, allowing unknown and mysterious powers to act on man and carry him on the wings of the night to a more than personal destiny?

(1930/50: §148)

Emotional terror induced by the horror experience is the antithesis of being glad to be alive. It is the antichrist of the life well lived.

References

Adorno, T. (1984) *Aesthetic theory*, eds G. Adorno and R. Tiedemann, trans. C. Lenhardt. London: Routledge.

Adorno, T. and Horkheimer, M. (1944/1986) *Dialectic of enlightenment*, trans. J. Cumming. London: Verso.

Burke, E. (1958) *A philosophical enquiry into the origin of our ideas of the sublime and the beautiful*, ed. J. T. Bolton. London: Routledge & Kegan Paul.

Conrad, J. (1902) *The heart of darkness*. London: J. M. Dent & Sons.

Crane, J. L. (1994) *Terror and everyday life: singular moments in the history of the horror film*. London: Sage.

Creed, B. (2004) 'Freud's worst nightmare: dining with Dr. Hannibal Lecter', in S. J. Schneider (ed.), *Horror film and psychoanalysis: Freud's worst nightmare*. Cambridge and New York: Cambridge University Press. pp. 188–203.

Day, W. P. (1985) *In the circles of fear and desire: a study of Gothic fantasy*. Chicago, IL: University of Chicago Press.

Docherty, T. (ed.) (1993) *Postmodernism: a reader*. Hemel Hempstead, UK: Harvester Wheatsheaf.

Edelglass, S., Maier, G., Gebert, H. and Davy, J. (1992) *Matter and mind: imaginative participation in science*. Edinburgh: Floris.

Frijda, N. (1986) *The emotions*. Cambridge, MA: Cambridge University Press; Frijda, N. (1988) 'The laws of emotion', *American Psychologist*, 43, pp. 349–58 (quoted in E. Tan, *Emotion and the structure of narrative film: film as an emotion machine*, trans. B. Fasting. London: Routledge).

Hodson, P. (2004) '"The void" a neurobiological approach', in P. W. Ashton (ed.), *Evocations of absence: multidisciplinary perspectives on void states*. New Orleans, LA: Spring Journal Books. pp. 125–45.

Hoxter, J. (1998) 'Anna with a devil inside: Klein, Argento, and the Stendhal syndrome', in A. Black (ed.), *Necronomicon: The Journal of Horror and Erotic Cinema* 2. London: Creation Books. pp. 99–109.

Jung, C. G. (1930/50) 'Psychology and literature', in *The collected works of C. G. Jung*, Vol. 15, *The spirit of man, art and literature*. London: Routledge, 1966.

Jung, C. G. (1931) 'The spiritual problem of modern man', in *The collected works of C. G. Jung*, Vol. 10, *Civilisation in transition*, 2nd edn. London: Routledge, 1970.

Jung, C. G. (1943) 'On the psychology of the unconscious', in *The collected works of C. G. Jung*, Vol. 7, *Two essays on analytical psychology*, 2nd edn. London: Routledge, 1966.

Ligotti, T. (2012) *The conspiracy against the human race: the contrivance of horror*. New York: Hippocampus Press.

Lovecraft, H. P. (1927) 'Supernatural horror in literature', *Collected essays Vol. 2: Literary criticism*. New York: Hippocampus Press.

Lyotard, J. F. (1993) 'The sublime and the avant garde', in T. Docherty (ed.), *Postmodernism: a reader*. Hemel Hempstead, UK: Harvester Wheatsheaf. pp. 244–56.

Metzinger, T. (2009) *The ego tunnel: the science of the mind and the myth of the Self*. New York: Basic Books.

Nietzsche, F. (2003) *Beyond good and evil*, trans. R. J. Hollingdale. London: Penguin Books.

Paini, D. (2001) 'The wandering gaze: Hitchcock's use of transparencies', in D. Paini and G. Cogeval (eds), *Hitchcock and art: fatal coincidences*. Montreal: Montreal Museum of Fine Arts. pp. 159–67.

Sarup, M. (1993) *Post-structuralism and postmodernism*, 2nd edn. Hemel Hempstead, UK: Harvester Wheatsheaf.

Schneider, S. J. (2004) *Horror film and psychoanalysis: Freud's worst nightmare*. Cambridge and New York: Cambridge University Press.

Tan, E. (2011) *Emotion and the structure of narrative film: film as an emotion machine*, trans. B. Fasting. London: Routledge.

Zimbardo, P. (1969) 'The human choice: individuation, reason and order versus deindividuation, impulse, chaos', in W. J. Arnold and D. Levine (eds) *Nebraska symposium on motivation*. Lincoln: University of Nebraska Press (quoted in E. Tan, *Emotion and the structure of narrative film: film as an emotion machine*, trans. B. Fasting. London: Routledge).

Online source

Longinus (2015) Wikipedia article [online]. Available at: https://en.wikipedia.org/wiki/On_the_Sublime [Accessed 25 May 2015].

Filmography

Alien. (1979) [film] Directed by Ridley Scott. USA.
Aliens. (1986) [film] Directed by James Cameron. USA.
Invasion of the body snatchers. (1956) [film] Directed by George Segal. USA.
Let the right one in. (2008) [film] Directed by Tomas Alfredson. Sweden.
Night of the living dead. (1968) [film] Directed by George Romero. USA.
Student of Prague, The. (1926) [film] Directed by Henrik Galeen. Germany.
Thing, The. (1982) [film] Directed by John Carpenter. USA.
Wolf Man, The. (1941) [film] Directed by George Waggner. USA.

12

HUNGRY CHILDREN AND STARVING FATHERS

Auteurist notions of father hunger in *American Beauty*

Toby Reynolds

Introduction

According to Bruzzi, currently the father in film studies is 'still "a bit like air" – omnipresent but rarely talked about' (2005, p. xi). As a key masculine archetype, the father is surely one of the most ubiquitous, yet rarely discussed or analysed, masculine presences within film studies. The centre point and launching place for 1,000 filmic narratives, yet at the same time one of the most ignored, the father has largely escaped critical attention until relatively recently.

In the film *American Beauty* (dir. Mendes, 1999), the figure of the father is portrayed as being essential to the construction of cinematic masculinities by virtue of what has been termed 'father hunger' (Bly, 2001; Biddulph, 1998; Maine, 2004). Father hunger, or the conscious and unconscious desire *for*, and/or to *be* a male parent, is central to the narrative drive and themes of the film. The film's director, Sam Mendes, presents the masculine as being in a state of severe disruption within *American Beauty*, causing father hunger both within children and the two fathers depicted. If we accept that the paternal is central to masculine gender identity, father hunger can be argued to be a symptom of damaged, or incomplete masculinities. Contextually, the film also powerfully demonstrates the cultural influence of the 1990s' men's movement with the figure of the father being located as a fundamental solution to the questions that surround gender identities and their constructions (Bly, 2001; Biddulph, 1998). This question of contextuality is also crucial when we consider the theoretical function of the auteur as practising a *technique of self*, outlined in more detail below.

Mendes also consciously uses and mediates archetypal and symbolic imagery to achieve this portrayal, and in so doing demonstrates his status as an *auteur* director. By focusing on the functions and role of the auteur from a post-Jungian perspective, we can reinvigorate the debates around auteurship in film studies as a whole. It is the proposition of this chapter that the auteur can be defined as a figure that demonstrates the conscious and unconscious mediation of archetypal imagery. It is this act of mediating imagery, both symbolic and semiotic, that distinguishes the auteur from other directors, both in the authorial signature of the imagery produced, and through the signature thematic areas explored by the auteur within the films.

This chapter is both a contribution to both the debates around the father (and on a wider level, masculinities in cinema) and the debates around the auteur as these discussions overlap in an academically fertile way within the film. As such, this argument will consist of a brief exploration of the theoretical landscape both of auteur theory and archetypal imagery and the ways in which they cross-pollinate. To link the theory with the film, *American Beauty*'s imagery and *mise-en-scène* will be closely analysed with the archetypes in mind to demonstrate how Mendes fulfils the role of auteur director. Lastly, the implications for wider debates around authorship will be explored. Before we can analyse the film and how it depicts the masculine in more detail, we first need to examine notions of auteurship and imagery, and how they interact.

Auteurs and authorship

In the early days of film theory, the auteur was utilised as a main entry point into film at first in order to better understand it; later theories demanded that the author was deconstructed: Caughie (1981), Stam and Miller (2000), Grant (2008), Sellors (2010). Currently, debates around the auteur have now gone past those totalising theories about the function (or not) of the author and have moved into the arena of post-structuralist concerns, where a multiplicity of meanings, or polysemous functions, appears to be holding sway in terms of defining authors and authorship. All this activity makes clear that authorship still matters. Gerstner and Staiger note in the introduction to *Authorship and Film*: 'although authorship may be subject to the wiles of humanism and capitalism, it also has functions for social action. Contemporary poststructuralist theory may be working to articulate a dynamics of agency not yet fully realised' (2003, p. xi). This resilience of auteur discourses within film theory strongly suggests the figure of the auteur is here to stay, despite the best efforts of, amongst others, Roland Barthes (1967) to downplay its importance. The idea of an auteur occupies an interesting position in that it was initially seen as an integral part of a film text, but also was widely understood to inhabit an unstable, or at the very least, an *uneasy* position within film theory due (in part) to the contradictory nature of the collaborative production process.

For some auteur theorists such as Schatz and Corrigan, rather than focus on who the author may or may not be (which also allowed accusations of auteurist filmic parlour games as to who the greatest director may or may not be), a more productive way to think about this question is to consider the question in terms of the function of *authorship*, rather than one individual *author*. This allows a film to have a number of claims made by its various authors (writer, producer, studio being the main claimants), each possessing a different function of authorship. The approach has a useful flexibility as it allows a consideration of many of the different factors that go into the creation and consumption of a film. However, a central identifying figure was usually sought, around which meaning could coalesce. In practice this was usually the director, as evidenced by the focus on this figure from many sources within both academia and within the film industry.

For his part, Mendes has worked fruitfully with screenwriters, in *American Beauty*'s case, Alan Ball (who won an Oscar for his efforts, along with the film winning Oscar for Best Picture). The film is a classic example of collaborative efforts and rewards, but also an example of the auteur director as being the final interpreter and mediator of the film. As such, the figure of the director keeps being mentioned in film theory, and in industrial contexts too, as not only a creative source of film but also as an important device for the marketing and consumption of cinema. For example, in reviews it is not unusual for a film to be described as 'Lynchian' in its atmosphere, 'Hitchcockian' in its suspense or containing 'Tarantinoesque' levels of swearing and violence; clearly directors can be adjectival! Whilst Mendes has yet to reach this level of recognition, even so the media chose to focus their attention on his status as a director when it was announced in 2012 that he would direct the James Bond film *Skyfall* (and consequently also directing the next film in the series *Spectre* [2015]) – this strongly suggests he has reached the status of a recognised auteur. To add to this industrial position that the director is usually perceived to be the main author of the film, is to also consider that the director possesses the power and decision-making ability to *direct* both the imagery and sound of the film. In other words, she or he literally points the way for the audience/spectator within a film for understanding or meaning to be received. If we accept that the director, in this case Mendes, does indeed possess this power to direct our attention to those images and aspects of the narrative that he particularly wishes us to see and absorb, then (for the most part) authorship can be legitimately claimed in the majority of films by the director. It is from this position that the arguments will be made.

Authors and techniques of self/Self

Having established the position of the director as the main author of the film, or at least the director laying claim to most of the functions of authorship, we can return to the current state of authorship studies. In *Authorship and Film* (2003), Janet Staiger offered seven broad definitions of authorship, namely, origin, personality, sociology of production, signature, reading strategy, site of discourses and, finally, but most important for our purposes, authorship as a *technique of self*. These definitions have a number of crossover potentials; it is a feature (as stated before) that authorship is a polysemous phenomenon. It follows then that it would be an error to focus wholly on one definition of authorship to the exclusion of others. Although this chapter will be focusing mainly on analysing authorship as a technique of self, authorship will also be referred to as also acting both as a *signature* and a *personality*, traits that have long been assigned to the author of any text. As a technique of self, authorship was first highlighted as having the power to give agency and power to voices in non-dominant societal positions. Answering theorists who would argue that it did not matter who was speaking, Staiger comments:

> but the point is to rescue the expression of the self as a viable, if contingent, act – a potent one with real effects. Thus, *the author is reconceptualised as a subject having an ability to act as a conscious analyzer of the functionality of citations in historical moments*.
>
> *(2003, p. 49, emphasis added)*

Authorship can be reframed as both commentary upon and reflection of, the mediation of social and cultural conditions. It is this power of authorship to address cultural issues that is of particular interest in this chapter (the films of Spike Lee, as an example, spring to mind when considering this definition of authorship). With *American Beauty*, Mendes fulfils the role of auteur as a conscious analyser, particularly in the ways he mediates filmic masculinities as a technique of self; in doing so he demonstrates how masculinities are constructed.

In addition to the above, authorship as *authorial signature* needs to be considered here in terms of both visual signature (achieved by distinctive use of cinematography, and *mise en scène*) and thematic signature, in terms of the themes that the film is concerned with. After a distinguished career as a theatre director, Mendes made his cinematic auteurial debut by virtue of a strong visual style, analysed in more depth below. These two aspects of authorship will be discussed in greater detail as the chapter progresses, suffice to say that it is the imagery of the film that is of paramount interest to us when we analyse the role of the director as author. Such a focus leads us to consider the post-Jungian position on the author. Within recent post-Jungian film theory, the auteur is a figure that has had, and is increasingly having, attention from, amongst others, Hauke and Alister (2001), Izod (2006), Singh (2009) and Rountree (2008). Whilst early Jungian and post-Jungian film analysis focused on analysing film usually via narrative and psychological symptoms and situations portrayed by onscreen characters, auteurs and auteurial signatures have now been analysed in greater depth and sophistication. From in-depth analyses and discussions about the films of Spielberg and Kubrick (Hauke and Izod) in terms of their relationship to gender and to societal and cultural commentary, to debates about the author's role as a shamanic figure (Rountree), the auteur has been central to the growing number of post-Jungian film theory discussions. This chapter will add to these debates in terms of highlighting the role of the auteur and how this figure achieves auteurship via the conscious mediation of imagery.

Imagery and affect

From the perspective of analytical psychology, imagery occupies a fundamental position when analysing any text. Hockley points out in *Frames of Mind* that for Jung imagery is central to the psyche: 'image alone is the immediate object of knowledge' (2007, p. 7). It therefore follows that any psychology which has this tenet at its heart, cinema would be a fruitful and rich source of images and worthy of analysis, 'it is through psychological images that it is possible to come to an understanding of ourselves and of our relationship to the world' (ibid., p. 7). This particular interpretation of the value of imagery and its relationship to externalities, resonates with our earlier definition of authorship as a *technique of self* with its emphasis on the analysis of cultural and historical moments, moments that in turn generate powerful images.

When it comes to the source of images and imagery with regard to analytical psychology, the idea of archetypes and their resulting imagery cannot be far behind. Jung defined archetypes as: 'typical forms of behaviour which, once they become conscious, naturally present themselves as *ideas and images*' (1947/54: §435). *A Critical Dictionary of Jungian Analysis* defines the archetype as, 'The inherited part of the psyche; structuring patterns of psychological performance linked to instinct; a hypothetical entity irrepresentable in itself and evident only through its manifestations' (Samuels *et al.*, 1986, p. 26). Archetypes, being unconscious psychic structures that cannot be consciously known, are largely discerned by the images and imagery that are produced by them. Put simply, we know when the archetypes are present from their imagery, or, perhaps more accurately, the archetypes *make themselves* known by the imagery they produce.

There is also need to clarify the archetypal imagery depicted within a text in terms of whether the images are symbolic or semiotic, or a mixture of both. Fredericksen helpfully differentiated between the two, stating that there were dangers inherent in an approach that only engaged with the semiotic, all images being subsumed into phenomena that can be 'known' as Freud, Marx and others, would have it. He comments, 'The [purely] semiotic attitude is ultimately limiting because it either denies the existence of the symbolic realm by definition, or denies its existence in practice by attempting to explain symbolic expressions semiotically' (2001, p. 27).

Fredericksen argues for an approach towards signs and symbols that, in his words, 'forge and keep a living tie between them' (ibid., p. 28). He maintained that failure to do so would mean any analysis, as Edward Edinger argues, would fall victim to (ibid.) 'the reductive fallacy', in other words the belief that all imagery, both signs and symbols, can be rationally explained. Fredericksen explains why symbolic imagery and images are so important noting, 'They carry large amounts of energy and have an energizing effect. These several qualities of the symbol make our symbolic experience numinous' (p. 29). It is then arguable that a large part of the power and numinosity of *American Beauty* is derived from the archetypal images and imagery that are presented to the spectator by Mendes. If we accept the concepts outlined by Fredericksen and Edinger above, we can start to appreciate the power of a film to create affect within the audience – a power that is wielded by an auteur director.

American Beauty or American ugly?

As mentioned at the start of this chapter, the auteur director is a figure that consciously mediates archetypal symbolic imagery to produce affect. With that in mind it is now possible to start to identify why auteur directors are considered and identified as such. This use of symbolic and semiotic imagery produces affect in service of whatever message, or ideology, is being communicated within the film by the director. In this case, *American Beauty* offers a dark but acutely comedic dissection of an unhappy middle-class American suburban family. The film unflinchingly tackles a number of major themes including: repressed sexual desires, both male and female that are normative and transgressive; capitalist societal failures; dysfunctional nuclear familial issues; and it offers challenges to normative gender roles. More specifically, the film deals with depictions of masculinities within recent contemporary American society and the difficulties that are purported to face contemporary American males. Where the film particularly stands out is in its deliberate and conscious focus on the *numinous*, and the thwarted spiritual and psychological journeys that are depicted in the film in several of the main characters. Its director Sam Mendes signals these throughout the film through the conscious use of specific and symbolic imagery and images.

Before we continue to consider this analytical angle, the question arises of whether the analysis of authorship as a technique of self is appropriate, given its interpretation as empowering hidden or non-dominant voices. Males and masculinities (the plural form is used advisedly) cannot, at first glance, be defined as a non-dominant group. However, masculine vulnerabilities and challenges facing masculine cultural and societal positions (which is what *American Beauty* examines) are worthy of attention and analysis because gender is a key aspect of cultural and personal identity. Emerging at a time of significant popular and academic debate around the crisis in masculinity that was widely held to be ongoing within American and Western societies from the early 1990s onwards, films such as *American Beauty* reflected these cultural shifts. Gender is a part of self, and from a post-Jungian perspective, it is also part of the larger archetype of the Self.

To enlarge this point, in a development of Staiger's original definition, *authorship can be defined as a technique of self/Self* and subsequently is appropriate to be used in this way when reframing and analysing filmic texts. This analytical angle now established, we need to also be mindful of the dangers of assigning too much to the authorial voice, dangers that Fredericksen was aware of: 'At other times an author may be known and accessible, but may refuse to provide associations – on the grounds that everything he or she wishes to say, or can say, is in the artwork itself' (2001, p. 37).

There is a danger with studies of auteur theory that too much meaning can be assigned to the supposed intent of the individual director, and assigned contrary to any original intent. If the focus is on the director as mediator of archetypal imagery, then it allows greater clarity around the balance of authorial intent and conscious circulation of historically specific discursive formations. It is with these thoughts in mind that more in-depth analysis of *American Beauty* and its varying symbolic and semiotic imagery and themes can be explored.

Hungry children

Thematically, *American Beauty*'s imagery and dialogue makes references to father hunger straight from the beginning, initially from the perspective of a teenaged girl at the turn of the twenty-first century. Opening with grainy home-video footage (this deliberate shift in filmic perspective happens several times throughout the film) of Jane Burnham (Thora Birch) who is lounging sulkily on her bed with her lover Ricky Fitts (Wes Bentley) an initially unseen presence whom we hear talking to Jane as he films her. In this opening scene, we have Jane's current situation and relationship with her father Lester Burnham (Kevin Spacey) summarised pithily as only a teenaged daughter can, with Jane dismissing her father as acting like a sexually frustrated teenager when he should be acting as a role model and a man she can respect.

The bitter speech strongly echoes Maine (2004) regarding the emergence of the daughter's sexuality clashing with the father's uncertainty and sexual self-doubt, brought on by age-related anxiety. The film sets up Lester Burnham's journey of self-discovery, both spiritual and sexual, coinciding with his daughter's own similar journey, with Jane's anger at her father for not being an adequate (or even a 'good enough parent', as D. W. Winnicott [1973, p. 10] has termed it) male adult. Lester, through his voice-over, another narrative device used throughout the film, is surprisingly aware of his daughter's troubles and he displays an acute sensitivity to his daughter's insecurities, anger and confusion. His observation ends, however, on a pessimistic tone when he notes to himself that he wants to be able to reassure her that these negative feelings will pass, but that he does not want to be dishonest with her.

This awareness of his daughter's needs and his own inability to connect with her is portrayed by Mendes at the first of two dinner table scenes. This domestic space is utilised by Mendes as a key location for family conflicts, the first of which is when Lester announces that his job is under threat, a key anxiety area for economic identity. The lack of reaction or concern from the other two people leads him to observe that no one cares about his situation. In response, Jane rejoinders tartly that just because he has had a bad day, he cannot suddenly become her best friend, especially after hardly communicating with her over the previous few months.

It is not made clear who is responsible for this decline in their relationship, but given the timing of the daughter's adolescence and Lester's slowly growing mid-life crisis, Maine's theory of the daughter's developing sexuality and adulthood clashing with the father's re-assessment of his life is particularly pertinent at this juncture. If we analyse the semiotic imagery that is used in this scene, it reveals auteurist flourishes. The *mise en scène* is carefully composed on a number of levels beginning with the deliberate seating of Carolyn Burnham (Annette Bening) and Lester opposite one another, with Jane being placed forlornly in the middle. Given what we have already experienced of the Burnham's familial unhappiness, the chances of a parental confrontation are high, and Jane is almost certain to be caught in the verbal and emotional crossfire. The scene also contains a number of photographs of the family in (presumably) happier times to give contrast to the drama that is being played out. The cinematography of the dining room (dark lighting, tightly framed composition of the Burnhams to enhance the sense of pressure, with red roses present, a constant palette choice and significantly symbolic motif, discussed in more detail later) is a dark *temenos* space and it forms an emotional cauldron within which the Burnham family dynamics are played out. This scene is thematically revealing in that it shows the state of the father's status as fallen. To paraphrase Bly (2001) and Moore and Gillette (1992), Mendes depicts Lester's King archetype as weak and lacking purpose: as the abrogation of paternal responsibilities, and the resulting weakness and lack of conscious presence within his family that his daughter identifies and complains about. Lester is shown to be dimly aware of the situation, but instead of recognising and confronting it, retreats. The scene ends with the Burnhams still unhappy, despite Lester's feeble attempts to connect with his daughter, and the attention cleverly shifting to Ricky Fitts as he films the unhappy family from his bedroom window. Lester is attempting to be a father (he also suffers from father hunger in that he wants to act like a father), but psychically he is unable to because of his emotional blockages and timidity. As Chachere put it:

American Beauty is a very American film and it is very American about the disaster of married life. It is also the all-American Jungian mid-life crisis film. In the story, Lester is having his mid-life crisis, and sure enough, the *anima* comes and pops him on the head. He looks stupid. He looks especially stupid to his daughter, Jane.

(2003, p. 5)

Lester's self-described emotional and mental somnambulant state is depicted as being damaging to both his marriage and to his daughter. Mendes consistently depicts Lester as unavailable to the people that need him to be available. The scene is set for a major shift in the consciousness of Lester as he begins to wake up from his spiritual and emotional torpor and starts to challenge the status quo of his family life. The catalyst for Lester's awakening in his initial encounter with Angela, Jane's friend and fellow high-school cheerleader. As Chachere above correctly identifies, Lester's *anima* is shown as striking him awake, both locating itself both within Angela, or to be more accurate, simultaneously projected *on to* her by Lester. This is a pivotal moment in the film on a number of levels, and raises a number of deeper thematic questions to consider, not least of which is that difficult issues of incestuous desire are raised when we consider that the object of Lester's desire is his daughter's friend. Andrew Samuels identifies what he terms the dynamic of *erotic playback* between the father and the daughter as being essential to a maturing daughter's sense of self. In *The Political Psyche* (1993) he argues that the father plays a number of roles to his daughter in that he enables (along with the mother) the daughter to become psychologically pluralistic. One feature of this pluralistic theory is that the father provides erotic communication of a sort to the daughter that affirms that she is not just a maternal, or potentially maternal. This erotic playback between father and daughter is a delicate matter and Samuels recognises the dangers inherent at this stage of a developing relationship:

> Quite understandable concentration on erotic excess, for example, child sexual abuse, has made it very hard to stay with erotic deficit … there is the risk of being misunderstood as advocating incest … we begin to think of *an optimal erotic relation between father and daughter and, hence, of the pathology of a failure to achieve that.*
>
> *(p. 54, emphasis in original)*

The daughter needs to be in the psychologically strong position of being able to sexually renounce the father and, paradoxically, be able to be close to him as an adult woman. In terms of her developing awareness of eroticism (both her own erotic potential and the erotic masculine, assuming heterosexuality), the father (as the primary man in her life) needs to have a safe sexual presence around the daughter so that her erotic boundaries develop in a healthy way, and that she gains an understanding of the erotic potential of the masculine, constellating and assimilating this aspect of life within her psyche. Erotic playback is one of the various functions and *presences* of the father. Father hunger arises when this erotic playback is either not provided, as in the fathers described by Maine who shy away from the reality of the evidence of their daughters' maturation, or when damaged fathers fall into their Shadow and take the erotic playback too literally, and sexually abuse their daughters. Relating this to *American Beauty*, Lester is depicted from the beginning as failing to provide sufficient presence to Jane (erotic, physical or otherwise) that consequently leads to Jane's feelings of father hunger, expressed at the beginning and throughout the film. Where Lester does provide erotic feedback, it is when he first encounters her best friend Angela Hayes (Mena Suvari) at the high school basketball game, beginning the narrative in earnest.

Analysis of this key scene reveals a mediation of symbolic, rather than semiotic, archetypal imagery in their raw form. The scene begins by the camera focusing on Carolyn and Lester as they take their place on the bleachers to the darkened interior of the basketball court, deliberately dull suburban clothes and all. We then switch to Lester's point of view (POV) as the cheerleaders, Jane and Angela included, begin their cheerleading dance to staccato music that mimics the ticking of a clock, reflected in their automaton-like dance moves and lit up to emphasise them and them alone. The camera switches back to Lester's POV as the deliberately dream-like image of Angela is revealed, prompting an accompanying deliberate and distinct change in tempo of music, colour, sound and camera angle as the *mise en scène* changes dramatically and explosively. This deliberately theatrical change (echoing Mendes' previous role as a theatre director) employing harsh lighting on both Lester and Angela to reinforce the psychic connection between the two, is deeply symbolic as Mendes mediates the initial archetypal image of Lester's *anima* awakening in all of its primal psychic power.

This is Lester's first encounter with the sexually powerful aspect of his *anima*, and it is this power that finally seizes his attention and begins his individuation process. After an increasing series of camera close-ups on Lester's comically astonished face, the sequence progresses with the main motif and image being depicted. Angela is shown as both objectified as Lester's focus of desire, her unambiguously sexual look towards him culminating in her opening her jacket to reveal not her body and breasts as an audience might think, but instead a shower of red rose petals which fly out at a shocked Lester, at which point his dream/revelation ends abruptly and he (and the audience) is shown as returning to the diegetic reality of the basketball court.

A rose by any other name ...

The rose marks the start of Lester's awakening. The film uses the rose, specifically red roses, to symbolise this change. The rose can be analysed in a number of different ways. The petals not only resembling female sexual organs, particularly the labia, the flower also carries a pleasing scent or perfume, both physical attributes that resonates strongly with desire, sexuality and life. On a more symbolic level, the rose has been linked to goddess worship, particularly goddesses of love and fertility, reflecting its pan-culturally recognised symbolism. The rose also has more mystical associations:

> For alchemists, the entire process of psychic transformation takes place sub rosa (under the rose).... In alchemy the crossed branches of the white and red rose not only allude to the 'love affair' of opposite natures, and to the albedo and rubedo as understanding and realisation of psychic processes, but also to the silence necessary to the interior nature of the work and the womb or 'rose' within whose petalled folds the Self is secretly conceived.
>
> *(Ronnberg and Martin, 2010, pp. 162–163)*

Mendes uses the rose as a strongly symbolic signifier of psychic transformation, in this case Lester's symbolic psychic re-birth and partial awakening from an immature and emotionally asleep father and husband to a more self-aware and mature man and parent. The imagery is developed and mediated in a number of ways, from our first glimpse of Carolyn Burnham tending to her ruthlessly controlled and pruned 'American Beauty' rose bushes (her handling of her flowers with gloves can be read as indicative of both a distrust of the symbolic power of the rose, hence the need for control, as well as an appreciation of their thorny nature), to their sexually symbolic power signalling the continuation of Lester's psychological journey. Returning to the scene after the basketball game, we are then shown an excruciatingly embarrassing (for Jane) first encounter with Angela where Lester and Carolyn are introduced to Angela. For her own part, Angela displays preternatural awareness of the true state of the Burnham's marriage, when she contradicts Jane's disgruntled assertion about her father being inadequate, with an acutely perceptive observation about the lack of sexual contact that the Burnham parents are suffering.

At this point Angela is depicted as fulfilling, at first glance, Lester's sexual fantasies about her. She is initially portrayed as worldly, aware of her sexual capital and power over men via the agency of her looks and her body, referenced particularly in a previous scene with Jane where she recounts her growing awareness of her sexuality, her beauty and the effect it has on men. This depiction of Angela as a Lolita-esque figure continues throughout the film, with her true state of virginity and sexual inexperience only revealed at the end in another pivotal scene with Lester. Returning to the scene after the encounter above, we are then shown Lester in bed in another symbolic dream sequence, grinning in amazement and wonder as red rose petals (presumably of the American Beauty variety) fall gently all around him from above. His POV then shows a numinous version of Angela floating above him on an inverted and literal bed of roses, her body coyly covered strategically with petals. Mendes deliberately stylises Lester's fantasies in all of the dream sequences within the film to a high degree. Directly referencing 'sub rosa' as quoted above, Lester is depicted as beginning his *anima*-inspired journey towards aware father and mature man. Lester is quite literally under the power of the rose (*anima*) and it is working its psychic magic upon him to bring him out of his mental and emotional torpor. Going further, the rose, is both a symbol of beauty (referenced throughout the film and on the film's publicity materials – adverts, posters etc. – upon its release) and spirit. As Stevens has noted it is also:

> The Western equivalent of the lotus (allegorical symbol of creation and individuation) … the individuation of the Self. For the Christians, it refers to the chalice, the blood of Christ, the promise of redemption and resurrection, and the certainty of divine love … Aphrodite caused the red rose to grow from the blood of her slain lover, Adonis.
>
> *(1998, p. 389)*

This Shadow side of the rose (that it sprang from spilled blood, and that its thorns can draw blood as in various fairy tales) and its accompanying psychic power is also explored by Mendes in the final scenes of the film in which the dramatic narrative comes to a climax. Deepening his auteurial signature, he also utilises a number of other symbols to generate affective power, namely rain (water), blood and doorways. The background to these scenes is dominated by rain, with darkness falling in the evening to add to the imagery. In terms of numinous symbolism, this is highly significant. As with later films such as *The Road to Perdition*, rain is a primal indicator of spiritual cleansing and soul revitalisation:

> Rain is a miraculous visitation of heavenly power…. The alchemists saw the falling rain as the 'washing' of the *nigredo* state, illuminating and reanimating what felt dead and dark. This divine intervention of grace occurring at the darkest point preceded a new *coniunctio*, a psychic union of emotion, body, imagination and mind in a new level of consciousness.
>
> *(Ronnberg and Martin, 2010, p. 62)*

Water is depicted as a transforming symbolic force within the film; rain in particular symbolising a renewal of Lester's psyche and his maturation towards individuation. The imagery

Mendes uses is also highly reminiscent of horror films. His encounter with Angela is lit with rain clearly visible on window and with stark shadows and occasional rumblings of thunder as well. This direct hint at the Shadow aspects (the *nigredo* state) is indicated by the *mise en scène* in its claustrophobic framing, close-ups of faces, a darker palette of colours and harsher expressions of Shadow from the actors; powerful forces, both repressive and expressive, are on the march here.

Within the house, Lester is in the position of having his sexual fantasies fulfilled with Angela as she needs reassurance from someone that she is not ordinary after her fight with Jane and Ricky. When he discovers that, far from being the rose-petalled numinous being his psyche woke him to, she is a virgin, his awakening as a man and father is complete. His fantasies about Angela (which are all they have been up to this point) have collided with the reality of his position that he finds himself in that he realises that his desires have led him not to pleasure but to a truth about himself. The erotic playback – as defined by Samuels earlier – with a girl his daughter's age that he nearly gets so wrong fulfils its role in jolting him awake to become a mature man. This awakening enables Lester to experience a brief moment of numinosity in his final scene. Lester is alone and absorbing what just happened. He looks like a man renewed, and picks up a family photo of his daughter and wife in happier times, murmuring to himself as he does. The camera then pans away to a silver pistol pointed at the back of his head. This then cuts to an arrangement of (blood) red roses, stark against a white wall. An excruciating pause, then a gunshot echoes out, followed by a bloody splatter against the wall.

This mature realisation and the deep joy it is hinted at bringing, is both underscored and catalysed by Lester's last action, that of picking up a photo of his family and studying it (despite the chaos his hitherto largely selfish actions have wrought within his family up until now). Mendes cuts this experience short with his violent death, the red and white colour scheme that has been used consistently throughout the film echoed in his last moments as his brains are spread across the wall by Colonel Fitts's (the Shadow father) bullet, accompanied by the ubiquitous roses. We are forcefully reminded that the rose was held as springing up from the blood of a slain lover; both petals and thorns are therefore present, a reminder of the dangerous aspects of desire and of *Eros* energy. Blood, the symbol for both death and life, of sex, desire, etc., is used here in conscious conjunction with the rose: 'Blood symbolises our feeling for the sacredness of life before we distance ourselves in bloodless, abstract thought – it is the soul of embodied life, forming our essential character' (ibid., p. 396). The joining together of matter and spirit is powerfully invoked in the image of Lester lying dead in a pool of dark red blood, smiling at an unseen joke. Symbolically, the blood acts as the *coniunctio*, invoked not only by the rain outside as quoted above, but the mortal fluid that Lester is losing. This 'psychic union of emotion, body, imagination and mind in a new level of consciousness' (ibid., p. 62) is expressed as the film concludes with Lester's voiceover reassuring us of the benevolent force behind everyday life (similar to Ricky Fitts's earlier realisation) we are led through a poignant montage of images from his life.

Lester, as a father, is portrayed as being redeemed by this display of the mature paternal, finally realising that his role as husband and father is in itself a sacralised and spiritual role that he is now fully ready to embrace and inhabit. Mendes portrays the solution to father hunger as a numinous awakening, with both children and fathers potentially benefitting from this transformation, benefits that, alas, are cut short by death. Mendes achieves Fredericksen's 'living tie' (2001, p. 28) connection between semiotic and symbolic imagery, resulting in strong audience affect, if we are to judge by the commercial success and overall critical reception of the film when it was released (two Oscars for Best Picture and for Best Original Screenplay).

In terms of auteurs and the mediation of imagery, both archetypal and other, there is room to go further. Future investigations around the auteur acting as a conscious mediator of both semiotic and symbolic imagery do not have to be restricted to the function of the auteur practising a technique of self/Self. Indeed it is arguable that all of Staiger's original seven definitions of authorship can be fulfilled by the author being recognised as an agent practising mediation of imagery, albeit with some definitions (signature, origin and personality) being more obvious to analyse and explore than others. This flexibility in definitions allows other agents, not just the director, to be credited as the author of a film (producer, studio, writer, actor, etc.), and echoes the concerns around industrial and commercial definitions from earlier. The other major area of interest that post-Jungian analyses of mediation of imagery would naturally lead to is affect and reception studies with Singh (2009, 2014) already fruitfully exploring this area. Bearing in mind the arguments and examples given in this chapter, more research in these areas is needed to contribute to the current and future debates that surround auteurship and affect; we can only hope that it will be forthcoming.

References

Biddulph, S. (1998) *Manhood: an action plan for changing men's lives*. Lane Cove, Australia: Finch Publishing.

Bly, R. (2001) *Iron John: men and masculinity*, 2nd edn. London: Rider.

Bruzzi, S. (2005) *Bringing up daddy: fatherhood and masculinity in post-war Hollywood*. London: British Film Institute.

Caughie, J. (1981) *Theories of authorship*. London: Routledge.

Chachere, R. (2003) *Jungian reflections on literary and film classics: opus I: American Beauty*. Lafayette, LA: Cypremort Point Press.

Fredericksen, D. (2001) 'Jung/sign/symbol/film', in I. Alister and C. Hauke (eds), *Jung and film: post-Jungian takes on the moving image*. London: Routledge. pp. 17–55. (Originally published as two essays in the *Quarterly Review of Film Studies*, 1979, 1980.)

Gerstner, D. A. and Staiger, J. (eds) (2003) *Authorship and film*. London: Routledge.

Grant, B. K. (ed.) (2008) *Auteurs and authorship: a film reader*. Oxford: Blackwell Publishing Ltd.

Hauke, C. and Alister, I. (eds) (2001) *Jung & film: post-Jungian takes on the moving image*. Hove: Brunner-Routledge.

Hockley, L. (2007) *Frames of mind: a post-Jungian look at cinema, television and technology*. Bristol: Intellect Books.

Izod, J. (2006) *Screen, culture, psyche: a post-Jungian approach to working with the audience*. Hove: Routledge.

Jung, C. G. (1947/54) 'On the nature of the psyche', in *The collected works of C. G. Jung*, Vol. 8, *The structure and dynamics of the psyche*, 2nd edn. London: Routledge, 1969.

Maine, M. (2004) *Father hunger: fathers, daughters and the pursuit of thinness*. Carlsbad, CA: Gurze Books.

Moore, R. and Gillette, D. (1992) *The king within: accessing the king in the male psyche*. New York: William Morrow & Company, Inc.

Ronnberg, A. and Martin, K. (eds) (2010) *The book of symbols: reflections on archetypal images*. Cologne: Taschen.

Rountree, C. (2008) 'Auteur film directors as contemporary shamans', *Jung Journal*, 2(2), pp. 123–34.

Samuels, A. (1993) *The political psyche*. London: Routledge.

Samuels, A., Shorter, B. and Plaut, F. (eds) (1986) *A critical dictionary of Jungian analysis*. London: Routledge & Kegan Paul.

Sellors, C. P. (2010) *Film authorship: auteurs and other myths*. London: Wallflower Press.

Singh, G. (2009) *Film after Jung: post-Jungian approaches to film theory*. Hove: Routledge.

Singh, G. (2014) *Feeling film: affect and authenticity in popular cinema*. Hove: Routledge.

Staiger, J. (2003) 'Authorship approaches', in D. A. Gerstner and J. Staiger (eds), *Authorship and film*. London: Routledge. pp. 27–60.

Stam, R. and Miller, T. (2000) *Film theory: an anthology*. Oxford: Blackwell Publishing Ltd.

Stevens, A. (1998) *Ariadne's clue: a guide to the symbols of humankind*. London: Penguin Books.

Winnicott, D. W. (1973) *The child, the family, and the outside world*. London: Penguin Ltd.

Online source

Barthes, R. (1967) 'The death of the author', *Aspen: The Magazine in a Box*, no. 5 + 6, item 3. Available at: www.ubu.com/aspen/aspen5and6/threeEssays.html#barthes [Accessed 10 December 2017].

Filmography

American beauty. (1999) [film] Directed by Sam Mendes. USA.
Road to perdition, The. (2002) [film] Directed by Sam Mendes. USA.
Skyfall. (2012) [film] Directed by Sam Mendes. USA/UK.
Spectre. (2015) [film] Directed by Sam Mendes. USA/UK.

13

BEYOND THE MALE
HERO MYTH IN
CLINT EASTWOOD FILMS

Steve Myers

Introduction

Jung saw little value in artistic analysis that focused only on identifying the archetypes in a work of art, or in demonstrating how such art conformed to a recognised myth, such as the hero. He argued that such an approach could sometimes disguise or 'cloak' the significant meaning the work contains (1930/50: §143). For Jung, the value of any form of art or literature lies not in reaffirming the myths we already know, but in promoting psychological health, transforming individual lives and relationships, and in the advancement of contemporary culture through the discovery of new meanings. It follows this is not achieved in cinema by highlighting the archetypal or mythical structures it contains, but by recognising how a film goes beyond and transcends previous versions of those myths.

In his brief references to cinema, Jung admitted that he had neglected the medium in his writings. He suggested cinema had two main roles: the first is to provide an outlet for the excitement, passion, and fantasy that is repressed in everyday life, which helps maintain psychological balance or psychic health; the second is to bring about a 'new self-appraisal, a reassessment of our fundamental human nature' (1928/31: §195) that enables the transformation of the individual, relationships, and society. The contributions made by Eastwood's films to Jung's first role for cinema – an outlet for repressed contents – are fairly clear. His ability to invoke various emotions has developed from the early days of creating excitement, fear, and amusement, to more recent work that touches deeper themes of tragedy, hope, and love. This development is due in part to his use of the hero myth but also to many other factors, including his attitude of continual learning, his and his collaborators' increasing artisanship, and the improving quality of scripts and other resources that became available to him.

The contribution of Eastwood's work to the second role – individual and cultural transformation – might not be so obvious, because it requires recognition of how he has gone beyond the hero myth. To describe the process of transformation, Jung used the term *individuation*. This came via Nietzsche (Jung, 1913: §876) from Schopenhauer's use of the old scholastic phrase *principium individuationis*, which denotes the background of time and space that enables something to appear as different (1969, pp. 112–13). Therefore, individuation involves differentiation from what has gone before (whilst maintaining some continuity and links with it). With regards to the hero myth, this means recognising what is unique about the contemporary

163

use of it, how it is changing, and how people and society are being transformed into something new that is more whole and unique.

This chapter will examine how Eastwood has gone beyond the hero myth and how this has contributed to individuation or transformation. In the first section, *Unforgiven* (dir. Eastwood, 1992) will serve as an example of how film can be related to individuation in four different ways. Those perspectives will then be used in the main body of the text to examine three main periods of development in Eastwood's career and work – heroic, transitional, and post-heroic. The chapter will conclude with a review of the impact his later work has had on the lives of various people, the cultural significance that has emerged, and how it has radically reshaped the perception of the hero myth itself.

Throughout the chapter, no attempt will be made to draw a clear distinction between Eastwood's on-screen and off-screen personas. Although the relationship between the two would be an interesting investigation, what concerns us here is the journey they have gone through together. For the first forty years or so, Eastwood followed a traditional path of differentiating and exploiting a one-sided heroic persona in both his private and professional life. But in the last couple of decades he and his films have arguably entered a more advanced stage of individuation. This has resulted in a more sophisticated cinematic contribution that has affected not only the lives and culture of his viewers but also many others.

Four ways of viewing *Unforgiven*

Unforgiven is a western film that opens with one of the prostitutes in a brothel being disfigured by a client. The Sheriff orders the offender to compensate the brothel owner for loss of income. The prostitutes then call for help and offer a reward to anyone who can dispense a fairer justice. William Munny (Clint Eastwood) answers the call – though his morality, motivations, and heroic nature become increasingly ambiguous as the film progresses. The film concludes with Munny dispensing justice to both the offender and the sheriff. *Unforgiven* is arguably Eastwood's best film. In 2016 it had a rating of 8.3 at IMDB, which is bettered only by *The Good, The Bad and The Ugly* (dir. Leone, 1966). Eastwood received an Oscar nomination for Best Actor, and won Best Director and Best Picture (through his production company Malpaso), which was matched only by *Million Dollar Baby* (dir. Eastwood, 2004). After adjustment for ticket price inflation, *Unforgiven* achieved his second highest box-office receipts as director (boxofficemojo.com, 2016), which was surpassed only by *American Sniper* (dir. Eastwood, 2014). And rotten tomatoes.com (2016) rated *Unforgiven* as his second best movie as director – surpassed only by *High Plains Drifter* (dir. Eastwood, 1973).

However, the quality of a film is not what makes it significant to a Jungian inquiry, because as Jung notes, 'products of highly dubious merit are often of the greatest interest to the psychologist' (1930/50: §136). Rather, the key question is how it helps the self-appraisal and transformation of individuals and society. For this task, there are four main ways to relate cinema to personal or cultural development – looking at its structure, deconstructing it, interpreting it, or using an alchemical approach. These perspectives are derived from two of Jung's important dichotomies.

The first is between *visionary* art, which emerges from contemporary activity in the collective unconscious, and *psychological* art, which is based on conscious sources (ibid.: §139ff.). The second distinction is from his model of personality development, which he described as *constructive* – concerned with 'becoming' – rather than *reductive* – concerned with explaining (1914: §399). Although Jung associated the latter with Freud's approach, he still saw it as helpful, as providing information that can support the constructive process of becoming (ibid.: §413).

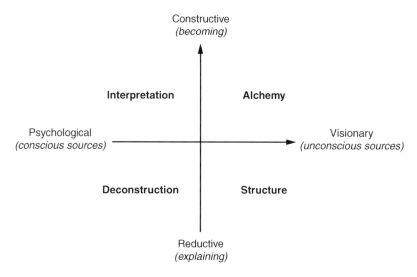

Figure 13.1 Four ways of relating to cinema.

If we focus on the underlying *structure* of a film, we show how it conforms to recurring unconscious (archetypal or mythic) patterns. *Unforgiven*'s conformity to Joseph Campbell's heroic monomyth has been demonstrated by Voytilla (1999). For example, Eastwood's character of William Munny starts out in the *ordinary world* of his farm, he receives a *call to adventure* to avenge a disfigured prostitute, he *refuses the call* by saying 'I ain't like that anymore' (Voytilla, 1999, p. 72). Campbell believed that the recognition of such patterns helps individuals and society to 'come to an understanding of the deep forces that have shaped ... both our private and public lives' (1993, p. 256). However, Jung saw little value in rediscovering age-old myths per se, because such structures are already well understood, and in the 'eternally repeated joys and sorrows ... there is no work left' (1930/50: §139).

A *deconstruction* of a film looks at the assumptions on which the film is based, particularly in terms of oppositional principles, and within a particular context. For example, the Sheriff's decision to compensate the brothel owner serves to problematise the relationship between morality and power in what was a pioneering system of justice. Deconstruction of this incident might lead to a better understanding of the various influences under which a nineteenth century Sheriff was appointed and made decisions. An *interpretation* of the film involves viewing its content subjectively, as reflecting aspects of the viewer or contemporary society, and interpreting what it means in terms of personal or cultural development. This can be seen, for example, in a PhD study that reads *Unforgiven* hermeneutically as examining ethical and existential problems that yield for the viewer a 'surplus of meaning' (Friedman, 2012). A practical example is that some viewers might see how the Sheriff has acted unfairly, and then reflect on how that can inform their own use of power and justice, or perhaps their experience of victimhood. Another interpretation, at the cultural level, is that *Unforgiven* undermines America's view of its own history by portraying the gun-slinging hero in unconventional and ambiguous terms. This could be viewed as reflecting the United States' uncertainty about its identity following the end of the cold war (Ruiz, 2011, p. 129).

Finally, *alchemy* is an interaction with film that results in some form of individual or societal transformation. Most of Jung's writings on alchemy referred to psychotherapy, in which the 'meeting of two personalities is like the contact of two chemical substances: if there is any reaction, both are transformed' (1933, pp. 49–50). *Unforgiven* had a transformative effect on Eastwood's career, with some reviews seeing it as his 'turning point' (Valero, 2011). However, as far as the hero myth and individuation are concerned, there are other turning points that are of greater cultural significance. We will discover these as we follow the development of the hero myth throughout Eastwood's life and work.

Clint Eastwood's oeuvre

Over a period of forty years, Eastwood developed a one-sided, sophisticated, and morally ambiguous heroic persona that mirrored his own personality to some extent. As one reviewer of a recent film put it, 'we can't quite be sure where the boundaries between character and actor lie' (O'Hehir, 2012). The unauthorised McGilligan biography – published in 1999 and revised in 2015 – not only recognised the admiration and loyalty that Eastwood engendered in others, but also exposed a controlling shadow of womanising, betrayal, disloyalty, and vengeful mistreatment of those who crossed him, in both his professional and personal relationships. During McGilligan's research for the book, he was 'struck by how many people … really hated Clint and made no bones about it … Clint … has left many broken friends and outright enemies in his wake' (1999, pp. 542–3). The closeness of on- and off-screen personas may be due to the significant influence Eastwood had over his characters, scripts, and films, even in his early career. Whatever the reason, some believe that many of the characters (not just his own) are his projections (e.g. ibid., p. 281).

Nevertheless, despite his significant personal influence, the films can still be viewed as largely a cultural rather than individual phenomenon. There were many external collective influences on the content of his films – such as the people and companies involved in each collaboration, expectations of audiences, need for commercial success, scripts/ideas provided by others, or inspiring world events such as the fall of apartheid that led to *Invictus* (dir. Eastwood, 2009). Eastwood is not being treated as an auteur in this chapter. His personal career is merely the gateway to discover the activities in the cultural layers of the collective unconscious.

Heroic period

The process of individuation begins with an undifferentiated personality, and Eastwood began his career as an unknown actor. Initially, he had a few minor roles that were not always credited including in *Revenge of the Creature* (dir. Arnold, 1955), *Lady Godiva* (dir. Lubin, 1955), and *The First Travelling Saleslady* (dir. Lubin, 1956). As his roles grew, he quickly began to differentiate and identify with an on-screen heroic persona, which is belied by his reaction to seeing *Ambush at Cimarron Pass* (dir. Coplan, 1958). Although it was his biggest part at that time, it made Eastwood feel 'really depressed' (McGilligan, 1999, p. 93), he considered giving up acting, and he regarded it as the low point in his career. The reasons for this are not immediately obvious. The film was a similar quality to his previous film, *Lafayette Escadrille* (dir. Wellman, 1958), and his portrayal of the character is fine. (This is both my subjective judgement and the evidence of reviews. *Lafayette* scores 5.8 at imdb.com and 33 per cent at rottentomatoes.com, whereas *Ambush at Cimarron Pass* scores 5.4 and 36 per cent respectively). What is different is the nature of the role he plays. In *Lafayette Escadrille* he has a smaller part, but it is a tough character. In *Ambush at Cimarron Pass* he plays a weak character that is petulant, ineffective, gets easily beaten in a fistfight, competes for the affections of a lady but loses out, and is referred to disparagingly as a boy.

Eastwood's embarrassment might be the first major hint that something visionary and of unconscious significance was occurring. In this case, it is probably related to the process of individuation, to his emerging need to identify with a cinematic hero. Jung summarised the process of individuation using the rather cryptic wording of the *Axiom of Maria*: 'One becomes two, two becomes three, and out of the third comes the One as the fourth' (1951: §237). Stage one is unconsciousness – i.e. lacking self-awareness and not discerning differences between the opposites. This relates to the period when Eastwood was an unknown actor. Stage two involves differentiating a one-sided conscious standpoint – in this case, a one-sided hero. It is one-sided because it seeks to triumph over its opposite in the world – e.g. good defeating evil, or truth prevailing over falsehood, or democracy taking the place of autocracy, or winning support for certain religious or political ideologies. In the case of *Ambush at Cimarron Pass*, Eastwood felt embarrassment because of his distaste for the role. It was the antithesis of the hero that he was differentiating and with which he, and a viewing public, wanted to identify.

Over the next forty years, Eastwood was able to differentiate/cultivate the persona of the one-sided, triumphant hero that he wanted, and for which society was looking. It was established through the television series including *Rawhide* (1958–66), the 'Man With No Name' spaghetti westerns, various other films, and *Dirty Harry* (dir. Siegel, 1971). These heroes were one-sided because they achieved something at the expense of others. In *The Good, The Bad and The Ugly* (1966), the Man With No Name acquires gold at the expense of the other protagonists (the characters played by Eli Wallach and Lee Van Cleef). In *Where Eagles Dare* (dir. Hutton, 1968), Clint Eastwood's character is part of the Allied force that steals secret information from the Nazis and exposes a high-level spy. And in *Dirty Harry*, Eastwood overcomes challenges of various sorts to get rid of an evil murderer.

In early films, Eastwood's heroes tended to be relatively shallow and 'what little back story there was to some of his characters would consist of mentioning that he was a decorated veteran' (McGilligan, 1999, p. 48). McGilligan explained this recurrence of the veteran theme as being 'fantasy projections, or wish fulfilment' (ibid.) because, during Eastwood's conscription in the early 1950s, he had managed to avoid serving in a war zone. This meant he was not in Korea for *Heartbreak Ridge*, the subject of 'one of his more jingoistic films' (ibid., p. 51). Over time, however, Eastwood increasingly tried to define himself (i.e. his on-screen persona) as being a morally complex hero as in the ambiguity of *Unforgiven*'s William Munny.

Although he deconstructed the hero ultimately Eastwood's heroes remained one-sided, through to the end of the century. The deconstruction was part of his ongoing differentiation of the hero, which continued to take the side of good in defeating the bad. Nevertheless, throughout this period there were increasing signs of the potential to move away from the one-sided 'good guy beats the baddies' plot. For example, *The Beguiled* (dir. Siegel, 1971) – which shows some signs of visionary material due to Eastwood being 'intrigued' (2013, p. 10) and engrossed by the book (McGilligan, 1999, p. 185) – demonstrated both the damage that war can do and the vulnerability of the veteran. In *Magnum Force* (dir. Post, 1973), Dirty Harry defends the baddies against an extreme form of police vigilantism. In *The Eiger Sanction* (dir. Eastwood, 1975), Eastwood's character stops short of killing his assassination target. At the end of *White Hunter Black Heart* (dir. Eastwood, 1990), he departs from (what is believed to be) the true story to pointedly undermine the morality of his cinematic, heroic macho (McGilligan, 1999, p. 454). And, in *Unforgiven* (1992), William Munny's face shows regret for having killed a harmless man – which for an Eastwood character seemed revolutionary at the time (Edelstein, 2003).

Transitional period

The heroic period in Eastwood's development occupied nearly forty years and involved greater differentiation and refinement of the one-sided hero. Despite the changes, and increased ambiguities, his persona always remained a hero, one for whom good ultimately triumphed over evil, albeit in more sophisticated and subtle ways. The most important stage of Eastwood's on-screen individuation was yet to come, and it begins after the turn of the century. For the *New York Times* film critic David Edelstein (2003), there was a watershed moment in *Mystic River* (dir. Eastwood, 2003):

> *Mystic River* was a watershed because in every film before this one, the vigilantism … was justified … Eastwood rigged the scenarios so that the right people always did get shot … Eastwood, who has confronted every variety of psychopath, has never regarded an evil so nebulous, so deep in the hearts of good men. It is as if he is looking into the abyss for the first time.

This suggests that Eastwood was entering the third stage of the *Axiom of Maria*, which involves abandoning the one-sided perspective and recognising the value of the opposite. This creates a tension between two opposing and contradictory principles, which reaches a conspicuous climax with the release of *Flags of Our Fathers* (dir. Eastwood, 2006) and *Letters from Iwo Jima* (dir. Eastwood, 2006). Originally, there was only meant to be one film, which examined the impact of using heroes to raise war funds. However, during the initial research, Eastwood grew 'curious' (2013, p. 207) about the Japanese general Tadamichi Kuribayashi whom the American generals seemed to regard with respect. As he investigated further, he was struck by the poignancy of a father writing to his children during the intensity of battle. Eastwood also found it an overwhelming experience to visit the island and (implicitly from the Japanese point of view) to visualise an armada of invading ships coming in. Emotions such as curiosity, poignancy, and being overwhelmed suggest that something visionary is happening – in this case, an unconscious drive to move from stage two, to stage three of the *Axiom of Maria*.

Eastwood's interaction with *Flags of Our Fathers* was alchemical – it led to a transformation of attitude from which emerged a second film. No longer were good people defeating evil people, but the good and evil was *on both sides*. Eastwood (now in his mid-seventies) had stopped differentiating the one-sided hero in film, and taken the individuating step of 'differentiation of the self from the opposites' (Jung, 1921: §183). He dispassionately treated what had previously been hero and enemy as now heroes of equal value in Western and Eastern culture. From this development two films emerged namely *Flags of Our Fathers* which provided the US perspective, and *Letters from Iwo Jima*, which Eastwood commissioned from scratch to provide the Japanese perspective. Film critic Ken Turan (2006), of the *Los Angeles Times*, wrote of the two films:

> Though each project stands on its own merits … they inevitably inform one another.… But while each film reinforces the other, it is 'Letters' that is finally the more remarkable accomplishment, a feat of empathetic cross-cultural connection that Eastwood … more or less willed into existence.… What Eastwood seemed to sense intuitively was the connection between his own themes of men being men and the challenges of masculinity, and the notions of honor, duty and heroism that are embedded in Japanese culture and tradition.

The cycle of the *Axiom of Maria* is not yet complete, however. Whilst the films recognised the value of the opposites in equal terms, they were kept very separate. They still needed to be transcended and reconciled, which is the fourth stage of the *Axiom of Maria*. Eastwood makes a significant move in this direction in his next film that touches on the theme of heroes – *Gran Torino* (dir. Eastwood, 2008). He plays a veteran of the Korean War (with Hmong neighbours) whom many reviewers saw as 'a complex and affecting compendium of all the Dirty Harrys that went before' (McGilligan, 2015, p. 572). However, from the perspective of the *Axiom of Maria*, such references to Dirty Harry focus on the old one-sidedness and miss the greater significance of the film, which is the move towards a post-heroic integration of Western and Eastern culture.

At the start of *Gran Torino*, Eastwood's character (Walt Kowalski) has a pejorative view of the Hmong. This is a one-sided perspective that corresponds to stage two of the *Axiom of Maria*. Over the course of the film, through various incidents, he begins to recognise their good side, which creates a paradox. How can a criminal who tries to steal his car also be his friend? The resolution of this type of paradox can only emerge from the unconscious. As Jung puts it: 'It would … be pointless to call upon consciousness to decide the conflict.… A conscious decision … could never supply … an irrational solution of a logical antithesis. For this we must go deeper; we must descend into the foundations of consciousness' (1921: §180).

This shows how consciousness must play its part in this process by holding the tension of opposites and waiting for an unconscious solution to emerge. This can be likened to a fire-fighter prising open the doors of a lift to allow its occupants to escape. In *Gran Torino*, Kowalski begins to hold the tension of opposites by accepting help from the Hmong neighbour who tried to steal his car. He then learns more about their culture and starts to value it as well as his own (stage three of the *Axiom of Maria*). Eventually, they develop a sense of mutual respect and establish a relationship that transcends their different cultures – which corresponds to stage four of the *Axiom of Maria*.

This fourth stage is also represented by the climax of *Gran Torino*, following an incident that creates a contradiction that can't be solved without compromising either legal justice or moral fairness. In previous films, such as *The Bridges of Madison County* (dir. Eastwood, 1995) or *Million Dollar Baby* (dir. Eastwood, 2004), there were often contradictions that needed to be resolved – such as who should Francesca choose, or should Frankie live or die? In those films, the conflict is dealt with by making a choice between the two opposites. In *Gran Torino*, however, a third option emerges – a *deus ex machina* – which is a previously unseen solution that transcends the two choices and resolves the conflict. The final act of the Eastwood character in *Gran Torino* reflects the wording of the final stage of the *Axiom of Maria* – out of the third (holding the tension between justice and fairness) comes the one (the initially unconscious solution, not apparent in the earlier plot) as the fourth (the conflict between justice and fairness is transcended and resolved without either being sacrificed). Eastwood's work had taken a new direction, beyond the classic hero myth. This was widely recognised (though not by all) and, towards the end of his transitional period before the release of *Gran Torino*, he was given a special award at Cannes – 'a combination of a lifetime achievement award and an acknowledgement of bold new work' (Dargis and Scott, 2008).

Post-heroic period

Having integrated these opposites, Eastwood's next film – *Invictus* (2009) – revisits the theme of heroism, but from the new perspective that no longer identifies with the one-sided hero. The lead character in this film (Nelson Mandela) sought to transform South Africa through holding the tension of opposites. The film sets the scene with Mandela being released and then elected as President. A TV commentator says 'there is a new hero in south Africa', but questions whether he can balance black hopes with white fears. Mandela's first action, when he moves into the presidential office, is to address the white staff who are expecting to be sacked – making them feel wanted and welcome. He forces black and white security staff that have a deep distrust of each other, to work together as his personal guard. He overcomes opposition on both sides to ensure that old symbols from both black and white cultures are used in the new South Africa. What emerged from this holding of the tension of opposites, and other examples such as the Truth and Reconciliation Commission (not depicted in the film), was a more united, tolerant, and collaborative South Africa.

Mandela's actions were not those of a one-sided hero because he rejected appeals to introduce black culture at the *expense* of the white. But he could still be viewed as a hero of sorts, because he helped to transform South Africa. In Eastwood's earlier years, his cinematic hero had provided an outlet for passion and fantasy. The sense of victory his hero gave, when good triumphs over evil in the world, relates to stage two of the *Axiom of Maria*. But if characters such as Mandela are still to be viewed as heroic then it is a different form of heroism. In stage three of the *Axiom of Maria* this type of hero maintains the tension of opposites (Samuels, Shorter, and Plaut, 1986, p. 66) and, in stage four, the ego obtains from the unconscious the new knowledge that is transformational. This is how analytical psychology reinterprets the hero myth, based on a subjective form of hero who 'does not seek to change the world ... but to transform the personality. Self-transformation is his true aim' (Neumann, 1949, p. 220). In Mandela's case, it was self-transformation of a whole country.

The next film to revisit the topic of heroism from Eastwood's new perspective was *J. Edgar* (2011). Based on another true story, the format of the film is a narrative within a narrative. Hoover dictates his life story to a biographer, which is enacted on screen through flashbacks. Early on in the film, Hoover says that it is important to clarify who are the villains and who are the heroes. Towards the end, he lists the various groups that he saved the country from during his lifetime. However, his lifelong friend Clyde Tolson points out that his story is exaggerated: Hoover had reconstructed his story to include heroic events in which he was not involved. The film is an example of someone identifying with the hero to such an extent that he remained stuck in stage two of the *Axiom of Maria*. He saw his role until the end of life as defeating the evil people in society. Where the reality didn't quite match up to the hero myth with which he identified, he changed his memory of the reality to fit his projections. This film was a cultural comment about over-identification with the hero archetype that Eastwood is unlikely to have made earlier in his career.

Eastwood's most recent film (at the time of writing) is *American Sniper* (2014). It is based on the true story of Chris Kyle, who served in four tours in Iraq and who was given a hero's funeral when he was killed in 2013. The film sparked a wide range of reactions, with some describing it as 'classic Clint Eastwood ... Dirty Harry vs the bad guys' (Dervis, 2015), as a shoot 'em up that praised war and warriors (Sharrett, 2015), or as the myth of the trauma hero (Scranton, 2015). For others, it generated intense emotions and launched a war of words, with some reviewers describing the film as repugnant, xenophobic, or an example of unexamined jingoism (McGilligan, 2015, p. 987). For example, Michael Moore tweeted that snipers are cowards, which prompted a bitter response from high-profile supporters not only of Eastwood but also of Kyle and US forces (Bash, 2015). The film had to be pulled from cinemas in Iraq because some members of the audience were deeply offended by it portraying Iraqis as terrorists (Sly, 2015). The *New York Times* also saw it in a one-sided way, as reaffirming Eastwood's commitment to the themes of vengeance and justice in a fallen world: 'violence is a moral necessity, albeit one that often exacts a cost from those who must wield it in the service of good' (Scott, 2014). Others viewed it as one-sided in the opposite direction, as anti-war – a characterisation with which Eastwood agreed (Kilday, 2015). *Film Journal International* thought that it seemed a straightforward war movie at the start, but then it showed Eastwood as deconstructing basic assumptions about warfare: it shows the Iraqis to be facing an inscrutable, capricious occupying force; Kyle is portrayed as broken by his experiences; it highlights the difficulty of veterans in adjusting to domestic life; and it leaves the viewer unsettled (Eagen, 2014).

Cultural significance

Although there have been various signs throughout Eastwood's career of both visionary and alchemical experiences, none is so clear and up-to-date as the reactions to *American Sniper*. It generated strong reactions in viewers in the US and indeed around the world. My suggestion is that these reactions were not due to Eastwood's film per se, rather they were the result of the film acting like a mirror in that it reflected the state of contemporary Western culture and its relationship with the Middle East.

One type of reaction to the film was that of Bradley Cooper, who played the lead role. He described the film as life-changing and has since been visiting military hospitals with Chris Kyle's wife. This has enabled veterans 'to express themselves in a format that they would never do normally' (Shields, 2015). Although Eastwood has sympathy for veterans and believes the film shows what veterans and their families go through (Galloway, 2015), the extent of its impact is not something that Eastwood could have envisaged. It is an example of an alchemical reaction to the film – Cooper and many veterans have interacted with it and been changed by it.

The film also had a significant impact by raising awareness of, and providing support to, certain veterans' causes. One significant issue is illustrated by a line in the film from Kyle's wife (played by Sienna Miller): 'I need you to be human again' (Hall, 2014). This reflects a very different type of experience to the previous two films. Throughout *J. Edgar*, it is clear that Hoover wanted to identify with the (one-sided) hero and defeat the villains, to the extent of distorting reality in his recollections. In the case of *Invictus*, the black majority wanted a one-sided hero who would defeat the white villains of apartheid. But Nelson Mandela recognised that the country needed something else – a transformative hero who could hold the tension of opposites; he was both able and willing to resist the heroic projections from black South Africans and avoid the trap of projective identification (unconsciously becoming what others wanted him to be). However, in the case of *American Sniper*, Chris Kyle just wanted to do his job. When society tried to project on to him the hero archetype, it was something that he was unprepared for. Projective identification with the hero *dehumanised him* and it robbed him of his individuality and his identity. *American Sniper* deconstructed the collective projection of the hero on to the individual (as did also *Flags of Our Fathers*), showing the struggle a veteran can have to remain normal. This aspect of the film was acknowledged by the organisation gotyour6.org (2015), who gave *American Sniper* an award for its normal depiction of veterans. Again, interaction with this aspect of the film was alchemical. Some people's attitudes towards veterans were transformed as a result of seeing the difficulties they faced when treated as heroes.

Alchemical reactions are not always positive, however, and a damaging impact can be seen in the withdrawal of *American Sniper* from cinemas in Iraq. In the film, the Iraqis are sometimes referred to using the term 'savages'. This word was not introduced by Eastwood but used by 'a lot of people' (Kyle *et al.*, 2012, p. 4) who were fighting the Iraqi forces. The use of this term in the film does not suggest that Eastwood has regressed from the valuing of other cultures that he demonstrated in *Letters From Iwo Jima*, or *Gran Torino*. Rather, it is Eastwood holding up a mirror to enable Western society to see what is contained in its own shadow. Much of Jung's theory about psychotherapy is concerned with establishing the right conditions under which a positive transformation of personality can take place. This involves having an appropriate vessel or container and a sequence of events that encourages a gradual transformation. Iraqi cinemas were not the right vessel for them to come face-to-face with such extreme Western prejudice and it created too much heat. Nevertheless, *American Sniper* has highlighted the pejorative view of Iraq that is held by some in the West. If attitudes are changed as a result then, along with the other reactions to the film, it will have contributed to a small thread of change in the tapestry of Western culture.

Conclusion

This chapter has gone beyond the hero myth in several ways. First, there is a psychological development that is evident in Eastwood's films. Until the turn of the century, although there was an increasing complexity and depth to the lead characters in his films, they usually portrayed heroes in a one-sided way. Their task was an objective one, to take the side of good and defeat evil in the world. But in more recent work he has gone beyond the one-sided hero myth and exposed it as a shallow psychological projection. In the case of *J. Edgar*, memories were reconstructed as a result of identification with the projected hero myth. In *Invictus*, one-sided heroism could have been an obstacle to cultural development, had Mandela not had the perspective and capability to resist it, while, in *American Sniper*, the one-sided hero myth is shown to be a dehumanising collective projection and the ongoing source of conflict within and between societies. Although what lies beyond the hero myth can also be described as heroic, it is a very different type of heroism. It has a subjective focus, seeking transformation of oneself, or one's own culture, and aiming to integrate evil rather than defeat it.

Further, the examination of Eastwood's films has gone beyond the limitations of identifying the underlying structure, which sees the hero myth as the central theme. Structures do have a role in a Jungian inquiry, but only as part of an initial reduction, as a starting point for information. They can point to the presence of heroes and other unconscious processes in film and in Western culture. Yet, film reviews that focus primarily on the remnants of Dirty Harry and other such characters take the cultural analysis backwards and miss its significance. When Eastwood's recent films are deconstructed, they challenge some of the widely held assumptions about heroes and war. They also highlight the ongoing intensity of political differences regarding the morality of warfare and military interventions overseas. These divides were also illustrated by the various interpretations of *American Sniper* where each side, whether for or against, used the film to reinforce their own one-sided viewpoint and attack those who took an opposing view.

There have been alchemical reactions to Eastwood's recent films but these have not always been productive. The 'hot-spots' of *American Sniper* have shown how exposing Western prejudices to other cultures can damage international cultural relations. Nevertheless, they have also been a vehicle of expression for veterans, and focusing on the heated reactions has shown how public acclaim of the hero can do damage to the private individual. Jung often warns of the damage that collective demands can do to the individual, and it raises the question whether celebration of the hero in film reinforces that type of damaging impact. This could be exacerbated by film reviews that fail to recognise the deconstruction, interpretation, and alchemy that flow from a film. If film reviews pay too much attention to the structure of the hero myth, and do nothing more than archetype-spotting, they may miss the more contemporary criticism that cinema makes of one-sided Western culture. It is the 'hot-spot' of a film, not the age-old myth, which reveals the contemporary developments in the collective unconscious, and takes culture and society forwards. Both individual and societal individuation requires that we go beyond the traditional hero myth.

References

Campbell, J. (1993) *The hero with a thousand faces*. London: Harper Collins Publishers.

Eastwood, C. (2013) *Clint Eastwood interviews: revised and updated*. Jackson, MS: University Press of Mississippi.

Jung, C. G. (1913) 'A contribution to the study of psychological types', in *The collected works of C. G. Jung*, Vol. 6, *Psychological types*, 2nd edn. London: Routledge. 1971.

Jung, C. G. (1914) 'On psychological understanding', in *The collected works of C. G. Jung*, Vol. 3, *The psychogenesis of mental disease*, 2nd edn. London: Routledge. 1972.

Jung, C. G. (1921) 'Schiller's ideas on the type problem', in *The collected works of C. G. Jung*, Vol. 6, *Psychological types*, 2nd edn. London: Routledge, 1971.

Jung, C. G. (1928/31) 'The spiritual problem of modern man', in *The collected works of C. G. Jung*, Vol. 10, *Civilisation in transition*, 2nd edn. London: Routledge, 1970.

Jung, C. G. (1930/50) 'Psychology and literature', in *The collected works of C. G. Jung*, Vol. 15, *The spirit in man, art, and literature*. London: Routledge, 1966.

Jung, C. G. (1933) *Modern man in search of a soul*. Abingdon: Routledge Classics, 2001.

Jung, C. G. (1951) 'The fish in alchemy', in *The collected works of C. G. Jung*, Vol. 9ii, *Aion: researches into the phenomenology of the Self*, 2nd edn. London: Routledge, 1968.

Kyle, C., McEwen, S., and DeFelice, J. (2012) *American sniper: the autobiography of the most lethal sniper in U.S. military history*. New York: Harper Collins Publishers.

McGilligan, P. (1999) *Clint: the life and legend*. London: HarperCollins Entertainment.

McGilligan, P. (2015) *Clint: the life and legend*, Kindle edn. New York and London: OR Books.

Neumann, E. (1949) *The origins and history of consciousness*. Princeton, NJ: Bollingen Paperbacks.

Ruiz, W. B. R. (2011) *American history goes to the movies*. New York and Abingdon: Routledge.

Samuels, A., Shorter, B., and Plaut, F. (1986) *A critical dictionary of Jungian analysis*. Hove: Routledge.

Schopenhauer, A. (1969) *The world as will and representation*. New York: Dover Publications.

Voytilla, S. (1999) *Myth and the movies: discovering the mythic structure of 50 unforgettable films*. Studio City, CA: Michael Wiese Productions.

Online sources

Bash, D. (2015) '"American sniper": Palin's attack on "Hollywood leftists" personal', CNN [online]. Available at: http://edition.cnn.com/2015/01/20/politics/sarah-palin-american-sniper-chris-kyle/ [Accessed 18 January 2016].

boxofficemojo.com (2016) 'Clint Eastwood', IMDB [online]. Available at: www.boxofficemojo.com/people/chart/?view=Director&id=clinteastwood.htm [Accessed 27 January 2016].

Dargis, M. and Scott, A. O. (2008) 'At glittery Cannes, a gritty Palme d'Or', *New York Times* [online]. Available at: www.nytimes.com/2008/05/26/movies/26cann.html?_r=0 [Accessed 18 January 2016].

Dervis, P. (2015) 'Fuse film review: "American sniper" – keep telling yourself … it's only a movie', Arts Fuse [online]. Available at: http://artsfuse.org/121751/fuse-film-review-american-sniper-keep-telling-yourself-its-only-a-movie/ [Accessed 16 December 2015].

Eagen, D. (2014) 'Film review: American sniper', Film Journal International [online]. Available at: www.filmjournal.com/content/film-review-american-sniper [Accessed 16 December 2015].

Edelstein, D. (2003) 'Dirty Harry wants to say he's sorry (Again)', *New York Times* [online]. Available at: www.nytimes.com/2003/09/28/movies/28EDEL.html?pagewanted=all [Accessed 2 January 2016].

Friedman, D. (2012) 'Unforgiven: a hermeneutical reading', PhD University of Melbourne [online]. Available at: www.film-philosophy.com/index.php/f-p/thesis/view/19 [Accessed 26 January 2016].

Galloway, S. (2015) 'Clint Eastwood describes his near-death experience, says "American sniper" is anti-war (Exclusive)', *Hollywood Reporter* [online]. Available at: www.hollywoodreporter.com/news/clint-eastwood-describes-his-death-781618 [Accessed 18 January 2016].

Kilday, G. (2015) 'Clint Eastwood on American sniper's "biggest antiwar statement"', *Hollywood Reporter* [online]. Available at: www.hollywoodreporter.com/news/clint-eastwood-american-snipers-biggest-766498 [Accessed 18 December 2012].

Got Your Six (2015) '6 certified projects' [online]. Available at: https://gotyour6.org/programs/6-certified/ [Accessed 18 January 2016].

Hall, J. (2014) 'American sniper' (screenplay), Warner Brothers [online]. Available at: http://pdl.warnerbros.com/wbmovies/awards2014/pdf/as.pdf [Accessed 18 December 2015].

imdb.com (2016) 'Unforgiven (1992)', IMDB [online]. Available at: www.imdb.com/title/tt0105695/ [Accessed 27 January 2016].

O'Hehir, A. (2012) 'After the chair: Clint Eastwood's tormented legacy', Salon Media Group [online]. Available at: www.salon.com/2012/09/22/after_the_chair_clint_eastwoods_tormented_legacy/ [Accessed 2 January 2016].

rottentomatoes.com (2016) 'Director Clint Eastwood's 10 best movies', Flixster [online]. Available at: http://editorial.rottentomatoes.com/article/director-clint-eastwoods-10-best-movies/ [Accessed 27 January 2016].

Scott, A. O. (2014) 'Review: "American sniper," a Clint Eastwood film with Bradley Cooper', *New York Times* [online]. Available at: www.nytimes.com/2014/12/25/movies/american-sniper-a-clint-eastwood-film-starring-bradley-cooper.html [Accessed 2 January 2016].

Scranton, R. (2015) 'The trauma hero: from Wilfred Owen to "redeployment" and "American sniper"', *Los Angeles Review of Books* [online]. Available at: https://lareviewofbooks.org/essay/trauma-hero-wilfred-owen-redeployment-american-sniper [Accessed 18 December 2015].

Sharrett, C. (2015) 'American sniper: war's glories', Film International [online]. Available at: http://filmint.nu/?p=14358 [Accessed 16 December 2015].

Shields, R. (2015) 'Bradley Cooper: why American sniper was "Life-Changing"', *People Magazine* [online]. Available at: www.people.com/article/bradley-cooper-american-sniper-chris-kyle-life-changing [Accessed 18 January 2016].

Sly, L. (2015) '"American sniper" misfires in Iraq', *Washington Post* [online]. Available at: www.washingtonpost.com/world/middle_east/american-sniper-misfires-in-iraq/2015/02/02/312a7fee-4e18-47f5-a823-4c8979d1df44_story.html [Accessed 2 January 2016].

Turan, K. (2006) 'Know thy enemy', *Los Angeles Times* [online]. Available at: http://articles.latimes.com/2006/dec/20/entertainment/et-letters20 [Accessed 18 January 2016].

Valero, G. (2011) '"Unforgiven" was Eastwood's turning point' [online]. Available at: www.rogerebert.com/far-flung-correspondents/unforgiven-was-eastwoods-turning-point [Accessed 26 January 2016].

Filmography

Ambush at Cimarron Pass. (1958) [film] Directed by Jodie Coplan. USA.

American sniper. (2014) [film] Directed by Clint Eastwood. USA.

Beguiled, The. (1971) [film] Directed by Don Siegel. USA.

Bridges of Madison County. (1995) [film] Directed by Clint Eastwood. USA.

Dirty Harry. (1971) [film] Directed by Don Siegel. USA.

Eiger sanction, The. (1975) [film] Directed by Clint Eastwood. USA.

First travelling saleslady, The. (1956) [film] Directed by Arthur Lubin. USA.

Flags of our fathers. (2006) [film] Directed by Clint Eastwood. USA.

Good, the bad and the ugly, The. (1966) [film] Directed by Sergio Leone. USA.

Gran Torino. (2008) [film] Directed by Clint Eastwood. USA.

High plains drifter. (1973) [film] Directed by Clint Eastwood. USA.

Invictus. (2009) [film] Directed by Clint Eastwood. USA.

J. Edgar. (2011) [film] Directed by Clint Eastwood. USA.

Lady Godiva of Coventry. (1955) [film] Directed by Arthur Lubin. USA.

Lafayette Escadrille. (1958) – a.k.a. *Hell bent for glory.* – [film] Directed by William Wellman. USA.

Letters from Iwo Jima. (2006) [film] Directed by Clint Eastwood. USA.

Magnum force. (1973) [film] Directed by Ted Post. USA.

Million dollar baby. (2004) [film] Directed by Clint Eastwood. USA.

Mystic river. (2003) [film] Directed by Clint Eastwood. USA.

Rawhide. (1959–65) [television series] CBS. USA.

Revenge of the creature. (1955) [film] Directed by Jack Arnold. USA.

Unforgiven. (1992) [film] Directed by Clint Eastwood. USA.

Where eagles dare. (1968) [film] Directed by Brian G. Hutton. USA.

White hunter black heart. (1990) [film] Directed by Clint Eastwood. USA.

14

TRUE DETECTIVE AND JUNG'S FOUR STEPS OF TRANSFORMATION

Stephen Anthony Farah

True Detective (2014) is an American crime drama, television series created and written by Nic Pizzolatto. The first season, which I focus on in this chapter, aired on HBO in 2014 and consisted of eight episodes, starring Matthew McConaughey and Woody Harrelson in the leading roles. (The cast also includes Michelle Monaghan, Michael Potts, and Tory Kittles.) The season received widespread critical acclaim and was a candidate for numerous awards. Beyond high production values, great acting and a tightly knit storyline, what sets *True Detective* apart is the brilliantly articulated nihilism of its central protagonist, Rust (Rustin 'Rusty' Cohle), played by McConaughey. In the golden age of television series *True Detective* stands out. It offers the aficionado a contemporary and psychologically astute version of the hero's journey. Taking its cue from films such as *The Road* (dir. Hillcoat, 2009), *Blindness* (dir. Meirelles, 2008) and *No Country for Old Men* (dirs Ethan Coen and Joel Coen, 2007) it presents viewers with a hero whose true challenge is to find redemption in a dystopian world.

Jungian theory offers a useful lens through which to focus *True Detective*'s mythological themes and developmental structure. The perspective provides an insight into how the series mirrors our human and challenging search for soul (Jung, 1933); more precisely, a relationship to soul and how that relationship acts out, not only intrapsychically – in inner psychic space – but also, intersubjectively, in our relationships in the world. This analysis utilises two key Jungian concepts to illuminate two dimensions of the series: the theme and the narrative structure. The first concept employed, for thematic analysis, is the 'anima' which is Jung's term for the soul image of the man, while the 'animus' refers to the soul image of women. 'Soul' here does not refer to the eternal soul that lives on beyond this mortal life, but the inner life of the subject (1921: §803–811). The narrative structure and development is analysed using Jung's 'Four Steps of Transformation'. This is my own coinage and is taken from Jung's essay 'Problems of modern psychotherapy' (1929) where Jung details the four psychotherapeutic steps or stages in psycho-analysis. These concepts, both uniquely Jungian, offer a valuable perspective not to be accessed without them. This interpretation affords us an insight into the archetypal frame of the narrative as well as the psychodynamic process and transformation of the two main protagonists. The light that such an analysis casts, enlightens not only the series in question but also the concepts themselves. This is a common feature of film analysis that uses psychoanalytic concepts and it is by virtue of such analysis that we embed the theory employed in the cinematic frame and thereby achieve a perspective that would otherwise have eluded us. The dramatis personae of the psychoanalytic concepts themselves reveal meaning in a way that is typically unavailable when encountered as abstracted theory.

The story of *True Detective* is ultimately a hero's journey, one that takes place not only in the world but, more significantly from the psychological perspective, in the inner, subjective space of the series' two protagonists, Rust and Marty (Char. Martin Hart, Woody Harrelson). It is a search for redemption and meaning, in a world brought to life by Pizzolatto and the production team, that reflects Rust's nihilism. A dystopia, devoid of beauty, and oppressive in its perverted character. A world populated by 'shit heels', criminals, monsters, the dim witted and irredeemably naive, victims, broken dreams, broken hearts and brutish reality. Where innocence is fragile and momentary, before the 'thresher' swallows it up. As the character of Rust comments, 'Think of the hubris it must take to yank a soul out of non-existence into this ... meat, to force a life into this ... thresher. That's ... so my daughter, she spared me the sin of being a father' (Rust, episode 2). This is a psychic landscape where, in Jungian parlance, the *anima* is either broken, lost, perverted or functions in only her negative aspect (Lirette, 2017); it is a place where Rust's only lifeboat is the function of the *animus* – of pure, cold, unfeeling, critical, reductive rationality. A world where the possibility of redemption lies in the journey out of the clammy embrace of the dysfunctional, oppressive, *anima* and through the dark heart of the shadow, to face the mythical monster.

As both a journey to redemption and a journey of transformation, *True Detective* can illuminate and, hopefully, educate us. Interestingly Jung was fascinated by another metaphor for change, namely the alchemical process which he regarded as an analogue for the process of transformation. As is apparent in the Four steps to Transformation he describes in psychoanalysis, and their mirroring of the process of transmutation in alchemy. Intriguingly, the storyline of *True Detective* and the narrative journey on which it takes the viewer, also mirror the psychoanalytic-alchemical process of psychological transmutation Jung describes.

The *anima*

Along with the *animus*, the *anima* is among Jung's more controversial concepts, as it is an essentialist and now arguably outmoded framing of gender identity. Jung offers the concepts of the *anima* (soul) and *animus* (mind) as being the contra-gender, internal other of men and women respectively. A soul image that compliments and completes the necessarily one-sided, biological and social identity of the subject. As we are now aware, however, gender identity, both in its expression in contemporary culture and through the lens of gender studies, appears more fluid and constructive or 'performative' than essential and fixed.

As just suggested, performative gender identity seemingly has a less essential and more constructed relation to biological gender than is suggested by Jung's *anima–animus* model. The last word on the extent to which gender determines certain essential social, relational and psychological characteristics has yet to be spoken. Even so the insights provided by gender studies challenge Jung's essentialist gender framing. Not wishing to abandon such a key concept in the Jungian universe, post-Jungians have reframed the original idea. In this reframing the archetypal masculine – the *animus* – and the archetypal feminine – the *anima* – are uncoupled from their essential relation to biological gender. They are instead understood as archetypal or primordial images of the masculine and feminine, possibly essential, or possibly mimetic, social constructions. Either way, in the practice of Jungian psychotherapy these ideas remain valuable tools (Samuels, 1985) and they can also be usefully applied to film analysis (Beebe, 2013).

With the above qualification stated, let us consider briefly the character of the *anima*. Jung locates the *anima* (or *animus*) as the inner attitude or face, turned to the unconscious, or inner world, complementing the face or 'persona' that faces the outer world:

> We can, therefore, speak of an inner personality with as much justification as, on the grounds of daily experience, we speak of an outer personality. The inner personality is the way one behaves in relation to one's inner psychic processes; it is the inner attitude, the characteristic face, that is turned towards the unconscious. I call the outer attitude, the outward face, the *persona*; the inner attitude, the inward face, I call the *anima*.
>
> *(1921: §803)*

Jung's view of the human being is that, psychologically, both men and women carry within their unconscious an implicit, complimentary and contrasting gender identity to their conscious, biological and explicit gender identity. Personhood then, at least psychologically, inclusive of both the conscious and unconscious self, is androgynous. This idea resonates with the biological fact of the presence of male and female genes in both sexes.

Development of the explicit, conscious gender identity has a corresponding and inverse development of the *anima* or *animus*. The relation to the *anima*, the specific focus of *True Detective*, concerns the subject's faculty to relate, both to himself and others, as well the world around him and in him – the world 'out there' and the world 'in here'. This function of the psyche determines the subject's capacity to relate, feel and empathise and also his ability to experience value, beauty and meaning. This inner *anima* image, through the mechanism of unconscious projection, is typically seen by the man as incarnated in the world through women. Such that, typically, the most common way for a man to relate to his own *anima* is through a relationship with a woman or women. It follows that relationship of men with women is coloured and influenced by the *anima* image and their relationship to it (1921: §803–811). This idea is vividly illustrated in the distorted, broken and perverse relationships of the various male characters to women, in *True Detective*.

The story of *True Detective* focuses on the relation of these stereotypically masculine men to the feminine principle. Both men, Rust and Marty, each in their own way, suffer from a disconnection to the feminine. In Jungian terms, in other words, they experience a disconnection from their *anima* or soul. Rust's suffering is symbolised by the loss of his daughter, who is killed in a car accident that additionally leads to the end of his marriage. Marty is unable to deal appropriately with the women who are in his life. Rust experiences himself as abandoned by the feminine and Marty is unable to conceptualise a relation to the feminine, beyond that of sexual objectification.

The consequence of this absent or displaced relation to the *anima* manifests itself symptomatically in both men's lives. Rust descends into cynicism to the point of nihilism, alienation and profound sadness. He is only able to operate in the realm of reason, the masculine function or *animus*, and is unable to access his feeling function or *anima*. Rust's feeling function is frozen as a self-defence mechanism to avoid being annihilated by the immense pain of losing his daughter and wife, an event which he has been unable to assimilate and come to terms with. In Marty's case, his inability to access a more mature relation to the feminine sees him grow ever further apart from his wife and daughters. Marty anaesthetises himself through his chronic alcoholism and indulges in serial infidelities with an increasing desperation as he attempts to reconnect with the feminine.

This displaced and wounded relation to the *anima* is symbolically represented in the first episode, with the discovery of the primal scene – the body of the murdered Dora Lange which has been elaborately and ritualistically displayed, naked and bound, on her knees in a position of prayer, appealing in vain to an unfeeling, monstrous god. Significantly she is found wearing a set of antlers that Rust later describes as a 'crown'. In other words, she wears a crown of horns. This is a metaphorically significant and presumably unconscious representation of the feminine gender by her killer, who, we can infer from this macabre display, not only tips the hat to some pagan god, but also reveals his inner image of the feminine as a horned, attacking, dangerous and potentially violent creature. She has been left on display by her murderer Errol Childress, known as 'the Lawnmower Man', his professional occupation, and also dubbed 'the Yellow King', by Dora Lange.

Childress is the series' primary antagonist and the monster who the two true detectives set out to capture, or destroy, over the lengthy period of their manhunt. Childress is the sharp edge of the Tuttle Cult, which includes elements of perverted revival belt Christian evangelism, along with ritual paedophilia, torture and murder within its ambit. In Childress' case this *anima* wound is so severe that he has descended into criminal insanity. His monstrous self is unmediated by a healthy feeling function. The normal function of empathy and an appreciation of the subjectivity, the inner life, of the other is seemingly absent. His narcissism, will to power and sense of personal inflation, combined with his dysfunctional or absent feeling function, are such that he feels entitled to objectify the 'other', and does so mercilessly with his victims. While the term 'other' has a specific technical reference in Lacanian psychoanalysis (Johnston, 2014) here it is used with reference specifically to 'other people' as a category of relatedness and symbolisation. This is a narrow adoption of the Lacanian 'other' that refers to both the ego itself as other and other egos out there as 'other/s'. In this case it is the *anima* as an internal and externalised other. Childress does not see other people as sovereign beings worthy of respect and embodying the transcendent principle and his disregard of the other reduces them to an exclusively utilitarian value; in Childress' case his victims are objects that allow him to act out his macabre rituals.

This barbaric display in human portraiture by Childress, symbolically reflects the wounded subjectivity and relationality of the two true detectives, Rust and Marty, who like Childress both display a displaced and wounded relation to the *anima* and the feminine gender. This is what Rust's and Marty's displaced *anima* functions can look like in a sufficiently deranged psychology, such as provided by Childress. The seeds of the wound in Childress are collectively carried by Rust and Marty. Rust, with his meaningless universe, devoid of any transcendent principle, and Marty with his sexual objectification of the feminine, converge in Childress. Childress, unfettered by any moral conscience, infers from these principles the 'not illogical' conclusion that self-gratification and assertion are the supreme good and logical aspirations of human existence. Might is always right.

With the theme in mind, namely the pathological and disconnected relationship to the *anima*, let us look now at how this dilemma evolves towards a resolution. This narrative evolution can be mapped using Jung's Four Steps of Transformation.

The Four Steps of Transformation and the alchemical metaphor

In an essay titled 'Problems of modern psychotherapy', published in 1929 Jung provides the reader with the meta-framework of his analytical psychology, the Four Steps of Transformation: confession, elucidation, education and transformation (§122). This essay is unique in providing a rare bird's eye view of Jung's psychotherapeutic model. Simultaneously it offers the reader an insight into 'modern psychotherapy' at the time or, more specifically, the various schools of psychoanalysis that had emerged and the essence of their respective psychotherapeutic approaches. The specific contributions Jung includes come from Josef Breuer, Sigmund Freud, Alfred Adler and Jung himself. The scope of Jung's ambition in writing this paper is clear. 'I would venture to regard the sum total of all our findings [in the emerging practice of psychotherapy] under the aspect of the four stages' (1929: §122). To the degree that Jung succeeds in his goal of offering us a concise description of the psychotherapeutic approaches of the main schools of psycho-analysis at the time, this essay is of considerable value to the student of psychoanalysis. To the degree that Jung concisely describes his own psychotherapeutic model, the paper is invaluable to the student of Jungian psychology. Beyond providing such a clear overview of the modes and structure of depth psychology, it also provides a valuable tool for the analyses of narrative devel-opment and the prima facie, quite mysterious phenomenon of 'transformation' in psychology.

Jung associates each step with one of the four main contributors to the psychoanalytic field at the time: confession with Breuer; elucidation with Freud; education with Adler; and trans-formation with his own school. One should not form the impression that this indexing of the four steps implies that each school is narrowly exclusive in its adoption of just one approach or method. Rather, the more modest claim is made that each school has an area of special-isation and focus. Clearly each practitioner, whilst focusing on a single approach, might well borrow from other approaches in his practice of psychotherapy. The development of these four steps can also be usefully viewed as reflecting the evolution of psychoanalysis from Breuer to Jung, with the final stage, the Jungian approach, encompassing all of the earlier approaches. This framing regards the Jungian approach as a more evolved method than its earlier antecedents, a proposition that remains unchallenged in Jung's essay. Whilst this chapter will not challenge this elevation of Jungian psychology above the other schools, the reader should not infer that such a challenge could not be made. Rather the focus here is on the use of the four step model as a tool of narrative film analysis. This is done as it offers an interesting perspective on the film in question and indeed the elegance with which the model can be applied speaks in its favour.

The four steps in Jung's Four Steps of Transformation echo the four stages of Western Alchemy that so inspired Jung and in which he found precedent for much of his psychological theory. The four stages of alchemical transmutation being (extracted from Jung, 1937):

Nigredo: the blackening. This process involves the burning away of the dross, seeking the 'Prima Materia', the original, pure, uncorrupted matter. This is symbolic of a rebirth, and fire is a critical element to achieve this. In psychotherapy this stage is represented by facing the Shadow. This stage refers to a blackening of mood, a depression, the 'dark night of the soul'. The process of internal conflict and facing one's undesirable qualities is intense and confrontational. This fire burns away the misconceptions, self-criticism and guilt. It is the death of the previous identity, creating the possibility of the birth of a new self.

Albedo: the whitening or emergence of the soul life. During this phase there is a withdrawal from the world, and intense reflection on the direction and purpose of the individual's life. The soul rises from the psyche and its essence is extracted. At the end of this stage, there is a height-ened spiritual awareness and purpose.

Citrinitas: the yellowing or rising of the sun. The rising sun is a symbol of a mystical experi-ence and contains aspects of revelation. It can be in many forms, but is experienced as a vision, a big dream or an intuition of our 'truth'.

Rubedo: the reddening. The spirit that was freed in the previous stage needs to be united with psyche again. The spirit that has been awakened now needs to be expressed appropriately and more authentically in the life and work of the individual. This is the stage of adjustment and re-alignment with authentic goals and purpose.

These four stages of alchemical transformation or transubstantiation mirror the four stages of psychotherapeutic transformation in some interesting ways. The rough analogue being: the stage of Nigredo with the stage of confession and catharsis; the stage of Albedo with the stage of elucidation or interpretation; the stage of Citrinitas with the stage of education; and the stage of Rubedo, the ripening, with the final stage of transformation.

The four steps in *True Detective*: confession and catharsis

Confession as a means of unburdening oneself of one's sins was an established practice in the Catholic Church long before its adoption by psychoanalysis. Confession as a psychotherapeutic method was introduced into the psychoanalytic method by Breuer and taken up by Freud. The principle behind the practice is the recognition that secrets held by the individual – whether, objectively speaking, virtues or vices – alienate the subject from his community. Whilst the secret remains unspoken, unconfessed and unarticulated, it functions at a lower level of consciousness, clouding the subject's psychology. As Jung puts it, 'All personal secrets, therefore, have the effect of sin or guilt, whether or not they are, from the standpoint of popular morality, wrongful secrets' (1929: §129).

These secrets or unspoken truths are comparable to the presence of the unconscious and its unconfessed role in the subject's psychology. Confession, then, is a way back for the alienated subject to a more fully participative engagement and connection with his community. It is worth noting that such an act of confession is effective even when the secret is shared only with a single individual in the sanctity of the confessional or psychotherapeutic practice. In the case of confession to the psychotherapist, the psychotherapist stands in for the community at large he or she represents, and symbolises the presence of the community. In Lacanian terms we might say that both the priest and psychotherapist, playing the role of master confessor, and representing God and the community respectively, stand in for and symbolise the 'big Other'.

This situation which the two protagonists, Rusty and Marty, face both in their inner worlds and in the Dora Lang case, presents us with the wound, the alchemical Nigredo, the dark night of the soul, the stone in the shoe. This is the constellated content that needs to be 'confessed' and that needs to be engaged with if there is to be the possibility of healing. This is the essential distress and archetypal situation that calls for rehabilitation through transformation. Secrets need to be shared and demons brought out of the shadows into the light of day. The act of confession is played out in the narrative of *True Detective* in two parallel confessionals. The container and set of the story is a confessional. The two detectives each separately undergo interviews by two other detectives in an interrogation room. These interrogations are filmed. Ostensibly this is for the two detectives, currently assigned to the case – long after Rust and Marty have left the service – to gather background information to assist them with their own investigation. As a dramatic tool employed by Pizzolatto it presents the story as confession which allows the audience to move between the unfolding events of the Dora Lange case and the reflective space of the two protagonists, Rust and Marty. This is the confession of the objective events of the Dora Lange case. The parallel confession takes place in the intersubjective space between Rust and Marty where they confess to each other the wounds they each bear. In the story it is mostly Rust confessing to Marty who acts as the master confessor hearing Rust's confession, albeit with much resistance and protest at times. At one point, unable to bear it anymore, Marty deems the car a 'place of silence'. Rust confesses precisely what Marty has repressed, namely they are living in hell. It is Rust's act of confession that shows Marty the ills that so trouble his own soul and that he desperately attempts to keep repressed.

As it always is with life's most profound challenges, in particular the experience of loss, there is no going back. There is no point of return despite our wish that there were. These situations always demand of us that we move forward – that we obey, in Jungian terms, the teleological imperative (1934: §798). Nothing will bring back Rust's family. And Marty, despite recognising the destructive force he has become in his own family and life, cannot by will alone, transcend his destructiveness. What is required is a coming to consciousness, an awakening, so that the scales that blind them may fall from their eyes. Like all great hero myths, they need to face the dragon, to be faced with a dilemma that takes them beyond their narcissistic, ego-centred perspectives into a meaningful engagement with the world. Individuation does not happen in isolation, but when we live in the world and engage with the archetypal processes we are called on to enter and grapple with. As is the case with such things, the dilemma is directly related to the wound. Rust and Marty's collective wound is the displaced relation to the feminine. What our two detectives are faced with in the story is a brutal, inhumane serial killer. A beast who preys on the helpless and the vulnerable. A man who has become so inflamed with his own masculine power, that he has quite literally become a monster. He represents in manifest form what lies latent in both our intrepid heroes – a corruption of the masculine principle and its relation to the feminine that, starting at alienation and taken far enough, leads to madness. A condition we are regrettably all too familiar with in the history of the world, with the litany of power-mad dictators and the savagery they have given us in the acting out of their inflated will to power as a corrupted and one-sided relation to the Other. This is also arguably the underlying archetypal issue at play in the total disregard of the biosphere and the ruthless exploitation of all natural resources, including human beings.

Elucidation: the interpretive method

Prima facie confession was seen as offering a complete cure in its initial adoption and application by psychoanalysis. However, Jung offers three problems with confession, which method seen on its own terms could constitute a complete cure of sorts, after which no further treatment should be needed, but is hindered by certain complicating factors. These are, first, the resistance of the patient to make a full confession, to admit previously unconscious content into consciousness. Repression and resistance often prevail, thwarting a full confession. The other two problems are related, both forms of fixation. The patient having made a confession to the master confessor, in this case the psychotherapist, transfers on to the psychotherapist forming a complicated relationship which frequently proves recalcitrant to dissolution. As Jung summarises:

> While the cathartic method restores to the ego such contents as are capable of becoming conscious and should normally be components of the conscious mind, the process of clearing up the transference brings to light contents which are hardly ever capable of becoming conscious in that form. This is the cardinal distinction between the stage of confession and the stage of elucidation.
>
> *(1929: §141)*

Finally, even in the relatively rare cases, where there is not a transference on to the psychotherapist, the patient frequently becomes fascinated with the 'hinterland' of his own unconscious mind. Such fascination binding him to the unconscious in a way that works contrary to the aim of the psychotherapeutic process, which has as its aim, greater adaptation and, for Jung at least, adherence to the teleological imperative (Jung, 1929: §135–138).

This transference which proves 'impervious to conscious correction' is fuelled by unconscious fantasy material. This fantasy material is correctly identified by Freud as being of an incestuous character. That such incestuous fantasy material should remain unconscious is entirely understandable within the social milieu in which we live. This incest fantasy is, if one accepts the Freudian perspective, which, we should note, Jung is unwilling to accept as axiomatic, however never denying its centrality and relevance, lies at the heart of what, perhaps necessarily, remains unspoken in the confession.

The interpretive method introduced by Freud is about uncovering and understanding what has been unsaid in the confession. Understanding the transference, the unspoken, unconscious:

supressed or repressed, remaining X, which is left over after the confession and is transferred on to the analyst. The method proceeds by the classical technique of psychoanalysis the examin- ation and interpretation of the subject's dream and fantasy material. Examining the associations of the subject, amplifying these within the context of the subject's psychology and interpreting the material that has emerged. (As a sidebar here, such amplification and interpretation, which at the adoption of this method by Freud was focused on the personal, is amplified into the realm of the collective and archetypal by Jung and the symbolic register by Lacan.)

In *True Detective*, this coming to consciousness, the Albedo, the whitening in alchemical terms, or the very first stages of elucidation in the four step model, is presented with Rust and Marty being assigned to investigate the murder of Dora Lange. In the narrative timeline, this is 1995. Although fortunately not always as dramatic as a murder, there is something valuable to be learnt here: coming to consciousness is usually not pretty. It involves facing something quite ugly and having the courage to look it in the eye. That is what it means to become conscious: not to avert your gaze; not to regress into the uncomfortable comfort of the wound or neurosis. Consciousness imposes the demand for a change in relation – a shift in perspective and is the first and critical step in the evolutionary process towards transformation.

What our two detectives Rust and Marty have to face when they confront and commit themselves to the investigation of the Dora Lange murder, are their own destructive capacities and symptomatic acting out of their own displaced relations to the feminine, which in each detective acts out destructively. Marty is destroying or 'murdering' his family with his pubescent sexual attitude and Rust is murdering the whole world with his nihilism.

Two quotations, both from Rust who is so eminently quotable, capture this destructiveness. In the recognition of their own evil, to Marty's question, 'Do you wonder ever if you're a bad man?' Rust answers, 'No. I don't wonder, Marty. World needs bad men. We keep the other bad men from the door.' Although that sounds good in the spirt of machismo parley, upon reflection its obvious logical flaw becomes apparent. The only reason there are bad men at the door, is because bad men exist. In other words, the only reason there is a need to protect against bad men is because there are bad men. They create their own need, a little like the old and bad joke about protection money: the men you are paying to protect you, protect you against them- selves. They create their own need.

The second quotation, also from Rust, epitomises his nihilistic attitude, this time in relation to his daughter's death:

> I think about my daughter now, and what she was spared. Sometimes I feel grateful. The doctor said she didn't feel a thing, went straight into a coma. Then, somewhere in that blackness, she slipped off into another deeper kind. Isn't that a beautiful way to go out, painlessly as a happy child? Trouble with dying later is you've already grown up. The damage is done. It's too late.

Education: the social reality

The process of re-educating the conscious personality requires the adaptation to social reality and the remedying maladapted behaviour. The intention is help the subject find better and alternative solutions and responses to the social issues that triggered the subject's neurosis. This broadly educative function derives from Adlerian psychology. As Jung notes:

> The Adlerian school begins precisely where Freud leaves off; consequently, they meet the needs of the patient who, having come to understand himself, wants to find his

way back to normal life…. [I]t is characteristic of Adler that he does not expect too much of the understanding, but going beyond that, has clearly recognised the need for social education…. Whereas Freud is investigator and interpreter, Adler is primarily the educator.

(1929: §152)

In *True Detective*, the ongoing process of elucidation, or, in alchemical terms, of Albedo and Citrinitas, takes place over the following seventeen years, a period where Rust and Marty become increasingly committed to finding the monster who is responsible for the murder of Dora Lange and countless others. In this process there is much conflict, to the point where they are completely alienated from each other for a period of years before they are finally reunited in the determination to complete their mission. The process exposes most of their bullshit for what it is: a facile, narcissistic defence, and each man pays dearly for the shortcomings of his own wound. In essence, they find themselves educated by Freud's reality principle. Neither one of them is able to sustain a relationship and each, in his own way, is obliged to face a life of loneliness and desperation. Even their friendship, which was presumably as close a friendship as either one of them is capable of, breaks down. They are obliged to face the inevitable consequences of their disconnection from the *anima* and in the process learn to understand themselves and their fallibilities better. They undergo the process of hard-won emotional and psychological maturity.

Transformation: the synthesis of the three previous steps

Transformation is the process of self-education of the analyst himself. As Jung puts it,

… who can educate others if he himself is uneducated? Who can enlighten others if he is still in the dark about himself? And who can purify others if himself impure? The step from education to self-education is a logical advance that completes the earlier stages.

(1929: §169–170)

The problem no longer exists out there; it is something within me that needs to be made whole. Transformation as an alchemical process of internal transubstantiation, which, notwithstanding the value of the three prior stages requires something more, something not wholly reducible to method. Transformation requires something intangible that, in the psychotherapeutic context of the analytical couple – analyst and analysand – happens in the transference. It is relational, alchemical and dialectical.

In *True Detective* this transference is acted out in the relationship of Rust and Marty and their extended dialogue. Like any relationship involving transference it is not smooth sailing. Their already challenging relationship boils over into violence after Rust has sex with Marty's wife. This incident causes a rift between the two men that lasts for many years. They finally turn a corner though, after a premature, false dawn is exposed – something that is not uncommon in transformation. Many years before they finally track down the serial killer, Childress, they were misled into believing they had already caught the culprit, which brought great honours on the two of them, but it turned out to be the wrong man – although no less deserving of justice. When they do finally reunite, after a long period of separation, to complete what they had left unfinished, each man discovers within himself a sense of humility and purpose. Their defining purpose becomes tracking this monster and they commit themselves to it absolutely. Their lives are now led in service of the self-archetype and not dictated by their wounds and this process of education is essential for transformation to occur. Of the Self, Jung comments:

I usually describe the supraordinate personality as the 'self,' thus making a sharp distinction between the ego, which, as is well known, extends only as far as the conscious mind, and the *whole* of the personality, which includes the unconscious as well as the conscious component.

(1941: §315)

Ultimately, both Rust and Marty find redemption in their own way, and one that restores the relation to soul that was the initial presenting condition. Crucially, though, this journey to redemption is only made possible by virtue of their relationship and their shared mission, which is the crucible of their transformation. Both men find this redemption not by going back or even by dealing with the issue in its presenting form, but by reconstructing their identities through this redemptive process which results in profound transformation.

In the final episode and penultimate scene of the series, we encounter Rust and Marty in hospital recovering from their near fatal wounds after their fight to the death with the monster Childress. They emerge victorious, killing Childress, but come very close to paying for this with their own lives. Symbolic of what it takes perhaps, to reconnect with the soul in a soulless dystopian world: only one who is willing to lose his life can gain his life. As the gospel of Matthew puts it, 'For whosoever will save his life shall lose it: and whosoever will lose his life for my sake shall find it' (Mathew 16:25). With this denouement realised, the longing for reconnection with soul, the displaced relation to *anima* is, at least temporarily, healed. We see Marty in his hospital bed, having just regained consciousness, surrounded by his ex-wife and his daughters, their love for him evident. He responds to his daughter's inquiry as to how he is, by smiling and protesting that he is well, whilst, simultaneously and incongruously, the tears stream from his eyes in response to the release of deeply pent up pain and fear, and his joy at being alive. (Possibly the single best piece of acting in Woody Harrelson's career.) Later, in the final scene, we find Rust and Marty under the night sky after Marty wheels Rust out of the hospital in his wheelchair. Here Rust speaks for the very first time about his daughter's death with real feeling and with a sense of forgiveness for himself, for fate and for the absent God. His reconnection with his soul being perfectly captured in the shot, the two men together experiencing a truly soulful connection, after their journey together which transcends words, under the clear, night sky, looking up at the stars.

Conclusion

The narrative development in *True Detective* sounds a note of truth for the viewer, offering something recognisable about the soul's journey to redemption. In so doing, it speaks for the value and archetypal truth of Jung's four step model. The critical acclaim and enthusiastic reception of the series supports this reading. It seems unlikely that when Jung wrote his paper 'The problems of modern psychotherapy' in which he describes the four steps to transformation that he intended it to be used for the purposes of mythological or narrative analysis. That noted, its mirroring of the stages of alchemical transmutation would no doubt have been significant for Jung and quite probably influenced his classification of the four steps.

The four steps, then, are not only a classification of the various schools of depth psychology, but express something archetypal about the journey to transformation. They also provide a useful frame in which to view the narrative structure of the journey to transformation as a 'hero's journey'. Its ability to illuminate the series *True Detective* allows us a deeper psychological insight into the unfolding events that enriches what we take from what could, at worst, be viewed as pulp fiction, or just another detective story. *True Detective*, in the elegance of its narrative structure as well as its sublime scripting, deserves the title of modern myth. It offers something much needed in a dystopian world: a view of the hero's inner subjective space and his journey of redemption.

References

Jung, C. G. (1921) 'Definitions', in *The collected works of C. G. Jung*, Vol. 6, *Psychological types*, 3rd edn. London: Routledge & Kegan Paul, 1971.

Jung, C. G. (1929) 'Problems of modern psychotherapy', in *The collected works of C. G. Jung*, Vol. 16, *The practice of psychotherapy*, 2nd edn. London: Routledge & Kegan Paul, 1966.

Jung, C. G. (1933) *Modern man in search of a soul*. London: Kegan Paul, Trench, Trubner.

Jung, C. G. (1934) 'The soul and death', in *The collected works of C. G. Jung*, Vol. 8, *The structure and dynamics of the psyche*, 2nd edn. London: Routledge & Kegan Paul, 1969.

Jung, C. G. (1937) 'Religious ideas in alchemy', in *The collected works of C. G. Jung*, Vol. 12, *Psychology and alchemy*, 2nd edn. London: Routledge & Kegan Paul, 1968.

Jung, C. G. (1941) 'The psychological aspects of the Kore', in *The collected works of C. G. Jung*, Vol. 9i, *The archetypes and the collective unconscious*, 2nd edn. London: Routledge & Kegan Paul, 1968.

Samuels, A. (1985) *Jung and the post-Jungians*. London: Routledge & Kegan Paul.

Online sources

Beebe, J. (2013) 'The anima in film' [online]. Available at: www.cgjungpage.org/learn/articles/film-reviews/666-the-anima-in-film [Accessed 15 July 2017].

Johnston, A. (2014) 'Jacques Lacan', in E. N. Zalta (ed.), *The Stanford encyclopedia of philosophy* (summer 2014 edn) [online]. Available at: http://plato.stanford.edu/archives/sum2014/entries/lacan/ [Accessed 15 July 2017].

Lirette, C. (2017) 'Men living in a brutally masculine world' [online]. Available at https://en.wikipedia.org/wiki/True_Detective_(season_1)#Themes_and_influences [Accessed 13 July 2017].

Filmography

Blindness. (2008) [film] Directed by Fernando Meirelles. Brazil/Canada.

No country for old men. (2007) [film] Directed by Ethan Coen and Joel Coen. USA.

Road, The. (2009) [film] Directed by John Hillcoat. USA.

True detective. (2014) [television series] Written by Nic Pizzolatto. Season 1, HBO. USA.

15

FILM FUTURISTICS

A forecasting methodology

Michael Glock

Introduction

Imagine that in 2020 you are tasked to understand and predict potential threats that existed in the world against your country. You decide to use *film futuristics* because its methodology is anchored in C. G. Jung's formulation of the collective unconscious and archetypes. It is a methodology where you research and analyze multiple films, synthesize the collected insights through a hermeneutic, heuristic process which is then followed by writing three fictional scenarios of possible, probable and preferable futures.

Jung describes the collective unconscious as 'a second psychic system of a collective, universal and impersonal nature which is identical in all individuals' (1936: §90). The collective unconscious appears in dreams as elementary and primordial images. When seen as a sequence, specific motifs dramatically appear. *Film futuristics* treats film as a dream sequence, a collection of systems that often reveal the collective unconscious at work.

Dreams operate in an altered state of consciousness and express themselves in a logically abstract way, often in the language of symbolic image, allegory, parable, metaphor and simile. They, theatrically operate below the threshold of awareness similarly to how films reveal hidden dimensions. Just like films, dreams have a language, a dramatic structure. As Jung puts it, 'a dream is a theater in which the dreamer is himself the scene, the player, the prompter, the producer, the author, the public, and the critic' (1916/48: §509). Dreams are a fundamental portal to the source and can be contemplated in terms of an unfolding dramatic sequence as expressed in classical Greek drama: 'exposition, peripeteia, crises, and lysis. These can be roughly translated as setting, walking about or development, crises, and outcome' (Whitmont and Perera, 1991 p. 69). Drama is an art form that has been consciously created and crafted to power pack the psychological allegories, symbolism and stories of human life to both entertain and teach forward. The dream on the other hand is the outcome of unconscious, non-rational processes in the individual. Both film and dream present unconscious dynamics and we relate to them both through the dramatic structure as an expression of the 'mythopoetic stratum of the psyche' (ibid., p. 69).

Film futuristics is a critical, action-orientated methodology that can be used to unpack the hidden dimensions and prospective probabilities within films and make the resulting knowledge and insight available to future planning. *Film futuristics* is a re-visioning of the original *cultural futuristics* methodology first proposed in 2007 by me (Glock, 2008). Unlike *cultural futuristics* where significant cultural events are analyzed, *film futuristics* primarily focuses on cultural artifacts such as films, video games, interactive media, virtual reality (VR), and similar moving image based narratives. Films are analyzed using an interdisciplinary approach including psycho and analytical approaches. The interdisciplinary approach is vital because *film futuristics* is fundamentally a forecasting technology and storytelling tool that interacts and informs the researcher, in order to enhance the depth and wisdom of the future histories that are created. *Film futuristics* is a close reading of the depths within artifacts, it is a heuristic phenomenological hermeneutic, whereby the researcher is implicated in the research and reanimates living within the analysis, synthesis and fictional future histories that are the outcome of the research. Such research requires the attitude of the '*smooth mind*' which brings into being 'flashes of acute intuitive insight [that] marks the presence of wisdom' (Basso, 1996, p. 147).

By focusing on the myths, symbols and powerful narratives within film, we can identify harbingers of events to come. Through psychologically understanding the symbolic material, and the disguised meanings communicated by these artifacts, *film futuristics* develops foreknowledge and oracular skills necessary for writing 'future history' that articulates possible, probable and preferable future conditions.

Practically consider this: films as I suggest can be understood as dreams, both have a dramatic structure and often present themselves theatrically. They offer access to the hidden dimensions of the collective unconscious by presenting archetypes as images, sequences of allegories and metaphors. Now, imagine tracking the development of the robots, or artificial intelligence (AI) as a character in four science fiction films, the original *Frankenstein* (1931) directed by James Whale and based on Mary Shelley's original story, the bodiless AI named HAL in *2001 A Space Odyssey* (1968) directed by Stanley Kubrick, the robots TARS and CASE in *Interstellar* (2014) directed by Christopher Nolan and the intelligent humanoid in *Ex Machina* (2015) directed by Alex Garland. By using the *film futuristics* methodology and doing a close reading of the films' texts and developmental arc of the androids and robots, it would be possible to conclude that a technological singularity will happen and is predicted within these films. The singularity 'is the hypothesis that the invention of artificial super-intelligence will abruptly trigger runaway technological growth, resulting in unfathomable changes to human civilization' (Wikiwand, 2016). The concluding three scenarios of this research would therefore expound on and explore the unfathomable changes confronting human civilization.

Film futuristics has been developed from Freud's metapsychology and Jung's models of how the unconscious is at work in human nature—via projection and shadow, the collective unconscious and collectively via the archetypes. Additionally, Jung's use of complexes, constellated opposites and alchemy provides the basis for *film futuristics*' analytical constructions. *Film futuristics* is further validated by Hillman's (1992) perspective that 'sickness is now out there' and a necessary focus for psychological inquiry. Hillman's emphasis on story and fiction confirms the value of *film futuristics*' precise and detailed attention to the fictional scenario-writing process itself.

Significance

The American event known and experienced as 9/11 was predicted and, because it occurred, it represents a failure of imagination. The powers in charge failed to perceive larger cultural patterns at work or to appreciate their implications. Peter Schwartz led the scenario team for the U.S. Commission on National Security/21st Century—the Hart–Rudman Commission—in 1998–2000. After the surprising end of the Cold War, the commission's task was to envision a new defense and security strategy. Their report, written 'a few months after George W. Bush was inaugurated in 2000, warned that terrorist incidents represented the greatest threat to the United States. In one scenario we anticipated terrorists destroying the World Trade Center by crashing airliners into it' (Schwartz, 2003, p. 4).

This demonstrates a poverty of expectations in policy enactment and an inability to grasp the collective capturing of the movement of psyche in cultural artifacts. Using cultural artifacts such as films, interactive video games or any type of moving narrative structure, a researcher and forecaster can imagine the unintended consequences to come and plan for and mitigate what Schwartz identifies as 'inevitable future surprises' a term that characterizes future events that 'can be anticipated now' (p. 2). Significant events and inevitable surprises are manifestations of humans' psychological lives and, as such, can be examined in order to fathom the future, because my contention is that the future is embryonically present within cultural artifacts.

Artifact, myth, metaphor, image and symbol

What movies signaled the first whisperings that terrorists might obtain a nuclear device for purposes of blackmail? Alfred Hitchcock's *Saboteur* (1942) projects a Nazi plot to sabotage American war industries at a time when public fears of espionage and industrial terrorism were at their peak. John Frankenheimer's *The Manchurian Candidate* (1962), depicts the assassination of a presidential candidate, masterminded by the Manchurian Corporation—perhaps a precursor of the powerful role special interest groups, lobbyists and big business has in American government today. The film appeared during a time of political killings; in fact, the movie was still in theatrical release when John F. Kennedy was assassinated in 1963. In Director Terence Young's *Thunderball* (1965), Sean Connery's James Bond character manages to thwart the terrorists, but the film's storyline seems remarkably prescient for post-9/11 times. George Seaton's *Airport* (1970) depicts a psychopathic kamikaze attempting to hijack an American airliner. At that time, the movie reflected the American public's growing anxiety over increasing airplane hijackings. These movies can be regarded as Hollywood's propaganda machine, producing cinematic terrorism for global consumption, as well as the collective capturing of the movement of the cultural psyche.

Video games, too, provide learning environments that teach a player how to control and often dominate, as well as providing an experiential environment that instructs a gamer to actually drive cars and fly planes within simulated environments. Violent editions of video games elicit aggressive solutions to conflict, 'priming aggressive thoughts and practicing new aggression related scripts that can become more and more accessible for use when real-life conflict situations arise' (Steyer, 2002, p. 90)

In fact, after 9/11, when Western journalists were visiting Al Qaeda safe houses in Kabul they: 'discovered packaging elements from the popular Microsoft *Flight Simulator*—a computer game that allowed users to simulate flight takeoffs from the world's largest airports and crash them into skyscrapers, including New York's World Trade Center' (ibid., p. 90). The attacks on 9/11 were eerily prefigured by Microsoft's *Flight Simulator* video game. The existence of the game can therefore be considered to have been a warning of imminent danger, a danger that went unnoticed because events tend to be seen in isolation and unconnected.

Prior to Microsoft's *Flight Simulator* video game, a spate of war movies prepared the collective American psyche for things to come, including *Tora! Tora! Tora!* (dirs Fleisher and Fukasaku, 1970), *Platoon* (dir. Stone, 1986), *Saving Private Ryan* (dir. Spielberg, 1998) and *Three Kings* (dir. Russell, 1999). Jarringly, *Three Kings* is about three American soldiers who went into the Iraqi desert to find millions in stolen Kuwaiti bullion and became involved in a democratic uprising. Their purpose was not to bring democracy to Iraq, in contrast to the Bush administration's main reason for going to war. The battle at Pearl Harbor on December 7, 1941, forced America's hand into the Second World War through a surprise Japanese-kamikaze attack. Eighteen ships were sunk, and 2,403 Americans were killed. The movie *Pearl Harbor*, released in 2001 was still fresh in the American cultural mindset when 9/11 occurred, thus preparing the country for rhetoric such as 'It's Pearl Harbor all over again.'

Another film that similarly was a psychological preparation and harbinger of a different form of catastrophe was *The China Syndrome* (dir. Bridges, 1979). The fictional story portrayed a near meltdown of a nuclear facility. Only weeks after the film's opening night, the Three Mile Island nuclear plant in Pennsylvania partially melted down and released radioactivity into Dauphin County. Was this an eerie coincidence or the silenced voice of a super-heated cultural psyche?

Reification

The event referred to as 9/11 is the result of myriad previous events, crises and historical decisions, all of which caused trajectories that careened into the present and continue onward into the future. This forgotten and unconscious material is a result of *reification*, a process described by Berger and Luckmann (1990) whereby the 'products of human activity' are apprehended 'as if they were something other than human products—such as facts of nature, results of cosmic laws, or manifestations of divine will' (p. 106). This implies, argue Berger and Luckmann that 'man is capable of forgetting his own authorship of the human world, and, further, that the dialectic between man, the producer, and his products is lost to consciousness' (p. 106). Berger and Luckmann further suggest that the reified world is 'a dehumanized world' and is experienced as a 'strange facticity, an *opus alienum* over which he has no control rather than as an *opus proprium* of his own productive activity' (p. 106).

Understood from this perspective of the sociology of knowledge, 9/11 is a critical-cultural event, a human construction and an event that we have forgotten that we authored. This necessarily results in an inability to bring essential meaning to the event, because we do not understand that it is a manifestation of our own psychological world, realized and made manifest. By using a rhizomatic model, as defined by Deleuze and Guattari in their book *A Thousand Plateaus: Capitalism and Schizophrenia* (1987), the researcher is able to counter this amnesia by unpacking the history and the current state of the official myths and hidden stories that comprised the human constructions in the preceding events that precipitated the current event. The rhizome unlike trees or roots

> connects any point to any other point … it is composed not of units but of dimensions, or rather directions in motion. It has neither beginning nor end, but always a middle (*milieu*) from which it grows and which it overspills.
>
> *(1987, p. 21)*

This process returns the dialectical possibilities to the event, where an exchange of propositions and counter-propositions may be exposed. This, in turn, generates the possibility of creating a synthesis through the exposure and articulation of opposing assertions, which invariably leads to remembering that we are the creators and authors of all the previous events. This knowledge produces a concomitant wisdom with reflexivity that garners foresight and insight into the future.

From a depth psychological perspective and methodology, one can etiologically return to and recover early culturally traumatic incidents. Similarly, a *film futuristics* researcher understands that reified material in a cultural artifact can cause a neurosis and a dysfunctional response to it, as occurred after 9/11 in America. In fact, the task of *film futuristics* is to remember what has been forgotten, to recover, and to unconceal hidden and unconscious constellated opposites, shadow material, projections and defense mechanisms. Bringing these elements to consciousness is the psychoanalytical healing process used in the consulting room in action and a core task of *film futuristics*.

Cultural complexes

The concern with fanatics, psychotics and neurotics is important to *film futuristics*, because the psychologically affecting and emotional power that exists around them leads inexorably toward the unexploded landmines of culturally unconscious complexes. If humans do not recognize how the unconscious is at work in culture, and if they remain unconscious of these under-ground, powerful, motivating forces, the conscious mind cedes control to the images and symbolic content. This implies the potential for dissociation, paranoia, systemized delusions and the projection of cultural conflicts ascribed to the supposed hostility of others. If unchecked, dissociation progresses to a cultural disturbance of consciousness and aggressive acts are rational-ized as holy missions. Or acts are committed in so-called self-defense, such as America instigat-ing a global war on terror because Saddam Hussein, the American people and the world are told, has weapons of mass destruction.

This disturbance of consciousness exists in present-day America. It was seen in the George W. Bush administration's 'holy mission of a global war on terror'. As Jung asserted:

> Today humanity, as never before, is split into two apparently irreconcilable halves. The pyschological rule says that when an inner situation is not made conscious, it happens outside, as fate. That is to say, when the individual remains undivided and does not become conscious of his inner opposite, the world must perforce act out the conflict and be torn into opposing halves.
>
> *(1951: §126)*

Jungian analysts Tom Singer and Sam Kimbles (2004), took Jung's theory of complexes and mapped them onto culture, coining the term *cultural complexes*. Cultural complexes deal with the cultural level of the psyche and the life of the group and how the life of the group exists in the psyche of the individual. Invariably, Singer and Kimbles suggest that the notion of cultural complexes will lead to an 'enhanced capacity to see more objectively the shadow of the group in its cultural complexes' (p. 4). Singer and Kimbles further suggest that:

> As complexes emerge out of the level of the personal unconscious in their interaction with deeper levels of the psyche and early parental/familial relationships, cultural com-plexes can be thought of as arising out of the cultural unconscious as it interacts with both the archetypal and personal realms of the psyche and the broader outer world arena of schools, communities, media, and all the other forms of cultural and group life.
>
> *(p. 4)*

The task now, Singer argues, is for every injured culture—be it American, Iraqi, Iranian, Balkan, Palestinian, Catholic, Jewish, Jungian, men, or women—'to learn to drink to the dregs of its own complexes, as well as those of its neighbors, allies and enemies' (p. 31). The emergence of a theory of cultural complexes suggests that an 'understanding of the individual psyche through its consciousness will not be enough. The group itself will need to develop a consciousness of its cultural complexes' (p. 31).

Through the postmodern fascination with the surface and its absorption in decoration, modern humans have lost knowledge of the cultural wounds that litter the global cultural psyche. Tribal, racial and ethnic wounds; gender mutilations and transformations; and religious, political and economic inequalities are all lost to the surface gaze. Like landmines, cultural complexes are buried under the surface and inside cultural artifacts, ready to detonate at the slightest provocation. Like dried-up riverbeds, these complexes are reminders of unresolved conflicts that have accumulated in the collective memories and emotions of generations. Like water that returns to a parched riverbed, critical and numinous events flow in as markers and expressions of deep wounds in the collective cultural psyche. These critical-cultural events explode and trigger chain reactions, because each is connected rhizomatically to all others. As each event explodes, the hidden invisible wounds grow.

Film futuristics delves into this fund of culturally unconscious images that often fatally confuse cultural consciousness. It is *film futuristics*' task to re-envision and return the 'matrix of a mythopoeic imagination which has vanished from our rational age' (Jung, 1989, p. 183).

There exists an unconscious, interdependent connection among all critical-cultural artifacts. When a researcher sees them this way, as an interconnected rhizomatic web, he or she is more able to visualize the affecting cultural-wounding effects, emotional power and destructive potential of the cultural unconscious within society's larger framework.

The power of opposites

Jung conceptualized the dynamism of the psyche by using the 'first law of thermodynamics which states that energy demands two opposing forces' (Samuels et al., 1986, p. 102). The key to understanding the psyche in critical cultural events and the key to the analysis used by *film futuristics* is in the revealing and understanding of opposites.

Pairs of opposites are by their nature considered to be in an undifferentiated state and diametrically opposed. Cultural life theoretically furnishes rules and limitations that of their own prevent excessive psychic disproportion: cultural 'wholeness implies a tremendous tension of opposites paradoxically at one with themselves' (Jung 1956: §460). However, the dissolution of any compromise reached between two halves of a pair renders the activity of opposition ever more intense, causing psychic disequilibrium and disassociation, such as that which is noticeable in psychosis. Alternatively, experiencing being at the mercy of one opposite extreme and then the other is the hallmark of an awakening consciousness. Ultimately, when the tension becomes intolerable, an alchemical synthesis occurs. Relief occurs because a reconciliation of the two opposites occurs at a 'different and more satisfactory level' (Samuels et al., 1986, p. 102). This is the *coniunctio* process that represents the most basic anatomy of the individual and collective psyche. The flow of libido, or 'psychic energy, is generated by the polarization of opposites in the same way that electricity flows between the positive and negative poles of an electrical circuit' (Edinger and Blackmer, 1994, p. 12).

The *coniunctio*, or sacred marriage of opposing constellations, can be 'conceived as opposites, [that are] either confronting one another in enmity or attracting one another in love' (Jung, 1955–6: §1). Either way, it indicates that the drama of the opposites is at play. Understood psychologically, consciousness requires the simultaneous experience of the opposites; similarly, the heart requires blood to pump full–empty, breath requires in–out. The more that consciousness can hold tension between oppositional forces or ideas, the greater consciousness is enhanced. Another fundamental aspect of opposites is that which is denied, repressed or activated by a complex can be brought into view via oppositional energies, a process that spawns advanced consciousness, which in turn cultivates forward-thinking wisdom, insight and clarity.

Opposition is 'the basic drama that goes on in the collective psyche. Every war, every contest between groups, every dispute between political factions, every game, is an expression of *coniunctio* energies' (Edinger and Blackmer, 1994, p. 15). Whenever one-sided identification with either one of a pair of warring opposites occurs, the tension between the opposites is lost; hence, the ability to enhance consciousness or to develop broadmindedness is lost.

The cultural-therapeutic goal of *film futuristics* is to strengthen and to support an expansion of personal and cultural consciousness—to rouse the personal unconscious of the *film futuristics* researcher, to reveal the unconscious within the event under study and expose the collective unconscious of culture at large. The intention is to produce insight, foresight and superior critical thinking with a concomitant wisdom, thereby lifting the fog caused by participation mystique. In a more modern sense, this is understood as removing the *projective identification* from between the researcher and the event under study. Essentially, this implies that knowledge of what is projected by the personality of the researcher onto the event is recognized and minimized. According to Jung, accomplishing this task 'integrates the unconscious, and gradually there comes into being a higher point of view where both conscious and unconscious [elements] are represented' (1946: §479). The collision of two opposing forces causes the unconscious psyche to produce a third possibility that becomes an 'ambiguous and paradoxical SYMBOL which is capable of attracting attention and eventually reconciling the two' (Samuels et al., 1986, p. 102).

Film futuristics recognizes that the critical artifact, as it acts out in the world, is indeed the result of secret springs of action. No matter how much information, dialog, news and media exist, cultural consciousness always remains the 'smaller circle within the greater circle of the [collective] unconscious, an island surrounded by the sea; and, like the sea itself, the unconscious yields an endless and self-replenishing abundance of living creatures' (Jung, 1946: §366). It is a wealth beyond our fathoming. For a long time, culture has been experiencing the effects and characteristics of these unconscious constellations without ever having understood their depths and 'potentialities, for they are capable of infinite variations and can never be depotentiated' (ibid.: §366). The function and task of *film futuristics* is to delve into the cultural unconscious' depths, examine some of its infinite variations and fathom the opposites that exist there, so as to bring forth wealth.

Sickness is now out there!

Freud and Jung both knew that analysis of neurosis would ultimately escape the therapy room and develop into a form of cultural analysis. James Hillman exemplified this possible future of analysis when he suggested bringing psychological meaning to what are often viewed as isolated cultural artifacts. Thus, this act of psychologizing is a 'process of seeing through' (Hillman, 1975, p. 140) into the underlying teleological factors, needs, values and archetypal impulses of the cultural psyche as they are expressed through numinous cultural events.

In accord with Freud and Jung, Hillman (1992) advocates that theories of neurosis and cultural pathology must be radically extended. He argues that psychology must re-envision the notion of subjectivity itself, because breakdown now exists in the world—in events like terrorism and the ecological and global climate change crisis—not just in people: 'We now encounter pathology in the psyche of politics and medicine, in language and design, in the food we eat. Sickness is now "out there"' (p. 96). Cultural breakdown is producing symptomatic fragments of paranoid politics, manic manufacturing and a loss of cultural vitality. *Film futuristics* aims squarely at understanding, and listening into, this symptomatic and ailing world in service to planning a better future.

Robert Sardello, a pioneer in understanding that an antidote to the 'subjectivizing tendencies of a psychological culture' (2004, p. 21) is imperative because we find ourselves further from the world. Sardello understands that 'therapy has shifted from the isolated chamber of the psychotherapist's office to the world' (p. 21). The organizing forms of buildings, economics, medicine, technology, energy, media and religion are making our culture. The result is that these are: 'making a pathological civilization.... The new symptoms are fragmentation, specialization, expertise, depression, inflation, cruelty, hardness, violence, and absence of beauty. Our buildings are anorectic, our business paranoid, detached and abstract, our technology manic.'

It is clear to both Sardello and Hillman that, psychologically, because of breakdown, the world 'is entering a new moment of consciousness: by drawing attention to itself by means of its symptoms, it is becoming aware of itself as a psychic reality' (Hillman, 1992, p. 97). The work of psychology ... 'consists of a re-evaluation of the domains of the modern world in terms of metaphor, image, story, and dream' (Sardello, 2004, p. 21). Hillman further argues that the world is in a state of 'gross chaos, exhibiting acute symptoms' (1992, p. 97) and observes that not only is pathology projected onto the world but that 'the world is inundating [us] with its unalleviated suffering' (p. 99). Hillman argues that it must become psychotherapy's task to take up the thread first initiated by Sigmund Freud (which is, fundamentally, *film futuristics*' task)—to analytically dissect cultural neurosis—which 'might lead to therapeutic recommendations which could lay claim to great practical interest' (p. 98).

The world is projecting its own repressed collective unconsciousness onto humanity through films, videos and virtual reality that humans make, witness and themselves live! Much of humanity is oblivious to this remarkable concept, yet it is nothing other than the cultural complexes as the *anima cultura mundi* at work in the world—behind and below the threshold of human consciousness.

Film futuristics seeks to perceive and to discern the hidden needs and voices of psyche that lie within significant films and to see underneath the repressive modernistic shroud of scientific and cultural materialism while conceptualizing the artifact as a rhizomatic web that interconnects meaning making threads with underlying unconscious components. This interlinking postmodern concept parallels Deleuze and Guattari's rhizome model, with its constantly emerging immanent space and place, versus the modern era's tree metaphor and idea of nomadic space. *Film futuristics* relies on Deleuze and Guattari's (1987) argument that a new nomadic space illustrated by the postmodern rhizomatic model is a 'map and not a tracing' (p. 12). 'The map is open and connectable in all of its dimensions; it is detachable, reversible, susceptible to constant modification. It can be torn, reversed, adapted, to any kind of mounting, reworked by an individual, group, or social formation' (p. 12).

Recovering, remembering or reconnecting the facades with the depths is therapy at work: in an individual context, therapy is the labor of restoring *the how*, to *the what*, bringing insight and vision to the invisible via the symptom that is in itself in disguise. This is what *film futuristics* does for the collective life of humanities future. It restores us to our place because it shows us that the cultural artifacts from which we seem to be apart is in fact a part of us, the visible expression of a story originated by us and continuing today and forming our future history.

Keith Basso: the smooth mind—wisdom and place

As a methodology, *film futuristics* requires the researcher to access a particular attitude in order to achieve maximum efficacy while conducting the analysis, synthesis and future history (writing

193

the three scenarios) on cultural artifacts. This required attitude can be found within the frame-work of indigenous wisdom, particularly in the idea of *smooth mind* as articulated in Keith H. Basso's *Wisdom Sits in Places* (1996). Basso explains how the Western Apache concept of land-scape and place is culturally significant and how they tell stories about places in order to foresee danger before it arrives from the future. Basso lifts the veil on the most elemental poetry of human experience—place. My move is to understand film as place.

For the Western Apache, certain places are significant and numinous. The stories told about those places are passed down from one generation to the next in order to pass on lessons learned from the events that occurred there. 'Drink from places, Apache boys and girls are told. Then you can work your mind' (Basso, 1996, p. 34). Drinking from places means that places have acquired the stamp of human events, meaning a consequential and liminal event has taken place there. Places that have greatly affected the Apache are named, and places are memorialized because they have become consecrated. Places with names are thus enhanced and endowed with hallowed force. The uncanny exists in these revered places, spaces and sites, and it is here that one experiences the soul shuddering, an 'experience [of] a religious humility' (Corbett, 1996, p. 12).

Places-of-occupation, combined with an elemental story and the stamp of a numinous event, mark place as an occupied field filled with wisdom. Consequently, places are like water that never dries up:

> You need to drink water to stay alive, don't you? Well, you also need to drink from places. You must remember everything about them. You must learn their names. You must remember what happened at them a long time ago. You must think about it and keep on thinking about it. Then your mind will become smoother and smoother. *Then you will see danger before it happens* [italics added]. You will walk a long way and live a long time. You will be wise. People will respect you.
>
> *(Basso, 1996, p. 127)*

Wisdom is, therefore, equated with survival; surviving is enhanced by having smoothness of mind, and smoothness of mind rests on two subsidiary conditions—'mental resilience and mental steadiness—which ward off distractions that interfere with calm and focused thought' (ibid., p. 132). Mental resilience is defined as a state of mind that is immune to chaos or affecting havoc. Even in horrifying circumstances, 'resilient minds maintain their ability to reason clearly and thus neither 'block themselves' nor 'stand in their own way' (ibid., p. 132). Resilience of mind is analogous to a tightly woven round basket—a container that has inherent flexibility because of its organic and natural fiber, yet is also strong because its shape yields to accom-modate that which it encloses. Resistant to the unnerving effects of jarring external events, resilient minds protect their interior spaces by shielding them against outside disruptions that threaten quiescent thinking.

By understanding these three mental conditions—smoothness, resilience and steadiness of mind—as a developmental model and applying this model to *film futuristics*, film as place becomes a transmitted story about place—a carrier of wisdom. Practically, knowledge is useful to the extent that stories about film/places can be swiftly recalled and turned rapidly into wise responses to the pending danger of significant and numinous events. This ability to recall stories under powerful affecting situations produces an uncanny ability to quickly and effectively respond, and is based on knowledge that has been passed from one generation to the next. This is the smooth mind and practical wisdom that defines foresight—an integral portion of *film futuristics*.

Film futuristics: praxis

Film futuristics requires the researcher to phenomenologically engage in a process of reliving history as a now experience. Significant cultural artifacts are understood to be manifestations of an age's psychological life, a mirror that returns an accurate picture of the forces at work behind the scenes. When tended by using *film futuristics*, the many-faceted symbols are uncovered in the symptoms, the countless myths are uncovered in the multitudinous meanings and the hidden dreams in the unfamiliar metaphors are revealed in the taken-for-granted truths.

The practice of *film futuristics* becomes a way home to the future, a method of 'way forward engineering' with soul in mind, because it includes that which has been forgotten, reified, repressed and exiled returning unconsciousness by reinserting soul into the fantasy of the future scenario—future history.

Film futuristics is constructed in three fundamental stages similar to the three principal stages of alchemy. The essence of *film futuristics* is in performing research, then separation and analysis on one hand, and synthesis and consolidation on the other. Numinous cultural artifacts are examined and explored phenomenologically, psychologically and mythically. Numinous artifacts as in the previous examples of robots and AIs in the science fiction films may be analyzed and then followed by writing future histories that predict, or forewarn or forearm policy makers and planners about (perhaps) a new age of leisure, or new teenage initiation rituals or a trans-modern world where all private ownership of motor vehicles is outlawed. Future histories act as narrative devices that condense and consolidate the analysis, which in turn produces synthesis. This is a fundamentally alchemical procedure that reunites opposing hostile and previously separated constellations by synthetically reintegrating them, and therapeutically transforming separation into unity.

The resulting future histories are written from a metaphorical perspective using the researcher's own activated transcendent function, functionally mediating, by way of the emerged symbols, the constellated opposites revealed during analysis. This perspective facilitates a transition from one psychological attitude or condition to another, by creating a linkage between 'real and imaginary, or rational and irrational data, thus bridging the gulf between consciousness and unconsciousness' (Samuels et al., 1986, p. 150). This is the therapeutic-healing function in action, oppositional forces, when held in tension, seek their compensation in unity. The confrontation of rational data with that of unconscious or irrational information is the transcendent function's task, resulting in an expansion of consciousness, a modification of standpoint and a transformation of perspectives.

It is important to iterate that *film futuristics* produces future histories that neither explain, nor develop, any unified or grand theories. *Film futuristics* makes the postmodern move from the need to cure and fix, to a deep honoring of the symptom in the dream of the film. Future histories are, thus, generative, intentional inquiries into symptom because (a) the teleological thrust of the hidden voice within a significant event has been understood as initially representing *coniunctio* energies, (b) the opposites have been held in tension and (c) future histories are written using the activated transcendent function of the researcher. The researcher is fundamentally implicated in the research process because the transferential field between the event under study and the researcher exists and affects both.

Futures studies vs film futuristics

The purpose of futures studies, or futuristics, is to discover or invent, examine and evaluate, and propose possible, probable and preferable futures. Futures studies' objective is to grasp today's landscape and how changes (or the lack thereof) may become tomorrow's reality. It includes the analysis of source patterns, that is, the causes of change and stability, in order to develop conceptual maps of alternative future conditions and states. The subjects and methods of futures studies includes the conceptualization of alternative formulations of the present social and natural environments, where *natural* is defined as independent of human impact.

Like depth psychology, future studies also uses a variety of methodologies to examine how forces at work in the world today are forming the future. Using multiple interdisciplinary perspectives, futurists seek to develop insight, foresight and maps of alternative futures. They construct narrative fictions called *scenarios* that explore tomorrow's possibilities. They call this process *scenario planning*. *Film futuristics* scenarios are differently constructed from the scenarios of futures studies. In cultural futuristics, scenarios A (possible future) and B (probable future) are written from the perspective of each constellated opposite, as revealed in the analytical phase. Scenario C (preferable future) is written from a metaphorical style of consciousness and from the perspective of the researcher's own activated, transcendent function. This scenario performs the alchemical-*coniunctio* function by reuniting the constellated opposites identified in scenarios A and B. This process, therefore, brings soul to scenario planning and consciousness to way forward engineering. This concept, method and approach currently does not exist in cultural analysis, cultural therapeutics or futures studies and are this chapter's contribution to the field.

Like Futurists, *film futuristics*' decisions and action are informed with futures thinking. Similar to van den Berg's Metabletica (1983), which attempts to explain what happened in the past and why, the efforts of futures studies and *film futuristics* are to examine, identify and propose responses to the embryonic potential that exists within the present as evidenced in film. This requires theoretical constructions of present conditions and how conditions might change.

Film futuristics adds several additional dimensions that are not currently included in futures studies. First, there is an unconscious motivating force existing within critical-cultural artifacts/films. Second, the rhizomatic interconnections of the unconscious components within multiple events can be utilized to expose the hidden, orphaned and exiled teleological directions as seen in the symptoms and complexes within the artifact. Third, the resulting scenarios after analysis can be written as future history. Future histories are designed to reveal the unconscious conflicts within the artifacts. They are revealed and released by focusing on the shadow projections, cultural complexes and constellated opposites witnessed within the artifact. The scenarios of future histories expand the consciousnesses of the researcher and the artifact, because future histories mediate the conflicted opposites within the event under analysis. Holding the tension between the opposites results in psychic growth and a concomitant wisdom, precisely because the opposites have a chance of being reconciled.

Two factors usually distinguish *film futuristics* studies from research conducted by other disciplines (although all disciplines overlap to differing degrees):

1 *Film futuristics* examines not only possible, but also probable, preferable and wildcard scenarios of future states or conditions.
2 *Film futuristics* endeavors to advance a holistic or general-systems view based on insights from a range of different disciplines.

It is important to note also that future histories are written through the lens of the *anima cultura futurus mundi* (the future cultural soul of the world), which recognizes that *coniunctio* forces are at work through collective-unconscious, and constellated complexes as seen in the cultural complexes. *Film futuristics* and future histories, as a two-part methodology, become an applicable process that benefits all the other methodologies that futurists use. Why? Because *film futuristics* offers radical insight into the cultural complex as a symptom and reveals the cultural soul within cultural artifacts.

The scenario

Ultimately, the end product of every futures methodology is the scenario. Scenarios are fictional stories about possible, probable and preferable futures. They are the optimistic, pessimistic or most probable outcomes, or a combination of all three. Often, there are numerous stories about possibilities for the future, each of which have different probabilities of transpiring under diverse and sometimes contradictory conditions. In this case, many more than three scenarios can be written. Scenarios propose goals and values that address the desirability or undesirability of various futures. Typically, they contain descriptions of available choices and a list of anticipated and unanticipated outcomes. They can include the formulation of unintended circumstances that could alter the scenarios dramatically. The scenarios may also include implicit and explicit recommendations regarding what 'choices and actions ought to be made now in the present to create the most desirable world in the future' (Bell, 1996, p. 317).

Even a brief example of this process will show how rapidly effective the method is and demonstrate the process. Imagine it is late 2020, and you decide to use *film futuristics* in a personal capacity to write a novella. But you face a blank page!

We will use the same films mentioned previously: *Frankenstein* (1931) directed by James Whale, *2001 A Space Odyssey* (1968), directed by Stanley Kubrick, *Interstellar* (2014) directed by Christopher Nolan and *Ex Machina* (2015) directed by Alex Garland.

Phase 1

Research begins with a steady, resilient and steadfast mind, anchored in place like earth packed around a post. You unpack the many meanings within the monster of Frankenstein. A being made up of the discarded and dead parts of previously living human beings. Frankenstein is constructed from what we have cast away, discarded, orphaned and exiled: Frankenstein is built completely of our shadows. In Mary Shelley's book *Frankenstein* (1996) we have a fundamental story of mankind becoming God by creating life. But the creator, Victor Frankenstein, of the so-called monster abandons his creature and refuses to take responsibility for his actions. The monster becomes marginalized, cast adrift and becomes the 'other', yet the whole story may also be understood as a prophesy. It is a modern retelling of the original mythic story of Prometheus and the Christian creation myth. It is a narrative construction that forces us to see our own psychological blindness and it is a haunting prescient rendering of the inevitable rise of technological power, artificial life and AI threatening to rival us.

In *2001 A Space Odyssey*, HAL, interestingly one letter of the alphabet removed from IBM, implies an immediate link toward evolution of the computer and perhaps the eventual enslavement of mankind by (IBM's) Watson technology. The film opens with primordial apes around a watering hole, a brilliant and unexpected beginning, considering the title of the film. Then we witness what logically must be the very beginning of bone as tool and weaponry. A tracking shot follows it up as it is flung into the air; revealing satellites circling the Earth. We recognize the configuration as preparation for space warfare. The soundtrack playing over this scene is the music of Johann Strauss's *Blue Danube*, it was also the name of Britain's first operational nuclear weapon. The fundamental plot is that we are not alone, humanity has found a mysterious monolith on Earth that when discovered sends a signal to another on the moon.

This is an evolutionary story. Sometime in the past, someone or something nudged evolution and placed monoliths on the Earth on the moon and Jupiter in order to warn or signal a maturity of human development. HAL 9000 and the human (Bowman) set off on a quest. A race to Jupiter begins with two fundamental players in competition to win a battle; whoever wins, and reaches the monolith creators achieves the next step in evolution, perhaps the final abyss.

Interstellar (2014) begins by showing us a near future where the apocalypse is approaching: blight, famine, major crops, such as corn, are ending their resource life cycles. Oxygen has begun to deplete, the 'dirt itself' has turned on mankind—man and the earth are cursed. Metaphoric, imagery, the wind torn dust of death is contrasted with our history of Eden. A possible reason for the blight and famine may be because we have genetically modified crops and geo-engineered the atmosphere. The narrative of *Interstellar* is perhaps a warning as well as proposing alternative responses for the resource crises afflicting humankind. This movie is a strategic warning scenario, with crucial components. Under the guise of fiction, it anticipates the way our society could 'choose to fail' yet *Interstellar* proposes that it is possible to invent the future and intervene in the present. We must accept the coming end of growth because of the finite resources and end of life cycle of everything. Space exploration suggests *Interstellar* holds the key to our civilization's survival through new off-world possibilities.

In *Ex Machina*, Ava is the mythical Eve, the first artificial super-intelligence to rival human capabilities. Caleb wins an online competition to spend time at Nathan's house/laboratory far away on an isolated mountainside. He arrives only to discover that he is to administer the Turing test. Conceived by Alan Turing to determine if a computer is as intelligent as a human, it requires that a human being should be unable to distinguish the machine from another human being by using the replies to questions put to both human and machine. Nathan says to Caleb 'If you've created a conscious machine it's not the history of man … that's the history of Gods' (*Ex Machina*, 2015). This is narcissism in action, a current cultural obsession. AI is a very narcissistic field of research. Are we not attempting to surpass ourselves? The central conceit is that creating human-like intelligence is both desirable and an ultimate achievement. Much more comes to mind, particularly, that Nathan is portrayed as the epitome of an all-too-real trope in high-tech, a typical silicon valley style, a hyper-masculine depiction of the male-dominated libertarian world where Ava is a stand in for women who are relegated to playthings, and as slaves and sex toys, seeking only to be free.

Phase 2

Now we separate and analyze on one hand, and synthesize and consolidate on the other. Inequality between the sexes exists; inequality of pay for the same work is rampant. Humankind is attempting to become God, as the Promethium myth suggests, stealing fire and mastering technology to create AI that rivals humankind is doomed. We have become obsessed with the idea that through AI we can create, or even become, God or a god. Our geo-engineering and resource depleting hydrocarbon society we have constructed is causing blight, famine and global climate change which threatens our very survival. We are entering an end zone, catastrophic apocalypse for planet Earth. Our only solution is to travel to the stars and experience the final abyss on Jupiter or wherever, or whatever that will be. Perhaps the only conceivable future is to advance the computer, into a genetic computer/human hybrid possessing the full capabilities of human masculinity and femininity that balances itself out and creates a third thing—a spiritual AI. This then becomes the ultimate combination, this is how we transcend death, as human beings.

This is how we leave Eden. The underlying narrative is that the singularity is pending. Humankind's key to defeating the real enemy—death—is to become Gods.

Phase 3

Now we write three scenarios and create future history. As previously outlined Scenario A is the possible future and Scenario B is the probable future. These are written from the perspective of each constellated opposite, as revealed in the analytical phase. Scenario C becomes the preferable future. This scenario performs the alchemical-*coniunctio* function by reuniting the constellated opposites identified simply: A plus B equals C.

Scenario A: the possible future

AI has found its way to Google/UBER. GoER is finding better ways for cities to move, work and thrive. Allowing drivers to earn money on your schedule with their own cars. A passenger hops into a GoER in Philadelphia, no human driver exists anymore only robots, good-looking robots. You, the passenger, have requested who you want, a gender neutral, jock or anime character. You have also chosen the conversation, a philosophical one, where the deepest questions are examined or the latest political news from the left, or right. It's all choices in the application. GoER used big data to collect it all, the brand mark on the dashboard is Teoogle (Tesla/Google).

Scenario B: the probable future

GoER's early adoption of AI is too early, several major incidents and massive deaths from autonomous accidents causes legislative delays. Tesla loses interest in domestic electric vehicle production and instead redirects focus on the first mission to Mars. One reason is because of the redirection of a pre-eminent first world democracy toward supporting right-wing dictators instead of shunning them and shutting them out. This combined with a reckless rebuilding of the oil and gas industry, and the reneging on the Paris Agreement, the United Nations Framework Convention on Climate Change. Combined with the gutting of the United States EPA (Environmental Protection Agency), and US Department of Education causes a generational retardation of well-informed citizens. Panic in the streets ensues, America destabilizes, China expands, Pacific Rim influence currying favor with Australia, New Zealand and Africa. Russia and America become the best of friends muscling the last of the planet's resources while plunging the Earth into an ever earlier apocalypse.

Scenario C: the preferable future

GoER and AirBnB and other sharing, gig type economies explode onto the global stage, disrupting the mega corporations, the global travel, hotel and the transportation industry. The nationalistic right-wing move from Brexit, to Trump in the United States, to Putin in Russia, rising nationalistic dictators in India, Germany, Japan, Venezuela, Poland and France all come to power because of globalization. It's the economy and the loss of jobs, loss of cultural vitality and soul. Globalization is stopped dead in its tracks. For now, but the pendulum swings away from the mega corporations and the mega rich who banked on a consuming pliable marketplace. Everyone on the planet begins to have less reliance on the corporate paycheck, on being or being used by big businesses or their offerings. Their power begins to wane, everything goes local and tribal, but is informed by the global, through social media. Peer to peer marketing, lending, financing, work and leisure become the new game in town. Thanks to robots taking over many of the menial manufacturing processes and service jobs leisure becomes the new industry and new models emerge that don't require an honest day's work anymore to live a full and well-structured, ordered, fulfilling life. Carl's Junior a fast food joint in America, boasts that it has the most robots serving customers in America.

Here we have three scenarios and the beginning of a skeleton from which to construct a prescient, fictional, fantastic story about a trans-modern human being, part-time GoER driver, part-time landlord with AirBnB, making money with bitcoin in peer-to-peer lending, leading a life of leisure.

This is an example of how *film futuristics* may be used as a tool to fathom ideas that lead to writing a novel, or advising a corporation on what products may be appropriate in the future. The method lends itself to helping advise NGOs and policy makers on the cultural shifts to come. A depth psychology beyond just analysis, away from the individual, but a combination of analysis, synthesis and extrapolation as future possibility with a focus toward group and community.

A future scenario becomes a compelling vision that then inspires policy makers and change agents to strive toward the future by remodeling the present in such a way as to achieve way forward engineering. Or not. The opposite is equally true; a vision can be so diabolical that an entire culture mobilizes to avert the potential disaster that is foreshadowed in the scenario. The scenario of global climate change is an excellent example of this.

Scenario planning delivers the ability to produce stout decision-making. It accomplishes this task by meeting three objectives. Kees van der Heijden, in his book *Scenarios: The Art of Strategic Conversation* (2005), argues that the first objective is to generate 'projects and decisions that are more robust under a variety of alternative futures' (p. 5). The second objective is to create better quality thinking about the future through unpacking and stretching mental models. With a lateral approach, new ideas and insights emerge that lead to new discoveries. The third objective is the search for predetermined elements, and the driving forces that produce predetermined elements.

Driving forces are forces that influence events. 'Often, identifying driving forces reveals the presence of deeper, more fundamental forces' (Schwartz, 1995, p. 103). When working on scenarios, it is imperative to identify the driving forces because they move the plot of the scenario forward. Schwartz identifies five driving forces: 'society, technology, economics, politics, and the environment' (p. 105). *Film futuristics* adds a sixth driving force—numinously significant cultural artifacts as film.

Conclusion

The bulk of this chapter has been devoted to arguments that validate *film futuristics* as a means to analyze the hidden dimensions and prospective probabilities in film to gain practical knowledge, insight, foresight and wisdom for future planning for both public and personal insight. It has articulated the required attitude necessary to perform *film futuristics*, outlined a process and methodological structure, and described how to write future histories, while also providing a brief personal example. Undoubtedly, there are ways of practicing *film futuristics* other than the way that I have outlined here. The more important issue is not the specific process involved or the methodology, even if the methodological questions may have some significance. What is important is to accomplish narrative fictions about the future that include the unconscious voice of soul in cultural artifacts. *Film futuristics* is one method of scenario writing that reanimates and functionally deals with future social and cultural issues. Following Keith Basso and the insights from indigenous wisdom, *film futuristics*' final outcome will be future histories, or medicine stories—powerful narratives that share with future generations the wisdom that sits in places.

Furthermore *film futuristics* exists to recover from critical-cultural events their possible future implications, constellations and dangers. If we look at America, for example, it can be argued that it has become entangled in its own *glory making*, unable to tear itself away and see the submerged messages and meanings that perhaps the rest of the world can clearly see. From a *film futuristics* perspective, the messages and meanings are eminently visible in movies, video games, political foreign policy stances and the rhetoric of anti-intellectualism. In this chapter, I have freely associated in an effort to connect prefiguring cultural artifacts with critical events. *China Syndrome* (1979) prefigured Three Mile Island. A video game maker not only provided the idea but also the training to destroy the World Trade Center on 9/11. For the highest levels of government and its military leaders to say that an attack of this complexity using jumbo jets as missiles to destroy the World Trade Center was impossible to imagine. That it was failure of imagination, is nothing short of pathological denial, consistent with a clinical diagnosis of what may be called cultural narcissistic personality disorder.

Ultimately, *film futuristics* has been designed to clarify and deliberate the problems and risks that cultures face, and to outline, through future history, how things might be done differently. This is presented in full knowledge that a precise envisioning of the actual future is impossible.

References

Basso, K. H. (1996) *Wisdom sits in places: landscape and language among the Western Apache.* Albuquerque, NM: University of New Mexico Press.

Bell, W. (1996) *Foundations of futures studies: human science for a new era.* New Brunswick, NJ: Transaction Publishers.

Berg, J. H. van den (1983) *The changing nature of man: introduction to historical psychology.* New York: W. W. Norton.

Berger, P. L. and Luckmann, T. (1990) *The social construction of reality: a treatise on the sociology of knowledge.* New York: Anchor Books.

Corbett, L. (1996) *The religious function of the psyche.* New York: Routledge.

Deleuze, G. and Guattari, F. (1987) *A thousand plateaus: capitalism and schizophrenia.* Minneapolis, MN: University of Minnesota Press.

Edinger E. F. and Blackmer, J. D. (1994) *The mystery of the coniunctio: alchemical image of individuation.* Toronto: Inner City Books.

Heijden, K. van der. (2005) *Scenarios: the art of the strategic conversation.* Chichester, UK: John Wiley.

Hillman, J. (1975) *Re-visioning psychology.* New York: Harper.

Hillman, J. (1992) *The thought of the heart and the soul of the world.* Dallas, TX: Spring.

Jung, C. G. (1916/48) 'General aspects of dream psychology', in *The collected works of C. G. Jung*, Vol. 8, *The structure and dynamics of the psyche*, 2nd edn. London: Routledge & Kegan Paul, 1969.

Jung, C. G. (1936) 'The concept of the collective unconscious', in *The collected works of C. G. Jung*, Vol. 9i, *The archetypes and the collective unconscious*, 2nd edn. London: Routledge & Kegan Paul, 1968.

Jung, C. G. (1946) 'The psychology of the transference', in *The collected works of C. G. Jung*, Vol. 16, *The practice of psychotherapy*, 2nd edn. London: Routledge, 1966.

Jung, C. G. (1951) 'Christ, a symbol of the Self', in *The collected works of C. G. Jung*, Vol. 9ii, *Aion: researches into the phenomenology of the Self*, 2nd edn. London: Routledge, 1968.

Jung, C. G. (1955–6) 'The components of the coniunctio', in *The collected works of C. G. Jung*, Vol. 14, *Mysterium coniunctionis: an inquiry into the separation and synthesis of psychic opposites in alchemy*, 2nd edn. London: Routledge, 1970.

Jung, C. G. (1956) 'The battle for deliverance from the mother', in *The collected works of C. G. Jung*, Vol. 5, *Symbols of transformation.* London: Routledge, 1956.

Jung, C. G. (1989) *Memories, dreams, reflections.* New York: Vintage Books.

Samuels, A., Shorter, B. and Plaut, F. (1986) *A critical dictionary of Jungian analysis.* New York: Routledge & Kegan Paul.

Sardello, R. J. (2004) *Facing the world with soul: the reimagination of modern life*, 2nd edn. Boca Raton, FL: Lindisfarne Books.

Schwartz, P. (1995) *The art of the long view: planning for the future in an uncertain world.* New York: Currency Doubleday.

Schwartz, P. (2003) *Inevitable surprises: thinking ahead in a time of turbulence.* New York: Gotham Books.

Shelley, M. W. (1996) *Frankenstein.* Charlottesville, VA: University of Virginia Library.

Singer, T. and Kimbles, S. L. (2004) *The cultural complex: contemporary Jungian perspectives on psyche and society.* New York: Brunner-Routledge.

Steyer, J. P. (2002) *The other parent: the inside story of the media's effect on our children.* New York: Atria Books.

Whitmont, E. C. and Perera, S. B. (1991) *Dreams, a portal to the source: a guide to dream interpretation.* New York: Taylor & Francis.

Online sources

Glock, M. (2008) 'Cultural futuristics: bringing consciousness to cultural complexes and soul to scenario based planning' [online]. Available at: http://pqdtopen.proquest.com/doc/275776990.html?FMT=AI [Accessed 9 September 2016].

Wikiwand (2016) 'Technological singularity' [online]. Available at: www.wikiwand.com/en/Technological_singularity [Accessed 18 October 2016].

Filmography

2001: A space odyssey. (1968) [film] Directed by Stanley Kubrick. UK.

Airport. (1970) [film] Directed by George Seaton. USA.

China syndrome, The. (1979) [film] Directed by James Bridges. USA.

Ex machina. (2015) [film] Directed by Alex Garland. USA.

Frankenstein. (1931) [film] Directed by James Whale. USA.

Interstellar. (2014) [film] Directed by Christopher Nolan. USA.

Manchurian candidate, The. (1962) [film] Directed by John Frankenheimer. USA.

Pearl harbor. (2001) [film] Directed by Michael Bay. USA.

Platoon. (1986) [film] Directed by Oliver Stone. USA.

Saboteur. (1942) [film] Directed by Alfred Hitchcock. USA.

Saving private Ryan. (1998) [film] Directed by Stephen Spielberg. USA.

Three kings. (1999) [film] Directed by David O. Russell. USA.

Thunderball. (1965) [film] Directed by Terence Young. UK.

Tora! Tora! Tora! (1970) [film] Directed by Richard Fleisher and Kinji Fukasaku. Japan, USA.

PART III

Transnational approaches

Edited by
Terrie Waddell

16

THE AUSTRALIAN LOST CHILD COMPLEX IN ADAPTATION

Kurzel's *Macbeth* and Stone's *The Daughter*

Terrie Waddell

The theory of a cultural complex in Jung-based psychology, as distinct from the idea of a collective shadow dominating a social group or nation state, is controversial and not uniformly supported by scholars in the area. I do, however, find some sympathy with Singer and Kimbles' (2004) concept of a 'complex' not only influencing the psyche of the individual, but also a culture, and have discussed this concept publicly in relation to a recurring theme that I argue dominates the cultural landscape of my country, Australia. *The lost child* motif predominately guides both the fictional narratives and reportage of our television, 115-year-old film industry, media, art and literature. It currently overshadows our internal politics in relation to harsh refugee policies that have contributed to the deteriorating mental and physical health of geographically displaced children, and the remorse now directed at policies that legislated for indigenous children (the stolen generations) to be taken from their families and placed in state and religious institutions.

When starting to research this area, I felt that the dominance of *the lost child* was so prolific that it would be verging on cliché to examine the phenomenon in depth. What surprised me most was that although scholars had long looked at the lost child in early Australian (nation making) literature, few had tackled the subject exclusively in relation to film (Menadue, 1975; Pierce, 1999; Torney, 2005; Tilley, 2012). When given a focus in screen texts, the concept was approached from either a sociological or a genre-based framework, rather than one drawing on the psychology of the archetype and its relationship to complexes. It seemed to me that the notion of a culturally collective complex that interweaves a persistent, almost compulsively surfacing, archetypal energy with an entangled history of individual and collective trauma, was highly appropriate to this phenomenon of the lost child that I had grown up with and been culturally enriched by. Its resurfacing can be traced back to our earliest cinema productions from *The Story of the Kelly Gang* (dir. Tait, 1906), the world's first feature film (Gaunson, 2013), to *Lion* (dir. Davis, 2016) based on the memoir of Saroo Brierley, an Indian child adopted by Australian parents who, as an adult, returned to his birth neighbourhood of Khandwa in search of the mother from whom he was separated as a five year old.

Although Australia has a highly creative and diverse independent film culture, my work focuses on mainstream cinema releases. Clearly identifiable lost child themes on screen that achieve commercial distribution, are robustly marketed and attract financial support by national and state-based funding bodies, and demonstrate the collectively compelling nature of this recurring motif. I argue that the lost child is archetypal in its depth and cultural reach; a psychological pattern dominant in Australian screen storytelling – the prime image-based medium through which we access the contemporary reworking of mythology and our collective archetypal rumblings.

What interests me for the purposes of this particular chapter is not how the archetype filters through Australian original and literary-based scripts, but how directors and screenwriters integrate and significantly accentuate the motif when adapting international work. To tackle this trend, I will concentrate on a small sample of two 2015 productions – Shakespeare's *Macbeth*, adapted for the screen by Justin Kurzel and the reworking of Hendrik Ibsen's *The Wild Duck* (1884), renamed *The Daughter* by Simon Stone. Before this analysis though, it is important to expand upon what I understand to be the nature of the lost child complex and raise some hypothetical reasons as to why it has captured the imagination of Australian screen culture.

The lost child complex on screen

As Singer and Kimbles argue, the cultural complex is shaped largely by the attachment of trauma to an archetypal pattern that resonates on a collective *and* personal level, capturing the culture as a whole and the individuals who contribute to shape its development. If we understand the Jungian inflected term *archetype* as collectively occurring unconscious patterns, breaking through to consciousness via projection (1934/54: §6) then it is easier to separate archetypes from *stereotypes* – intentionally created categories, driven by a variety of cultural agendas. In my previous books (Waddell, 2006, 2010) I analysed how archetypes filter through and influence film and television content. This kind of interweaving is not just simplistically related to character embodiments of these psychological energies, but can permeate structural elements of a screen 'text': Christopher Nolan's *Memento* (2000), in relation to the motif of *trickster*, is, as I have suggested, a particularly clear-cut example (Waddell, 2006).

When talking about cultural complexes, it is important to grapple with the cultural breadth of a particular archetypal projection, from the arts to politics, and the undercurrents of trauma that give it sustenance. The lost child has particular currency in Australia. Colonised directly through penal settlement, starting with the first fleet of 11 ships in 1788, the first UK settlers were convicts, crew and their families, with free settlers arriving in 1793 (Currey, 2006). It is therefore possible to argue that white Australia was founded on the trauma of transportation: a kind of separation anxiety that one might argue was later projected on to indigenous communities through the removal of children from families into institutional 'care' (Human Rights and Equal Opportunity Commission, 1997). These legislated mass abductions, often leading to physical and emotional child abuse, ushered in an irreconcilable grief that continues to unnerve the culture, despite social and political attempts at national healing. Founded by a collective of what might be called 'lost children' seized from the British motherland, who later imposed lostness on those they in turn displaced, it is not surprising that coloniser and colonised became, as Peter Pierce has titled his sociological/historical study on the phenomena, *The Country of Lost Children* (1999).

It is as if the child has historically and politically, shifted to a symbol of both trauma and futurity that continues to shape a challenging and abiding aspect of national identity. To grapple with the nature of this psychological fixation on a cultural level, it is important to explore how the lost child – reflected in Australian culture from the stolen generations to UK orphans transported en masse to Australia in the 1950s and often abused (Independent Inquiry into Child Sexual Abuse, 2017), the sexual exploitation of children in religious institutions and the ever declining mental health of refugee children held in detention centres on Manus Island and Naru by Australian authorities (Australian Human Rights Commission, 2014) – translates into a shared symbol that dominates our reported, biographical and fictional storytelling on screen.

The symbol in Jungian-based analysis, or what is more commonly referred to as depth psychology, departs from 'the symbol' as we understand it in the work of early structuralists as fixed within a network of established cultural meanings and representations, nor is it directly related to post-structuralist thought that argues for signs as fluid and socially negotiated. Rather, symbols in depth psychology are thought to be rooted in the archetypal – unconscious and therefore beyond the social; as Don Fredericksen explains, symbols 'escape our attempts to enclose them within the wholly or essentially personal, and irrevocably link us to the transpersonal' (2001, p. 37). They can be individually and collectively significant, recognized by their *affect* or emotional reverberation and yet never quite enclosed within a definitive meaning. The lost child is one such unknowable symbol. One might argue, as does Luke Hockley (2014), that this phenomenon can also arise unwittingly in cinema through psychological hooks, distinct from direct references to specific images or conscious directorial manipulations. Emotions related to the lost child, can therefore also be aroused independently of its direct representation. This 'third image' as Hockley terms the 'apperceptive response to films in which collective inscribed meanings are overwhelmed by unexpected, unanticipated personal and emotional responses', is formed largely in the liminal space between the artefact of screen or projected image and the viewer (p. 9).

Archetypal psychologist James Hillman helps to clarify the symbol of the child when carried in the image of actual children, often the case in Australian cinema: 'Whatever we say about children and childhood is not altogether about children and childhood … Clearly, some realm of the psyche called "childhood" is being personified by the child and carried by the child for the adult' (1975, p. 8). To use Hillman's language, a more therapeutic response involves addressing what it is that we are collectively 'carrying' in our cultural, creative and persistent attachment to the lost child. Adopting images, narratives and histories of this motif suggests a powerful collectively unconscious symbol at work – one that, in various cultural projections, compels us to face the largely unknowable psychological state that urges this image forward. In discussing the phenomenon of what he calls 'the orphan' archetype, relevant to ideas of the lost child, Hillman avoids arguing for a solution or easy escape from this unconscious entanglement. Rather he sees the need to *live with* the attachment:

> By giving favour to this idea of the child that is not meant to grow, we might imagine the child's abandonment and need for rescue as a continuous state, a static necessity that does not evolve towards independence, does not evolve at all, but remains as a requirement of the fulfilled and matured person.
>
> *(1991, p. 31)*

It is therefore important to draw attention to the dominance of the cultural complex on a number of artist levels, where it is most clearly projected.

Analysis of the lost child in Australian literature is perhaps the most prolific area of study with screen analysis less represented and, if discussed, only largely to support a more broad exploration of the phenomenon or another aspect of film culture (Collins and Davis, 2004). By concentrating on Australian film adaptations of Norwegian and English plays, I wish to discuss the broader reach of the symbol and the complex that allows for its continual resurfacing. A close, textual, analysis of *Macbeth* and *The Daughter* reveal the most potent aspects of this phenomenon – those that in their original form were less emphatic in presenting a combination of trauma and the lost child. For those caught by this motif, it is as if, like two strangers meeting through an unconscious acknowledgement of, and attraction to, each other's vulnerabilities, an acute identification between reader/viewer and text takes place; even, from the briefest presence of the lost child, as in Shakespeare's *Macbeth*. This identification suggests a return to the complex, which in the case of both films, comes to dominate the narrative.

Kurzel's *Macbeth*

Justin Kurzel trained as a set designer at Sydney's National Institute of Dramatic Art before directing television commercials. His debut feature *Snowtown* (2011), based on a series of violent murders in Kurzel's home state of South Australia was followed by 'Boner McPharlin's Moll', a piece in the 18 short-film compilation *The Turning* (2013), *Macbeth* and *Assassin's Creed* (2016) adapted from Ubisoft Entertainment's video game of the same name (2007). The most haunting aspect of *Snowtown*, is its focus on the corruption of vulnerable 'lost' and previously abused boys and men by the sadist John Justin Bunting who defleshed and dismembered eight victims in 1999 before hiding the bodies in barrels that he later stored in a disused bank vault (Anderson, 2014). While applying the same level of uncompromising brutality to *Macbeth*, *Snowtown*'s intensity was augmented by the distressing revelations of the Bunting case and trial 12 years earlier (*R* v. *Bunting and Wagner* 2004 SASC 235).

It was a film I felt obliged to watch given the buzz surrounding its release, but sitting in the centre of a tightly packed cinema, the experience was claustrophobic and profoundly disturbing. Even as I write this chapter, Kurzal's introductory scene of troubled brothers being photographed naked and in underwear by a male neighbour their mother entrusts with their care, stirs the spectre of *the lost child* complex in its darker aspect. These foreboding images that hint at the trauma-induced futures of these disadvantaged children, particularly 16 year old 'Jamie', later manipulated into Bunting's circle, produce an uncomfortable mixture of pathos and disquiet. I felt the kind of heat rising in my body that used to come with watching particularly gory horror films in crowded cinemas.

Macbeth opens similarly with a sense of archetypal haunting as the grief stricken Macbeths (Marion Cotillard and Michael Fassbender) enact cremation rites for their small child. Mentioned only briefly in Shakespeare's text where Lady Macbeth convinces her conscience-plagued husband to commit to their plan of murdering King Duncan, are we offered any suggestion of a 'lost' infant:

> I have given suck, and know
> How tender 'tis to love the babe that milks me.
> I would, while it was smiling in my face,
> Have plucked my nipple from his boneless gums
> And dashed the brains out, had I so sworn as you
> Have done to this.
> *(Shakespeare, 1980, 1.7.54–9)*

From this introduction to grief, perhaps signalling the brief window of unconditional love allowed to an eleventh century Scotland defined by war, revenge and, for Kurzel, post-traumatic stress disorder (Barnes, 2015), the child dominates as a presence of both irreconcilable loss and the cyclic repetition of that loss. It has also been claimed though, that the above dialogue suggests not a fusion of trauma, mourning and loss, but the infertility of the couple and the fantasy of infanticide: 'the smiling babe she indifferently plucks from her gall-filled breast comes to represent nothing less than Macbeth's aborted patrilineal line' (Chamberlain, 2005, p. 85). Kurzel's focus, however, allows for a re-evaluation of Lady Macbeth's seeming maternal ambivalence. Not only does she emerge as a mother steeped in loss, but one whose actions, while not excused upon her death, are, through Cotillard's poignant performance, at least tempered by a sense of sympathy for her moral and maternal anguish.

The focus on the child in *Macbeth* is not Kurzel's invention – lost children are embedded in the original play. For Clare Asquith (2005), Shakespeare's text, first performed for the court in 1606, makes conspicuous allusions to the foiled Catholic inspired 'Gunpowder plot' a year earlier, which aimed to destroy the House of Lords. Had the rebellion been successful, Robert Catesby, Guy Fawkes and their co-conspirators would also have killed Queen Anne and Prince Henry. This leads Asquith to suggest that, 'Images of dead children and murdered boys fill the play, echoing one of the chief talking points of the time, the callousness of including [King] James's popular young heir, Prince Henry, among the victims' (p. 217).

In relation to the child in Polanski's (1971) and Kurzel's versions, Gemma Miller finds Kurzel's adaptation in particular, 'saturated with children – dead, alive, human and supernatural. He takes the all-pervasive trope of childhood in *Macbeth* and turns it into a visual image that permeates the landscape of his film' (2016, p. 11). Her convincing analysis concludes that Kurzel's child challenges the twentieth century's investment in children as beacons of optimistic futurity and innocence by reinterpreting them as omens of 'a future dogged by uncertainty and fear' (p. 4). Drawing on leading scholarship in the area of childhood, she questions the traditional romanticism of the child, suggesting that the concept of childhood in the twenty-first century has become coloured by a sense of the 'ambiguous' and 'alien'. In setting aside definitive interpretations, she inadvertently identifies the child as *a symbol* in the Jungian sense, of individual and collective projection (p. 4). While not contesting Miller's analysis, I would like to extend the discourse by reading Kurzel's film through the various manifestations of the lost child complex that he relocates from the wastelands of South Australia's rural Snowtown to the blooded soil of the Scottish Highlands.

Children as irreconcilable loss

The opening scene of bereavement, set against a harsh Highland winter, offers us an initial close-up image of a Christ-like child draped in white and peacefully resting on a straw covered bed/manger. The shot widens to reveal a scene of ritual mourning – the child is dead and the straw of the 'manger' serves as fuel for a cremation pyre. The grief of Macbeth and Lady Macbeth gives way to imagery of the three witches, who like a Greek chorus will come to preside over the narrative. Rather than reducing these characters to demeaning physical travesties of formulaic femininity as in Polanski's (Playboy produced) vision, they come to us as three generations of 'observers' – a middle-aged woman, a younger woman with a child approaching puberty and a younger woman carrying an infant. Each bear three ritualized horizontal scars on their forehead, evoking an impression of medieval Druidesses – healers, herbalists, midwives or oracles. The gender of the Macbeths' child is unknown, but given the fate of men and male children in Kurzel's *Macbeth*, as will be discussed, we might assume this dead, lost child is male. The witches in contrast, a collective image of female knowing, come to represent the enduring presence of girls and women forced to bear witness to the cyclic folly of male warfare.

This is the first scene to encapsulate the idea of irreconcilable loss for the Macbeths, who according to Kurzel and Australian production designer Fiona Crombie, deal with the trauma of war and childlessness by substituting parenthood for ambition (*Bold Bloody and Resolute: The Making of Macbeth*, 2015). In opening on their grief, the scene is set for a drama of thwarted ambition, woven around the image of the child, now firmly established as a symbol of loss. Two other critical scenes in the film play a significant role in cementing this premise: the slaughter of Lady Macduff and her children, and Lady Macbeth's final sleepwalking soliloquy.

The turning of Lady Macbeth and the 'sleepwalking' scene

I have always struggled to reconcile the turning of Lady Macbeth from co-conspirator and accomplice in the death of Duncan, to a suicidal woman tormented by conscience. With the exception of enduring her husband's intensifying megalomania and paranoia, no direct personal repercussions or accumulative torment result from her role in the initial regicide, unlike the well paced escalation of Macbeth's instability. Perhaps though, Kurzel has merely made the catalyst for Lady Macbeth's nascent madness, the killing of the Macduff family, more transparent. While this appears to be the pivot point in the text, Kurzel manages to highlight the gravity of the scene, by reenergising the symbolism of the lost child.

It has always been a disturbing turn of Macbeth's desperation, that having ordered the death of Banquo and his son Fleance who manages to escape the ambush, he then turns his sights on Macduff (Sean Harris), who he attempts to psychologically destabilise by ordering the murder of his wife and their three young children. Rather than have this carried out by henchmen in the Macduff castle, as in the play (Shakespeare, 4.2), Kurzel has the family captured as they flee Macbeth's court and then jointly burnt at the stake, with Macbeth igniting the pyre in a public, almost ceremonial, show of ruthlessness. Lady Macbeth does not bear witness to the killings in Shakespeare's text, but here Kurzel positions her as a central spectator. With Fleance's (Loch-lann Harris) resourcefulness in fleeing from the murder of his father and subsequent protection by the pre-pubescent young witch who magically appears to usher him to a safer place, with the Macduff family Macbeth's attempts at child killing are finally successful.

As Miller points out, 'The ritualised slaughter of the Macduff family ... recalls the opening frame sequence' (2016, p. 12). From the close-up of the Macbeths' initial grief for their child, presumably (as we later learn) cremated because of disease – Lady Macbeth's inconsolable tears dominating the screen – we are now witness to a parallel inconsolable grief and psychologically inward retreat via the burning of the Macduff children and their protesting mother. Lady Macbeth glances to and from the two small angelic boys jointly bound to a shared stake – echoes of her cremated child. For Macbeth, the burning sequence can be read as an act of vengeance for his childlessness, conveniently projected and inflicted on to Macduff. All players in this lost child triad – the Macbeths' child, the Macduffs' children, and now finally Macduff himself (through caesarean section) – have variously been 'untimely ripped' from their mothers (Shakespeare, 5.8.14–16). The separation of mother and child becomes a cyclic pattern of loss with the surviving, and victorious child in this mix, Macduff, nevertheless carrying the lost child within to an even greater degree than the mourning Macbeths.

Kurzel makes it clear that this is the catalyst for Lady Macbeth's decline. We see her wandering the harsh landscape of her castle in thinly woven clothing, impervious to the bitter cold, those around her and her own physical well-being. This inward retreat takes her not to an overly played out rubbing of imaginary blood from her hands, but a more haunting and sympathetic fantasy. The popularly known 'the sleepwalking scene', takes place in the large church enclosure in the original village, now deserted, where she cremated her child and conspired to murder Duncan. The shape of a crucifix is carved high in the wall to emit crucifix-like rays of light. But this is a still, tranquil reworking of the somnambulant, hand-wringing convention of past Lady Macbeths. Unaccompanied by her carers, the worried doctor and gentlewoman (Shakespeare, 5.1), she sits alone, Madonna-like figure, cloaked in a white-blue tinted robe with the rays of the cross streaming around her, as she delivers in monologue the mutterings that originally interspersed the doctor and gentlewoman's dialogue.

Kurzel and Cotillard shape the scene as a melancholic insight into Lady Macbeth's delusional withdrawal into lost child complex. The line connecting her to the pivotal Macduff murders – 'The thane of Fife had a wife; where is she now?' (5.1.42) – takes on a haunting quality able to transport the spectator back to her horror at the stake burnings, while also presaging her own death and hoped for reunion with the lost child. This notion of reunion becomes clear, when at the end of Cotillard's speech, performed in long-shot then unedited head-shot as if addressing another character off-camera, or speaking to herself while fixing on a distant area of the hall, it is revealed that she is talking to the ghost of her child, sitting in front of her but gazing out of the open church door. He does not acknowledge her presence and in the turn of his little face we see the left side of his exposed neck covered with smallpox-like blisters. The instructions in this speech – 'wash your hands, put on your nightgown, look not so pale, to bed, to bed' – originally staged as if Lady Macbeth is directing herself as to what she must do, are now directed at the child who seems to be ushered into her awareness with the imagery of gentle falling snowflakes. The line 'there's knocking at the gate, come give me your hand' now becomes an invitation to death – to join her child, or ask her child to take her with him. In the next shot she walks in a thin night shift towards the three witches and their pre-pubescent and infant children with the line 'to bed, to bed' as if she is being called to join them (as did Fleance) in the safety of another dimension. It is Fleance though, who, for Kurzel, re-emerges in the battlefield to seize Macbeth's discarded sword and so reignite the cyclic power-play for kingship and loss, while Lady Macbeth has been presumably shepherded to the afterlife to be reunited with her child.

Kurzel's adaptation of *Macbeth*, as yet another expression of the Australian lost child complex through the medium of cinema, talks predominantly to an inability to 'hold' the inner child; to, as Hillman argues, find and form a relationship with the lost child within. This calling to acknowledge shadow material that the complex embraces and periodically throws at those in its thrall, provides an opportunity to reconcile with that which either torments us, or that which we disavow. Kurzel argues that the lost child is replaced, or misplaced, by something that might eclipse grief, namely ambition and power. As a symbol of the unreconciled emotional conflict that underlies his ambition and guilt, toxic ambition, the fantasy dagger that Macbeth tries and fails to grasp after he has killed Duncan is analogous to the child as a haunting symbol of an unanchored, ungraspable aspect of the self. For me the sleepwalking scene, most predominantly, demonstrates the need to reconcile loss. The real tragedy of Lady Macbeth in this version, is that death is her only means of abiding in the child … and still one wonders, if even there, this little boy will prove to be as imaginary as the dagger.

Stone's *The Daughter*

Simon Stone's *The Daughter*, inspired by Ibsen's play *The Wild Duck*, also reworks the original to more fully incorporate a sense that the central characters are driven by an internal lost child complex. An earlier Australian film version of *The Wild Duck* (dir. Safran, 1984), featuring internationally distinguished actors Liv Ullmann and Jeremy Irons, takes a more direct approach in adapting the text to film so that unlike Stone's work, as is clear from his title, the lost child character is not positioned as the central focus. Although the archetypal motif is addressed from a less heavy-handed approach than we see in Kurzel's *Macbeth*, the idea of lostness guides Stone's narrative of secrets that disrupt the lives of an adolescent girl Hedvig, her father and, in particular, his childhood friend Christian (or 'Gregers Werle' in the original). Each carries the burden of the lost child. The wild duck in both stories, winged by a misfired gunshot from the pivotal patriarch Henry (Werle, Greger's/Christian's father), and Hedvig who nurses the animal back to health, overtly embody the complex that eventually forces them to confront their own displacement. The newly created back-story of Christian, even more than the maturing of Hedvig to create a less naive and parentally coddled 14 year old, allows us to more clearly see how in this adaptation, the lost child aspect of the original is not only tenuously reinforced but reinvented – as if to suit the purposes of the *archetypally* themed, and *complex driven* popular cinema of Australia.

Stone originally directed and adapted the play for the Belvoir St Theatre in Sydney (2011) before revising the text further for film. Ibsen's nineteenth century Norway is updated to the contemporary Snowy Mountains foothill town of Tumut in New South Wales: 'The play's emphasis was on the dialogue' according to co-producers Jan Chapman and Nicole O'Donohue, 'so the challenge in adapting from stage to screen was to open up the world and create atmosphere and tension through locations and the use of camera and sound' (Screen NSW, 2017). The tragedy of Ibsen's more wordy text and *The Daughter*, with Hedvig committing suicide in the original and barely surviving her self-inflicted gunshot wound in Stone's version, is that only until her death/near death, is there any sense of claiming, owning or reconciling with the lost child. Unlike *Macbeth*, where the archetype presages a cyclic pattern of suffering and disavowal, there is a sense that the complex embedded in *The Daughter* is eventually acknowledged and reconciled by those closest to Hedvig. For others drawn into her story though, it still functions as a firmly fixed source of continuing trauma.

Stone remains faithful to the basic narrative of the play and the dramatic tension created by the secrecy underpinning Hedvig's final act of agency. The unfolding history, revolves round Henry (Geoffrey Rush) the owner of a contentious timber mill marked for closure, his adult son Christian (Paul Schneider), recently returned from America for his father's wedding to their much younger housekeeper, and the Finch family (or Ekdal in the original), Hjalmar renamed Oliver (Ewen Leslie), his wife Gina now Charlotte (Miranda Otto), Oliver's father Walter, originally Old Ekdal (Sam Neil) and their teenage daughter Hedvig (Odessa Young). The connection between the two families develops from Walter's former business partnership with Henry, and Charlotte's previous employment as Henry's housekeeper before her marriage and Hedvig's birth. The accentuated affection between Oliver and Hedvig functions as a red flag for their later rift. Charlotte's revelation that Henry is Hedvig's birth-father rather than Oliver, exposes the tenuous nature of her early marriage and relationship with both Oliver and Hedvig. The more tragic consequence of this deceit is Oliver's inability to reconcile his daughter as Henry's child, and Hedvig's overwrought reaction to her abandonment: 'Let me go, I can't look at you, I can't fucking look at you' he says, paraphrasing Ibsen's dialogue – 'Don't come near me Hedvig! Go away-go away! I can't bear to see you' (Ibsen, 1958, p. 145). Oliver's abrupt dismissal of, and seeming willingness to desert, his wife and child in the light of this revelation, seems contrived and jarring in Stone's version, but, as in the play, the depth of his renunciation serves as the catalyst for Hedvig's suicide/attempted suicide.

Neither Charlotte nor Oliver seem to be able to reconcile the deceit that has rendered a once secure triadic family relationship, into one that is not simply fractured and fragile, but defined by the archetypal shadow of the lost child. To understand how the updating has centralised and exacerbated the lost child theme, like the *Macbeth* analysis above, I will examine two key instances in the film – the reimagining of Christian and the repositioning of Hedvig's relationship to the wounded duck.

The reinvention of Christian and the redrawn parallels between Hedvig and **The Wild Duck**

The relationship between Hedvig and Christian is pivotal to the climax in both versions. In Ibsen's work we see an idealistic and self-righteous Gregers (Christian), revealing the truth of Gina's (Charlotte's) pregnancy to his close childhood friend Hjalmar (Oliver) through a

misguided and largely theoretically driven sense that truth-seeking and the exposure of deception will strengthen any relationship. He later tells Ibsen's 'innocent' Hedvig that she should
shoot her beloved duck as a gesture of sacrifice to her father and so secure his acceptance.
Instead she sacrifices herself. This final act reveals not only the inability of Gregers to understand
the intricacy of interpersonal relationships, but his manipulative pitting of a lost/estranged child's
love for a parent against the creature to which she has become a parent – referred to as the 'little
wild-duck mother' (Ibsen, 1958, p. 152) – for both an ideological principle and as revenge
against the father that betrayed his mother through, as is intimated in Act four, the pursuit and
rape of his then housekeeper, Hedvig's mother Gina.

In *The Daughter* we see a more fleshed out version of Gregers in Stone's 'Christian'. As in the
play Christian calculates early into the drama that Hedvig is in all likelihood his father's daughter, and therefore his half-sister. It is more clearly spelt out in the film, that Charlotte's (Gina's)
pregnancy most likely contributed to Christian's mentally unstable mother's suicide when he
was in university. While Hedvig is most obviously positioned as a symbol of the lost child in *The
Daughter*, Christian, caught in his own childhood memories of loss, deception and loathing for
his indifferent father, can be read as an even more intense embodiment of the complex. He is
given a backstory beyond Ibsen's characterisation of alcoholism, a strained marriage and a short-
lived university life with his friend Oliver. On returning to his father's home after living in
America, we see his life unravel – his current sobriety giving way to bouts of binge drinking,
and a wife who eventually abandons him for another man, much as his father emotionally abandoned his mother for Charlotte. As both he and Oliver drink to the point of inebriation in a
university pub, Christian vomits in the adjoining laneway. Collapsing into Oliver's arms says, 'I
don't want to grow up … lets never grow up' – 'It's too late mate' says Oliver, 'it's too late'.

What we see in Christian is the pivotal lost child, or orphan in Hillman's work, prohibiting
any sense of futurity or individuation. The complex, as Jung would say of this kind of psychological roadblock 'has' him, or grips him beyond conscious control: 'Everyone knows … that
people "have complexes". What is not so well known … is that complexes can *have us*' (1934:
§200 – emphasis as original). After drunkenly staggering through his father's mansion-like house,
he crouches by the old bath where he found his mother's body. Although a young adult when
this occurred, he and Hedvig are positioned as children arrested in adolescence. While the
complex operates on an intensely personal level for Christian, as an example of contemporary
Australian filmmaking, we are yet again made aware of how the personal journey of one character tends to magnify the wounds of those in their orbit. This then speaks to bigger picture
thinking and how the lost child is not only pivotal to an individual's traumatic history, but
simultaneously bound to a collective that recognises the motif as intrinsic to its own identity.

Unlike Christian who we sense is fixed firmly within the complex, unable to form a relationship with his inner lost child, Hedvig is an entirely different animal so to speak. He suggests that
her duck, a transparent allegory of Hedvig, should be called 'Lucky', because 'my father shot her
and she survived'. There is a sense of redemption and bitter revenge in both this statement and
his bourgeoning relationship to Hedvig: a longing to bond with this living projection of his
inner lost child, and a problematic impulse to inflict further pain and estrangement on this
'innocent' source of his mother's suffering.

In the play, Olivia Noble Gunn argues that the duck acts as a floating symbol for a variety of
meanings – one of which is Hedvig, representative of 'the romantic child, an icon of idealized
life and innocence' and that as a 'sacrificial subject' becomes 'an over-symbolized creature – one
that retains more similarity to the duck than many critics would like to admit' (2013, p. 47).
Rachel Price similarly discusses the duck in relation to Hedvig through the prism of human–
animal aesthetics where 'animals are often understood to perform absorption without any

awareness or illusion. They are authentic because they cannot deceive, because they are not theatrical' (2006, p. 800). The artificial enclosure, a facsimile of the environment outside, where Walter (Oliver's father) keeps the duck, along with other wounded or lost animals, creates pets of these creatures. As Price suggests of the play, Hedvig too is confined to an artificial life as a protected part-orphan: 'The wild duck's transformation into pet explains in part its function as foil for Hedvig, which culminates in the very real identification through which Gregers's incitation to kill the bird translates into Hedvig's suicide' (pp. 804–5).

The Daughter does not reproduce the motherly overtones we see in the play between Hedvig and the duck – the symbolism therefore is much less bound by a simple semiotic premise. The notion of sacrifice, also does not translate clearly in the film, rather one senses that Hedvig's abandonment, by her boyfriend and school friends whose parents must leave the town to find work now that the mill has closed, and finally her own father, bring her despair and rejection to a tragic climax. Before stealing her grandfather's gun, she takes the bird from the enclosure, telling the creature that she can't look after it anymore – 'You'll survive for me' she says. With a few attempts to ease the bird into the air, it is finally forced to fly away. Critically wounded as she lies in hospital, her very lostness galvanizes the family bringing Oliver back to her side and, one senses, forcing all the characters to redefine the reality and responsibility of their relationship to this lost child which increasingly becomes a symbol in the Jungian sense, of their own displaced, floundering and unreconciled child within. The notion of sacrifice in the play is therefore clearly replaced with notions of grief, abandonment and lostness, through deceptions revolving around the conception, birth and attempted death of the 'innocent' Hedvig who, in surviving the gunshot, is, like the duck – lucky. And in being Lucky, the assumption that she too will heal and escape her wounds – reconcile her lostness – is clearly embedded in the final scene of the film where we see her in close-up lying on a hospital bed – an oxygen mask strapped to her face.

It all comes back to the land

Both Australian cinema and the lost child share an almost symbiotic relationship with landscape. From the early settler and twentieth century literature/reportage of lost children in the bush to versions of this narrative theme in cinema, the landscape has provided a sense of continuity, place and embrace: popular examples include *Walkabout* (dir. Roeg, 1971), *Picnic at Hanging Rock* (dir. Weir, 1975), *Evil Angels* (dir. Schepisi, 1988), *Strangerland* (dir. Farrant, 2015) and *The Dressmaker* (dir. Moorhouse, 2015). Kurzel's and Stone's work is no exception. From locations limited by their necessary containment in the theatre, *Macbeth* and *The Wild Duck* have been given a uniquely Australian twist in the rich and dominating backdrops of the Scottish Highlands and the high country of NSW. Also characteristic is the dwarfing of each character against the atemporal and ultimately unpredictable land that both embraces and consumes the lost. The Macbeth and Macduff children die on the land, and Hedvig often retreats to the surrounding pine forest for comfort and finally to her favourite deserted bush warehouse with her shotgun.

The landscape then is perhaps the only character which forms an enduring relationship with the lost child and continues to frame, what I argue, is one of the most defining and problematic psychological knots of Australian culture. The predominance of allusions to the child in theatrical adaptations to film, might be understood as a way to not only bring the complex forward for acknowledgement as an element of our collective selves, but I would like to hope, as a way of – even if unconsciously – abiding in it, as we abide in the land despite its resistance to containment and modification. The almost obsessive focus on the lostness of the child, suggests a need to change our relationship to it, recognize it as both ungraspable and within reach: an ever-present cycle of rediscovery and opportunity. I can predict that the coupling of the lost child and the land, that in varying ways claims her/him, will endure in future cinematic expressions of this interweaving Australian struggle with displacement, abandonment and possibility. Australia is, after all, often called the 'lucky' country – a winged duck perhaps, seeking freedom through the nurture of a lost child.

References

Asquith, C. (2005) *Shadowplay: the hidden beliefs and coded politics of William Shakespeare*. New York: Public Affairs.

Brierley, S. (2015) *A long way home*. New York: Berkley.

Chamberlain, S. (2005) 'Fantasizing infanticide: Lady Macbeth and the murdering mother in early modern England', *College Literature*, 32(3), pp. 72–91.

Collins, F. and Davis, T. (2004) *Australian cinema after Mabo*. Port Melbourne: Cambridge University Press.

Currey, John (ed.) (2006/1793) *The first fleet journal of John Hunter, October 1786–August 1788*. Malvern, Victoria: Colony Press.

Fredericksen, D. (2001) 'Jung/sign/symbol/film', in I. Alister and C. Hauke (eds), *Jung and film: post-Jungian takes on the moving image*. London: Routledge. pp. 17–55. (Originally published as two essays in the *Quarterly Review of Film Studies*, 1979, 1980.)

Gaunson, S. (2013) *The Ned Kelly films: a cultural history of Kelly history*. Chicago, IL: Intellect.

Gunn, O. N. (2013) 'A scandalous similarity? The Wild Duck and the romantic child', *Ibsen Studies*, 13(1), pp. 47–76.

Hillman, J. (1991/1975) *Loose ends: primary papers in archetypal psychology*. Dallas, TX: Spring Publications.

Hockley, L. (2014) *Somatic cinema: the relationship between body and screen – a Jungian perspective*. London: Routledge.

Ibsen, H. (1958/1884) 'The Wild Duck', trans. R. Farquharson Sharp, E. Marx-Aveling and L. Hannas, *A doll's house, the wild duck, the lady from the sea*. London: J. M. Dent & Sons Ltd.

Jung, C. G. (1934) 'A review of the complex theory', in *The collected works of C. G. Jung*, Vol. 8, *The structure and dynamics of the psyche*. London: Routledge & Kegan Paul, 1960/69.

Jung, C. G. (1934/54) 'Archetypes of the collective unconscious', in *The collected works of C. G. Jung*, Vol. 9i, *The archetypes and the collective unconscious*. London: Routledge & Kegan Paul, 1959/68.

Menadue, J. E. (1975) *The three lost children 1867–1967*. Victoria: Daylesford and District Historical Society.

Pierce, P. (1999) *The country of lost children: an Australian anxiety*. Cambridge: Cambridge University Press.

Price, R. (2006) 'Animal magnetism: theatricality in Ibsen's The Wild Duck', *New Literary History*, 37(4), pp. 797–816.

Shakespeare, W. (1980) *The complete works of William Shakespeare*. London: Octopus Books.

Singer, T. and Kimbles, S. L. (2004) *The cultural complex: contemporary Jungian perspectives on psyche and society*. London and New York: Routledge.

Tilley, E. (2012) *White vanishing: rethinking Australia's lost-in-the-bush myth*. Amsterdam: Rodopi.

Torney, K. (2005) *Babes in the bush: the making of an Australian image*. Fremantle: Curtin University Books.

Waddell, T. (2010) *Wild/lives: trickster, place and liminality on screen*. London and New York: Routledge.

Waddell, T. (2006) *Mis/takes: archetype, myth and identity in screen fiction*. London and New York: Routledge.

Online sources

Anderson, P. (2014) 'How Australia's worst serial killers John Bunting and Robert Wagner stained Snowtown with their sadistic kill games', *Herald Sun* [online]. Available at: www.heraldsun.com.au/news/law-order/true-crime-scene/how-australias-worst-serial-killers-john-bunting-and-robert-wagner-stained-snowtown-with-their-sadistic-kill-games/news-story/7a8f5f816349f60b8eeee2e06b23b2a4 [Accessed 23 November 2016].

Australian Human Rights Commission (2014) 'The forgotten children: national inquiry into children in immigration detention', Canberra [online]. Available at: www.humanrights.gov.au/our-work/asylum-seekers-and-refugees/publications/forgotten-children-national-inquiry-children [Accessed 6 March 2017].

Barnes, H. (2015) 'Michael Fassbender: "Macbeth suffered from PTSD"', *Guardian*, 23 May [online]. Available at: www.theguardian.com/film/2015/may/23/michael-fassbender-macbeth-suffered-from-ptsd [Accessed 3 March 2017].

Human Rights and Equal Opportunity Commission (1997) 'Bringing them home: national inquiry into the separation of Aboriginal and ToresStrait Islander children from their families', Commonwealth of Australia [online]. Available at: www.humanrights.gov.au/publications/bringing-them-home-report-1997 [Accessed 6 March 2017].

Independent Inquiry into Child Sexual Abuse (2017) 'Public hearing in the child migration programmes', UK [online]. Available at: www.iicsa.org.uk [Accessed 6 March 2017].

Miller, G. (2016) '"He has no children": changing representations of the child in stage and film productions of *Macbeth* from Polanski to Kurzel', *Shakespeare* [online]. DOI:10.1080/17450918.2016.1174728.

Screen NSW (2017) 'Interview: co-producers Jan Chapman and Nicole O'Donohue: The Daughter' [online]. Available at: www.screen.nsw.gov.au/news/interview-co-producers-jan-chapman-and-nicole-o-donohue-the-daughter?enews=220 [Accessed 3 February 2017].

R v. *Bunting and Wagner* (2004) SASC 235 [online]. Available at: www.austlii.edu.au/au/cases/sa/SASC/2004/235.html [Accessed 3 March 2017].

Filmography

Assassin's creed (2016) [film] Directed by Justin Kurzel. UK, France, Hong Kong, USA, Taiwan, Malta, Canada.

Bold bloody and resolute: the making of Macbeth (2015) [DVD featurette] Directed by Justin Kurzel. UK, France, USA.

'Boner McPharlin's Moll' in *The Turning* (2013) [film] Directed by Justin Kurzel. Australia.

Daughter, The. (2015) [film] Directed by Simon Stone. Australia.

Dressmaker, The. (2015) [film] Directed by Jocelyn Moorhouse. Australia.

Evil angels. (1988) [film] Directed by Fred Schepisi. Australia, USA.

Lion. (2016) [film] Directed by Garth Davis. Australia, USA, UK.

Macbeth. (1971) [film] Directed by Roman Polanski. UK, USA.

Macbeth. (2015) [film] Directed by Justin Kurzel. UK, France, USA.

Picnic at hanging rock. (1975) [film] Directed by Peter Weir. Australia.

Snowtown. (2011) [film] Directed by Justin Kurzel. Australia.

Story of the Kelly gang, The. (1906) [film] Directed by Charles Tait. Australia.

Strangerland. (2015) [film] Directed by Kim Farrant. Australia, Ireland.

Walkabout. (1971) [film] Directed by Nicholas Roeg. Australia, UK.

Wild duck, The. (1984) [film] Directed by Henry Safran. Australia.

17

NUMINOUS IMAGES OF A NEW ETHIC

A Jungian view of Kieslowski's *The Decalogue*

Judith R. Cooper and August J. Cwik

Introduction

If a man is endowed with an ethical sense and is convinced of the sanctity of ethical values, he is on the surest road to a conflict of duty. And although this looks desperately like a moral catastrophe, it alone makes possible a higher differentiation of ethics and a broadening of consciousness. A conflict of duty forces us to examine our conscience and thereby to discover the shadow. This, in turn, forces us to come to terms with the unconscious.

(Jung, 1949: §1417)

Visionary Polish film director Krzysztof Kieslowski, who died suddenly in 1996 at the age of 54, has been called a filmmaker of the ineffable. His 1987–1988 series *The Decalogue*, made for Polish television, has been recognized as one of the major achievements and masterworks of modern cinema. It has been included among the top 100 'Essential Films' of all time by the National Society of Film Critics (n.d.) and ranked #36 in *Empire* magazine's 'The 100 Best Films of World Cinema' (2010/2017). Other international awards include winner of the International Federation of Film Critics (fipresci) at the Venice Film Festival in 1989.

Each one-hour segment of the ten film series encompasses an active imagination, a meditative reflection on one or several of the Ten Commandments, filled with transcendent, numinous, affect-laden images. The ten films focus on inner ethical struggles and personal dramas situated in contemporary situations and modern contexts. Kieslowski professed his goal was to capture the soul and make the inner world of emotions more tangible. The films can evoke intense reactions in the viewer, uncovering the universal in the particular and the spiritual in the mundane. The images and stories are grounded in profound experiences of loss and alienation, but also reveal the redemptive power and mystery of human connection and possibilities for transcendence. In them we see the complexity and difficulty of acting out of a place of connection with the Self. The films deeply explore ideas of interconnectedness, synchronicities, and 'not knowing' – what Jung called '*mysterium tremendum et fascinans*' or energies of the Self.

Ironically, Kieslowski was a professed spiritual agnostic. 'I'm somebody who doesn't know, somebody who's searching' (Stok, 1993, p. 194). His characters frequently echo Kieslowski with the statement 'I don't know.' He has been called a mystical philosopher, an 'agnostic mystic,' and is considered part of the Polish movement, the Cinema of Moral Anxiety. He began his career as a documentarian, making films of social consciousness when Poland was still under Communist rule. One of his last works, *The Double Life of Veronique* (1991), is considered an examination of the intangible essence of what constitutes a soul.

The Decalogue grew out of a collaboration between Kieslowski and his co-writer, lawyer, Krzysztof Piesiewicz. Many of the situations on which the stories revolve derive from legal or personal experiences. Piesiewicz is quoted as stating, 'The most important things are people's dreams and their sufferings' (Insdorf, 1999, p. 151). They took as their starting point the Old Testament's Ten Commandments, the core of western ethics, which might also be thought of as the embodiment of an Archetype of Ethics. Then they were interwoven into specific situations, secular, everyday dilemmas of ordinary people struggling to understand themselves and their world, confronted with and enacting dramas of moral choice and what it means to be human. Interestingly, Kieslowski resisted linking each film to one specific Commandment; he wanted the viewers to work it out for themselves. Mood, texture, and the inner life and landscape of the characters are key to understanding his films. That they are supremely unsentimental seems to account for some of their emotional power. Recurring themes are interconnectedness (characters from one film appear in others and the action mostly takes place in and around one apartment building/housing complex in Warsaw); manifest images of the mysterious and unexplainable contained in quotidian, mundane existence; active compassion for the world of the absurd, subject to the logic of chance; and universal motifs of love, betrayal, forgiveness, helplessness, despair, alienation, and redemption.

We view these films as having the potential to influence the viewer's ideas of the spiritualized psyche. Despite being tied to the Ten Commandments, they carry a more catholic, if you will, universal viewpoint, rather than arguing for any particular religious belief system. The Ten Commandments offer a starting-off point to weave archetypal stories of the ethical struggles which arise from real world experience – what it means to accept our human limitations while still attempting to connect with, and be in relationship to, the transcendent.

In Jung's psychology, the psyche expresses itself in the language of images. He posits that 'every psychic process is an image and an "imagining," otherwise no consciousness could exist' (1939: §889). In our view, the moving image lends itself to portraying the realm of the unconscious, both personal and collective. Film images can constellate the transcendent function in the viewer. Mediating between the conscious and the unconscious they are what Jung terms 'visionary' (1930/50). *The Decalogue* is an exemplar, offering images that act as living symbols, full of affect and meaning.

Return of the repressed: film criticism, style analysis, and the re-introduction of emotion and the numinous

It has been noted that film criticism and film theory often display a level of anxiety and ambivalence toward the role of interpreting film through a lens of emotion, as if it could and should be contained, as if affect could derail and disrupt the major significance of a film (Groves, 2003; Plantinga and Smith, 1999). The more appropriate or accepted stance for the film theorist or critic is to split off the emotional impact of a film. Their stance is that the affective, more subjective dimensions of a film, be 'quarantined' and 'theories be insulated against the dangers of cinephilia' (Groves, 2003, n.p.). However, a small number have insisted, 'If psychoanalysis is to have any future in film theory, the emphasis must shift to include, dissect, and integrate visceral experiences and self-vision, a post-structural mission if ever there was one' (Groves, 2003, n.p.). In other words, film analyses should be openly inclusive of and acknowledge the more embodied, visceral experiences of emotions in the critic, or lack thereof, with this self-examination becoming part of the critical discourse.

How are we to consider emotion in the arena of inquiry or discourse in psychoanalytically informed film analysis and criticism? Historically, this has mostly been grounded in Freud's work. According to Plantinga and Smith (1999), Freud's writings do not contain a sufficiently developed theory of emotions for this purpose. For Freud, the foundation of human behavior resides in the instincts, especially the sexual instinct that drives his psychic economy. Emotional expressions are seen merely as mechanisms to release and dissipate this energy. In this view, it is not particularly important to study the specifics of how the drives discharge emotional energy or to what content the emotions are connected; 'By reducing cinematic emotional response to its drive component, Freud's followers in psychoanalytic film theory deemphasize the richness of that (emotional) response' (Plantinga and Smith, 1999, p. 13).

Jung's concepts of the complex, the living symbol, archetypes, and archetypal resonance inherently contain a more central place for the presence of the emotions, in affective intensity as well as content. For Jung, affect is the central organizing principle of psychic life because it links together sensations, ideas, memories, and judgments, lending them a common basis in feeling-toned complexes which are the basic functional units and building blocks of the psyche. Every complex is an 'affect-image' (Perry, 1976, p. 28), or image of a personified affect (Kalsched, 1996, p. 90). In this way of thinking, emotion is the chief source of consciousness (Jung, 1938/54a: §179) and therefore Jung's concepts are particularly well-suited to illuminate the power of Kieslowski's cinematic style.

Contemporary film theory has mostly remained focused on 'issues of meaning, representation, and their ideological implications' (Plantinga and Smith, 1999, p. 10). When film studies have examined the affective experiences of spectators, they usually discuss them in terms of 'pleasure' and 'desire' effectively by-passing the emotions to offer broader and more reductive explanations that are void of deep explanatory power (see Plantinga and Smith, 1999, for a more detailed history and critique of film criticism, especially, pp. 1–47).

In *Camera Lucida* (2010) Roland Barthes posits affect as *the* key criterion to judge the essence of a powerful artwork. Barthes, a celebrated French philosopher, critic and literary theorist, explores the role of emotion and the unconscious to account for the power of photography. This book has appealed to cinephiles, as well as lovers and practitioners in other artistic media. Barthes' concepts of *studium* and *punctum* have been appropriated as standards of critical evaluation. In *Camera Lucida*, Barthes distinguishes between two different categories of photographs. One category exhibits what he names the *studium*, photographs that purely demonstrate a particular time and place with obvious historical or cultural elements. Photographic images that possess a *studium* have an intellectual value for the viewer, but they do not trigger emotional reactions or disturbances. They interest us, but we do not love these pictures. These could be likened to Jung's description of a 'dead symbol' that only possesses historical significance. By contrast, those photographs which contain an essence Barthes names the *punctum* and they are subjective, personal, and can 'pierce' or wound in a way which enlivens and disturbs the viewer with potent emotional impact and resonance. *Punctum* is Latin for wound, as 'trauma' is wound in Greek. A *punctum* has an ineffable quality, a disruptive energy, an arresting uncanniness in the image that carries tremendous affective power. The *punctum* is that surprising but essential detail in a photographic work of art that attracts, distresses, and fascinates the observer. Barthes writes, 'The *punctum* is induced by an element which rises from the scene, shoots out of it like an arrow, and pierces me … this wound, this prick, this mark made by a pointed instrument, a sting, speck, cut, little hole' (2010, p. 26). These photos contain emanations from the unconscious, sparks that animate the photo for the viewer with a living quality and vibrant energy analogous to Jung's *living symbol*. A photograph with a *punctum* contains an unconscious element that becomes a force for transformation, a catalyst that is affectively bruising – an elusive detail that is emotionally charged.

When Jung wrote that 'the experience of the [archetypal] Self, is always a defeat for the ego' (1955–6/70: §778), he is pointing to an experience of the ego being stung and wounded, in Jungian parlance 'relativized.' But Barthes succeeds in amplifying 'defeat' with the more evocative language of body sensations or a knowing body. When we experience art, including the cinema, through the body, through the emotions, it can be more effecting, more transcendent. Kieslowski's *The Decalogue* creates cinematic *punctums* of transcendent power.

Erich Neumann's *Depth Psychology and a New Ethic*

Erich Neumann's *Depth Psychology and a New Ethic* (1990) as well as Jung's ideas of the religious function of the psyche, are helpful concepts in exploring the psychological themes and ethical conundrums raised by the films. The religious function of the psyche confers meaning, longs to connect with the transcendent, and privileges the numinosum (a divine presence) and its dark side. This chapter explores how Kieslowski's series defines a moral and psychological attitude grounded in behaviors and attitudes which appear to long for, and allow unconscious motivations and greater connection with, the Self, thus, the embodiment of the *New Ethic*, as defined by Neumann, grounded in Jung's ideas of psyche and its purposeful growth toward individuation.

Neumann's *Depth Psychology and a New Ethic* differentiates between what he names the *Old Ethic* and the *New Ethic*. The *Old Ethic* is an ethic of conscious attitudes only, a one-sidedness, a partial ethic that fails to consider the existence of an individual unconscious with its particular demands and needs. This denial of the negative (i.e., the shadow), contains an absolutism and perfectionistic morality, of shoulds and oughts that lead to a collective authority, or cultural superego which defines the norms of the culture and the individual in the culture. This denial of the negative is achieved primarily through the defenses of suppression, repression, and dissociation. In fact, Neumann stresses that the *Old Ethic*, based as it is on the primacy of collective needs, *demands* suppression and repression of individual conscience in the service of the culture, such that an illusory code of ethics forms in the collective, excluding the reality of the individual unconscious in its unique individuality. It does and has produced a set of codified laws governing human conduct in a universal manner. Neumann argues that dangers can arise from split off complexes – a consequential hubris of ego inflation and deflation can develop, i.e., an over-identification with these split-off parts. The individual is subsumed and identified with the group, deferring to and accepting the voice of a leader, not returning to the source of one's own experience and conscience. Neumann concluded that this *Old Ethic* has lost its psychological efficacy due to violence in the culture. This conscious denial of the negative becomes contagious because the negative is not accepted by the individual, assimilated, transformed, lived, and suffered. Rather it is split off from consciousness, with the potential of overwhelming the ego with these repressed unconscious contents: a *return of the repressed* then contaminates the culture.

The *New Ethic* is the ethic of Individuation that accepts the existence of a powerful unconscious, endeavoring to bring conscious and unconscious into responsible relationship. It is centered on awareness and acceptance of the shadow in which the ego has been relativized, i.e., ego-consciousness allows for and submits to the greater power of the unconscious. There is therefore not a denial of the negative, but an acceptance of a confrontation, a fight with the shadow, and relatedness to the negative/shadow, with the recognition that these individuals can change collective consciousness. *The Decalogue* films demonstrate just how challenging, complex, and difficult this process can be. Moral law then is not just something imposed from the outside. A conscience forms like the Freudian superego, but in the form of an authentic inner voice. Acceptance of this internal voice does not involve indiscriminate approval of everything that comes from inside, any more than acceptance of the negative side involves acting out the negative without resistance. It is not to be worse or better than one actually is. Ambiguity, mystery, and uncertainty are present and always prevail.

The *New Ethic* is more encompassing in the sense that it is orientated toward wholeness, i.e., no longer only individualistic by taking into account the ethical situation of the individual, but also considers the effect that the individual's attitude will have upon the collective. This may entail doing evil, but does not always entail external action, what Edinger names as 'necessary crimes' for individuation (1972, pp. 25–26). Edinger states that what is a crime, or unethical, at one stage of psychological development may be lawful at another. He also emphasizes that 'one cannot reach a new stage of psychological development without daring to challenge the code of the old stage' (p. 21).

Some level of innocence and unambiguous certitude must be sacrificed to progress to the *New Ethic*. An authentic inner voice of conscience is developed, consulted with, and relied upon. We each can go to the Source (Self) and have an experience of the Divine Other. It is a reflective process that considers individual context. That is the religious function of the psyche.

General considerations of *The Decalogue* series

As mentioned above, Kieslowski's expressed filmmaking goals are related to metaphysical concerns: explorations of capturing what constitutes the soul, existence of a deity, salvation and redemption, and ideas of good and evil. Despite his avowed ambivalence regarding the existence of a transcendent source or deity, his films veer toward and attempt to embrace the numinous, which is imbued with affectivity. His use of abstraction through his pared-down images, finds a sense of universality in the particular, thus pointing to a transcendent reality (see Kickasola, 2004, pp. 41–89). His editing process eliminates extraneous, unnecessary details to better allow for increased mystery, uncertainty, and ambiguity, inducing the viewer to struggle along with the film's characters.

Recurring images in the series include mundane items like spilled liquid, milk, glass, broken glass, mirrors, windows, and reflections. Kieslowski denies any symbolic content in these images, and yet many of these images seem to carry the call for greater inner reflectiveness, potentially leading to behaviors that are associated with more ethical outcomes. Kieslowski's filmmaking style mediates a liminality wherein he creates in narrative, music, and cinematography, a tension between matter and spirit, the articulate and the ineffable. In the specificity of images, the universal is unmasked, revealing the spirit within matter, echoing Jung's valuing of alchemy as a template of human relationship couched in archetypal images. The power of his filmmaking style facilitates access to deeper emotional experiences. It humanizes the drama, highlighting the vulnerabilities, imperfections, and struggles the characters experience of these ethical dimensions. His directing style focuses on extreme facial close-ups. These serve to emphasize relational contexts and the attendant emotional fields, creating deeper connectedness between the characters and drawing viewers deeper into the drama. These living symbols act like Barthes' *punctum* to create highly charged images.

A recurring theme of the series is the importance of the life of a child – a child's life becomes an image of *punctum*, a powerful symbol of innocence, hope, and renewal – a motif filled with poignant suffering. Kieslowski's expressive film images embody archetypal resonances from the deep unconscious, bypassing ego consciousness and knowledge, thus inviting the viewer into a deeper emotional place. It evokes a transcendent, mysterious, meaningful, numinous experience, that can take on a spiritual sense.

The role of the Watcher

We think this spiritual sense is especially relevant as a means by which to highlight one particular character that appears in eight of the ten episodes. He functions as a witness, a silent observer, identified by some as 'an angel' or a Christ-like figure. In an anecdote regarding the origin of the figure, Kieslowski and Piesiewicz had worked on screenplays for a year but felt something was missing. One day, Kieslowski's literary agent told him a story about an author commenting to a film director, that he liked the guy in a black suit in a certain scene. When the director denied that there was any such figure, the author protested. He had seen him, on the left-hand side of the frame, he then walked across to the right-hand side and moved off. The author was adamant that not only had he seen him, but that that particular moment was the best part of the film. When Kieslowski heard this, he understood what was missing from the screenplay: 'He doesn't have any influence on what's happening, but he is a sort of sign or warning to those whom he watches' (Stok, 1993, pp. 158–159). He is called the Young Man in *The Decalogue* screenplays and Kieslowski denies any religious significance to his appearance at critical moments and key turning points. He has been called by various names including Theophanes ('appearances of God,' Kickasola, 2004, p. 163), eternal witness, the Watcher, an angel (Insdorf, 1999, p. 74). He is 'Pure Gaze' like a film camera recording human folly or suffering but unable to alter the course of the lives it witnesses. He creates an emotional presence as well. The moments when the Witness appears are intense periods of reflection, where the action is slowed down, with an almost meditative moment-to-moment hyper-reflectiveness. Kieslowski stated; 'He has no influence on the action, but he leads the characters to think about what they are doing … his intense stare engenders self-examination' (Insdorf, 1999, p. 73). Despite the non-religious nature of the figure and Kieslowski's intention, this idea exists in some theologies, i.e., the idea that God mourns and suffers with us but is helpless to intervene. The Watcher figure's presence seems to carry this reflective energy, a pause and ponder dynamic which could potentially lead to greater freedom of choice, conscious understanding, and, in turn, individuation and wholeness. He is a non-intervening moral conscience – pulling us toward contemplation, responsibility, and accountability – drawing viewers to the space he occupies – demanding the ego evaluate, assess, reflect.

The episodes

The ten installments of *The Decalogue* are informed by the Ten Commandments, though they do not necessarily align episode by episode:

    I   I am the Lord thy God: thou shalt not have other gods before me
   II Thou shalt not take the name of the Lord thy God in vain
  III Remember the Sabbath day, to keep it holy
  IV Honor thy father and thy mother
   V Thou shalt not kill
  VI Thou shalt not commit adultery
 VII Thou shalt not steal

VIII   Thou shalt not bear false witness against thy neighbor
 IX   Thou shalt not covet thy neighbor's wife
  X   Thou shalt not covet thy neighbor's goods

We will illustrate our thesis using two of the ten films: Decalogue IV and VIII – interpreting the ethical issues and dilemmas presented, through the lens of the relationship to Neumann's ideas of an *Old Ethic* versus a *New Ethic*. These two stories deeply affected us. We believe they provide evidence of Kieslowski's genius and craft in exploring these moral and psychological realms.

Decalogue IV: honor thy father and thy mother

In an ironic but significant twist, *Decalogue IV*: 'Honor thy father and thy mother,' is about incestuous longings and fantasies. A young woman has been raised since birth by a man whom she has always suspected was not her biological father. From the opening scene there is tremendous erotic tension between them, and the viewer is uncertain about the nature of their relationship. The drama centers around a letter written by the young woman's deceased mother, marked 'To be opened only after my death,' and 'for my daughter Anna,' that carries the possible question of whether Michal is her real father or not. It, thus, becomes an examination of the nature of parenthood and the ability to follow and obey this Commandment.

The daughter confronts her father with a perceived certainty that he is not her biological father, thereby liberating her incestuous love feelings for him, and her belief that he holds similar desires and longings toward her. With this, erotic feelings explode and erupt between them, bursting forth with the full archetypal force of the transgressive, regressive incest impulse that constellates the need for the taboo.

The Commandment is usually interpreted as urging us to honor our parents by showing them respect, obedience, and love. Respecting our parents is one of the most fundamental human duties and imperatives. However, what is overlooked is present in a commentary to this portion of the biblical injunction: that the 'greatest achievement open to parents is to be everfully worthy of their children's reverence, trust, and love' (Hertz, 1960, p. 299). It appears that this unstated corollary is what Kieslowski is imagining in this film. Parenthood is not just a biological relationship – it is a supremely psychological relationship as well. This is increasingly relevant with today's blended and varied, multi-constructed families of adoption, surrogacy, and donor egg and sperm.

In the *Old Ethic*, there is no conscious place for the erotic in the context of parent–child dynamics that follows some imposed rule of law. This can lead to repression of authentic feelings and a greater possibility of acting out of sexual feelings due to that repression; there is no conscious place for *Eros*. The *Old Ethic* stresses the taboo, but ignores the impulse that could lead to acting out. In the *New Ethic*, by contrast, one reflects on feelings, however uncomfortable, contradictory, or dangerous and acknowledges these feelings, at least to oneself, though not necessarily to or with the other. In this manner, there is recognition of the shadow in which lies the existence of the incest impulse. With this increased consciousness, there is greater potential for the incest prohibition or taboo to force the libido out of its sexual channel and into a deeper psychological purpose.

Unlike Freud, Jung viewed incest impulses and fantasies from a symbolic or psychological perspective, differing from Freud's purely literal or biological stance. Jung emphasized the symbolic function of incest fantasies as representing union with one's own being, pointing toward individuation and becoming one's self (Jung, 1946: §419). Jungians are well aware that this difference in theoretical understanding led to the eventual split in the Freud/Jung relationship.

In *Decalogue IV* we watch the 'father' initially deny his feelings, hesitate, struggle with, and then, at his daughter's urging, finally acknowledge his own erotic feelings and longings. He states that he 'wished for the impossible.' Once he is able to admit to these feelings of sexual longing for his 'daughter,' he can renounce them, respecting her and not acting on his feelings, and is able to turn away from her desires.

There is tremendous erotic tension in this confrontation. One author (Judith Cooper) was witness to a loud collective gasp in a crowded movie theater audience as these scenes dramatically unfolded. Her father exhibits a quiet strength and is able to mediate these powerful instinctual erotic energies and not be frightened by them. Once they both consciously admit to and then renounce these longings, what follows is a renewed father–daughter connection between them, a parent–child bond that is sensuously tender and loving. He cradles her and they hum together a childhood song. Her father, by acknowledging his romantic longings, but refusing to act on them by sexualizing their filial love, becomes a carrier of the *New Ethic*, holding the tension of the impossible wish and the longing to connect sexually but also the renouncing of these desires. This change in relationship opens up the possibilities for Anna to better live her own life, with her father's blessing, knowing herself to be a sexually desirous woman. Letting go of sexual fantasies toward her father, she can allow her libido to be present for another.

The Witness/Watcher appears at two key crucial moments: as the daughter contemplates opening her deceased mother's letter, and also when the daughter finally confesses to her father that she had not opened her mother's letter and had fabricated the scenario she had hoped for. The deceased mother's letter is highly symbolic and numinous, it could be thought of as the 'letter of the law' – do they obey the truth of this outside declaration or discover their own truth. The Self exists outside one's self in the letter of the law. Once they confront each other and resolve this tension, they both agree and decide to burn the letter, to live as father and daughter no matter what the letter reveals as the truth. It is a graphic example of destroying the *Old Ethic*, i.e., letting the mother decide for them how they want to relate to each other, without acknowledging and processing their feelings. They are now in the *New Ethic*, discovering their own truth by confronting and examining their own individual shadows. The essence of the *New Ethic* is that one does not do something just because it is a bad thing or just because the law states, 'thou shalt not.'

This dynamic is applicable to the analytic relationship. Harold Searles's seminal article 'Oedipal love in the counter-transference' (1959) powerfully addresses this. Searles posits an understanding of mutual longing and mutual renunciation between analyst and client. Searles argues for the inevitability of *Eros*, erotic feelings and fantasies in both patient and analyst, toward one another, reenacting familial dynamics and the powerful pull toward the incest wish. He states that this acknowledgment, without repression or suppression, promotes individuation, echoing Neumann's *New Ethic*. Legitimatizing and valuing these energies in relationships whether father–daughter, mother–son, father–son, mother–daughter, or analyst–client can more likely inoculate potential dangers of acting out, as feelings are not unconsciously repressed. In the film this process of the father's capacity to show respect and love toward his psychological daughter affirms the daughter's healthy erotic viability and selfhood. This is what Jung refers to as kinship libido – the desire for connection and the search for wholeness through relationship.

Clinically, we have noted the damage done to children when, at puberty, fathers (and mothers) can become sarcastic, mocking, ignoring, or rejecting of children's incipient development out of fear or envy of their children's youth and energy and their aliveness around sexuality. Andrew Samuels, on the relationship between fathers and daughters and the incest myth, has written that we can find psychological meaning and purpose in incestuous fantasies. Samuels argues for fathers' erotic involvement without acting out, terming this 'erotic playback' (1989, p. 82). Samuels, following Jung, states that these incestuous fantasies are symbolic, a symbolic expression of longing for rebirth of one's Self through contact with the beloved, trusted parent. This can lead to transformation as this incest pull is a numinous experience to return to the Self as a way of rejuvenating one's personal self in relationship to the archetypal Self initially carried by our parents.

Decalogue VIII: thou shalt not bear false witness against thy neighbor

In many ways this episode represents the essence of Kieslowski's ethical vision – it is the jewel of the set. Here he even brings into question his own thesis of the child being of the utmost importance.

In this segment a Jewish woman, Elzbieta, who is doing research on survivors of the Second World War, presents a dilemma during an ethics class. Our Watcher figure appears as one of the students in the class, acting as a reminder that something of an important ethical order is going to unfold. We gradually become aware that it is the history of the young woman and the older ethics professor, Zofia. As a very young girl Elzbieta was to be baptized to protect her from persecution by the Nazis, and then given to another couple with the baptismal certificate as protection while sheltering the girl. At the last moment Zofia, who agreed to sponsor the baptism, backs out invoking the Eighth commandment: thou shalt not bear false witness – basically the injunction against lying. She never knew the fate of the little girl until that moment.

What ensues is a confrontation of the deepest moral order. We find out that Zofia suspected the adopting couple of being Nazi collaborators, and that the baptism was intended to entrap the underground movement of which she was a member. This turned out not to be true and Zofia suffered for the rest of her life with the guilt that she likely had sent Elzbieta to her death. It is this individuation crisis that forms the defining moment of Zofia's life and was instrumental in her dedication to becoming a writer and professor of ethics. In one of their dialogues Elzbieta asks about her students, 'Are you trying to get them to lead good lives?' Zofia replies, 'I'm trying to help them find themselves.' She describes her class as an ethical hell.

Kieslowski's psychological movie-making art is beautifully demonstrated in several subtle details of the interaction and story. After the confrontation in the class Zofia takes Elzbieta back to the apartment in which the drama unfolded many years before. Questionable in itself, this return to the 'scene of the crime' evokes intense tension in both the participants and the film's viewers. We see an altar to the Virgin Mary in the window of one of the apartments as a paradoxical reminder of the failure of the archetypal mother to incarnate on this exact spot. Elzbieta then emotionally turns the table on her abandoner/persecutor by hiding out, frightening Zofia into feeling that once again she had caused her harm. The enactment of this sado-masochistic psychodrama highlights the dynamics of trauma by portraying Elzbieta's attempt to 'put into' her persecutor the same powerful feelings of fear and abandonment that she felt as a child, a process that psychologists call projective identification.

In Zofia's apartment there is a painting that repeatedly ends up hanging unevenly on the wall. She rights it one time and Elzbieta another. A subtle metaphor that leading a balanced life takes effort and that it is never done once and for all – one often goes out of kilter, and balance needs to be consciously returned. As Jung states:

> The right way to wholeness is made up, unfortunately, of fateful detours and wrong
> turnings. It is a *longissima via*, not straight but snakelike, a path that unites the opposites

in the manner of the guiding caduceus, a path whose labyrinthine twists and turns are not lacking in terrors.

(1944: §6)

Zofia's life is portrayed as a constant striving for balance in body, mind, and soul as she is seen exercising, dieting, teaching, and how she takes responsibility for her past decision. She says to Elzbieta 'about good, I believe everyone has it in them. The world gives birth to either good or evil. That particular evening in 1943 did not bring out the good in me.' Elzbieta questions just who is the ultimate judge of good and evil, and Zofia indicates that there is an inner source in all of us without having to resort to the notion of God – 'perhaps we can leave God out of it.' Here Zofia supports our thesis that one can make moral choices from one's own inner center.

Zofia demonstrates a certain strength of character that John Beebe would describe as integrity. Quoting Erickson he states,

> Ego strength in the old means the ability to maintain the wholeness of the personality even as the body gradually falls apart and again becomes a conglomerate of parts, which now weaken as they once matured at different rates. Only a certain integrity can save the old from annoying despair. But if a certain vigor of mind combines with the gift of responsible renunciation, some old people can envision human problems in their entirety which is what integrity means, and express the principles involved.

(1992, p. 126)

While out running Zofia has an interesting, almost Felliniesque, interlude in the woods with the 'rubber man' – a man preparing for a television appearance by bending over backwards and placing his head between his legs. She is amused and makes a half-hearted attempt to emulate him but this woman is solid, she cannot 'bend over backwards.' The *New Ethic* does not mean that anything goes and that one can be so adaptable and bendable, able to move in any direction.

In the final scene Zofia is contrasted with a tailor – part of the couple that was to shelter Elzbieta as a child. Elzbieta wants to meet him and thank him for his efforts. But this man had refused to talk with Zofia following her apology to him for mistakenly thinking he was a collaborator, and does not want to talk to Elzbieta either. He is portrayed as closed, rigid, and only able to make clothes that are out-of-date. We might imagine that he also felt guilty that he needed a baptismal certificate to feel safe even though it brought others into jeopardy. As Jungians might say, he was stuck in an outdated persona – never recovering from his own woundedness related to the war.

In naming her Zofia, the Greek word for wisdom, Kieslowski is suggesting that she is the embodiment of what we are calling the '*New Ethic*' – an individual living from his or her own inner moral center. She admits that like any of us she can do, and choose, what is not always considered to be a morally *right* action. We also hear a story that she is estranged from her son. She is far from perfect, but consciously working toward wholeness. And, sometimes, even if it is never exactly *the* right moral action, a child must be sacrificed for the greater good, a 'necessary crime.'

Conclusion

In the two episodes under analysis we noted that in IV the 'right' thing to do was to uphold the intent of the commandment, while in VIII the exact opposite was necessary – 'correct' ethical action involved breaking the commandment. The commandments as concretizations of the *Old Ethic* have become too rigidified as a new depth psychological approach has entered into consciousness:

> Through the New Ethic, the ego-consciousness is ousted from its central position in a psyche organized on the lines of a monarchy or totalitarian state, its place being taken by wholeness or the self, which is now recognized as central.
>
> *(Jung, 1949: §1417)*

Kieslowski's profound psychological insight and *punctum* in *The Decalogue* highlights the need for and acceptance of mystery and ambiguity in approaching any type of moral 'should.' Jung emphasized the need for individuals to confront collective laws that do not do justice to complicated psychological situations. He said, 'I do not write for believers who already possess the whole truth, rather for unbelieving but intelligent people who want to understand something' (in Edinger, 1984, p. 62). We could say the same for Kieslowski: his movie making is not for the believer but for the questioner.

The development of consciousness goes hand-in-hand with the development of conscience. It is hard to imagine there was ever a time in human history when moral structures were not necessary and certainly a codification of rightness was necessary early in history. But particularly during chaotic times, such as we are now experiencing, the fundamentalism of the 'believers' somehow must be confronted and questioned, as Kieslowski models in *The Decalogue* series, to find a *New Ethic* honoring the individual. The observing consciousness of the Watcher is necessary, but not sufficient in critical moral moments. Awareness that something new is being called for might allow for 'right action' in a given situation. Or as Viktor Frankl posits in *Man's Search for Meaning*, 'Between stimulus and response, there is a space. In that space is our power to choose our response. In our response lies our growth and our freedom' (2006, p. 95).

Edinger (1984) offered depth psychology as the new dispensation, that is, a new system of spiritual order. He stated,

> *The new psychological dispensation finds man's relation to God in the individual's relation to the unconscious.... In essence the Jewish dispensation was centered in the law, the Christian dispensation was centered in faith and the psychological dispensation is centered in experience.*
>
> *(p. 90, authors' italics)*

As Zofia might say, 'we all have good in us, but sometimes circumstances bring out the bad.' When they do we must own and take responsibility for them. Kieslowski grasps this notion at an elemental level and provides us with numinous images of this *New Ethic*.

References

Barthes, R. (2010) *Camera lucida: reflections on photography*. New York: Hill & Wang.

Beebe, J. (1992) *Integrity in depth*. College Station, TX: Texas A&M University Press.

Coates, Paul (ed.) (1999) *Lucid dreams: the films of Krzysztof Kieslowski*. Trowbridge, UK: Flicks Books.

Edinger, E. (1972) *Ego and archetype*. New York: Penguin Books.

Edinger, E. (1984) *Creation of consciousness: Jung's myth for modern man*. Toronto: Inner City Books.

Frankl, V. (2006) *Man's search for meaning*. Boston, MA: Beacon Books.

Hertz, J. H. (ed.) (1960) *Pentateuch and haftorahs*. London: Soncino Press.

Insdorf, A. (1999) *Double lives, second chances: the cinema of Krzysztof Kieslowski*. New York: Hyperion.

Jung, C. G. (1930/50) 'Psychology and literature', in *The collected works of C. G. Jung*, Vol. 15, *The spirit in man, art and literature*. London: Routledge & Kegan Paul, 1966.

Jung, C. G. (1938/54a) 'Psychological aspects of the mother archetype', in *The collected works of C. G. Jung*, Vol. 9i, *The archetypes of the collective unconscious*, 2nd edn. London: Routledge & Kegan Paul, 1959/68.

Jung, C. G. (1934/54b) 'Archetypes of the collective unconscious', in *The collected works of C. G. Jung*, Vol. 9i, *The archetypes of the collective unconscious*, 2nd edn. London: Routledge & Kegan Paul, 1959/68.

Jung, C. G. (1939) 'Forward to Suzuki's "introduction to Zen Buddhism"', in *The collected works of C. G. Jung*, Vol. 11, *Psychology and religion: east and west*. London: Routledge & Kegan Paul, 1958/69.

Jung, C. G. (1944) 'Introduction to the religious and psychological problems of alchemy', in *The collected works of C. G. Jung*, Vol. 12, *Psychology and alchemy*. London: Routledge & Kegan Paul, 1944/53.

Jung, C. G. (1946) 'The psychology of the transference', in *The collected works of C. G. Jung*, Vol. 16, *The practice of psychotherapy*. London: Routledge & Kegan Paul, 1954/81.

Jung, C. G. (1949) 'Forward to depth psychology and a new ethic', in *The collected works of C. G. Jung*, Vol. 18, *The symbolic life*. London: Routledge & Kegan Paul, 1954.

Jung, C. G. (1955–6/70) 'The conjunction', in *The collected works of C. G. Jung*, Vol. 14, *Mysterium coniunctionis*. London: Routledge & Kegan Paul, 1955–6/70.

Kalsched, D. (1996) *Inner world of trauma: archetypal defenses of the personal spirit*. New York: Routledge.

Kickasola, J. G. (2004) *Films of Krzysztof Kieslowski: the liminal image*. New York: Continuum.

Neumann, E. (1990) *Depth psychology and a new ethic*. Boston, MA: Shambhala Press.

Perry, J. W. (1976) *Roots of renewal in myth and madness*. San Francisco, CA: Jossey-Bass.

Plantinga, C. and Smith, G. M. (eds) (1999) *Passionate views: film, cognition, and emotion*. Baltimore: MD: Johns Hopkins University Press.

Samuels, A. (1989) *The plural psyche: personality, morality, and the father*. New York: Routledge.

Searles, H. F. (1959) 'Oedipal love in the counter-transference', *International Journal of Psychoanalysis*, 40, pp. 180–90.

Stok, D. (ed.) (1993) *Kieslowski on Kieslowski*. London: Faber & Faber.

Online sources

Empire (2010) 'The 100 best films of world cinema' [online]. Available at: www.empireonline.com/movies/features/100-greatest-world-cinema-films [Accessed 21 July 2016].

International Federation of Film Critics (fipresci) (1989) 46th Venice Film Festival, 4–15 September [online]. Available at: www.fipresci.org/festival-reports/1989/venice-film-festival [Accessed 18 November 2017].

National Society of Film Critics (n.d.) '100 essential films' [online]. Available at: www.filmsite.org/alist.html [Accessed 18 November 2017].

Groves, T. (2003) 'Cinema/affect/writing', *Senses of Cinema*, March (25) [online]. Available at: www.sensesofcinema.com [Accessed 24 May 2003).

Filmography

Decalogue, The. (1988) Directed by Krzysztof Kieslowski. Poland, West Germany.

18

THE *HAN* CULTURAL COMPLEX

Embodied experiences of trauma in New Korean Cinema

Amalya Layla Ashman

Introduction

The documentary film *The Cinema on the Road* (*Gil-wi-ui yeonghwa*, dir. Jang Sun-woo, 1995) suggests that the South Korean cinema of the 1990s constituted a national cinema that sought to overcome the traumatic events of the twentieth century. He likens this cinematic representation of the historical reconciliation of the nation's anger and suffering, to a traditional shamanic exorcism, known as a *gut*, of *han*. *Han* is an emotion specific to Korean culture that is both a personal and collective expression of suffering. It ranges from righteous anger, rebellion and vengeance, to depression, melancholy and nostalgia. This chapter extends Jang's proposition by examining *han* as an instance of what post-Jungians term a 'cultural complex' in 'New Korean Cinema', which is considered to be filmmaking of the post-democratisation period, from 1992 to present. Conceived as a cultural complex, this chapter argues that, more than a feeling, *han* is a culture-specific, psychosomatic expression of societal trauma, which has been shaped by the events of the twentieth century and the emerging South Korean national identity.

Like many emotions, *han* is socially constructed. This chapter starts with a summary of some of the recent scholarly, literary, religious and political attitudes that have defined the current notion of *han* in South Korea. Common to all these opinions is the belief that twentieth century events including colonisation, war, national division and authoritarian rule have intensified the people's *han*. The chapter will then highlight the parallels between the inter-generational transfer of this suffering through to the new century, and explore Thomas Singer and Samuel L. Kimbles' (2004) definition of the cultural complex. As with other cultural complexes, *han* is associated with certain archetypal images; however, one of its unique aspects is the physical manifestation of suffering, which leads me to emphasise its psychosomatic nature. Drawing on Susan Rowland's (2002) discussion of the 'subtle body' in post-Jungian thought and Luke Hockley's (2014) writing on the viewer's somatic experience of cinema, this chapter proposes that *han* is also an 'embodied experience' of trauma. This operates on various levels, as literal physical pain in the body while experiencing *han* and as wounds that symbolise the mental anguish of *han*.

To illustrate this last point, I will look at three ways in which the psychosomatic trauma of the cultural complex *han* is expressed in New Korean Cinema through wounding or defiling the body. This will be illustrated through the examination two films that feature self-harm and suicide as a response to the violent, authoritarian oppression of citizens from the 1960s to the

1980s. These films address specific events in South Korean history that constitute historical injustices: the suppression of the labour movement in the 1960s and 1970s depicted in *A Single Spark* (*Areumdaun cheongnyeon Jeon Tae-il*, dir. Park Kwang-su, 1995), and the complicity of the ordinary citizen in the authoritarian regime of the 1980s in *Peppermint Candy* (*Baka satang*, dir. Lee Chang-do, 1999). Next, the chapter will highlight recurring archetypal images of the *puella* (eternal girl) in the work of Kim Ki-duk, whose self-confessed interest in the nature of *han* has informed many of the films he has written and directed. Financially and sexually exploited women populate Kim's films (and many other texts in New Korean Cinema), which, I suggest, channel the energies of the *puella* into images of defiled female bodies that symbolise the exploitation of the people by the state. Lastly, the chapter will analyse how the body is used as a canvas in *The Vegetarian* (*Chaesikjuuija*, dir. Lim Woo-seong, 2009) for creatively expressing the degradation – or passive *han* – of our everyday lives. As the injustices of the past begin to recede in public awareness and are replaced by the subtle inequalities of the democratic South Korean state, this chapter argues, that representations of the *han* cultural complex have become more abstract and divergent from Western portrayals of trauma.

Defining *han*

While all emotions are shaped to some extent by the culture in which they occur, the complexity of feeling and the specific cultural signifiers inferred by *han* make it unique to the Korean people. In fact, the specificity of *han* to the societal attitudes and events of South Korea means it is important to summarise the modern history of the state and opinions of cultural commentators. (One caveat is that this research cannot speak for the expression of *han* in North Korea.)

Lee Jae-hoon offers the following basic definition of *han*, '[it] is not a single feeling, but many feelings condensed together, including resentment, regret, resignation, aggression, anxiety, loneliness, longing sorrow, and emptiness' (1994, p. 2). The closest word to *han* is the Chinese 恨 (pronounced 'hen'), which also signifies hatred, but does not possess the same multilayered feelings or cultural prominence. *Han* has two main aspects in Korean culture: first, *won-han* describing hatred that strives for justice or revenge, and *jeong-han* denoting a passive acceptance of 'sorrow, distress, and unresolved sentiment' (Yoon and Williams, 2015, p. 41). Various scholars, artists, religious leaders, and even statesmen, have thought of *han* as being inherent to the national character of South Korea: 'we Koreans often think of ourselves as a *han*-ridden people' (Hyun, 1982).

In spite of the rapid globalisation of South Korean popular culture (often referred to as *Hallyu*), there has been little vernacular use or academic analysis of this defining concept of South Korean nationality. In the 1990s and 2000s, the first texts discussing the metaphysical and psychological aspects of *han* were translated into English. Perhaps serendipitously, these first translations – *The Explorations of the Inner Wounds: Han* (Lee, 1994) and *Haan of Minjung Theology and Han of Han Philosophy* (Son, 2000) – both referred to Jungian models of the psyche in their explanations of *han* to a non-Korean audience. However, a number of key works remain Korean only resources, such as *Haneui Gujoyeongu* (Cheon, 1993) and *Haneuihakjejeokyeongu* (Kim *et al.*, 2004). In Western scholarship, *han* has been cited in terms of film and popular culture, beginning with Isolde Standish (1994), Nancy Abelmann (1996), Eungjun Min *et al.* (2003) and Darcy Paquet (2010). The most recent, and thorough, writing on *han* by Park Myoungkyu appeared in the volume *Civilising Emotions: Concepts in Nineteenth Century Asia and Europe* (2015), where he discussed the evolution of *han* into a sentiment of nationalism, while Keumsil Kim Yoon and Bruce Williams address the prevalence of *han* in contemporary South Korean cinema in their book, *Two Lenses on the Korean Ethos: Key Cultural Concepts and their Appearance in Cinema* (2015).

To understand *han*, it is necessary to look at its origins, or, at least, the history ascribed to it by prominent voices in South Korea. The poet, Ko Un speculated in 1990 that *han* united the nomadic tribes of Northeast Asia, from which, it is widely believed, Koreans are descended. He surmises that this community found solidarity in the qualities of *han* common today by raging against their enemies and resenting hardships when times were bad, all the while celebrating the good with shamanic displays. South Korean historians, like Kim Won-yong (1983), support a theory that a Manchurian tribe, known as the *Yemaek*, settled the Korean peninsula around 1000 BC, and that contemporary Korean culture has 'retained its northern traits throughout her history largely due to a remarkable ethnic homogeneity' (pp. 2–3). From this perspective, not only is *han* distinctive, it is also a distinguishing quality that can be traced back to Korea's pre-historical peoples. In a sense, Ko (1990) is suggesting that Koreans are the product of an 'emotional community', a term associated with Barbara Rosenwein, who studies the emotions of medieval Europe, defining 'emotional communities' as groups 'animated by common or similar interests, values and emotional styles and valuations' (quoted in Plamper, 2010, p. 253).

While this is a neat explanation, it is in fact problematic. As we know from research into the history of emotion, all human feelings, and the communities created around them, are subject to change brought about by the society and culture of their age (Matt and Stearns, 2014, p. 42). Thus, it is 'utterly unhistorical', in Rosenwein's words, 'to assume that our emotions were also the emotions of the past' (quoted in Plamper, 2010, p. 253). The historical accuracy of the origins of *han*, might be questionable, but what is not, as Yoon and Williams point out, is the belief that a recognisable iteration of the emotional concept of *han* appears throughout centuries of historical documents, oral traditions and literature in South Korea (2015, p. 40). Even though the notion of 'being Korean' held little traction with the people of the peninsula prior to the turn of the nineteenth century, by the late twentieth century it quickly became ' "politically incorrect" [within South Korea] to question the eternal and natural essence of the Korean ethnic unity' (Eckert quoted in Shin, 2006, p. 3). In the mythology surrounding *han*, not only is it treated as an 'eternal' trait of Korean culture, unchanged by the centuries, it is also inferred that *han* transformed a group of nomads into a 'people' destined to nationhood.

Despite this false start, we can of course take the current political landscape in South Korea as a starting point to examine the contemporary concept of *han*. Yoon and Williams (2015), as in my own research, preface their definitions of *han* with a list of tragic twentieth century events: the annexation and occupation of Korea by Imperial Japan (1905–1945); the devastating civil war (1950–1953) that resulted in the division of the country into the Communist North and capitalist South; decades of political suppression of the South Korean people causing multiple protests; and the massacre of citizens in Gwangju in 1980. Gi-wook Shin (2006) cites these same events to explain how the South built a state around a central belief in ethnic nationalism.

In some measure, South Korean national identity is predicated on the shared suffering, or *han*, of these events. The nature of *han* in South Korean national identity is clear in the self-reflective filmmaking of the post-democratic era from 1992 onwards. The transfer of power from military to civilian rule that took place between 1988 and 1992 is known as the democratisation of South Korea. Decades of authoritarian governments had suppressed the rights of South Korea's citizens, which united various civic, religious and literati groups to oppose the state under the umbrella term of the *minjung* [trans. 'the common people'] movement (Lee, 2007, p. 214). The movement rallied people by creating an ideology around the notion of *han* as an inherited trauma that propelled the Korean people to protest for justice (Abelmann, 1996, p. 37). This drive for historical justice continued in the 1990s, and initiated numerous state investigations into corruption and human rights abuses by former regimes headed by Chun

Doo-hwan and Roh Tae-woo. In terms of cinema, democratisation heralded what Julian Stringer calls, a 'cultural phenomenon' of 'qualitatively different' filmmaking from 1992 onwards (Stringer and Shin, 2005, pp. 2–3). Due to key structural changes to the cinema industry – new distribution patterns, more versatile sources of funding, dedicated film schools and the softening of censorship – domestic film production yielded higher quality, more commercially successful films (Stringer and Shin, 2005, p. 6). Thematically, the films of the 1990s and 2000s in South Korea encouraged reflection on the past, including, what Stringer and Michael Robinson (2005) consider a quasi-postmodernist questioning of the 'grand narratives' that dominated pre-democratic South Korea: patriarchal power, colonial politics, and modernisation.

Han as a cultural complex

The inspiration to define *han* in this research as a post-Jungian cultural complex came from a particularly prescient description by the analytical psychologist J. H. Lee:

> *han* is not only a personal complex but also a collective complex of the Korean people inherited from past generations. It is the product of social and cultural conditions throughout Korean history. These are repeated foreign invasions, political oppression by powerful elite, and interpersonal conflicts among family members in the large family system.
>
> *(1994, p. 13)*

Lee's comments were published ten years before Singer and Kimbles' 2004 work on reviving the concept of the cultural complex in post-Jungian thought; however, the parallels are clear. Singer and Kimbles define a cultural complex as:

> based on repetitive, historical group experiences which have taken root in the cultural unconscious of the group. At any ripe time, these slumbering cultural complexes can be activated in the cultural unconscious and take hold of the collective psyche of the group and individual/collective psyche of individual members of the group.
>
> *(2004, p. 7)*

They refer to a model of the psyche devised from Carl Jung (1936) and Joseph Henderson's (1988) interpretations, which feature separate layers of the unconsciousness, including a cultural layer specific to the individual's group identity. For Singer and Kimbles, the post-Jungian psyche flows from the archetypal foundation of the collective unconscious to the cultural unconscious, followed by the personal unconscious and individual ego-based consciousness.

There are several points of comparison between that description of the behaviour of a cultural complex and this interpretation of the nature of *han*. To begin, the delineations between the layers of the post-Jungian psyche are not strict. As Kimbles explains, both personal and cultural complexes 'arise out of archetypal aspects of the psyche and provide affect, image, structure, and dynamism to individual and group life. Cultural complexes function between the personal and archetypal psyche by linking the two realms in group and individual life' (2006, p. 98). Thus, the distinction between individual and cultural experiences, emotions and identities are as fluid as the complexes that underlie personal and collective archetypal images. Similarly, we repeatedly see examples of conscious and unconscious connections forged between an individual's *han* and that of the nation's past and present struggles.

As emphasised above, many commentators regard *han* as an indicator of Korean-ness. Cultural complexes also provide a sense of belonging by connecting personal experiences of the individual with group expectations of ethnic, racial, religious or social identities (Kimbles 2006, p. 99). The interpretation of twentieth century events as *han*-ridden political oppression corresponds to Kimbles' description of how complexes are built upon cultural histories shaped by the group's ideology and storytelling traditions (p. 102). Finally, and especially relevant to *han*, cultural complexes involve 'complicated group processes that include memories of perpetration by a particular group, survival strategies, woundedness, and retaliatory and vengeance dynamics' (p. 102). Of these, 'woundedness' stands out as a principal metaphor for the trauma of the *han* cultural complex in South Korean film, as examined below.

Witnessing, testimony and historical injustice in the 1990s: *A Single Spark* and *Peppermint Candy*

Political leniencies for New Korean Cinema in the 1990s allowed filmmakers to directly address specific, historical instances of political oppression of the *minjung* in previous decades. These events formed part of the cultural history of the *han* cultural complex, as they were interpreted by protesting civilians as a legacy of state-sponsored violence that not only curtailed the rights of South Koreans, but personally and collectively traumatised citizens. Most notable for their direct representation and criticism are: *A Single Spark*, which tells the story of protestor, Jeon Tae-il, who committed suicide in the name of workers' rights in 1970, and *Peppermint Candy*, which features an ordinary man traumatised by, and complicit in, government-sanctioned violence against citizens, first as a soldier, and later as a policeman. Connecting these films is Lee Chang-do, who wrote the script for Park Kwang-su's *A Single Spark*, and also wrote and directed *Peppermint Candy*. *A Single Spark* was the fifth feature film Park Kwang-su directed on the theme of working class struggles. His films *Chilsu and Mansu* (here Chilsu and Mansu are the names of the titular characters) (*Chilsu-wa Mansu*, 1988) and *The Black Republic* (*Geudeul-do uri-cheoreom*, 1990) are considered by Standish (1994), as prime examples of a new realism in South Korean cinema that became known as the Korean New Wave.

Park's filmmaking aligns him with many values of the *minjung* movement, including the use of *han* as an emotional impetus to 'feel' its place in history as the next generation of protestors seeking justice for past traumas (Abelmann, 1996, pp. 36–37). In the comparatively 'uncensored' period of New Korean Cinema brought about by democratisation, films could creatively address the contentious topics of earlier decades. By 1995, with *A Single Spark*, Park was able to depart from allegorical narratives to dramatise historical figures from previous working class generations and student revolutionaries. In *A Single Spark*, the fictional protagonist, Kim Young-soo, is an academic and activist on the run from police in 1975. He is intent on keeping the memory of the real protestor, Jeon Tae-il, alive through a biography he is writing and the protests he helps stage. Throughout the film, the narrative cuts between Kim's life on the run shot in colour, and black and white scenes depicting Jeon Tae-il's political awakening in the 1960s. Jeon's 1970 suicide by immolation, in support of the labour movement, provides the film's climax.

In spite of the fact that only five years separate the fictional Young-soo's efforts (which purportedly takes place in 1975) to record Jeon's life for younger generations, and Jeon's death in 1970, the film employs a number of devices to memorialise Jeon. First, the use of black and white film stock exaggerates the sense of 'pastness' – a pre-colour document of historical events – that differentiates it from the fictional, colour story concocted by Park Kwang-su and Lee Chang-do as a vehicle to narrate Jeon's biography. Second, Young-soo learns more of Jeon by talking to Jeon's mother, whose voice-over narrates turning points in Jeon's life that led him to become increasingly dedicated and self-sacrificing towards his co-workers. Third, the viewer enters these black-and-white flashbacks to Jeon when a place, person or sound reminds Young-soo of him, and he slips into what appears to be his memories of Jeon's story. Young-soo, however, has never met Jeon, so his 'memories' are perhaps better interpreted as a form of imaginative, historical storytelling.

In this film, testimony in the form of a mother's personal account and Young-soo's biography looms large as a device through which it is possible to connect to the *han* of past protestors and the reconstruction of history. Testimony and witnessing are, of course, a mainstay of Dori Laub's (Felman and Laub, 1992) writing on trauma. Laub considers testimony to be 'the process by which the narrator (the survivor) reclaims his position as a witness' and 'a conceptual break-through as well as a historical event in its own right' (p. 85). Thus, as biographer, Young-soo positions himself as 'witness' to Jeon's life, and by extension, each viewer of *A Single Spark* becomes another witness in this chain, carrying the 'memory' and the *han* of Jeon's sacrifice with another generation. Laub writes that traumatic events often take 'place outside the parameters of "normal" reality', which 'lends to it a quality of "otherness"' and a 'timelessness' (p. 69). The slow-motion, black-and-white scene depicting Jeon consumed by flames as he runs, screaming 'Comply with labour laws! We are not machines!' into the gathered protestors, is intended to leave this same lasting impression on the viewer.

A colourised still from this episode is also used on many posters and DVD covers for the film. Despite its iconic status, this is not the final scene. The narrative ends with Young-soo visiting the street where Jeon burned to death, to mark the anniversary of his last protest. Young-soo allows himself a small smile when he spots a trendy, 'Westernised' youth, dressed head to toe in denim, who bears a striking resemblance to Jeon (he is played by the same actor, Hong Kyoung-in), carrying a copy of Young-soo's biography. The message, the film suggests, is not that Jeon's death was merely tragic, but that it is a tragedy that must be remembered as part of South Korea's traumatic history and passed along to future generations. The film appears to acknowledge that this (or any) biography of Jeon is an act of imagination, such that the cultural inheritance in South Korea of both the political struggle and *han* is indebted to the creative and unconscious influences of cultural complexes.

A Single Spark ends with the suicide of an impoverished protestor: by contrast *Peppermint Candy* begins with the suicide of a cruel, and dishonest, ex-policeman with a history of torturing political activists. The film opens at a reunion picnic of university friends, where a drunk and belligerent Yong-ho climbs up on to the railway tracks and screams out before a train hits him 'I want to go back!' From here, the film narrates Yong-ho's life in reverse chronological order, beginning with his attempted suicide three days prior to the picnic, and chronicling his business losses in the Asian Financial Crisis of the 1990s and his desertion of his wife and daughter. Going back to the 1980s, Yong-ho is a fresh recruit to the police force who is taught by experienced police offers how to torture prisoners. The violence of his new profession appears to spark traumatic memories for Yong-ho.

One night, drinking after work with fellow policemen, Yong-ho appears to be intoxicated and cycles on a bike in endless circles outside the restaurant, until he points the vehicle into the dining area. Once inside he starts screaming and attacking his superiors with a broken broom, insisting that they follow army orders and fall into formation. The drinkers are uncertain whether to take him seriously or not – as his desperation suggests this is more than a drunken prank and more akin to a psychic breakdown. The latter is proved to be the case in the final flashback to Yong-ho's conscription to the army. The date is May 1980, and Yong-ho's unit is called to Gwangju to participate in quelling a civilian protest, which results in a bloodbath. Yong-ho, a young, terrified recruit, is shot in the leg almost as soon as he touches down in Gwangju. He crumbles to ground in tears at a deserted train station. A young teenage girl emerges from the shadows and pleads with Yong-ho to let her run across the tracks home, he agrees and fires some shots in the air to hurry her along. He is distracted by the sound of other soldiers from his unit coming to rescue him, and when he turns back he finds that one of his bullets has hit and killed the girl.

Peppermint Candy presents a dark picture of the consequences of participating in a society that uses its citizens to oppress the rights of others. Both dissenters and supporters of the state are represented as victims, traumatised by authoritarianism. Yong-ho's loss of innocence and empathy for his fellow citizens is clearly linked to the decisions of the government to call the army into suppressing a student protest, and to later deter political radicalism through police brutality. By the end of his life, Yong-ho's trauma – his *han* – is turned to bitterness, and a strong sense of victimhood. Yong-ho lashes out at anyone who comes close to him, blaming everyone for his shortcomings in life. Eventually he comes to realise that the only way to alleviate his *han* is suicide. While Jeon's impulse to kill himself lies with an altruistic desire to transform the rebellious anger inside him into a political statement, Yong-ho's suicide is an antidote for the resentment and self-hatred he carries. It is important to note that here suicide is not presented as the unfortunate by-product of a curable mental illness, it is instead the physical manifestation of a person consumed inwardly by *han*. These films suggest *han* accumulates until it reaches a point when it is no longer tolerable by the sufferer, who must then turn against the body as a way of acting out their trauma.

Rape, rivalry and symbolic incest: Kim Ki-duk's abused young women

Desperate men driven to suicide by *han* also appear in the films of director, Kim Ki-duk, notably, the crazed young soldier patrolling the border between North and South Korea in *The Coastguard* (*Haeanseon*, 2002), and the suicidal, mixed-race teen, Chang-guk, of *Address Unknown* (*Suchwiinbulmyeong*, 2001), abandoned by his African-American military father. But it is not only men who are depicted as ending their lives because of mental anguish as increasingly con-temporary South Korean films address the subject of female (teenage) suicide. In *Thread of Lies* (*Uahan geojinmal*, dir. Lee Han, 2014) extreme bullying pushes the middle-schooler, Cheon-ji, to hang herself, meanwhile in *Han Gong-ju* (dir. Lee Su-jin, 2013) the titular character, throws herself into the Han river in Seoul after it becomes clear that she will never be able to lead a normal life as a rape survivor. Based on real events from 2004, Han Gong-ju is 14 years old when she was gang-raped by up to 41 male high-school students, whose family later pressure the victims, and the legal system, to drop serious charges against their sons. Sexually abused women are frequently the subject of New Korean Cinema, not least in the work of Kim Ki-duk, who has been active in the film industry since 1996.

Kim Ki-duk has gravitated towards narratives that explore feelings of *han* and historical traumas through the, often sexual, exploitation of his female protagonists by violent male characters. In *Crocodile* (*Ageo*, 1996) the man who saves a suicidal woman, rapes her and so begins a strange rela-tionship between them, much like that of Han-gi and Sun-hwa in *Bad Guy* (*Nappeun namja*, 2002), who become a couple after Han-gi, a pimp, tricks Sun-hwa into prostitution. Prostitution holds a particular fascination for Ki-duk, not least because it evokes an extreme view of how women's lives can be ruined by economic hardship and misogyny. The teenagers Yeo-jin and Jae-young both turn to prostitution to pay for a holiday in Europe in *Samaritan Girl* (*Samaria*, 2004), while the prostitutes servicing tourists and locals at backwater fishing resorts, like Jin-a in *Birdcage Inn* (*Paran daemun*, 1998) and the mute Hee-jin *The Isle* (*Seom*, 2000), have no such optimism for the future.

It is not merely their profession, but more importantly the treatment of these women, especially Jin-a, by other men and women who scorn or trick her into financial predicaments, that position them as representative of the politically oppressed *minjung*. Kim also repeatedly draws on the Christian imagery of female suffering, first in the publicity for *Samaritan Girl*, featuring a naked girl dressed in a white nun's habit, and later with *Pieta* (2012), which, as the name suggests, depicts a weeping mother as the Virgin Mary holding her dead son. These symbolic, religious images that play upon the sexuality of women, demonstrate a conscious effort on the director's part to explore the archetypal imagery evoked by his female protagonists.

Kim Ki-duk explores the physical and sexual exploitation of such characters through relationships that blur the line between sexual and familial bonds that result in actual, or implied, incest. Interwoven with the symbolism of incest, the figures that represent mothers and daughters evoke archetypal images of the 'mother' and the '*puella*'. *Address Unknown* (2000), *Pieta* (2012) and *Moebius* (*Moebiuseu*, 2013) all explore inappropriate sexual contact (and even cannibalism) between mothers and sons. In *Address Unknown*, Chang-guk strips his mother naked, bathes her, cuts off her breast and kills himself. His mother discovers his frozen body in a field and eats flesh from his corpse as she burns to death, in a suicide bid. In *Pieta* the loan shark Kang-do tortures and disables debtors and is reunited with a woman claiming to be his mother. Their relationship takes a dark turn when Kang-do rapes his mother, and forces her to eat flesh cut from his thigh. *Moebius* is a particularly literal adaptation of Oedipal desire and castration anxiety. A mother catches her son masturbating to a scene of his father having sex with another woman. Incensed, she takes a knife to castrate her husband, but is fought off, so instead she castrates her son and eats his penis. In almost all of these films, these examples of sexual and physical abuse are not in fact the source of the characters' *han*, which instead comes either from personal history of suffering or emerges as a consequence of some societal ill. Curiously these traumatising events intensify yet also paradoxically alleviate *han*.

To illustrate this point let us turn to a symbolic alternative to the literal forms of incest mentioned above, via Kim Ki-duk's drama, *The Bow* (*Hwal*, 2005). In the film a 60-year-old fisherman lives on a boat with a 16-year-old girl, who is promised to become his wife when she turns 17. Due to a paucity of dialogue in the film, no further backstory is provided, so it is uncertain whether the girl's betrothal to the man is voluntary or not. Or even if the minimal affection she displays for him is familiarity, or perhaps a form of love for him, maybe as a father figure, or a future husband. At the very least, the film promotes a sense of ambiguity regarding sexual coercion and incest. To make money, tourists come aboard to fish, some drawn by the story of this beautiful, mute girl. Although their relationship is platonic up to this point, the old man is violently possessive of the girl, and threatens to kill a young man who tries to help smuggle her off the boat.

With the rival male banished, the film concludes with the 'betrothal' of the old man and the girl, both dressed in expensive, traditional Korean wedding attire, alone on a rowing boat, staring lovingly into each other's eyes. The old man undresses his bride on a white mattress. He serenades her with a *haegeum* (a traditional stringed instrument made out of a hunting bow), while she lies down smiling. He then dismantles the instrument and cocks an arrow to the bow, which he releases high above them into the sky, before he dives into the water and disappears. Some time passes and the girl rolls over, spreads her legs and begins to mime sexual intercourse. The arrow falls from the sky piercing her white dress between her legs. Her sighs and love-making climax, until blood seeps from around the arrow. All the while her boat is adrift, until she is discovered by the same young man who fell in love with her and tried to smuggle her back to land. Still in the throes of lovemaking, the girl pulls the confused boy into an embrace, as if it were him making love to her. As shown, through the magical-realism of *The Bow*, Kim indicates that the sexual act – whether tinged with negative allusions to rape or incest – is also a positive symbol of initiation and renewal. These connotations appear in Jung's analysis of incest, as well. He writes that, 'whenever this drive for wholeness appears, it begins by disguising itself under the symbolism of incest', which in the context of *han*, denotes a psychic desire to compensate for the unconscious traumatic contents of the cultural complex, and therefore bring the psyche into balance and towards 'wholeness' (1946: §471). Thus, the defiled female body in New Korean Cinema serves as a metaphor in two senses. First, it represents the exploitation of the people by the state and, second, it stands for the (re) traumatised South Korean cultural psyche. In Kim Ki-duk's films women are victims largely of male aggression, however next we will look at the book and film adaptation of *The Vegetarian* and see how one woman channels her *han* into abstinence until her body becomes yet another type of symbol, this time for suffering.

Feeling *han* through the body: *The Vegetarian* (2009)

In *The Vegetarian*, the female body is a canvas on to which men project their desires, at times these desires are sexual but for the most part they are controlling desires that seek female compliance and subordination. In the film, *han* appears in abstract forms: as the social injustice of sexism; the patriarchal organisation of the family in South Korea; and the human cruelty of eating animals. Written by Han Kang in 2007, *The Vegetarian* was adapted to the screen by Lim Woo-seong in 2009. The main character, Young-hye, is a bland and inoffensive wife who has a vivid nightmare one night that causes her to renounce meat and become a vegetarian. The invasive dream seems to have stemmed from a childhood memory. It depicts a chained dog being brutally beaten by a man, who is probably her father. Young-hye's husband and father are particularly incensed by her refusal to eat meat, which leads to an altercation at a family meal-time. Young-hye stabs herself with a knife in protest at being force fed food she doesn't want. Her erratic behaviour lands her in hospital and her husband divorces her. However, Young-hye is unperturbed as she becomes increasingly thin and withdrawn from all relationships.

Young-hye's sister, In-hye, tries to tend to her by delivering food and keeping her company, and asks her husband to help. In-hye's husband becomes obsessed with Young-hye and re-kindles his problematic art career with a secretive video project featuring Young-hye and himself, naked, with flowers painted on their bodies, having sex on camera. Young-hye agrees to the video because she is intrigued by the floral camouflage, but seems disconnected from the moral implications of sleeping with her brother-in-law. Young-hye is eventually placed in a mental asylum, mute and dying of starvation, out of a desire to cease being human and transform into a tree. The exact motivation, or set of fears, behind Young-hye's actions is not clearly articulated to the viewer or the other characters. Regardless, Young-hye's decision is contextualised as an act of resistance to patriarchal desires. Despite the apparent passive means of resistance (refusing to eat, dress or speak) and the tranquil image of plants, the novella suggests that despite appearances the symbolism of plants is more charged: 'the trees by the side of the road are blazing, green fire undulating like the rippling flanks of a massive animal, wild and savage' (Han, 2007, p. 188). It is as if her *han* comprises a deep-seated disgust for human cruelty and that this aversion has translated into self-hatred and the destruction of her own body.

Healing *han* creatively through the body

Suggesting that their characters do not heal psychologically by talking about their feelings of *han*, both *The Vegetarian* and Kim Ki-duk's work in general are notable for their lack of dialogue. In Yoon and William's overview of *han*, they describe three means in which this type of suffering is dealt with socially: first, by turning to shamanic rituals to dispel *han*; second, by passing desires and frustrations on to the next generation; third, by cultivating drive and self-discipline to pursue difficult paths (2015, pp. 46–47). On the final point, they elaborate that frequently the will to succeed takes on an artistic element: venting *han* through literature, music or art. Depictions of creative expressions of *han* appear in several texts in New Korean Cinema. The vocal tradition of *pansori* is explored in *Seopyeonje* (*Seopyeonje* refers to a style of singing *pansori* that originates in the southwestern region of South Korea, Jeolla-do) (dir. Im Kwon-taek, 1993), and its sequel *Beyond the Years* (*Cheonnyeonhak*, 2007), while *Painted Fire* (*Chwihwa-seon*, 2001) by the same director features the work of the nineteenth century painter, Jang Seung-up. Most recently, *Dongju: Portrait of a Poet* (*Dong-ju*, dir. Lee Joon-ik, 2016) recounts the poet Yun Dong-ju's efforts to resist the Japanese occupation of Korea, culminating in his imprisonment, which inspired poems to describe his suffering. In *The Vegetarian*, Young-hye's brother-in-law directs his feelings of inadequacy, as an artist, a husband and a 'man', into his artistic and sexual excitement over Young-hye's self-imposed misery. Their sexual tryst is the only episode during Young-hye's withdrawal from society that animates her. However, it is not the human connection that excites her, it is the symbolism of the painted flowers, as she explains: ' "I really wanted to do it", she said carefully. "I've never wanted it so much before. It was the flowers on his body … I couldn't help myself. That's all" ' (Han, 2007, pp. 113–114). The painted flowers do not halt Young-hye's retreat from humanity, in fact they seem to intensify her behaviour and she is eventually admitted to a mental institute. In the asylum, Young-hye is silently euphoric, spending her days in a handstand as she imitates the trees she wants to become. Eventually her body fails her.

The *subtle body* and *embodied experience*

Susan Rowland (2002) offers a description of the role of the body in the Jungian psyche, which she calls the 'subtle body'. The subtle body encapsulates the means by which the psyche conceives of the body physically and psychically, and suggests that the archetypes bridge this divide because they are psychosomatic (p. 35). Rowland explains that, on the one hand, 'archetypes make the body psychological by representing it through archetypal images', while, on the other, 'the body expresses the physical aspect of the psyche: bodily experiences and needs can reflect psychological experiences and needs' (p. 35). In spite of the centrality of the psyche in Jungian thought, Rowland adds that the body is necessary to 'ground' the ego, to avert the unconscious from overwhelming consciousness (p. 134). In this sense, the 'subtle body' plays a part in the identity of the individual, and also links the psyche to social and cultural influences (p. 134). Jung often undervalued social and cultural factors in psychic imagery; nonetheless, the subtle body is a means for socio-cultural input into archetypal images because these images are formed by what Rowland refers to as 'bodily impressions' (p. 135). In this way, we can say that Jungian symbols are shaped by the subtle body through the instinctive archetype, bodily sensations and, importantly, the social, cultural and affective world we are situated in (p. 144).

Luke Hockley's *Somatic Cinema* makes a similar argument with his synthetic concept of the 'third image', which denotes an intersubjective space where meaning is negotiated between viewer and text, intellect and emotion, and conscious and unconscious cognition (2014, p. 133). Writing about the integrity of the individual viewer, he argues that 'the psychological meaning of films involves a somatic experience', which is to say that the viewer's interpretation of the text is intellectually construed, but physically and emotionally felt (p. 1). Unlike many descriptions in analytical psychology about conceiving archetypal images, Hockley highlights that fact that:

for Jung, a psychological image is not necessarily visual … [the image] contains the psychological meaning of a given moment: [via] the interplay of the unconscious with consciousness through the mediating presence of the body and it creates an embodied awareness that feels, thinks, and intuits the psychological meaning.

(p. 5)

Hockley did not explicitly intend to address cultural complexes, yet, through the notion of 'embodied experience', *Somatic Cinema* provides a model for understanding how collective emotions and complexes are transmitted via affect from individual to individual. Feeling, in the Jungian sense, is a form of value judgement, and guides others to attach emotions to the same objects. Kimbles points to the same notion as Hockley that, in relation to the cultural complex, intergenerational trauma: 'operate[s] at the level of the group and are communicated among individuals in families (or groups) who have experienced historical trauma and whose descendants receive the effects of these events through *unconscious communication*' (2006, p. 105, italics added). To my mind, this 'unconscious communication' implies the psychosomatic sensing of the emotional state of others, which is to say, we are not only mentally present in the cinema and in society, we are physically present, as well.

Embodied experiences of trauma

In the emotional community surrounding *han* in South Korea the body is a medium for sensing the suffering of others, as well as a site to physically manifest grief and symbolise mental anguish. This relationship between the body and trauma is described by Ananya Jahanara Kabir (2014) as 'embodied trauma', and presents new challenges to Western trauma theory in the humanities. Kabir's recent work on song, music and dance related to the trauma of the Kashmir conflict has led her to prioritise the body and affect as key sites of producing meaning. Given that the inception of trauma theory began with Cathy Caruth's assertion that trauma is 'a bodily wound', it follows, according to Kabir, that the body must be central to our investigations in cultural trauma (2014, p. 72). As alluded to by Rowland, Hockley and Kimbles, Kabir argues that this idea of embodied trauma, whereby the body 'does not exist in a vacuum: its return to the space of trauma is an act of reclamation', must take into consideration how 'the work of trauma embeds the body in place, as well as the processes which have displaced it' (p. 72).

Han is likewise 'embedded' in place, its specificity to South Korean history and culture is such that the notion of *han* as a cultural complex can only be construed through the particularities of post-democratic South Korean society. However, our *emotional* proximity can no longer be assured by our *physical* proximity to others in emotional communities. Our increasingly globalised societies allow displaced cultures (and peoples) to engage with their identities and histories online and mediated through cultural texts. This complicates the collectively embodied nature of *han*, which in the past was dependent on physical presence for emotional literacy in the community. As a consequence, the cultural complex is instrumental in displacing the visceral trauma of *han* into a cinematic language of symbols and emotions in South Korean film, literature and media and in so doing it depicts the body of the individual as a metaphor for the suffering of the many. The unconscious contents of the *han* cultural complex, capable of flooding our bodies with painful wounds and assaults, can now be corporeally experienced through the affect of film. As such, in homes and cinemas across the globe, the audience's psychic and physical experience of the *han* cultural complex via New Korean Cinema denotes a new 'affect world', which Kabir claims, 'lead us, time and again, to the traumatised subject using the resources of the body to re-embed itself in place' (2014, p. 73).

References

Abelmann, N. (1996) *Echoes of the past, epics of dissent: a South Korean social movement*. Berkeley, CA: University of California Press.

Cheon, I. (1993) *Haneui gujoyeongu* (A study on the structure of *han*). Seoul: Munhakgwajiseong.

Felman, S. and Laub, D. (1992) *Testimony: crises of witnessing in literature, psychoanalysis and history*. New York: Routledge.

Han, K. (2015 [2007]) *The vegetarian*, trans. D. Smith. London: Hogarth.

Henderson, J. (1988) 'The cultural unconscious', *Quadrant*, 2(2), pp. 7–16.

Hockley, L. (2014) *Somatic cinema: the relationship between body and screen – a Jungian perspective*. New York: Routledge.

Hyun, Y. K. (1982) 'Minjung: the suffering servant and hope', Paper presented at Union Theological Seminary, New York, 13 April.

Jung, C. G. (1936) 'Wotan', *The collected works of C. G. Jung*, Vol. 10, *Civilisation in Transition*, 2nd edn. London: Routledge, 1970.

Jung, C. G. (1946) 'The psychology of the transference', in *The collected works of C. G. Jung*, Vol. 16, *The practice of psychotherapy*. London: Routledge, 1966.

Kabir, A. J. (2014) 'Affect, body, place: trauma theory in the world', in G. Beulens, S. Durrant and R. Eaglestone (eds), *The future of trauma theory: contemporary literary and cultural criticism*. Hoboken, NJ: Taylor & Francis. pp. 63–76.

Kim, J., Sudong, J., Changwhan, H., Myunggon, Y., Gwangho, Y., Yungpil, K., Hyodeok, I., Daeseok, G., Jeongheui, P., Jeonguk, S. and Gangwha, Y. (2004) *Haneuihakjejeokyeongu* (A multidisciplinary study on *han* emotion). Seoul: Cheolhakgwahyeongsil.

Kim, W. Y. (ed.) (1983) *Recent archeological discoveries in the Republic of Korea*. Paris and Tokyo: UNESCO and the Centre for East Asian Cultural Studies.

Kimbles, S. L. (2006) 'Cultural complexes and the transmission of group traumas in everyday life', *Psychological Perspectives*, 49(1), pp. 96–110.

Ko, U. (1990) 'I ttangeso haneun mueosinga?' (What is *han* in this land?), *Gyeogan Sasang*, 5, pp. 36–89.

Lee, J. H. (1994) *The explorations of the inner wounds: han*. Atlanta, GA: Scholars Press.

Lee, N. (2007) *The making of minjung: democracy and the politics of representation in South Korea*. Ithaca, NY and London: Cornell University Press.

Matt, S. J. and Stearns P. N. (eds) *Doing emotions history*. Chicago, IL: University of Illinois Press.

Min, E., Joo, J. and Kwak, H. J. (2003) *Korean film: history, resistance, and democratic imagination*. Westport, CT: Praeger.

Nelson, S. M. (2010) 'The politics of ethnicity in prehistoric Korea', in R. W. Peucel and S. A. Mrozoski (eds), *Contemporary archaeology in theory: the new pragmatism*. Oxford: Blackwell Publishing. pp. 290–300.

Paquet, D. (2010) *New Korean cinema: breaking the waves*. London: Wallflower.

Park, M. (2015) 'From shame to sympathy: civilization and emotion in Korea, 1860–1920', in M. Pernau (ed.), *Civilising emotions: concepts in nineteenth century Asia and Europe*. Oxford: Oxford University Press. pp. 269–87.

Plamper, J. (2010) 'The history of emotions: an interview with William Reddy, Barbara Rosenwein, and Peter Stearns', *History and Theory*, 49, pp. 237–65.

Robinson, M. (2005) 'Contemporary cultural production in South Korea: vanishing meta-narrative of nation', in J. Stringer and C. Y. Shin (eds), *New Korean cinema*. New York: New York University Press. pp. 15–31.

Rowland, S. (2002) *Jung: a feminist revision*. Cambridge, UK: Polity.

Shin, G. W. (2006) *Ethnic nationalism in Korea: genealogy, politics, and legacy*. Stanford, CA: Stanford University Press.

Singer, T. and Kimbles, S. L. (2004) *The cultural complex: contemporary Jungian perspectives on psyche and society*. New York: Brunner-Routledge.

Son, C. H. (2000) *Haan of Minjung theology and Han of Han philosophy in the paradigm of process philosophy and metaphysics of relatedness*. Lanham, MD: University Press of America.

Standish, I. (1994) 'Korean cinema and the new realism', in W. Dissanayake (ed.), *Colonialism and nationalism in Asian cinema*. Bloomington, IN: Indiana University Press. pp. 65–89.

Stringer, J. and Shin, C. Y. (2005) *New Korean cinema*. New York: New York University Press.

Yoon, K. K. and Williams, B. (2015) *Two lenses on the Korean ethos: key cultural concepts and their appearance in cinema*. Jefferson, NC: McFarland & Company, Inc.

Filmography

Address unknown. (2001) [film] Directed by Kim Ki-duk. USA.

Bad guy. (2002) [film]. Directed by Kim Ki-duk. USA.

Beyond the years. (2007) [film] Directed by Im Kwon-taek. South Korea.

Birdcage inn. (1998) [film] Directed by Kim Ki-duk. Denmark.

Black republic, The. (1990) [film] Directed by Park Kwang-su. South Korea.

Bow, The. (2005) [film] Directed by Kim Ki-duk. UK.

Chilsu and Mansu. (1988) [film] Directed by Park Kwang-su. South Korea.

Cinema on the road, The. (1995) [film] Directed by Jang Sun-woo. UK.

Coastguard, The (2002) [film] Directed by Kim Ki-duk. USA.

Crocodile. (1996) [film] Directed by Kim Ki-duk. Denmark.

Dongju: portrait of a poet. (2016) [film] Directed by Lee Joon-ik. South Korea.

Han gong-ju. (2013) [film] Directed by Lee Su-jin. South Korea.

Isle, The (2000) [film] Directed by Kim Ki-duk. USA.

Moebius. (2013) [film] Directed by Kim Ki-duk. USA.

Painted fire. (2001) [film] Directed by Kim Ki-duk. USA.

Peppermint candy. (1999) [film] Directed by Lee Chang-do. South Korea.

Pieta. (2012) [film] Directed by Kim Ki-duk. USA.

Samaritan girl. (2004) [film] Directed by Kim Ki-duk. USA.

Seopyeonje. (1993) [film] Directed by Im Kwon-taek. South Korea.

Single spark, A. (1995) [film] Directed by Park Kwang-su. South Korea.

Thread of lies. (2014) [film] Directed by Lee Han. South Korea.

Vegetarian, The. (2009) [film] Directed by Lim Woo-seong. South Korea.

19

THE OUTSIDER PROTAGONIST IN AMERICAN FILM

Glen Slater

Introduction

Cinema is art that permeates the everyday world, and American cinema has in no small part defined this art. Hollywood films instill a widely recognized narrative of human experience. This narrative comes in various shades of what is a single dominant theme: a heroic encounter with extreme inner challenges and outer obstacles, most often ending in success against the odds. It is a way of imagining life, reflecting the history and character of the American nation, where tradition and tribe are repeatedly left for personal self-making, perpetually poised to become a divinely sanctioned quest. Hollywood has thereby shaped and promoted a decidedly American condensation of a wider Western pursuit of liberty and the elevation of willful endeavor.

In psychological terms American cinema reflects the growth of an egocentric stance that draws both admiration and condemnation from the rest of the world. This stance sets up great tensions and oppositions in the psyche, reflected in a lengthy roster of memorable screen heroes and villains, battles against the forces of darkness, personal victories over authority, and elevation of the gifted and unique over the unremarkable. On the screen and in the psyche we see a distinct conundrum playing out: how to recover significance and meaning when separated from the past, nature and the wider reaches of being? How to live for one's self while furthering the deeper human story? For better or worse America has become the great Western experiment in the face of this conundrum, and its movies portray this effort. The heroic self-making of the American film protagonist becomes a kind of ideal encounter with the tumult of life. They epitomize the agency that has always defined this dramatic position, but do more than reiterate an archetypal root of storytelling. When these characterizations do not fall into stereotype, which they often do, they reflect a nuanced negotiation of modern existence. We study these characters to find out who we are, and we are drawn to them by far more than their willful drive.

In more complex and layered expressions, screen protagonists are shaped not only by conscious striving, but also far more by the backstory of their lives, by hidden flaws and desires, by other characters and unforeseen events. Films are able to reveal significant depths of character, explore the hand of fate and show us how timeless archetypal patterns continue to shape contemporary events. When the thoroughly imagistic, symbolic qualities that define a well-made film are added, we find ourselves standing in a vast field of potential psychological insight. A concentration of these wider considerations can be found in a certain type of American screen protagonist, the *outsider*, that has gained prominence in more recent decades and offers both a more defined window onto the American psyche and a more fitting exemplification of what Jung meant by the individuation process.

We begin this attempt to convey something of the essence of American film with two main premises. The first, is that Hollywood-derived screen stories epitomize a critical feature of the modern Western psycho-cultural situation, in which the individual, estranged from traditional sources of meaning and behavioral guidelines, negotiates inner and outer encumbrances to discover a unique and ultimately meaningful path. The second premise is framed by Jung's model of individuation and related concepts that provide a fitting means to comprehend these stories, not only in terms of their dramatic elements, but also their imagistic, cinematic presentation. Further, the Jungian approach prompts us to translate these considerations into an understanding of the key psychological tasks that confront us at various historical moments. This approach exemplifies a 'hermeneutics of amplification' (Frederickson, 2001, p. 30), pertaining more generally to a Jungian 'hermeneutics of hope' (Jones, 2003), which discerns a goal or purpose – a teleology – within the imagery and thematic architecture of the film. It emphasizes the way 'neurotic symptoms and symbolic art draw attention to the fact that a change of conscious standpoint is necessary' (Frederickson, 2001, p. 35). Frederickson underscores this shift in awareness when he suggests that amplification is not 'a "merely academic" activity.... If it is not taken up by a felt necessity, it is better left alone' (p. 40). As Izod describes the process, 'it elaborates the reading of characters, plots, settings and images in a given movie or screen drama by extending it through comparison with the language and symbolism of pre-existent texts' (2001, p. 7), especially by 'setting them against the backdrop of legends and myths both ancient and modern' (p. 7). This exposure of psychic patterns and propensities also attunes us to the psyche's innate self-healing tendency, that can be detected at both personal and collective levels. The perspective employs what Jung called the *synthetic* or *constructive method* of interpretation, which he contrasts with the reductive mode (1921, p. 701). The outsider protagonist takes the story from here.

Light through darkness

Innovative striving, personal reinvention and the transcendence of external limitations define the American experience. This forthright face of the world's movement west is captured in ideas of America as the New World, the land of opportunity and the frontier. Baudrillard has called this movement 'a violent extraversion' and a 'pragmatic exotericism' (1988, p. 75). As the image-making capital of this frontier, Hollywood sits, geographically and culturally, at the very edge of the movement west and has galvanized its cinematic prominence with *The Western* as its signature genre. However, this is only half of America's story. The other half contains dark historical episodes and deep national wounds: a decimation of indigenous peoples, bloody battles for independence and unity, a major segment of its population starting out enslaved, fraught struggles for civil rights and women's rights, assassinations of masterful and promising leaders, Vietnam, and 9/11. These events/movements *also* underlie the American character and shape its screen protagonists. Hollywood's most poignant and critically embraced characters reflect both sides of this American situation, prompting a reclamation of the dark shadows that lie behind the 'shining city on a hill.' Providing psychic containers for what those around them cannot hold, these characters exemplify the imperative Jung named as an ultimately inescapable dynamic in the human psyche, namely the push to embrace the totality of lived experience.

The *outsider* dimension of key protagonists involves feelings of being set apart and distinctly alienated from society and the flow of everyday life. A prominent feature is some form of dominant wound. This wound is less overcome and more woven into their final accomplishment, which is a hard-won vision of what surrounds them, in its light and dark totality. We find the outsider protagonist anchoring Hollywood classics through characters like Atticus Finch in *To Kill a Mockingbird* (dir. Mulligan, 1962), Rick Blaine in *Casablanca* (dir. Curtiz, 1942) and Vigil Tibbs in *In the Heat of the Night* (dir. Jewison, 1967). All are celebrated heroes, but their gravitas comes more from the endurance of inner strife than poised external action. Each comes to carry a great chunk of the fraught world in which they find themselves. The dark undercurrent that runs through their psyches does not simply lend complexity and pathos to their character, but it becomes part of their very handle on prevailing circumstances, which is why these films tend to end on notes of irony and sobriety rather than distinct triumph. It is this darkened perspective and maturated conscience that the audience is drawn into and perhaps find themselves challenged to take on. The outsider element is thus a more pointedly *internal* feature, even if it coincides with an external expression of the theme. This coincidence is most evident, for example, in characters like Jake Gittes in *Chinatown* (dir. Polanski, 1974), Conrad Jarrett in *Ordinary People* (dir. Redford, 1980) or Clarice Starling in *The Silence of the Lambs* (dir. Demme, 1991), each of whom have found themselves marginalized at some point before we meet them, and before they have become attuned to what lies at the margins of their culture and sensitized to what this culture dismisses or suppresses.

Atticus Finch and Vigil Tibbs may bear witness to a more overt outcropping of this shadowland, as do Benjamin L. Willard in *Apocalypse Now* (dir. Coppola, 1979) and William Munny in *Unforgiven* (dir. Eastwood, 1992). However, more often this shadow relation is indirect, and the outsider appears in stories pervaded with the smell of unfinished business or the feeling of impending fragmentation. Luke Hockley conveys this quality in his Jungian reflections on one particularly American genre, 'the world of *film noir*, with its dark streets … canted camera angles, and alienated characters,' which, he adds,

> was not just the result of war-time restrictions on film budgets…. It can equally be seen as an embodiment of psychological symbolism that represented the growing unrest felt in American society, at again being involved in the horrors of international warfare.
>
> *(2001, p. 63)*

Light and dark in the American character took yet another turn after the Second World War, with the sense of noble victory forced to contend with the atomic destruction of Hiroshima and Nagasaki, the fire bombings of Dresden and other Japanese cities, not to mention the way the dead tend to linger in the warrior's mind. Entry into a long Cold War with the Soviets was also creeping upon the nation, conjuring images of widespread destruction. In *film noir* light and dark form stark visual contrasts, but the latter always seems to take the upper hand.

War might well be archetypally geared for moral ambivalence, but America has so often converted that ambivalence into an entrenched dissociation, clinging to ideals like freedom and democracy on one side while disowning destructive impulses and paranoid projections on the other. The more that ambivalence cries out for recognition, the more those who come home after seeing the action up close tend to be disowned. The Vietnam War and its cinematic portrayals explore this dynamic, with protagonists who mirror a schizoid reality that the nation as a whole has not been able to overcome. It is not merely the horror of war that is being witnessed, but also the hypocrisy and madness of its execution and the inability of the collective to hold its heroic ideals alongside its shortcomings. As Chris Taylor of *Platoon* (dir. Stone, 1986) says at the end of the film, 'I think, looking back now, we did not fight the enemy; we fought ourselves. And the enemy was in us.'

The outsider protagonist comes to carry an awareness those surrounding them cannot, which points the way to the coexistence of previously incompatible realms. In their psyches light and dark, upper world and underworld undergo a collision, opening a portal into the realm of collective wounding. Notable realizations of this dynamic in American films often take place in everyday urban settings, showing that this collision often surfaces here too. Benjamin Braddock of *The Graduate* (dir. Nichols, 1967), Thelma Dickerson and Louise Sawyer of *Thelma and Louise* (dir. Scott, 1991) and Lester Burnham of *American Beauty* (dir. Mendes, 1999) all become psychic vessels for what is unconscious in the collectivity surrounding them. Secondary characters in these films, such as the iconic Mrs. Robinson, nearly every male character in *Thelma and Louise* and Lester's wife Carolyn in *American Beauty*, are contrasting casualties of the larger split, which can manifest as repression, possession, fragmentation or a combination of these processes. Benjamin Braddock's quest to save his integrity from a future in plastics first requires an inoculation, through an encounter with the cynical and manipulative existence of Mrs. Robinson. Thelma and Louise must confront and then overpower the misogynist objectification that has dogged their lives, eventually raising the value of bonded womanhood above that of life itself. They take a road trip as a temporary reprieve, but find themselves forced to confront a rapist, which catapults them far beyond their socially constructed female identities. Lester Burnham also eventually loses his life, but not before seeing through the emptiness of middle class materialism and midlife escapism. To do this, however, he must fully enter his malaise and stop outsourcing his inner vitality to an adolescent cheerleader and a driven, gun-toting wife.

These characters are forced to acknowledge the cultural problems that grip them and realize they can no longer escape by means of the defended, hyper-masculinized striving that surrounds them. Sometimes they survive the immersion in their particular social affliction, surfacing in an authentic way, only to finally meet with another order of intolerance because of what they have awakened. The juxtaposition with the repressed and defended world they inhabit is too great and, as we see with Thelma, Louise and Lester, their lives are sacrificed once they expose the psychological splits in those around them. We are left looking straight into the American shadow.

Although outsider protagonists can face an insurmountable opposition to their countercultural endeavors, and end their quests in a pool of awareness rather than a blaze of glory, from the psychological point of view, in terms of individuation, they start at an advantage. Here I am reminded of James Hillman's assertion that human lives are placed in service of the soul rather than the other way around. He writes, 'our lives are on loan to the psyche for a while. During this time we are its caretakers who try to do for it what we can' (1975, p. 180). This is a more radical statement of Jung's perception of an autonomous psyche at work, something beyond the ego that orientates our experience in the direction of a deeper calling, meaning or principle. The organizing factor that Jung placed at the center of this movement, which he calls *the Self*, sometimes feels like the hand of fate at work. Hillman preferred the notion of a *daimon*, a personified figure within, conducting our lives with an alternate agenda. The outsider protagonist, unable to find a comfortable footing in the everyday world or escape the pull of their own wounding, is thrust more directly into the hands of this subterranean factor. While their ego may suffer, a deeper purpose has more room to make itself known. In *Ordinary People* (1980) the young protagonist, Conrad, attempts suicide after losing his brother in a boating accident. But the deeper problem, which he must finally overcome, belongs to the atmosphere of denial and persona perfection imposed by his mother, Beth, who is unable to reconcile events with her upper middle class version of the American Dream. These protagonists may go through their own resistances and wrong-turns; they may push against what must, in the end, come through them. But they are, from the beginning, equipped to question habitual perspectives and explore what others cannot or will not perceive. If, as Delbanco suggests, 'Americans have tried to save themselves from the melancholy that threatens all reflective beings' (2000, p. 10), these are characters that, in the end, cannot or will not do so.

Jung on American culture

My reading of these themes relating to the deeper function of the outsider protagonist also draws upon Jung's psychology of modernity, in which his view of the American psyche plays a critical part. Christopher Hauke (2014) has previously assembled Jung's analysis of the American situation, and has considered its bearing on cinematic offerings. In terms of resonance with the themes I've been laying out in this chapter, one of the most pertinent passages comes from a *New York Times* interview with Jung. He is quoted as saying:

> When I see so much refinement and sentiment as I see in America, I look always for an equal amount of brutality. The pair of opposites – you find them everywhere. I find the greatest self-control in the world among the Americans – and I search for its cause. Why should there be so much self-control, I ask myself, in America, and I find for an answer brutality. I find a great deal of prudery. What is the cause, I ask, and I discover brutality. Prudery is always the cover for brutality. It is necessary – it makes life possible until you discover the brute and take real control of it. When you do that in America, then you will be the most emotional, most temperamental, the most fully developed people in the world.
>
> *(Hauke, 2014: 61/Jung, 1978 [1912], pp. 13–14)*

Hauke introduces this passage by noting a critical psychodynamic, which underlies Jung's formulation:

> The compensatory nature of the unconscious means that the self-control and prudery Jung finds in the American are both covers for the inherent brutality (the leitmotif of the Western film) once required for conquering the New World, and which is still barely managed in the American psyche.
>
> *(2014, p. 61)*

The return of the repressed is in Jung's thought extended into the more nuanced notion of compensation – an understanding that the unconscious can supplement and balance the one-sided attitudes of consciousness. Such unconscious tendencies gather additional strength when they're ignored by the conscious mind, and a vicious cycle can ensue. The antidote to this process comes at the end of the passage, where Jung suggests that America 'discover the brute and take real control of it.' (Hauke 2014: 61/Jung 1978 [1912], p. 14). Without this more conscious negotiation, however, the subterranean brute might also rise up and take charge.

A path of development around this theme is precisely what the most visionary American films invite – a discovery of the subterranean character of the culture through an alignment with the compensatory dynamic at work in the psyche. Whereas some films no doubt reinforce conscious values and defensive dynamics, and others just exploit the shadowlands, those that expose the underbelly of a culture in order to challenge the habitual cultural mindset exemplify the psychodynamics of Jungian thought. This is what the American outsider protagonist models for us: a reconfigured relationship with the inner brute. It is for this reason that Hauke highlights a scene towards the end of *In The Heat of The Night* (1967) where Tibbs, a black Chicago police officer, slaps a white Southern plantation owner immediately after this man has slapped him (2014, pp. 57–58). It parallels the moment in *Thelma and Louise* (1999) when the pair now reveling in their rebellion ignite the oil-filled tanker of a male trucker whose repeated objectifying gaze and predatory habits have become intolerable. It is as if they have been waiting their whole lives to put this kind of man in his place. In both cases, the outer character also represents the inner antagonist, and the real accomplishment is overcoming the internalized cultural complex. The antagonizing element is not eradicated or banished in the typical heroic style, but out-maneuvered through an inner familiarity with its influence, suggesting a certain interpenetration of conscious and unconscious factors.

This psychological achievement is vividly contrasted by the way in which disowned aspects of the American psyche can be projected onto the face of the other. We have already touched on this scapegoating process in terms of the zeal to fight enemies at a distance, but it pertains even more so to the racial divisions shaping the country. Despite Jung's own racial insensitivities, he saw how this played out, especially in the South, amplifying the general psychic opposition set out above by describing the coexistence of 'cruelty and chivalry.' He continues:

> The Southerners treat one another very courteously, but they treat the Negro as they would treat their own unconscious mind if they knew what was in it. When I see a man in a savage rage with something outside himself, I know he is, in reality, wanting to be savage towards his own unconscious self.
>
> *(Hauke 2014: 56/Jung 1978 [1912], p. 16)*

Hauke suggests that 'many of the aspects of American life identified by Jung are indeed those that America has faced – with varying results – since 1960' (Hauke 2014, p. 63). Many films have worked hard to expose dark chapters of American history. However, whereas a certain style of repression may have been lifted by 'America's own reflexivity' (ibid.), resulting in a more widely exposed underbelly, the culture still suffers from an oscillation of extremes and has yet to find a way to contend with its dual nature. Slavery was not only an abominable, inhuman source of labour, it was also a psychic management system, a ready-made method of avoiding all manner of contradiction within the psyche of slave-owners and the society supporting them. The deep-seated resentment of Civil War defeat, reignited during the Civil Rights struggle of the 1960s, was fueled by the removal of this scapegoating mechanism. Since this time the psychic splitting and projection, pervasive in the history of this region, has continued to give rise to a defensive outlook. For example, what is known as the American Bible Belt directly overlays the map of former slave-owning states. This coincidence might be considered a response to a long period of darkness, but the fundamentalist obsession with the light and associated Biblical literalism breeds an ominous dissociation. The anti-intellectualism, suspicion of East Coast Liberals and 'Hollywood-types' that runs through the American Evangelical movement is not just focused on perceived moral differences; it is about the intolerance of social and psychological complexity. In Robert Duvall's *The Apostle* (1997), we find a preacher who tries to live with integrity but cannot seem to escape the cultural undertow. Writing from inside the southern religious scene, one reviewer noted: 'I have known many preachers just like Sonny (Duvall's character) over the years who have preached a hot Pentecostal gospel with seeming success only to fall into the very sins that they so fervently denounced from the pulpit' (Synan, 1998). This dissociation from the devil within continues to exert a determinative effect on the American political scene.

Another increasingly pervasive psychological style that manages to circumvent the complexity of the American soul is narcissism. In this posture we find an attempt to fabricate a false and highly rigid ideal that seeks success and greatness while doubling down on splitting and projection, typically resulting in an 'us and them' mentality. While on the screen and also in life this syndrome inevitably winds its way to a destructive conclusion, it has nonetheless proven to be useful in getting ahead in American culture (Lasch, 1978). *Citizen Kane* (dir. Welles, 1941) is an early cinematic expression of the pattern. The way the film sees through the grandiosity of its protagonist Charles Foster Kane is perhaps one reason it is often claimed to be the best American film ever made. In what is undoubtedly one of the most famous scenes in cinema history, Kane's final utterance of 'Rosebud,' and the recollection of the simple pleasure he enjoyed playing in the snow as a child, instantly pierces the lifelong attempt to become an outsized personality and live an outsized life. Memorable characters like Gordon Gekko of *Wall Street* (dir. Stone, 1987) and Daniel Plainview of *There Will Be Blood* (dir. Anderson, 2007) are cut from the same cloth.

Through its cinematic offerings America might have begun to follow 'Jung's recommendation that America should "face itself"' (Hauke, 2014, p. 49); however, it is here we need to see the difference between the mere return of the repressed and the embrace of the compensatory dynamic Jung placed at the heart of the psyche. Whereas the former releases a certain amount of psychic tension and frees libido for more creative expression, the latter requires another level of awareness. Namely, what returns from the unconscious does not do so in a willy-nilly fashion, but offers shapes and forms, symbols and metaphors for the path ahead.

Sunset Boulevard

An enduring and celebrated example of film noir that also offers a rich array of symbolic and metaphorical potential in terms of the themes we are exploring here is *Sunset Boulevard* (1950), directed and co-written by Billy Wilder. The opening is a perfect example of the dreamlike capacity of cinema to alert our imagination to the territory it is about to enter:

> *Sunset Boulevard* begins with a shot of the famous street name, not high on a sign, but down in the gutter where street names are sometimes stenciled. The choice is not arbitrary. While this street already conjures an arterial sense of Hollywood high and low life, 'sunset' points to the theme of death that pervades the film. Seeing this name in the gutter builds these associations into a potent metaphor for a story of failure, desperation, and faded stardom.
>
> *(Slater, 2005, p. 5)*

The underworld character of the film is established, not only by the layered meanings of this opening shot, but by the very framing of the entire story, which is narrated from the grave. More precisely, the film quickly moves to an image of its protagonist, Joe Gilles, floating facing down in a swimming pool, and it is his story, prior to this event, that we are about to enter. We soon realize the pool belongs to an aging silent film star, Norma Desmond, on the grounds of a Sunset Boulevard mansion that was once majestic, but has become a crumbling monument to a bygone era, dedicated to her former self. The pathetic attempts to preserve that self now cover a crippling underlying emptiness. Her inner state is on full display in her surroundings.

Whereas Norma Desmond reveals a garish, grandiose narcissism, her 'victim,' our protagonist, is carrying a more recessed narcissistic wound, wanting to overcome his weak personality by making it as a screenwriter in Hollywood. Down on his luck and maybe his talent, Joe's weakness lies in wanting a share of the limelight. He ends up in Desmond's driveway, fleeing the repo men; it seems like a good place to hide after his tire blows out, but we ultimately come to see it was fated. In a wonderfully subtle addition to the start of this early sequence, Joe pulls into the street from his parking spot behind Rudy's Shoe Shine and, as he passes the black man doing an honest day's work, he narrates: 'Rudy never asked any questions about your finances, he'd just look at your heels and know the score.'

The film is a meditation on how Joe's inner world is reflected in the spider web of Norma's existence, how her largely transparent means of escaping decrepitude aligns with Joe's attempt to circumvent his own sense of emptiness. Norma becomes both an accurate externalization of Joe's *anima* and, by extension, a portrayal of the dark *anima* at work in the high-octane version of the American Dream that is Hollywood. When they first meet, after he has managed to stow his vehicle in her overgrown garage, she mistakes him for the undertaker she is expecting to measure her recently deceased pet monkey for a coffin. It is an omen, as Joe will, in many ways, soon take the place of the monkey. Recognizing her for the first time, he says, 'You used to be big.' And in one of the great lines from the film, she replies, 'I *am* big. It's the pictures that got small.'

Norma is constantly suppressing and denying the encroaching reality, in the same way she tortures her face and body with beauty treatments to slough off the years. But when Joe threatens to finally leave and return to his smaller life in the Midwest after facing his own manipulative enabling of the façade, the dam finally breaks and the gun finishes things off. Norma's final, psychotic return to the movies occurs as she descends her stairs playing Salome, with news cameras rolling and members of the press witnessing the haunting spectacle: 'You see, this is my life,' she says. 'It always will be. There's nothing else. Just us, and the cameras, and those wonderful people out there in the dark. Alright Mr. DeMille, I'm ready for my close-up.'

The character of Norma Desmond offers insight beyond the femme fatale stereotype by showing us the way the soul turns rancid when the only concern is the persona field. This is obviously a distinct syndrome of show business, but it is also a sizable trap of general American psychology. Joe unknowingly creates the conditions of his own demise and becomes a kind of sacrificial lamb on the altar of a place obsessed by pseudo divinities. When the persona-shadow split becomes too great, it is always the shadow that wins, because one-sided investment in a perfected, god-like self-image is met by a compensatory demand of the psyche for an imperfect whole. And here we see a large portion of the American problem in close up. The true faith, the real religion of America, is the cultivation of the persona field, combined with the ability to self-make and remake, to craft an image and convey substance where, very often, there is none.

Los Angeles is a place where the American Dream exerts its most outlandish claims, where the 'radicalization of the utopian demand' (Baudrillard, 1988, p. 75) is most radically displayed. Fittingly, it is the most fabricated of cities – a paved desert that must beg, borrow or steal life-sustaining water from neighbors. Filmmakers like David Lynch, the Coen brothers and Quentin Tarantino, troll its underworld and deconstruct its idealism in very effective ways. In *Mulholland Drive* (2001), Lynch uses a dreamlike obscuration, which has been noted by Terrie Waddell, who calls the film 'a dark and complex myth' (2006, p. 62). It begins with a car crash on the notorious twisting thoroughfare, a consistently effective metaphor for the way life unravels going into or out of Los Angeles, and the surviving figure stumbling into an apartment on Sunset Boulevard. Waddell's description of the way the title sequence introduces the protagonist (of sorts) tunes us into the movement that is about to take place. We see first the 'overexposed image of "Diane Selwyn" … with a synthetic "ingénue-in-Hollywood" giddiness,' and then 'Diane, falling into the pillow, the dream, the unconscious' (p. 52). Waddell suggests further that the ensuing dream 'provides a form of compensation for the malleable and fluctuating state of Diane's fragile ego' (p. 54). Fragile egos are very often drawn to the heightened version of the dream this city seems to offer, but it is the compensatory dream that moves things from the self-making to the Self-making – from the ego to the larger totality.

The Coen brothers pack *The Big Lebowski* (1998) with noir allusions, altered states and a good slice of the LA underworld, as they canonize slackers who linger in the cracks of this west coast 'paradise.' Offerings by the Coens like *Blood Simple* (1984), *Fargo* (1996) and *No Country for Old Men* (2007) show the flipside of cultural ideals in other locales, their characters always seeming to emerge from some deep America mythos. Tarantino's *Pulp Fiction* (1994), also serves as a punctuating point for these reflections. Lydia Lennihan's reading of the film (2001) highlights the juxtapositions between the white and black characters, the everyday world and the criminal underworld, as well as the alchemical patterns that seemingly direct events. It's an unlikely set-up for an individuation process, but Lennihan convincingly argues that Jules, played by Samuel L. Jackson, undergoes a psychic transformation wherein the sense of 'good and evil, darkness and golden, [and] a union of sublime complexities' (p. 67) takes hold. She notes: 'What is happening to Jules is also happening to us as we view the film' (ibid.). It is this vicarious encounter with the compensatory movement of the unconscious and the creative reshaping of the rejected cultural elements this movement generates that invites a reshaping of our own vision.

Reframing the cinematic hero

It must be clear by now that the outsider protagonist does not fit the mold of the traditional hero, and that Campbell's model of the hero's journey (2008 [1949]), which is often turned to as an interpretive key for many American films, is inadequate for understanding this figure. The most telling feature that differentiates the two is that the outsider does not 'return' from their 'Night-Sea Journey' in the typical hero manner. Sometimes they are more apt to stay in the underworld or be so affected by its gravity that a large part of their psyches never leave it. Too, the 'helpers' and 'mentors' that Campbell identifies as appearing once the hero has heard the 'call to adventure' (p. 210) are typically scarce if non-existent. This also reinforces the alienation of this figure. And rather than depart from the community and then return with a gift or 'boon' (p. 211), the outsider protagonist begins and ends in a largely separate state. The boon is perhaps a psychological state, which is what they and we come to see at a distance.

We must keep in mind that Campbell's hero is an abstraction, even if a helpful one. The abstract hero is an attempt to see what Jung called the archetype per se, which he also admitted was something we can never glimpse. It is the fleshed-out version we always see, which is a particular character in a particular story. What is most interesting, psychologically, is not the skeletal form of the timeless, universal structure, rather where and how these universals have been remade by the prevailing social and cultural situation.

One critical feature of the hero, which *does* apply to the outsider and is often circumvented by stereotypical Hollywood offerings, is what Campbell called 'self-achieved submission.' He immediately follows the naming of this quality with the question: 'But submission to what?' (p. 11). Before Campbell, Jung had taken up the theme of the hero in his first major publication, *Wandlungen und Symbole der Libido*, revised and republished in English as *Symbols of Transformation* (1956). Here he discusses the way the mythic hero must first sacrifice the regressive tendency to remain unconscious and avoid the challenges of life. But he goes on to describe another kind of sacrifice, a kind of purposeful, willing regression. He refers to this as a sacrifice of power and also a sacrifice of the libido. Much of Jung's psychology emanates from this early insight, which he describes in terms of 'an unconscious transformation of energy, of which the ego becomes aware in much the same way as sailors are made aware of a volcanic upheaval under the sea' (1956: §669). He later adds: 'Through sacrifice man ransoms himself from the fear of death and is reconciled to the demands of Hades' (§671).

The character of Frankie Dunn in *Million Dollar Baby* (dir. Eastwood, 2004) is an outsider protagonist who embodies this process. A common mistake in looking at this film, especially if one looks too hard for the heroic element, is to see Maggie Fitzgerald, the female fighter played by Hilary Swank, as the protagonist. But in the end Maggie is the vehicle for Frankie's evolution of consciousness. In this film the boxing ring, the fight and the training are all metaphors for the challenges of life, and, as the voiceover tells us at the start, 'everything in boxing is backwards.' Conscious intentions are reversed; everything has a flipside. The film itself is telling us how to read the film – to discover what's behind every willful action.

For example, known in the boxing world as a 'cut-man (an expert at repairing open facial wounds) Frankie's own wounds remain open, especially those surrounding an apparent estrangement from his daughter. However, he is suffering the situation in a largely defended way, and is initially unable to break the guilt-ridden cycle of returned letters and attending daily Mass. Frankie is forced to make two sacrifices. The first occurs when he agrees to train Maggie, a trailer park escapee from the Ozarks, still waitressing in her mid-thirties to make ends meet. The second takes place when he must surrender to her wish to die. Between these two sacrifices, their bond grows, and he seemingly regains a 'daughter.' The hyper-masculinized world of boxing is also reversed to reveal a story of deep relatedness, devotion, loyalty and love.

The second sacrifice finally upends Frankie's life. He can no longer hold on to Maggie and must fight every instinct to help her escape the suffering of feeling trapped on artificial life support. No more heroics of the striving kind, only a submission to a deeper imperative and the full realization of what he himself says to Maggie at the start: 'Tough ain't enough.' It seems like a bleak ending, but his gym custodian, Eddie 'Scrap-Iron' Dupris, has been tracking and narrating the bigger picture. When Frankie returns from talking to the burnt-out Catholic priest, he 'confesses' to Scrap, the real priest in the story. And then Scrap sets him straight: Maggie was given her shot in life, and achieved something she'd not dare imagine, because of Frankie. He had cleared a path for Maggie's genius and effectively became the father she had lost.

We are left to imagine how Frankie might now be carrying the restored feminine presence that had been working its way into his psyche. Reading Keats and learning his ancestral Gaelic was not enough; neither was daily Mass. He had to become 'reconciled to the demands of Hades.' The subtext of the ending, where Frankie walks away from it all, contains a hint of accepting life in all of its backwardness, unfairness and contradiction. A closing image of the diner he and Maggie had visited, with the telling name of 'IRA's,' the one that served 'the best lemon pie around,' implies a movement toward an acceptance of the bittersweet. Further, Scrap's voiceover narration of the letter he has been writing to Frankie's actual, estranged daughter, plants the seed for some kind of renewal.

The reconciliation to Hades that Jung described and Frankie embraces through a self-imposed sacrifice, is at the core of what Jung referred to as the *religious function* (1921: §150). This concept is constantly woven into Jung's various reflections on the psyche, and provides a basis on which to assess the ultimate significance of the outsider protagonist in American film. Jung wrote:

> Religion appears to me to be a peculiar attitude of mind which could be formulated
> in accordance with the original use of the word *religio*, which means a careful con-
> sideration and observation of certain dynamic factors that are conceived as 'powers':
> spirits, daemons, gods, laws, ideas, ideals, or whatever name man has given to such

factors in his world as he has found powerful, dangerous, or helpful enough to be taken into careful consideration, or grand, beautiful, and meaningful enough to be devoutly worshipped and loved.

(1938/40: §8)

The heart of the individuation process is the effective embrace of the religious function. The ego shifts the locus of concern away from itself and recognizes the powers and values operating beyond its direct influence. It pertains to Campbell's refinement of the authentic hero's 'self-achieved submission' as well as to Hillman's attempt to restore our sense of the original mythic hero's ties to the underworld (1979: 110ff).

The outsider protagonist emulates this deeper essence of the hero by giving themselves over to something that is trying to make its way out of the shadows and into awareness. By contrast, the hero that has been untethered from an underworld orientation personifies much of America's habitual attitude. Always preferring action to thinking, as this culture also tends to use action as a way to avoid soul-searching. Hillman addresses this problem in his *Re-Visioning Psychology* stating: 'Sometimes we act in order not to see … to avoid knowing what my soul is doing.' He adds, 'Without ideas the soul is more easily compelled, more compulsively active' (1975, p. 116). The compulsiveness of action increases in direct relation to the lack of insight. Along such lines, the stereotypical action hero of American cinema might be regarded as more an emblem of neurotic defense than an accurate expression of a timeless archetype.

The underworld is not only a place, it is also a perspective. In an earlier encounter with the underworld quality of these films I had suggested that both 'possession by the dark' and 'the darkened eye' which 'sees more deeply, less naively' are recurrent features (Slater, 2005, p. 14). Many of the protagonists we find in these cinematic offerings function as psychopomps for a culture in desperate need to awaken to its denied darkness. Their outsider status becomes a shamanic gift for the rest of us. Jung's call to individuation is too often framed as elitist navel-gazing, confined to the world of weekly analysis. However, it is more aptly considered an individual assent to a movement that corrects society's one-sidedness and hosts archetypal values that may be indispensable for a viable future. The necessity of this movement is more glaringly apparent against the American backdrop for, as I indicated at the beginning of this chapter, it is here the modern experiment has reached its zenith. American cinema, considered through this perspective, provides a stark, often thrilling, sometimes moving response to the dilemmas of Westernized cultures. We are transported to a psychic field in which victory and defeat, justice and injustice, love and lamentation rub together, and we are given a glimpse of something noble and dignified about the human spirit as it emerges from the fray.

References

Baudrillard, J. (1988) *America*. New York: Verso.

Campbell, J. (2008 [1949]) *The hero with a thousand faces*, 3rd edn. Novato, CA: New World Library.

Delbanco, A. (2000) *The real American dream: a meditation on hope*, 2nd edn. Cambridge, MA: Harvard University Press.

Frederickson, D. (2001) 'Jung/sign/symbol/film', in C. Hauke and I. Alister (eds), *Jung & film: post-Jungian takes on the moving image*. Philadelphia, PA: Brunner-Routledge. pp. 17–55.

Hauke, C. (2014) *Visible mind: movies, modernity and the unconscious*. New York: Routledge.

Hillman, J. (1975) *Re-visioning psychology*. New York: Harper & Row.

Hillman, J. (1979) *The dream and the underworld*. New York: Harper & Row.

Hockley, L. (2001) *Cinematic projections: the analytical psychology of C. G. Jung and film theory*. Luton: University of Luton Press.

Izod, J. (2001) *Myth, mind and the screen: understanding the heroes of our time*. Cambridge: Cambridge University Press.

Jones, A. (2003) 'Teleology and a hermeneutics of hope', in *Cambridge 2001: proceedings of the fifteenth international congress for analytical psychology*. Einsiedeln, Switzerland: Daimon Verlag.

Jung, C. G. (1921) 'Definitions', in *The collected works of C. G. Jung*, Vol. 6, *Psychological types*. London: Routledge & Kegan Paul, 1971.

Jung, C. G. (1938/40) 'Psychology and religion', in *The collected works of C. G. Jung*, Vol. 11, *Psychology and religion: west and east*. London: Routledge & Kegan Paul, 1956.

Jung, C. G. (1956) 'Sacrifice', in *The collected works of C. G. Jung*, Vol. 5, *Symbols of transformation*. London: Routledge & Kegan Paul, 1956.

Jung, C. G. (1978) 'America facing its most tragic moment', in W. McGuire and R. F. C. Hull (eds), *C. G. Jung speaking*. London: Thames & Hudson Ltd. pp. 32–43. (Originally published *New York Times*, 19 September 1912.)

Lasch, C. (1978) *The culture of narcissism*. New York: W. W. Norton & Co.

Lennihan, L. (2001) 'The alchemy of *Pulp Fiction*', in C. Hauke and I. Alister (eds), *Jung & film: post-Jungian takes on the moving image*. Philadelphia, PA: Brunner-Routledge. pp. 56–69.

Slater, G. (2005) 'Archetypal perspective and American film', *Spring*, 73, pp. 1–19.

Waddell, T. (2006) *Mis/takes: archetype, myth and identity in screen fiction*. New York: Routledge.

Online source

Synan, V. (1998) '*The Apostle*, directed by Robert Duvall. October Films, 1997', *Journal of Southern Religion* [online]. Available at: http://jsr.fsu.edu/synan.htm [Accessed 19 October 2016].

Filmography

American beauty. (1999) [film] Directed by Sam Mendes. USA.

Apocalypse now. (1979) [film] Directed by Francis Ford Coppola. USA.

Apostle, The. (1997) [film] Directed by Robert Duvall. USA.

Big Lebowski, The. (1998) [film] Directed by Joel and Ethan Coen. USA.

Blood simple. (1984) [film] Directed by Joel and Ethan Coen. USA.

Casablanca. (1942) [film] Directed by Michael Curtiz. USA.

Chinatown. (1974) [film] Directed by Roman Polanski. USA.

Citizen Kane. (1941) [film] Directed by Orson Welles. USA.

Fargo. (1996) [film] Directed by Ethan Coen and Joel and Coen. USA.

Graduate, The. (1967) [film] Directed by Mike Nichols. USA.

In the heat of the night. (1967) [film] Directed by Norman Jewison. USA.

Million dollar baby. (2004) [film] Directed by Clint Eastwood. USA.

Mulholland drive. (2001) [film] Directed by David Lynch. USA.

No country for old men. (2007) [film] Directed by Joel and Ethan Coen. USA.

Ordinary people. (1980) [film] Directed by Robert Redford. USA.

Platoon. (1986) [film] Directed by Oliver Stone. USA.

Pulp fiction. (1994) [film] Directed by Quentin Tarantino. USA.

Sunset boulevard. (1950) [film] Directed by Billy Wilder. USA.

Silence of the lambs, The. (1991) [film] Directed by Jonathan Demme. USA.

Thelma and Louise. (1991) [film] Directed by Ridley Scott. USA.

There will be blood. (2007) [film] Directed by Paul Thomas Anderson. USA.

To kill a mockingbird. (1962) [film] Directed by Robert Mulligan. SA.

Unforgiven. (1992) Directed by Clint Eastwood. USA.

Wall street. (1987) [film] Directed by Oliver Stone. USA.

20

SPIRITED AWAY AND ITS DEPICTION OF JAPANESE TRADITIONAL CULTURE

Megumi Yama

It is rare that a film talks directly to an idea of the psyche developed by Jung. In *Spirited Away*, written and directed by Hayao Miyazaki and produced by Studio Ghibli (2001), audiences are exposed to a realm of the imagination populated by spirit elements and loosely guided by a mixture of lesser male and more dominant female energies that align to notions of earthiness and spirituality. The narrative is set in a threshold realm that takes the form of a Bathhouse; a contained, yet meandrous alchemical and transformative space that equates to the Jungian unconscious where archetypal energies work to drive a sense of individuation, or psychological development. Many of the mercurial beings inhabiting the Bathhouse represent concepts of alignment, compensation, equilibrium and the changing nature of these energies as they work together to harness a sense of wholeness. For the lead character, 'Chihiro', a young girl on the threshold of adolescence who accidentally stumbles upon this other world, the Bathhouse presents as dream-like place – an unconscious fantasy – that challenges her fear of change. Not only is she transformed on a personal level, but those in her orbit also find themselves evolving. While *Spirited Away* has become a global success, touching on concepts of the unconscious from a Western perspective, it also speaks to a particularly Japanese sensibility that I wish to explore in this chapter.

Japanese animated film, or *anime*, an abbreviated version of the English loanword *animeeshon*, evolved from, and still bears, the echoes of traditional Japanese culture. The form originated from *emakimono* (literally 'picture scroll'), often simply called *emaki* – long, horizontal illustrated narrative forms, popular before and since the Heian era (794–1185). One views these scroll parchments from right to left, as with written Japanese, by reading the text in sections of about an arm's length. The preface of the 2006 catalogue to the *Emaki Unrolled: Masterworks of Illustrated Narrative Handscrolls* exhibition, held at the Kyoto National Museum, describes the artifact as, 'Forming a unique mode of expression in which a tale unfolds on a long, horizontal sheet of paper, the *emaki* parallel [*sic*] of modern movies and animation in their spatial and temporal presentation of narrative.' Dating back to these picture scrolls, the *anime* audience is, albeit in an abstract way, engaged in a form of time travel: sharing the pleasures of fantastical characters, narratives and action sequences that entwine early and contemporary Japanese culture and spirituality.

The very style of *anime* is particularly well aligned with the Japanese cultural tendency towards ambiguity. By this I mean that concepts are often projected through obscure and fluid objects that eventually give rise to a sense of wholeness. Such an expressive style encourages audiences to immerse themselves in the power of the image. For better or worse, this is how some communication styles in Japanese society are created, as Kate Matthews hints at in *Logic and Narrative in Spirited Away* (2006) when she asks: 'Why does Spirited Away appear to lack "logic" and what, aside from "logic", gives it structure?' (p. 135).

I have chosen *Spirited Away* (Japanese title: *Sen to Chihiro no Kamikakushi*), the highest-grossing film in Japan to date, because of its reputation as a masterpiece of storytelling. A globally recognized work, it won a number of accolades including an Academy Award for Best Animated Feature Film (2003), a Golden Bear at the Berlin International Festival (2002) and a nomination by the British Film Institute as one of the top ten films you should see by the age of fourteen. After its Japanese release, *Spirited Away* was broadcast on television roughly every two years. The ratings figures for each rerun achieved a staggering 20 per cent, suggesting that even fifteen years after its release, the film is still enjoyed by adults and new generations of children alike. It has arguably 'captured' many viewers and now occupies a place as deep in the psyche as myth or fairy tale. The fluidity of the images, as they transcend and morph from their original forms, allows us to not simply view the film objectively from the outside, but engage in the screen images, as if we have been invited into the scene, and somatically experience the events developing around us.

The story begins with ten-year-old Chihiro and her parents travelling to their new home. She seems an ordinary pre-adolescent girl struggling with the shift from the security of her former environment. When her father tries to make a short-cut and ends up taking a wrong turn, they pass an old *torii* (a gateway to a Shinto shrine) which stands at the entrance to an unpaved mountain path scattered with numerous *hokora* (small shrines or spirit houses). These mystic symbols suggest a threshold into the spirit realm. As they arrive at a tunnel-like entrance of what appears to be an abandoned amusement park, the unusual and almost numinous atmosphere of the deserted fairground awes Chihiro. After leaving the car and walking through a long tunnel together, her parents set out to explore, and as they walk around the empty town they find a deserted stall piled with food. Seeing this as an invitation, they begin to devour the various offerings voraciously, but Chihiro is wary of possible repercussions and abstains.

While wandering around the town, she comes across a traditional Japanese building, a public Bathhouse, accessed by an ornate bridge. Here she meets the first character that appears to belong to another realm; a boy dressed in robes warning her to leave before dark. When she returns to her parents, to her horror she finds that they have metamorphosed into pigs and as night falls, shadowy figures fill the once deserted street. It is revealed that we have entered a Spirit World – home to myriad beings (*yaoyorozu no kamigami*, literally 'the eight million Gods and Goddesses') who gather to request comfort and luxurious treatments.

The boy, Haku, who seems to have known Chihiro in another dimension, advises her to ask the Bathhouse boiler man, Kamaji (lit. 'iron pot old man') for a job as a means of surviving her journey and eventually finding her way back home. Descending a very long, steep, rickety set of stairs at full speed, almost as if falling beyond her will, Chihiro arrives at the basement where Kamaji is working. A hybrid of human and spider with six arms, his job is to stoke the fire that boils water for the Bathhouse tubs. Kamaji directs Chihiro to Yubaba (lit. 'hot water old woman'), the tyrannical owner of the Bathhouse who lives on the upper floor. Yubaba initially refuses to offer her a job, but finally relents.

On signing a contract, Yubaba steals some of the characters that make up Chihiro's name (千尋), renaming her Sen (千). There are several different readings for Japanese kanji characters, some of them are originally from Chinese readings, and others are from native Japanese readings. The *Chi* from *Chihiro*, becomes *Sen* when Yubaba 'steals' the other character from her name, giving our protagonist a new identity for the spirit realm and allowing Yubaba to exert control over her. Eventually after many adventures in the bathhouse Chihiro finds her way back to her parents, now returned to their human form, reclaims her name – her sense of self – and feels prepared to confront her new life.

English vs original Japanese versions: 'kami' in Japan

To begin an analysis of the film, I would like to look at its Japanese title, *Sen to Chihiro no Kami-kakushi* – which in a literal translation reads, 'Sen and Chihiro are hidden by *kami*'. Although *kami* is often translated as 'god' and is used to describe deities such as Christ or Yahweh, its Japanese meaning is more complex and non-monotheistic. For an explanation of the phenomenon of *kami-kakushi*, I will turn to Japanese folklorist Kazuhiko Komatsu and his 2002 work *Kami-kakushi to Nihonjin* (*Kami-kakushi* and the Japanese). Komatsu explains that historically, Japanese believed in the existence of an 'other world', and the possibility of being transported to, or 'hidden' within, this dimension by someone or something that has entered the everyday. '*Kami*' is ambiguously used as a generic term for these kinds of trespassers. With Japan's modernization in the 1960s and 1970s, such superstitions and beliefs gradually disappeared, but did not die out entirely. Komatsu (2002) adds that we have lost sight of this realm where *kami* (there is no distinction between singular and plural in Japanese) dwell.

Kami might also be thought to refer to phenomena that inspires a sense of awe and wonder. This can be compared to Otto's (1917 [2010]) description of the '*Numinoese*', *mysterium tremendum and fascinans*. I would argue that this relates to Chihiro's sense of foreboding when she first stepped into the Spirit World – sensations that her parents were not sensitive enough to perceive. That the unconscious yearns for some essence of the mystical might contribute to the global success of *Spirited Away*. In the film *kami* are explicitly described as *yaoyorozu no kami*; literally the 'eight-million *kami*', which are thought to be the *kami* of Shinto, the native religion of Japan based in the ancient worship of nature and the ancestors. In truth, most Japanese do not identify as Shintoists although many attend Shinto shrines and pray to the *kami*. There are no formal rituals for Shinto, but its primary beliefs are deeply imbued in the culture. *Kami* also refers to the divine or sacred essence that manifests in multiple forms. Sites in the landscape are said to host unusually sacred spirits and are therefore considered to be places of worship – mountains, rocks, trees, rivers and waterfalls, as well as the naturally occurring phenomena of wind, lightning, earthquakes, volcanic eruptions and so on. *Kami* has been translated to mean more than just 'God' in English – no single English word is able to express its full meaning. In the translation of *Spirited Away* the word 'spirit' replaces *kami*, which seems to be an appropriate and, for the most part, helpful choice.

The Bathhouse: a multilayered structure

Spirited Away is likely to be read as a narrative about a ten-year-old girl grappling with adolescence through a series of adventures in the Spirit World, but the text also reads as a story of a transformation for each character. The Bathhouse, as the locus for the narrative, especially in the first act, becomes an alchemical vessel, hence its relationship to metamorphosis. The building is grandiose and opulent and traditionally Japanese in style. However, the red, green with semi-dark tones of brown and gold in the overall colour scheme take on a gaudiness that is not common in Japanese taste; this aesthetic offers the Bathhouse an exotic, otherworldly ambience. The most important characteristic of the structure is its multilayered design, making it possible for characters to move effortlessly between multiple floors above ground level – numbered to incorporate the words *ten* and *chi* ('heaven' and 'earth' respectively). In this spirit and somewhat spiritual environment, the audience may unconsciously experience a sense of embodied movement in sync with the characters as they transition from space to space.

The Top Floor (天: heaven) has two doors – the right leads to Yubaba's office, adjacent to Boh's bedroom, her spoiled overprotected giant baby, while the left door is permanently closed. The room is opulently built, lined with expensive vases, accentuated by magnificent architecture and followed by twisting hallways. The Boiler Room is located below ground, and is home to Kamaji and countless *susuwatari* (soot sprites), who are ordered to maintain the fires for cooking and the bathing of customers. An imposing furnace dominates the room and the walls are lined with drawers of herbs that filter herbal water to the baths. The Bathhouse has a set of old unstable stairs jutting outside the building, leading directly to the Boiler Room and bypass the usual means of internal elevator entry. There is also a shaft connecting the Boiler Room to Yubaba's office.

The Ground Floor (*chi*) is ostensibly composed of kitchens and baths for the customers' use while the Second Floor (*niten*, lit. 'second heaven') comprises traditional Japanese tatami-matted dining rooms for customers. A long hallway with spaces separated by *shoj* (rice paper sliding doors) runs the length of the second floor. Large stages for entertainment are also incorporated into the design. The floor is popular and crowded with customers, as well as Bathhouse staff who bring food and drink to the clients. The building as a whole, takes the complex form of a multilayered maze, where most of the characters, including Chihiro, repeatedly descend and ascend via stairs, elevators or shafts.

Jung (1987 [2010]) pays particular attention to 'the stairs' and notions of ascent and descent in the dreams of children, associating these various planes with different levels of consciousness. The Japanese Jungian analyst, Hayao Kawai, in his work on thirteenth century Japanese priest Myoe (*The Buddhist Priest Myoe: A Life of Dreams*), writes that 'ascent and descent are very important themes in dreams' (1987 [1991], p. 137). He refers to Jung's account of a near-death experience where he felt himself rising to a great height causing a separation from the world of his everyday reality. Through this narrative, Jung alludes to the importance of descent, or, in other words, finding a sense of reconciliation with the body. Comparing *Spirited Away*'s spirit world to the dream experience, the frequent climbing and falling in the Bathhouse facilitates transformation, and for Jung and Kawai, in a symbolic sense, this movement relates to various psychic stages and the transition between these realms.

I think it might be difficult for Japanese, accustomed as they are to a polytheistic culture, to understand the concept of a single transcendent absolute. In the film Chihiro's transformation and growth comes about not through a single transcendent experience, but through multiple encounters with creatures in the Bathhouse. In the process of developing a sense of maturity, or individuation, she affects a number of other characters, facilitating both their change and their rescue. Her encounters and experiences suggest a form of symbolic death and rebirth that in analytical psychology constitutes the basis for growth and self-knowledge.

The mother and the father

The mothers – Yubaba and Zeniba

There are two significant elder female figures in the story – both are witches who reign over the Spirit World; one is Yubaba, the tyrannical proprietor of the Bathhouse who lives in the penthouse, and the other is her identical twin sister Zeniba, who lives at a place called Bottom Swamp. Although the extravagant Yubaba (lit. 'hot-water old woman') is obsessed with gold, her sister Zeniba (lit. 'money old woman') lives a simpler, more frugal life. The name Yubaba evokes the image of an affectionate elderly woman – the opposite of her overbearing and intimidating personality. On the other hand, Zeniba shows warmth and hospitality to Chihiro and her companions. It seems that their names and personalities work in balanced opposition to each other.

Yubaba is an overprotective mother, almost 'swallowing' her giant baby son with affection, but she also has the capacity for occasional acts of compassion, similarly Zeniba initially appears to be as cruel as Yubaba, but her actions are driven by a sense of justice. Unlike many traditional Western narratives, where good and evil are neatly personified, the two *Mothers* display various aspects of the Great Mother *and* the paternal. The *Mother* who sometimes also embodies the *Father* is overwhelmingly dominant in the Spirit world the film creates.

Eating, vomiting and limitlessness

In *Spirited Away*, appetite becomes a significant theme and a link between the act of ingesting food with a sense of integration and a desire for unity indicative of the Great Mother. From the opening scenes, Chihiro's parents complain of hunger and when they happen upon the food stall in the deserted amusement park, they immediately devour its contents, as if under the influence of this archetypal energy. No-Face, a dominant spirit character in the film, also displays a strong sense of appetite and tempts a frogman working at the Bathhouse with the offer of gold before swallowing him. As greedy workers, hoping to be tipped, swarm around him with endless plates of food, he begins to adopt their personalities in the hope of attracting Chihiro's attention. As he increasingly reflects the negative qualities of the workers, his desire becomes limitless and he grows larger and larger by ingesting enormous amounts of food, gradually transforming into a monstrous creature. When fed the last of the magic dumplings (*niga dango*, lit. bitter dumpling) gifted to Chihiro, he regurgitates everything he has eaten, returning to his original timid self. As eating brings unity and vomiting suggests separation, No-Face would seem to embody these qualities (the Stink-spirit is another example of this process).

The father – Kamaji (lit. 'boiler old-man')

With no significantly featured father-figures in the film, the strong, commanding all-devouring Great Mother dominates the Bathhouse with her excessive and even limitless power. Although *Spirited Away* features characters that carry notions of the *Father*, they are inconspicuous and weak. The character of Kamaji, the old man with six spider-like arms who operates the boiler room in the basement of the Bathhouse, sleeping and eating his meals there, provides a stark contrast to Yubaba's opulence and extravagant living space. This impoverished paternal figure though is related to the Great Mother who according to Kawai (1995), is often symbolized by the spider. Furthermore, the spinning and weaving of spiders, reminiscent of Moira the Goddess of Fate who weaves the cloth of fortune and Arachne in Greco-Roman mythology who challenged Athena to a weaving contest and was consequently transformed into a spider as punishment for hubris. Soot Sprites (*susuwatari*, lit. 'travelling soot'), the only beings that are under Kamaji's rule, carry coal to his furnace. In contrast, Yubaba runs the Bathhouse with vast numbers of frogmen employees and slug-women who are forced to work feverishly.

The walls of his room are lined with large cabinets where he keeps herbs for the guests' baths, crushing them into powders with an alchemist's mortar. The use of herbs is usually associated with witches, or female energy, and his dwelling in the lowest floor of the Bathhouse suggests a groundedness associated with the maternal. It therefore appears that Kamaji embodies both the *Father* and the *Mother*, and despite his less prestigious role in the running of the Bathhouse, it is only through him that the enterprise is physically able to function.

If we regard baths as similar to alchemical containers, and the Bathhouse as a place where alchemical transformation takes place, it is also possible to read Kamaji as an alchemist, who diligently maintains the fire required for these sacred vessels. According to von Franz, one of the rules of alchemy is to, 'see that fire never goes out … otherwise you can start again' (1997, p. 18). As mentioned above, while the power of Yubaba and Zeniba is overwhelming and absolute, without Kamaji the Bathhouse itself would cease to operate. What is more, because he encouraged Chihiro to visit Zeniba, and gave her 'Ocean Railway tickets' to do so, we can also see glimpses of the Wise Old Man archetype manifest in this character. At first, Kamaji seems cold and abrupt, much like Zeniba, but gradually he begins to show maternal warmth and kindness to Chihiro, helping to facilitate both her escape from the Bathhouse and a reunion with her parents.

Symbolically speaking, we can theorize a vertical axis within the Bathhouse between Yubaba (embodying the *Mother/Father*) and Kamaji (embodying the *Father/Mother*/Old Wise Man). While these roles compensate each other, maintaining a subtle balance, the *Mother* emerges as the dominant energy. The relationship between these compensating aspects of each character is fluid and changeable, much like the action within the Bathhouse – a continuous flow of movement through the various spaces over the duration of the narrative.

Three Heads (the three 'Kashira')

Apart from Kamaji, the Three Heads are also examples of male figures in the narrative – a trio of men that live with Yubaba and Boh in the penthouse/office. Heads without bodies, they move together by bouncing and rolling on the floor, often closely following Yubaba, like bodyguards, servants or even bizarre pets. However, it is possible to read these characters differently. It is clear that Yubaba is Boh's mother, but the story does not give any clues as to who the father might be. Considering that Yubaba, Boh and Three Heads share a living space, the Three Heads could possibly be Boh's father. If this is the case, the father is once again exceedingly disempowered compared to the mother.

From another quite different, if not cynical viewpoint, the Three Heads might be considered to display one of the unique past aspects of Japanese masculinity. The Three Heads' only verbalization is the single syllable 'Oi', a word associated with chauvinist behaviour. The effect of Three Heads jumping in a group, uttering 'oi, oi, oi', is quite comical. The word is mostly used by Japanese men when trying to draw attention to themselves. In Japanese family scenes, it is not uncommon for middle-aged husbands to summon their wives with the phrase 'oi' as a way of indicating that they wish a certain task to be carried out. For example, when they want a bath prepared, usually they just say, 'Oi, furo [bath]' and waiting at the table for dinner, 'Oi, meshi [meal]' is a term commanding to their wives to serve food. This ordering sounds arrogant, but stems from the traditional idea that men need few words to maintain a presumably 'dignified' position in the family.

It might sound contradictory, but the idea of male domination over women still prevails in all aspects of contemporary Japanese society, and is largely accepted as *natural*, or, more accurately, *unconsciously lived*. A man behaving arrogantly towards his wife, is often likened to a demanding infant responding to a more powerful mother figure. When the Three Heads grunt, 'oi, oi, oi' it brings to mind a scene of traditional Japanese domestic life. That Three Heads do not have a body suggests the ostensible patriarchal temperament of the Japanese *Father* is simply a facade and, in reality, he is cut off, or even separated from, a more whole sense of self – something is missing; a self consisting of both compensating male and female attributes. Kawai (1995) suggests that attempts to maintain a fine balance between various pairs of opposites were common throughout the historical periods described in the *Kojiki* (*Record of ancient matters*: the oldest Japanese mythology) and despite more ideologically driven gender roles, this need for equilibrium continues today.

The Western and Japanese ego

Finally, I'd like to turn to a rather personal experience. Since living in the US during my adolescence, I have felt as if I had two different egos: one is Japanese and the other is Western. I have had opportunities to go back and forth between Japan and Western countries such as the UK, US, Australia and Europe, and through my experience as a psychotherapist in Japan, I have been deeply interested in the difference between the Western and Japanese psyche. For instance, I have previously stated that:

> Modern Western consciousness seems to have spread across the world as a result of globalization, and Japan has certainly been affected by this influence. However, ego consciousness and the establishment of a subject in the Japanese psyche have evolved differently and have roots that go far back into a rich cultural history.
>
> *(Yama, 2013, p. 68)*

Furthermore, I attempted to explore the way in which the ego emerges in the Japanese psyche by returning to the narrative embedded in the oldest layer of Japanese culture. This was done through an analysis of *Kojiki*, the earliest Japanese myth, in order to present another way that the ego may develop distinct from its evolution in the West.

In *Spirited Away*, Chihiro takes on a series of complex problems, which she confronts in the hope of curing her transformed parents. Finally, she decides of her own free will to go to Zeniba in order to help her wounded friend Haku, an action which might psychologically be considered to demonstrate autonomy. It is noteworthy that in *Spirited Away* there is no separation from the Uroboros (the circular image of a snake eating its own tale — a symbol of death and rebirth), no birth of the Hero and no dragon to contend with as described by Neuman (1949 [1993]) in *The Origins and History of Consciousness*, where the story of the development of Western ego is beautifully depicted. Chihiro remains in a Mother-dominant world. Everything takes place in the Spirit World, a realm accidentally breached by Chihiro and her family. As we have seen, this reality consists of some ambiguous opposites maintaining a fine balance making up the Whole, despite, in a cursory reading of the film, an impression of chaos, or at least disorder.

Reading the narrative objectively, the story makes little sense, but staying *within* the story, experiencing it subjectively, helps us to understand its significance. In traditional Japanese culture, the ego seems not to have an a priori existence. Through various experiences within a Great Mother-dominant world, a sense of subjectivity is only established after a lengthy process, which individuals seem to undergo quite passively. In my opinion this sense of passivity equates to an inability to articulate and take direct action in unfolding this process (Yami, 2013).

As mentioned above, through my attempt to read the beginning of *Kojiki*, I showed that there is a long process before the first tangible personified pair of deities appears in Japanese mythology; in contrast, gods in Greek mythology are more clearly defined and developed. This process might be seen to overlap with the process that Chihiro undergoes in the narrative of *Spirited Away*, in which she begins as ordinary, sulky adolescent girl and ends as a strong willed individual.

A model proposed by Kawai (1976) which shows the difference between the structure of the Japanese psyche and that of Westerners might be helpful (Figure 20.1). The ego is the centre of the conscious personality and the Self is the unifying centre of the total psyche in Western Jungian thought.

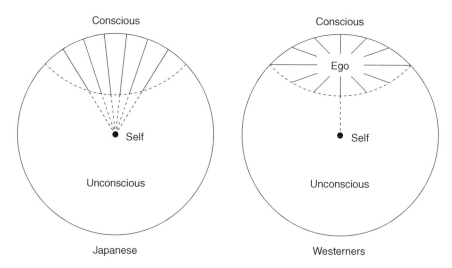

Figure 20.1 Two models of Japanese consciousness and Western consciousness according to Kawai.
Source: Pictorially interpreted by Yami, 2013, p. 58.

According to Kawai, in the Japanese psyche, the boundary between consciousness and unconsciousness is much less defined. The ego is buried in the unconscious depths of the psyche. As it is usually difficult to articulate what is taking place in the unconscious, we need to be involved *within*. *Spirited Away* gives us a beautiful story that shows what might happen in the illogical unconscious realm. Logic in general is based on rational thought, yet it is quite difficult to follow the film in a linear fashion. Events are somewhat incoherent and many characters merely acknowledge and attempt to understand what is happening to them, in a non-linear manner, without questioning the processes of transformation that they are under-going or actively directing it through a more ego-led, self-determining, sense of heroism. The Japanese word *jinen* is helpful here – it denotes a state in which various elements flow spontaneously. It might be interesting to suggest that the narrative developed in accord with *jinen*, which interestingly shares the kanji characters with *shizen* (nature). In Japanese, fate and nature seem to go hand-in-hand.

Conclusion

The Bathhouse is like an unconscious melting pot, populated by images and spirits that talk in a visual and somatic language to our consciousness. That is, it is as if, like archetypal energies in the dream landscape, these projected elements of another realm, function as drivers of change – psychopomps if you like – for transformation. Chihiro's most immediate need, on entering the amusement park, or spirit world, on the journey to her new life and school in a distant town, was to develop a stronger sense of self-awareness and resilience; to integrate conflicting energies at play in this very difficult emergence from childhood into adolescence. While the story does not adopt a hero's journey paradigm, it taps into a Japanese sensibility of *jinen* that in its seeming chaos and fluidity is able to facilitate transformation. The embrace of this concept through the enthusiastic support of Miyazaki's work here by non-Japanese audiences, suggests a form of collective unconscious recognition of *jinen* – of nature and fate, so entwined in contemporary anime and its historical picture scroll counterpart.

Acknowledgement

I would like to express my gratitude to Stephen Richmond, who helped revise my manuscript and gave much valuable feedback.

References

Jung, C. G. (1987 [2010]) *Kodomo no yume*. Kyoto: Jinbun-shoin. (*Children's dreams: notes from the seminar given in 1936–1940*, Jung Seminars. Princeton, NJ: Princeton University Press.)

Kawai, H. (1976) *Boseishakai Nihon no Byori* (Pathology of Japan as a society of maternity). Tokyo: Chuokoron-sha.

Kawai, H. (1987 [1991]). *Myoe yume wo ikiru*. Kyoto: Shohaku-sha. (*The Buddhist priest Myoe: a life of dreams*. Culver City, CA: Lapis Press.)

Kawai, H. (1995) *Dream, myth and fairy tales in Japan*. Einsiedeln, Switzerland: Daimon.

Komatsu, K. (2002) *Kamikakushi to nihon jin*. Kadokawa Sophia bunko. Tokyo: Kadokawa-shoten.

Kyoto National Museum (2006) 'Emaki unrolled: masterworks of illustrated narrative handscrolls'. Kyoto National Museum, Japan.

Matthews, K. (2006) 'Logic and narrative in *Spirited Away*', *Screen Education*, (43), pp. 135–40.

Miyazaki, H. (2006 [2013]) *Kaze no kaeru basho: naushika kara chihiro made no kiseki*. Bunshun jiburi bunko. (*A place where the wind return: trajectory from Nausicaä to Chihiro*. Tokyo: Bungeishunju.)

Neumann, E. (1949 [1993]) *The origins and history of consciousness*. Princeton, NJ: Princeton University Press.

Otto, R. (1917 [2010]) *Das Heilige: über das Irrationale in der Idee des Göttlichen und sein Verhältnis zum Rationalen*. Breslau: C. H. Beck. (*Sei naru mono*. Iwanami-Bunko. Tokyo: Iwanami-shoten.)

Von Franz, M. L. (1997) *Alchemical active imagination*. Boston, MA and London: Shambhala.

Yama, M. (2013) 'Ego consciousness in the Japanese psyche: culture, myth and disaster', *Journal of Analytical Psychology*, 58, pp. 52–72.

Filmography

Spirited away. (2001) [film – animation] Directed by Hayao Miyazaki. Japan.

21

COLD COMFORTS

Psychical and cultural schisms in *The Bridge* and *Fortitude*

Alec Charles

Introduction

This chapter explores two popular television takes on the genre of Nordic noir: the Danish–Swedish co-production *The Bridge* (2011–) and the British-led international collaboration *Fortitude* (2015–). Each series hinges upon a brilliant and enigmatic central character, a personality so obscure as to appear almost empty, all-seeing yet somehow invisible: Sofia Helin's Saga Norén and Stanley Tucci's Eugene Morton. These two figures maintain degrees of professional and emotional detachment which might be thought to resemble states of social or psychical alienation or conversely to align with processes of individuation – the process of approaching wholeness. As such they advance the possibility of the interdependence of those two conditions. In doing so individuation is seen as a product of alienation, and also vice versa. It follows that the two figures provide a potential symbiosis of what seem to be contrary states. Jung hinted at this paradoxical reconciliation of alienation and integration when he wrote that, 'individuation does not shut one out from the world, but gathers the world to oneself' (1947/54: §432). Norén and Morton negotiate, mediate and interpret the irrational flux of their narratives, transforming the arbitrary chaos of the violent worlds they inhabit into meaningful (and indeed archetypal) structures: transforming a sense of absurdity into comprehensible systems of motivation and meaning. Both detectives perform the role of semiotic analyst to the psyche of their respective societies. While this might be seen, obviously enough, to be the province and function of the fictive detective, the heightened absurdities of the situations they face and the mysteries they solve, emphasize the transformative power of their ability to rationalize such phenomena. This chapter offers a Jungian perspective on this hermeneutic. It is one that suggests the evolution towards well-being or meaningfulness and the reconciliation of psychical conflictedness, may necessarily remain provisional and traumatic. It explores whether these figures represent valid analytic paradigms, as individuating and integrating subjects. In doing so the chapter examines if they are figures of ancient and natural wisdom, or if they are no more than mental conjuring tricks that offer the illusion of such perspicacity.

Both series have achieved significant levels of international popular and critical success. The series pit their especially eccentric and enigmatic detective leads against particularly alienating and often surreal situations and environments. In doing this, they significantly advance the televisual detective genre, which may account, in part, for their success with audiences. They extend the genre's possibilities for the exploration of psychological scenarios and personality types, and therefore reveal insights of such interest under the lens of Jungian analysis.

This chapter will explore the first three seasons of *The Bridge* (at the time of writing the producers have promised a fourth and final season), and the first season of *Fortitude* (at the time of writing a second season is in production).

Saga's archetypes

The Bridge's Saga Norén (Sofia Helin) is a detective-hero unlike most others. Similar to her Nordic counterpart Sarah Lund (Sofie Gråbøl) in *The Killing* (2007–12), she seems detached from those around her – but that detachment is (in contrast to the cliché of the maverick cop) mirrored by an obsessive attachment to the institutional processes of police procedure. Gilbert (2015) notes that 'her character sits somewhere on the Asperger's spectrum, although the script is careful not to diagnose her'. Townsend (2015) adds that 'while the writers of *The Bridge* have never confirmed that Saga has Asperger syndrome … it has been generally assumed to be the case'. (In this respect she seems an elaboration on Stieg Larsson's Lisbeth Salander.)

As one of her colleagues observes in the series' opening episode, 'she's a bit odd'. Another notes that 'she's very different … in every way'. Her Danish partner (in the first two seasons) Martin Rohde is a rule-bender; Saga is rigid in her rule-compliance. Early in their relationship Martin suggests that one need not apply rules indiscriminately in all cases: 'it's an unwritten law'. To which Saga responds: 'I don't know any of those.'

In the third season another colleague explains that some kinds of 'police intervention require a great deal of empathy' and adds that 'this kind of interaction with other people is not [her] forte'. A few episodes later Saga parrots these words: 'empathic interaction with others is not my forte'. When she is told that she has a history of complaints from witnesses she has questioned – complaints that she has been 'unpleasant' and 'insensitive' – Saga appears nonplussed and upset by this revelation. When offered 'the option of sensitivity training' she says that she is well aware of her limitations. When a lifestyle guru asks her if she is happy, she asks him to 'define happiness' which he says is 'a permanent feeling of well-being, independent of external factors, be they positive or negative'. Saga does not respond, but looks troubled.

Saga sometimes seems almost inhumanly distant. As Martin says in the first season, she 'doesn't share her feelings'. At the start of the second season Martin asks her how she can 'shut out' painful memories: 'I only think about what I want to think about', she says. Another colleague suggests she 'doesn't get irony' and compares her to an 'over-analytical robot devoid of any emotion'. Henrik, Saga's partner (and lover) in the third season, calls her 'Wikipedia' – or 'Wiki' for short. As a result of this introspection another character supposes she is 'totally and utterly uninterested in everything outside [her] own world'. To her acquaintances her autism (if that is what it is) gives the misleading appearance that she is something of an automaton.

The first three seasons of *The Bridge* concern her transnational investigations into acts of serial terror. She is accompanied by a Danish co-investigator in the first two seasons, the down-to-earth but increasingly troubled Martin Rohde (Kim Bodnia), and in the third season by the profoundly grieving Henrik Sabroe (Thure Lindhardt). Both Martin and Henrik exude a boyish charisma (allied to a prodigal sexual charm): in that sense, they exhibit aspects of the archetypal figure of the '*puer aeternus*' or '*filius sapientiae*' whom Jung (1954b: §193) witnesses accompanying the 'Great Mother' and sharing her wisdom ('the grace of Sophia'). But Saga is not simply, in her naturalness and insightfulness, that Great Mother; as we shall see. She represents a more complex and conflicted amalgam. For much of the time Saga is supported by her boss the senior police officer Hans Petersson (Dag Malmberg) who acts as an emotional advisor and a father figure. In Jungian terms he is something of a *senex*, 'the father of the soul' (Jung, 1954a: §74). While Saga aspires to that ancient sagacity, she remains her own eternal child, a hero who, in Jung's terms, 'signifies the potential anticipation of an individuation process which is approaching wholeness' (1951a: §281); but she is also an uncompromising rationalist, liable (under extreme pressure) to irrational reactions, a rule-keeper prone to turn trickster. (I will return to the notion of the trickster later.)

Family and friends

We discover in the first season that Saga had a younger sister who committed suicide at the age of 14 by jumping in front of a train after having left her parents and moved in with Saga. The sister figure serves as a constant but barely articulated shadow in Saga's psyche: her opposite (she was, as Saga says, not like her: her sister was 'normal') and a projection of Saga's hopes, fears and regrets. 'The shadow', writes Jung (1939: §513), 'personifies everything that the subject refuses to acknowledge about himself and yet is always thrusting itself upon him.' Her memories of her sister underpin feelings of shame which distances her from the possibility of emotional proximity with others; her sister represents both everything she is not (a victim of abuse, a victim of her own self-imposed alienation, a figure of potential social and psychical integration and normativity) and everything that she will not acknowledge about herself (a victim of abuse, a victim of her own self-imposed alienation, a figure of potential social and psychical integration and normativity). Saga's condition appears to be exacerbated by this psychological trauma.

We are later informed that Saga's sister had been the victim of Munchausen Syndrome by Proxy. In the third season, Saga reveals that she had unjustly accused her parents of sexual abuse in order to save her sister from her mother's maltreatment. Saga, the epitome of guilelessness and legalistic compliance, perpetrated an act of deception which continues to trouble her conscience. It is her inability to come to terms with (or to articulate) her sister's loss or her own crime against her parents (her almost Oedipal transgression) which impedes her own individuation. Yet it is through her natural transparency, and also through the proxy therapy of her analysis of other tricksters' transgressions, that she seeks her atonement. The result is that her acts of criminal detection underpin her path towards psychological reconciliation or redemption.

When asked if her sister had shown signs of depression, she responds: 'I don't pick up on signs.' Her talent of course is to do precisely that. It is a contradiction that her lack of psychical empathy allows her an extraordinary degree of insight. Her ego is not so opaque as to obscure the purity of her vision; on the contrary, her own transparency allows her to see clearly. If she is something of an *idiot savant*, then the one quality predicates the other. She has made it her vocation to pick up on signs because at that critical moment in her life (the time of her sister's suicide) she failed to do so; she has devoted her life to the enforcement of the law because she once, as she says, 'committed a crime' for which she is unable to atone. This response to trauma is itself traumatic as it lacks the transcendent 'leap of faith' (Kierkegaard, 2005, p. 95). In its place comes a type of acceptance, in the style of Camus (1975, p. 53). It brings with it an awareness of how life can be lived more truthfully once we accept that it 'has no meaning' – no transfigurative meaning beyond the imposition of Saga's regulations and repressions.

In the opening episode Saga attempts to console a man apparently about to die in a bomb blast by pointing out that, as an atheist, he knows 'everything will just stop. The body won't have time to register pain.' Five episodes later the same character is resuscitated after a drug overdose: upon his recovery he says that he saw no light or tunnel as he died: 'there was only darkness'. In the next episode he dies alone in his car. An existential emptiness occupies the heart of this drama – as Martin observes in the first episode, it is no wonder that Ingmar

Bergman came from Sweden. It is, by contrast, Martin, the cop from the land of Søren Kierkegaard, whose relationship with Saga offers to restore to her existence some sense of temporal faith: he affords the possibility of a faith not in Kierkegaard's God and not in all humanity but at least in other people – in the validity and value of trust in certain individuals other than herself.

Jung (1939: §511) wrote that 'in the unconscious of every man there is hidden a feminine personality, and in that of every woman a masculine personality'. Rohde and Saga respectively demonstrate key aspects of the *anima* and *animus*: intuitive sensitivity and 'hidden wisdom' (Jung, 1954a: §64) on the one hand, and analytical knowledge, inflexibility and 'critical disputatiousness' (Jung, 1928: §335) on the other. They complement each other psychically: or as Rhode puts it, they 'work well together' – and she 'does [him] good'. He is, as she says, her 'only friend'. The unique value of their relationship is based not upon their gender difference (which a simplistic interpretation of the *anima/animus* relation might suggest) but upon the specific complementarity of their personalities (for which the *anima/animus* relation provides a useful model). Each represents the condition of possibility for the other's individuation and yet it is their adversary, the so-called Truth Terrorist, who not only brings them together (who like the psychoanalyst establishes the conditions for coming into psychical well-being) but also divides them, withholding the possibility of such redemption – therapist and terrorist at the same time. That is the ultimate betrayal, the ultimate terrorism: to purport to offer truth and thereby psychical reconciliation but in fact to promote violence, disintegration and alienation.

Saga, however, loses Martin at the end of the second season when she reports him for an apparent homicide – the murder of the Truth Terrorist, his former police partner, a monster created by Martin's own transgressions, the man who killed his son, and who has in turn become Martin's inescapable shadow, haunting his waking dreams. 'A man who is possessed by his own shadow', writes Jung (1950a: §222), 'is always standing in his own light and falling into his own traps'.

Troubled water

Nordic Noir and its Anglophone offshoots in recent years have increasingly focused on the supernatural. There are clear hints of this in the works of Scandinavian crime writers such as Johan Theorin and Yrsa Sigurðadottir, and this literary trend has influenced the televisual genre. In the Swedish–German co-production *100 Code* (2015), for example, an English detective in Sweden (Dominic Monaghan) is haunted by the image of his deceased girlfriend, similarly Stellan Skarsgård, a Swedish detective in England, sees visions of the dead in the British series *River* (2015). In the third season of *The Bridge*, Saga Norén's partner Henrik (like Bruce Willis in *The Sixth Sense* [1999, dir. Shyamalan]) also sees dead people: 'I see them [his dead wife and daughters] – they're here in the house with me. All the time. I talk to them. And they talk to me.'

This then is a place for ghosts, the realm of the dead. The bridge between Copenhagen and Malmö (which links the lands of the living and suspends the living above the dead) is itself transformed by the events of *The Bridge*'s first season into a site of death. It is the place from which the deaths, years before the series began, of the first season's antagonist's wife and son have provoked his cycle of killing (his family 'ended up in the water'). The bridge is also the scene of the discovery of his first murders (parts of two corpses are found halfway across the bridge). Finally, it is the site of his murderous revelation where Martin Rohde discovers the killer has murdered his son. This Truth Terrorist claims to expose the hypocrisies and delusions of civilization, and the bridge itself represents one such delusion in its symbolic and actual attempt to impose an artificial structure over nature's flow and entropic tides. This bridge does not then in the end defer death but bridges the gap between the living and the dead – like Zoroastrianism's Chinvat Bridge or the As-Sirāt bridge in Islam or the bridge to Hel in Norse mythology (or even Charon's ferry). The bridge itself as an architectural psychopomp lies somewhere between the wise old man, green man or great mother, and the figure of the trickster. It offers to raise humanity above the raging madness of the flow and tides of the natural world, or at least to reconcile human rationality with that madness, but it becomes the site in this narrative of insanity and violent destruction. The Truth Terrorist makes similar promises, and conspires in this betrayal. By contrast Saga in her emotional simplicity and moral purity promises nothing and yet comes closer to delivering the possibility of rationalization and reconciliation.

If the Truth Terrorist tries to conjure his own Ragnarök by crossing Bifröst, the bridge from Earth to Asgard, and transforming himself into the giant who slays and supersedes the gods, then he fails to understand that this Nietzschean venture like other delusions he exposes cannot transcend the natural order of the living and the dead. It is Saga's more lucid sagacity that deconstructs her own apocalyptic and hubris-laden apotheosis: she sees the self-serving mundanity behind his self-aggrandizing revelations. This serial killer has undergone cosmetic surgery to transform his features, but, though he may assume the role of the Truth Terrorist (a trickster which promises to transcend his dissembling nature and reveal the absolute truth), it is Saga who comes to represent the true shaman, the figure of Odin, the one-eyed god. Saga's own perceptual impairment, like Odin's, in fact underpins her perspicacity; her emotional scars afford her a transformational power beyond the scope of the Truth Terrorist's cosmetic artifice. Saga does not hide her scars, and may overcome or become reconciled to them. Her opponent, in submerging or repressing his, *becomes* them. The closing moments of the third season see Saga, as she confronts past trauma, in the early stages of psychical readjustment. The Truth Terrorist, by contrast, lies about himself to the world and to himself; he transforms his appearance and veils his lies and motives in a guise of transformative truth, but he cannot escape the corrosive influence of the trauma that will come to define him.

The Norse god Odin – 'wise and shrewd, benevolent and terrible' (Anderson, 1989, p. 138), 'master-by-force-of-knowledge-and-intellect' (Hodge, 1988, p. 40) – recalls Jung's *senex*, that 'wise old man ... who symbolizes the pre-existent meaning hidden in the chaos of life' (Jung, 1954a: §74). But insofar as Odin and the trickster Loki evolved from the same figure (Charles, 2013, p. 93) the proximity between Saga and her nemesis, the Truth Terrorist, remains problematic. Saga negotiates a traumatic and perilous route towards her own individuation, even as she meets opponents travelling in the opposite direction.

Saga herself inadvertently terrorizes with the truth. In the series' third episode a psychologist's profile of the Truth Terrorist seems to mirror her own personality:

> This person is extremely focused on a single project, he's not in a relationship, he is or has been very successful professionally. He has experienced something traumatic ... he's trying to regain balance and make sense of the world again. Everything is meticulously planned and executed.

Later in the episode Saga repeats details of this profile to her boss (the wise father-figure): 'extremely focused, single, successful, clearly defined targets, good at planning'. For a moment he appears to think she is describing herself. It is, however, Saga's lack of guile (her absolute truthfulness, reflected in her inability to tell a lie) which distinguishes her from the terrorist who only purports to speak the truth.

Forces of nature

In the opening moments of *The Bridge*'s second season a crewless ship of lost souls (five missing people chained below decks, four unconscious and dying, one already dead) runs adrift against the great sea bridge between Denmark and Sweden, the construction which gives the series its title and its defining metaphor: Charon's ferry abandoned by its pilot, rudderless. The five have been infected with a deadly strain of pneumonic plague.

The opening of this season revolves around a 'cell' of 'pathos-driven eco-terrorism' agents who wear animal masks to deliver environmental messages (Saga stresses that it is a *cell* – clearly that biological metaphor matters). They are transformative tricksters assuming to be an empathic embodiment of nature, a version of the 'green man' which Hockley (2007, p. 115) observes as being common in the reporting of 'stories on ecology' and which Anslow (2001) specifically relates to the British press coverage of an environmental campaigner who became known as *Swampy*. The trickster can transform into an animal, a familiar of nature, but is neither the *senex* nor the green man (the figure neither of ancient nor of natural insight) yet may present the semblance of both. *The Bridge*'s petty eco-tricksters are themselves swiftly out-tricked by their superiors: within three episodes these faux-natural spirits have been murdered by their puppet-masters. Thus a corporate psychopath who, as we are later informed, 'doesn't give a fuck about nature' manipulates the environmentalists. Yet he himself is controlled (and eventually killed) by a further conspirator who ensures that everything he does is done 'for the environment'. In turn she is controlled and eventually killed by a shadowy mastermind whose motives and identity are never revealed.

In this resistance to closure, the televisual text becomes its own trickster, following in the footsteps of more complex *film noir* classics like *The Big Sleep* (1946). Its director Howard Hawks famously cabled Raymond Chandler during filming to ask who committed one of the murders; the author responded 'no idea' (Hiney, 1999, p. 163). *The Bridge* fosters a similar indeterminacy. Saga represents the truthfulness of innocent transparency; her enemies claim to represent an absolute truth. *The Bridge* reveals the deceptive nature of such deterministic closure, deferring solutions to questions like, what was the fate that befell Henrik's family? Did Martin murder the Truth Terrorist? Was Saga right about her sister's abuse and did she murder her mother?

These narratives tangentially enact age-old and ongoing conflicts between the forces of social order and the natural order. While *The Bridge* pits its heroes against terrorists who purport to be inspired by nature or natural justice, its generic counterparts *Fortitude* and *Jordskott* revolve around the anarchy of *hypernatural* environments.

Swedish television's *Jordskott* (2015) tells the tale of how a rationalist police detective faces a series of fantastical events prompted by 'Nature's revenge' in a time when people have 'made an enemy of the forest'. Donaghey (2015) has dubbed it a 'fairytale-noir […] eco-friendly journey into a heart of darkness'. While *Jordskott* witnesses the slow transformation of people into plants (a transformation which, though traumatic, seems ultimately redemptive), *Fortitude*'s first season depicts the catastrophic aftermath of 'something incredible [that has] come out of the ice, something ancient, something that's going to cause a hell of a lot of trouble'. This primal force of nature takes the form of a species of parasitic wasp that has lain dormant since pre-history. *Fortitude* capitalizes on the extreme climate of its Nordic setting to present a generic hybrid somewhere between the *film noir* echoes of David Lynch's *Twin Peaks* (1990–91), its own most immediate Nordic Noir heritage and John Carpenter's 1982 remake of that Antarctic science fiction horror classic *The Thing*.

The series, set in the remote arctic settlement of Fortitude, suggests it is not human civilization but the force of nature, which demonstrates the most overwhelming resilience. The re-emergence of monstrous living fossils have a parasitic influence on their human hosts, which evokes a sense of monstrosity. Foucault (1974, p. 155) witnesses the way in which the exposition of the fossil record reveals not only the distance but also the 'continuity of nature' between human civilization and that 'absolutely archaic prototype, buried deeper than any history'. *Archaic prototypes* such fossils are, as Foucault's phrasing suggests, the archetypes of the earth. Like Jung's archetypes they are symbolically loaded images, ancient and steeped in human culture, which surface as a way of confronting us with particular psychological challenges. As one resident of the frozen community of Fortitude says, 'nothing buried in permafrost ever decays. Disease doesn't die in the ground.' Or as another points out, 'there are bodies in the cemetery that still have plague in them. This place is a forensic treasure-house.'

What has emerged in Fortitude is, as the first season's policeman-protagonist DCI Eugene Morton (Stanley Tucci) puts it, 'a profound psychosis … inhuman savagery'. It is his task, like the psychoanalyst's, to divine the source of the problem. The insightful yet distant Morton is a transnational outsider, an American working for Scotland Yard dispatched to this arctic wasteland to investigate the frontier forces of law and order. Like all (psycho)analysts, Morton is something of a shaman, or a trickster masquerading as a shaman (a sham shaman). In this respect he contrasts with the character who appears genuinely in touch with the natural history of this frozen world, the town's only indigenous resident, 'a powerful man with powerful connections to the old world of darkness and grudge … a shaman'.

If DCI Morton is something of a trickster, we may note that Stanley Tucci is also known for having played Puck in Michael Hoffman's film of *A Midsummer Night's Dream* (1999), another trickster figure. His job, as he says, is to 'interpret' the scene of the crime. But as Morton investigates the first murder, a clue hints at the morphic ambiguity both of the settlement and of its prospective saviour. Morten finds that Henry Koster's *Harvey* (1950) has been paused on a television screen: James Stewart explains that his imaginary friend Harvey is a *pooka* or a sprite that adopts the form of animals. It is, in other words, another trickster: 'a bestial and divine being' (Jung, 1954c: §472). With the forces of nature running riot, civilization's last best hope, it appears, resides not in the *senex* but in trickster.

'Abandon hope all ye who enter here', warns the terminally ill Henry Tyson (Michael Gambon) in *Fortitude*'s fourth episode. There is a strong sense that this isolated community represents an infernal fantasy, a hell frozen over, one only slightly less surreal than the realm which the late passengers of Oceanic Airlines Flight 815 experience in *Lost* (2004–10). The Wild North town of Fortitude is a realm at the edge of reason and at the edge of law: in the tradition of such tales (geographical, social and moral frontiers), its sheriff takes the law into his own hands, performing an act of justice, the execution of a rapist: a murder conducted by means of a contrived polar bear attack.

The Bridge and *Fortitude* both offer accounts of transnational convergences as does *Lost* but while the former is based on Danish–Swedish relations, the latter portrays an arctic settlement populated by Norwegian, British, Spanish, American, Russian and Eskimo residents and visitors. Indeed even its ostensibly Norwegian characters are portrayed by Danish, Icelandic, English and northern Irish actors. It includes Romanian, Singaporean and Tanzanian actors. This transcultural diversity underpins a sense of late postmodern dislocation that characterizes existence in this imaginary, pre-apocalyptic community.

Michael Gambon's Henry Tyson observes that 'there's something very bad going on in this place', but his mistake is that he imagines that the 'something very bad' has supernatural origins, a daemonic spirit struggling against human encroachment rather than the arbitrary resurgence of indiscriminate forces of nature. *Fortitude* is, like the world of *The Bridge*, a godless realm dangling above the abyss of natural chaos and destruction. The parasitic wasps which menace and transform the colony's human population merely expose existential precarity. Upon the discovery of the wasps, a local scientist notes that 'Charles Darwin considered their life cycle to be inimical to the notion of a benevolent creator. A loving God could not have created something so wicked.' Another character responds: 'It is not wasps that should make one doubt the existence of a benevolent God. It is us, his children.' *Fortitude's* wasps are merely nature's way of exposing the transgressions of an encroaching civilization.

Intuition and insight

C. G. Jung (1921: §610) describes intuition as 'not mere perception … but an active, creative process that puts into the object as much as it takes out'. The intuitive is, in a psychical process which mirrors Heideggerian *Dasein*, constantly projecting herself forward into future possibilities, insofar as it is 'only through envisioning possibilities [that] intuition [is] fully satisfied' (Jung, 1921: §612). As the newness of such possibilities is swiftly exhausted, 'in a very short time every existing situation becomes a prison for the intuitive, a chain that has to be broken (Jung, 1921: §612). Jung continues:

> Because he is always seeking out new possibilities, stable conditions suffocate him. He seizes on new objects or situations with great intensity, sometimes with extraordinary enthusiasm, only to abandon them cold-bloodedly, without any compunction, and apparently without remembering them, as soon as their range is known and no further developments can be divined.
>
> *(§613)*

These characteristics of a specifically extravert intuitive type in the world of fiction might summon the image of Sherlock Holmes and his various reincarnations like *Fortitude's* Eugene Morton. As Jung (1921: §613) suggests, the kind of extravert intuitive epitomized by Holmes or Morton 'has his own characteristic morality, which consists in a loyalty to his vision and in voluntary submission to its authority. Consideration for the welfare of others is weak. Their psychic well-being counts as little with him as his own' (§613). This type, for Jung (§615), exhibits a 'ruthless superiority' – 'not that he means to be ruthless or superior – he simply does not see the object that everyone else sees and rides roughshod over it.' Jung (§613) notes that 'since his intuition is concerned with externals and with ferreting out their possibilities, he readily turns to professions in which he can exploit these capacities to the full'. Jung points out vocations in business, finance and politics but fails to mention literary detection. It seems clear, however, that the likes of Morton and Holmes spend their careers exploiting their capacities to ferret out what lays beneath external appearances; reading a crime scene or interpreting the emotional states of the recently or soon-to-be bereaved.

If Holmes is an extraverted intuitive, then other fictive detectives might exhibit characteristics of Jung's other psychological types. Sarah Lund, for example, in the Danish–Swedish co-production *The Killing* (see Charles, 2015), demonstrates traits of the introverted intuitive who 'moves from image to image, chasing after every possibility in the teeming womb of the unconscious, without establishing any connection between them and himself' (Jung, 1921: §658).

The savant qualities of this 'wise simpleton' (Jung, 1921: §661) are echoed in the rationally insightful characters lacking emotional intelligence, like Saga Norén in *The Bridge*. Norén seems to approximate Jung's 'introverted thinking type' whose personal traits 'tend to disappear and get concealed' and, like the intuitive extravert, case judgements that seem 'cold, inflexible, arbitrary, and ruthless' (Jung, 1921: §633). Jung continues:

He usually has bad experiences with rivals in his own field because he never understands how to curry their favour; as a rule he succeeds in showing them how entirely superfluous they are to him. In pursuit of his ideas he is generally stubborn, headstrong, and quite unamenable to influence.

(§634)

Jung adds:

In his personal relations he is taciturn or else throws himself on people who cannot understand him ... The better one knows him, the more favourable one's judgment becomes, and his closest friends value his intimacy very highly. To outsiders he seems prickly unapproachable and arrogant.

(1921: §635)

This introverted thinker has much in common with aspects of the intuitive, but the former remains grounded in solid reason and remains focused upon single sets of possibilities, rather than leaping to the next idea. Her insights develop more from painstaking rigour and persistence rather than flights of imagination. The apparent naturalness, or lack of artifice, in her emotional transparency is balanced by the conscious constructedness of her intellectual processes. Her position within the orthodox structures of Jung's psychological typology contains its own contradictions. Her conflictedness is further revealed by Jung's archetypal model, which is underpinned by the conflict and the capacity for reconciliation, between such psychical contraries. The striking reality of her paradoxical character is that she is both an alienated redeemer and an integrated outsider.

Intuition for Jung involves an ability to comprehend archetypal symbolism:

... the images arising from the *a priori* inherited foundations of the unconscious. These archetypes ... are the precipitate of the psychic functioning of the whole ancestral line; the accumulated experiences of organic life in general, a million times repeated, and condensed into types. In these archetypes, therefore, all experiences are represented which have happened on this planet since primeval times.... The archetype would thus be ... the noumenon of the image which intuition perceives and, in perceiving, creates.

(1921: §659)

Intuition then apprehends, reveals and interprets those culturally antique archetypes, which underpin the unconscious mind. This process of discovery is also a process of creation, or of perpetuation or reinvention. Intuition recognizes these profound and ancient truths for what they are in themselves, because it is from human intuition that these symbolically weighty images have sprung. Intuition can come to demonstrate a 'prophetic foresight ... explained by its relation to the archetypes' (Jung, 1921: §660); and thus the intuitive type can come to appear something of a 'mystical dreamer' or 'seer' (§661). This ability to identify and comprehend psychological iconography from the past allows the intuitive to interpret the present and therefore to project the possibilities of the future. This mystical intuition underpins the revelation of apparently preternatural and primordial phenomena in such serials as *100 Code*, *Fortitude* and *Jordskott*. For example, it is only as *Jordskott*'s police detective Eva Thörnblad (Moa Gammel) moves from her professional rationalism to be guided first by her emotional history and then by the atavistic forces of the forest themselves, that she comes intuitively to recognize the impact of primordial archetypes, forces so profoundly natural as to appear preternatural.

It's not easy being green

Jung (1945: §406) writes of the archetype of the old man who 'represents knowledge, reflection, insight, wisdom, cleverness, and intuition'. Jung therein recounts the Russian fairy tale of the 'King of the Forest', an old man whose 'green beard hung down to his knees'. He explains that

> the King of the Forest is here a vegetation or tree numen who reigns in the woods and … also has connections with water, which clearly shows his relation to the unconscious since the latter is frequently expressed through wood and water symbols [from Thörnblad's forest through to Morton's glacier to Norén's Øresund strait].

Jung reminds us here that forest and sea, and indeed icy wasteland, represent the implacable and irresistible dominion of the natural world. Sometimes the violent chaos which these narratives' villains attempt to harness is perverted in the process and it comes to corrupt and control them. This in turn provides the chaos out of which these narratives' detective-protagonists seek understanding, rationalization or reconciliation. If detective and villain represent two sides of the same coin, their distinction lies in a crucial difference of emphasis, dependent on degrees of self-awareness: the difference then between the lighter and darker sides of the trickster, fraudster or saviour, and the related figure of the green man.

The green man figure resembles what Varner (2006, p. 154) calls 'the woodland god … or green man', a figure 'found throughout world mythology' (p. 119) who emphasizes 'humanity's close relationship to nature' (p. 149). This green man, for Curran (2007, p. 23) represents the 'memory of a time when men had actually been an equal part of the natural world'. Invoking Jung, Curran (p. 23) witnesses in this cultural memory the possibility of opening up 'a great body of consciousness to which we have no immediate access'. Anslow writes that:

> the green man archetype … represents mankind's connection with nature, with all its capricious implications … Puck … Loki … the mischievous spirit of life where the rational justice of humanity melds into the undeniable but often cruel and amoral rightness of the natural world.
>
> *(2001, pp. 19–20)*

Banks and Wein (1998) suppose that the green man 'symbolizes the union of humanity and the natural world' and stands as an advocate for, and embodiment of, 'the laws of nature'. As such, however, this figure can also demonstrate the potential catastrophic disunity that can arise (witnessed in *Jordskott* and *Fortitude*) when civilization overturns natural laws.

The green man converges with the Great Mother. Cheetham notes:

> For Jung the Great Mother is not only the destroyer of worlds, she is also the womb and the very substance of their matter. The darknesses of the Mother are tied to the earthly, to the mortal, and to the unconsciousness of matter and of the human psyche. It is into her realm that we descend during the dark night of the soul. But after this death there may come a rebirth that signals the redemption of the soul and of the world.
>
> *(2005, p. 34)*

Jung's 'primordial image of the mother' (1954b: §149) – the 'Primordial Mother and Earth Mother' (§309) – inscribes both the 'benevolent goddess and one who is malevolent and dangerous' (§189) – 'something alien … filled with the imagery latent in the unconscious'

(§192). The Earth Mother is, for Jung (§312), 'always chthonic' – a figure of the underworld of the unconscious, of 'the dark side of the human psyche' (§313) – a figure which carries out 'various tortures and obscenities' including 'drinkings of blood and bathings in blood' (§311). Women can 'identify directly with the Earth Mother' (§193): 'the Earth Mother plays an important part in the woman's unconscious' (§312). Saga Norén, though she explicitly denies her maternal instincts, shares both this figure's insightfulness and her darknesses.

Anderson, invoking Jung, argues:

> An archetype will reappear in a new form to redress imbalances in society at a particular time when it is needed. The green man is rising up into our present awareness in order to counterbalance a lack in our attitude toward nature.
>
> *(1990, p. 25)*

Anderson's interpretation of this archetype may in this context be seen as the latest stage of what Jung calls 'the conflict between "culture" and "nature"' (1950b: §680).

In *Jordskott* Eva Thörnblad is afforded by the green man (who is the incarnation of the forest and who *is* the forest) the possibility of a transformation which is at once an individuation (a coming into being and an atonement) and a disindividuation (a coming into nature as an at-one-ment). By contrast, it is not redemptive but a retributive sense of nature which in *Fortitude* fatally disrupts both DCI Eugene Morton's attempts to rationalize this atavistic chaos and the plans of Governor Hildur Odergard (Sofie Gråbøl) to tame the glacier and transform it into an ice hotel – a situation which may remind us of the great unconscious mass which lies forgotten and feral beneath the surface of the ice. Meanwhile in *The Bridge*, as the delusions of murderous tricksters seek to expose the delusions of civilization, it is only the naive naturalness of the series' unlikely heroine who might deconstruct both sets of lies, and offer a traumatic and problematic route which is at best, a purgatorial route to her eventual reconciliation with the shadows that haunt her present and past, and her transformation from trickster to healer.

Jung (1954c: §456) writes of the trickster's 'powers as a shape-shifter, his dual nature, half animal, half divine, his exposure to all kinds of tortures, and … his approximation to the figure of a saviour'. He adds that 'there is something of the trickster in the character of the shaman or medicine-man' (§457). But if the trickster is a healer then s/he is, like Derrida's *pharmakos* – like Christ, Odin or Norén, one whose healing powers are intrinsic to her/his capacity for suffering: 'the wounded wounder is the agent of healing … the sufferer takes away the suffering' (§457).

Jung (1954c: §465) observes that 'this phantom of the trickster haunts the mythology of all ages'. He sees the trickster as representing an atavistic yet vital recurrence:

> Now if the myth were nothing but an historical remnant, one would have to ask why it has not long since vanished into the great rubbish-heap of the past, and why it continues to make its influence felt on the highest levels of civilization.… In many cultures his figure seems like an old river-bed in which the water still flows. One can see this best of all from the fact that the trickster motif does not crop up only in its mythical form but appears just as naïvely and authentically in the unsuspecting modern man – whenever, in fact, he feels himself at the mercy of annoying 'accidents' which thwart his will and his actions with apparently malicious intent.
>
> *(§469)*

The trickster is then simultaneously responsible for, and responsible for exposing, every malaise of contemporary life.

Stanley Tucci offers a Puckish and Holmesian performance as Eugene Morton in *Fortitude*, which seems to fit the model of trickster. Tucci is an actor also known for playing a serial killer in *The Lovely Bones* (dir. Jackson, 2009), and we may see in the figure of the trickster a character not dissimilar from those self-aggrandizing serial killers repeatedly faced by Sofia Helin's Saga Norén: figures which may advance claims to be societal healers, figures of justice or nature, but who are no more than counterfeit medicine men, homicidal charlatans.

Yet the trickster also seems homologous with the green man: the trickster is, after all, 'god, man and animal' – a medicine man who procures and purveys the remedial herbs of the forest – and even on occasion the progenitor of vegetation: 'from his penis he makes all kinds of useful plants' (Jung, 1954c: §472). He is, like the green man and the Great Mother, a creature associated with and attached to a primordial unconscious: 'a primitive cosmic being of divine-animal nature … unreason and unconscious'. He is, though, a lesser such figure: caught between nature and culture, he displays those 'defects … the marks of his human nature which is not so well adapted to the environment as the animal's' (§473). He is not a creature of unreconstructed atavism, but he offers through his intuitive extraversion an empathic connection with that atavism and in so doing provides a way to negotiate with it. Thus the trickster offers a 'gradual civilizing … of a primitive daemonic figure' (§475) while at the same time serving as a reminder to the 'so-called civilized man' that 'his own hidden and apparently harmless shadow has qualities whose dangerousness exceeds his wildest dreams' (§478). He is a reminder of the fact that 'outwardly people are more or less civilized, but inwardly they are still primitives' (§482).

There remains a fine line in these archetypal structures between the presentation of a divine spirit of nature and the shadowy, daemonic figures that seek to represent spirit. It seems to be no coincidence that the killers of these narratives are often police officers. In, for example, the first seasons of *The Bridge* and *Fortitude* and the second season of *The Killing*. Neither is it coincidental that the heroic detective protagonists tend to become emotionally detached (Sarah Lund and Saga Norén), delusional (Martin Rohde and Henrik Sabroe) or even homicidal (Martin Rohde, Sarah Lund and perhaps even Saga Norén). The secret of the detective is therefore to pursue a path towards societal atonement and personal individuation by finding the divine humanity within the trickster. They represent the need to address the archetypal directly by seeing these structures as signposting routes to fulfilment, rather than modes of being in themselves.

References

Anderson, P. (1989) 'The archetypal Holmes', in P. Shreffler (ed.), *Sherlock Holmes by gas lamp*. Zionsville, IN: Baker Street Journal. pp. 135–41.

Anderson, W. (1990) *The green man: the archetype of our oneness with the earth*. London: HarperCollins.

Anslow, J. (2001) *Myth as news: Jungian archetypes in press stories*. Southampton: Southampton Institute.

Banks, A. and Wein, E. (1998) 'Folklore and the comic book: the traditional meets the popular', *New Directions in Folklore*, 2.

Camus, A. (1975) *The myth of Sisyphus*, trans. J. O'Brien. Harmondsworth: Penguin.

Charles, A. (2013) 'Three characters in search of an archetype', *Journal of Popular Television*, 1(1), pp. 83–102.

Charles, A. (2015) 'Sarah Lund and the crime of individuated happiness', in L. Hockley and N. Fadina (eds), *The happiness illusion: how the media sold us a fairytale*. London: Routledge. pp. 181–98.

Cheetham, T. (2005) *Green man, earth angel: the prophetic tradition and the battle for the soul of the world*. Albany, NY: State University of New York Press.

Curran, B. (2007) *Walking with the green man: father of the forest, spirit of nature*. Franklin Lakes, NJ: New Page Books.

Donaghey, J. (2015) 'Murder, mystery, evil Swedish forests', *Guardian*, 14 July.

Derrida, J. (1981) *Dissemination*, trans. B. Johnson. London: Athlone Press.

Foucault, M. (1974) *The order of things*, trans. A. Sheridan. London: Routledge.

Gilbert, G. (2015) 'Sofia Helin on The Bridge and why she based Saga Noren on a cross between Dirty Harry and a goat', *Independent*, 9 November.

Heidegger, M. (2010) *Being and time*, trans. J. Stambaugh. Albany, NY: State University of New York Press.

Hiney, T. (1999) *Raymond Chandler: a biography*. New York: Grove.

Hockley, L. (2007) *Frames of mind: a post-Jungian look at film, television and technology*. Bristol: Intellect.

Hodge, J. (1988) 'New bottles, old wine: the persistence of the heroic figure in the mythology of television science fiction and fantasy', *Journal of Popular Culture*, 21(4), pp. 37–48.

Jung, C. G. (1921) 'General description of the types', in *The collected works of C. G. Jung, Vol. 6, Psychological types*, 3rd edn. London: Routledge, 2014.

Jung, C. G. (1928) 'The relations between the ego and the unconscious', in *The collected works of C. G. Jung, Vol. 7, Two essays on analytical psychology*, 2nd edn. London: Routledge & Kegan Paul, 1966.

Jung, C. G. (1939) 'Conscious, unconscious and individuation', in *The collected works of C. G. Jung, Vol. 9i, The archetypes of the collective unconscious*, 2nd edn. London: Routledge & Kegan Paul, 1968.

Jung, C. G. (1945) 'The phenomenology of the spirit in fairytales', in *The collected works of C. G. Jung, Vol. 9i, The archetypes of the collective unconscious*, 2nd edn. London: Routledge & Kegan Paul, 1968.

Jung, C. G. (1947/54) 'On the nature of the psyche', in *The collected works of C. G. Jung, Vol. 8, The structure and dynamics of the psyche*, 2nd edn. London: Routledge & Kegan Paul, 1969.

Jung, C. G. (1950a) 'Concerning rebirth', in *The collected works of C. G. Jung, Vol. 9i, The archetypes of the collective unconscious*, 2nd edn. London: Routledge & Kegan Paul, 1968.

Jung, C. G. (1950b) 'Concerning mandala symbolism', in *The collected works of C. G. Jung, Vol. 9i, The archetypes of the collective unconscious*, 2nd edn. London: Routledge & Kegan Paul, 1968.

Jung, C. G. (1951a) 'The psychology of the child archetype', in *The collected works of C. G. Jung, Vol. 9i, The archetypes of the collective unconscious*, 2nd edn. London: Routledge & Kegan Paul, 1968.

Jung, C. G. (1951b) 'The psychological aspects of the Kore', in *The collected works of C. G. Jung, Vol. 9i, The archetypes of the collective unconscious*, 2nd edn. London: Routledge & Kegan Paul, 1968.

Jung, C. G. (1954a) 'Archetypes of the collective unconscious', in *The collected works of C. G. Jung, Vol. 9i, The archetypes of the collective unconscious*, 2nd edn. London: Routledge & Kegan Paul, 1968.

Jung, C. G. (1954b) 'The psychological aspects of the mother archetype', in *The collected works of C. G. Jung, Vol. 9i, The archetypes of the collective unconscious*, 2nd edn. London: Routledge & Kegan Paul, 1968.

Jung, C. G. (1954c) 'On the psychology of the trickster-figure', in *The collected works of C. G. Jung, Vol. 9i, The archetypes of the collective unconscious*, 2nd edn. London: Routledge & Kegan Paul, 1968.

Kierkegaard, S. (2005) *Fear and trembling*, trans. A. Hannay. London: Penguin.

Larsson, S. (2005) *Män Som Hatar Kvinnor*. Stockholm: Norstedts Förlag.

Sigurðadottir, Y. (2013) *I remember you*, trans. P. Roughton. London: Hodder.

Theorin, J. (2008) *Echoes from the dead*, trans. M. Delargy. New York: Doubleday.

Townsend, L. (2015) 'How The Bridge's heroine became a role model for women with autism', *BBC News*, 9 December.

Varner, G. (2006) *The mythic forest, the green man and the spirit of nature*. New York: Algora Publishing.

Filmography

100 code. (2015–) [television series] Created by Robert Moresco. Sweden, Germany.

Big sleep, The. (1946) [film] Directed by Howard Hawks. USA.

Bridge, The. (2011–) [television series] Directed by Henrik Georgsson. Sweden, Denmark, Germany.

Fortitude. (2015) [film] Created by Simon Donald. UK.

Harvey. (1950) [film] Directed by Henry Koster. USA.

Jordskott. (2015–) [television series] Created by Henrik Bjorn. Sweden, Finland, UK, Norway.

Killing, The. (2007–12) [television series] Created by Soren Sveistrup. Denmark, Norway, Sweden, Germany.

Lost. (2004–10) [television series] Created by J. J. Abrams, Jeffrey Lieber and Damon Lindelof. USA.

Lovely bones, The. (2009) [film] Directed by Peter Jackson. USA, UK, New Zealand.

Midsummer night's dream, A. (1999) [film] Directed by Michael Hoffman. Italy, UK, USA.
River, The. (2012) [film] Created by Oren Pell and Michael R. Perry. USA.
River. (2015) [television series] Created by Abi Morgan. UK.
Sixth sense, The. (1999) Directed by M. Night Shyamalan. USA.
Thing, The. (1982) [film] Directed by John Carpenter. USA.
Twin peaks. (1990–91) [television series] Created by David Lynch and Mark Frost. USA.

22

CULTURAL HEGEMONIES OF FORMS AND REPRESENTATIONS

Russian fairy tale women and post-Jungian thought

Nadi Fadina

Mirror, mirror on the wall, can't you see, they know it all?

Myths, folklore and fairy tales are an integral part of our life-long search to understand who we are and how we want to be in the world – what Jung calls individuation. Jung also argues those same stories can provide a means of amplification through which to come to view and understand the interplay between social and psychological constructions of ourselves and, by extension, our gender.

Numerous philosophers and academics of different countries, movements, schools and approaches, have debated the multifaceted questions of myth and folklore during the twentieth century. From psychology, both Freud (1900) and Jung (1959) drew heavily on myths and as might be expected so too do their followers. In terms of world mythology there is the work of Campbell (1949), while the investigation of folktales in the national contexts is the province of Propp (1928, 1946), Jacobson (1966), Haney (1999) and Johns (2004). Taking an international perspective there is Eliade (1963), Warner (2014) and Zipes (1991, 1994, 2000, 2012). Propp (1946) and Nikiforov (1938) adopt a formalist approach that was later to be developed in the structuralist work of Lévi-Strauss (1969, 1978) and the post-structuralism formulations of Barthes (1957). A more recent formalism is offered by Lüthi (1974, 1979). Bettelheim (1976) revives and develops psychoanalytic formulations and from the perspective of analytical psychology there is the foundational work of von Franz (1970, 1972, 1993, 1996). Feminist theory has also examined myth and fairy tale as in the work of Bottingheimer (1987a, 1987b, 2009), Lieberman (1972), Rowe (1979), Gilbert and Gubar (1979, 1987) and Bell *et al.* (1995). Anthropological and sociological approaches have been taken by Anderson (2000) and Baker-Sperry (2007) respectively, while Zipes has taken a neo-Marxist approach to the subject (1979, 1983, 1997). There is an abundance of research into fairy tales as scholars continue to explore the power of these cultural products in ancient and modern contexts.

Such a deep engagement with fairy tales in such a diversity of disciplines, discourses and domains is probably due to the nature of the material itself, as it provides a productive base on which theories can thrive. Indeed fairy tales represent a distinctive mixture of national and simultaneously universal stories, as common motives reappear again and again in different cultures and epochs.

As the origin of fairy tales is a subject of ongoing debate we are left only with speculation as to why countries separated by geography and different time periods have developed similar narratives. Hence Theodor Benfey's theories about the monogenesis of fairy tales (in Leeming, 1997) and on the other hand those of Joseph Bédier on their polygenesis (in Ziolkowski, 2010). Nevertheless, fairy tales have undergone an interesting historical trajectory travelling back-and-forth from low-culture to high-culture and from the adult domain into the children's domain (Zipes, 2006), thus blurring the boundaries of class formations and target demographic groups. Their seeming simplicity and 'depthlessness', as Lüthi (1979) puts it, is multiplied by common wisdom and possible sacral symbolism. If we are to add to this complexity the ability of fairy tales to explore the personal and collective (both conscious and unconscious) then it is apparent that the philosophical and academic debates around the subject are justified.

It might seem as though we have already learnt everything about these old stories. Dissected them inside and out. After the decades of research into fairy tales they might seem like a mundane subject devoid of new insights. Further, there has clearly been a distinct misconception in academia that revolved around the mistaken belief that fairy tales are intrinsically sexist. Although the peak of the debate took place at the end of 1970s and the beginning of 1980s (Lieberman, 1972; Zipes, 1983, 1986; Rowe, 1979; Gilbert and Gubar, 1979), over the years this understanding seemingly became axiomatic. However, in the last decade some research and arguments have started appearing that are shining a light on ancient fairy tales, which can actually provide us with narratives that function as alternatives to dominant patriarchal discourses (McVey, 2011). That said, the debate on the matriarchal aspects of fairy tales is still ongoing (Zipes, 2012), and speculation around the existence and significance of earlier matriarchal cultures continues to inform many thinkers (Ucko, 1968; Fleming, 1969; Gere, 2009).

Throughout the twentieth and twenty-first centuries, new fairy tales in different media formats have been emerging. It is widely argued, especially by the Frankfurt school, that modern media adapted and appropriated these ancient stories, which have now formed deep roots in the patriarchal ideologies of contemporary cultures (Addison, 1993; Zipes, 1995; Bell *et al.*, 1995). As Bacchilega suggests:

> In the middle ages, folk tales served more of an emancipatory function because they expressed the problems and desires of the underprivileged; in modern times, the fairy tale has more often than not been 'instrumentalised' to support bourgeois and/or conservative interests.
>
> *(1997, p. 7)*

However, a question remains unanswered – do the new mediated tales adapted from the old narratives have the capacity to offer fresh opportunities and perspectives about what it means to be a modern man and a woman in our ever changing but also paradoxically rigid world? This chapter sets out on a journey to explore the ways in which post-Jungian thinking around gender can be reformulated and used in the analysis of Soviet and Russian animated fairy tales.

The pathway is thorny though. The Jungian approach to film studies is gradually becoming an integral part of the current exploration of contemporary mediated fairy tales, as analytical psychology is establishing itself as a well-honed research tool for screen studies. However, this has not always been the case. While von Franz (1970, 1972, 1993, 1996), Stein and Corbett (1995) and Jung (1959) explored the cultural and psychological aspects of myths and fairy tales, when it came to film analysis, depth psychology was something of an outcast in the academic world.

From the perspective of a scholar working within a broadly feminist approach to film theory there are multiple problematic issues with Jung's views on gender and sexuality – he is notoriously famous for his conservative understanding of both femininity and masculinity. Therefore, if Jung's thinking was a quintessence of patriarchy can his legacy be of *any* benefit in challenging the doctrines and discourses of the established gendered order? The answer is complex and multi-layered. It might well be that viewing film through a Jungian lens could reveal some of the psychological mechanisms at work that would not otherwise be visible. Some of the post-Jungian iterations strive to develop a more inclusive model of human sexuality, adopting less rigid readings of gender (Hockley, 2015; Rowland, 2002; Wehr, 1997). When this new approach is coupled with thinking around myth, fairy tales and film as ways of amplifying underlying psychological structures, Jung's more adaptable theories can then be mobilised as fertile ground for further feminist analysis.

So how can analysing what are seemingly conservative fairy tales and their media adaptations, and applying a somewhat patriarchal Jungian perspective be helpful in dissecting patriarchy and providing us with the tools to challenge it? By analysing several animated adaptations of ancient Russian fairy tales this chapter demonstrates the transformative effect these narratives offer audiences. It will examine gender representations in Soviet and post-Soviet cinematic fairy tales and debate the applicability of Jungian and post-Jungian theories to the analysis of the female imagery produced under totalitarian regimes and emerging democratic societies. Using extracts from animated fairy tales, most of which are unknown in the West, such as *Poidi Tuda, Ne Znayu Kuda – Mashini Skazki* (animation series Masha's Fairy Tales, dirs Gazizov and Chervyatsov, 2012), *Poidi Tuda, Ne Znayu Kuda* (Go There I Don't Know Where, dirs Ivanov-Vano and Danilevich, 1966), *Pro Fedota Streltsa Udalogo Molodtsa* (About Fedota-the-Shooter, the Fine Young Man, dir. Steblyanko, 2008), *Tsarevna Lyagushka* (The Frog Princess, dir. Tsekhanovsky, 1954) and some others, this chapter will show how notions of gender appear to change but actually remain static, how gender politics plays an essential role in what I see as a contemporary identity crisis, and how individuation can become a driving force in overcoming these challenges.

Liminality: at the crossroads of who we are

Much has been written about the construction of identities and the representation of gender in the works of the fairy tale monopolist of the twentieth century, namely Disney (Bell *et al.*, 1995; Zipes, 1995). Feminist discourse in this field, however, has mainly focused on well-known western fairy tales by noted authors like the Brothers Grimm and Charles Perrot. By contrast, ancient Slavic fairy tales remain less researched. This is significant as Slavic fairy tales provide unique examples of liberating female and male representations, unique imagery, ambiguous liminality, as well as what Jungians term *individuation*.

The word 'liminal' comes from the Latin *limen*, or threshold, and is a concept traditionally related to anthropology. It was first developed by the French ethnologist and folklorist Arnold van Gennep (1909) and subsequently adapted by British cultural anthropologist Victor Turner (1967, 1974). Both Gennep and Turner researched small tribes and used the idea of liminality to describe people undergoing initiations into adulthood. Those undergoing these rituals were considered to be 'liminal beings'; they did not belong to any particular group of the tribe, standing 'in-between' culturally established categories of identity.

The term, however, has also been adopted by psychoanalysis and analytical psychology. In this context liminality refers to a transitional phase in a person's psychological development. Liminality is considered to be a place of great intensity, as one is stepping outside his or her comfort zone by tearing apart the cocoon of old life patterns. Liminality is relevant to our attempt to understand individuation, which as Jungian and post-Jungians argue is a deeply transformative psychological process that involves discovering, accepting and integrating one's identity. It requires a journey through liminal 'lands' that are actual and metaphorical spaces of uncertainty and ambiguity. The process of individuation in its turn, as described by Jung, leads to a more transpersonal understanding of inner and outer worlds that often exists beyond conscious awareness. In fact, individuation requires an engagement of the personal and collective unconsciousness. It is here that fairy tales can play a crucial role.

So how is it that fairy tales and their modern adaptations can help us resolve psychological dynamics that might otherwise have gone unnoticed or unresolved? Slavic fairy tales are heavily rooted in imagery of liminality and in its multiple manifestations. The fairy tale itself takes place in the liminal, unknown and uncertain time and space – in an unknown kingdom far, far away, or in a time long, long ago. The fairy tale usually starts with a hero or heroine embarking on a journey during which they inevitably find themselves traversing deep dark forests. This form of liminal space suggests entry into a threshold experience. In the Russian fairy tale tradition, heroes typically find themselves at a crossroads marked by a Stone of Direction and Destiny. There are different versions as to what the Stone says, but it always offers a choice and states the consequences that each choice will bring. For example: 'Go to the right – you lose the horse but save yourself; go to the left – you lose yourself, but you save your horse; go straight you lose your life and your horse.' Most likely all of us at some point in our lives come across not dissimilar dilemmas accompanied by a moment of hesitation during which we must make a choice. We might have very mixed and complex feelings of fear and excitement. How afraid are we to choose the wrong road, especially when the stakes are high and the outcomes are unclear? But the heroine or hero takes the step, and so the fairy tale tells us that while we might have been feeling safe on the familiar road, it is now necessary to turn to a different path. Fairy tales often demonstrate that the experiences we go through follow a common pattern of human existence and crucially provide an opportunity for change. Understanding and recognising these liminal spaces and times encourages us to embrace and integrate liminality into our life.

Russian fairy tales also present us with an abundance of liminal characters who do not adhere to strict gender differentiations, identities or behaviours. For example, male heroes in Russian fairy tales often express qualities traditionally considered female. They cry and show emotions; they are sometimes praised for their passivity. Therefore, I would argue that fairy tales show a range of emotions that transcend cultural gender ascriptions. While in the West nature was associated with women, male heroes in Russian fairy tale films are always rewarded for being in harmony with it. As for female heroines, indeed some remain as classical princesses waiting to be rescued. However, there are narratives in which female characters are rulers of kingdoms and active subjects (*Marja Morevna, Bogatyr-Maiden*, etc.). There is also a unique character in Russian fairy tale tradition that embodies the notions of liminality and individuation in a way that might appear to transcend gender. It is Baba Yaga.

Baba Yaga: burn the witch

Baba Yaga plays a distinctive role in Slavic culture and is one of the most well researched characters in Russian national fairy tales. Like many fairy tale characters, her origins are complex and uncertain. She has been compared to other mythological female characters including: the Indian Goddess of Death Kali; Fate; the Great Mother Goddess; the Indo-European Goddess of Death and Winter. Baba Yaga is an anchorite; she lives in the woods and is the all-powerful mistress of nature and of the four elements, earth, wind, water and fire. She is also the mistress of the three riders: Morning, Day and Night. Her omniscience resembles Dante's description of Love that 'moves the sun and the other stars' ('l'amor che move il sole e l'altre stelle') (Paradiso 33), which as Barolini (2015) argues is a periphrasis for God. Baba Yaga emerges as a numinous and liminal figure, who lives on the threshold between this world and the other world, inhabiting the border between consciousness and the unconscious.

Famously she lives in a house on chicken legs and has many animalistic characteristics such as sharp teeth. She also has both male and female characteristics such as a huge nose rooted in the ceiling (phallic) and exaggerated breasts which she hangs on a hook. She flies in a mortar, navigating it with a pestle, which in Russian culture was traditionally associated with a sexual intercourse. This again underlines her liminal and androgynous qualities.

Baba Yaga has the power of transmutation and transfiguration; she puts people into her stove, as if to bake them. While the Russian folklorist Vladimir Propp (1946) argued that this baking could be a ritual of cremation or initiation (and here again we can consider the stove to be somewhat a liminal object or place), I would argue that it could also well be a ritual of healing and immortalising, similar to the practice of the Egyptian goddess Isis, and later Demeter, who put children into a stove to make them immortal. Could Baba Yaga be a Slavic 'version' of a spouseless goddess? Developing this point, if we remember that generally Russian myth 'has its roots in a period long before the formation of a distinctively Russian language' (Warner, 2002, p. 7), comparing Baba Yaga to Demeter offers an interesting perspective. Analysing the Russian myth of Mother Damp Earth – the ultimate sacral object for agricultural societies – Joanna Hubbs compares it to Demeter, who fertilises herself without a spouse (1988, p. 54), hence is an androgynously liminal being. Baba Yaga might well stand for the Earth itself and so supports the view that she is a possible incarnation of earlier female, liminal and divine beings.

This latter observation is important because it points towards the Great Mother Goddess of the Pre-historic, Palaeolithic and Neolithic period. The argument that Baba Yaga could be a mythological trace of the Great Goddess is supported in Analytical Psychology, hence von Franz's reference to Baba Yaga as the Great Mother Archetype (1993). However, if we consider the Great Goddesses outside the scheme of gender (Fadina, 2015), it becomes possible to reposition this Slavic witch as an archetype of liminality. Rather than being a female deity, Baba Yaga might well be closer to 'Zoe' – life itself that is neither male nor female, but rather an incorporation of both, or neither – an ungendered concept.

Summing up, most researchers agree that Baba Yaga has a complex nature. She performs the function of both a donor (helper) and a villain; she rewards and punishes. Indeed she helps the young characters (female or male) although she traps, kidnaps and eats people. She is a trickster of sorts, and is therefore closely associated with liminality. What remains important is that Baba Yaga is intimately connected to the liminal journey on which a hero or heroine embarks. She is often the initiator of change and coming across her hut on chicken legs is a signal that the hero or heroine is entering a transitional realm where the distinction between the conscious and unconscious is blurred.

The way that Baba Yaga has been depicted in cinema has undergone a radical change, no less radical than the changes in Russian society. In Soviet films from the middle of the twentieth century, Baba Yaga was represented as a powerful carrier of secret knowledge. Yet in contemporary cinema she has become a caricature of her former self, and an object of ridicule. In the animated film *Tsarevna-Lyagushka* (The Frog Princess, 1954) Baba Yaga retains her magical powers as she embodies nature through her animalistic characteristics. Although the film was created during the heyday of Socialist Realism on screen, Baba Yaga was not stripped of her magic. Over time, in Russian animated fairy tale films she began to lack power, significance and respect, especially from male heroes and has often been excluded entirely from the screen. When she does appear she is portrayed as someone to be pitied as in the following examples: two somewhat different animated versions of the fairy tale *Go there, I know not where; find what I know not* (classified by Aarne and Thompson (1961) under number 465 – 'The man persecuted because of his beautiful wife and Supernatural tasks'). As is commonplace with fairy tales this story has several regional variations, but a brief storyline, summing up the main elements and events, might help to clarify cinematic adaptations of the fairy tale and Baba Yaga.

Once upon a time a royal hunter was ordered to provide game for the tsar's dinner. He shot a bird. Wounded, the bird talked to him and begged him not to kill her but to take her home. The hunter did so, and the bird turned into a beautiful maiden who suggested they marry. After the wedding, the tsar fell in love with the hunter's wife and started devising ways to get rid of the husband by giving him three impossible tasks.

The first was to make a carpet with the whole of Russia on it, or be executed. The hunter's wife summoned two magic helpers and together they made the carpet. The second task was to catch a deer with golden horns. Again his wife conjured up the deer. The third time, the tsar sent the hunter to 'go I know not where and bring back I know not what'. The wife's magical servants could not help her this time. The wife then gave the hunter a magic ball showing the road and a handkerchief to wipe his face and told him to go around the world searching for the wonder himself. The moment the hunter left, the tsar went to propose to the hunter's wife, but she turned back into a bird and flew away. Meanwhile the magic ball led the hunter to a hut on chicken legs, the house of Baba Yaga. The witch first wanted to bake the hunter in the oven and eat him, but saw a handkerchief embroidered by her daughter. After the hunter told the witch that her daughter was his wife, she summoned all the beasts and birds to see if they knew how to 'go I know not where and bring back I know not what'. They did not. Then Baba Yaga went out to sea and summoned all the fish. Last of all to arrive was a limping frog who knew how to complete the task.

The frog carried the hunter across sea and land and brought him to a secret place where he met with an invisible magic force 'Shmat Razum' (which literally means a Gob of Mind).

Shmat Razum returned the hunter to the kingdom, and through a cunning trick gifted the hunter with a fleet of ships and an army. Upon arriving home Shmat Razum built a castle for the hunter and the hunter's wife returned to him. When the tsar discovered that the hunter had been 'where I know not where, brought back what I know not', had reunited with his wife and that they were now living in their own castle, he immediately ordered the army to go to the coast, burn the palace to the ground and execute the hunter and his wife. The hunter, however, summoned his fleet and the army and defeated the tsar. In a happy ending, the hunter was chosen to be the king of these lands and lived happily ever after.

Although there are significant differences between the versions of this fairy tale produced during the Soviet and post-Soviet periods, in all versions Baba Yaga is either shown in a humiliating manner or excluded from the screen completely. In the 1966 animation directed by the most authoritative figure of Soviet animation Ivanov-Vano, the figure of Baba Yaga is completely missing. The same is true of the most recent 2012 adaptation (dirs. Chervyatsov and Gazizov), while in the adaptation by the famous Soviet actor and writer Leonid Filatov, *Pro Fedota Streltsa Udalogo Molodtsa* (About Fedot-the-Shooter, the Fine Young Man, 2008), Baba Yaga is represented as a mean older woman obsessed with her appearance. It transpires that she had an affair with the king's general, and as the story unfolds she conspires with him to defeat the hunter, but fails. Baba Yaga is not portrayed in a way that mirrors her Soviet era counterpart from *Tsarevna Lyagushka* (The Frog Princess). Instead she is represented as a well-groomed older lady, manicured and made-up, wearing a short dress that matches her quirky head-band decorated with skulls. We also see photos of Baba Yaga when she was younger in which she resembles a model with accentuated breasts and an over the top, diva-style appearance.

Typically, in contemporary imagery she no longer has her youthful good looks (she therefore loses the only and most desirable option available in patriarchy − to be a sex/love object of

The Man). Even animals (over which she had total power in the original fairy tale) laugh at her. Though Baba Yaga comes up with devious plans to get rid of the hunter, she no longer has her magic powers. Neither does she engender respect from the film's heroes. Gone are the animalistic features, androgynous qualities, liminality and superpowers. It is disheartening that the film is directed by a woman.

This tendency to ridicule and devalue Baba Yaga in the second part of twentieth and beginning of the twenty-first centuries is also present in adaptations of other fairy tales, including *Tsarevna Lyagushka* (The Frog Princess, dir. Yelisseev, 1971), *Letuchii Korabl* (*Flying Ship*, dir. Bardin, 1979), *Dva Bogatyrya* (Two Strong Knights, dir. Davidov, 1989) and *Ivan Tsarevich i Seriy Volk* (Prince Ivan and the Grey Wolf, dir. Toropchin, 2011) to name a few. Tellingly, in *Prince Ivan and the Grey Wolf*, Baba Yaga trades her secret knowledge for a box of make-up, as if underlining society's ongoing obsession with maintaining the youthful appearance of women.

From Russia with love: Russian roots of individuation and the *anima/animus* dichotomy

Once again in an uroboric move we return to where we began – individuation. Since this chapter discusses Russian fairy tales, it is interesting to note a possibility, namely that the idea of individuation, as well as the contrasexual concepts of Jung's philosophy, are reminiscent of regressive Russian notions of the feminine. Recently a debate is taking place concerning Jung's Russian patient Sabina Spielrein and her influence on Jung's theory of individuation (Launer, 2015). Previous academic work has suggested that Spielrein might have provided Jung with the inspiration for his formulation of the contrasexual *anima* archetype (Carotenuto, 1982; Kerr, 1993). However, recently Spielrein's role in the development of Jung's thinking around the concept of the *anima* has been challenged by Launer (2015) who gained full access to the Spielrein Literary Estate in Russia and where he conducted extensive research on the subject. Launer notes that Spielrein, 'was preoccupied with the idea that she had a "higher calling" and that her life would only be fulfilled if she discovered what it was' (p. 190). This sense of responding to a personal higher calling, in which one lives life in an authentic and personal manner, does indeed sound somewhat like Jung's concept of individuation. (The core of the idea of which is to live as the people we are, as opposed to settling for what life turned us into.)

It is illuminating to note that the idea of both androgyny (as in the *anima/animus* archetypes) and also the concept of individuation has clear parallels in Russian philosophical thought of the nineteenth century and Russian fairy tales. While Spielrein was certainly on her own psychological journey, part of the cultural baggage she carried with her must have come from Russian philosophy, literature and mythology. She was an educated Russian woman from a well-to-do family who graduated with a golden medal (the equivalent of an honours diploma) from an elite high school in Rostov-on-Don, so there is always a strong possibility that she encountered the popular rhetoric of the period.

There have been a few attempts to draw parallels between Jung's ideas and Russian philosophy but none of them have examined Spielrein's role. For example Georg Nicolaus in his book on Berdyaev and Jung (2011) explored their different understanding of individuation, drawing parallels in the works of two male thinkers. The book did not mention Spielrein or her possible influence/involvement in the theory of individuation at all. This demonstrates how Spielrein continues to be marginalised in the history of the subject. It transpires that unfortunately Spielrein is a member of a large group of women whose scientific findings have variously been hidden and appropriated by male colleagues, or who have historically been dismissed. Of course it is nothing new, as Luce Irigaray (1981) would argue, Western patriarchy is based on a history of matricide. Somewhat similar to the fairy tale Baba Yaga (once a carrier of sacred knowledge and now a parody of femininity), Sabina Spielrein – a brilliant scientist and thinker – was stripped of her powers and downgraded to the status of the sex/love object of Jung.

Until recently Spielrein's work was largely forgotten, but was resurrected as part of the pre-existing conceptual frameworks of her male colleagues, Freud and Jung. It is equally unfortunate that the personal relationship between Spielrein and Jung has received more attention than her theoretical contributions to the development of psychoanalysis. Cinema, too, particularly David Cronenberg's *A Dangerous Method* (2011) has marginalised Spielrein's intellectual contribution by focusing on her sadomasochistic sexual relationship with Jung.

We have seen how liminality and androgyny operates in Russian fairy tales. Let us now briefly undertake an overview of how philosophy opens up the potential for a new perspective on the subject. Of course the constraints of this chapter do not allow for a full retrospective analysis of the parallels found in Jung's writing with Russian philosophy. This is speculative in nature, as one cannot actually prove or disprove if Spielrein deliberately informed Jung about the Russian philosophical developments of the nineteenth and twentieth centuries and what her views were on the subject. While some commentators consider Russian philosophy as reactionary and lacking originality (Berlin, 2008 [1948]), let us assume there was at least some merit and progressive thinking in the works of the best Russian minds of the time.

Importantly the question of gender became central in the writing of prominent Russian intellectuals in the nineteenth century. It seems almost every intellectual, every writer and every social activist debated the issue of femininity and women's position in society (Chernishevsky, Soloviev, Berdyaev, Leo Tolstoy and Dostoevsky to name but a few). The nineteenth century Russian intelligentsia was intensely interested in women and the feminine. As Riabov (1999) notes, the old idea of femininity in Russia was mainstream discourse (as in the works of Khomyakov, Herzen, Kavelin). The Russian messianic idea, and woman as a saviour (Dostoevsky), was another popular theme at the time. The female image was deeply bound to the idea of national identity in and through myth, archetype and romantic fantasy. These ideas continued to exercise their power during the following pre-revolutionary Silver Age and into the post-revolutionary period: as Costlow et al. note, 'Silver Age culture, ... is marked by the repudiation of the materialist ethos of the 1890s, and by the advent of unprecedented freedoms' (1993, p. 11).

Some thinkers of the nineteenth century can be considered forerunners of feminism. Chernyshevsky (1828–1889), in the last quarter of the nineteenth century was writing about the curse of gender division. He regarded the dominance of men as a source of all exploitation and injustice. In his view this could have been overcome through the abolishment of gender ascribed behaviour, when there would be just people, neither women nor men (Chernyshevsky, [1878] 1939–1953) (all translations of the abstracts are done by Nadi Fadina).

Most of the thinkers who argued about the feminine continued a discourse in terms of the already well-established paradigm of binary opposition and gender differentiation. Like their future Western 'counterparts' of the twentieth century (Freud and Jung, for example), most of the intellectual male elite adhered to the old traditions of gender differentiation and their male fantasies of femininity. For example, a famous Russian scientist Bakunin (1820–1900), wrote in 1881: 'In order to learn man kills life, and so he knows all the voices of death. Woman, in order to learn, lives and loves, and therefore, knows all the voices of life' (p. 391). It is important to underline that while being an active supporter of the abolition of social gender and inequality, Bakunin like many other male theorists saw the feminine as empty, fluid and volatile, making women strangers in the masculinised world of order and *Logos*.

These ideas are somewhat similar to the distinction that classical Jungian psychology used to make between *anima* and *animus*. Jung suggested a contrasexual principle in which the feminine side in men is composed of the *anima* and the masculine side in women the *animus*. He speculated that we are both drawn to and anxious about these contrasexual elements. We are attracted to them as they are important elements in our psychological growth yet we also distrust them as they are culturally transgressive. Less helpfully, Jung assigned certain qualities to 'anima possessed' men (overly moody and emotional), and 'animus possessed' women (overly intellectual and emotionally cold). In this formulation the thinking side of women is never in balance with her intellect. Similarly men's emotional lives are always out of kilter with their thinking. It also sets up an unfortunate dichotomy between body and mind, or psyche, which is actually not typical of Jung's somatic orientation. A more contemporary formulation would be to see the *anima* and *animus* as not directly linked to biological sex and instead offering ways of understanding human behaviour. Unfortunately Jung adopted a more essentialist approach. His helpful insight is that regardless of gender, we all have access to a full range of human emotions, capabilities and functions. However in ascribing them with either a female or male principle he was reductive and limiting.

Returning to Russian philosophy, there was another popular trend at the time. At the end of the nineteenth and the beginning of the twentieth centuries there was also a tendency to aspire to an ideal unity of both genders – androgyny. Soloviev in *Plato's Drama of Life* in 1898, argued that the true fullness of a human's ideal personality cannot be only man or woman, but should be the result of a unity of both. In the early twentieth century another famous Russian thinker, Berdyaev (1916), supported the idea of androgyny in his work *The Meaning of the Creative Act*, looking at the concept of human transformation based on the idea of the androgyne. While Hellenic thinking naturally influenced Jung's ideas of an androgynous unconscious – the *anima* and *animus* – it also strikingly coincides, and correlates, with the Russian philosophical thought of the nineteenth century.

These attempts to challenge a long-standing tradition and patriarchal order could have been considered progressive, but they have binary opposition at their core and cannot be considered as pro-feminist (Fadina, 2015). The same holds for Jung's theory of contrasexuality, which he was developing at roughly the same time. As Costlow *et al.* note, 'The accounts of Karlinsky and Berdyaev shape familiar oppositions (familiar, one notes, not only in Russia): of body versus spirit, of celebration versus repression, of homosexuality versus heterosexual love' (1993, p. 11).

The preceding brief overview of the epoch that Sabina Spielrein was born into makes it tempting to redress this imbalance and to speculate that she brought the core ideas of androgyny, *animus/anima* dichotomy and individuation to Jung. Indeed the suggestion of this chapter is that Spielrein's Russian origins, her cultural heritage partially composed from the narrative and philosophical contexts in which she was educated, like Ariadne's thread, offer a guide through this cultural labyrinth to the origin of the idea of individuation and the contrasexual aspects of Jung's theories.

Conclusion

It is important to underline that historically fairy tales have played a significant role in humanity's discourses and practices and so were integral to social and ideological ways of thinking. Today audiences are more likely to see fairy tales as entertainment and naive stories for children, rather than vehicles for adult insight. Meanwhile, as scholars of fairy tales have pointed out, these same stories and their mediated adaptations walk hand-in-hand with our psychological identities, sense of gender, ethnicity, class and sexuality. Jungians and post-Jungians have also made significant progress in understanding how Jung's ideas on the androgynous nature of the unconscious and the process of individuation are inextricably linked to cultural products and artefacts; however, there is still progress to be made on how exactly Jung's theories of individuation have been influenced.

Post-Jungian approaches continue to explore the ways that all of us can experience the full range of emotions, regardless of our biological sex. This insight into the inclusivity of gender is of enormous value in our quest to better understand both our psychological selves and also our relationship with screen media.

While Jungian thought is at times flawed particularly in the way it tends towards an essentialism that emphasises difference in gender, this can be remediated by considering the concepts around androgyny and sexual identity that were pioneered in the nineteenth and early twentieth century through Russian philosophy and the influence of Jung's Russian patient Sabina Spielrein. This is a two-edged sword, for while it normalises many of Jung's theoretical elaborations, it also renders them less novel and innovative. Nonetheless, post-Jungian writing on sexuality is a useful tool for film research (and maybe sometimes even a magic wand) with which to transform our understanding of the critical approaches to film and fairy tale analysis. It also offers a means to turn them into something that is at the same time remarkably old and fascinatingly new.

The analysis of Baba Yaga both in its ancient form and on-screen representation, helps us to reflect on regressive screen gender representations that were and still are taking place today. It raises questions as to what 'fairy tales' (including the fairy tale of gender) should we tell ourselves and listen to? What does the rejection and disintegration of the all-powerful and liminal female figure of Baba Yaga tell us about ourselves, and what we reject in ourselves and in society?

To answer these questions it is important to understand the psychological dynamics of liminal space and time, as well as the liminal characters themselves as they appear in myth and fairy tale; both factors are instrumental in initiating the transformational change process, which by definition happen at the deeper levels of self-identity. Such archetypal liminality in Slavic fairy tales draws attention to who we are and where we are going. It questions what spaces are being left and which ones are being entered. By identifying these elements it is possible to work with archetypal processes and figures, and in so doing create new possibilities for ourselves. We might take our cue from the fairy tale figures as we cross the threshold to the mysterious, unknown and unexplored terrain of human potential.

References

Aarne, A. and Thompson, S. (1961) *Types of folktale: a classification and bibliography*. Helsinki: Academia Scientarum Fennica.

Addison, E. (1993) 'Saving other women from other men: Disney's Aladdin', *Camera Obscura*, January/May, 11, pp. 4–25.

Anderson, G. (2000) *Fairytale in the ancient world*. London: Routledge.

Bacchilega, C. (1997) *Postmodern fairytales: gender and narrative strategies*. Philadelphia, PA: University of Pennsylvania Press.

Baker-Sperry, L. (2007) 'The production of meaning through peer interaction: children and Walt Disney's Cinderella', *Sex Roles*, 56(11/12), pp. 717–27.

Bakunin, P. (1881) *Zapazdalyi Golos Sorokovikh Godov: (Po povodu zhenskogo voprosa)* (A belated voice of '40s: about women's question). St Petersburg.

Barthes, R. (2009 [1957]) *Mythologies*. London: Vintage.

Bell, E., Haas, L. and Sells, L. (eds) (1995) *From mouse to mermaid: the politics of film, gender and culture*. Bloomington, IN: Indiana University Press.

Berdyaev, N. (1916) *Smysl Tvorchestva: Opyt Opravdanya Cheloveka* (The meaning of the creative act: experience of discharging a human being). Moscow: Izdatelstvo G. A. Lemana i S. I. Sakharova.

Berlin, I. (2008 [1948]) *Russian thinkers*. London: Penguin Group.

Bettelheim, B. (1976) *The uses of enchantment: the meaning and importance of fairytales*. New York: Knopf.

Bottigheimer, R. B. (1987a) *Grimm's bad girls and bold boys: the moral and social vision of the tales*. New Haven, CT: Yale University Press.

Bottigheimer, R. B. (ed.) (1987b) *Fairy tales and society: illusion, allusion and paradigm*. Philadelphia, PA: University of Pennsylvania Press.

Bottigheimer, R. B. (2009) *Fairy tales: a new history*. Albany, NY: State University of New York Press.

Campbell, J. (2008 [1949]) *The hero with thousand faces*. Novato, CA: New World Library.

Carotenuto, A. (1982) *A secret symmetry: Sabina Spielrein between Jung and Freud*. New York: Random House.

Chernyshevsky, N. (1939–1953 [1878]) 'Pismo Pypinoi [25 fevr. 1878]', in *Polnoe sobranye Sochinenii*, in 15 volumes, vol. 15 (Letter to Pupina in collection of writings). Moscow.

Costlow, J. T., Sadler, S. and Vowels, J. (eds) (1993) *Sexuality and the body in Russian culture*. Stanford, CA: Stanford University Press.

Eliade, M. (1963) *Myth and reality*, trans. W. Trask. New York: Harper & Row.

Fadina, N. (2015) 'The second loss of androgyny: the fairytale of dualism', in L. Hockley and N. Fadina (eds), *Happiness illusion: how the media sold us a fairytale*. London: Routledge. pp. 50–70.

Fleming, A. (1969) 'The myth of the Mother-Goddess', *World Archaeology*, 1(2), Techniques of Chronology and Excavation (October), pp. 247–61.

Freud, S. (1997 [1900]) *The interpretation of dreams*. Ware, UK: Wordsworth Editions Ltd.

Gennep, A. (1960 [1909]) *The rites of passage*. Chicago, IL: University of Chicago Press.

Gere, C. (2009) *Knossos and the prophets of modernism*. Chicago, IL: University of Chicago Press.

Gilbert, S. M. and Gubar, S. (1979) *The madwoman in the attic: the woman writer and the nineteenth-century literary imagination*. New Haven, CT: Yale University Press.

Gilbert, S. M. and Gubar, S. (1987) 'The queen's looking glass', in J. Zipes (ed.), *Don't bet on the prince*. New York: Routledge. pp. 201–8.

Haney, J. (1999) *An introduction to the Russian folktale*. Armonk, NY: M. E. Sharpe.

Hockley, L. (2015) 'Snow White and the huntsman: the fairytale of gender and the female warrior', in L. Hockley and N. Fadina (eds), *The happiness illusion: how the media sold us a fairytale*. London: Routledge. pp. 33–49.

Hubbs, J. (1988) *Mother Russia: the feminine myth in Russian culture*. Bloomington and Indianapolis, IN: Indiana University Press.

Irigaray, L. (1981) *Le corps-à-corps avec la mere*. Montréal: Les Editions de la pleine lune.

Jacobson, R. (1966) *Selected writings*, vol. 4. The Hague and Paris: Mouton.

Johns, A. (2004) *Baba Yaga: the ambiguous mother witch of the Russian folk tale*. New York: Peter Lang Publishing Inc.

Jung, C. G. (1959) 'The phenomenology of the trickster in fairytales', in *The collected works of C. G. Jung*, Vol. 9i. *Archetypes and the collective unconscious*, 2nd edn. London: Routledge, 1968.

Kerr, J. (1993) *A most dangerous method: the story of Jung, Freud, and Sabina Spielrein*. New York: Alfred A. Knops.

Launer, J. (2015) 'Carl Jung's relationship with Sabina Spielrein: a reassessment', *International Journal of Jungian Studies*, 7(3), pp. 179–93.

Leeming, D. (ed.) (1997) *Storytelling encyclopedia: historical, cultural and multiethnic approaches to oral traditions around the world*. Phoenix, AZ: Orix Press.

Lévi-Strauss, C. (1969) *Mythologiques*, in 4 volumes, vol. 1: *The raw and the cooked*, trans. J. Weightman and D. Weightman. London: J. Cape.

Lévi-Strauss, C. (1989 [1978]) *Myth and meaning*. London: Routledge.

Lieberman, M. R. (1972) 'Some day my prince will come: female acculturation through the fairytale', *College English*, 34(3), pp. 383–95.

Lüthi, M. (1974) *The European folktale: form and nature*, trans. J. D. Niles. Bloomington, IN: Indiana University Press.

Lüthi, M. (1979) *Once upon a time: on the nature of fairytales*. Bloomington, IN: Indiana University Press.

McVey, D. (2011) 'And they lived queerly ever after: disrupting heteronormativity with Russian fairy tales', *Queer Scope*, 2, pp. 17–29.

Nicolaus, G. (2011) *C. G. Jung and Nikolai Berdyaev: individuation and the person: a critical comparison*. New York: Routledge.

Nikiforov, A. (1938) *Zhanry Russkoi skazki* (Genres of Russian fairytale). St Petersburg: Uchen.zap. Leningradskogo GPU imeni M.N.Pokrovskogo.

Propp, V. (1968 [1928]) *Morfologia Skazki* (Morphology of folk tale). Austin, TX: University of Texas.

Propp, V. (2004 [1946]) *Istoricheskie Korni Volshebnoi Skazki* (Historical roots of magical fairytale). Moskva: Labirint.

Riabov, O. (1999) *Russkaia Filosofia Zhenstvennosti XI–XX veka* (Russian philosophy of femininity). Ivanovo: Yunona.

Rowe, K. (1979) 'Feminism and fairytales', *Women's Studies: An Interdisciplinary Journal*, 6, pp. 237–57.

Rowland, S. (2002) *Jung: a feminist revision*. Cambridge: Polity Press.

Soloviev, V. S. (1898 [1988]) *Zhiznennaya drama Platona* (Plato's drama of life). Moscow: Mysl'.

Stein, M. and Corbett, L. (1995) *Psyche's stories: modern Jungian interpretations of fairy tales*. Asheville, NC: Chiron Publications.

Turner, V. (1967) *The forest of symbols: aspects of Ndembu ritual*. Ithaca, NY: Cornell University Press.

Turner, V. (1974) *Dramas, fields, and metaphors: symbolic action in human society*. Ithaca, NY: Cornell University Press.

Ucko, P. J. (1968) 'Anthropomorphic figurines of predynastic Egypt and neolithic Crete, with comparative material from the prehistoric Near East and mainland Greece', in *Royal Anthropological Institute Occasional Papers*, 24. London: Andrew Szmidla. pp. 68–9.

von Franz, M. L. (1970) *An introduction to the psychology of fairytales*. New York: Spring.

von Franz, M. L. (1972) *Problems of the feminine in fairytales*. Dallas, TX: Spring Publications.

von Franz, M. L. (1993) *The feminine in fairytales*. Boston, MA: Shambhala.

von Franz, M. L. (1996) *The interpretation of fairytales*, revd edn. Boston, MA: Shambhala.

Warner, E. (2002) *Russian myths*. London: British Museum Press.

Warner, M. (2014) *Once upon a time: a brief history of fairy tale*. Oxford: Oxford University Press.

Wehr, D. S. (1997) *Jung and feminism: liberating archetypes*. New York: Routledge.

Ziolkowski, J. (2010) *Fairy tales from before fairy tales: the Medieval Latin past of wonderful lies*. Ann Arbour, MI: University of Michigan Press.

Zipes, J. (1979) *Breaking the magic spell: radical theories of folklore and fairytales*. London: Heinemann.

Zipes, J. (1983) *Fairy tales and the art of subversion: the classical genre for children and the process of civilization*. New York: Wildman Press.

Zipes, J. (ed.) (1986) *Don't bet on the prince: contemporary feminist fairytales in North America and England*. Aldershot, UK: Gower Publishing Company Ltd.

Zipes, J. (ed.) (1991) *Spells of enchantment: the wondrous fairy tales of western culture*. New York: Vikings.

Zipes, J. (1994) *Fairytale as myth/myth as fairytale*. Lexington, KY: University Press of Kentucky.

Zipes, J. (1995) 'Breaking the Disney spell', in E. Bell, L. Haas and L. Sells (eds), *From mouse to mermaid: the politics of film, gender and culture*. Bloomington, IN: Indiana University Press. pp. 21–43.

Zipes, J. (1997) *Happily ever after: fairytales, children, and the culture industry*. New York: Routledge.

Zipes, J. (ed.) (2000) *The Oxford companion to fairytales: the western tradition from medieval to modern*. Oxford: Oxford University Press.

Zipes, J. (2006) *Fairytales and the art of subversion: the classical genre for children and the process of civilization*. New York: Wildman Press.

Zipes, J. (2012) *The irresistible fairytale: the cultural and social history of a genre*. Princeton, NJ: Princeton University Press.

Online source

Barolini, T. (2015) '*Paradiso 33: invisible ink*', Commento Baroliniano, Digital Dante. Center for Digital Research and Scholarship. New York: Columbia University Libraries [online]. Available at: http://digitaldante.columbia.edu/dante/divine-comedy/paradiso/paradiso-33/ [Accessed 28 November 2016].

Filmography

Dangerous method, A. (2011) [film] Directed by David Cronenberg. UK/Canada.

Dva Bogatyrya (Two strong knights). (1989) [animation] Directed by A. Davidov. Russia.

Ivan Tsarevich i Seriy Volk (Prince Ivan and the Grey Wolf). (2011) [animation] Directed by V. Toropchin. Russia.

Letuchii Korabl (Flying ship). (1979) [animation] Directed by G. Bardin. Russia.

Poidi Tuda, Ne Znayu Kuda – Mashini Skazki (Masha's fairy tales, go I don't know where). (2012) [animation series] Directed by R. Gazizov and D. Chervyatsov. Russia.

Poidi Tuda, Ne Znayu Kuda (Go there I don't know where). (1966) [animation] Directed by I. Ivanov-Vano and V. Danilevich. Russia.

Pro Fedota Streltsa Udalogo Molodtsa (About Fedot-the-shooter, the fine young man). (2008) [animation] Directed by L. Steblyanko. Russia.

Tsarevna Lyagushka (The frog princess). (1954) [animation] Directed by M. Tsekhanovsky. Russia.

Tsarevna Lyagushka (The frog princess). (1971) [animation] Directed by Yu. Yelisseyev. Russia.

PART IV

Clinical approaches

Luke Hockley

23

FEELING FILM

Time, space and the third image

Luke Hockley

Introduction

The first two words of this chapter's title take us to the heart of the phenomenology of the cinematic experience. When writing about 'feeling film' there is an ambiguity in what is meant and this lack of certainty around meaning itself will prove to be central to the argument as it unfolds. The sticky question of meaning and where it resides along with its role and function in the cinema, and indeed in the consulting room too, adheres to this argument as indeed it does to much of this book as a whole. Does 'feeling film' mean to engage and apprehend the physical stuff itself in a tactile manner, as a substance in our hands, as though we were editing the traditional celluloid material? Or perhaps it is that we have an intensified experience of the surface textures of the cinema. We notice its screen, seats, décor and lighting as we experience the contrast between foyer and auditorium. We become aware of the tactility of ticket booths, the food concessions and how the smell of musty popcorn contrasts with the subdued lighting and the racked comfortable seating of the theatre itself. The implicit movement from one psychological space to another imprints on our bodies that we have entered an area that is different from the quotidian geography of the everyday world. We feel differently, even as we enter the cinema.

Or does 'feeling film' mean we have an emotional reaction to the films we watch? Certainly there are films that cause us to feel, to have emotional reactions to their images and sounds. Certainly films set out with all the artifice of the seductive look, the sly eye or the visceral thump in the gut to engage us. Looked for or not, the emotional is always present in the cinema. Yet, cinema is not always so overly flirtatious. Oftentimes feelings sneak up on us unexpectedly. Before we know it we are happily, sadly and yet inevitably in love with a film. Such seduction is what brings us back to the cinema repeatedly, evening after evening. We hope that in some way we will learn and gain insight from this relationship as we find ourselves not just 'looking for the heart of a Saturday night' (Waits, 1989) but for some heart-felt insight into how we are in the world.

Finally does the film itself feel? It seems unlikely. Yet with Sobchack (1992, 2004), Marks (2000) and Shaviro's (1993) work in mind, is there a sense in which the film body 'feels', that in some way the film itself responds emotionally as a reaction to our own emotions? Is it possible the film body when in relationship with the body of its viewers reacts, almost as a lover? Psychological therapists know that one of the ways that it is possible to build empathy with clients is through what is referred to as 'therapeutic attunement' – the aligning and adjustment of oneself, psychologically and physically with the other person. Perhaps too the interplay between the feelings in the body of the film and the feelings of its viewers are in a state of flux, and the complex matrix of that relationship is much more unpredictable, intimate and unstable than is often assumed.

So here we have it. The question is whether this chapter is concerned with the tactility of the filmic experience, or the emotional reaction to the films we watch, or the relationship between our bodies and the body of the films themselves? The answer is that feeling is significant because it is simultaneously all these individual elements and also a composite of them – this what I term 'The Third Image' – not the image on the screen, not the images in our interpretative imagination, but a third image that somehow comes to occupy the space between viewer and screen as we enter into a relationship with the film itself. This is the cinematic psychological corpus, the body of meaning, this chapter will explore. To do so we start not with a phenomenological encounter, though it is in part that, but with the writings of Henri Bergson and, in particular, the section in his 1911 work *Creative Evolution* headed 'The cinematographic mechanism of thought and the mechanistic illusion'. We will return to more obviously phenomenological concerns, and some structural matters, later.

Background

To set the scene, in 1899 Sigmund Freud published *The Interpretation of Dreams*, where he famously set out the mechanisms of dream work and the need of the psyche to disguise the true sexual meanings of its nocturnal fantasies. The mechanism of repression and the emphasis on childhood and its oedipal drama meant that while a dynamic psychology the optic orientation of Freud's thinking work was backwards. It was by looking through and into dreams, and indeed other somatic activities, that it was possible to see their origins in the early years of life. Meanwhile, Carl Jung had met with Freud in 1907 while he was working on *The Psychology of Dementia Praecox* and in 1910 he published *The Symbols of Transformation*, just three years before his split with Freud. In contrast to Freud, Jung's psychological look was to the future. While acknowledging the importance of one's life experiences he came to regard the psyche as fundamentally teleological. Thus a symbol was only a symbol so long as it contained the psychological germ of some future insight. At the moment of understanding the flower blooms while the symbol itself withers.

If Freud had one eye on the past, and Jung on the future, then Bergson was clearly focused on the present. His concern was with what it means to 'be' in the moment. Here it is possible to discern a hint of what will later morph into the rather different viewpoints of existentialism and phenomenology. That said, Bergson chooses not to write about 'being' (as both existentialism and phenomenology would) and instead opts for the term 'duration' (or in the original French, *durée*). It follows for Bergson what he is interested in is the combination of consciousness and time as it is the conscious experience of time and awareness that is encapsulated by *durée*. As we will see, Bergson argues that duration makes itself known through a series of images, each of which offers only a part of the whole. The entire picture itself, as it were, cannot be grasped by consciousness, or the rational mind alone. A complete sense of the present moment requires intuition and creativity. Even so the complexity and changing nature of duration means that it can never be fully understood or comprehended.

It might already be apparent that there are some points of contact here with Freud and Jung's psychoanalytic formulations of the self and consciousness. Freud regarded the events of an individual's life as a series of pictures, if you will, that built sequentially to form a composite of an entire life in the present moment. For neurotic patients, this expressed itself in a particular image or symbolic mode of behaviour (a perversion) the meaning of which was unavailable to the patient's conscious mind. Understanding its meaning required the creative engagement of the analyst in disassembling the composite into its individual life events. By contrast Jung regarded the symbolic image as the best possible encapsulation of the present. Like Bergson, he thought its meaning could not be grasped by the conscious mind. Unlike Bergson, Jung looked beyond the present as for him everything psychological is part of a life-long psychological parabolic trajectory under whose penumbra life is lived. Bergson's conception of image is somewhat different. Understanding it is important in order to see what it can add to and differentiate from Jung's ideas about image, and also because the ideas provide two of the pillars for Deleuze's writing on cinema, namely the movement-image and the time-image.

Bergson and time

The first part of Bergson's argument is concerned with 'nothing' – a state which he reasons cannot exist (1911, p. 294). He postulates it cannot exist because the body is always engaged in the act of perception as it registers the existence of external events in the world. If such stimulation is removed then perception shifts to the internal world and its thought processes. It follows for Bergson that there is always something, either from without or within the body and this constant state of perception is perceived by the body as a dynamic condition in which it is constantly coming into being. As Bergson observes, 'Matter or mind, reality has appeared to us as a perpetual becoming. It makes itself or it unmakes itself, but it is never something made' (p. 287).

For Bergson this understanding is central to his larger project which is the search for a 'philosophy more nearly approaching intuition' (ibid., p. 293). Intuition here is important as it is only by and through intuition that the flux of coming into being in the present moment (*durée*) can be apprehended. Even then such apprehension will only be partial for when the conscious mind freeze frames the present moment the image is jolted out of the flux of *durée* and loses its rich unknowable sense of being in the present.

Bergson seeks to illustrate this idea through the metaphor of the cinematic apparatus. It is unfortunate that this has frequently led to a mistaken view of Bergson's opinion of cinema as a mechanistic and psychologically impoverished medium. Notwithstanding, Bergson argues that cinema is a good example of a failed attempt to achieve *durée*. He observes that films are composed from a series of still images, which when one follows the other provides the illusion of movement. The frames never interpenetrate one with the other and instead offer only the illusion of coming together. In so doing they create a sense of meaning in the present moment. For Bergson this illustrates how the rational and conscious mind attempts to understand the world. It appears to have a full and good understanding of the conditions of being; actually it is an impoverished understanding because it fails to comprehend the flux of *durée* and its essential unknowableness as past interpenetrates the present from second to second. Cinema offers only a partial view of the world because it is a composite of still images that have been extracted from the flow of *durée*. As Bergson puts it, cinema fails to acknowledge the imminence of the past in the present.

This point is going to be important as it will show how this idea of constantly coming into being in the present moment can help to understand one aspect of the 'cinematic condition' that we enter into when we engage in the activity of watching a film. I will be arguing that this is akin to the 'psychotherapeutic condition' in which therapist and patient are likewise engaged in a fluid process of coming into being and in which both enter into a unconscious yet transformative flux. For Bergson this fluid state is *durée* and it demands the active engagement of our creativity. In a somewhat similar vein, Jung sees the life-long process of psychological development that he termed individuation as something that likewise cannot be grasped by just the intellect. As with Bergson, Jung too asserts that to be fully the people we are and to fully realise our potential to 'be' we need to deploy our intuition. Where Jung parts company with Bergson is in the role that the unconscious plays in the process of being: for Bergson the idea of a structuring core in the psyche is superfluous, while for Jung it is crucial.

When it comes to the key concepts that we have just encountered, 'intellect' and 'intuition', Jung and Bergson have somewhat different views. We will start with Bergson who sets up an epistemological dualism between the two ideas. He uses the term 'intellect' to refer to the way that we understand the state of inert objects as immobile and static, from which it follows that their state of being is no less fixed. Significantly for Bergson the cinema falls into that category of being, as the appearance of movement (of flux or fluidity) is created by the passage of what are a series of still images. By contrast 'intuition' is the true flux of reality as it is the coming into being that arises from movement and change – this is the state of *durée*. Unlike the intellect, it does not require conscious awareness. For example, objects in nature such as plants or trees are in a state of flux, of change and growth. As such they are in *durée* but clearly they are not consciously aware of themselves.

Similarly for Bergson 'Real Time' is equivalent to *durée* as it flows. Significantly such real time is different from objective or scientific time. Such mechanical time (as measured by clocks, for example) is not part of *durée* as the seconds proceed one after the other and, crucially, they do not interpenetrate each other. Scientific time marches on but it does not flow as it cannot merge the past with the present. *Durée* on the other hand is subjective. It requires the diminution of the intellect and immersion in intuition. As Bergson notes, 'It is no use trying to approach duration: we must install ourselves within it straight away. This is what the intellect generally refuses to do' (1911, p. 315). The idea is reminiscent of Jung's assertion that:

> We must be able to let things happen in the psyche. For us, this is an act of which most people know nothing. Consciousness is forever interfering, helping, correcting, and negating, never leaving the psychic processes to grow in peace. It would be simple enough, if only simplicity were not the most difficult of all things.
>
> *(1929: §20)*

Bergson and image

To recap, Bergson uses the metaphor of the cinematographic apparatus to provide an illustration of how the intellect apprehends reality, namely one frame at time, as it were. Had Bergson undertaken a different project, namely to examine watching films in light of his arguments about images and their flow in *durée*, then he would have presented a rather different commentary on the cinema. However he did not, and for him film is a good example of what constitutes 'intelligence', conscious apprehension and more generally the rational mind making sense of the world. Essential certainly, but equally it is insufficient, as it serves to reconstruct reality rather than to enter into it. As Bergson puts it: 'Instead of attaching ourselves to the inner becoming of things, we place ourselves outside them in order to recompose their becoming artificially … *the mechanism of our ordinary knowledge is of a cinematographical kind*' (1911, pp. 322–3, emphasis in original).

It is worth pointing out that for Bergson the same problem exists with other artistic media, for example music. In Bergson's terms music is not in flow, but in fact is composed from a series of individual notes – horizontally in melody and vertically for harmony. The two structures are combined in various ways and in so doing give the illusion of progression or flow. Crucially they do not constitute *durée*. It follows that music, like film, fails to interpenetrate consciousness and requires the engagement of rationality. In this sense, it follows that film music is a willing accomplice with the cinematic screen in keeping us out of *durée*. One concern with Bergson's argument is it fails to adequately account for the emotional experiences we undoubtedly experience when watching films or indeed when listening to music. Quite clearly, such feelings are not fully explained by deploying rational consciousness, even in Bergson's particular definition. Here Jung's conception of the image will be of great help in articulating the ways in which emotions and images can be bound together. As will become clear, the Third Image offers a particular somatic example of how *durée* can be experienced in both the cinema and in therapy, and while listening to music for that matter.

Deleuze and image

Interestingly Deleuze in *Cinema 1* and *Cinema 2* (2005) takes his cue from Bergson but argues against Bergson's assertion that cinema should not be understood as a series of still images. It is important to notice what has happened here. Deleuze on the one hand takes Bergson's commentary as in part passing judgement on cinema, while on the other he offers up a taxonomy that can be applied to cinema. Both are problematic as rendered by Deleuze, although there remains another way Bergson can be of use in providing a fresh perspective on space and time, both in therapy and for an understanding of the cinema. As we have seen, Bergson used one of the mechanisms of cinema (its physical existence as series of separate images on a strip of celluloid) to illustrate his concept of what was in *durée* and what remained outside that state. That is significantly different from asserting something about the nature of cinema. Deleuze is aware of this distinction and uses it to assist in his formulation of the movement-image. This idea suggests that it is the continuity of movement that defines the whole. (The concept as applied to cinema in itself marks a new twentieth century rendering of Zeno's arrow.) As illustrated by Deleuze, cinema offers specific and numerous examples of the movement-image. To be clear, Deleuze acknowledges that Bergson was not studying cinema itself, and so has to work hard to connect up his own ideas about the status of the image in cinema with Bergson's formulations. However, as we will argue, Deleuze would have been well advised to bypass the cinematic image as used by Bergson and to move more directly to his more potent concept of *durée*. In other words, unlike Deleuze, we will avoid the illustration and instead focus on the process.

That said, what Deleuze does take successfully from Bergson is his taxonomy of image: the perception-image, the affection-image and the action-image. In Bergson's formulation, it is perceptions that cause affects, which in turn lead to actions. For Deleuze this illuminates the movement-image of the cinema. In practice, what intervenes between affect and action is memory and it is this that Bergson refers to as a series of 'conditions' that provide automatic connections to the present. For example, I know how to play the piano and I remember it. However, another less automatic response concerns memory that is evoked by the act of remembering. Clearly at any one time we do not remember all the events of our life, as the present intervenes in the act of selection and editing. The closest we get to a sense of a total set of life memories is when we are dreaming. Here, anticipated or not, consciously remembered or not, events from our past emerge once more in our dreams. So too in the cinema our consciousness fades as we find ourselves entering the cinematic condition that enables seemingly forgotten memories to be experienced. I want to suggest that to experience such acts of unlooked for recall is actually to enter the state of *durée*. Further, that being in *durée* is a precondition for the creation of the Third Image – in this way, when watching a film the present is indeed pregnant with the past.

Deleuze goes on to argue in *Cinema 2* that movement is subordinate to time. While cinema does of course move, both the material of film itself and the resultant images on screen, these are subsumed by the flow of time. (In the digital age we might wish to think of the movement of pixels as they alternate between their on and off states.) The movement-image is the ability to sense the world as it changes, while the time-image is concerned with subjectivity, reflection and questioning. For Deleuze the movement-image characterises cinema before the Second World War, while the time-image typifies the cinema that followed. Deleuze was interested in how film, first, puts movement into our mind and, second, how the time-image comes to alter our perceptions of ourselves and by extension the world. In distinction to Bergson's image of cinema as a series of still images, Deleuze sees our perception as fused into the film itself, as encapsulated in time. If Bergson uses a cinematic metaphor to explain *durée*, Deleuze sees cinema as a reality that alters our perception. It follows for him in our minds, even when a film has finished or is paused, we complete the act of movement, as it is though we need to stick with it and in so doing we continue the forward propulsion of the 'movement-image'.

At this point it seems right to reposition Bergson and bring him back into the fold of cinematic thinking. As argued above, Bergson was not writing about cinema itself and was instead using the mechanics of cinema to illustrate a philosophical point. If cinema had been his interest he would surely have dwelt more fully on the act of perception rather than the materiality of the cinematic apparatus. Had he switched track to focus on the viewer, then he would have seen that the state one enters into while watching a film (the cinematic condition) has numerous points of similarity with the fluid state of *durée*. To develop this point it is interesting to note how films often blur the difference between reality and dream, or hallucination. Christian Metz went so far as to characterise cinema as more powerful than dreams as it manages to delude its viewers while they are still awake (1977). A slightly different take is offered by Deleuze who explores the ways cinema blurs reality through both the movement and time images, or as Bergson might have said, though he did not, through *durée*.

It would be misleading to suggest that all films at all times allow for, or facilitate entry into, *durée*. Though I am towards the end of the chapter going to suggest that the entry into *durée* while sometimes facilitated by the formal properties of cinema is also a result of the interaction between personal unconscious complexes with the images and sounds of films. Here it is helpful to draw on Deleuze's reformulation of some Bergsonian derived ideas. In particular the movement-image and the time-image. Deleuze is intrigued by the way that certain sequences in films slip between different types of time: between Scientific Time, and Real Time, as Bergson might have it. Many of the examples he uses are taken from European 'Art house' cinema which indeed is replete with such examples.

However, mainstream films also offer slipways into *durée*. Further, it is worth noting that contrary to the suggestion made by Bergson about the qualities of the static image, actually still images do encapsulate both time and movement. While in one sense these are indeed frozen there is another more meaningful way in which still images also contain the implication of past movement (what has happened leading up to the moment the image was taken) and future movement – what might happen after the moment depicted in the image. Such movements, into which the image intervenes, apply to both the moment that is recorded and also to the subjectivity of the photographer, the moments before and after the press of the shutter or the start and end of cinematographic take. In this way, the creative act is the result of the interaction between form and subjectivity.

Deleuze extends this to examine the formal properties of the images themselves and how such devices as deep focus cinematography constitute elements of the time-image. He observes how the cinematic technique in which some characters at the back of the image are kept in sharp focus along with those in its foreground, indicates a certain sense of temporality in space. This echoes Bergson's image of the inverted cone, whose tip is in the present moment and whose gradually thickening base forms the layers of memories that come from the past. It is also richly suggestive of the ways in which our previous cinema going experiences come to inform any given viewing of a film. As Bergson might put it: the past is always there in the present, and the present image also contains its past. In other words, the present is always splitting. So too in the cinema we need both our previous experiences of films, our expectations, and we also need to let them go. A genre film is in part comprehensible because we have learnt its syntax and structure, and this type of literacy once acquired over years makes the viewing experience meaningful. But it also enables us to let it go, and to allow our own psyche to interact with the film and in so doing to enter into a non-rational but meaningful relationship with the film. As viewers we bring our experiences to bear on the current film, locating it within a broad discourse of similar films. In other words, we create a type of family of films, a genus or genre, which requires a systemic set of relationships to create a field within which to generate a hermeneutic set of meanings (c.f. Izod and Dovalis, 2015).

So too in therapy we need to understand the ways in which our life patterns repeat themselves. This becomes embodied in the therapeutic relationship and once experienced and understood it becomes possible to let that relationship go as we enter into a state of 'being' who we are, less confined by past behaviours. Such breaks are not without their pain, and as changes happen in therapy they also manifest themselves in relationships outside the consulting room. While in therapy erratic behaviour and non-rational feelings are part and parcel of the daily work, when they impact on actual relationships they can be destructive, bizarre and frightening. So too in the cinema, the emotional relationship we have with films can be perplexing to others, appearing as it is, to be irrational. However, in therapy, cinema and personal life all is not lost for if the ego-strength of all involved is strong enough such dark and frightening events in life offer the potential to transform unconscious material into conscious insight, though often at some cost.

The emotional effect of entering into *durée* as it is experienced in the cinema is certainly not confined to rarefied films and is actually more pervasive than is often assumed. Indeed, its ubiquity is one of the reasons that popular cinema continues to be an enduring and psychologically rich medium. As examined by Deleuze (*Cinema 2, pp.* 58–60) a good example of this is offered by the film genre of the musical. Take a moment to consider those points in a film when a character leaves the 'real world' of the film and enters a state of reverie. It is significant that the exact point of such a transition (from the world of the intellect in the film to *durée*) is often unclear. Deleuze analyses the well known scene in *Singin' in the Rain* (1952) when after giving Kathy (Debbie Reynolds) a goodnight kiss Don Lockwood (Gene Kelly) performs the famous song and dance sequence from which the film takes its title. Of interest here is the problem of exactly when it is that Don leaves the world of the rain-drenched sidewalk and enters into the fantasy of singin' and dancing in the rain. Of course, it is not clear, as the one slips into the other. To make this transition is to make the transition from walking to dancing, it is to move from intellect to intuition and it is to shift from mind to body – this is the blurred sense of entering *durée*.

To elaborate, the point here is surely that cinema is both in and outside *durée* and can be so at the same time. The image that Bergson offers for this duality is of a crystal in supersaturated solution. The 'past' liquid is in a condition of coming into being in the present, in the form of its crystal state. This is *durée*. Liquid and solid – *durée* is a crystalline image. In the cinema too the past is in the processes of crystallising in the present moment, both the past of the film (other films that have gone before it) and the past within the film, which exists in the narrative life of its characters. So too as viewers, our past life experiences, include our film viewing history, is both liquid and crystal as we are psychologically suspended in the unconscious fluidity of the present moment.

There are then several different types of past at play here. The first concerns the life of the characters off screen – what happens to them in their fictional worlds while not on the screen? What too of their lives before the narrative start of the film and after its ending. These phantasmal thoughts open a way for the spectoral images of cinema to have at least an implied existence outside the frame of the film. However, and crucially, to do so they need the viewer or spectator, for it is the act of looking into the film that gives its characters spirit – it brings them together as spectator and film are brought to life. This again is to enter into a type of *durèe* and it does not matter if we are conscious of it or not. Indeed, Bergson might suggest it would be advantageous if we were unaware of what it is we are doing.

So too in therapy, the past of the client in the presence of the therapist crystallises into something new – something that enables the client to trust in their unconscious processes sufficiently to live in an independent manner. Indeed quite possibly one of the central aims of therapy is for the patient to develop a robust set of internal resources within which to live in an authentic and fulfilling manner. Here then the ego takes the form of the crystalline structure in the fluid state of *durèe*. As it forms it requires the liquid of the unconscious to surround it, being partly in both the conscious and the unconscious and totally in a state of coming into being. It follows that past, present and future are all elusive concepts, for what matters here is the precondition of *durèe* as a state within which to facilitate the process of fully being.

Conclusion – feeling film

The idea of an elusive present is as much Jungian, or at least post-Jungian, as it is Bergsonian. For Jung the collective aspects of our psyche exist in a trans-historical and trans-rational realm. In this regard the archetypal patterns that Jung postulates are central to our psychological health, growth and maturity remain unknowable and incomprehensible to consciousness, at least fully. It is reasonable to regard the experience of archetypes, their affect and somatic as existing within the realm of *durée* – at least they can be seen as offering one way of stepping outside the realm of rational consciousness and into the flow of being that is *durée*. Jung draws on images from Heraclitus to illuminate the psychic flow of the process of individuation (the lifelong mission to live in the manner that is right for us) that is the province of the archetypes themselves. In particular the image of the river into which we can never step into twice (a result of its flow, and changes in ourselves from moment to moment). The same image also seemingly acts a precursor to some of Bergson's thinking around *durée*. Jung took the image and found in it a confirmation of his idea that the psyche is always in a state of change and, or, transition. He also interpolates from Heraclitus' river that the psyche is flowing somewhere, namely down the ancient archetypal riverbeds of individuation.

The movement of the river is significant in our consideration of cinema, which after all is largely a medium of movement (tracks, pans, zooms, edits, crane shots, images from drones, shifts in camera position and so forth). As we have argued it is these formal properties of cinema films that in part facilitate our entry as viewers into *durée*. Further understanding the points at which we enter *durée* in life show that like the experience of watching a film these too are moments of affect invasion. Therapy partly helps us to understand that periods of being under the influence of an affective image are not necessarily deleterious (even though they might seem that way at the time) as for the conscious mind to no longer prove sufficient and to enter into an bodily relationship is to slip into the healing flow of *durée*. But of course, being dipped into the river Styx is both protective and also renders oneself vulnerable to the cluster of feelings that surround the complex: shame, fear, regret and so forth are commonly attached to the dissolution of such complex material. This builds on the ideas discussed earlier, namely that the cinema enables us to enter a state of *durée* by suggesting that the movements in the image reflect (as in our glassy reflections) movement in the psyche. Or put in a more Bergsonian manner: the apparatus of cinema enables us to enter *durée* by suspending the crystalline logicality of conscious mind by replacing it within the grasp of intuition.

That both therapy and the cinema allow us to slip into the stream of *durée*, that both elicit in us a 'will to dream' suggests the therapeutic qualities of films. The sense of temporality, and its lack of fixedness is often missed in the analysis of the so-called 'look' of cinema where it is frequently conceived of as a type of mirror. On the one hand this is seen rather like an actual mirror that offers a doubled image – an actual doubling of the world. While the image is tempting, it is actually rather difficult to see how the technologically constructed world of a film in any meaningful way mirrors the physical world. An alternative view is offered by viewing film as a type of Lacanian mirror, which, as imagined by cinema theory, fragments the body, offering tantalising glimpses of the potential for an idealised sense of wholeness. This too is for numerous reasons unsatisfactory, failing as it does to recognise that no one has ever reported being fragmented by watching in film. Nor does it capture the psychological insights that clients frequently report from watching films that are surely true more generally for film audiences.

This chapter opened with a brief consideration of what 'feeling film' might mean. As it has unfolded we have argued that feeling is polyvalent, working as it does in agency with both the unconscious and consciousness. Both nocturnal and diurnal, feeling is our consciousness aware-ness of the unconscious in the present moment. To facilitate its expression and containment, our bodies encode these deeply experienced moments of affect. Sometimes these offer moments of pleasurable insight while at other times the invasion of the unconscious threatens to overwhelm us, resulting in distressing feelings, thoughts and behaviours. The process of reflection allows for the integration of such material by and into the ego.

What happens when we watch a film is that forgotten personal complexes become activated. They do so if the formal properties of film have slipped us into the state of *durée*. This is some-what unpredictable, as it requires the meeting of unconscious personal material with a film, in an unplanned and unlooked for manner. It is not possible to 'prescribe' a film to allow for psychological healing, any more than it is possible prescribe a dream. That said, it is possible to change our orientation and to approach our inner life with a spirit of enquiry and openness. If we see film in only materialist and historical terms then the opportunity for such insight is closed down. By contrast, if when we watch a film we do so as part of a psychological orientation that assumes life experiences can be psychologically informative then we are more likely to have filmic encounters that offer us moments of personal illumination. It is worth underscoring that such 'third image' moments are often not pleasurable and it seems that the older and deeper the complex is that gets encapsulated in the third image the greater is the affect. Films can cause considerable personal distress when they activate old unconscious material and this can in turn have a considerable effect on those around us as well as ourselves (c.f. the chapter by Kalsched, in this volume.)

Feeling film requires us to establish a personal relationship with a film. It means to suspend the scientific logic of everyday life and instead to enter into an intuitive relationship with images and sounds that is not predicated on their representational qualities and meaning. It is to lose the plot, and to slip into *durée* as we are drawn into the cinematic flow of a film. In one of the imaginative dialogues in C. G. Jung's *Red Book*, a fantasy figure named 'He' comments:

> 'You can go to the cinema in the evenings. That's great and it's cheap. You get to see everything that happens in the world'. [Jung muses] I have to think of Hell, where there are also cinemas for those who despised this institution on earth and did not go there because everyone else found it to their taste.
>
> *(2009, p. 233)*

Fortunately, we do not have to share Jung's struggle with his attraction to what he saw as the meretricious appeal of cinema. We can avoid his fantasy of a hell full of cinemas to punish the snobbish and instead see cinema as both meritorious and delightfully seductive. We noted in the opening paragraphs how to enter a cinema is to make a transition into another realm, it is to enter the underworld of the unconscious in which our collective fantasises and fears are brought to life. So too the act of ordering a movie on-line, or playing it on a DVD or Blu-ray disk has its ritualistic qualities. As well as being a collective experience such activities facilitate our readiness to enter into the psychological flow state of *durée*. It is there that our personal anxieties and complexes find expression. Hopefully in due course the ego is able to integrate such experiences and in so doing 'feeling film' becomes a way of finding ourselves. In so doing we allow ourselves to experience what happens in the world, be that the world of the film, or more potently the personal inner world of our psyche.

References

Bergson, H. (1911) *Creative evolution*, trans. R. Mitchell. London: Macmillan & Co Ltd.
Deleuze, G. (2005) *Cinema 1: the movement-image*. London: Continuum.
Deleuze, G. (2005) *Cinema 2: the time-image*. London: Continuum.
Freud, S. (1899) *Die Traumdeutung* (The interpretation of dreams). Leipzig and Vienna.
Izod, J. and Dovalis, J. (2015) *Cinema as therapy: grief and transformational film*. London: Routledge.
Jung, C. G. (1929) 'Commentary on the "secret of the golden flower"', in *The collected works of C. G. Jung*, Vol. 13, *Alchemical studies*. London: Routledge, 1967.
Jung, C. G. (1956) *The collected works of C. G. Jung*, Vol. 5, *Symbols of transformation*, 2nd edn. London: Routledge, 1970.
Jung, C. G. (2009) *The red book: liber novus: a reader's edition*. New York and London: Norton.
Marks, L. (2000) *The skin of film: intercultural cinema, embodiment and the senses*. Durham, NC, and London: Duke University Press.
Metz, C. (1977) *Psychoanalysis and cinema: the imaginary signifier*. London: Macmillan Press.
Shaviro, S. (1993) *The cinematic body*. Minneapolis, MN: University of Minnesota.
Sobchack, V. (1992) *The address of the eye: a phenomenology of film experience*. Princeton, NJ: Princeton University Press.
Sobchack, V. (2004) *Carnal thoughts: embodiment and moving image culture*. Berkeley, CA: University of California Press.

Filmography

Singin' in the Rain. (1952) [film] Directed by Stanley Donen and Gene Kelly. USA.

Audio CD

Waits, T. (1989) *The heart of Saturday night*. USA: Atlantic Records.

24

GETTING YOUR OWN PAIN

A personal account of healing dissociation with help from the film *War Horse*

Donald E. Kalsched

Introduction

This chapter presents a healing, albeit painful, personal encounter with a recent film *War Horse* (dir. Spielberg, 2011) and how it came to 'unlock' a long-dissociated pocket of childhood experience. In so doing the experience of watching the film helped me recover a piece of my personal story that had been lost in obscurity. To borrow the language of another film about dissociation *Equus* (dir. Lumet, 1977) it was instrumental in 'getting my own pain.' To put it another way the film helped to uncover a lost piece of my *personal* story that had been lost in the *generic* story of my life as I knew it thus far. Fifteen years of Jungian analysis with three different analysts and other psychotherapists before that, had never touched this un-remembered all-too-personal pain, nor had the symptoms which clustered around this dissociated complex ever been satisfactorily interpreted. Thanks to the triggering effect of a powerful scene in *War Horse*; thanks also to my dreams that night; and thanks especially to the tender but insistent ministrations of my wife Robin (who is also an analyst), I was able to re-visit this 'story within a story' and feel its emotional impact for the first time. My experience illustrates how modern cinema can provide a *via regia* (royal road) into the dissociated contents of the unconscious, bypassing resistances and defenses that had cordoned off the relevant material for decades. This ability of cinema to connect us to personal complexes carries important therapeutic implications and these are explored briefly at the end of the chapter.

Jung: implicit verses explicit stories

In a memorable interview with Laurens van der Post (1986, p. 15) at his Bollingen retreat, Jung once confessed that his work as a healer did not take flight until he realized that the key to the human personality was its story: 'Every human being at core, he held, had a unique story and no man could discover his greatest meaning unless he lived and, as it were, grew his own story' (ibid.). Jung did not complete the telling of his own personal story until he was 83 years old when he decided to write his autobiography, *Memories, Dreams, Reflections* (1963). It was a difficult undertaking because he discovered that as he directed his attention inward, and let the light of his consciousness illuminate the obscure darkness of certain aspects of his early childhood, feeling-experiences began to emerge that were painful to him. Understandably he resisted the process of recovering these memories.

Jung described this struggle in a letter to an anonymous friend:

> Dear N,
> You must bear with my peculiar mental state. While I am writing this I observe a little demon trying to abscond my words and even my thoughts and turning them over into the rapidly flowing river of images, surging from the mists of the past, portraits of a little boy, bewildered and wondering at the incomprehensibly beautiful and hideously profane and deceitful world.
>
> *(1975: §408)*

This bewildered and awe-struck little boy comes alive in the pages of Jung's autobiography and much of what he recovered of this child's memories carries the mark of trauma and dissociation (c.f. Kalsched, 2013, Chapter 8). The act of writing was a healing act in which he gathered together some of the previously dissociated pieces of his life and wove them into a coherent narrative that made sense out of his otherwise fragmented experience. He was, in effect, 'getting his own pain.' In the process, Jung discovered that he had two autobiographies not one—the first one known and familiar, made up of explicit memories and conscious experience, the other unknown and unfamiliar, made up of memories and experiences that had previously been unconscious. Jung named these his number one and number two personalities.

In completing his autobiography, Jung was re-discovering in his own life the importance of untold stories, just as he had earlier discovered in the lives of patients he treated as a young psychiatrist at the Burgholzli Mental Hospital in Zurich. Looking back over many years of experience, Jung offered the following reflection:

> In many cases in psychiatry, the patient who comes to us has a story that is not told, and which as a rule no one knows of. To my mind, therapy only really begins after the investigation of that wholly personal story. It is the patient's secret, the rock against which he is shattered. If I know his secret story, I have a key to the treatment ... but how to gain that knowledge? In most cases exploration of the conscious material is insufficient. Sometimes [projective techniques] can open the way, so can the interpretation of dreams, or long and patient human contact with the individual.
>
> *(1963: p. 117)*

While films are not projective techniques in the classic clinical sense, they are imaginative, artistic products of the human psyche. Like a collective dream, films can give us access to orphaned parts of ourselves and their 'stories'—what Theodore Reik (1964) called 'voices from the inaudible.' We all have secret stories. Sometimes these stories are secret because they contain shadow contents and feelings which constitute those parts of our experience we are ashamed of or embarrassed by. When we get in touch with those parts of the story, we blush or change the subject. Even so we recognize the difficult truths they contain. Eventually, if we are in a trusting environment, we learn to include their repressed contents in our overall autobiographical narrative about ourselves. Such an acknowledgment represents a major part of the process of psychotherapy and involves filling in the gaps in our personal story ... integrating the shadow as Jung would say and in so doing becoming more 'whole.'

Then there are some stories that are so secret that they are unknown even to ourselves. In that case, they are the implicit memories that follow the kind of emotionally 'shattering' experiences that Jung refers to. Another word for this shattering is trauma. Trauma creates unbearable pain and anxiety and it leads to defenses that are more primitive than repression. The main such primitive defense is *dissociation*. When traumatic parts of our experience are split off from the ego by dissociation, we do not 'make sense' to ourselves. We cannot tell an emotionally coherent story about our lives. We may have flashbacks or major gaps in experience and are left with blacked out places that frighten us. Or, strange symptoms may defy interpretation because they seem un-related to the known places where we are injured. In short, major pieces of the puzzle remain in what neuro-scientists call 'implicit' memory (see Siegel, 2010, pp. 148ff.) in which they are out of reach of our storytelling capacity, of our 'autobiographical memory.' This is the reason why trauma survivors must often lead a double life with one apparently normal story 'on the surface' but inwardly haunted by another unformulated implicit story. This is an untold and un-tellable story and is composed of the painful memories of abuse, neglect or betrayal that remain a shameful secret.

In what follows, I would like to describe how a dissociated complex of my own forgotten childhood experience was 'triggered' by a sequence of dramatic scenes I watched in the film *War Horse*. This micro-complex of dissociated material had apparently lain dormant for over 60 years, including around 20 years of psychoanalytic work on myself plus almost 50 years of attention to the psyches of my patients. My story illustrates how the healing of trauma is a life-long adventure and how the story we tell ourselves, and others, about our lives can have holes in them big enough to drive a truck through!

My experience of the film

Shortly after the film version of Steven Spielberg's *War Horse* started showing around town in Albuquerque, New Mexico, my wife Robin and I went to see it. Based on the Tony award-winning Broadway play, the film is set in the beautiful farm country of rural Great Britain before the First World War, and features a close friendship that develops between a young boy named Albert and a horse named Joey. Albert's drunken father Ted was supposed to bring home an inexpensive plow horse, instead spent a whole month's rent on Joey—sleek thoroughbred, purchased from the town's auction. A deep bond develops between Joey and Albert, as he trains the horse not only to ride but also to accept a harness and plow, and together they set about saving the family farm, which ultimately they do. When the First World War breaks out, Albert's father, drunk as usual, sells Joey to the Army not to pull a farmer's plow but to haul cannons. Albert is crushed but enlists himself in the army and vows he will see Joey again.

The film then follows the separate stories of Joey and Albert for several years, as they endure the horrors of the War. Joey pulling weapons and surviving only because of his strength and endurance, as well as the respect and care he evokes from his soldier caretakers on both sides. Albert meanwhile suffers the horrors of trench warfare wounded by machine-gun fire and temporarily blinded by exploding mortar shells.

In one of the final scenes of the movie, the events of the war bring Joey and Albert together in the same front line, facing the German enemy across no-man's land. Albert, temporarily blind and slowly recovering from his wounds behind the lines, does not know that Joey is nearby. In a dramatic scene, Joey is startled to madness by exploding shells and charges off into no-man's land. He crashes through stanchions and barricades until he collapses in coils of barbed wire, unable to rise, slowly dying. Looking up with his soulful luminous brown eyes, he seemingly implores both sides to stop this senseless carnage. A British soldier erupts out of his trench and, heedless of the danger, runs to the dying animal trying desperately to free the horse from the wire. German machine guns are trained on him and we expect that at any minute he'll be gunned down. Instead, from behind the German lines, wire cutters are thrown and several enemy soldiers come out to help free the animal. For one remarkable moment, a mini-truce is declared and soldiers on opposite sides are united through the compassion for this innocent and beautiful animal. All through this moving scene, which results in the badly wounded horse being freed and returned to the British lines, all I could think of were Joey's eyes. They spoke directly to me, although I don't know what they are saying. What I am certain about is that I'm convulsed with sobbing and that I'm struggling to contain my unbidden emotions in this public theater.

Slowly I got control over myself and sat quietly for a few moments, until the next scene broke me open again … the 'reunion' scene. Covered with mud and bleeding from his wounds, Joey is led back to the British lines. The commotion alerts Albert, who is now near by. Albert hears the unmistakable sounds of his beloved, long lost and almost un-recognizable animal. Yet the Army veterinarian, who has examined the horse's wounds, orders the horse to be put down. Reluctantly following orders, the sergeant draws his pistol and Joey lowers his head as if accepting his fate. There is a deafening silence. Then, instead of the death-dealing report of the gun, we hear Albert's whistle in the near-distance. It is the same whistle that Joey learned from the boy as they forged their bond so many years earlier on the farm. Joey jerks his head up in recognition, as everyone is amazed and looks around. And again those beautiful eyes! This scene is repeated two more times and each time the pistol is aimed and the whistle comes instead of the shot. Finally Albert comes stumbling along the trenches into the scene, his half blind eyes bandaged, his long-lost soul animal obviously overjoyed to see him again. And again I am convulsed with sobbing. This time I couldn't stop until the final scene of the movie.

The closing scene of the film is shot against a deep red-orange sunset in which a lone rider appears on the horizon, approaches and dismounts. He embraces a woman and a man. Then all three embrace the horse's head. Music swells and we know that Joey and Albert have returned to the family and the farm where their relationship began. As Robin and I sat in the darkened theater, I slowly returned to a more or less regulated state. Like us, most people were deeply moved by the film and stayed in their seats until the credits finished.

Resistance to feeling and a final breakthrough

We filed out of the theater hand in hand, everyone in silence. On the drive home Robin and I talked about what a good anti-war film this was and about the beauty of the 'truce' scene where soldiers dedicated to killing each other paused and together freed an innocent animal. We talked about the terrible violation of innocence between man and animal. Then, for some reason (we both had previously studied theology), the question came up of 'where God was in this film.' I had an immediate surge of conviction and said emphatically (and probably a little arrogantly) that 'God was in the luminous eyes of that horse … that's where God was.' (I was thinking, when I said this, of a moment described by Elie Wiesel [1982] in his book *Night* that I had never forgotten, where he and other inmates at the Auschwitz concentration camp were forced to watch as three prisoners were hung on the gallows, and among them was a small child. The child did not die when the chairs were tipped over and dangled from his noose writhing in agony for half an hour as Wiesel was forced to watch. A prisoner behind him asked in agony 'So where is your God now!?' And at that moment from deep within himself, Wiesel heard a voice answer 'where is He? He's up there hanging from the gallows.')

Wiesel's horrific story and the scene of Joey dying in the mud and barbed wire, his innocent eyes looking imploringly at us before the fire went out of them, both seemed to capture the terrible paradox of the human condition described by Jung's little boy – 'bewildered and wondering at the incomprehensibly beautiful and hideously profane and deceitful world' (1975,

p. 408). This agony, I thought to myself, is what God must have suffered in 'coming down' into this world in the Christian incarnation story and also somehow it is what we must take on if we are to let God take up residence in the human heart.

Of course I was not conscious of all this at the moment but my conviction that 'God was in the eyes of that horse' was as close as I could get to what I felt. However Robin was not convinced. She was on another track. She was struck by the fact that the same patriarchal God was worshiped by both sides in the First World War and it was in His name that all the killing was going on and, she wondered, 'where was the feminine in all this horror?' Robin was furious about the waste of lives depicted in the film and not very sympathetic to what I considered my poetic and mystical interpretation and it seemed to me she dismissed it out of hand. This irritated me further and I expressed my chagrin that she was stuck in a shallow feminist argument against the patriarchy and by the time we got home we were both irritated. I was fuming and agitated while she was quiet and withdrawn.

Feeling misunderstood and alienated, I stormed downstairs to get away from Robin as she got ready for bed. I opened my computer and started writing, trying to process for myself what had just happened and why I was so upset. Was it the film? Was it the horse? Was I just in the wrong marriage? What was going on? No conclusion.

When I came back up and sullenly went about my bedtime ritual, Robin approached me and said something like 'sweetheart, I'm sorry if I hurt your feelings ... I didn't realize you felt so strongly about this. I've been thinking about it,' she continued:

> Could it be that you're so moved by that scene in the movie because your Dad put a gun in your hands when you were only five years old and took you hunting animals a year later ...? Do you think maybe that could be part of your reaction? You must have watched many animals die and you were so young....

I cut her off quickly. 'Of course not,' I said. 'You don't understand the context of that early hunting!' Now I felt even more misunderstood and angry. Here were my intense vulnerable feelings—my conviction that the soul of the whole world was in the eyes of that innocent animal and all this was now being interpreted and reduced by my psychoanalyst wife to a stupid childhood experience.

I was incredibly defensive and more than a little self-righteous. I explained how my early hunting experiences were an important initiation into my own manhood and the significance for me of the many weekends hunting with my Dad, my Grandfather and my Uncle, in the woods of northern Wisconsin. I described how I was a crack shot by age five and how proud I was of that and what self-esteem this gave me with my father and grandfather. I described the beautiful days I had afield with them, the lunches along the logging roads in northern Wisconsin, the stories about our adventures after ruffed grouse, the late afternoons listening together to the Wisconsin Badgers football games. I explained how cool I was with other boys my age and how we never shot game we didn't eat, how my father taught me the ethics of safety and conservation ... not just how to kill animals but how to honor and respect them and end their suffering immediately. I went on to say how nowadays nobody knows where their meat comes from and how most of it is raised in cages and packaged in cellophane, and how it was a good thing that I learned how to kill and clean animals for the table. At least I wasn't a part of this miserable disconnected culture. And besides, I said, hunting is an archetypal experience and I turned myself over to it with enthusiasm like generations of young men before me. It was formative of my very being!

'Well I just wondered,' Robin said:

I've always felt you were too young to be your Dad's hunting buddy at five years old. You told me you were five when you shot your first squirrel. You were so innocent at that age. This is too early for masculine initiation rituals! Some part of you would have still been identified with those animals. It might have torn you apart.

Somehow that last point reached me. I was just completing a book in which a whole chapter was devoted to innocence and how much it has been neglected in our field of therapy and how traumatic it can be for innocence to gain experience too early. I began to wonder whether this chapter could possibly have something to do with me? (Kalsched, 2013).

So, partially reconciled, we went to bed. But I couldn't sleep. I tossed and turned and in the hypnagogic images that came up in that twilight of sleep, I started to get fragments of memories that upset me. Then it was like a secret file opened in my brain and images spilled out that were painful and shame-filled memories of animals dying. The first was a dream of my father with his famous 'varmint rifle' having just shot a porcupine out of a tree. There was an image of this animal with its blood and guts spilled all around and I realized as I woke from this dream that the imagery constituted a partial memory of being dragged by my proud father to see his massacred trophy when I was only three years old. There was no feeling to the dream, just the image but there was the vague memory of fainting and throwing up when I had seen this poor animal and of feeling embarrassed that I had disappointed my father with my 'weakness.'

Then there were owls shot out of trees, and a great blue heron wounded at 500 yards that I had to go and tackle and kill. I was only eight. There was the rancher's feral cat that I shot for him across the road in the sagebrush and the way that animal wailed and clawed at me and the image of its eyes before I shot it a second time … there was the time when at nine years old I led a gang of younger boys on a mission to climb a tree in a neighbor's yard and kill baby robins by bashing them on the ground … and the punishment that followed from my mother which I didn't understand. Wasn't I my father's son? Wasn't I supposed to be a hunter and a killer? Finally, I remembered the time in my thirties when, on a visit home to Wisconsin with my two-year-old son, I was cleaning some mallard ducks that my father and I had shot on the Mississippi River. I had their gutted carcasses laid out on the basement ping-pong table and was preparing to take off their heads, wings and feet. I picked up a drake mallard and readied the scissors when my son suddenly looked upset: 'Poor little fella, he said … gone from the sky.' I remember being shaken by this moment and again the familiar tears from I-knew-not-where. What I did feel was shame that I had exposed my beautiful little boy to such butchery at the age of two. At the time I did not connect this moment to my own violated innocence but I remember how a fleeting thought crossed my mind that maybe I should stop hunting.

By the time morning came I felt exhausted. I needed to talk about all this with Robin who, thank God, was willing to listen. I poured out the dream images and memories that had come to me, crying intermittently the whole way through, realizing that this had truly been a trauma that I had covered up. It was one I couldn't afford to feel because I loved my father so much and because I was embedded in an heroic narrative that left excluded all this pain and grief. Now I felt heartsick for the little boy that was me, and rage at his violation, however well-meaning and unknowing it had been. This wasn't about me, it was about my father, and having my adoring eyes on him and my being just like him. Why had he not honored my boyhood innocence? Was he so desperate for a hunting buddy that he had to make a child soldier out of me at age of five or six? I was furious at him for this, and also sad for him that his life was so permeated with a culture of guns and killing that it left him terribly empty at the end.

In retrospect, I realize that memories of these experiences were dissociated because they were in some ways unbearably shameful and incompatible with my story about myself—my ego-ideal

… and my story about my wonderful childhood as the beloved son of a loving father. That story is not false … it just didn't include the underlying truth of how my sensitivities as a small child were injured and unconsciously even exploited. The surface story of my Number 1 personality required that I divide myself in two, growing up too fast, leaving a part of my story behind in the un-remembered past beyond the influence of reflective self-awareness or subsequent experience. Back there and orphaned by my precociously grown up narrative was the young seeker of beauty in the world, the young boy linked to the mystery of animals, the lover of all life, identified with the beautiful soulful eyes of dogs and horses, torn away from his own soul by prematurely learning how to kill.

As Robin and I talked, further parts of my 'forgotten' life-story came into focus. For example, as a young man, I had a bothersome 'symptom' of being afraid to have my own blood drawn and I would also get queasy in films where there was a lot of blood spilled—for example if someone was shown helplessly wounded or having cut their own wrists. This symptom worried me a good deal because I originally went to college to become a doctor and on several occasions I had fainted during various 'demonstrations' for pre-medical students. I remembered one in particular where dogs were shaven and cut open, their hearts exposed with heart–lung machines pumping their blood through tubes. I fainted dead away and had to be carried out. This seemed to my naïve mind to spell the end of my future medical career and I was depressed for weeks afterwards.

In my original Jungian analysis this problem was labeled my 'blood complex' and because blood is frequently symbolic of affect and feeling it was interpreted as my fear of strong feeling in general. While that made sense to me the interpretation didn't really help much. My symptom continued. The only thing it did was make me feel bad that not only was I afraid of blood, I was apparently afraid of what blood represented, i.e., strong emotion! Never were my early childhood experiences of traumatically violated innocence and the guilt about the blood I had spilled, explored.

These memories remained implicit and were encoded in parts of my brain that did not connect to higher cortical centers that would have allowed me to reflect on the experience and bring it back into autobiographical memory. Instead these traumatic memories lay in wait, ready to be triggered. This was equivalent to a filmic flashback, the irruption of the past into the present, not yet recognized as the past but only taken in as a 'symptom.' That's what my fainting episode in the surgical demonstration represented. It is like re-living an earlier injury right now but without recognizing it as a past injury. The threat of helpless animals being sacrificed (no matter how justified the rationale) was one I had already seen countless times at my own hand, but never explicitly known. Such is the defense of dissociation which cements the memories in the lower right hemisphere where they remain implicit and unprocessed by higher cortical centers. I was overwhelmed by tears looking into the eyes of Joey the War Horse, but I didn't know why. I didn't know I was looking into the eyes of my own impossible experiences. When Robin and I went through our argument together these early implicit memories were processed in the storm and stress of relationship and became explicit, conscious for the first time.

Getting your own pain

As I was preparing the manuscript of this chapter for publication, I was reminded of a scene from another film, *Equus*, which struck me as uncannily relevant to the experience I have just reported. And it has to do with finding one's way to a uniquely personal—as opposed to a generic (mythic or collective)—life.

Equus, the 1977 film, directed by Sidney Lumet and starring Richard Burton as the psychiatrist and Peter Firth as his young patient, is an adaptation of Peter Schaffer's award-winning (1973) play *Equus*. I had seen the film in New York at a special screening for the C. G. Jung Institute where I was training to be an analyst. Remarkably enough, both the play and the film constitute a drama about the killing of innocent animals (horses) by a young stable boy (Alan Strang), and about the 'god' he sees reflected in the eyes of the horses, one of which (Nugget) he rides naked at night in what amounts to a Dionysian ritual of orgiastic ecstasy followed by the boy prostrating himself before his 'god' Equus.

Tragically, and, unlike my own experience in War Horse, the 'god' that Alan sees staring back at him from the horses' eyes is a wrathful Deity, mocking him (in Alan's twisted projection) for his failed love-making attempt with a beautiful young woman in the stable the night before. The shame he feels is so intolerable that the boy blinds the horses with a steel spike in a horrific scene, killing them, while at the same time 'killing' his own consciousness of his erotic arousal, his shame about it and his unbearable 'failure' as the lover of a real woman. The unbearable personal humanity of the story, now mixed with the crime of killing the animals he had worshiped, became dissociated and the result was complete psychosis. The rest of the play is about the slow therapeutic abreaction of Alan's dissociated crime and the uncovering of his 'true story.'

While I remember being horrified by the images of the boy killing the horses (for reasons that the previous narrative makes understandable), the particular scene that riveted my attention and stayed with me for more than 40 years was a piece of dialogue between Alan, who is now in a psychiatric hospital, and his treating psychiatrist, Martin Dysart (Richard Burton). Dysart is cast as an obsessively intellectual man living a conventional life in a loveless marriage with florid fantasies of unlived erotic and 'primitive' life in which he indulges, in sublimated form, by reading Greek mythology. From his repressed state of sclerotic rigidity he is mesmerized by his young patient's archetypal revelries. Alan's ritual enactments of Dionysian ecstasies have a fascination for him that parallel Jung's fascination with what he called 'living one's own myth,' a parallel and confusion I will attempt to sort out in a moment.

In the following scene, Dysart is talking to Hesther Salomon, a nurse, about the boy's suffering and about whether he has any right to take his pain away from him. In the particular dialogue that I found unforgettable, Dysart is trying to explain to Hesther what it means to 'get your own pain' (following is from the text of the play *Equus*, 1974, p. 94):

HESTHER: …but he's in pain Martin. He's been in pain for most of his life. That much, at least, you know.
DYSART: Possibly
HESTHER: Possibly?! … That cut-off little figure you just described must have been in pain for years.
DYSART: [doggedly] Possibly.
HESTHER: And you can take it away.
DYSART: Still—possibly.
HESTHER: Then that's enough. That simply has to be enough for you, surely?
DYSART: No!
HESTHER: Why not?
DYSART: Because it's his.
HESTHER: I don't understand.
DYSART: His pain. His own. He made it.
PAUSE.

[EARNESTLY] *LOOK ... TO GO THROUGH LIFE AND CALL IT YOURS— YOUR LIFE—YOU FIRST HAVE TO GET YOUR OWN PAIN. PAIN THAT'S UNIQUE TO YOU. YOU CAN'T JUST DIP INTO THE COMMON BIN AND SAY 'THAT'S ENOUGH!'....* HE'S DONE THAT. ALL RIGHT, HE'S SICK. HE'S FULL OF MISERY AND FEAR. HE WAS DANGEROUS AND COULD BE AGAIN, THOUGH I DOUBT IT. BUT THAT BOY HAS KNOWN A PASSION MORE FEROCIOUS THAN I HAVE FELT IN ANY SECOND OF MY LIFE. AND LET ME TELL YOU SOMETHING: I ENVY IT. [EMPHASIS ADDED]

HESTHER: You can't.

DYSART: [vehemently] Don't you see? That's the Accusation! That's what his stare has been saying to me all the time *'At least I galloped! When did you?'* ... [simply] I'm jealous, Hesther. Jealous of Alan Strang.

HESTHER: That's absurd.

Hesther is not happy with Dysart's analysis and we shouldn't be either. When he says we all have to 'get our own pain, pain that's unique to us' ... he's right. That would be equivalent to 'growing our own story' as Jung suggested to Laurens van der Post (above). When he says 'You can't just dip into the common bin' he's right again. We can't just live a generic life, fitting in with the common bin of so-called everyday suffering as it is defined for us by the narrative about ourselves that we adopt from others and from the prevailing culture. But when he says that the boy has 'done that' i.e., gotten pain that's unique to him, Dysart has got it exactly backwards.

In Jungian terminology, Alan has been possessed by an archetypal image of the God Equus and is burying his own repressed sexuality and twisted personal pain in a mythic enactment that keeps him away from the deeper unbearable story and his consciousness of it. Similarly my own generic 'mythic' story of myself as a heroic young hunter masked the deeper personal pain that was unique to me and would have to be discovered through the difficult process of remembering that is described above.

In the same way, for Alan Strang 'getting his own pain' meant recovering those dissociated and shameful personal experiences lying behind his archetypal enactment of his crime of blinding the horses. That involved recovering the pain of his own violently repressed and distorted sexuality and recovering this from the shaming defenses that he's projected onto the horses whose huge eyes watched him while he tried to make love in the stable, are leering and mocking and preventing him from loving a real woman. It is as if he has turned his painful personal story over to an archetypal enactment, in order not to feel it. He is living a myth instead of his own life. Discovery of his painful personal story and the violent rejection of his own sexuality lies ahead of him in the film—just as it lay ahead for me, in the unbearable reality of my own childhood killing of animals. It is the difference between living a personal limited life and being lived by a generic mythic one.

As a young man studying to be a Jungian analyst when I saw Peter Shaffer's play and the later screenplay by him. I was captured by the same romantic vision of 'getting your own pain' as was Dysart along with the surrendering of oneself to archetypal affects and the living out a kind of possession by one's own personal daimon. This was made even more confusing for me by the way Jung himself sometimes spoke positively about finding one's own myth ... the myth that you live by, as if this was an important part of individuation.

In his autobiography, Jung even describes his envy of people who are unconsciously embedded in the archaic and the mythic. Specifically, Jung described his encounter with a Taos Pueblo Indian chief Ochwiay Biano who lived inside a mythic worldview in which he believed his ritual worship of the sun would actually help the fiery orb cross the sky. Jung felt that this belief, 'primitive' as it was, gave his life dignity and a meaningful place in the cosmos. Jung envied him for it:

311

It springs from his being a son of the sun; his life is cosmologically meaningful, for he helps the father and preserver of all life in his daily rise and descent. If we set against this our own self-justifications, the meaning of our own lives as it is formulated by our reason, we cannot help but see our poverty. Out of sheer envy we are obliged to smile at the Indians' naiveté and plume ourselves on our cleverness; for otherwise we would discover how impoverished and down at the heels we are. Knowledge does not enrich us; it removes us more and more from the mythic world in which we were once at home by right of birth.

(1963, pp. 247–252)

Here Jung is lamenting the same impoverishment of modern life and objective 'knowledge' that Dysart felt with Alan Strang. Fortunately, Jung finds his way out of his 'mythological envy' with a new understanding. Dysart is not so lucky. Here's Jung, description of his envy of Ochwiay Biano and its resolution:

I had envied him for the fullness of meaning in that belief, and had been looking about without hope for a myth of [my] own. [But] now I knew what it was, and knew even more: that man is indispensable for the completion of creation; that, in fact, he himself is the second creator of the world, who alone has given to the world its objective existence—without which, unheard, unseen, silently eating, giving birth, dying, heads nodding through hundreds of millions of years, it would have gone on in the pro-foundest night of non-being down to its unknown end. Human consciousness created objective existence and meaning, and man found his indispensable place in the great process of being.

(ibid., p. 256)

Jung resolved his envy of his Pueblo friend's mythic embeddedness through the discovery of a new myth, namely the myth of consciousness in which he could participate enthusiastically even as a modern man. He thus deepened the integration and connection between his inner symbolic life on the one hand and his personal/professional life as a psychiatrist and scientist on the other. Dysart in Schaffer's play, and later film, is unable to make this transition. Reluctantly he treats the boy and helps relieve the unbearable pain that was being enacted in (and disguised by) his archetypal symptoms. But even in the film's final farewell to Alan Strang, Dysart is full of ironic regret: 'you won't gallop any more, Alan. Horses will be quite safe … [but] you'll be without pain. More or less completely without pain' (*Equus*, pp. 124–125).

Of course the playwright and his character Dysart, have it backwards again. The process of recovering his traumatic memories (as depicted in the last third of the film) is extremely painful for young Alan Strang and it is precisely this that constitutes his 'getting his own pain'—not galloping to a frenzy in the fields at night in an archetypal ritual that shames him and that he does not understand. Granted, he will not be carried away by the same volcanic affect or riveted by the same passionate obsessions, but he will be living a personal life and not a generic or mythic one. In the same way, my discovery that the archetypal and heroic rituals of hunting that had so obsessed and enthralled me as a young man, had to be given up, was its own form of initiation … initiation into my own greater consciousness, into my own personal pain and into my own individual and authentic suffering.

It is possible that we all start out living a generic life and eventually, if we're lucky, slough off our collective, mythological envelope so to speak, finding our way with help to 'getting our own personal pain.' This is undoubtedly a pre-requisite for what Jung meant by the 'vocation' of personality and why he said (1932: §284) that 'the ultimate aim and strongest desire of all mankind is to develop that fullness of life which is called personality.'

Final thoughts

As I look back over the process of writing this story two things occur to me. First, just as Jung got some help with a coherent autobiography by writing his story at 83 years old, with help from his dreams, I too, at age 73, have benefitted from this process of writing and integration and helped along the way by the memory-triggering impact of a contemporary film. I hope that this narrative of my experience in the film *War Horse* helps underscore how helpful movies can be in opening up ('triggering') early un-remembered trauma and, in this way, helping us to both 'get our own pain' and also our own greater consciousness.

Since this experience I have paid particular attention not only to my patients' dreams, but to the films they find compelling and especially to the particular scenes they find themselves returning to … sometimes year after year for decades. I make an effort to see films that are important to my patients and we discuss them. I have found this cinematic attention rewarded many times with profound insights into their lives and a deep resonance in the transference as we have, in effect, shared a common dream.

Second, my story demonstrates that dissociation is an amazing thing. It can encapsulate a complex of memories and keep the shame associated with them out of consciousness for 60 years! This encapsulated 'complex' of affects and images was like a cyst in the musculature of my life. While it did not dramatically hamper my overall development, it was a secret source of embarrassing symptoms during my formative years and constituted a gaping hole in any coherent personal narrative of my life. It also helped change my direction from medicine to psychology and (in retrospect) informed my interests in trauma and dissociation as well as the emphasis I have placed in my recent book (Kalsched, 2013) on violated innocence. As a so-called expert helping other people with their trauma histories I was humbled to find this missing piece of my own forgotten personal history.

References

Jung, C. G. (1932) 'The development of personality', in *The collected works of C. G. Jung*, Vol. 17, *The development of the personality*, 3rd edn. New York: Bollingen Foundation, Inc., 1954.

Jung, C. G. (1975) *Letters, Vol. 2: 1951–1961*, ed. G. Adler, trans. R. F. C. Hull. Princeton, NJ: Princeton University Press.

Jung, C. G. (1963) *Memories, dreams, reflections*, ed. A. Jaffe, trans. R. Winston and C. Winston. New York: Vintage Books.

Kalsched, D. (2013) *Trauma and the soul: a psycho-spiritual approach to human development and its interruption.* London: Routledge.

Reik, T. (1964) *Voices from the inaudible: the patients speak.* New York: Farrar, Straus, & Co.

Schaffer, P. (1974) *Equus.* New York: Avon Books.

Siegel, D. L. (2010) *Mindsight: the new science of personal transformation.* New York: Bantam Books.

Van der Post, L. (1986) 'The story is the wind', *Resurgence*, 117, July/August, pp. 14–17.

Wiesel, E. (1982) *Night*, trans. S. Rodway. New York: Bantam Books.

Filmography

Equus. (1977) [film] Directed by Sidney Lumet. UK.

War horse. (2011) [film] Directed by Steven Spielberg. USA.

25

HEALING THE HOLES IN TIME

Film and the art of trauma

Angela Connolly

Introduction

The relationship between film and the practice of psychotherapy has a long and complicated history, which goes as far back as Freud himself and the doubts he expressed to Abraham and Sachs at the time of the making of *Secrets of a Soul* (dir. Pabst, 1926) as to the capacity of film to create an accurate representation of the reality of what goes on in the room of the analyst. As Glen Gabbard remarked in a 2002 interview for the *New York Times*, all too often Hollywood's depiction of mental illness and its treatment 'has mostly preferred distortion and stereotype over more true-to life representations'. Indeed, according to Gabbard, out of over 400 films depicting psychiatric treatment, fewer than five could be described as accurate. This is even truer of the way popular cinema has depicted the treatment of trauma. From Hitchcock's *Spellbound* (1945) onwards, the message is that what cures trauma is the cathartic recovery of the traumatic memory, and success is assured if the therapist falls in love with the patient. Given all this it is hardly surprising that until recently most analysts of all schools would agree that films have very little to teach us about how to practise psychotherapy.

However, this conclusion has changed with the upsurge of interest in the way that aesthetics can provide important insights into the practice of psychotherapy and into the analytical process itself. A greater awareness of film aesthetics allows us to reflect in very different ways on its relevance to the narrative reconstruction of traumatic memories. Developing this observation this chapter explores how the specific aesthetics of trauma films can help in clinical work with the survivors of severe trauma. It will begin by examining the relationship between aesthetics and analytical practice. It will then define some of the effects of severe trauma that lead to profound alterations in memory and in imaginative and metaphoric capacity. It will also examine how trauma destroys the empathic bond with the other that is essential for any meaningful dialogue. The final result is the impossibility of reconstructing and representing the trauma, of creating a meaningful personal narrative which can be told to an 'other'. Finally the chapter focuses on some of the particular aesthetics of successful trauma films to show the way in which they can offer us insights into how clinicians need to modify clinical technique when working with trauma victims.

The aesthetics of analysis

As John Beebe noted in a 2010 article, 'Psychotherapy in the aesthetic attitude', because of Jung's own extreme ambivalence towards aesthetics, 'aesthetics has remained, theoretically, a bit off limits for our psychology, and it has rarely been seen as applying to what we might do with patients' (p. 170). Beebe, perhaps because of his lifelong engagement with film, feels that an aesthetic attitude is an important part of the therapeutic tools at the analyst's disposition and that the aesthetic attitude

> confronts both analyst and patient with the problem of taste, affects how the therapy is shaped and 'framed' and can grant a dimension of grace to the analyst's mirroring of the struggles that attend the patient's effort to be a more smoothly functioning human being
>
> *(p. 165)*

Beebe delineates three specific aesthetic dimensions which he feels have been all too often neglected in psychotherapeutic work: taste, shape and grace. Mark Winborn too, in an important article from 2015, suggests that, 'many of the experiences associated with analytical process – such as the experience of depth, the emergence of meaning, transcendence, coherence, narrative flow or moments of meeting – can be viewed through the lens of aesthetic experience' (p. 94). In particular, Winborn focuses on three distinct aesthetic experiences – the aesthetics of the setting, the aesthetics of interpretation and, finally, the aesthetics of narrative, and it is this last on which I will concentrate attention. In the therapeutic treatment of trauma, it is exactly the narrative reconstruction of the causative traumatic reality rather than the analysis of the inner world that many analysts working with trauma victims consider to be fundamental. As Bohleber notes, 'the analysis of the transference and the countertransference in the here-and-now of the analytical relationship carries the risk of failing to help the patient to distinguish between phantasy and reality, and in the worst case, of retraumatizing her' (2007, p. 343).

Spence in his 1982 work, *Narrative Truth and Historical Truth*, suggests that in analysis, what is at stake is narrative truth rather than the recovery of historical fact and, as Winborn writes, when we work with narrative truth, 'the emphasis is on coherence, continuity, fit, pattern recognition and pattern making areas of focus that are as much about aesthetics as meaning' (2015, p. 103). Intense and prolonged trauma, which rips apart the very fabric of the psyche leaving a space whose nature is best expressed in metaphors such as the empty circle or the black hole, brings us to the limits of representation. Trauma narratives are all too often incoherent, confused and full of lacunae and distortions. When we are dealing with trauma therefore we have to grapple with a different aesthetics: the aesthetics of the negative Sublime. The negative Sublime is an aesthetics of uncertainty and indeterminacy but at the same time, as I have written in a previous paper, 'the sublime moment attests to the infinite possibilities of the human subject and its struggle against the limits of human knowledge' (Connolly, 2003, p. 410). According to Lyotard in 'The sublime and the avant-garde', the sublime corresponds to the moment when:

> The faculty of presentation, the imagination, fails to provide a representation corresponding to this Idea: This failure of expression gives rise to a pain, a kind of cleavage between what can be conceived and what can be imagined or presented. But this pain in turn engenders a pleasure … the impotence of the imagination attests *a contrario* to an imagination striving to figure even that which cannot be figured.
>
> *(1984, p. 202)*

Analysts have something to learn from films in this work of the struggle to represent that which cannot be figured.

Defining trauma

Severe trauma such as that undergone by the victims of genocide or by the survivors of the Nazi death camps and of the Stalinist gulags, profoundly impacts the capacity to remember and to find categories of images and words to represent such experiences to oneself and to others. Current research on the relationship between trauma and memory suggests that traumatic experiences are stored in memory in a different way from those utilized for non-traumatic events. Van der Kolk for example hypothesizes that the intense excitation produced by trauma interferes with the explicit-declarative memory system situated in the hippocampus which permits the conscious recall of experience but does not inhibit the implicit-procedural memory system, the memory system that controls conditioned emotional responses, skills and habits, and sensori-motor sensations related to experience (1994, p. 258). These implicit memories correspond to actual events but they cannot initially, at least, be integrated into a narrative memory or worked on by the symbolic function. Laub and Auerhahn in a 1993 paper suggest that the possibility of remembering and knowing trauma can be organized along a continuum according to the distance between the ego and the traumatic experience. As they note:

> The different forms of remembering trauma range from non knowing; fugue states (in which the events are relived in an altered state of consciousness); retention of the experience as compartmentalized, undigested fragments of perception that break into consciousness (with no conscious meaning or relation to oneself); transference phenomena (where the traumatic legacy is lived out as one's inevitable fate); its partial, hesitant expression as an overpowering narrative; the experience of compelling, identity defining and pervasive life themes (conscious and unconscious); its organization as a witnessed narrative, to its use as a metaphor and vehicle for developmental conflict. These different forms of knowing ranging along the continuum of psychological distance from the trauma, also vary in the degree of encapsulation versus integration of the experience and in the degree of ownership of the memory – i.e. the degree to which an experiencing 'I' is present as subject. Variations in distance dictate variations in the presence of imaginative elaboration and play.
>
> *(pp. 289–290)*

It is exactly when the traumatic event or events are too close to the experiencing 'I' that the narrative 'I' fails and in this failure it becomes impossible to bring into play any imaginative elaboration of the event. The other devastating effect of severe trauma is the way in which it destroys the empathic bond between self and other, between self and world. This is what Laub and Podell call 'the primary empathic bond' (1995, p. 991) and without it there is an abyss between the sufferer and the human community. As Jean Amery, a survivor of Auschwitz who later killed himself, wrote in a chilling comment cited in Primo Levi's *I Sommersi e i Salvati*,

> whoever has been tortured remains tortured ... whoever has undergone torment is no longer at home in the world ... the faith in humanity which is already fractured with the first blow to the face and then demolished by torture, can never be regained.
>
> *(2003, p. 14)*

All this suggests that working with trauma requires a particular attention to the aesthetics of the negative sublime and the ability on the part of the analyst, to allow 'the structure-shattering psychotic universe' (Gubrich-Simitis, 1984, p. 313) to reach her without losing her imaginative capacity or her empathic stance.

The aesthetics of trauma films or the art of trauma

The result of massive, extreme trauma as seen, renders impossible any representation of the experience due to 'the collapse of the imaginative capacity to visualize atrocity', as Laub and Auerhahn put it (1993, p. 288). Narrative requires the capacity to use metaphor in order to fashion the experience into a form that will be comprehensible and meaningful to others, yet as these authors point out, 'because of the radical break between trauma and culture, victims often cannot find categories of thought or words for their experience' (p. 287). The result is that all too often, the accounts of traumatic experience remain at the level of chronicles, detailed factual, historical accounts which, as Laub and Podell state, 'are able only to convey the surface of the experience, they lose their power to impact on the present living world ... they precludes the establishment of a dialogical relationship and hence hinders the reconnecting to others and to oneself in the present' (1995, p. 997).

Trauma victims need to be able use imagination and metaphor to create effective trauma narratives and this requires what Laub and Podell term 'the art of trauma', which they regard as a particular form of artistic representation that is capable because it is 'indirect, unaestheticised and dialogic nature' (1995, pp. 991–998). As such it creates the possibility of 'witnessing at an internal level' and it does so through the recreation of a dialogical space with the other. However, the representation of traumatic experiences and memories, whether direct or transmitted, also requires a very particular form of narration if, as Bohleber points out, 'the core and the truth of the experience is not to be distorted' (2007, p. 344).

However it is my contention that the art of trauma is not 'unaestheticised'; in fact it requires a rather particular aesthetic approach, capable of blending together reality and imaginative fiction. In the words of the Spanish writer Jorge Semprun, a survivor of Buchenwald:

> I don't want to do a plain eyewitness account. Right from the start I mean to avoid, to spare myself any recital of suffering and horror ... so I need a narrative 'I' that draws on my experience but goes beyond it, capable of opening the narrative up to fiction, to imagination.... Fiction that would be as illuminating as the truth to seem convincing.
>
> *(1997, p. 165)*

To be successful in its attempt to convey the reality of trauma without betraying the experience requires the creation of new aesthetic forms that bring together and creatively blend different literary categories in such a way as to bring imagination to bear on reality, such as in the historicized literary fiction of Shalamov in *Kolyma Tales* and of Richard Flanagan in *The Narrow Road to the Deep North* or the documentary fiction of the Nobel prizewinner, Svetlana Alexievich in *Voices from Chernobyl*.

Trauma films too require a particular use of cinema technique if they are to be successful in conveying the reality of the trauma. Janet Walker in her study on trauma documentary films, suggests that the principle characteristic of successful trauma films is the way in which the traumatic events are depicted 'in a non-realistic mode characterized by disturbance and fragmentation of the film's narrative and stylistic regimes' (2005, p. 19). Paradoxically it is exactly this blend of the dispassionate, detached and objective style of the documentary with the imaginative and affective power of the visual images that works to convey both the reality of the traumatic event in a way that no traditional aesthetic form can do and at the same time open up the 'real' facts to the creative power of the imagination in such a way as to offer the possibility of representation and integration. This is even more true of any attempt to create representations of the

Holocaust which in its unspeakable horror seems to defy and delegitimize all attempts at representation. As Huyssen argues in his text on Art Spiegelman's use of mimesis in his documentary cartoon, *Maus* based on his own father's experiences in Auschwitz:

> Maus acknowledges the inescapable inauthenticity of Holocaust representations in the 'realistic' mode, but achieves a new and unique form of authentication effect on the reader precisely by way of its complex layering of historical facts, their oral retelling, and their transformation into image-text. Indeed, it is as animal comic that Maus, to quote a typically Adornean turn of phrase ... 'preserves the legitimacy of the image ... in the faithful pursuit of its prohibition'.
>
> *(2001, p. 35)*

To illustrate these points I will refer to two trauma films, Claude Lanzmann's 1985 *Shoah* and the 2008 animated documentary of Ari Folman, *Waltz with Bashir*.

Shoah

Very few events in history have attracted so much attention from film and documentary directors as the Holocaust. Annette Insdorf in her masterly analysis of the filmography of the Holocaust, *Indelible Shadows*, cites over 100 documentaries and over 170 fiction films made before 1989 and around another 170 films made after this date, all of which attempt to represent the reality of the Holocaust.

However it is Claude Lanzmann's *Shoah* (1985) that marks a watershed in the filmography of the Holocaust in as much as its director was among the first to reflect not so much on *what* to represent but on *how* to represent the horrors of the death camps, in an ethical and efficacious manner. When Lanzmann began working on the film in 1974, he found himself faced with the difficulty of thirty or so years later how best to make the viewer reflect emotionally and intellectually on what risked being reduced to a purely abstract fact: the reality of the extermination of six million Jews in the Holocaust. This is in line with the ideas of Luke Hockley who, working from a Jungian vision of cinema, suggests that there are three different ways of reacting to film images: the perception of the image on the screen, the conscious intellectual and cognitive engagement and, finally, and most relevant, the unconscious embodied affective response to the screen images. As Hockley states, 'Meaning comes from the intermingling of our individual psychology with the film, its narrative, images and sounds in order to create a new meaning' (2014, p. 7). Successful trauma films whether fiction or documentary, need therefore to be able to impact an audience aesthetically, intellectually and viscerally, in an embodied affective response.

Lanzmann needed to create a narrative capable of representing to an audience the horrendous reality of the death camps which would be neither a mere commemoration of something past and thus incapable of affectively impacting the present, nor a trivializing or mythologizing fiction which all too often finishes by sanitizing and denying the horrors of the Holocaust. Relevant here for example is the NBC 1978 television mini series *Holocaust* with its distorted depiction of a cultured, middle class family of Berlin Jews that go to their deaths in a dignified manner, a representation that is totally at odds with the reality of the mass of half-starved, half-mad, men, women and children who were driven into the gas chambers with whips and blows. At the same time Lanzmann's difficulties were compounded by the fact that all he had to work with was, in a certain sense, sheer nothingness, fragments of vanishing traces. As he himself declared in 1985 in an interview published in *L'Express*, in directing *Shoah* he was faced with the problem of 'making a film with traces of traces of traces'. In opposition to the aesthetics of Resnais's famous documentary, *Nuit e Brouillard* (1956) which made full use of black and white archival photographic clips interspersed with present-day colour shots of the empty present day camps, Lanzmann chose to avoid any use of archival documents, preferring rather to use imagination to transform the bare facts; in his own words, 'to invent everything' (1985a, p. 12).

Even Resnais, when he came to make *Hiroshima Mon Amour* (1959), revised his position in light of his experiences depicting the Holocaust in *Nuit e Brouillard* and, as Cathy Caruth notes,

> The possibility of knowing history, in this film, is thus also raised as a deeply ethical dilemma: the unremitting problem of how not to betray the past…. In his refusal to make a documentary on Hiroshima, Resnais paradoxically implies that it is direct archival footage that cannot maintain the very specificity of the event.
>
> *(1996, p. 27)*

Lanzmann spent eleven years seeking out and collecting 350 hours of the testimony of individuals who had witnessed the extermination process at close hand – Jewish members of the *Sonderkommandos*, Nazi perpetrators and Polish eyewitnesses – while at the same time visiting and making himself familiar with the sites on which the camps stood, sites that he refers to as 'non-sites of memory' (2007, p. 15). Non-sites of memory according to La Capra, are, 'traumatic sites that undermine the work of memory' (2007, p. 198). Lanzmann then condensed all his material into nine-and-a-half hours through careful montage that deliberately eschew an overarching grand narrative. Instead, he stitches together a patchwork of small individual narratives without a sense of temporal or spatial coherence, and in so doing communicates the destruction of temporality and the sheer sense of meaningless the inmates of the camps experienced.

Despite the commonly held opinion that *Shoah* is a documentary, Lanzmann insists it must also be seen as an original work of art with its own particular aesthetics. As noted above, attempts to represent in a realistic mode, the horrors of the death camps such as the works of fiction created in film studios or even the archival documentary shots taken by the American, English and Russian military photographers in the liberated camps, are inevitably doomed to failure. Interestingly enough, Lanzmann refers to this type of archival material as 'images without imagination' (cited in Liebman, 2007, p. 16). Paradoxically it is exactly Lanzmann's use of subtle compositional and *mise-en-scène* techniques that allows him to convey the emotional and corporeal feel of a reality that in a certain sense, defies representation. In the same way, he insists on knowing in advance the stories of his key witnesses, the Jewish members of the *Sonderkommandos* in order to carefully stage their testimony in such a way as to bring home to the audience the narrative truth of their experiences.

We can see this in the harrowing scenes with Simon Srebnik as he and Lanzmann converse while they walk through the empty spaces of Chelmno, or when we see them in a boat floating down the river Narew, as Srebnik talks about his experiences when, as a thirteen-year-old boy, he was forced to sing as the Germans scattered the ashes of the cremated Jews into the river. These scenes 'make present in an almost carnal, physically tangible terms the experiences beyond any human limits evoked by these witnesses', as Liebman states (2007, p. 17). At the same time Lanzmann is careful to avoid any sense of a full mimesis and to preserve the distance and the distinction between the obscene reality of the gas chambers and its representation. This is clearly shown in the scene with Abraham Bomba, the barber who cut the hair of the naked women waiting to enter the gas chambers, who narrates his experiences in a men's barber shop in Tel Aviv. As Lanzmann commented in a 1990 seminar using a woman in his scene, 'would not have transmitted … it would have been obscene' (cited in Liebman, p. 166). *Shoah* is about the ethical impossibility of a full mimetic representation of traumatic reality. As Fred Camper states it is 'Lanzmann's knowledge of the limits of representation, his willingness to acknowledge the impossibility of a full cinematic mimesis of his subject, that is at the heart of the film's aesthetic and moral position' (2007, p. 105).

Lanzmann teaches us that working with trauma is working with 'traces of traces' and the aesthetic attitude we need to develop is that of the negative sublime, that capacity to tolerate uncertainty and indeterminacy while accepting the fragmentary and incomplete nature of any authentic representation of the traumatic event. Lanzmann's imaginative work is very similar to that particular faculty of the psyche which César and Sara Botella call 'figurability' (*Darstellbarkeit*), 'an instinctual process whose quality derives from a property of intrapsychic movement of convergence and hallucinatory intelligibility, the dream being its most successful manifestation' (2005, p. 1). Figurability is not representation, perception or hallucination but a fourth form of intelligibility implying and implicated in the other three. It requires a very particular kind of empathy which the Botellas call, 'working as a double'. As they state,

> The outcome of this *mode of working as a double (travail en double)*, so to speak, reveals that which already exists in the analysand in an irrepresentable state, as a negative of the trauma, and can at last have access to the quality of representation.
>
> *(p. 49)*

This is neither sympathy, feeling for the other, nor what Stefano Bolognini in 1997 termed empathism, a defensive hyperconcordant attitude (cited in Bisagni, 2013, p. 616). Rather, it is closer to Francesco Bisagni's definition of empathy as a 'complex mental state (we could say emergent) that involves conscious, preconscious and unconscious levels of both patient and analyst and which leads to the possibility of getting close to unpredictable/as yet un-nameable/as yet undeveloped psychic content' (p. 627).

This leads us on to one of the most troubling aspects of *Shoah*. Various critics have objected to the somewhat aggressive interviewing technique Lanzmann uses when he presses the survivors of the *Sonderkommandos* to remember and narrate the memories that they have so desperately tried to forget. Indeed as Domenic La Capra writes, his purpose seems to be to 'provoke the repetition of the trauma in the other' (2007, p. 195). As we can see from the interviews with Richard Glazar and Flip Muller the moment of emotional catharsis is very clear when the survivors break down as they remember that which they have repressed – it is a re-traumatization. In other words, while Lanzmann is able to make use of his own traumatic survivor guilt in order to carry out a work of figurability and render representable the dissociated memories of the Jewish survivors, his aim is not to act as the therapist of his witnesses but rather to represent the narrative truth of the victims. This would suggest that while Lanzmann has profound feelings of sympathy and empathy for the survivors he does not exorcise their guilt and in a certain sense he cannot. Instead, his purpose is to give voice to the dead victims, those whose voices have been lost forever and whose very traces were cancelled by the Nazi perpetrators. In order to allow the dead victims to speak, to recreate their narrative truth, Lanzmann is prepared to re-traumatize the survivors and in this sense the film could be seen as anti-therapeutic.

Waltz with Bashir

Waltz with Bashir (dir. Folman, 2008) too struggles with the problem of how to represent the effects of trauma by bringing imagination to bear on the real facts but here the film is profoundly therapeutic. As well as presenting one of the most accurate filmic examples of the effects of trauma, the film is also a moving account of the way in which the director Ari Folman strives to overcome the holes in his memory through the dialogical space he creates in his conversations with his fellow soldiers and therapists.

The idea for *Waltz with Bashir* came to Folman in 2002 when he agreed to undergo a series of eight sessions with a military therapist about his experiences in the war in Lebanon of 1982 in which he had participated at the age of nineteen. In the course of these sessions, Folman realized for the first time that he had never before told his own personal story to anyone and that there were 'black holes' in his memories. The film begins in 2006 when Folman meets up with an old friend and fellow veteran of the Israeli Defence Force, Boaz Rein-Buskila who tells him about a recurrent nightmare in which he is pursued by twenty-six terrifying black dogs which he feels is connected to a traumatic episode he experienced during the Lebanese war. Folman suddenly realizes that he has no memory at all of that war although he knows he took part. That night, however, he experiences a kind of hallucinatory flashback in which he and an old friend Carmi Cnaa'n together with some fellow soldiers emerge naked from the sea on to a beach in West Beirut, pull on their uniforms, take up their weapons and move towards the city streets where Folman sees a photograph of Bashar Gemayel and then a group of Palestinian women and children moving blindly towards him. Puzzled and disturbed by the hole in his memory and by this vision, he turns for help to Ori Sivan, his best friend who is a filmmaker as well as a therapist. Sivan suggests to Folman that he contact his fellow soldiers to try to reconstruct his memories and Folman decides to visit Carmi who lives in the Netherlands. Carmi's life has been completely devastated by his war experiences to the point that he has abandoned his dream of becoming a nuclear physicist and, having made his fortune selling falafel, he has withdrawn from his previous life to live with his family in an isolated country house. In Carmi's own words, 'By the time I was twenty it was over. I couldn't become anything.' Carmi denies any memory of being present on the beach but he does tell Folman about a surreal image that he had on the boat that was taking him towards Lebanon when he imagined himself floating in the sea on the belly of an enormous woman while he watched the boat exploding into flames.

As he returns towards the airport in a taxi, Folman suddenly begins to remember some of his experiences, and through his dialogues with his fellow veterans and with Professor Zahavi Solomon, an expert in post-traumatic stress disorder, he begins to partially reconstruct some of his missing memories. He continues however to have the same flashback and is still unable to remember his role in the massacre of Palestinian civilians in the camps of Sabra and Shatila at the hands of the Christian Phalangists to avenge the killing of Bashir. He returns to Ori Sivan who tells him that he is obsessed with this massacre as it reminds him of other camps and other massacres as both his parents were survivors of Auschwitz. Sivan suggests that he seeks out individuals who were present at the massacre and as the film proceeds, through his dialogues with a tank commander, Dror Harazi, and with Ron Ben Yishai, a journalist, the story of the massacre begins to unfold. He returns once more to Sivan who tells him that he cannot remember because he feels that even if he only shot the flares to help the Phalangists in the massacre, he feels that he was behaving exactly like the Nazis. In one of the final scenes Ben Yishai tells him that when he saw the column of women and children coming out with their hands up, it reminded him of the famous photograph of the little boy with his hands up, shot during the clearing of the Warsaw Ghetto. In the final scene of the film, Folman once again sees the column of screaming women and children coming towards him as they emerge from the camps having witnessed the full horrors of the massacre. He now remembers everything and the animation gives way to real archival photographic shots of the piles of dead corpses of men, women and children and the anguished lamentations of the surviving Palestinian women.

To make this film about his journey of self-discovery, Folman was clear from the beginning that he wanted to create an animated documentary, a technique he had already begun to explore in a previous film made for Israeli television. The animated documentary has a long history and is particularly able, as Hoeness Roe writes, 'to broaden and deepen the range of what we can learn from documentaries' (2011, p. 217). As she suggests, animation has, 'a unique representational function for the non-fictional moving image, one that could not be fulfilled by the conventional live-action, photographic-based alternative' (p. 219). Folman began by using the internet to ask for stories from anyone who had participated in the Lebanese war. Using these stories, in six days he created a ninety-page screenplay which he then shot in a sound studio and edited it to make a ninety-minute video film. This was utilized to create a storyboard which formed the basis for the 2,300 illustrations created by the art director David Polonsky and his three assistants. It was next animated by Yoni Goodman and his collaborators in the studio of the Bridgit Folman Film Gang, using a mixture of Flash cutout animation, classic animation and 3D animation. Animation gave Folman the freedom and the tools to begin to present, represent and recreate the actual experience of trauma. In this way Folman brings alive for the viewer the affective embodied experience of what it actually feels like to be severely traumatized. The faces and upper bodies of the protagonists are animated through Flash and this gives a particularly static quality to the faces, while the legs and lower bodies are animated using classical animation in order to give a much stronger feeling of movement and activity. This dynamic quality is particularly evident in the pivotal scene of Frenkel's waltz where the whole body of the character is animated using the classic technique as in a kind of trance like state he spins around wildly shooting. This allows Folman to begin to convey something of the dissociation between mind and body that is typical of extreme trauma. In the same way, Folman uses colour to convey the difference between reality on the one hand and fantasy and dissociated memories on the other. The scenes with the interviews and also those where he wishes to represent conscious memories are coloured in a more realistic way and are sharply defined. By contrast the flashbacks, dreams, hallucinations and screen memories are depicted using black and ochre to mark their surreal qualities and representing the uncertain and incoherent quality of traumatic memories and experiences they are also much less defined.

Like Lanzmann, therefore, Folman too is able to recreate the narrative truth of trauma with its fragmentation of the narrative 'I' and its uncanny incompleteness and incoherence. As Vilijoen notes,

> As an animated documentary, and a graphic novel, *Waltz with Bashir* is an example of a contemporary text that deliberately attempts to present the viewer/reader with representations that allow for an encounter with the tentativeness, incompleteness, fracturing and surreality of trauma in the narrative context. As such it seems to stand somewhere between experience and representation.
>
> *(2014, p. 40)*

Unlike *Shoah*, however, *Waltz with Bashir* is a film about therapy and, even more, it is film as therapy. In fact at the beginning of the film Boaz Rein poses the question to Folman, 'Can films be therapeutic?' and it would seem that Folman does indeed believe this to be the case. As he himself states in the interview on the DVD, 'A journey trying to figure out a traumatic memory from the past is a commitment to long term therapy', and during the six years he dedicated to exploring his memories he experienced a period of 'dark depression' which required therapy. By his own admission, however, he does not believe that his therapy was particularly efficacious and indeed he is not a believer in the effectiveness of psychotherapy. He does however feel that making the film was therapeutic for him and that viewing it can be therapeutic for others. In the interview he describes how the film allowed many Israeli veterans to begin to recuperate their own repressed memories. In his words, 'they had scars and they scratched the scars with the film and the memories came out'.

Even more importantly the film illustrates how the work of filling in the black holes in memory created by trauma requires a very particular dialogical and intersubjective space in which Folman is able to take in and make use of the memories of others, no matter how fragmented and partial they were, to allow him to restore, piece-by-piece, his own memory. In other words, in trauma work, the restoration of memory is a co-creation that can only emerge from the empathic dialogue between therapist and patient. Here the therapist is required to work as a double or substitute for the patient and he or she has to be capable of accessing and utilizing empathically, his or her own traumatic experiences to understand and represent those of the other.

Conclusion

According to Janet Walker in *Trauma Cinema*, 'certain films and videos advance our understanding of the etiology and sequelae of trauma by elaborating the links between, and the consequences of, catastrophic past events and demon memories' (2005, p. xvi). The aesthetics of trauma films like *Shoah* and *Waltz with Bashir* help us to understand that when we work with traumatized patients we must help them reconstruct the holes left in memory and represent their experiences in ways that are meaningful to them. It is necessary to respect the incoherent, fragmentary and incomplete nature of their narrative truth, without reaching out for any premature understanding or narrative coherence. All this requires the use of negative capacity, the ability to tolerate uncertainty and to accept the impossibility of ever fully 'knowing' the reality of intense trauma. As Laub writes,

> in the case of massive psychic trauma, knowledge can be reconstructed only to a certain extent and though one sense and feels that one remains cut off from certain knowledge, one cannot go beyond these limits ... the empty circle remains but can no longer wield such acute and inexplicable power over one's life choices.
>
> *(1998, p. 527)*

Waltz with Bashir goes further and shows the kind of analytical relationship and the kind of imaginative work that is necessary if we are to work effectively with trauma.

From the work of the Botellas onwards, psychoanalysts of all schools have become increasingly aware that trauma requires a capacity on the part of the analyst to create a dialogical space in which it becomes possible to co-create through the empathic and imaginative reverie of the analyst an adequate representation of the negative of the trauma which the patient alone is incapable of. This requires, however, the capacity to tolerate a good deal of psychic pain and distress. As Christian Maier puts it in his article, 'Intersubjectivity and the creation of meaning', where, as he describes his work with a traumatized patient, he comments that

> [when we work with trauma] we are up against two psyches working together as a team against great psychic distress. This mutual representational work results in visual images that reflect the traumatic experience of both parties and enable them to find a meaning that can be named.
>
> *(2014, p. 632)*

References

Alexievich, S. (2006) *Voices from Chernobyl: the oral history of a nuclear disaster*, trans. K. Gessen. New York: Picador.

Beebe, J. (2010) 'Psychotherapy in the aesthetic attitude', *Journal of Analytical Psychology*, 55(1), pp. 165–86.

Bisagni, F. (2013) 'On the impact of words: interpretations, empathy and affect regulation', *Journal of Analytical Psychology*, 58(5), pp. 615–36.

Bohleber, W. (2007) 'Remembrance, trauma and collective memory: the battle for memory in psychoanalysis', *International Journal of Psycho-analysis*, 88, pp. 329–52.

Bolognini, S. (1997) 'Empathy and empathism', *International Journal of Psycho-analysis*, 93(3), pp. 279–93.

Botella, C. and Botella, S. (2005) *The work of psychic figurability: mental states without representation*. Hove and New York: Routledge.

Camper, F. (2007) 'Shoah's absence', in S. Liebman (ed.), *Claude Lanzamann's Shoah: key essays*. Oxford and New York: Oxford University Press. pp. 103–12.

Caruth, C. (1996) *Unclaimed experience: trauma, narrative and history*. Baltimore, MD: Johns Hopkins University Press.

Connolly, A. M. (2003) 'Psychoanalytical theory in times of terror', *Journal of Analytical Psychology*, 48(4), pp. 407–33.

Flanagan, R. (2013) *The narrow road to the deep north*. Sydney: Vintage Books.

Gabbard, G. (2002) 'A conversation with Glen Gabbard', *New York Times*, 5 February.

Gubrich-Simitis, I. (1984) 'From concretism to metaphor', *Psychoanalytic Study of the Child*, 39, pp. 301–19.

Hockley, L. (2014) *Somatic cinema: the relationship between body and screen – a Jungian perspective*. London and New York: Routledge.

Hoeness Roe, A. (2011) 'Absence, excess and epistemological expansion: towards a framework for the study of animated documentary', *Animation: An Interdisciplinary Journal*, 6(3), pp. 215–30.

Huyssen, A. (2001) 'Of mice and mimesis: reading Spiegelman with Adorno', in B. Zelizer (ed.), *Visual culture and the Holocaust*. New Brunswick, NJ: Rutgers University Press. pp. 28–44.

Insdorf, A. (2003) *Indelible shadows: film and the Holocaust*. Cambridge: Cambridge University Press.

La Capra, D. (2007) 'Lanzmann's Shoah: here there is no why', in S Liebman (ed.), *Claude Lanzmann's Shoah: key essays*. Oxford and New York: Oxford University Press. pp. 199–221.

Lanzmann, C. (1985a) *Le Matin de Paris*, 29 April.

Lanzmann, C. (1985b) *L'Express*, 10 May.

Laub, D. (1998) 'The empty circle: children of survivors and the limits of reconstruction', *Journal of the American Psychoanalytic Association*, 46, pp. 507–29.

Laub, D. and Auerhahn, N. C. (1993) 'Knowing and not knowing massive psychic trauma: forms of traumatic memory', *International Journal of Psycho-analysis*, 74, pp. 287–302.

Laub, D. and Podell, D. (1995) 'Art and trauma', *International Journal of Psycho-analysis*, 76, pp. 991–1005.

Levi, P. (2003) *I sommersi e i salvati*. Torino: Einaudi.

Liebman, S. (2007) 'Introduction', in S. Liebman (ed.), *Claude Lanzmann's Shoah: key essays*. Oxford and New York: Oxford University Press. pp. 3–27.

Lyotard, J-F. (1984) 'The sublime and the avant-garde', in A. Benjamin (ed.), *The Lyotard reader*. Oxford: Blackwell. pp. 196–211.

Maier, C. (2014) 'Intersubjectivity and the creation of meaning in the analytical process', *Journal of Analytical Psychology*, 59(5), pp. 624–64.

Semprun, J. (1997) *Literature or life*, trans. L. Coverdale. New York: Viking.

Shalamov, V. (1994) *Kolyma tales*, trans. J. Glad. Harmondsworth: Penguin Books.

Spence, D. (1982) *Narrative truth and historical truth: meaning and interpretation in psychoanalysis*. New York: W. W. Norton.

Spiegelman, A. (1996) *Maus*. London: Penguin Books.

van der Kolk, B. A. (1994) 'The body keeps the score: memory and the evolving psychobiology of post-traumatic stress', *Harvard Review of Psychiatry*, 1, pp. 253–65.

Vilijoen, J.-M. (2014) 'Waltz with Bashir: between representation and experience', *Critical Arts*, 28(1), pp. 40–50.

Walker, J. (2005) *Trauma cinema: documenting incest and the Holocaust*. Berkeley and Los Angeles, CA: University of California Press.

Winborn, M. D. (2015) 'Aesthetic experience and analytical process', *International Journal of Jungian Studies*, 7(2), pp. 94–108.

Filmography

Hiroshima mon amour. (1956) [film] Directed by Alain Resnais. France.

Holocaust. (1978) [television mini-series] Directed by Marvin J. Chomsky. USA.

Nuit e brouillard. (1956) [film] Directed by Alain Resnais. France.

Secrets of a soul. (1926) [film] Directed by Georg Wilhelm Pabst. Germany.

Shoah. (1985) [film] Directed by Claude Lanzmann. France.

Spellbound. (1945) [film] Directed by Alfred Hitchcock. USA.

Waltz with Bashir. (2008) [film] Directed by Ari Folman. Israel.

26

DISCOVERING THE MEANING OF A FILM

John Beebe

Introduction

This chapter draws on approaches C. G. Jung pioneered in his lifelong engagement with psychologically generative images as well as processes I have developed for working with imaginal material in clinical settings. It describes a method of film contemplation that involves letting a certain image in the film support a view of the entire experience. To find this image places demands on the viewer of a film: it requires engaging in a continuous search for what resonates within while the film is viewed from beginning to end. It also necessitates re-seeing the film, not only by viewing it again, but also by replaying the film in one's mind, as one would a dream, until images linger that can function as keys to the film as a whole.

What I will describe here is organized around three stages of experiencing a film in this viewing and reviewing process. These are:

1   Accepting the film as *prima materia* (the base or starting material with which alchemists work). This term, taken from a natural philosophy tradition that stretches from Anaxagoras and Aristotle to spiritual alchemy and analytical psychology (Jung, 1944: §26), reminds us that to extract meaning from any experience, including the watching of a film, is to make our way from an initial chaos toward a gradual perception of pattern and priority. In befriending a film, we must open ourselves to the sometimes-overwhelming welter of material that the film presents. In this way, we can begin to locate something in ourselves that is seeking transformation and that cries out in response to the film.

2   Finding a central or core image in the film as a point of orientation. By image, here, I do not mean anything that can be captured by a still photograph of the kind that is not infrequently used for publicity shortly after a film is released, and used again by a film archive once the film has achieved the status of a classic. Rather, a central cinematic image is an object, place, or situation that the film itself enables us to see over time from different angles and perspectives. Identifying such an image from which proceeds all else that works on us in the film requires developing an ability to distinguish image from story, and to allow the film image to speak to our own imagination apart from its role in telling the story.

3   Returning to the story, with this now more spiritually 'grounding element' (Pessin, 2013, pp. 22–27) of its central image in mind, we watch for that image's capacity within the film

to support transformation. We also notice the way it transforms the film within our own mind by becoming a key to the other images.

Following these steps enables the Jungian viewer to apply imaginal theory in a manner that is not reductive. The goal is to explore the film in such a way that insights will continue to unfold upon successive viewings, rather than become folded up in one's mind like the images on an old-fashioned painted fan that one is fond of but may no longer see the point of reopening.

Prima materia

Accepting a film-watching experience as one's *prima materia* means that a movie one decides to experience and engage with long enough to take up the question of its meaning cannot be explained by reducing it to any other material thought to be more primary, such as its literary or stage or previous film source, but must be taken as it is presented to the viewer. Here, *prima materia* is meant to suggest that the film one has selected to work on, deploying a Jungian alchemy that relies on association, amplification, analogy, and attention to what produces awe, has a ground to which we can return both to start any interpretative process and to verify what then emerges. Often watching a film will reawaken a complex related to something unusually painful experienced by the viewer, who then projects it back into the film. This may be a dis-integrative experience many viewers have had in common, such as facing the aftermath of a war, experiencing a love affair complicated by betrayal, or coming uncomfortably near to a process of death. The universal human problem becomes a starting point for the experience of watching the film, just as the patient's perception of an original problem begins an analytical psychotherapy, in the hope that the suffering of it can at last be mirrored and understood. One expects this from a film about a subject that touches one's own life. Naturally a viewer's prior experience in film-watching will also contribute to how the *prima materia* of this film's viewing manages to consolidate itself. In all these ways, the viewer co-creates the ground of the film, participating in what the film has made visible as to what it has in mind (Hauke, 2014). All the imaginal content – the archetypes and complexes that the film generates and manipulates – stems from an interaction between viewer and what is on offer to be viewed (Hockley, 2001, pp. 2–3). Nevertheless, in watching a film, the viewer will try to suspend a priori expectation so as to experience what seems to him or her to be foregrounded by the filmmaker in the acting, music, script, and editing.

The insights of C. G. Jung, taking up a project inherited from Freud – dream interpretation – as to the creative intelligence of visual fantasy were greatly amplified through his discovery of active imagination (Jung, 2009, pp. 198–202), a rather cinematic method, which has led many Jungians to make a similar effort to see what can be learned about the imaginative process at the heart of filmmaking (Izod, 2000). My personal path to broadening the scope of Jung's work in just this way proceeded, rather naturally, from a lifetime love of movies, begun (I am told) when at 18 months old I was held up to see my first film, a 1940 movie starring American radio's funniest man, Bob Hope. I believe I enjoyed hearing his already familiar voice. The first movie I can recall seeing, however, comes from the year I turned six, when my mother took me to see *Wonder Man* (dir. Humberstone, 1945) starring a far more cinematic comedian, Danny Kaye, playing a dual role. In that well-titled film, one of the twin brothers Kaye was playing managed also to split himself. Edwin, the more bookish of the brothers, is writing a history book, and is engaged, pencils in both hands, with taking notes from a reference book. Both pencils were necessary for efficiency because, as played rather matter-of-factly by a serious, bespectacled Kaye, Edwin could write the first half of a note with one hand while his other hand was writing the second half of the same entry. Perhaps this was the first time it dawned on me that two meaningful processes could be happening at the same time in a film without ultimate loss of coherence.

I was an avid filmgoer through all my years of growing up, but it was when I started analytic training and was waiting for patients to fill the individual therapy hours I had to offer, that I became most dedicated. In need of binding my anxiety about having so little work to do, I found it helpful to go and watch movies as often as daily. This was in the early 1970s in San Francisco when there were at least four repertory cinemas. The same nostalgia boom that led to such first-release movies as *Cabaret* (dir. Bob Fosse, 1972) and *That's Entertainment* (dir. Jack Haley, Jr., 1974) was giving film buffs like me a chance to sample Hollywood's entire oeuvre: silents with Chaplin, Keaton, Garbo, and Gish; dramas of the 1930s and 1940s from each of the major Hollywood studios, retrospectives of major directors. Going every day, one could see a full week each of Capra, Hawks, and Ford; of Joan Crawford, Bette Davis, and Judy Garland; of Cary Grant, Gary Cooper, and Humphrey Bogart. Imitating the way such films were originally shown in American theaters, first-run, one could view the same film twice and get to memorize it.

My goal, though, was to use Jungian thought to extend the aesthetic sense I was cultivating. I was reading a lot of Hillman and von Franz in those days, and I see now I was trying to gain both the 'image-sense' (Hillman, 1979, p. 130) and the ability to trace archetypal motifs (von Franz, 1970) that I knew I would need to be adequate to the dreams patients would be bringing me.

This link between the cinematic and the depth psychological had been made explicit to 1940s film audiences by Hitchcock's *Spellbound* (1945), which had Ingrid Bergman working her way through the vicissitudes of a psychological cure that she often faced in her movies. She looked as if she was in analysis even when she was playing an analyst herself, and my eager, intense *anima* could identify with her fascinated, frightened discovery of the unconscious. For her character, the psyche was not only a mystery she needed to sophisticate herself to solve, it was clearly a reality that she tracked with great excitement. It was the intensity of her devotion to that task that carried the meaning she lent to her Hitchcock movies of 1945 and 1946, *Spellbound*, and the infinitely superior *Notorious*. This is what *anima* means, I told myself, watching her in them. Recognizing the vulnerability in her attentiveness to psychological discovery got me to reflect upon the pluses and minuses of the intensity I brought to my own work.

I was not as quick to realize how cruel the film medium's flirting with the shadow can be. Having watched Welles' *Touch of Evil* (1958) and Hitchcock's *Psycho* (1960) first-run as an undergraduate and, feeling how these films' mythic power was built around attacks on the body, I was not immediately afraid of violent imagery in film. I thought of the murders in these two films not only as witty humiliations of the body, but also as ways to construct anxiety in the viewer over shadow issues. Within noir film, an unsatisfied longing for closure seemed to me a corollary to the power that Greek tragedy depended upon – what we imagine when the violent actions occur offstage. The 'cinema of loneliness' (Kolker, 1988) epitomized by *Taxi Driver* (dir. Martin Scorsese, 1976) taught me that shadow is not always a route to redemption. Robert Altman's *The Long Goodbye* (1973) was a shocking discovery, that a film image can disrupt even the wish to go on contemplating a film sequence – in this case, the smashing of a coke bottle across a young woman's face. My subsequent work using film images to reflect a developing feminine containing capacity in both men and women (Apperson and Beebe, 2008) is necessarily shadowed by the recognition that film images can also jar and wound, kindling the imagination to the point of becoming traumatic.

I bring these fragments of autobiography forward because of my conviction that film-watching, like filmmaking, is a process with a developmental history. At first, one only can know that one wants to go on seeing movies. The movies one saturates oneself with in those early days of falling in love with the medium are the *prima materia* for what will eventually become an alchemical *opus*. In the case of the Jungian analyst of film, the aim is a philosophic understanding through the art of contemplation, which, given that film is already a contemplative medium, is to wash the material, as the alchemist would say, 'in its own water.'

Core image

It is sometimes said that the greater part of filmmaking is done in the meltdown of the cutting room where a director and editor work together to see what can be made of the material that has been shot. In a film that succeeds, however, we may find that the filmmaker has realized an intention to approach the material in the light of a central image that was there from the start. The essence of the *prima materia* can be summed up in a single image, which, though static, is numinous, like the ruby slippers in *The Wizard of Oz* (dir. Viktor Fleming, 1939). I have discovered in contemplating great films that it is often possible to locate just one image that seems to have served as the lodestone for its auteur, containing the spiritual essence of the *prima materia*.

In recent years, I have returned to one of my early favorite films, *Rashomon* (dir. Kurosawa, 1950), drawn, I think, by the creativity with which it engages us in relating to the traumatic aftermath of war. The film's central image is Rashomon Gate, the large, ruined city gate outside Medieval Kyoto that we see at the outset of the film, and to which we return after each of the stories told by a series of narrators about a rape and a murder that have recently been perpetrated. These stories almost seem to emerge from the gate itself, because three men – a priest, a woodcutter, and a cynical commoner – are sitting together under it, waiting for the rain to end, passing the time by talking. Many viewers have wanted to downplay the image of the lofty gate that is so broken that it can barely shelter the men. It is usually seen as a rather uninspiring frame for the real interest of the film, which, for most people, is the way we lie in recounting traumatic experiences – the so-called '*Rashomon* effect.' That focus makes the film fashionably self-reflexive, because film is a medium of storytelling that is essentially tendentious, though it can try to get us to believe that its point of view, because it is a photographic medium, is objective.

But Rashomon Gate holds more significance than merely being the place where we learn about point of view. My basic reading of *Rashomon* is that the woodcutter who observed the rape and murder, about which each of the participants lied, gives us a reasonably accurate picture of what happened. His account is more believable than that of the bandit who pretends to a trickster's capacity not to care about anything but his chance to assert his masculine prowess, the wife who is raped and then insists that her husband try to avenge her, and that the bandit fight for her as well, and the dead samurai himself, whose spirit is summoned by a shamanistic witch. The cynical commoner who seizes upon the one bit of truth that the woodcutter leaves out – that he stole a pearl-handled dagger from the crime scene – to conclude that the overarching lesson of the story is that everyone lies, has himself missed the moral focus of the film. That focus is what we do with the shame caused by the fact that we are not always true to our values.

The cynical commoner leaves the gate – and the film – after stealing the clothing from a baby who has quietly been abandoned there. All the cynic can see is that everyone connected with the rape and murder has managed to tell a self-serving version of what occurred. Such behavior is in accord with what the social psychologist Norman Alexander postulated for 'situated identity theory' (Alexander and Lauderdale, 1977) that, in any public human situation, people will behave in such a way as to select, and if necessary lie to construct, the most favourably viewed identity that is available within that situation. People lie because no one is just the most favorable role that they select as persona – there is too much else to the self in all of us.

Kurosawa's addition, as scenarist, to the Akutagawa story, 'In a grove' (1952) that the film is based on, was the action at the gate, a locale that he took from another Akutagawa story, 'Rashomon,' the plot of which he discarded. This choice turned out to be crucial to the meaning of the story. *Rashomon* literally begins and ends with the image of the ruined gate. The Continuity Script for *Rashomon* starts as follows:

> The title sequence consists of some ten shots of the half-ruined gate, Rashomon, in the rain. Superimposed over these are the titles and credits, including, in some prints distributed in the United States, vignettes (oval-shaped insets) showing the major characters in action. Various details of the gate are seen: its steps, the base of a column, the eaves of the roof, puddles on the ground. Everywhere, there is evidence of the downpour. *Gagaku*, traditional court music, is heard during the credits, then the sound of the torrential rain.
>
> The final title reads, 'Kyoto, in the twelfth century, when famines and civil wars had devastated the ancient capital'.
>
> *(Richie, 1987, p. 35)*

In his recent book, *Kurosawa's Rashomon: A Vanished City, A Lost Brother, and the Voice Inside his Iconic Films*, Paul Anderer (2016) devotes an entire chapter to 'The Gate.' In it he tells us:

> The gate, lashed by driving rain, stands in the middle of nowhere. It is the first image we see. We don't know how it fell into ruins. No structure is visible to the right or to the left of it, behind it or in the foreground, beside what we can see: a fallen pillar, splintered shards of wood, a soupy expanse of mud.
>
> *(p. 10)*

Yet this simple-enough sounding image, largely static in a film that is elsewhere noteworthy for the fluidity of its movement, including the movement of the camera itself, was the most elaborately constructed element of Kurosawa's film. Anderer comments:

> Kurosawa, to the exasperation of his producers, had spent nearly the whole of his set and design budget on this single, dilapidated structure. He stretched for some justification, saying he meant it to represent the Rajo Gate that stood at the southern entrance to the imperial capital of Kyoto during the Heian period (784–1185). But the original was long since demolished (there is speculation it was never completely built, or had been destroyed already by 950). Despite their efforts, Kurosawa's design team could find no extant paintings or screens from the period that took this gate as a focal point. Armed with text references only and nothing visual to faithfully replicate, Kurosawa had a free shot to imagine the gate's shape and mass.
>
> The result, he later confessed, was that 'the Gate just kept growing in my mind's eye.' It took his crew twenty-five days to build.... Because of its scale – almost sixty feet wide, forty feet deep, thirty-five feet high – a generic, traditional gate design was abandoned entirely in favor of one that simulated a grand Buddhist temple ... [a] type of *sanmon* ... resembling the still extant Nanzenji Temple in Kyoto.... But this visual nod to Buddhist temple architecture would carry spiritual weight, too, giving the structure before us a solemnity beyond anything a merely secular gate could have borne.
>
> *(pp. 10–11)*

I identified the gate as the central image of the film before knowing any of this, because the most significantly transformative transactions occur there, especially the interaction between the Buddhist priest and the woodcutter after the cynic has left. The gate itself already seemed to me, from my first sight of it, the signifier of a damaged integrity, and the stories recalled from the magistrate's inquiry into the murder of the Samurai, as heard by the priest and the woodcutter at the inquest and retold to the commoner at the gate, for me merely exemplified the truth of a time of decomposing moral structures.

Part of the imaginal power of the gate is that, though massive, it is in a state of extreme breakdown. Nevertheless, it retains its power to summon a sense of the moral authority it must have once possessed, to decide what was permissible to enter the city and what must be kept out. In its role as delimiter and protector of the city, the gate and its original keepers served the archetypal process we call *discrimination*. When the ability to make appropriate discriminations is impaired, as symbolized by the broken gate, integrity is bound to suffer.

The film invites us to see this late Heian period as a mirror of how shattered Japan's morale was after the Second World War. We have to recall that when *Rashomon* was first shown in the West in 1951, there was a crisis in moral philosophy. The post-Holocaust moral philosopher Levinas (1989), in a paper that year titled, 'Is ontology fundamental?' had begun a critique of the notion that philosophy should begin with an exploration of being and epistemology. Rather, he asserted, philosophy should start with ethics and our relation to the reality of the Other.

Kurosawa's gate, therefore, is not only an image of a shamed Japan: it can just as well represent the crisis in moral discrimination that the Second World War had revealed. The gate signifies, in a cinematic way, the breakdown of criteria of value by which we are in a position to determine which behaviors are admissible. That the gate is damaged and defaced suggests an injury to *Logos* itself, in the sense Jung gives that term (which he sometimes describes as the 'masculine' principle): 'discrimination, judgment, insight' (Jung, 1955–6: §224). Yet Kurosawa uses this decrepit gate to signify a place where men brought together in a heavy storm are forced to decide if there is such a thing as human goodness. This can only be decided by using one's own ethical sense to discriminate, and *Rashomon* tests whether it is still possible to do that.

The long rain, like an alchemical operation (Edinger, 1985, pp. 44–81), offers a process of deliverance, a washing and dissolving of shame, with the gate as the grounding element that, though damaged, can endure the downpour. The great moment at the gate comes when the cynical commoner has gone off, having pilfered the kimono and amulet from the abandoned baby. This theft is too much for the priest, who concludes that human nature is beyond repair. At that point the woodcutter, still suffused with shame at having been exposed for taking the dagger, starts to pull the baby away from the priest who is holding the crying child in a posture of impotent containment. The priest, says the continuity script, 'violently resists' the woodcutter's impulsive gesture of rescue, which he entirely misunderstands.

> PRIEST: What are you trying to do? Take away what little it has left?
>
> *(Richie, 1987, p. 90)*

At this point, comes the part of their exchange most critics of *Rashomon* have ignored. The woodcutter humbly shakes his head to refuse the shabby intent the priest has just attributed to him. His face reveals that he is at least as embarrassed for the priest as ashamed that the priest can only imagine that he would steal again, even from a baby. In compassionate sorrow for how the priest has gotten his intention wrong, yet recognizing that his past behavior has earned him the opprobrium of being seen as nothing but a thief, he slowly but firmly refuses the cynical inference. And then, in words, he reveals his true intent, his face in pain from knowing how ashamed the priest will become when he hears what that really is.

331

WOODCUTTER: I have six children of my own. One more wouldn't make it any more difficult.

The priest, now faces the woodcutter as abashed as the woodcutter has just faced him. The script is terse:

PRIEST: I'm sorry. I shouldn't have said that.
WOODCUTTER: Oh, you can't afford not to be suspicious of people these days. I'm the one who ought to be ashamed. I don't know why I did a thing like that [referring to his theft of the pearl-handled dagger].

(ibid., pp. 90–91)

It is almost a silent movie, at this moment, their faces carrying the meaning of the alchemical dissolving that is their deliverance from the false belief that there is no integrity to be found in the world, and nothing but suspicion, even in the heart of a priest. They are both ashamed, and they hold each other's shame at participating in the general mutual suspicion of the times. They embrace each other's shame (Beebe, 1992, pp. 59–61) and it is dispersed in a moment of mutual compassion. As the woodcutter departs with the baby who has stopped crying, we can see that the downpour has abated. It is as if the baby has given the woodcutter a future he can be proud of.

No wonder that Kurosawa needed to make the gate, which has become a portal to new possibilities, resemble a Buddhist temple. The real effect of *Rashomon* is to show us that compassion for the cynicism we all develop in the face of the betrayals we suffer and perpetrate facilitates the maturation of our integrity more than pure adherence to principle would have done. When both men know they are flawed and can still recognize each other's ethical instincts, the woodcutter can be trusted to take the new Japanese child into a somehow restored world.

Looking at archetypes in the light of the central image

With this core image as the symbolic key to the picture, the stories that viewers remember being told by the principals to the rape and murder are relativized by the fact that our entry into them is as damaged as the gate at which they were told. What we have seen take place at the gate makes us realize that even if it is the signifier of a damaged *Logos*, it also can support the possibility of restoration of what it originally stood for through *Eros*, which Jung defines as 'the capacity to relate' (1955–6: §224).

We could not know that integrity has been breached were there not an archetypal basis in all of us that feels when this has happened. We are usually more galvanized to integrity by the discovery of its absence than by its plentiful presence. We imagine an earlier time when there must have been much greater integrity in the collective (Beebe, 1992, p. 7). The once great gate, now fallen on hard times, captures this sense very well. Fortunately, damaged integrity is exactly what summons the reparative effort to assert the energy remaining in the archetype.

The promise of cinema is that it makes the archetypal which can normally not be seen, visible. It lets us see for ourselves what happens, as Kurosawa's camera seems to do, bringing the stories to life as they are presented to us exactly as if they were happening in the present. On reflection, we can realize that what we have seen in *Rashomon*, is not the truth of lived emotion, but the uncanny fiction of a continuous excess of emotion. The characters' accounts inspire sympathetic identification with extremes of dismay in the face of being set upon during peaceful travel, being raped, being mocked, being shamed, and finally being killed. These events are acted out for us in extremes of theatrical style ranging from Kabuki to romance to farce. They have been visualized for us to match how the different characters would like us to believe they were affected in the roles they want us to believe they assumed.

Trauma, responsible for the excesses with which the characters recall their emotions, has turned their very persons into archetypes. Their stories are too one-sided to be real. Their humanity has devolved into dynamisms of shame, so that one is shameless, one is shamed, and another is shaming. The bandit has much too much agency, the samurai is far too pragmatic, the lady, while sending out a storm of histrionic emotion, is only too willing to leave decisive self-assertion to the men. Each enacts his or her role in a way that accentuates the posture she or he has chosen to affect, so that even their desires to preserve dignity, chastity, and the possibility of enduring love exemplify how little they can access their humanity: their bodies have become ruined gates to the integrity that would be needed to try to take up their former identities again.

If we were to try to see these characters as allegorical of key components of the psyche, naming them as persona, *anima*, and shadow, we would still have to notice how little these archetypes cohere. They have no relationship to an organizing center, a person within this psychic maelstrom, that would enable them to cooperate around their common interest in remaining human. The archetypes are presented in *Rashomon* as hyper-individual personalities, rather than aids in becoming an effective person. Although essential to the action of the film, they do not comprise its essential meaning. Reducing our search for meaning in the film to the self-servingly mythic personages the characters would like to have been cannot unify in our minds what we have also glimpsed, which is how human these people turned out to be, despite their actorly striving to be archetypal.

The turn of these rather ordinary Japanese people to Kabuki level stylized theatrics as well as to the physicality of American movies, in an uneasy join of recently opposed forces in the world, emphasizes a common self-importance between the warring parties in both the film and the recent history that was its proximate background. A clear message of the story as related by the principals is that this is what humanity looks like when overtaken by narcissism. The bandit, the lady, and the samurai realize that fact themselves, and theirs is the clarity of shame. How people remain human, even after a human process motivated by greed that has led to an inevitable defeat, is not shown to us by this dramatic story, however. Listening to the different stories told by the principals, we are not unlike the cynical commoner pulling off parts of the decomposing wood structure of the gate to light a fire. We get emotion to warm us, but at the expense of respect for what we are observing.

On the other hand, if we watch *Rashomon* to the end and let its central image unlock the meaning of the story for us, we are made to see that our humanity is more than this. We are *not* made of nothing but archetypes. Rather, we have an equally archetypal capacity to discriminate archetypes. This is our integrity, a *Logos* threaded with *Eros* like the electrical system that enables a heart to beat. At its heart, integrity will not let us fail to care about the others with whom we interact. The awkward but heartfelt mutual forgiveness of priest and woodcutter, because of the absence of charisma in the persons of these men, is so strikingly different from the bravura with which the principals in the story have presented themselves, that many viewers are disappointed by how the film ends. It is true that the movements of the priest and woodcutter are also slow and stylized, as if to underline the steps of their transformation in a sort of Noh drama. Yet though the story devolves into just the image of these simple men's interaction, their ritual bowing to each other outlines a little gate through which life can issue forth again, now that the rain has stopped. Like the baby taken into the woodcutter's care, humanity in Japan can still develop and once again offer hope.

There is a strong echo, at the end, that the woodcutter and the baby are like an old and a new Adam leaving an Eden of illusion for a realistic second chance at integrity. Despite its Japanese overlay, Kurosawa is retelling the Genesis story of the Western Bible. There has been a visible fall from the glamor and grace of the now forgotten principals. But ordinary life is going forward with a renewed sincerity, and what has now been returned to recognition is the healing reality of human life's interdependence, the truth that was ironically brought home by its lack in the grove where the crimes occurred.

There is, as often in Kurosawa, a Buddhist addition to what might otherwise be more Western in its spiritual attitude than immediately meets the eye (Lu, 2005, pp. 39–40). Because he has taken his scenario back to the gate where the story of Japan's fall from samurai grace has been told, he has made of that broken structure an enduring place of contemplation. If we let ourselves rest our reflections just on that image, we can entertain the meaning of what we have seen. The dissolving of shame effected by the temple-like gate being soaked by the rain no longer seems at all pitiless: it has made possible the compassionate gestures of forgiveness of self and other that the priest and woodcutter make toward each other, as they hold what they know about themselves and each other with as much caring as sorrow. They come together through the recognition of their shared imperfection.

At the heart of their shame is the knowledge that we all manage to lose sight of our integrity. That the film allows the two men to witness that happen in each other, and generates forgiveness rather than cynical judgment is an epiphany for us. Seeing them recognize each other as human breaks the spell the film has cast previously in suggesting that the only alternative to self-idealization is cynicism. Rather, we have seen illusion dissolved in favor of a transcendent humility. The gate that has demanded that we see what compromised integrity looks like now allows us to move beyond the limitation of its border into another story, the baby's, which is just about to begin. It is as if the gate has given birth to the baby.

The return to possibility brings creative energy to the restored integrity. It tells us that there is a way not to fail at human life, even after a serious failure of integrity. This way is to return not just to being as simply human as possible, but also to the risks and the wonder of new attachments. At the end of the film, the woodcutter, carrying the baby, comes toward us, entering our space and passing beyond us, as if inviting us to contemplate something that will occur that exceeds our present capacity to keep on imagining it.

Summary

I hope that at least some readers will feel drawn to experiment with seeking the meaning of a film of their choosing by applying the three-step process I have demonstrated here. Accepting the film as *prima materia* requires that we submit fully to the film itself, living a complete emotional and associative experience rather than protecting and distancing ourselves as we watch. To identify the central image, we take the time to experience in memory how the different images of the film impact us, looking for the one that most opens, rather than limits, future possibilities.

Contemplation of the entire film in light of the central image also takes time, but it is rewarding because it helps us to make sense of all the interesting moments that were out of focus so long as the film was merely a set of imaginal materials rather weakly strung together by a story. When it does this, we have the uncanny feeling that we have gone through a process that was designed to unfold from the start, rather like the unspooling of the film that has made the entire experience possible.

References

Akutagawa, R. (1952) *Rashomon and other stories*, trans. T. Kojima. New York: Liveright.

Alexander, C. N. and Lauderdale, P. (1977) 'Situated identities and social influence', *Sociometry*, 40(3), pp. 225–33.

Anderer, P. (2016) *Kurosawa's Rashomon: a vanished city, a lost brother, and the voice inside his iconic films*. New York and London: Pegasus Books.

Apperson, V. and Beebe, J. (2008) *The presence of the feminine in film*. Newcastle: Cambridge Scholars Publishing.

Beebe, J. (1992) *Integrity in depth*. College Station, TX: Texas A&M University Press.

Edinger, E. (1985) *Anatomy of the psyche: alchemical symbolism in psychotherapy*. LaSalle, IL: Open Court.

Hauke, C. (2014) *Visible mind*. London and New York: Routledge.

Hillman, J. (1979) 'Image-sense', *Spring*, pp. 130–43.

Hockley, L. (2001) *Cinematic projections*. Luton: University of Luton Press.

Izod, J. (2000) 'Active imagination and the analysis of film', *Journal of Analytical Psychology*, 45(2), pp. 267–85.

Jung, C. G. (1944) 'Introduction to the religious and psychological problems of alchemy', in *The collected works of C. G. Jung*, Vol. 12, *Psychology and alchemy*, 2nd edn, trans. R. F. C. Hull. Princeton, NJ: Princeton University Press, 1968.

Jung, C. G. (1955–6) 'Mysterium coniunctionis', in *The collected works of C. G. Jung*, Vol. 14, *Mysterium coniunctionis*, trans. R. F. C. Hull. Princeton, NJ: Princeton University Press, 1963.

Jung, C. G. (2009) *The red book: liber novus*, ed. S. Shamdasani, trans. M. Kyburz, J. Peck and S. Shamdasani. New York & London: W. W. Norton.

Kolker, R. P. (1988) *A cinema of loneliness: Penn, Kubrick, Scorsese, Spielberg, Altman*, 2nd edn. New York and Oxford: Oxford University Press.

Levinas, E. (1989) *The Levinas reader*, ed. S. Hand. Cambridge, MA: Blackwell.

Lu, F. (2005) 'Personal transformation through an encounter with death: a study of Akira Kurosawa's *Ikiru* on its fiftieth anniversary', *Journal of Transpersonal Psychology*, 37(1), pp. 34–43.

Pessin, S. (2013) *Ibn Gabirol's theology of desire: matter and method in Jewish medieval neoplatonism*. Cambridge: Cambridge University Press.

Richie, D. (ed.) (1987) *Rashomon*. New Brunswick, NJ: Rutgers University Press.

Von Franz, M. L. (1970) *Interpretation of fairytales*. New York: Spring Publications.

Filmography

Cabaret. (1972) [film] Directed by Bob Fosse. USA.

Long goodbye, The. (1973) [film] Directed by Robert Altman. USA.

Notorious. (1946) [film] Directed by Alfred Hitchcock. USA.

Psycho. (1960) [film] Directed by Alfred Hitchcock. USA.

Rashomon. (1950) [film] Directed by Akira Kurosawa. Japan.

Spellbound. (1945) [film] Directed by Alfred Hitchcock. USA.

Taxi driver. (1976) [film] Directed by Martin Scorsese. USA.

That's entertainment. (1974) [film] Directed by Jack Haley, Jr. USA.

Touch of evil. (1958) [film] Directed by Orson Welles. USA.

Wizard of Oz, The. (1939) [film] Directed by Victor Fleming. USA.

Wonder man. (1945) [film] Directed by Bruce Humberstone. USA.

27

UNDER THE SKIN

Images as the language of the unconscious

Joanna Dovalis and John Izod

Introduction

When aliens come to our planet, one thing which science fiction audiences learn to expect is that, whether for better or for worse, and whether they take up residence here or move on, visitors who traverse galaxies to reach Earth rarely leave things here unchanged. With the exception only of the tiny number of Earthlings who claim intimate knowledge of incomers, the physical being of extra-terrestrials, if any, is entirely unknown to humanity. Therefore (whether found in dreams, legends, myths or fictions), images of and ideas about such visitors are impregnated with fantasy. *Ipso facto* these beings are vehicles for energy sourced outwith consciousness. The anxiety that surrounds them is one sign of that characteristic.

UFOs as living myth

In a time of international crisis at the end of the 1950s, C. G. Jung wrote a short book about Unidentified Flying Objects (UFOs). Its publication coincided with the intensification of the Cold War to the point where, terrifyingly, global annihilation through nuclear conflict was becoming an all too present danger. Living through the decade when populations of many nations felt imperilled, Jung observed that UFO phenomena, whether physically real or imagined, had been sighted in much increased numbers. He realised they had become a living myth such that 'in a difficult time for humanity a miraculous tale grows up of an attempted intervention by extra-terrestrial "heavenly" powers' (1959, p. 14).

This flurry of UFO sightings chimed in Jung's imagination with his observation that by that date the old gods were dead or dying. Associating UFOs with symbols arising from both the individual and the transpersonal unconscious, he concluded that these round, shiny objects seen in the sky could be regarded as archetypal images. In every age in the Western world, circles, being complete and perfect, had played an important role as both symbols for the unity and wholeness of the soul, and as images of God (1959, pp. 20–1).

A circle in the sky is the first discernible form in the pre-title sequence of *Under the Skin* (dir. Jonathan Glazer, 2013). The film actually opens in pitch dark while a rasp-like, creaking music of scouring energy thrusts into consciousness. Only then is a pinprick of light born in the black screen's centre. Gradually it swells into circular form, undecipherable (because beyond human

336

experience) whether it be a spacecraft, a planet moving through a field of aligned moons, a ring formed by the play of immense energy, a deity's probing eye – or just conceivably the archetypal vehicle for them all. As it nears, repeated chuffing breaks through the wracking buzz. Something alien, straining to vocalise like a human baby, prepares to communicate with Earthlings. Could the strange music carry, on a parallel communication channel, signals incomprehensible to us? At all events, before characters' actions introduce a degree of narrative direction, Mica Levi's fearful soundtrack suggests not only terror but also the subjective loss of spatial coordinates. It does not encourage the hope, whether this twenty-first century UFO be transportation for creatures or a deity, that they might be more benign than the incoming hostiles who fed rampant paranoia in Hollywood's Cold War science fiction.

Myth and art

Why might all this matter to us as we engage with *Under the Skin*? Joseph Campbell explains that 'it is the artist who brings the images of mythology to manifestation, and without images (whether mental or visual) there is no mythology' (1986, p. xxii). When art produces the visionary images necessary to perceive the world differently, it taps into dominant psychic archetypes that hold the potential healing energy to transform the individual *and* transpersonal psyches. One of the attractions of this extraordinary film is that, although its aesthetics and structure do at times invite a naturalistic reading (for example, scenes filmed in Glasgow resemble a *vérité* representation of the city), their utilisation quickly shatters the plausibility of that outer space and refers sound and images to inner space, 'the wonderland of myth' (ibid.). In effect reading this film cannot, even at entry level, be satisfactory unless one looks for something beyond a clinically reductive interpretation. 'Amplification is the *conditio sine qua non* which *cannot* be left out in mythological interpretation' (von Franz, 1990, p. 146). Myth is the language of the psyche. Thus our aims are to engage at depth with *Under the Skin* to discover whether it reveals changes in dominant archetypes and, if it does, to bring their potential meanings towards the consciousness of individuals and, should the gods favour our labours, a wider culture.

> Watching this film feels like a genesis moment – of sci-fi fable, of filmmaking, of performance – with all the ambiguity and excitement that implies. It's as if director and star have gone into some alien space to discover what embodies a person, exposing the interior dynamic of psyche and soul and its relationship to the exterior.
>
> *(Sharkey, 2014)*

Creation mythology

Erich Neumann notes that, for all peoples in all religions, creation first appears as the coming of light. 'The coming of consciousness, manifesting itself as light in contrast to the darkness of the unconscious, is the real "object" of creation mythology' (1954, p. 6). This primordial state of being is perfect because it is self-sufficient and independent. It is also 'the place of origin and the germ cell of creativity' (p. 10).

When in *Under the Skin* light pierces the darkness, it takes a constantly changing circular form which evolves into and then beyond an energy-charged doughnut ring. It recalls the uroboros (the Great Round), the circular snake of ancient myths that bites its own tail, thus slaying, wedding and impregnating itself (ibid.). The uroboric period is that initial phase of psychic identity in which all things are fused together in *participation mystique* (Neumann, 1971, p. 109). It is the state of mystic identity that precedes the emergence (in an individual or a collective) of reflective consciousness. This is the phase in which the movie begins. It brings to mind both the moment of universal creation and the beginning of an individual's life before differentiation commences and the betrayal of separation is first encountered. As Aldo Carotenuto notes, it is at this precise moment of birth that each living creature experiences betrayal for the first time (1996, p. vii). This first phase of separation brings the principle of opposition into being, initiating the earliest stages of self-awareness. Love and hate, light and darkness, conscious and unconscious enter into conflict with one another. Read in this mythologised context, the film's opening invites us to realise that we are witnessing a moment of creation, whether of a lone individual, a new world, or both.

Glazer introduces his alien eyes wide open to a revelation beyond words, the utter wonder and terror of being. Campbell calls such revelation another essential service of mythology (1986, p. xx). From the moment of the alien's entry to the Earth's sphere, a creature not identifiable as either male or female, what we see and hear is mainly formed by her developing perceptions. Access to language initiates the process of differentiation entailed in both making and discerning meaningful variants between sounds: it thereby introduces reflective consciousness. Consciousness may select what a speaker intuits to be the most appropriate words for a given scenario; but those words also reveal the input of the personal and cultural unconscious. Conversely, language deployed consciously begins to change the unconscious. So when the alien incarnates, she must use human language to carry out her mission which impacts on her unconscious, something neither she nor her cohort seem to have anticipated. Losing the plot and losing our minds before we investigate them both can prove a necessary abandonment in starting to pursue an alien!

Liminal being: Johansson the alien

As most reviewers of *Under the Skin* revealed, the audience do not know for some time what to make of the new arrival, except that she both is and is not Scarlett Johansson. As film star she is, by virtue of the juxtaposition between the narrative and her socio-cultural position in the audience's imaginal world, both a virgin goddess and a seductive *anima* figure. As such, she is 'a mediatrix to the unknown, the unconscious. She mediates through images, not words or dialogue' (Douglas, 2000, p. 183). That said, 'Mica Levi's dissonant score creates a pervasive sense of dread, teetering on the brink of madness' (Gray, 2014). What the alien/Johansson embodies remains for us to discover or perhaps co-create.

The Earth-based plot commences at night. The camera surveys a ribbon of wet road that winds through the Scottish Highlands. Reprising the film's opening, a second pinprick of light emerges out of the dark. A powerful bike hurtles down the long glen and an unrelenting electronic chord carried through from the pre-title sequence envelopes the barely visible biker in mystery and speed. He descends towards human habitation, a ruthless messenger who could conceivably have been given power by god-like creatures newly landed in the mountains. As his machine tears through a town, the pumping grind resumes that we heard in space, and the rider (Jeremy McWilliams) heads into the outskirts, stops at a bungalow and disappears beyond the streetlights' reach into the garden. After a moment he comes out, the corpse of a young woman (Lynsey Taylor Mackay) slung over his shoulder. It has been speculated that she is a cadaver found at the side of the road, but the biker is an efficient killer who knows where he is going and why, witness the van ready for him and his cargo.

When the biker dumps the body in the van we cut hard from a deep night-for-night shot into a brilliant light box with the victim's face in close up. As so often in Glazer's films, the aesthetics surprise no less than the form. Where is this blinding, unearthly place? The alien, now embodied in Johansson's naked human form, strips the dead woman of her clothes and dons them. Director of Photography Daniel Landin holds both the living and the dead in blue-black monochrome, sometimes in images recalling Lotte Reiniger's paper cut silhouettes. This woman (the only female whom the aliens kill) has been targeted because her clothes will fit one particular alien's body, and that body must be sexily female. Cladding herself in the feminine, 'she' mimics the hero of classical myth preparing for war. Her performance of dressing also embodies an attitude she intends to adopt in her new earthly surroundings as she aims to seduce the human males whom she will target. Carotenuto emphasises the central role of seduction in human experience, designating it as a particular circular space where the Me is placed in relation to the Other (2002, p. 2). Implicated in this alien Psyche's disarming attire is the possibility that she may become a new collective dominant in a specific new feminine form, offering a more complete realisation of ego and Self, where the ego experiences the Self and becomes one again with it.

Landin's camera takes up the alien's point of view in shots where, gathering information, she turns an equally cool gaze on the cadaver and an ant marooned on the body. She picks up the insect, peers at it and notices a tear leaking from the corpse's eye. This bizarre juxtaposition will acquire meaning retrospectively for the audience and for the alien herself who gathers information randomly as it impinges on her. Ants have long represented communities that function in an orderly, efficient yet instinctive manner, in contrast to the great difficulty that societies of human beings (endowed with consciousness) experience in trying to behave comparably. This lone ant brings to mind an autonomous complex emerging from the collective unconscious: perhaps a new cultural consciousness.

Meanwhile, the corpse's tear returns us to Carotenuto's thoughts on betrayal. People come into the world exposed to 'the betrayal of life by death, betrayal through hate, betrayal of the primary unity through birth itself' (1996, p. 85). Individual psychological birth is impossible without the experience of betrayal (ibid.); but the young woman's sacrifice may allude to something beyond her individual murder, namely the rupture of an old way of feminine relating. One kind of betrayal is to reveal inadvertently a person's identity or character that should be secret. In this sense, the victim's corpse reveals the shadow side of the female as lacking in psychic energy. Being impoverished, it must come to life again. Thus her death signals metaphorically the victim's unlived part of the feminine element and simultaneously implies potential qualities yet to become part of the alien's character and actions. We shall discover through the female alien's mysterious power, that only a conscious and responsible attitude transforms the shadow into a friend (von Franz, 1996, p. 139).

A hard cut takes us from the ant in extreme close up to the foot of a residential tower where demolition is under way. The awkward juxtaposition of the crumbling tower and the wrecked homes that it contains can be taken as another emblem of decaying human culture and consciousness in both their masculine and feminine aspects. Overhead, lights flare briefly: the UFO lifts away from the skyscraper's top while the alien/Johansson exits via a dilapidated stairwell and takes possession of the van. Her disguise, chosen by the male biker (his victim's denim miniskirt and torn fishnets), does not suit her purpose and she needs to hit Aphrodite's temple, a brightly lit mall redolent with the aura of desire, to fine-tune her appearance for seduction or warfare. Filmed *cinéma vérité* style as she walks among shoppers in her 'slatternly mop of dark hair' (Anderson, 2014), the working girl ignored by the crowds is also Johansson the unseen dark goddess and now Laura, the alien/human. (The dark side of goddesses is the one most intimately associated with transformation [Downing, 2007, p. 110]). In one context, Laura's Earthling name associates her with triumphant Roman generals through their laurel garlands. Yet we notice on her calves the rip in the murder victim's fishnet tights. It suggests a feminine wound arising from the unstable nature of an overly adapted self, a female mask that has been defined by Western civilisation. This adaptive part of the personality must always avoid something, and therefore uses the primitive defence of splitting as a coping mechanism. As a result, the person behaves in ways not in relationship to their whole psyche. Only when the personality maintains a certain plasticity can the ego be sufficiently influenced by the Self and healthfully adapt to the whole psychological system.

Exploiting liminality

In the mall alien/Laura observes women being shown how cosmetics alter their personae. She buys stand-out lipstick on the saccharine side of scarlet and complements it with a faux-fur jacket and acid wash jeans. Her attraction to make-up and clothing both covers up and reveals her instinctual desires. Thus re-equipped in 'low-rent French Connection chic' (Anderson, 2014), she appears both more obvious and bordering on the false: a working-class Brit but posh too, as her middle-class English accent suggests (see Romney, 2014). Her tacky fur, neon lips and van could be the cover of a middle-class woman away from home, prowling Glasgow to pull men. Equally, the weird combination might reveal a common theme of science fiction, the extra-terrestrial's necessary adaptation to her destination. Anthony Morris catches the character's strange, doubled quality:

> Usually in film, women – especially a movie star like Scarlett Johansson – are presented as sexy and attractive, whether the story requires it or not. That's part of what makes you a movie star: people like to look at you. Here that's reversed: Johansson is shown as sexy in the story we're watching – the men she picks up look at her with barely concealed lust – but both the film and Johansson herself work hard to present her (or her body at least) to the audience as something unsettling and remote. She seems human to the leering men around her, but she's an alien to herself, and Johansson gives a brilliant performance as a creature always slightly horrified to be who she is.
>
> *(2014)*

The shimmering of her roles against each other penetrates, in an almost hallucinatory manner, into the celebrated quasi *vérité* sequences filmed when the alien/Johansson drives around Glasgow picking up young working–class men and flirting with them. In fact the aesthetics differ from the purely observational style that orthodox *vérité* aspires to. Take, for example, two effects which can be interpreted, because of their unfamiliarity, as revealing what the alien hears and sees. Where *vérité* would favour direct sound, we hear a sophisticated, mixed sound spectrum: a pump, one stroke heavier than the other, labours under a subaltern buzz that is pierced occasionally by screeching violins. Except for its mechanical rhythm, the beat might recall a limping human heart. The visual perspective disquiets too: though the van prowls slowly, it sometimes swerves across the traffic lane and Landin's camera pans a bit too far, as if controlled by a poorly programmed machine.

Romney (2014) notes that the men lifted from the streets do not realise what they are being sized up for:

> the actual men in front of the camera, non-professionals picked up on the spur of the moment, don't realize that they're in a movie – and that they're being chatted up by none other than Scarlett Johansson.... Thus the film becomes on one level a documentary about how these men react to Johansson, and on another, about how unsuspecting earthlings might behave just before being killed.

Alien as *anima*

The associations of 'Laura's' pseudonym with the garland of a victorious general befit the alien's ambivalent nature. In selecting her victims, she discriminates in two ways: she never kills women; and she does not take men who have a family. Her acts resemble the methodical harvesting of a natural resource. When killing her first victims she seems no more emotionally engaged than a farmer offloading sheep ready for market at the abattoir. Yet, by the laws of our planet, her business is meditated serial murder. James Hillman notes that the unconscious *anima* is a creature without relationships, an autoerotic being whose aim is to take total possession of the individual (1985, p. 116). The untouchable element of the alien/Laura's personality has just this characteristic. Such women, Esther Harding comments,

> conquer men not for love of the man, but for a craving to gain power over him. They cannot love, they can only desire. They are cold-blooded, without human feeling or compassion. Instinct in its daemonic form, entirely non-human, lives through them.
>
> *(1990, p. 118)*

In Carotenuto's terms, she incarnates perfectly

> The type of woman-Anima Jung first described – a woman able to impersonate the projections of the man she seduces so perfectly that … [she] assumes the countenance of our fantasies, becoming the shadow onto which we project the internal image of *our* sexual counterpart.
>
> *(2002, p. 11)*

Yet Laura's robotic quality implies that she herself does not yet possess the psychological characteristic of projection because she is imbedded in an archaic identity (not the only such personality in the screenplay). In writing of these large areas of unconscious identity, Jung says that only if a necessity has arisen to dissolve the identity can one begin to speak of projection, but not before (1923: §783).

Only when Laura starts picking up men is minimalist dialogue first heard. If she spots a potential victim she engages with him easily, but mostly she asks questions, as Chris Knight notes. 'When she makes statements they are repetitions of earlier answers, intending to elicit more data. She speaks like a chatbot, a computer program designed to fool human operators into thinking it has sentience' (2014). (Johansson voiced a comparable role as an intelligent computer operating system in Spike Jonze's *Her* [2013].) More than one reviewer found the men's Glaswegian accents indecipherable, but accepted that could be how our world sounds to an incomer (Martin, 2014). And the characters played by non-actors reveal their sensual awakening through body language.

If naturalism is the more obvious shaping influence in the street scenes, fantasy once again dominates when the alien leads all-too-willing men into what they take to be her home. Once through the door, walking backwards steadily over a reflecting black surface while discarding one garment after another, Johansson/the alien leads each new captive into immeasurable space.

> Reflecting objects have [had], … from time immemorial, a numinous significance for human beings. The oldest experience of a reflecting object may well have been that of the surface of water … Ninck shows that in the world of antiquity water was always

thought of as chthonic, as having sprung from the earth, and that it was always associated with what he calls the 'night conditions' or 'night states' of the soul: intoxication, dream, trance, unconsciousness, and death.

(von Franz, 1995, p. 183)

Throwing off their clothes, the priapic fellows advance towards her, snared by lust for the splendid body that recedes before them, completely unaware that the mysterious surface sustaining her is deluding them. John Berger compared representations of the naked body and a nude via spectators' use of their images. The former is the image of someone wearing no clothes; the latter of a naked person clad in spectators' desire (1972). In the alien's slaughterhouse, her aroused victims see her as nude, dressing her in cocksure anticipation that she reciprocates their lust; but the audience sees a naked woman walking backwards purposefully over a reflecting black surface. The men are *pueri aeterni* (eternal youths) whose erotic longings reflect that they have been captured by their own shadow projections. The shadow, the repressed or neglected part of consciousness that has split off into the unconscious, contains the overwhelming power of irresistible impulses and actions. As we have seen, it conceals the personal *anima*, embodying the feminine psychological propensities in a man's psyche and his relation to the unconscious. In a sense, the *anima* is the male's experience of the feminine unconscious. Its most frequent manifestation takes the form of erotic fantasy with the present scene exposing its most dangerous negative aspects. These are the destructive illusions which distort men's decision making and thereby drag them into the *anima*'s lair. The victims plod ever deeper into something that, weirdly, neither ripples nor instantly drowns them. Neither the characters nor the audience can make out what it is – and that's the point.

Instinct

One night, when she is driving the city, a lacy veil of shadow falls and lifts again and again across alien/Laura's face as she motors under the streetlights, a fascinating image that pulses like oscillating consciousness. Through it mixes the sound of heavy seas, deep water leading into a scene of naked horror. It is daylight when Laura parks the van above a gravel beach where an Atlantic gale whips spume from powerful waves, a veil occluding the bay. She watches a vigorous swimmer exit the turbulent waves, engages him with her chat-up routine, establishing that he is a lone Czech visitor (another alien in Scotland) and a good target for seduction. But suddenly his attention snaps away from her to the far end of the bay where a family man trying to save his wife from drowning has put himself at risk. Unmoved, Laura the alien looks on while the Czech, facing extreme peril, drags the husband to safety. But the rescued man cannot abandon his wife although high seas have pulled her far beyond reach. He staggers back into the waves, where both drown.

The family disaster commenced when the wife leapt into the ocean to save their dog. As von Franz reminds us, animals are the bearers of human projections: 'As long as there is still an archaic identity, and as long as you have not taken the projection back, the animal and what you project onto it are identical; they are one and the same thing' (1996, p. 36). By rushing to her death in the oceanic waters of the unconscious, the woman vividly portrays the failure of her maternal instinct and its connection to the deeper feminine. In complete identification with the animal, she has projected her disavowed instinctual nature on to the dog, impulsively following it to her death. Plainly she lacked conscious connection to the *Eros* principle, 'an opener and a uniter, the wisdom of Eros encompassing bitterness together with its life-giving power acquired by feeling-experiences' (ibid., p. 130). That lack made her unable to judge soundly and sacrifice the dog. Driven by overwhelming emotions – love, terror and anguish – both parents acted impulsively, as humans do in a crisis, unconsciously forgetting their baby. Jung reminds us that

> The autonomy of the unconscious … begins where emotions are generated.… In a state of affect a trait of character sometimes appears which is strange even to the person concerned, or hidden contents may irrupt involuntarily. The more violent an affect the closer it comes to the pathological, to a condition in which the ego-consciousness is thrust aside by autonomous contents that were unconscious before.
>
> *(1939: §497)*

The emotional reactions of this married couple reveal disturbing relationships both between their individual conscious and unconscious and in the interpersonal aspect of the unconscious relationship between their *animus* and *anima*. How, then, could the feminine principle of *Eros* and relatedness conceivably be redeemed by this robotic, murderous incomer?

What follows could not express more graphically the difference between murder and self-sacrifice motivated by tenderness for life. When the baby's anguished wails pierce the racket of storm on stone, alien Laura notices it stranded on the rocks. Contrary to the affect-driven nature of humans (and to the deep shock of the film's audiences) she completely ignores the infant as its cries rise to helpless screams of terror – further evidence that the alien does not possess that human quality of projection which reveals the subjectivity of a personal psyche and interior life. Instead, witnessing the exhausted Czech collapse unconscious on the gravel, she strides purposefully along the roaring water's edge and cracks his skull with a large stone before delivering him to the biker and death. This, her first physically aggressive act, may be a reaction to a kind of betrayal, her first failed attempt to seduce. It's an early sign that her experiences on Earth may be changing alien/Laura, a development that her tribe did not anticipate.

Abandonment and the patriarchy

From a depth-psychological and cultural perspective, Laura/the alien's indifference frames the baby's abandonment in the context of a crisis of our time. On the personal level, the baby's fate is clearly due to the neurotic components of the parents' personalities and lack of connection to their instinctual natures.

> If however, one leaves it embedded within its archetypal context, then it takes on a deeper meaning, namely that the new God of our time is always to be found in the ignored and deeply unconscious corner of the psyche.
>
> *(von Franz, 1996, p. viii)*

Understanding the archetype of the feminine is essential to comprehending the *anima* as the archetype of life and its connection to what Jung calls the Self, that is, the psychic totality of an individual and the regulating centre of the collective unconscious. Thus the baby's cry gives direct voice to the abandonment content of our dangerously narrow, one-sided culture whose instinctual life has been oppressed and repressed. Having no parents, everything for the orphaned baby lies ahead in an unknown future. So who is this 'child'? Clearly it personifies some realm of the psyche, and is not altogether about the infant per se. For Jung, 'The "child" is all that is abandoned and exposed and at the same time divinely powerful; the insignificant, dubious beginning and the triumphal end' (1951: §300).

Neumann reminds us that the development of consciousness in the West is a history of masculine, actively oriented consciousness whose achievements led to a patriarchal culture.... The different nature of the female and feminine psyche must be discovered anew not only if women are to understand themselves, but also if the patriarchally masculine world that has fallen ill thanks to its extreme one-sidedness is again to return to health (1994, p. xi).

As long as our female alien continues acting ruthlessly, her masculine side dominates, noticeably so while her deeds resemble the biker's. *Under the Skin* in this phase is a piercing tale about a heroine's problem with the shadow and her destructive *animus*. The *animus* is an internal image of the masculine in the unconscious, entwined with the shadow and associated with *Logos*. It has both bad and good qualities. Until now we have seen only its negative aspects, the one-sided, collectively masculine-driven universe that alien/Laura comes from. In this negative form the *animus* leaves a woman where *Eros* is lacking, separated from life. In its positive aspect it builds a bridge to the Self and, ultimately, enables transformation to spiritual wisdom. Where *anima* reaches backwards by its reflective nature, *animus* is concerned with the present and the future.

The biker conscientiously removes the drowned family's tent to destroy signs of their presence but leaves behind the hysterical infant tottering in near complete darkness along the water line. Its wailing does not distress these dangerous visitors because, as an innocent (still held in the archetypal realm of the mother), it has no relevance for their mission. Only when alien/Laura notices a black baby drowsing contentedly in a car does the sight get under her skin. Although the audience don't know it, she too is black beneath her adopted hide. With this sighting, the mirroring image of the black baby may have initiated a connection with her own unconscious. The language of images is that of the unconscious therefore, we can never reach beyond the symbolic images which the unconscious produces. Psychologically interpreted, the contact appears to have sparked her *potential* to develop the psyche's creative activity because as soon as there is a tendency for self-reflection and doubt, projection appears. Nevertheless, whatever latent metamorphoses may be stirring within, they do not immediately unsettle her mimetic human persona. As long as she remains the efficient killing machine, there is complete cold objectivity in the way the alien lives, manifesting no feeling life. But, as Ean Begg notes, repressed parts of the archetype both in individuals and history tend to 'take their captors captive' (1986, p. 37).

It becomes possible, as the narrative unfolds, to compare Laura/alien with the males who populate the world she moves in. When she first sets about entrapping Glaswegians, they resemble each other under the skin despite obvious (delusory) differences between her adopted human gender and theirs. She chooses from the city streets only men all of whom are dead in spirit and come to life only at the prospect of a primitive sexual encounter. Their zombie-like personas are filled with unconscious contents which have been rejected and killed off, neither grieved over nor buried. Asking them if they have family, she chooses only those who are not connected to anyone. Lacking relationship to their internal feminine, they are vulnerable to seduction. Their isolation contrasts with the way a group of women partygoers cheerfully sweep Laura into their vivacious collective. But she is not one of them. As yet in her alien being undifferentiated from the biker, she selects victims who, with their dumb, biddable energy, would augment a totalitarian power structure – possibly the destination to which she despatches them.

Approaching feminine consciousness

We have noted that alien/Johansson arrives on Earth in a psychological state of *participation mystique*. A moment that initiates her development occurs when, after she has sunk some men in her pool, she examines what is not her own but Laura's face in a mirror, acquiring perhaps via her adopted persona some glimmer of feeling for the human Self that it masks.

As Jung said many times, it is through a mirror that the unconscious becomes aware of its own face (1954: §43).

The biker is unsettled by his colleague's moment of introspection. Sensing danger, he addresses her intently, though on a channel to which we cannot tune. Hitherto (despite their differently gendered human forms), they have lived in a collective world of sameness. But step-by-step she is now breaking out from *participation mystique*, commencing the individuation process, coming to consciousness and, in consequence, equally bewildered by human kindness and cruelty. The biker does not and will not change, his body-integral backpack declaring his robotic otherness.

Meanwhile sunk in the surreal bath to which alien/Laura has led them, two of the Glaswegian men touch, causing a bang like an electrical short circuit. The shock hurls them back from each other, tinfoil manikins wrinkling into nothingness. Interpreted psychologically, the moment when they reach out and touch in the indescribable bath of the unconscious exposes them to the devastation of coming to consciousness too late. 'Whenever the psyche is set violently oscillating by a numinous experience, there is a danger that the thread by which one hangs may be torn' (Jung cited by Stein, 2006, p. 45). For example, in Ovid's *Metamorphoses*, when Earth's inhabitants cry out for Zeus to intervene in their crises, he responds with apocalyptic lightning strikes. Like those ancients exposed to the divine presence for which they lusted, these flaccid and unprepared victims are destroyed, sucked along a blood-red beam down which white light sears. Their obliteration is confirmed by Levi's rasping music that develops material first heard in the pre-title sequence: all change can only take place in the unconscious.

Laura the alien takes another step differentiating her from her minder when the lonely vulnerability of a facially disfigured young man (Adam Pearson) attracts her. Like this sufferer from neurofibromatosis, she too is alone and misshapen, concealed in a woman's form to carry out the aliens' collective mission. She gazes at the unfortunate man and seems, like a lover, to take him into her inner world. She is in contact with the feminine aspect of a human, albeit in a deformed male body which elicits the nascent feminine in her. That shows in her compassion and sense of his beauty when she identifies with him as a positive mirror of her own shadow. The encounter will draw out her instinctive impulse to awaken the feeling connection with the depths of the unconscious and with nature, since in life it is the task of the feminine to renew feeling values.

This does not happen instantly, for when she takes him to her slaughterhouse, she begins as usual to strip and (while surfaces dissolve and stressed violins wail) draws the unfortunate fellow into the deeps over which she presides. But as he descends, she discerns (barely perceptible in the dim light) a submerged human form, not his body wracked by neurofibromatosis, but an image of perfected humanity, momentarily superimposed on her gazing profile. Everything changes. The ugly man has stirred vivid affect beneath consciousness and it has generated a dark idealisation of human potentiality in her mind – a transformational archetypal image. The shock breaks her seduction ritual and draws her once more to the mirror where her watching face scrutinises its reflection, her slight, questioning movements out of synch with those in the mirrored image. Her reflection gradually clarifies as the gloom that first obscured it lifts. It is an expressionistic rendering of the metamorphosis she is undergoing: the shadow redeemed by being made conscious. Hillman says that *anima* consciousness brings the possibility of reflection in terms of awareness of one's unconscious and that is why *anima* is the archetype of the psychological calling (1985, p. 137).

A frantic housefly scrabbles to escape from a frosted window. In chilly dawn light alien/Laura unbolts her door and shepherds the naked man out of the tomb prepared for him. Fleeing his seducer for dear life, he flounders barefoot over a marshy field as panicky as the fly. Meanwhile she drives away in the van, knowing full well that her demonic minder is already hammering along open roads in pursuit. The biker first slays the poor fellow and dumps his corpse unceremoniously. Then he hunts Laura who now imperils the aliens' mission. For the first time her movements signal fear, a further lurch towards consciousness in a creature that, before cladding herself in woman's form, never knew feelings.

Trying out humanity

Finding herself in the Scottish Highlands, alien/Laura drives past a mountain loch where the wind curls spume above the water, a stunning image that recalls the sea bay where the family drowned, but this time without horror. Given the changed context, these shots lay bare to her eyes the wonder of nature and, thanks to the wind, bring to mind the potentially inspiring spiritual quality of the unconscious. She enjoys only a glimpse of this strange beauty before a chill fog of unknowing maroons her. She abandons the van and, now unprotected by her fellow aliens, mimics people in order to pass as human. But she cannot emulate these alien creatures perfectly. Taking afternoon tea in a café, she discovers she cannot swallow Earthlings' food: unlike David Bowie's *The Man Who Fell to Earth* (dir. Roeg, 1976), she has not come for food to sustain physical life on her planet. Since eating is often implicated in emotional life, it seems she cannot yet digest the human experience. She walks on, lost and alone, tracking the ribbon of tarmac until local resident Andy (Michael Moreland) advises her to catch the rural bus with him. Although she cannot find words to respond to people's concern about her inadequate clothing, she gradually recognises Andy's kindness and accepts the loan of his leather jacket and an invitation to his bachelor home.

She continues exploring her nascent emotions, beginning to unlock the unconscious albeit, shorn of her pre-set chat-up programme, she remains wordless. She watches Andy move around his kitchen to the rhythm of a pop song and tries to copy him but cannot hit the beat. Nor can she eat the meal he prepares. But later, alone in his spare bedroom, she strips off and looks cautiously at the reflection of her human body. What she sees intrigues her and she flexes the strange limbs, discovering with a hint of erotic awakening their appealing softness.

By absconding, 'Laura' has slighted the biker's power as enforcer. Deploying his only resource and thereby confirming his one-sidedness, he calls up three more bikers as reinforcements. The four clones, a quasi-military contingent, pound country roads through the night to find and eliminate her, edgy violins again scratching at the machines' roar. These clones belong in the pre-conscious unity, the undifferentiated collective, their mono-vision locked on safeguarding the mission. As part of the totalitarian collective that swallows its victims, they fear separateness and the uncontrollable vitality that self-awareness brings. Ironically they constitute a male quaternity; but where the number four should symbolise wholeness, here it represents only the *Logos* principle dominating their collective attitude. *Under the Skin* thus continues to emphasise the missing feminine by dwelling on a dominant collective attitude in which the principle of *Eros* – of relatedness to the unconscious, the irrational and the feminine – has been lost. The *anima*, on the other hand, serves life and entangles a man in it (von Franz, 1996, pp. 169–70).

The edge of liminality

Laura meanwhile has commenced a heroic journey oriented towards emancipation through rebirth. She soon encounters further challenges. Andy becomes her guide and leads her across the countryside to explore a ruined castle. For her the main feature is not archaeology but paralysing vertigo: the intergalactic traveller is living between two worlds and must depend on this gentle man to lead her down the dark steps of an ancient tower. In so doing, Andy draws her down from the high wall whence she witnessed one of the bikers speeding past. Acting as psychopomp, he mediates between the conscious and unconscious and shows her the way. By assisting her to find shelter in the dark, he demonstrates *puer* consciousness and his positive relationship with his *anima* to make the unknown safe. In this context he is also the positive *animus*, unconscious awakening in Laura. That night they share the bed and Laura begins to learn how two humans express affection for each other. But when their pleasure rises, he finds it impossible to enter her. She jumps up to examine her groin. A virgin in her alien human form, she is perhaps checking whether lovemaking has torn her skin. Be that as it may, the sweet bond that was emerging between the man and his visitor breaks. Evidently the aliens know nothing about human sexuality or desire.

Daylight finds Laura marching across open country into a dark forest plantation. Compared with her fear when navigating the castle stairwell, she moves confidently between dripping trees and, covered by one of Andy's heavy jackets, picks a way over sodden earth and fallen lumber. But when a truck driver approaches through the trees, he tells her needlessly that the forest is safe, with well-marked but slippery paths. And while speaking he takes note of the attractive, defenceless woman. As she scrambles on, one of the bikes tears along a wet road flanking the forest, menacing in its noisy speed. She is still the males' quarry.

Dystopia and hierophanies

Deep among the trees she comes on an empty bothy and decides that it is a safe place. She stretches out on the floor, her awkward preparations revealing that sleep is another human experience still new to her. Yet she does sleep while the wind rises, which recalls Hillman's observation, 'Breezy wind and shifts of atmospheric pressure all belong to anima' (1985, p. 25). The gusts waltz the treetops and an image of her dozing form emerges softly couched and nested tranquilly high among rocking branches. The picture invokes rich associations with the naiad Daphne, a woodland character and virgin nymph in ancient Greek myth whose name meant 'laurel'. Just as Laura in the superimposed shot looks whole unto herself, ensouled, lovely and more human than ever, Daphne's beauty was widely celebrated. On seeing the nymph, the sun god Apollo fell irredeemably in love. However, his unswerving passion for her beauty was not stronger than her determination to live alone. When after long pursuit Apollo was about to catch her, she appealed to a river god, to 'work some transformation, and destroy this beauty which makes me please all too well!' (Ovid, 1955, pp. 43–4). Thereupon she metamorphosed into a laurel tree. The disappointed Apollo, still in love with her, decreed that laurel leaves should (as we noted earlier) garland victorious generals when they led triumphal processions through Rome (ibid.). Whereas Daphne becomes a nature goddess, the film's closing images manifest a different but no less archetypal transformation awaiting Laura.

The ambivalent associations of forests are rich. Who can fail to be reminded, as Laura wanders, of Dante's evocation of the lost soul's confusion in the dark woods of the unconscious? Nor can we forget the menace of goblins, trolls and malevolent animals concealed within its deep shadows. On the opposite side, the forest represents nature and the place where pure instinct and healing reside. Jung, looking beyond such familiar metaphors in European myths and fairy tales, observed that forests symbolise the layer in the unconscious that lies close to the somatic processes (1948: §241); and von Franz parses this as the psychosomatic area of the unconscious (1997, pp. 63–4). Likewise, writing as it were on the body, skin is the liminal barrier between inner and outer, not just flesh but psyche too.

Taken together, these perspectives prepare the ground for Joseph Cambray's post-Jungian interest in the ecology of psyche. Recognising that the world is diseased, he advocates that Jungians should explore this darkness. He offers as inspiration the observation that scientists have become myth-makers, shifting their focus from objects to the ways in which those very objects are interconnected and thereby change each other. Cambray instances the complex adaptive system of rhizomes (part of the underground structure of certain plants) that send out roots and shoots to interact with other subterranean life forms ('Rhizome', Wikipedia). He speaks of a mode of interaction beyond mere survival, an altruism or cosmic generosity of great trees which support smaller plants in the forest that could not otherwise survive in their shadow. Thus, when forests are slashed and burnt to make way for cash crops, not only the woods, but the unseen life-support systems under the surface are wrecked too (Cambray, 2016).

From a depth-psychological perspective, psyche and soma are actively engaged and interconnected, a reaffirmation that everything co-originates. On the personal level, bodily symptoms act as mouthpieces for the personal unconscious. Hillman (2005) notes that the Greek roots of the word 'symptom' refer to anything that has befallen one, a happenstance or chance (p. 108.) As a symptom, our planet's dis-eased ecology speaks of what has been violently extracted from mother earth and consequently requires that we descend into the psyche's underworld to deal with it. At its conclusion, *Under the Skin*, with its machining of trees and rape of nature, comes flat out into contact with what Vandana Shiva calls the myth of our time – limitless growth (2016). This poisonous myth feeds the greed-driven id of a one-sided culture that is arrested in the illusionary state of limitlessness, continuing to live in the psychic realm of *participation mystique* with its addictive attractions.

The magical emblem that gives rise to these speculations, the vision of 'Laura' blessed by nature, hints that she too might experience transformation into a tree. But any idea that she might metamorphose completely into a woman is erased violently when back in the bothy she is shocked awake by the truck driver stroking her leg with indecent intent. She rushes into the woods and takes refuge behind a fallen tree's mossy roots which look uncannily like a green giant's massive foot. Von Franz might have seen this as an emblem of Laura's assailant, when describing giants as half-human archaic beings that represent emotional factors of crude force which have not yet emerged into the realm of human consciousness (1996, p. 123).

The beleaguered woman runs on and finds a forest track where a massive articulated vehicle waits to be loaded with logs; but the driver has taken its keys and blasting the horn to summon help simply reveals her whereabouts. She races back through the trees with her attacker in pursuit until strength fails. Two millennia after its origin, the Daphne myth plays out again, this time running on to the conclusion that the nymph had dreaded, when the truck driver, no effulgent Apollo but the latest brutalising male in *Under the Skin*, catches his quarry.

The same halting music resumes that played when, as alien, she lured her victims into the fatal pool. When she did so, the instinct emerging from her alien tribe's mission possessed her, as part of the group's single mind. Then, *participation mystique* excluded any personal intention. The trucker, in contrast, is dominated by the ego's appetite to exercise personal power. He knocks Laura to the ground and tears at her clothes. When she resists as best she can, thereby spurring his frenzy, he tears the blouse from her back and, appallingly, rips humanoid flesh, her secret pink costume.

While the enraged trucker, stymied in his intended rape, hastens back to his lorry, Laura/alien, now the victim, peels off her split skin to reveal under it a black body and aquiline head. She staggers towards open ground beyond the trees, her alien eyes gazing at the Laura mask now cherished and cradled in her hands. The ascetic black face is strange but neither less beautiful nor less feminine than the lush mask in which 'Laura's' eyes blink, not yet defunct, still engaging with her alien mistress. As her persona, the Laura mask has done more than conceal the alien's own face, healing and helping birth the latter's positive *animus* with all its spiritual wisdom. This, the only image of the two together, personifies the relationship that now exists between the alien's inner and outer worlds. In the instant before transformation, mutual compassion bonds them, a final reversion to mirroring. The trucker returns from his vehicle hefting a can of petrol, splashes fuel over the couple, lights it ... and scurries away.

Too late, the lead biker stands on a snowy ridge posing like a titan commanding the Highland landscape. Pretending irresistible masculine power, he (like the trucker a moment earlier) shows no trace of *anima* culture. Blind to what is happening beneath him as the conflagration rages and then dies to cinders, he has, since his protégée escaped him, become powerless. His coldness freezes him in the land of the dead. As a character type, however, his significance perseveres, linking masculine dominance to the spiritual totalitarianism that amplifies this century's crisis. Hillman saw the semi-human titan as a mythic emblem of the contemporary Western world's grotesque, overblown and greedy nature:

> There is a huge and ugly, and evil, empire at work day and night to keep us this way. Manically charged, hyper-loud and strong TV, sensationalist media news; ... the health industry building muscles not sensitivity; the medical industry as drug dispensers; ... and shopping, shopping, shopping.
>
> *(1988, p. 154)*

Hillman identified three interlocking prerequisites to finding a cure for 'titanism'. 'Reawakening the sense of soul in the world goes hand in hand with an aesthetic response – the sense of beauty and ugliness – to each and everything' (ibid.). That demands integration of the opposites whereby both individuals and societies learn to live with their shadows. In turn, that necessitates 'trusting the emotions ... as the felt immediacy of the gods in our bodily lives, and their concern that this world, our planet, their neighbor, does not become the late great planet earth' (ibid.).

As flames consume the duo when they stagger out of the trees to collapse in snow, they fill each other's gaze lovingly. Alien/Laura cannot escape death nor, unlike Daphne, transform into a tree. Yet, once in the clearing, they do metamorphose. Something occurs analogous to the Toltec ritual of dismembering and re-membering (to this day the deep crux of a shamanic practitioner's initiation rites). While the duo burn, black smoke rises thickly through the falling snow that covers the boggy landscape. They are a sacrifice offered for transformation, not as before through the death of a person like the girl killed when the aliens landed, but of collective *personal* values: the one-sided culture filled with unyielding longings and ossified ways of being. *Anima* has successfully discriminated itself from the feeling life. Psyche has become one with Nature and is transformed. White and black, when presented as archetypal images, evoke 'the remotest depths of the unconscious, where it becomes an almost abstract, pure structure with no human feeling' (von Franz, 1997, p. 49). Immersed in nature's opposites, the beautiful relationship between them embodies a newly developed feminine attained through the act of reflection. All is changed utterly and 'a terrible beauty is born'.

We have arrived at a most powerful conjunction presenting itself to viewers puzzled by the twofold nature of Alien/Laura. As Campbell wrote, 'The life of a mythology derives from the vitality of its symbols as metaphors delivering, not simply the idea, but a sense of actual participation in such a realization of transcendence, infinity and abundance' (1986: xx). When the inner eye of viewers is awakened and a revelation arises from their inner space to meet impressions brought to mind by the senses from outer space (here, the film), 'the significance of the conjunction is lost unless the outward image opens to receive and embody the elementary idea – this being the whole sense of the transformation of nature in art' (p. 8).

Mercea Eliade observed that

> The very dialect of the sacred tends to repeat a series of archetypes, so that a hierophany [a revelation of the supernatural or sacred] realized at a certain historical moment is structurally equivalent to a hierophany a thousand years earlier or later.
>
> *(1964, p. xvii)*

Therefore, to revert to Hillman, a symptom can be interpreted as a *kairos* moment. 'There is a meaningful pattern in the precisions of a symptom itself, its picture, its immediate effects. Then a case is not only an abnormality, nor is a symptom merely a disorder. They are opportunities' (2005, p. 108). For Eliade, such revelations tend to show the sacred in its totality,

> even if the human beings in whose consciousness the sacred 'shows itself' fasten upon only one aspect or one small part of it. In the most elementary hierophany *everything is declared*. The manifestation of the sacred in a stone or a tree is neither less mysterious nor less noble than its manifestation as a 'god'.
>
> *(1964, p. xvii, emphasis in original)*

In a development of Hillman's project for combatting titanism, Cambray invites us to consider our visions of the cosmos, understanding that they are limited by the dominant archetypes of an era (both personal and collective). Our souls get hidden in the world of the collective unconscious where images interact; but the human imagination is capable of understanding these visions because they give rise to beauty, and beauty puts us in touch with complexities. Furthermore, beauty is an embodied way to experience complexity since soul may be hiding in the images themselves (2016). If it is ever to be found, soul must be in the integration of a renewed feminine. Little wonder that the dying alien gazes on Laura's not quite dead mask before both are caught in the flames set by a man. This lasting image epitomises the psychological reality that the persona presides over the collective conscious, as the *anima* rules the inner world of the collective unconscious.

Snow falls on the lens and gradually obscures every object that lies in front of it, but lets light seep through. Symbols, as Susan Rowland tells us, unite the human psyche to the animism of the non-human world (2015, p. 91); for the psyche is the only immediate reality we are able to experience. The process of individuation, both personal and cultural, leads us towards wholeness, towards uniting our inner and outer worlds. Images, then, are the language of the unconscious which *Under the Skin* (in its final shot from beneath the snowy membrane) encourages us to persevere bringing to consciousness – perhaps birthing through hierophany a new living myth.

References

Begg, E. (1986) *The cult of the black virgin*. London: Penguin.

Berger, J. (1972) *Ways of seeing*. London: BBC; Harmondsworth: Penguin.

Cambray, J. (2016) 'Climates and ideas in crisis: perplexing questions', Unpublished conference paper presented at 'Climates of Change and the Therapy of Ideas' Pacifica Graduate Institute, Santa Barbara, CA.

Campbell, J. (1986 [2002]) *The inner reaches of outer space: metaphor as myth and as religion*. Novato, CA: New World Library.

Carotenuto, A. (1996) *To love to betray: life as betrayal*. Asheville, NC: Chiron Publications.

Carotenuto, A. (2002) *Rites and myths of seduction*. Asheville, NC: Chiron Publications.

Douglas, C. (2000) *The woman in the mirror: analytical psychology and the feminine*. Lincoln, NE: iUniverse. com, Inc.

Downing, C. (2007) *The goddess: mythological images of the feminine*. New York: Authors Choice Press.

Eliade, M. (1964) *Shamanism: archaic techniques of ecstasy*, Bollingen Series LXXVI. New York: Pantheon.

Harding, E. (1935 [1990]) *Woman's mysteries: ancient and modern*. Boston, MA: Shambhala.

Hillman, J. (1985 [2007]) *Anima: an anatomy of a personified notion*. Putnam, CT: Spring Publications.

Hillman, J. (1988 [2007]) '…And huge is ugly: Zeus and the Titans', in *Mythic figures*, Uniform Edition 6.1. Putnam, CT: Spring Publications.

Hillman, J. (2005) *Senex & Puer*, Uniform Edition 3. Putnam, CT: Spring Publications.

Jung, C. G. (1923) 'Psychological types', in *The collected works of C. G. Jung*, Vol. 6, *Psychological types*, 2nd edn. Princeton, NJ: Princeton University Press, 1971.

Jung, C. G. (1939) 'Conscious, unconscious and individuation', in *The collected works of C. G. Jung*, Vol. 9i, *The archetypes and the collective unconscious*, 2nd edn. London: Routledge & Kegan Paul, 1968.

Jung, C. G. (1948) 'The spirit Mercurius', in *The collected works of C. G. Jung*, Vol. 13, *Alchemical studies*. London: Routledge & Kegan Paul, 1967.

Jung, C. G. (1951) 'The psychology of the child archetype', in *The collected works of C. G. Jung*, Vol 9i, *The archetypes and the collective unconscious*, 2nd edn. London: Routledge & Kegan Paul, 1968.

Jung, C. G. (1954) 'Archetypes of the collective unconscious', in *The collected works of C. G. Jung*, Vol. 9i, *The archetypes and the collective unconscious*, 2nd edn. London: Routledge & Kegan Paul, 1968.

Jung, C. G. (1959 [1977]) *Flying saucers: a modern myth of things seen in the skies*. London: Routledge & Kegan Paul.

Knight, C. (2014) '*Under the skin* reviewed: Scarlett Johansson's sexy alien thriller hits all the right spots', *National Post*, 8 May.

Neumann, E. (1954 [1973]) *The origins and history of consciousness*. Princeton, NJ: Princeton University Press.

Neumann, E. (1956 [1971]) *Amor and psyche: the psychic development of the feminine. A commentary on the tale by Apuleius*. Princeton, NJ: Princeton University Press.

Neumann, E. (1994) *The fear of the feminine*. Princeton, NJ: Princeton University Press.

Ovid (1955 [1967]) *The metamorphoses*, trans. M. M. Innes. Harmondsworth: Penguin.

Rowland, S. (2015) 'Jung, art and psychotherapy re-conceptualized by the symbol that joins us to the wildness of the universe', *International Journal of Jungian Studies*, 7(2), pp. 81–93.

Shiva, V. (2016) 'Healing: from the Self to the planet', Unpublished conference paper presented at 'Climates of Change and the Therapy of Ideas' Pacifica Graduate Institute, Santa Barbara, CA.

Stein, M. (2006) *The principle of individuation*. Wilmette, IL: Chiron Publications.

Von Franz, M. L. (1990) *Individuation in fairytales*. Boston, MA: Shambhala

Von Franz, M. L. (1995) *Projection and re-collection in Jungian psychology*. Chicago and Las Salle, IL: Open Court.

Von Franz, M. L. (1996) *The interpretation of fairy tales*, revd edn. Boston, MA: Shambhala.

Von Franz, M. L. (1997) *Archetypal patterns in fairy tales*. Toronto: Inner City Books.

Online sources

Anderson, M. (2014) 'Scarlett fever', *Artforum*, 4 January [online]. Available at: www.artforum.com/film/id=46042 [Accessed 27 January 2015].

Beebe, J. (1992) 'The anima in film', *The Jung Page* [online]. Available at: www.cgjungpage.org/learn/articles/film-reviews/666-the-anima-in-film [Accessed 3 April 2015].

Gray, A. (2014) 'Review: *under the skin*', *Shiznit*, 10 March [online]. Available at: www.theshiznit.co.uk/review/under-the-skin.php [Accessed 12 February 2015].

Martin, P. (2014) 'Review of *Under the skin*', *Arkansas Online*, 25 April [online]. Available at: www.arkansasonline.com/news/2014/apr/25/under-skin-20140425/ [Accessed 29 January 2015].

Morris, A. (2014) 'Scarlett Johansson creeps in *under the skin*', *Vine* [online]. Available at: www.thevine.com.au/entertainment/movies/scarlett-johansson-creeps-in-under-the-skin-20140528-281683/ [Accessed 27 January 2015].

'Rhizome', *Wikipedia* [online]. Available at: https://en.wikipedia.org/wiki/Rhizome [Accessed 4 May 2016].

Romney, J. (2014) 'Film of the week: *under the skin*', *Film comment*, 3 April [online]. Available at: www. filmcomment.com/entry/under-the-skin-jonathan-glazer-review [Accessed 27 January 2015].

Sharkey, B. (2014) 'Review: Scarlett Johansson mesmerizes while getting *under the skin*', *LA Times*, 3 April [online]. Available at: www.latimes.com/entertainment/movies/moviesnow/la-et-mn-under-the-skin-20140404-story.html#page=1 [Accessed 11 February 2015].

Filmography

Man who fell to Earth, The. (1976) [film] Directed by Nicholas Roeg. UK.
Under the skin. 2013. [film] Directed by Jonathan Glazer. UK.

PART V

Approaches post-cinema

Edited by
Greg Singh

28

BEYOND THE SECOND SCREEN

Enantiodromia and the running-together of connected viewing

Greg Singh

Introduction

In his influential 1948 essay 'Le Camera Stylo', Alexandre Astruc writes that:

> Up to now the cinema has been nothing more than a show…. The day is not far off when everyone will possess a projector, will go to the local bookstore and hire films written on any subject, of any form…. From that moment on, it will no longer be possible to speak of the cinema. There will be *several* cinemas.
>
> *(1968, p. 19, emphasis in original)*

Although writing from the technological perspective of the 1940s, here Astruc is remarkably prescient: for not only is he speculating the extension of film distribution and viewing beyond cinema theatres (and into homes and libraries), he is also commenting on new developments in portability, as well as the evolution of film culture itself and, crucially, the possibilities in what people would do to actively seek out infotainment experiences, given the access to technology and the opportunities afforded. The predictions discernible in Astruc's statement range from video hire (from both municipal and commercial sources) and interaction between technology (Web-based infrastructure) and distribution networks and apparatus (historical examples include Blockbuster and lovefilm, superseded by Netflix and other popular streaming sites and content providers; but also the continuation of municipal systems such as public library loans in the UK). Therefore, one may say that in terms of delivery, film narrative and the kinds of storytelling to which so-called Classical film narrative lends itself, has always relied upon multiplicity of access, novel innovation, and technological development. In Astruc, there is also a useful theoretical precedence which this chapter seeks to use: to realise a theory of 'several cinemas' in the context of convergent, multiplatform viewing cultures, and through the post-cinematic concept of 'connected viewing'.

In their editorial introduction to a special issue of *Convergence* on the theme of connected viewing, Holt *et al.* (2016) state that 'Connected viewing essentially refers to the multiple ways viewers engage with media in a multiscreen, socially networked, digital entertainment experience' (p. 342). Media scholarship has tackled this in a number of ways according to specific themes and approaches. These might include audience engagement and participatory culture

(Jenkins *et al.*, 2013; Shirky, 2008; van Dijck, 2013), power relations in connected media environments (especially Andrejevic, 2011), and the political economy of the digital world (Allmer, 2015; Fuchs, 2013, 2015; Labato and Thomas, 2015). In all of these themes and approaches, however, there are a couple of important constants that underpin the principle of connected viewing. The first is the acknowledgement that this arena of academic study is fast-moving, and often seems quite ephemeral when compared with other traditional academic areas in the Arts and Humanities. Second, to me it is clear that the active role of the participant in driving the development (and indeed contributing to the accelerating pace of change in this area, thanks to the power of demand-driven evolution of converged media cultures) is crucial. As a media and cultural studies scholar whose main task is to address this connected media environment and the place of cultural production within this context, in a critical way, the challenge is clear. This is complicated by the fact that I am also a media and cultural studies scholar who seeks to understand some of the crucial questions around active participation through the lens of depth psychology. This emerging area of post-Jungian media studies is very young, but not without precedent.

Participative and connected viewing and the post-Jungian studies context

In the summer of 2009, *Screen* gave Luke Hockley, Chris Hauke, and I the opportunity to form a panel to present papers on the theme of 'Film Analysis and Post-Jungian Approaches to Participative Viewing' at the annual conference in Glasgow. Although there may have been papers given from classical perspectives in years gone by, to our knowledge this was the first time that a panel had convened around the theme of post-Jungian film analysis at *Screen*. The session was (to our delight) oversubscribed in terms of audience attendance, and provided a rare and most welcome opportunity to engage colleagues working in film and media studies at an international level. At that event, we had decided to address a specific problem, identified independently by each of us in very different ways: the problem of participatory viewing. Surprisingly, perhaps, for an approach that places such an emphasis on human psyche, Jungian film analysis often forgets that there is a flesh-and-bone human being at the heart of the viewing act; and, further, that the co-production of meaning-making in the relationship between viewer and viewed tends to get lost in acts of interpretation when conducting close textual analysis, especially when using a derivative of classic Screen Theory in the analytic process and even more so when the primary object of analysis is the author, and authorial intentionality.

Indeed, this problem of participatory viewing (and the attendant issues associated with Jungian textual analysis) was one of the centrepieces of my argument in *Film After Jung* (Singh, 2009), a monograph dedicated to rethinking film theory in relation to concepts driven through analytical psychology. We discussed our different approaches to the cultural and psychic dimensions of subject and agency in contemporary, participatory viewing practices and touched upon how the notion of co-creation of meaning, particularly in the world of post-cinematic technologies and repeated viewing practices tends to get utterly lost. What we uncovered through discussion that day in 2009, arguably a touchstone for so much work in post-Jungian media and cultural studies since, is what I would describe as the need to acknowledge the 'warm psychology' of the contemporary cinematic encounter (Singh, 2014). This contemporary cinematic encounter has remained participatory in its aspect but, through shifts in media ecologies, has more recently come to resemble something that can be described as 'connected viewing'. I argue that these participatory, connected viewing practices, often discernibly technological in character, embody a warm psychology, driven through what post-Jungians describe as the 'third image' (Hockley, 2014; Singh, 2014, pp. 4–6).

Admittedly, it is all too easy to slip into an interpretative mode of film criticism when using the tools of analytical psychology. In close textual analysis, the temptation might be to unpick meaning from thematic devices in cinematic texts – artefacts that seem 'pregnant with meaning' or somehow 'ripe'. This rather literal approach to analysis reflects a tendency that characterises some of the more influential Jungian-influenced film criticism published to date (e.g. Fredericksen, 2001; Izod, 2001). In the past, I might have been vocal in my criticisms of this kind of classical approach (2009, 2011, 2014). With hindsight, however, I can acknowledge that there is still work to be done where classical Jungian film criticism can provide real insights for close textual analysis, as well as for traditional modes of film criticism. A rather good example of this can be found in Izod and Dovalis's remarkable book *Cinema as Therapy* (2015), and there are many shorter examples in the present volume.

However, there are a number of reasons for my erstwhile position. In many ways, although softened through the years, my criticisms of such approaches maintain the same logic. Jungian analysis has always concerned itself with images, and, in particular, the psychological production of images in relation to the individual's experience. It therefore makes sense that the 'canon' of work relating to Jungian film analysis has devoted itself to (especially) visual interpretation as its main analysis object. (The field – if it can be called such – is now maturing and subsequent generations of work are beginning to emerge exponentially as attested to by this volume.) This specular-ocular focus is, of course, not without its own problems. I will touch upon this in relation to my subject later on in this chapter, but a full discussion of this issue in relation to the phenomenology of affective viewing may be found elsewhere (Singh, 2014; Hockley, 2014).

I have argued (2009, 2011, 2014) and extend the argument here, that there are a number of ways that post-Jungian approaches seek to move beyond the classical position as a matter of course – 'classical' in the textual traditions of both Jungian film criticism and British film criticism; and to embrace the lived, embodied, affective aspects of the cinematic encounter as the main object for analysis. There are plenty of examples (Hockley, 2014; Hauke and Hockley, 2011; Hockley and Fadina, 2015) to evidence a concerted effort in post-Jungian theory and criticism to extend the methodological tools and conceptual frameworks of analytical psychology beyond what might be described (albeit rather harshly) as a rather *passive* textual approach. I would say that this is especially so in the context of post-cinema encounters, where the notion of texts as isolated incidents of cultural production and consumption makes little sense.

My own perspective is shaped by innovations in the field of post-Jungian depth psychology and its potential to provide an understanding of the psychic, unconscious, and archetypal processes at work in the production and consumption of culture. Post-Jungian ideas have been applied to a number of Arts and Humanities fields, but perhaps most successfully in film theory and criticism. The rapid growth in this scholarship is an indicator of the speed at which the very different fields of film studies and post-Jungian studies are moving (see, for example, Hauke and Alister, 2000; Hauke and Hockley, 2011; Hockley, 2007, 2014; Bassil-Morozow, 2010; Izod, 2001, 2006; Izod and Dovalis, 2015; Singh, 2009, 2014). This growth might reasonably be extended to more traditional forms of television and media studies, which are also continued from post-Jungian perspectives (Hockley and Gardner, 2011; Waddell, 2006; Hockley and Fadina, 2015). However, there are at present still very few post-Jungian or depth-psychological interventions in the field of contemporary digital media cultures. Notable exceptions being edited collections, e.g. Weitz, 2014; a special issue of the *Spring* journal on the theme of technology, cyberspace, and psyche, Winter 2008; and book-length studies by Balick, 2014; and Singh, 2017, and forthcoming.

To summarise, the post-Jungian approach that I am taking in this chapter is to extend the frame of analysis in a number of crucial directions, using the Jungian and post-Jungian concepts of *enantiodromia*, and the phenomenology of the 'third image', as tools for conducting critical inquiry into the cultural practices of connected viewing. In doing so, I consider the warm psychology of the post-cinematic encounter that exists *beyond the text* (in the third image, co-produced sense of meaningfulness in the psychological space between viewer and viewed); *beyond the high/low cultural distinction* so often found in the choices of objects in more traditional, Jungian-inflected close textual reading; and finally, in conclusion, *beyond cinema* itself in contemporary converged multiplatform entertainments. I consider how the contemporary media ecosystem provides post-Jungian approaches to analysis and criticism a frame for rethinking the 'post-cinema' concept, especially given the contexts of home cinema technologies, shared cultural practices, and the consumption practices of 'second-screening' that accompany connected viewing today.

Connected viewing: beyond the text

As I have noted elsewhere, there are many challenges facing film and media studies today (Singh, 2017). I argue that one of the most important challenges to acknowledge is the rapid acceleration of a media ecosystem in popular culture through which people communicate, share, and seek escape from everyday life. Indeed, this seems to be a central driver for media studies. In particular, the sub-discipline of celebrity studies seeks to explore the parasocial and participatory aspects of these phenomena, with a focus in this context on online streaming and Video on Demand (VoD) services (see, for example, Cunningham *et al.*, 2016; Lashley, 2013). While it may be clear that the contemporary media ecosystem is both an extension and continuation of more traditional media forms, the acceleration effect that accompanies this connectivity presents a set of specific problems. In particular, in relation to the way that media scholars now need to approach innovations in technology, institutions, financial arrangements, and consumer or end-user behaviours as fundamentally connected and part of a holistic, intra-related ecosystem (Singh, 2017; Krüger and Johanssen, 2014).

To an extent, this was certainly always the case. Cinema studies, for example, has recognised for some time now, the need to engage narrative encounters across multiple access points and migratory content across convergent platforms, industries, and audience behaviours (King, 2002; Jenkins, 2006; Singh, 2014). Locating this within a sustainable conceptual framework robust enough to stand up alongside the rapid changes in technology and consumer practice has proven difficult, but a number of commentators have attempted to do so.

Henry Jenkins has termed the kind of narrative world-building and flow of content across media delivery platforms found in connected media environments as 'transmedia storytelling'. Put simply, this is 'a process where integral elements of a fiction get dispersed systematically across multiple delivery channels for the purpose of creating a unified and coordinated entertainment experience' (2007). As Jenkins notes, 'Moving characters from books to films to video games can make them stronger and more compelling' (2003). However, the primary concern here is commercial. Building a stronger story-world, according to Jenkins, 'can sustain multiple characters (and their stories) and thus successfully launch a transmedia franchise'. Additionally, as Jenkins states in the online *Technology Review* (2003):

> We have entered an era of media convergence that makes the flow of content across multiple media channels almost inevitable.... Everything about the structure of the modern entertainment industry was designed with this single idea in mind – the construction and enhancement of entertainment franchises.

One can see how Jenkins has arrived at this conclusion, but his most telling insight with regard to the strength of transmedia storytelling is that 'Reading across the media sustains a depth of experience that motivates more consumption.' This suggests that the structure of the modern entertainment industry and its convergence of delivery platforms has not merely a creative-, but also a commercially orientated tendency. However, in terms of the audience's encounter with narrative, such multilayered, convergent delivery enables 'a more complex, more sophisticated, more rewarding mode of narrative to emerge within the constraints of commercial entertainment' (2003).

The narrative strategies employed in mainstream media productions, engaging the services of online content producers, digital advertising, and mobile media therefore seem to fit Frederic Jameson's idea of the 'megapicture': an idea that describes a postmodern, hypertextual event within popular cinema cultures, rather than a discrete, hermetic, or 'pure' text or set of singular texts (1992). There are other scholars who give equal emphasis to event or ritual to content, and these ideas have become fairly influential in the field of cinema studies. For example, in *Visible Fictions*, John Ellis states that two things are bought and sold through ticket sales at the box office: the film as a differentiated commodity, and the cinema as a familiar cultural practice (1992, pp. 25–27). This suggests that, in the context of viewing film in a cinema theatre, the 'event' or ritual of 'going to the movies' is a valuable commodity itself. It is clear that two of the things that differentiate a film from its viewing context are the viewing experience itself and the anticipation of what that experience promises to be. Thus, the duration of the narrative (and the work of the narrative, in a psychological sense where anticipation holds so much emotional investment in readiness) can be said to extend beyond the duration of the screening of a text, and can be associated with the external world of ritual as well as the internal world of imagination. In this sense, narrative encounter can be configured, at least conceptually, as a kind of running-together – an *enantiodromic* movement – between ritual and imagination.

This differentiation between text and viewing context is a powerful commercial device that has been exploited time and again in cinema, and can lead to a cultural association with the event of the theatrical release as a more 'valuable' experience than home viewing. However, it should be noted that this is not to generalise the home viewing process as an inferior process, nor to suggest that people generally prefer to see a film at the cinema theatre. In fact, the historic advent of television (and, therefore, television culture) brought with it certain viewing pleasures specific to that medium regarded as both separate from, and fundamentally tied-up with, the fate of cinema. What this valuation does suggest is that media ecology has become increasingly undifferentiated due to convergence both of technologies and of the experience of viewing within several viewing contexts. Indeed, television culture today is saturated with example of 'event TV' where live broadcasts are promoted through the opportunity for viewers to participate in the broadcast as it unfolds through their use of social media and apps on hand-held or mobile devices (see, for example James Blake's description of *Coronation Street Live*, 2017). As I will go on to discuss, this most often happens concurrently in practices of 'media stacking' in multitasking scenarios: a usually simultaneous mixing of large, small, and hand-held screen media (most often used in social media and connected environments), defined by more recent terminology such as second-screening and connected viewing.

Media convergence, and digitality in particular, has posed some obvious challenges for film theory for some time now, particularly in relation to how one necessarily approaches the notion of film-as-text in contemporary contexts. As Dan Harries acknowledged some time ago in *The New Media Book*, 'The material differences between media technologies have increasingly eroded and subsequently converged, and any discussion of a particular media technology will almost certainly rub up against other forms of technology' (2004, p. 1). In his essay 'The business of new media' in the same volume, John T. Caldwell noted that:

> The old media corporations – defined historically by the entertainment experience of the screen, the narrative, the star, and the genre – now work to calculate, amass, repackage, and transport the entertainment product across the borders of both new technologies and media forms.
>
> *(2004, p. 63)*

Although these two perspectives are quite dated in the specific media that they use as case studies, they are both very useful in thinking through the problem of media convergence, because they were written at a time when convergence as a concept was first gaining traction in orthodox cinema studies. These commentators highlight, one might say, a notion that convergence as a concept is itself a *convergent* problem. It has technological dimensions certainly, but these dimensions are impacted upon *by* shifts in media business as much as they are reflected *by* shifting business practice, and the artistic, aesthetic, and textual aspects of cultural production associated with the practice of filmmaking and cinematic storytelling. It is an infinitely complex area already, and this is before we take into consideration (as a matter of necessity) the act of viewing and the cultural practices shared by audiences and user communities.

This is where the concept of connected viewing comes into its own. Holt and Sanson use the phrase to describe 'a larger trend across the media industries to integrate digital technology and socially networked communication with traditional screen media practices' (2014, p. 1). However, this trend emerges through a wider aspect of convergent media culture that has become prevalent in popular culture. In their important intervention piece 'YouTube, multichannel networks and the accelerated evolution of the new screen ecology', Cunningham *et al.* outline the emergence and virtual domination of multichannel networks (MCNs) as 'Arguably one of the most challenging and innovative elements of the evolving screen ecology … a low-budget tier of mostly advertising-supported online channels driven mainly by the professionalization and monetization of previously amateur content creation' (2016, p. 377).

Given this, further extension of this complexity into post-Jungian frames and concepts (indeed, in my view framed as what Singer and Kimbles, and others, have described as a 'cultural complex' (2004)) is not without its challenges either. However, the approach that I took in *Feeling Film* (2014) attempted just that within the context of the affective and psychic economy of the all-around-all-at-once of the 'cinematic glance' (2014, especially Part II). It is also further complicated when one takes into consideration the pleasures of repeated viewing and the pleasurable recognition of archetypical elements through cultural familiarity with certain story-worlds (Singh, 2011). Arguably, this recognition process has gone into overdrive in the era of accelerated media evolution.

Film histories and analyses of films as formal systems (such as those proposed by David Bordwell 1985, 1996, 2006), tend to neglect the political implications of the varying modes of engagement with textuality available to the contemporary viewer over time. Textual analysis as a methodology in its classic mode requires an elucidation of what is on the screen, what happens within the frame, and what happens to the elements within the frame, in time. When one takes as the co-created relationship of viewer and viewed as an object of analysis, however, a number of issues present themselves as having an immediate impact upon what is being analysed, and why. For example, if the way that people ordinarily watch films they love repeatedly (either via carrier media such as DVD or Blu-ray, or via a streaming service – although this does not discount the fact that people still sometimes go to see movies at a theatre more than once), it fundamentally changes one's approach to textual analysis. What is being viewed within the frame is not only transformed through time, but also via medium, spatial context, and viewer proximity (both in the sense of physical proximity to a screen, but also in the sense of cultural proximity, as in, their familiarity with the film's narrative). The foregrounding of the experience of the cinematic encounter is thus dialectically presented as an almost-simultaneous object for analysis alongside the 'film text' itself. The formal system of the text, and the phenomenological encounter of the co-created third image between viewer and viewed in the encounter are intertwined, and running-together in co-sequence.

There are precedents to this way of thinking around the primacy of textual analysis as an approach. An overview and comprehensive application of Bordwell's approach to texts as formal systems for example may be found in particular, in his 2006 book, *The Way Hollywood Tells It*. In this account, Bordwell demonstrates an understanding of the sophisticated synergistic business practices of media corporations, referring to Wasko (2003), Compaine and Gomery (2000) and Klinger (2006) amongst others in framing what he describes as a 'middle-level approach'. He demonstrates that there is a clear relationship between the conglomeration of the media and the film production system as big business, and the storytelling strategies employed by the products themselves. However, whereas there is much in this middle-level approach to be admired, not least in its rejection of hermeneutic analysis and polarisation of culturalism/determinism, there are a number of problems. The most important criticism to raise is that Bordwell stops short at the mechanistic political economy of Hollywood production. He never really considers why this is such an important factor, and fails to elaborate upon this mechanism as a determining factor (or not). Such an account of production economics is superficial, and does not negotiate the complexities of capitalist logic – a logic that operates visibly in multinational corporate practice, but largely invisibly within the relationship between the commodity, the consumer, and the implicit content of the product itself.

To articulate this within a theoretical framework, Bordwell does not engage with the impact of form upon content in any meaningful way, and thus can never get to the notion of the articulation of form and content, one in the other, in the relationship between viewer and viewed – a point that currents in recent film theory have attempted to address in various ways. For example, in a phenomenological tradition following Vivian Sobchack's *The Address of the Eye* (1992) and *Carnal Thoughts* (2004), and Laura Marks' groundbreaking work, *The Skin of the Film* (2000), Jennifer M. Barker (2009) seeks to engage film's embodiment (as an articulation of form and content in the visceral viewing experience); Angela Ndalianis has identified a similar articulation of industry and aesthetics, noting that the morphing of the film industry itself into multiplatform content providers (of more generalised entertainment experiences) 'increased adeptness and reliance on digital technology' (2000, p. 253); and Stephen Keane (2007) has noted, in all but name, the articulation of form and content (one in the other) in film cultures, through matrices of technology, digital aesthetics, fandom, interactivity, and branding.

According to Paul Lunenfeld, film narrative as encountered through convergent media through which access to content is enabled, regulated, and modified, is characterised by 'sheer plenitude of narrative, exemplified by the glowingly accessible archive of everything' (2004, p. 151). The crucial step-change since Lunenfeld's piece was written is in the ways that connectivity, accompanied by the acceleration effects of connected viewing practices and cultural convergence, has altered the character of media ecology and one's experience as a viewer. YouTube and MCNs have been subject to accelerated evolution – and lying at the heart of contemporary, connected viewing ecology, this suggests that the MCN-driven ecosystems themselves are subject to secondary acceleration effects. Cunningham *et al.* state that 'the accelerated rate of change, in particular its professionalizing–amateur commercialization strategies, has now reached a level that demands critical analytical attention without such strategies being normatively framed against the brief period of pure YouTube amateurism and informality' (2016, p. 378). This would suggest a new strand of critical inquiry focused upon MCNs, but fully aware of the historical dimensions that accompany somewhat nostalgic normative frames of medium purity. Indeed, in some ways, MCNs represent an accelerated form or extension of Jameson's hypertextual event, mentioned above in relation to historical popular cinema practices.

These shifts have far-reaching implications in the study of convergence – in the deregulation, concentration, and divestment of media ownership, but also in the ways that such industrial level shifts run-together with cultural practices focused around connected viewing. Cunningham *et al.* mainly focus on the aspects of MCN-connected viewing practices that reflect new multilevel industrial models of production, and control of content flow dominant in the corporate concentration/diversification models of the intermediary industry (in both so-called NoCal and SoCal production cultures). When one adds to this the complexity of the connected viewing encounter, and the third image movements that exist within such encounters, then this state of affairs suggests that the objects of analysis in popular media cultures are obscure, amorphous, and multivalent.

Enantiodromia and mediated personality: beyond high/low cultural distinctions

This situation precipitates a major concern for media studies scholars who are interested in psychological and humanist approaches to media. Accessibility of convergent media content, in its various formats, using various platforms and hardware, and from an array of access points, is becoming open to increasingly individual, personalised choices. This condition lies at the very heart of what might be described as a Web 2.0 ethic of connectivity: the notion that media forms are inclusive, participatory, writable from the perspective of an end-user, immediate, and, ultimately, democratised through practices of access, sharing, and gift economies. At the front-end of these services, it would seem that the extent of that freedom of choice, of paramount importance in a deregulated media ecosystem, signifies an agency that is at once participatory and empowering. However, this has increasingly become prone to criticism from a number of disciplinary approaches where, even at this front-end of service provision, choice has an illusory dimension (see, for example, Zelenkauskaite, 2016). I refer here to the algorithms associated with streaming services, for example, Netflix, or YouTube, which operate within economies of attention and affect to present the consumer with front-end suggestions according to not only personal preferences based upon prior consumer choices (a narrowcast-based, 'pull' tendency), but also complexities associated with third-party arrangements for profile and data monetisation, and content provision (a more ostensibly broadcast-based 'push' tendency based on long-tail economic models and AI prediction technology).

A case in point here: various algorithms have been developed to increase market potential for YouTube content producers – note the use of that term, producers, which is a professionalised recuperation of the more interactive, amateur-ish produsage model often referred to in Web 2.0 scholarship (e.g. Bruns, 2008). To illustrate the extent of this recuperative turn, for example, intermediary firms DigitasLBi and Outrigger Media, have recently developed OpenSlate – a YouTube and social media analytics application designed to anticipate stars of the future before they break. The results of analysis guide investment choices for corporate players to develop new online talent, and decrease risks of such investments whilst simultaneously increasing the chances of return on investment. Essentially, according to Learmonth (2013), OpenSlate produces predictive, qualitative data of a kind not available from YouTube's own analytics systems. Webster (2014) states that OpenSlate tracks over 50,000 channels, and twenty-five million individual videos on YouTube, giving scores based upon specific qualitative criteria: audience engagement, frequency of new content added, influence, and reach. For Webster:

> It's possible the talent identified in this way would hit it big without intervention. But using metrics to identify winners can create winners. Unlike the weather, social

predictions can change outcomes; and, unlike in the physical world, predictive algorithms powered by big data have the potential to create 'self-fulfilling prophecies' in the social world.

(p. 93)

One of the more radically infused book-length critiques of this logic can be found in the work of Deborah Lupton. Her *The Quantified Self* (2016), studies the forms and practices of self-tracking via various lifestyle applications powered by Web 2.0 connectivity, from a critical sociological perspective. These are popular self-tracking practices – the phenomenon of FitBit, for example, or any number applications associated with measurements of body-mass indexing, jogging-route mapping, stepometers, and other wearable technologies or mobile phone applications all form familiar aspects of everyday media engagement, and with various connected screen interactions. The implications of Lupton's work also necessitate that one considers ways in which such practices partake of a broader culture associated with self-improvement, modification, and technologies of well-being or work productivity within relations of power. I have discussed some of the intimate correlations and dialogues between self-image, lifestyle, and cultures of self-improvement elsewhere (Singh, 2015) so I do not wish to repeat too much on that here, but it is noteworthy that such questions have begun to be addressed from a post-Jungian critique (indeed, for the range of subjects and positions taken on self-improvement and transformation, see the whole collection within which that specific work sits: Hockley and Fadina, 2015). The aspect of Lupton's work that I would like to develop here through dialogue with post-Jungian ideas is how connected viewing articulates, in practice, her emphasis on the ways in which practices of self-tracking are 'spreading from the private realm into diverse social domains, and the implications of the self-tracking phenomenon for the politics of personal data, data practices and data materialisations' (2016, p. 1).

The contradictory elements suspended in this personality-driven media ecosystem are intertwined spectacle and everyday life, in the form of public and private identities. The contradictions are both tense (running-against) and complementary (running-together). One of the ways that post-Jungian approaches examine contradictions of this sort, is through the conceptual frame of *enantiodromia* – a 'running-together' of seeming opposites. In his essay *Psychological Types*, Jung described *enantiodromia* as the emergence of the unconscious opposite in the course of time and is a term used to designate the play of opposites in the course of events (1971). *Enantiodromia* is a term taken from Heraclitus, whose philosophy was largely predicated on the constancy of change. However, Heraclitus recognised that, whereas change is a predominance, it is not chaotic. Rather, it operates along continua; a running-together, running-against tension. For Sue Mehrtens (2012), in the field of psychology of personality, the more an attitude is repressed the more it acquires a fanatical character, and the nearer it comes to conversion into its opposite: an *enantiodromia*. Throughout his work, there are examples where Jung recognised the value of the concept of opposites, and particularly their interrelatedness in explicating the workings of the psyche. Indeed, in many ways this thinking forms the basis of Jungian psychological theory itself. There are many familiar examples in Jung where the emergence of unconscious material occurs when an extreme one-sided tendency dominates conscious life. In all instances, the common thread is that, over time, a countertendency builds, eventually breaking through conscious control, in the form of psychological union or accommodation.

For Luke Hockley (2014), this allows a psychological space of consideration for the messy, lived complexity of social phenomena, and the way that humans as intersubjective beings tend to engage contradiction in our dealings with one another. This lived complexity is as important for spaces of imagination as it is for social spaces of communication, and, by extension, the co-produced relationships between individuals and groups in the social and the imaginal realms. In the context of cinema, for example, Hockley states that:

> Jung used the term *enantiodromia* ... to suggest that opposites, far from pulling in different directions, in fact turn out to run into each other. When seen in this light it is apparent that the cinema is both a place of psychological encounter yet equally provides a safe space for this encounter to happen.
>
> *(p. 35)*

Whereas cinema may be argued as a space par excellence of the social imaginary, so it would seem an almost natural exemplar of *enantiodromia* in its playful inhabitation of both the social and the imaginary; of ritual and imagination. YouTube is not cinema. Indeed, one must always be mindful of the qualitative differences and medium-specific character of each medium under discussion. It is additionally worth noting here a specific distinction, in that YouTube and other SNSs are not necessarily 'safe spaces' for these kinds of encounters, in contrast with the relatively safe spaces of cinema. One might include here the sorts of toxic disinhibition effects of online communications described by the social psychologist John Suler (2004), which are now part of the everyday fabric of social media communications – trolling, baiting, doxing, and general use of threatening language is a problem so common that it is difficult to see a way to even begin to tackle it. In what follows I touch upon this issue.

Just as for analytical psychology individuals exist within and contain contradictions and forces that are at odds, so too the personalities and performances for implied audiences on YouTube embody contradiction and complexity. We might say that YouTube is both *anthropocentric*, in the sense of *for* human consciousness, in all its playful contradiction and complexity, and in the way it plays with our productive need to connect as social beings and share stories; and *enantiodromic*, in the sense that it embodies (and in an everyday, normal sense, pathologises) misrepresentation, through what is essentially the presentation and containment of two powerful contradictory forces which run-together, without distinction: a mediated self, and a physical and conscious human subject.

Bringing these contradictions to the surface in considerations of media consumption, and suspending them in tension, is part of what Hockley describes as an *enantiodromic* exercise (2007). He writes that this pulling together of seemingly contradictory terms is essential to engage the role of culture in determining the expression of collective psychological encounters: 'in keeping with post-Jungian theory, which aims not to establish a lack (as in Freudian and particularly Lacanian theory) but rather to find a productive tension in bringing what might appear to be opposites together' (p. 14).

Perhaps the most productive tension in the context of YouTube personalities and celebrity cultures within connected media environments is the blurred distinction between public and private in the identification, construction, and mobilisation of self. The immediacy and sheer speed of exchange, amplified through emotionally charged celebrity culture, and engaged with by consumers of popular culture who are not only fans (or haters) of the celebrity figures themselves, means that consumer-users tend to be adept with the discourses featured in the communicative practices of platforms. Things tend to escalate very quickly under such intense circumstances. The voracity, extremity, and self-belief, for example, that during the #Gamergate scandal, Gamergaters displayed in their dedication to discrediting female videogame developers, critics, and commentators through multichannel engagement was deeply troubling in its aggression (Singh, 2017). Well-known examples of this practice of trolling-as-lifestyle goal include the relentless attacks upon 'Tropes vs. Women in Video Games' YouTuber and 'Feminist Frequency' vlogger, Anita Sarkeesian.

Indeed 'meninist' men's rights activist YouTubers such as NateTalksToYou, Thunderf00t, and dozens of others, have devoted entire YouTube *series* to discrediting her work. Comments on their posts often appear to endorse crossing multiple social boundaries to attack Sarkeesian on a personal level, punctuated with sexually violent language towards her or her family.

The *enantiodromic* movement works on two levels in this example. In the first place, the position of Sarkeesian as a public intellectual rests upon her professionalised use of Web 2.0 technologies to pursue and leverage audience reach. Her success is such that demands for content have Sarkeesian crowdfunding future work through social media campaigns. This itself has led to criticisms of her work ranging from drifting away from her video essay DIY roots, to criticisms of her using fans' money for her own private gain. At this purely technical level, Sarkeesian cannot win: her opponents use the same production conventions as weapons to undermine her position. At another level, the professionalised nature of her opposite numbers is in itself astonishing. Using the same levers and monetisation tactics as those attacked, these YouTube commentators have established norms in harnessing parasocial mechanisms of both identification and alienation to facilitate parallel careers.

They present as 'reality' – the logic of such right-wing critics relies on appeal to facts, logic, and 'keeping things real' to succeed. Reality in this sense is a discursive and aesthetic principle through which the ritual of familiarity and belonging (specifically, in engaging a fanbase using a mode of address that is peer-to-peer) solicits emotional responses articulated as comments on video and textual content. The presentation of personae on the part of the content producers and the commentators tends to be that of a straightforward, authentic self-presentation. But even at a superficial level, analysis uncovers processes of self-presentation by bloggers and commenters alike to be well-established (generic) practices. This occurs as a textual phenomenon for the YouTubers themselves (reflecting the tension between realism and spectacle in presentation and self-conscious performance). It also occurs as an interactive communications practice for end-users via comments, posts, and even their own tribute video posts dedicated to YouTubers (activities reflecting the imaginal space of end-users in terms of their alignment, emotional investment, and parasocial relationships with the celebrities). In the Sarkeesian case, as in other right-wing YouTuber cases, this even produces instances where fan videos are made in tribute to the critics of so-called 'Social Justice Warriors' (e.g. fan videos dedicated to NateTalksToYou). The point here is that the escalation into what can only be described as hate-filled practices on free speech platforms, ironically predicated on a perceived need to shut someone down, is sped up through the connected capabilities of the platforms themselves, without really tending to the damage such oscillation between extreme opposites can have upon collective consciousness. In cases of celebrity YouTuber–user interaction, because of public visibility, interaction is viewed by fan 'others' who tend to judge to standards in a 'defensive' style; due in part to their own emotional investment in those parasocial relationships, and partly due to collective dimensions of the *enantiodromic* movements described here.

Enantiodromia and convergence: cinema beyond cinema

There are other aspects of connected viewing that relate to this idea of emotional investment and parasocial identification with 'real' others where, clearly, mediation occurs at multiple levels. In their work on 'Second-screen theory', Lee and Andrejevic (2014) claim that early instances of interactive television as it has developed through the emergence of digital television, provided a precedent for data collection through consumer activity (which, in the historical context of the UK in the early 2000s to give an example, included Teletext, red button content, and emergent time-shifting and PVR technology such as Sky+ and, later, Smart TV tech).

In other work, drawing from reports from CEA and NATPE, Zelenkauskaite (2016) has noted a number of emergent patterns in relation to second-screening as a popular cultural practice. First, that second-screening has for some time now been a very popular practice: for example, Zelenkauskaite notes that in 2014, cross-platform viewership of television in the US included 79 per cent of viewers interacting through a second screen as they watched a television screen, be it mobile phone, laptop, or tablet. In addition, the reasons given for using a second screen while watching television were less likely to be programme related, and, more likely, as devices of distraction either to facilitate multitasking, serve as a distraction during commercials, or to view when the programme itself became less engaging (2016). Here, I feel, is where the importance of re-thinking the relationship between viewer and viewed, and the spaces between the social world of ritual and the psychic world of the imaginary, become crucial in the connected context. Television studies has long recognised this in principle – Skeggs and Wood, for example, pointing to television as an affective technology 'of the social that works through encouraging intensity, intimacy and belonging' (2012, p. 71). The same authors also found evidence that showed that what happens in collective viewing spaces especially around reality TV and factual programming facilitates a sense of *interconnectivity* (2012). This word – interconnectivity – is of special interest here, as it acknowledges the interdimensional axes along which the technological, social, psychological, and industrial-commercial intersect in real-world experiences, and where the ritual and the imaginative run-together.

As Sherryl Wilson has pointed out, television studies research has often engaged with this intersectionality (2016). To my mind, the contradictions inherent in the televisual as a conceptual category do seem to embody the oppositional aspects driving these dimensions. Indeed, this is a sentiment borne out in post-Jungian approaches to screen culture more generally. For instance, Hockley suggests that, in suspending seemingly opposite ideas of the commercial and the psychological in association, what one discovers is that 'it is the very sense and idea of commodity that provides the entry point into the *enantiodromaic* world of the other' (2014, p. 37, emphasis in original). Hockley uses the deep imagery of the Ferryman as symbolic of the psychological journey to the underworld, as simultaneously symbolic of the commercial rituals associated with the cost of admission to the cinema: 'As such, it [the box office transaction] is partly a ritualistic act, and one that gives us access to the transformative experience of the underworld' (p. 37).

Hockley is primarily thinking about the act of going to the movies here, and the specific pleasures and associations found in that highly ritualistic process reminiscent of John Ellis's extra-textual aspect of cinema-going, outlined above. In Hockley's statement, what can seem at first glance a little far-fetched in terms of drawing analogy actually helps us to apprehend what is, at an allegorical level, a very useful way to engage screen culture beyond cinema. Jungian thinkers are probably quite used to the notion that a cinema screen can be thought of as a sort of allegorical container of psychic material, whether they might be persuaded of that notion or not. The interesting thing about post-cinematic modes of viewing is that they amplify what already exists in traditional media forms. So, for Hockley, just as change occurring as a result of the release of affect during psychotherapy consultation can have lasting effect, so what happens in the space between viewer and viewed stays with us beyond the duration of a screening (2014).

In connected viewing contexts, and within connected media ecologies, the character of this ongoing change is a perceptible *open-ended-ness*. This is a sort of *opera aperta* of narrative work that, as a direct consequence of the technological and cultural aspects of what is known as being 'always-on' (Turkle, 2011; Boyd, 2012; Singh, 2017), means that the extended duration of narrative encounter that happens through our engagement with linear media texts is amplified indefinitely. This imagined social space of engagement has a powerful psychological dimension because it opens up the potential for social and psychological fulfilment through persistent connectivity, and for an active media agency (engaging with content and story) in full interaction with extraordinary means for accessing information and engaging other people (social media connectivity). Connected viewing, particularly in modes of connected viewing where there are strong elements of social networking site activity, has the potential for this. And yet, at the same time, in an *enantiodromaic* movement, pulls this back forcefully in collision with a contrary force – passive, event experience for what appears to resemble a mass audience, in a rather traditional mode of distracted viewing. My point here is that connected viewing embodies both at once.

Lee and Andrejevic state that 'One of the persistent challenges of the digital era for television broadcasters has been how to make a notoriously "passive" medium interactive. [… the authors note] productivity of interactivity as a means of generating real-time data about viewers' (2014, p. 40). This seems inherently contradictory to most discourse around interactivity which sees a baseline of active, participatory viewing as an essential, almost default prerequisite to connected viewing. This challenges the fantasy of control that viewers have of process, interaction, and choice in connected media environments. They go on to write that:

> While [Internet Television – on-demand streaming services] provides greater possibilities for viewers to access an abundance of content on the web and fulfils interactive television's promises of flexibility, customization, and personalization, it also collects a great amount of data generated by viewers through their browsing, search, and selection behaviors.
>
> *(p. 41)*

There is logic to this contradiction that seems to feed into a counter-narrative to the assumed participatory conditions of contemporary popular culture. When put simply, a second screen can be thought of as any companion device (mobile, handheld) that people use when watching television. If the television set itself is no longer considered by the consumers themselves to be the primary interactive interface, then the television can be synchronised, through wired or Wi-Fi connectivity, to that second screen to enable real-time monitoring, customization, and targeting. It is in this sense that Lee and Andrejevic (amongst others, including van Dijck, 2013) have either implied or explicitly stated that television piggy-backs on to other forms of interactivity in connected media environments, drawing from constant flow of online commentary associated with social media feeds generated through consumer interaction. However, the fundamentally linear push of the narrative sequencing here tends to simulate traditional narrative media forms, and foreground this linearity. Second-screening thus lends itself to certain kinds of 'event TV' (such as the *Coronation Street Live* example mentioned above, which saw a special live broadcast to mark the anniversary of the longest-running soap opera in television history in 2015) where something resembling a mass audience appears to be engaging with the textual material in real-time. At once, the real-time engagement is with the textual material *and* with one another, at the same time. Lee and Andrejevic also note that the trend to turn viewing into a 'networked social event' bucks a counter trend for on-demand and time-shifted viewing, where programming is deferred in favour of personal convenience.

There is an appetite for 'event viewing' that in some sense turns the contemporary cultural image of niche time-shifting, and the placement of control in the hands of the viewer, on its head. This conclusion, from a narrative running decidedly counter to the popular story inherited from Web 2.0 logic – that all media is interactive, and that tech-savvy consumers are active participants in a connected media ecology – rubs dramatically against the cultural image of control, choice, and participation in popular culture, and provides yet another instance of opposites in the contemporary media ecology.

References

Allmer, T. (2015) *Critical theory and social media: between emancipation and commodification.* London: Routledge.

Andrejevic, M. (2011) 'Surveillance and alienation in the online economy', *Surveillance and Society,* 8(3), pp. 278–87.

Astruc, A. (1968) 'The birth of a new avant-garde: le caméra-stylo', in P. Graham (ed.), *The new wave.* London: Secker & Warburg. pp. 17–23.

Balick, A. (2014) *The psychodynamics of social networking: connected-up instantaneous culture and the Self.* London: Karnac.

Barker, J. M. (2009) *The tactile eye: touch and the cinematic experience.* London: University of California Press.

Bassil-Morozow, H. (2010) *Tim Burton: the monster and the crowd – a post-Jungian perspective.* Hove: Routledge.

Blake, J. (2017) *Television and the second screen: interactive TV in the age of social participation.* Abingdon: Routledge.

Bordwell, D. (1985) *Narration and the fiction film.* Madison, WI: University of Wisconsin Press.

Bordwell, D. (1996) 'Contemporary film studies and the vicissitudes of grand theory', in D. Bordwell and N. Carroll (eds), *Post-theory: reconstructing film studies.* London: University of Wisconsin Press. pp. 3–36.

Bordwell, D. (2006) *The way Hollywood tells it: story and style in modern movies.* London: University of California Press.

Boyd, D. (2012) 'Participating in the always-on culture', in M. Mandiberg (ed.), *The social media reader.* New York: New York University Press. pp. 71–6.

Bruns, A. (2008) *Blogs, Wikipedia, second life, and beyond: from production to produsage.* New York: Peter Lang.

Caldwell, J. T. (2004) 'The business of new media', in D. Harries (ed.), *The new media book.* London: BFI. pp. 55–68.

Cater, N. (ed.) (2008) 'Technology, cyberspace, and psyche' [Special issue], *Spring: A Journal of Archetype and Culture,* 80.

Compaine, B. M. and Gomery, D. (2000) *Who owns the media? Competition and concentration in the mass media industry,* 3rd edn. Mahwah, NJ: Lawrence Erlbaum Associates.

Cunningham, S., Craig, D. and Silver, J. (2016) 'YouTube, multichannel networks and the accelerated evolution of the new screen ecology', *Convergence: The International Journal of Research into New Media Technologies,* 22(4), pp. 376–91.

Ellis, J. (1992) *Visible fictions: cinema, television, video,* 2nd edn. London: Routledge.

Fredericksen, D. (2001) 'Jung/sign/symbol/film', in C. Hauke and I. Alister (eds), *Jung & film: post-Jungian takes on the moving image.* Hove: Brunner-Routledge. pp. 17–55.

Fuchs, C. (2013) *Social media: a critical introduction.* London: SAGE.

Fuchs, C. (2015) *Culture and economy in the age of social media.* London: Routledge.

Harries, D. (ed.) (2004) *The new media book.* London: BFI.

Hauke, C. and Alister, I. (eds) (2000) *Jung & film: post-Jungian takes on the moving image.* London: Routledge.

Hauke, C. and Hockley, L. (eds) (2011) *Jung & film II: the return.* Hove: Routledge.

Hockley, L. (2007) *Frames of mind: a post-Jungian look at cinema, television and technology.* Bristol: Intellect.

Hockley, L. (2014) *Somatic cinema: the relationship between body and screen – a Jungian perspective.* Hove: Routledge.

Hockley, L. and Fadina, N. (eds) (2015) *The happiness illusion: how the media sold us a fairytale.* Hove: Routledge.

Hockley, L. and Gardner, L. (eds) (2011) *House: the wounded healer on television – Jungian and post-Jungian reflections.* Hove: Routledge.

Holt, J. and Sanson, K. (eds) (2014) *Connected viewing: selling, streaming, & sharing media in the digital era.* New York: Routledge.

Holt, J., Steirer, G. and Petruska, K. (2016) 'Introduction: the expanding landscape of connected viewing', *Connected Viewing,* special issue, *Convergence,* 22(4), pp. 341–7.

Izod, J. (2001) *Myth, mind and the screen: understanding the heroes of our time.* Cambridge: Cambridge University Press.

Izod, J. (2006) *Screen, culture, psyche: a post-Jungian approach to working with the audience.* Abingdon: Routledge.

Izod, J. and Dovalis, J. (2015) *Cinema as therapy: grief and transformational film.* Hove: Routledge.

Jameson, F. (1992) *Signatures of the visible.* London: Routledge.

Jenkins, H. (2006) *Convergence culture: where old and new media collide.* New York: New York University Press.

Jenkins, H., Ford, S. and Green, J. (2013) *Spreadable media: creating value and meaning in a networked culture.* New York: New York University Press.

Jung, C. G. (1971) 'Psychological types', in *The collected works of C. G. Jung,* Vol. 6, *Psychological types,* 3rd edn. Princeton, NJ: Princeton University Press.

Keane, S. (2007) *CineTech.* Basingstoke: Palgrave Macmillan.

King, G. (2002) *New Hollywood cinema: An introduction.* London: I. B. Tauris.

Klinger, B. (2006) *Beyond the multiplex: cinema, new technologies, and the home.* London: University of California Press.

Krüger, S. and Johanssen, J. (2014) 'Alienation and digital labour: a depth-hermeneutic inquiry into online commodification and the unconscious', *Triple C – Communication, Capitalism and Critique,* 12(2), pp. 632–47.

Labato, R. and Thomas, J. (2015) *The informal media economy.* Cambridge: Polity Press.

Lashley, M. C. (2013) *Making culture on YouTube: case studies of cultural production on the popular web platform.* PhD. University of Georgia.

Lee, H. J. and Andrejevic, M. (2014) 'Second-screen theory', in J. Holt and K. Sanson (eds), *Connected viewing: selling, streaming, & sharing media in the digital era.* Abingdon: Routledge. pp. 40–61.

Lunenfeld, P. (2004) The myths of interactive cinema', in D. Harries (ed.), *The new media book,* 2nd edn. London: BFI. pp. 144–54.

Lupton, D. (2016) *The quantified self.* Cambridge: Polity.

Marks, L. (2000) *The skin of the film: intercultural cinema, embodiment and the senses.* London: Duke University Press.

Ndalianis, A. (2000) 'Special effects, morphing magic, and the 1990s cinema of attractions', in V. Sobchack (ed.), *Meta-morphing: visual transformation and the culture of quick change.* Minneapolis, MN: University of Minnesota Press. pp. 251–72.

Shirky, C. (2008) *Here comes everybody: the power of organizing without organizations.* London: Penguin Press.

Singer, T. and Kimbles, S. L. (2004) *The cultural complex: contemporary Jungian perspectives on psyche and society.* New York: Brunner-Routledge.

Singh, G. (2009) *Film after Jung: post-Jungian approaches to film theory.* Hove: Routledge.

Singh, G. (2011) 'Cinephilia: or, looking for meaningfulness in encounters with cinema', in C. Hauke and L. Hockley (eds), *Jung & film II: the return.* Hove: Routledge. pp. 163–84.

Singh, G. (2014) *Feeling film: affect and authenticity in popular cinema.* Hove: Routledge.

Singh, G. (2015) 'The myth of authentic self-actualisation: happiness, transformation and reality TV', in N. Fadina and L. Hockley (eds), *The happiness illusion: how the media sold us a fairytale.* Hove: Routledge. pp. 162–80.

Singh, G. (2017) 'YouTubers, online selves and the performance principle: notes from a post-Jungian perspective', *CM: Communication and Media,* 11(38), pp. 205–32.

Singh, G. (forthcoming) *Death of Web 2.0: ethics, connectivity and locked-in psyche in the twenty-first century.* London: Routledge.

Skeggs, B. and Wood, H. (2012) *Reacting to reality television: performance, audience, value.* London: Routledge.

Sobchack, V. (1992) *The address of the eye: a phenomenology of film experience.* Princeton, NJ: Princeton University Press.

Sobchack, V. (2004) *Carnal thoughts: embodiment and moving image culture.* London: University of California Press.

Suler, J. (2004) 'The online disinhibition effect', *International Journal of Applied Psychoanalytic Studies,* 2(2), pp. 184–8.

Turkle, S. (2011) *Alone together: why we expect more from technology and less from each other.* New York: Basic Books.

Van Dijck, J. (2013) *The culture of connectivity: a critical history of social media.* Oxford: Oxford University Press.

Waddell, T. (2006) *Mis/takes: archetype, myth and identity in screen fiction.* Hove: Routledge.

Wasko, J. (2003) *How Hollywood works*. London: Sage Publications.

Webster, J. G. (2014) *The marketplace of attention: how audiences take shape in a digital age*. London: MIT Press.

Weitz, P. (ed.) (2014) *Psychotherapy 2.0: where psychotherapy and technology meet*. London: Karnac.

Wilson, S. (2016) 'In the living room: second screens and TV audiences', *Television and New Media*, 17(2), pp. 174–91.

Zelenkauskaite, A. (2016) 'Remediation, convergence, and big data: conceptual limits of cross-platform social media', *Convergence*, 22(1), pp. 1–16.

Online sources

Jenkins, H. (2003) 'Transmedia storytelling: moving characters from books to films to video games can make them stronger and more compelling' [online]. Available at: www.technologyreview.com/s/401760/transmedia-storytelling/ [Accessed 17 January 2017].

Jenkins, H. (2007) 'Transmedia storytelling 101' [online]. Available at: http://henryjenkins.org/2007/03/transmedia_storytelling_101.html [Accessed 17 January 2017].

Learmonth, M. (2013) 'Digitas unveils tool to find YouTube stars before they're stars: a long tail of YouTube stars is out there but how to find them?' *Advertising Age*, 2 May [online]. Available at: http://adage.com/article/special-report-tv-upfront/digitas-unveils-tool-find-nascent-youtube-stars/241262/ [Accessed 18 July 2016].

Mehrtens, S. (2012) 'Jung on the enantiodromia: part 1 – definitions and examples', *Jungian Center for the Spiritual Sciences: Whole Person Learning in a Jungian Context* blog [online]. Available at: http://jungiancenter.org/jung-on-the-enantiodromia-part-1-definitions-and-examples/ [Accessed 11 October 2016].

29

ANIMA LUDUS

Analytical psychology, phenomenology and digital games

Steven Conway

Introduction

I drive the Batmobile through downtown Gotham. Activating its turbine jet engine I reach enormous speeds of over 200 miles-per-hour (mph) in a matter of seconds; my vision blurs. As my sense of control lessens, anxiety emerges as a three-dimensional object spreading from stomach into shoulders and upper back. A strip of road undulates unexpectedly and I am fired into the air; reaching the trajectory's apogee I lean back in my recliner chair pulling the *Play-Station 4* thumbstick downwards; using the chair's momentum I sling myself forward as the Batmobile begins its descent; I squash the thumbstick upwards as I land.

Later, I am caught up in a fistfight with Penguin's henchmen; Tim Drake, a.k.a. Nightwing, is at my side. Leaping over, smashing heel and fist into, grappling with foes, an enormous sense of power and alacrity emanates forward from my chest, hands gripping the *PlayStation 4* controller tightly, expertly. In rapid sequence I press X, SQUARE three times, X and SQUARE simultaneously: I enact a special 'takedown' move, permanently eliminating one enemy, and encounter a surprise; I am now Nightwing, not Batman. I continue as Nightwing, twirling a pair of batons, decimating opponents with acrobatic flair.

Playing *Batman: Arkham Knight*, I do not encounter the recliner chair as a chocolate brown object; I do not encounter the television as its pixels or resolution; I do not experience Gotham City and its inhabitants as 3D models and post-processing effects such as per-object motion blur or occlusion mask darkness; I do not encounter the analogue stick as rubberised plastic; I do not experience the X or SQUARE button. I rest upon and simultaneously move beyond them as I encounter the Gotham city streets at enormous speed; as I encounter the Penguin's minions; as I encounter feelings of anxiety, power, fluidity, control and domination through embodiment as the Batmobile, as Batman and Nightwing. As Hillman (1997) remarks:

> Let us imagine the *anima mundi* neither above the world encircling it as a divine and remote emanation of spirit, a world of powers, archetypes and principles transcendent to things, nor within the material world as its unifying panpsychic life-principle. Rather, let us imagine the *anima mundi* as that particular soul-spark, that seminal image, which offers itself through each thing in its visible form.
>
> *(p. 101, emphasis as original)*

371

Similarly let us imagine games, through the *gestalt* effect of their various narratological, ludo-logical, ideational and material systems, as having an innate *anima ludus* present within the moment of play itself. My Being is being-in-the-world: I do not encounter Jungian archetypes only in a world of Platonic forms, but *as my everyday existence*. In Heideggerian phenomenology, existence is an ontological clearing through which things are lit up (*Lichtung*), i.e. in meaning-fulness. As Roger Brooke articulates:

> [T]his imaginal depth of things is their reality … from the Heideggerian point of view, it is not so much 'wrong' for Jung to speak of images as simply superfluous … It is not the case that things are actual whereas images are fantasised.
>
> *(1991, p. 90)*

Phenomenologically, existence is innately fantastical. To be is to be essentially hermeneutic: there is no World without interpretation. Therefore 'World' in phenomenology is, as Sheehan describes, 'a specific context of significance, such as the world of the business woman or the world of the cleaning staff' (2015, p. 118) and 'the lived world is present not as a thing or object, but as meaningfulness' (p. 122). I do not need to ponder the signification of the Batmobile's colour, or its storied owner's penchant for chiroptera, for it to have meaning. Instead, I am always-already in meaning as an ontological feature of my Being; being-in-the-world is being-in-meaning as Sheehan further notes:

> I do not perceive things as objects standing over against me. Rather, I am involved and concerned with them. In fact, structurally I *am* concern (*Sorge*), and this structure cuts across the disastrous mind-body split … I am a bodily minding, which is the same as a minding body.
>
> *(p. 115, emphasis as original)*

Artwork is poetic and therefore a making (*poesis*); providing shape and structure to World. Great art is a holding open of the tension between one's World (stable structure of meaning) and the Earth (all potential meaning). The greatest poetic work is as an embodied rupturing of stability where new truth is unconcealed (*a-letheia*) for one's being-in-the-world. Brooke describes the dynamic well in a blending of Heideggerian and Jungian terminology:

> The unconscious [Earth] is that absence which nevertheless calls for appropriation so that the one-sidedness and limitations of consciousness [World] may be compensated. This can be best done with an attitude of steadfast receptivity to that which seeks to show itself.
>
> *(1991, p. 135)*

All artwork is therefore a building of meaning which can afford dwelling as Heidegger defines, '[P]oetic creation, which lets us dwell, is a kind of building' (1971, p. 213). Dwelling is this 'attitude of steadfast receptivity' Brooke advocates (1991), opening one to what Heidegger describes as hearing the call of conscience (outlined below) or, in more Jungian terms, the call of the Self. Both are essential to self-understanding, growth and maturity.

Being-in-the-game-world is then, *in potentia*, a psychologically significant experience, but it can never be reduced to recliner chairs, button presses, the screen, the sound, the mind, the body. It is all of these, and more; an altogether third image, a *gestalt* of Being and World, as Luke Hockley points out (2014). In playing a game, not only do I 'stick with the image', to use Hillman's distinctive mantra, but I *am* the image, and experience the game as an embodied being-in-the-game-world. In the proceeding discussion, we articulate what digital games mean via an *anima ludus*, and how this affords or deters psychological reactivity as described by Hockley (ibid.); finally, we come to a set of criteria for game design which may amplify this quality.

I/Eye is essence

'[T]he dimensions of Lara Croft's body ... are irrelevant to me as a player, because a different-looking body would not make me play differently ... When I play, I don't even see her body, but see through it and past it' (Aarseth, 2004, p. 48). So states Espen Aarseth in what has become a famous broadside on behalf of ludology (the study of games primarily as rules, mechanics and dynamics of play, in opposition to narratology's focus upon representation).

Aarseth's claim is, however, paradoxical. On the one hand, he decries the 'visualism' and other approaches that attempt to 'read' games as texts, yet, the next moment, affirms it: Lara Croft's body is not important, nor is any body in the game space, he ultimately qualifies, because he does not *see* it. Therefore, in his very own formulation, *seeing* remains the metric for meaning. Indeed he carries the metaphor: seeing is valid, it is simply that Aarseth 'sees through it and past it' (ibid., p. 48). To what, one asks? To some essential 'it' not described, yet prominent. In so doing, he inadvertently subscribes to the very visualism he seeks to negate.

Throughout the cited article, Aarseth certainly *intends* to dispel the notion that games are 'texts', which, in his view, is dangerously close to a narratological reductionism. Instead, he offers, games are a kinaesthetic pleasure. Again, a contradiction arises. Unless Aarseth contends that pleasure arises simply from fine motor skills, minor adjustments of neck, back, fingers or arms (as in board or video game) as one simply flicks sticks and presses buttons, he must admit the kinaesthetic pleasure is intertwined with the game's audio-visual and haptic feedback: any kinaesthetic pleasure comes from my use of a game controller to manipulate Lara's movement, and Lara's movement *feels* great because of the gestalt effect of 3D modelling, animation, the physics engine, sound design, controller ergonomics and more. *My* kinaesthetic pleasure is intertwined with *Lara's* kinaesthetic performance.

Sadly, advocates of Aarseth's perspective took up the clarion call: representation is trivial, the play's the thing. This was taken to a bizarre extreme in Jesper Juul's book, *Half-Real: Video Games between Real Rules and Fictional Worlds* (2005): rules are real, fictional worlds are somehow not. This barometer for 'real' is never explicitly stated, but taken for granted as apodictic. Whilst it is certainly sustainable to argue rules are an ontological feature of 'game', it is peculiar to further explicate that rules exist independently of representation, as some kind of Platonic form or material substrate of reality.

Juul's strong ontological claim is perhaps the most straightforward example of Game Studies' confused, egregious and outdated metaphysical foundations, which tend towards dualism. Yet it is evident too in Johan Huizinga's notion of the 'magic circle', in his work *Homo Ludens: A Study of the Play Element in Culture* (1949), viewed as a principle text for Game Studies scholarship. Within, Huizinga describes the 'magic circle' of play as a realm of existence somehow outside reality and all its messy social, cultural, political and altogether historical baggage: 'Inside the play-ground an absolute and peculiar order reigns ... play ... creates order, *is* order. Into an imperfect world and into the confusion of life it brings a temporary, a limited perfection' (p. 10). We are, it would seem, confronted by many old-fashioned Cartesian dualisms in Game Studies: mind vs body, subject vs object, play vs reality, reading vs playing, game rules vs game fiction, simulation vs representation, narratology vs ludology.

This ontology follows the Cartesian delineation of meaning, synonymous with a form of 'seeing' via the only trustworthy apparatus left after hyperbolic doubt: mental representation (*res cogitans*, 'thinking thing'). This view, arguably beginning with Plato's *eidos* ('forms', from the Greek *eidein*, 'to see'), reaches its apotheosis in Edmund Husserl's phenomenology, where, following Franz Brentano, 'intentionality' is the defining characteristic of consciousness, as McIntyre and Smith clarify:

> When I see a tree … my perception is a perception *of* a tree; when I think that $3 + 2 = 5$, I am thinking *of* or *about* certain numbers and a relation among them … Each mental state or experience is in this way a *representation* of something other than itself … This representational character of mind or consciousness – its being 'of' or 'about' something – is 'intentionality'.
>
> *(1989, p. 147, emphasis as original)*

The later Husserl would bind the terms *noesis* and *noema*, both descended from the Greek *nous* (mind), to his concept of intentionality, to highlight the cardinal relation between acts of consciousness and meaning; for something to *mean* it must be *seen* in the mind. As with Descartes, human consciousness is sovereign lord of Being, dictator (literally and figuratively) of meaning. Thus it makes perfect sense in such a metaphysical position to ask, as Aarseth does, 'what meaning do I give the game?', and to locate this process in a mental representation that neglects the body.

This Cartesian dualism is also often true of Jung's work. At times invoking phenomenology explicitly (1959), Jung's use has much in common with the older Kantian or Hegelian application, wherein 'phenomenology' means 'an experiencing consciousness'. This follows an epistemological rather than ontological trajectory; the focus is upon '*how* do we experience?' rather than the more fundamental 'what *is* experience?'. Consequentially, the answer to 'how' (by seeing an image in a mind) became the answer to 'what' (an act of consciousness). Such a perspective implies the same Cartesian dualisms as listed above. As Brooke (1991, 2009) has outlined, it is clear at times that Jung wished to escape this ontology; indeed, Jung himself states in *The Spiritual Problem of Modern Man* that 'we are still caught in the old idea of an antithesis between mind and matter … recognition of the body cannot tolerate a philosophy that denies it in the name of spirit' (1928/31: §195). However, due to Jung's reliance on philosophers such as Kant, he was inevitably caught up in a metaphysical trap of his own making.

Martin Heidegger's phenomenology and his inheritors, however, whom we briefly turn to below, offer a radical questioning of these assumptions: Being is being-in-a-world, which is to say always in-a-body with pre-reflective meanings, and in-a-situation with felt possibilities and affordances. In Heidegger's philosophy the meaning of something is not 'transcendent to things' (Hillman 1997, p. 101), as with Plato, Descartes, Kant and so on, but instead immanent within the experience itself.

To riff on Hans-Georg Gadamer's pithy phrase, if 'all playing is a being-played' (2004, p. 106), then the question is not 'what meaning do I see in this game?' but instead 'what *is* being-in-the-game?'

Existence is essence

Cartesian metaphysics provides a deceptive bed which both Jung and the field of Game Studies often fall into, one that Procrustes would applaud: chopping, stretching and manipulating the *corpus* of the field with little justification. To briefly summarise: for something to *mean* in this metaphysical view, it must be *present*, usually as cogitated upon, i.e. seen in the mind and processed by some form of established conceptual grouping. For example in playing *Batman: Arkham Knight*, instead of describing the embodied experience of play and building from there (as in my introduction), I would instead move adroitly to focusing upon the symbolic significance of bats, apply a cognitivist model of decision-making, or perhaps an Aristotelian model of tragedy. I move away from 'the things themselves', i.e. the experience, to its categorical abstraction.

It is this mode of impersonal, abstract knowing that Heidegger (2008) termed presence-at-hand (*vorhandenheit*). It is from this kind of understanding that theory, and in Heidegger's view, Western metaphysics, takes its cue. In this manner, presence-at-hand can also be described as uncritical adherence to a metaphysical system. As McManus describes:

> Our talk is confusedly informed by an inconsistent set of crude – 'neutral', 'faded' – metaphors or models … Heidegger may have interpreted phenomenology as targeting such confusions, the 'return to the things themselves' being an attempt to make us aware of the influence of metaphors and models in our thinking and of the amount of active interpretive work – unrecognized because embedded in the philosophical tradition in which we are 'brought up' – that is needed in order to impose them.
>
> *(2012, pp. 218–219)*

Indeed in *The Self*, Jung is similarly critical of this mode of understanding in psychology when he remarks:

> The intellectual 'grasp' of a psychological fact produces no more than a concept of it, and that a concept is no more than a name, a *flatus vocis*. These intellectual counters can be bandied about easily enough. They pass lightly from hand to hand, for they have no weight or substance. They sound full but are hollow; and though purporting to designate a heavy task and obligation, they commit us to nothing.
>
> *(1959: §60, emphasis as original)*

In perhaps Heidegger's most widely discussed contribution to philosophy, he highlighted another mode of understanding forgotten by Western metaphysics: readiness-to-hand (*zuhandenheit*). In his famous tool analysis, Heidegger regards a hammer. We may speak of it in the present-at-hand mode (*vorhanden*), in the 'as' structure, e.g. hammer *as* a certain material, length, weight, colour and so on, using metrics supplied by others in pursuit of a mundane 'correctness'. Such literal facts 'level off' the hammer's individual meaning to some public standard.

The originary or 'pre-ontological' mode, however, which allows the emergence of the *vorhanden*, is ready-to-hand (*zuhanden*): this is evidenced simply in picking up and using the hammer, accessing its equipmental aspect (its 'in-order-to', e.g. 'in-order-to' hang a picture). This is all performed in a manner unique to my current *Da-Sein* (There-Being or Being-There), a term Heidegger coined to emphasise the centrality of context to Being. For example, picking up a hammer in a workshop, a circus or through my avatar within a digital game may hold vastly different meanings and felt possibilities: Being is always a Being-There.

Further, in readiness-to-hand (*zuhandenheit*) the hammer *withdraws* phenomenologically, which is to say it moves beyond the 'levelled', categorical understanding of its being, the *vorhandenheit* mode, and instead becomes *my* understanding, sensitive to my specific context and needs. If I am skilful with the hammer, it becomes part of my bodily schema (Merleau-Ponty, 1962); I literally in-corpor-ate the hammer as a felt extension of my arm.

In such skillful coping (Dreyfus and Dreyfus, 1980) my focus is not upon the hammer, but upon the nail I hit, the picture I hang; with the tennis racquet not upon the racquet handle but upon the ball; in video games, not upon the game controller but the gameworld I inhabit. In this mode my relationship to the hammer, the racquet, the game controller *is innately fantastical*, in the psychological sense: I imbue each with emotion, meaning and corporeality far beyond the literal understanding of the iron, carbon fibre or plastic object. Again, in line with a pheno-menological approach, as Sipiora (2000) pithily states, this fantasy is 'not, however, the move from the concrete to the abstract. Quite the opposite, it is the literal which is seen to be abstract, while the fantasy-image is always concrete' (p. 67).

Consequently, as with post-Jungian cinema studies (Singh, 2014; Hockley, 2014), the body should be understood as our foundational hermeneutic apparatus; our initial means of having a world. Therefore, we must comprehend affect, mood, feeling etc. as cardinal modes of attuning our being-in-the-world, and thus in meaning. As Jung and Heidegger would perhaps agree, it is not that we 'have feelings', but that feelings *have us*: most have experienced, in states of high anxiety, deep depression and so on, a sense of meaningfulness and connection to the world 'recede', or, more pointedly, the world recedes from us. As Matthew Ratcliffe remarks, 'we experience the world through our feeling bodies, and that distinctions between internally dir-ected bodily feelings and externally directed intentional states should be rejected … moods … constitute the experienced meaningfulness of the world' (2009, p. 350).

Meaning is existence

Though Heidegger's thinking has many repercussions for philosophy, let us maintain focus on the issue that concerns us: contra Aarseth (2004), and to a degree Jung (1959), just because a thing like Lara Croft's body *withdraws* from conscious circumspection, this is not *ipso facto* evid-ence of a diminution in meaning. Rather it is an alternate mode of understanding and, further-more, may lead us towards a conclusion which flows in the opposite direction of Aarseth's claim: as the thing becomes part of my bodily schema, accessed through my specific context and needs, I become more attuned to it, more sensitive to its polyvalence, and therefore the thing is not less but more meaningful.

Observing the game controller on my table as a present-at-hand phenomenon, it is under-standable *as* a piece of plastic, *as* a certain weight, *as* an ergonomic and aesthetic design appro-priate to our historical period; this is all meaningful of course. But *using* the game controller to play a video game is also meaningful, indeed it is an enormously affective experience: holding the controller tightly, thumbs on analog sticks and index fingers wrapped around trigger buttons I feel powerful and in control; my *animus* is not just *in* me but *pervades* and *expands* through my being-in-the-game-world. Other times being-in-the-game-world is an anxious and vulnerable experience. Once more this is not just an 'internal' state, but is diffuse through my world, affecting my understanding and interaction with all kinds of entities located outside my body. Such meaning is only accessible through my using the gamepad in a *zuhanden* manner originary to *Dasein*, which allows my sense of embodied attunement with the gameworld.

Once more: comprehending the way in which the world intrudes, persists and insists upon Being (*Sein*), Heidegger coined *Dasein/Da-Sein* (There-Being or Being-There); another way of saying this, as above, is being-in-the-world. In doing so Heidegger intended to accomplish two things: first, to highlight the inextricability of one's understanding with one's historical, social, cultural, carnal situation; one's thereness as *con*-text, so to speak. Second, and following, to illus-trate the untenability of Cartesian dualism or indeed any ahistorical philosophical system that de-contextualises and prioritises one essential thing (for example Democritus' atoms or Descartes' mind), criticised by Heidegger (2008) as 'ontotheology'. It is in such respects, as has been noted by others (Brooke, 1991, 2009; Hillman, 1997; Hockley, 2014; Levin, 2000; Mook, 2000; Sipiora, 2000), that we see particularly fruitful links between phenomenology and analytical psychology.

The game-play complex

Incorporating analytical psychology into an existential phenomenological approach informed mainly by Hans-Georg Gadamer and Paul Ricoeur, Bertha Mook remarks:

> [P]lay is ontologically prior to the player. The player in turn discovers his own self-presentation in his play by subordinating himself to it and listening to what it has to say. In the therapeutic context, we could say that the imaginative play of a child has a story to tell to the child and his therapist as it reveals meanings about the child and the life-world that were previously concealed.
>
> *(2000, p. 245)*

Play is, then, complex in every sense of the term: as constituted by different parts, as a bringing together, as a rich phenomenon with depth and revelation, and as encouraging abnormal behaviour (i.e. the lusory attitude) which may reveal, and aid, in healing psychic conflict. However, before we further discuss relations between play and psychotherapy, we must offer a clarification: *play is not synonymous with game*. Both are ways of framing behaviour, imbuing one's world with meaning alternate to an 'everyday' experience, yet the permissions, dynamics, identities and relationships differ markedly, as has been discussed in game studies for many years. If play is fluid, game is rigid; if play is ephemeral, game is reified; if play is to deviate, game is to adhere; if play's cardinal injunction is yes, game's is no. Phenomenologically, play is felt as an extreme, almost vertiginous freedom: possibility pours forth as I follow my whim. Conversely, game generates and simultaneously denies possibility: I can now do *this* (score a goal in soccer) but not *this* (use my hands to touch the ball).

Game is, to paraphrase Garry Whannel, a 'parallel universe with its own values, its own institutions, structures and practices. Indeed this is part of its pleasure ... a gateway to the mythic' (2002, p. 54). As mythopoetic, i.e. story-making activities, games are a cohesive set of values structured in a way to generate a finite set of expressions comprehensible to an audience, not least of which is the player herself. These values, structures and practices broker much less deviation than unregulated play; whether enforced by judge, referee or computer code, the ontology of game is essentially bound up with, to counter Juul's (2005) separation, rules-as-expressed.

This is what Gadamer refers to when he quips that 'all play is a being-played', going on, '[t]he attraction of a game, the fascination it asserts, consists precisely in the fact that the game masters the players ... What holds the player in its spell, draws him into play, and keeps him there is the game itself' (2004, p. 106). Games establish a phenomenological lifeworld (*lebenswelt*), wherein the playful experience is a gestalt coming together, both as co-llision and co-llusion. As opposed to unregulated play, which we call paidia (Caillois, 2001), games (*ludus*) are a phenomenon wherein the *anima ludus* becomes uniform, managed and, therefore, shareable; the player is not in control but, more accurately, under control. As noted, it is interesting this ontological discussion of games is similar to Jung's rumination upon complexes. Jung contemplates:

> Everyone nowadays knows that people 'have complexes'. What is not so well known
> ... is that complexes *have us*. The existence of complexes throws serious doubt on the
> naive assumption of the unity of consciousness ... and on the supremacy of the will.
>
> *(1934: §200, emphasis as original)*

As complexes are patterns of abnormal behaviour, wrapped up in values, emotions and perception sharing a common theme, so are games similarly a system designed to encourage patterns of conduct. If to play is to engage in active imagination, then we might refer to digital games as systems for amplification of specific images, with all of the dangers and benefits inherent in amplification as therapeutic strategy.

As with the playing of a game, the working out of complexes is not an objectified process of knowledge processing (*vorhandenheit*): one could no more play a game just by reading a rulebook than one could read a dictionary definition and be cured of a complex. Instead, both complexes and play are unique expressions of one's being-in-the-world, and therefore a *zuhanden* (ready-to-hand) approach is suitable to exploring such phenomena before one attempts further layers of theoretical abstraction, as Mook recommends (2000).

Thereness

This is where Heidegger's discussion of guilt is of conceptual use. Guilt (*Schuld*) is not to be understood here in any traditional moral sense, but as an ontological feature of *Dasein* that makes any and all moral systems possible; it is a foundational indebtedness or 'being responsible for'.

Guilt is embodied in the call of conscience to understand one's specific situation (one's *Da*, thereness), one's finitude and to take ownership over one's possibilities. This is counterposed against another ontological feature of *Dasein*, its 'thrownness' (*Geworfenheit*) into the World, which is to say one's being 'thrown' into existence: body, society, culture, language, i.e. one's history, or, more pointedly, one's ego. Part of this is an inescapable 'fallenness' (*Verfallen*) into the world, experienced as being absorbed in the practices of *Das Man*, the public standards of a 'they-self' informing the construction of the ego-complex. As the seat of consciousness, the ego is very fluid and adaptable, sensitive to history, opposed to the relatively static archetypes. Therefore, the constant temptation for the ego to carry on one's life 'as one does' without reflection or critical contemplation is part of this fallenness. Guilt is a counterbalance, as Heidegger advises, '[c]onscience summons Dasein's Self from its lostness in the "they"' (2008, p. 319).

Inauthentic guilt happens when one responds by fleeing from the call of conscience, identifying the call as some mundane fear, communicated via the 'idle chatter' of *Das Man* which admonishes one for 'not doing what one does': 'do this instead!' *Das Man* commands. Conversely the authentic response, when one does not run from the call of conscience but instead dwells, is a deeply held anxiety (also translatable as angst, or perhaps in Hillman's oeuvre as depression), providing no advice on how to proceed: the 'call does not report events; it calls without uttering anything. The call discourses in the uncanny mode of *keeping silent*' (ibid., p. 322, emphasis as original).

The authentic call shakes one out of a complacent attitude to take a stand on oneself, face up to one's potentiality-for-Being. It is not in a panic heard as 'lazy!' or 'disgusting!', the super-ego of *Das Man*, but instead held authentically as an ambiguous, altogether uncanny, feeling where one's world withdraws, as a stable structure filled with significance and meaning, and one no longer feels 'at home' (a rather straight translation of Heidegger's term, *Unheimlichkeit*, is unhomeliness). In this mode of experience one is compelled to comprehend one's situation, finitude, individuality and potentiality, and must make an existential decision on what one is to become, which Heidegger calls resoluteness. Again, one may draw fruitful links here with Jung's discussions on the Self and individuation, Hillman's on depression and, indeed, Joseph Campbell's description and analysis of the monomyth (1949).

Complexes in the Heideggerian view, then, are inauthentic interpretations of the call of conscience: heard and reacted against as the call of they-self (*Das Man*) to act, rather than the authentic call of the Self to dwell. It follows a specific design can afford a therapeutic working through of complexes by the design acting as a call to conscience through amplification of particular behaviours. A game that provokes anxiety and encourages one to dwell would tend towards authenticity; a game that provokes common fears and pleasures, and strongly prescribes what to do, would tend towards inauthenticity.

Put another way, a design that allows one to 'stick with the image' in a *zuhanden* (ready-to-hand) mode can provide an authentic call to conscience, more so than one which constantly objectifies and dictates the user's engagement in a *vorhanden* (present-at-hand) mode. In practice, we might say that as a rule, *to play* is a priori more authentic than *to game*, as the latter attempts to enforce a mode of understanding via all kinds of insistences: 'go here!', 'do this!' and so on via its narratological and ludological systems, as outlined by Ruggill and McAllister (2011).

A poetic space

Yet, that is not to say that games are without value. As outlined, the digital game medium can amplify and emphasise dwelling. Though ruminating specifically on films that are psychologically effective (i.e. of therapeutic utility), Luke Hockley's *Somatic Cinema* is informative here:

> [I]ts meaning is sufficiently fluid for individuals to find space for their own understanding … to allow for the activation of unconscious material. Again, the parallel with dreaming is instructive … texts and images that tend towards the psychologically polysemic which allow for the possibility of personal psychological meanings. In contrast, those texts where the meaning is relatively anchored to closely prescribed ideas are less available for individual negotiation.
>
> *(2014, p. 20)*

Hockley thus introduces the concept of the 'third image', which 'exists between the film's effects on the viewer and the viewer's own affects and projections onto, and into, the film' (p. 137). Amplifying this spatial metaphor, there must be a substantial enough gap, between person and artefact, through which the 'third image' can emerge. To offer a vivid example from mythology, Narcissus chased his own voice (represented by Echo), then moved so close to the water he allowed no space between understanding of self and reflection upon self: this is a sure recipe for psychic disaster, death even.

As mentioned, bridging existential phenomenology with Jungian approaches for play therapy, Mook (2000) offers a compatible description where player and play meet, 'the child can be seen as carrying out imaginative variations on reality which is kept at a distance and metamorphozed in the process … The power of imaginative play lies in this metamorphosis and redescription of reality' (pp. 247–248). In phenomenological terms, this is *poesis*, a making, which unconceals (*a-letheia*) Being.

Crucially, for this to happen there must be a depth of fantasy offered through interaction: 'depth' here is an effect of encountering the previously concealed (*lethe*), for if one only encounters that which is already known, there can be no profundity. As Heidegger articulates, 'poetic images are imaginings in a distinctive sense … visible inclusions of the alien in the sight of the familiar … By such sights the god surprises us' (1971, pp. 223–224).

Tied to this, the design must facilitate a dwelling with the being of the work. Heidegger defines dwelling as a form of measuring, 'a taking which at no time clutches at the standard but rather takes it in a concentrated perception, a gathered taking-in, that remains a listening' (p. 221). As opposed to the idle measuring of *Das Man*, this measuring is a circumspective, poetic pursuit: a careful listening. In ludic terms this is autotelic, rather than paratelic engagement: playing within and for the moment, rather than in pursuit of a future reward. If a game is to be psychologically effective then, phenomenologically, there must be a certain gap between gamer and game; there must be a fluidity and depth of meaning for player access; the design should facilitate dwelling. Taken together, this generates the opportunity for a phenomenological revelation that persists for one's being-in-the-world.

This revelation is a truth beyond a simple *vorhanden* 'correctness' or 'coherence', such as checking the relationship between statements and facts, for example between the taste and aesthetic principles of *Das Man*, as in the Kantian tradition. Revelation is instead a *zuhanden*, embodied truth, which again Heidegger used the Greek term *aletheia* to denote; it is a lighting up of Earth, that which contains within it all possible meaning, into the World. The Earth, as pure potential, is always partially hidden, as only certain meanings come through into the World at any particular moment. The Earth is therefore deep, the World, as current structure of significance, is relatively shallow; again in Jungian terms, we find correspondences between World and consciousness, Earth and the archetypes (as structuring agent for all possible experiences).

The essence of all artwork in the Heideggerian view (1971) is this tension (or 'strife') between Earth and World, wherein new meaning is alighted. Unconcealment (*aletheia*) is therefore a vertiginous rupturing of one's being-in-the-world as the Earth momentarily protrudes, and one's sense of existence is fundamentally altered through this encounter. Similar to Hockley's third image (2014), this tension between Earth and World, reified in the artwork, is the crucial ingredient to *aletheia*.

Let us take this hypothesis, blending together Heideggerian phenomenology with Jungian phenomenological approaches, and apply it briefly in the next section to a few popular dynamics of play in digital games, illustrating first failures and then a success of psychologically reactive design. As touched upon above, the myth of Narcissus provides a resonant image for contemplation, and, following the tradition of myth as hermeneutic aid in Archetypal Psychology, will be used to structure discussion. As Hillman notes, the 'hermeneutic begins with myths and mythical figures (not with a case), reading them downward for psychological understanding of the fantasies going on in behaviour' (2015, p. 43).

Chasing echo

The myth of Narcissus begins with the love of Echo, a wood nymph cursed to have no speech but that which is spoken to her. In love with Narcissus, she shadows him. One day she shows herself partly, peaking interest. 'Who's there?' he calls out. 'Who's there?' she returns, slipping away. 'Come here!' he commands; 'come here!' she teases. Narcissus, fascinated gives chase: 'Let us join one another!' Echo shows herself, throwing her arms around him. Narcissus, disgusted, shuns her love; Echo, devastated by rejection, dies of grief.

Echo is, of course, the first reflection Narcissus encounters, as repetition of his own speech. Fascinated by this reflection, he follows single-mindedly. Finally encountering Echo, the gap closes, depth falters, as Echo can only give back what she receives; the third image, promised by the momentary chase, becomes impossible. Though often viewed as a symptom of Narcissus' psychological immaturity, this is in fact a correct rejection. In recognising Echo for what she is, a repetition of his own making, Narcissus is justified in refusing what could only ever be a psychologically stultifying relationship: to return Echo's love would only be to reinforce his love of self. The problem is simply that Narcissus answers the call of conscience inauthentically: he dwells not in the authentic 'why do I feel hate for this person?' but fearfully interprets the call as 'she is disgusting!'; an immature reaction to his Shadow.

In other words, though Narcissus made the right decision, it is performed hatefully, and for the wrong reasons: he remains unconscious of his Shadow, overidentifies as his shallow Persona, and is therefore ignorant of his eponymous disorder. We are reminded of Jung's consistent lesson regarding the symptom, aptly summarised by Brooke's phenomenological approach:

> There is gold in the symptom which weighs us down like lead, and a prince in the beast … the beast has to be loved as a beast before his princely qualities can be revealed. In other words, we do not change the image; if befriended, the image heals us.
>
> *(1991, p. 133)*

This shallow chasing of reward is a very popular design dynamic in digital games, introduced by behavioural psychology via B. F. Skinner's eponymous 'Skinner box' experiment. The details of the test are unimportant for the concerns of this chapter; all one need know is the investigation focused upon the optimal frequency of reward to motivate desired behaviour. Ultimately, this optimum was defined as 'variable', which is to say one is rewarded sometimes but not always, either as a ratio (x actions to reward) or intervals (x time to reward). As long as the frequency of reward is variable, there is a much greater chance of consistent conduct because, experientially, the participant is induced to believe the reward for enacting the prescribed behaviour may just be around the corner. For a classic example, casino slot machines work on this principle.

This has filtered through to video games in many formulations but is most commonly referred to as a 'loot' system: goods rewarded through discovery of new areas, opening of containers, or defeating enemies. ('Lut' comes from a Hindi word that means goods taken from an enemy.) The loot can be represented as some form of currency, weapon, armour, ability, vehicle or experience point system relevant to the game's diegesis. Though finding its heritage in tabletop gaming, implementation of loot is now prominent in many mainstream best-selling digital games such as the *Call of Duty* series and Massively Multiplayer Online Games (MMOGs) such as *World of Warcraft*.

The overarching dynamic is, phenomenologically, experienced as a push to rectify deficiency. The specific deficiency is clearly outlined by the game's representational and ludic framework: one must collect experience points, weaponry, armour, land, life, the Princess and so on, the more the better. Critical reflection is discouraged by such design, buried beneath the constant glimpsing of achievement upon the horizon: the game insists one either chases or fails. In this manner the autotelic aspect of play is undermined: one is encouraged not to dwell within the moment of play but instead to look forward to some promised moment of satiation. This is an illusory sense of completeness exacerbated by reward systems, for example *Xbox* and *Steam* 'achievements', *PlayStation* 'trophies' and so on, encouraging overidentification with the Persona. Promoting overall a paratelic engagement, such design insists upon the user to labour rather than play; a dynamic of infinite accumulation, rather than finite dwelling, encouraging mundane fear (I don't have enough!), rather than existential anxiety (Why am I compelled to collect?). This dynamic of chasing reward is game-as-distraction, rather than game-as-revelation.

Narcissus *ex machina*

In *The Culture of Narcissism*, Christopher Lasch opines '[p]rudence, caution, and calculation, so prominent in everyday life but so inimical to the spirit of games, come to shape sports as they shape everything else' (1991, p. 123). This overbearing, Apollonian rationality has certainly held true for sports such as baseball for many years, yet has reached its proper zenith in the digital game incarnation where everything is present in *vorhanden* statistics: the athlete-avatar is athlete-as-numerical-resource. In digital games such as the *FIFA, MLB The Show, NBA 2K* series and more, the player is tasked with optimisation: manipulating athlete-avatar tactics, formations and positions according to an extraordinarily broad suite of numbers associated with specific abilities (speed, accuracy, strength, stamina etc.) to find, in the rather mathematical sense, a 'winning formula'. This is the antithesis of poetic measuring, which is dwelling; instead, this is a literal measuring 'with ready-made measuring rods' (Heidegger 1971, p. 224), a mundane *metron* of *Das Man*.

'The coming to presence of technology threatens revealing, threatens it with the possibility that all revealing will be consumed in ordering and that everything will present itself only in the unconcealedness of standing-reserve' (1977, p. 33), so frets Heidegger considering the essence of technology. In his view, the essence of technology is nothing technological, but its power of Enframing (*Ge-Stell*), encouraging the experience of one's World in a certain way: to conceal the Earth and reveal World only as a supremely ordered *vorhanden* 'as' structure, being-*as*-commodity, which Heidegger calls *Bestand*, often translated as 'standing-reserve', as above. For example, previously romantic landscapes become landscape-*as*-commodity (mineral resource, hydroelectric resource, tourist resource), a person is diminished to person-*as*-commodity (human resource, financial resource, biological resource) and so on. (There is much more to Heidegger's discussion; see Conway (2016) for an in-depth exploration.) The poetic capacity of Being, inherent within the phenomenological Earth, to reveal Worlds in new, surprising, creative ways, critical for authenticity and understanding, is nullified by Enframing; everything is instead ordered as homogeneous resource, e.g. the database, and only one World is possible, that of consumption and this points towards a neurotic *Animus*.

To offer a recent, popular example from digital games, *No Man's Sky* represents the endpoint of this mode of Being. The game offers a procedurally generated Universe, containing over 18 quintillion planets. The player can freely explore, flying between worlds, solar systems and galaxies using faster-than-light travel. In doing so the player must repair, fuel and maintain her spacecraft, spacesuit and weaponry by 'mining' resources from the planets landed upon. This is achieved through 'shooting' rocks with a 'mining laser' weapon held in the avatar's right-hand. As the player fires the mining weapon, the land feature targeted slowly dissolves and a certain amount of resources are awarded, displayed as a number associated to a chemical element (e.g. '12 Polonium'). Thus the main dynamic of the game revolves around slowly moving across a planetscape, 'dissolving' it into a numerical resource, then transmogrifying that resource into another resource: energy for one's engine, shields or the mining laser itself.

As Narcissus gazing into the pool, this is game-as-mirror, emulating the everyday working World of *Das Man*. As mirroring labour practices of knowledge economy workers and consumption cycles of consumers, this kind of game dynamic does not encourage critique or contemplation, but instead reinforces a superficial *vorhanden* attitude complicit with the Jungian Persona: wear the mask required by the knowledge economy; apply the conventions of *Das Man* and repeat *ad infinitum*, as the nine-to-five World of *Das Man* feels like an infinite loop. Appropriately, there is no formal end designed within such games, and features such as 'quick save' and 'quick load', so inimical to contemplation, expand this sense of infinity.

Solve et coagula

One of the grand ironies of Narcissus' tale is that in both verbal and physical reflection he is, metaphysically, unreflective. The lesson is clear: to achieve maturity, one must engage in deep critical reflection. As critical, this is necessarily a destructive process as much as it is constructive, and extends both to Jung's articulation of the Self and to Heidegger's notion of authentic *Dasein*. One is reminded of Jung's exploration of alchemy and the alchemists' maxim, *solve et coagula* (dissolve and coagulate), which Jung interpreted as a guideline for psychic growth (1963): constant dissolution and renewal of self should be practised.

As the mythopoetic space one engages with, how can the game medium facilitate, rather than obfuscate, critical self-reflection? How may it encourage, in Heideggerian terms, an authentic dwelling within the call of conscience, which, in Jungian terms, is a move towards Selfhood and psychological maturation? As discussed, to do so the design must facilitate *zuhanden* dwelling over *vorhanden* calculation; finitude over a sense of infinity; autotelic rather than paratelic play. Overall there must be a phenomenological gap between player and game, Earth and World, for psychological reaction to occur: too far away and the reaction is a dissipation, too close and the reaction is a replication. Both extremities are, as shown above, forms of shallow distraction that tend towards psychological stasis, whilst we are looking for deep provocation to generate a robust third image, catalysing *aletheia*.

One method of provocation is subversion: to draw one into conventional understanding, a taken-for-granted World, before violently rupturing it by holding open the tension between World and Earth. It is interesting to note both Heidegger, in *The Question Concerning Technology* (1977), and Jung, in 'The spiritual problem of modern man', quote the same line by German poet Friedrich Hölderlin, 'where danger is, Arises salvation also' (1928/31: §195).

Simply put, the psychologically a/effective artefact does not require an entirely new mode of existence. Instead, as indicated by Hölderlin, one may simultaneously represent and undermine convention, illuminating the idle chatter of *Das Man* whilst critiquing it; a simultaneous dissolution and coagulation. In doing so the Earth opens up, tension with World is held in place, and a third image becomes possible.

Ek-static design

As widely available, commercially popular and critically acclaimed, Jonathan Blow's *Braid* makes for an exemplary illustration. Initially, Blow's design seems to regurgitate the 'damsel in distress' trope often seen within two-dimensional platformer games such as the classic *Donkey Kong* and *Super Mario Bros.* series: *Braid*'s controllable character, 'Tim', is understood by the player as the hero rescuing the generic 'Princess', snatched by the 'Monster' at the end of each discrete level. Towards the end of the game Tim is instead revealed as the Princess's stalker, the Monster as not stealing but saving her, utterly changing the player's comprehension of game activity; a Dionysian dissolution of the player-avatar relationship. Phenomenologically, the chase dynamic and calculated puzzle-solving dissolves as heroic endeavour, congealing as an anxiety-inducing, tentative lingering.

This is a design decision emphasising *ek-stasis* 'outside of place': the stable structure of meaning (World) is stretched to breaking by the emergence of the Earth, and this tension is held in place. Every movement forward becomes a questioning on behalf of the player, every solution to a puzzle congeals with Tim's lecherous motivation, provoking discomfort. Further, the player can access a hidden ending which involves the reading of a set of story books poetically referencing scientific endeavour and the Manhattan Project. The only limitation is the hard drive (or cloud) space of one's computer to store saved files. This reframes play once more, draping the game in Promethean metaphor: the princess is the atom bomb, the player is the scientist; the princess is knowledge, the player is humanity. Phenomenologically, the player's understanding of the character undergoes many Dionysian vivisections.

As existential psychologist Mary Watkins remarks,

> [a] *dwelling with* that careful noticing requires opens pathways to the depths of a phenomenon and to participation with it ... such attention finds ways of caring action that are not superimposed, but arise from the ground of relationship spawned by careful attention.
>
> *(2005, p. 7, emphasis in original)*

Tim's singleminded application of an *animus*-driven *Logos* has undermined his comprehension of and relationship to humanity, to his *anima*. In Hillman's terms, this is a classic case of the heroic ego, a purely conscious mindset 'which attempts to deny and silence this multiplicity [of Psyche] and assume power and control' (ibid., p. 7).

The character can only understand *his* world through *vorhanden* deduction, an application of crude categories generated by *Das Man* which levels off the uniqueness of his situation, his *Da* (thereness), generating a fundamental misunderstanding. In some ways Tim represents the Enframing of modern technology described by Heidegger wherein all is viewed through an Apollonian gaze as an ordered, homogeneous resource. Appropriately, the main mechanic of *Braid* is time control: the player rewinds, fast-forwards and slows-down time to solve puzzles. As with all else in the *Dasein* of Tim, time is simply another resource for consumption. It cannot be understood in a *zuhanden* manner, a multiplicity of one's unique thrownness (past) and projection (future), but instead as the levelled off 'present' of *Das Man*. To quote from one of the game's hidden story books:

> Ghostly, she stood in front of him and looked into his eyes. 'I am here,' she said. 'I am here. I want to touch you.' She pleaded: 'Look at me!' But he would not see her; he only knew how to look at the outside of things.
>
> *(Braid, 2008)*

As the game ends, it begins anew: exiting the door of the final level, Tim appears back at the start of the game, and so the cycle continues until the player decides to stop. As with the World of *Das Man*, time takes on the appearance of a never-ending, infinite loop, and even death becomes an abstract event 'in one's future'. Yet Blow attempts to subvert this reception of *Braid*'s design through the revealing of Tim as stalker: the entire chase dynamic is unveiled as fable illustrating the perilousness of an overbearing *animus*; the heroic ego its avatar. In Heideggerian terms, this is the danger of fallenness into *vorhanden* understanding, the idle chatter supplied by *Das Man*: death, as the Nothing (*das Nichts*) upon which all authenticity is founded, becomes impossible.

This is simply one of many readings for, appropriately, an explicit, *vorhanden* approach to interpretation is always partial, as Blow describes in an interview:

> The narrative in *Braid* is not being obscure just for obscurity's sake. It's that way because it was the only way I knew how to get at the central idea, which is something big and subtle and resists being looked at directly. If I were to make some kind of statement about what the game is about – even a very long, elaborate and well-considered statement – it would miss.
>
> *(McElroy, 2008)*

Instead, *Braid* demands a *zuhanden* undertaking, a mode of Being not wholly captured by written word and mental representation: understanding is reached primarily in the moment of play. Through subversion, the game's design holds open the tension between Earth and World pivotal to psychologically affective artwork. The ek-static nature of *Dasein*, as always-already standing partially outside, between worlds, between past and future, is amplified; a third image becomes possible as the *anima ludus* shakes the foundation of the player's being-in-the-world, and dwelling is encouraged.

This form of game design is *aletheia* in the form of *enantiodromia*: the restoring of balance through introduction of an opposite. In *Braid* this is implemented by the game's core design, as convention is simultaneously presented and critiqued. To reiterate: 'where danger is, Arises salvation also' (Hölderlin in Jung, 1928/31: §195).

References

Aarseth, E. (2004) 'Genre trouble: narrativism and the art of simulation', in P. Harrigan and N. Wardrip-Fruin (eds), *First-person: new media as story, performance and game*. Cambridge, MA: MIT Press. pp. 45–55.

Brooke, R. (1991) *Jung and phenomenology*. London: Routledge.

Brooke, R. (2009) 'The Self, the psyche and the world: a phenomenological interpretation', *Journal of Analytical Psychology*, 54(5), pp. 601–18.

Caillois, R. (2001) *Man, play and games*. Urbana, IL: University of Illinois Press.

Campbell, J. (1949) *The hero with a thousand faces*. Princeton, NJ: Princeton University Press.

Dreyfus, S. E. and Dreyfus, H. L. (1980) 'A five-stage model of mental activities involved in directed skills acquisition', Paper to Air Force Office of Scientific Research.

Gadamer, H-G. (2004) *Truth and method*, eds J. Weinsheimer and D. G. Marshall, 2nd edn. London: Sheed & Ward.

Heidegger, M. (1971) *Poetry, language, thought*, ed. A. Hofstadter. New York: Harper & Row.

Heidegger, M. (1977) *The question concerning technology and other essays*, ed. W. Lovitt. New York: Garland Publishing, Inc.

Heidegger, M. (2008) *Being and time*. New York: Harper Perennial Modern Thought.

Hillman, J. (1997) *The thought of the heart and the soul of the world*. Woodstock, CT: Spring Publications, Inc.

Hillman, J. (2015) *Volume 1: archetypal psychology*, ed. M. McLean. Woodstock, CT: Spring Publications, Inc.

Hockley, L. (2014) *Somatic cinema: the relationship between body and screen – a Jungian perspective*. Hove: Routledge.

Huizinga, J. (1949) *Homo ludens: a study of the play-element in culture*. London: Routledge & Kegan Paul.

Jung, C. G. (1928/31) 'The spiritual problems of modern man', in *The collected works of C. G. Jung*, Vol. 10, *Civilisation in transition*, 2nd edn. Princeton, NJ: Princeton University Press, 1970.

Jung, C. G. (1934) 'A review of the complex theory', in *The collected works of C. G. Jung*, Vol. 8, *The structure and dynamic of the psyche*, 2nd edn. Princeton, NJ: Princeton University Press, 1969.

Jung, C. G. (1959) 'The Self', in *The collected works of C. G. Jung*, Vol. 9ii, *Aion: researches into the phenomenology of the Self*. Princeton, NJ: Princeton University Press, 1959.

Jung, C. G. (1963) *The collected works of C. G. Jung*, Vol. 14, *Mysterium coniunctionis*. Princeton, NJ: Princeton University Press, 1963.

Juul, J. (2005) *Half-real: videogames between real rules and fictional worlds*. London: MIT Press.

Lasch, C. (1991) *The culture of narcissism*. New York: W.W. Norton.

Levin, D. M. (2000) *Eros and psyche: a reading of Merleau-Ponty*, ed. R. Brooke. London: Routledge.

McIntyre, R. and Woodrow Smith, D. (1989) 'Theory of Intentionality', in J. N. Mohanty and W. R. McKenna (eds), *Husserl's phenomenology: a textbook*. Washington, DC: Center for Advanced Research in Phenomenology and University Press of America. pp. 147–79.

McManus, D. (2012) *Heidegger and the measure of truth*. Oxford: Oxford University Press.

Merleau-Ponty, M. (1962) *The phenomenology of perception*. London: Routledge & Kegan Paul.

Mook, B. (2000) 'Phenomenology, analytical psychology, and play therapy', in R. Brooke (ed.), *Pathways into the Jungian world: phenomenology and analytical psychology*. London: Routledge. pp. 233–51.

Ratcliffe, M. (2009) 'The phenomenology of mood and the meaning of life', in P. Goldie (ed.), *The Oxford handbook of philosophy of emotion*. Oxford: Oxford University Press. pp. 347–72.

Ruggill, J. E. and McAllister, K. S. (2011) *Gaming matters: art, science, magic, and the computer game medium*. Tuscaloosa, AL: University of Alabama Press.

Sheehan, T. (2015) *Making sense of Heidegger: a paradigm shift*. London: Rowman & Littlefield International.

Singh, G. (2014) *Feeling film: affect and authenticity in popular cinema*. Hove: Routledge.

Sipiora, M. P. (2000) 'THE *ANIMA MUNDI* AND THE FOURFOLD: Hillman and Heidegger on the "idea" of the world', in R. Brooke (ed.), *Pathways into the Jungian world: phenomenology and analytical psychology*. London: Routledge. pp. 64–81.

Whannel, G. (2002) *Media sports stars: masculinities and moralities*. London: Routledge.

Online source

McElroy, J. (2008) 'Joystiq interview: Blow unravels Braid in postmortem', *Engadget* [online]. Available at: www.engadget.com/2008/09/25/joystiq-interview-blow-unravels-braid-in-post-mortem/ [Accessed 2 October 2016].

Watkins, M. (2005) 'On returning to the soul of the world: archetypal psychology and cultural/ecological work' [online]. Available at: www.pacifica.edu/gems/watkins/OnReturning.pdf [Accessed 15 October 2016].

Ludography

Batman: Arkham Knight. (2015) [video game] Warner Bros. USA.

Braid. (2008) [video game] Designed by Jonathan Blow. USA.

Call of Duty. (2003–) [video game] Activision. USA.

Donkey Kong. (1981–) [video game] Nintendo Co. Ltd. USA.

FIFA. (1993–) [video game] Electronic Arts. USA.

Lara Croft: Tomb Raider. (1996) [video game] Created by Toby Gard. USA.

MLB The Show. (2006–) [video game] Sony Interactive Entertainment. USA.

NBA 2K. (1999–) [video game] Dreamcast. USA.

No Man's Sky. (2016) [video game] Hello Games, Sony Interactive Entertainment. USA.

Super Mario Bros. (1985–) [video game] Nintendo Entertainment. USA.

World of Warcraft. (2004) [video game] Blizzard Entertainment Inc. USA.

30

CINEMA WITHOUT A CINEMA AND FILM WITHOUT FILM

The psychogeography of contemporary media consumption

Aaron Balick

Introduction

It is widely reported that Freud did not like the moving pictures very much. When approached by Samuel Goldwyn with an offer of $100,000 to consult on *Secrets of a Soul* (dir. Pabst, 1926), a film about famous historical love stories that would start with Anthony and Cleopatra, Freud politely declined. Surprisingly, however, Freud was not at all affronted by the idea. According to Ernest Jones (1957), 'he was amused at this ingenious way of exploiting the association between psychoanalysis and love' (p. 114). Despite this unique opportunity Freud's 'disbelief in the possibility of his abstract theories being presented in the plastic manner of a film' (ibid.) prevented him from going ahead with Goldwyn's plan. Rather than abandoning it all together, he left it in the hands of his capable associate Karl Abraham. It did not turn out well. Despite the fact that Freud delegated the task, the production company nevertheless included in its publicity, without Freud's consent, that the film was 'planned and scrutinized by Dr. Freud'. This came to the delight of the English press, highly suspicious of Freudian theories at the time, who reported that 'Freud, having failed in securing support for his theories among professional circles, has in despair fallen back on the theatrical proceeding of advertising his ideas among the populace through film' (ibid., p. 115). This must have been very disturbing for the professor, who was continually working to promote psychoanalysis as a 'proper science' against intense resistance within the public and its institutions. As an aside, let's not forget the oft quoted phrase, 'There's no such thing as bad publicity' is associated with P. T. Barnum, whose life overlapped with Freud's for more than thirty years. It would seem that bad publicity was as much a boon for psychoanalysis as it was for Barnum and Goldwyn.

As it turned out, the plastic manner of film would be more amenable than anyone expected as an expression of the abstract theories of psychoanalysis. We can presume that Samuel Goldwyn might have seemed crass to Freud (such was his opinion of all things American) but Goldwyn was certainly not stupid. He saw quite clearly how a theory of unconscious human motivation could aid the creation of a gripping film with which his audiences might identify. Presumably he felt he could get the edge on his competitors by consulting the father of psychoanalysis himself.

Ultimately, psychoanalysis not only became a method for analysing film but also a great trove of source material for narratives that would express themselves through it. Never is the link between psychoanalysis and popular film more obvious than it is with Hitchcock, either through direct representations of psychoanalytic practice through a film such as *Spellbound* (dir. Hitchcock, 1945) or, as is more frequently the case, how psychoanalysis informs the underlying character motivations in a film like *Psycho* (dir. Hitchcock, 1960). Hitchcock's films emerged within a culture long over the scepticism of psychoanalysis that was so prevalent in Freud's own time.

Over the prevailing years psychoanalysis had become both institutional and mainstream. In order to gain such respectability, just as Freud had feared, much of American psychoanalysis had shed its early associations with childhood sexuality and libido theory in exchange for the more socially acceptable Ego Psychology that focused on normative adaptation to work and marital life. It was not the same in the UK where Object Relations became dominant, in France where it became heavily seduced by Lacan, and in other parts of the world that took psychoanalysis in a variety of different directions. Psychoanalysis would change and adapt with time and culture as it spread and evolved around the globe. In parallel we see film production and analysis making use of the varieties of explanatory systems the different schools of psychoanalysis have to offer. Whether this is in the continued representation of therapy itself on the large or small screen (Bainbridge, 2011), or the underlying narratives or interpretations being read through the eyes of one's preferred theorist in isolation or combination.

Today, as evidenced by the title of Part V 'Approaches post-cinema', we approach our understandings of film in a late modern period under the moniker 'post'; that prefix pointing to the de-centred paradigm indicative of all things postmodern (in relation to Jung in particular see Jones (2007) and Hauke (2000)). Rather than focusing on content, I shall be approaching post-cinema in a way that highlights the manner of a film's consumption and what happens during and after the film is consumed by way of associated technologies; outside a couple of small examples, I will mostly leave content analysis to others. In this way I will be reversing the usual approach in which content is usually figure and context is usually ground. A post-cinematic engagement as experienced today goes beyond the content of a film in that it also refers to films that are available to watch at any time (via streaming or DVD/Blu-ray) in any space (via a smart phone or tablet), during or after which thoughts about them shared almost immediately through *posts* on social media, blogs, Twitter, or on fan sites. In relation to the seeking of meaning as provoked by film, this extra-cinematic motivation is resonant with the post-Jungian perspective taken by Singh (2011) who looks at cinephilia as a meaning-making activity that extends beyond film itself, and Hockley (2011) who invokes 'the third image' to represent a register of meaning that exists outside the dyad between viewer and film to create something that is not immediately available to consciousness. (In contemporary relational psychoanalysis this is referred to as the 'analytic third' (Ogden, 1994) in a clinical setting.) Post-cinematic experience may express itself through the will to search items of interest on the Internet Movie Database (IMDB), or the online seeking out of the 'answer' to the burning question with which one leaves the cinema. Alternatively and paradoxically, post-cinema can contradict engagement with a film with reference to a search for meaning instead drawing one towards *distraction from* meaning or the deeper experiencing of the self by compulsive watching of nearly *anything* that will take attention away from internal psychological and emotional experience: media as distraction from self. All of these actions are available immediately and in real time, though seemingly outside time, at an arm's reach; if this isn't a culture of radical immediacy, I don't know what is (this hypermediation already goes back some time, see Bolter and Grusin's 1999 book *Remediation*). If 'post', as in postmodern is also a matter of things being de-centred, disintegrated, and subversive to traditional means of production and consumption, then it seems to be all that as well. In a contemporary context, content may be relegated as secondary, or at least wholly dependent on the context in which the film is consumed. As Denson and Leyda (2016) suggest:

Post-cinema asks us to think about new media not only in terms of novelty but in terms of an ongoing, uneven, and indeterminate historical *transition*. The post-cinematic perspective challenges us to think about the affordances (and limitations) of the emerging media regime not simply in terms of radical and unprecedented change, but in terms of the ways that post-cinematic media are in conversation with and are engaged in actively re-shaping our inherited cultural forms, our established forms of subjectivity, and our embodied sensibilities.

In the spirit of this I would again highlight not just in the content of films or the ways in which they are analysed, but even more importantly in the way in which we watch film, talk about film, understand it, converse about it, and engage with film in order to better understand ourselves as well as how we engage with film and other media in order to disengage with ourselves.

It's personal

Today filmmakers and film theorists alike have a variety of psychoanalytic angles from which to choose their approach to film, that is, if they choose psychoanalysis at all. The matter of one's approach is ultimately a personal choice, in much the same way that the bodies of work of any given theorist is also arguably a representation of their personal style. As Jung (1995) himself noted, 'philosophical criticism has helped me see that every psychology – my own included – has the character of a subjective confession' (p. 136). As the author of this chapter who clearly buys into the role of one's personhood in one's approach to film, it seems imperative to take a reflexive approach here and disclose up front that I do not approach cinema as a film scholar, as I am not one. Rather I am a clinical psychotherapist with a serious interest in applying psychotherapeutic thinking to a variety of media, and have chosen to share these thoughts regularly through my blog. I have found that film and television offer a unique insight into the human condition because they are deployed in a way that makes human meaning-making and emotional experience highly accessible to psychoanalytic thinking from a clinical 'real people' perspective. For me, this bridges the object of inquiry (cinema) with its mode of interpretation (contemporary psychoanalysis) without abstracting (too much) psychotherapeutic theory from its application towards actual people. Because I operate in a digital environment that allows me to easily disseminate these thoughts through blogging, I have found that this activity of blogging about films after I watch them has become part and parcel of how I watch film, think about it afterwards, and almost simultaneously share those thoughts with my readers: a kind of engagement that was previously unavailable to me. Heath (1981) covers resonant themes in his chapter on 'Narrative space' in *Questions of Cinema* when he makes a distinction about what is held within the film's frame, and what is outside it. While Heath does not explicitly discuss what might be done by the subject outside the cinema in reference to what is possible digitally (after all, this was written in 1981), he does interrogate the nature of the relationships between viewer and various registers of the film:

> A constant welding together: screen and frame, ground and background, surface and depth, the whole setting of movements and transition, the implication of space and spectator in the taking place of film as narrative. The classical *economy* of film is its organization thus as organic unity and the *form* of that economy is narrative, the *narrativization* of film.
>
> *(p. 43)*

Today, the viewing, analysis, and sharing have all become components of this narrativisation of film, a new kind of deployment of this economy from the subject of the viewer. For many of us, this greatly expands what 'engaging in film' encompasses within a post-cinema environment. My theoretical approach to film might be described as 'integrative psychoanalytic' because I can choose from a variety of theoretical schools to apply to a given film depending on its subject matter or the felt experience of the watching itself. Here we have two more elements that make this contribution 'post' – the deployment of a variety of psychoanalytic theories that implicitly undermine the conception of any schoolist or dogmatic psychoanalytic 'truth' alongside the fact that though I'm contributing to a part on post-cinema, my main expertise lies in another discipline. This very much reflects the way I approach psychotherapeutic practice too, drawing upon models that seem appropriate to both the material that any individual is bringing, alongside the uniquely characteristic inter-subjective dyad we create in the room together.

Like a patient, a film requires an approach personal to it and its viewer. For example, though *We Need to Talk About Kevin* (dir. Ramsay, 2011) and *Alien* (dir. Scott, 1979) are profoundly different kinds of films, I found that a Kleinian analysis offered the most favourable access to meaning (Balick 2011, 2012a); *Gravity* (dir. Cu>

arón, 2013) surprisingly leant itself to a classical Freudian reading (Balick, 2013b), however not by way of the texts one might expect, but rather through tracking the protagonist's journey as a parable of grief outlined in Freud's eloquent essay 'Mourning and melancholia' (1917). A more classical Freudian reading arises from a modern film like *Skyfall* (dir. Mendes, 2012) precisely because it so clearly and explicitly harkens back to a Hitchcockian aesthetic (Balick, 2012b), while another set of divergent films, *Her* (dir. Jonze, 2013) and *Blue Jasmine* (dir. Allen, 2013) required a contemporary relational approach (Balick, 2014b, 2013c). The variety of ways in which all manner of psychoanalysis and film come together are as myriad as the ways in which there are pairings of therapist and patient in the consultation room – each one trying to understand the other using an idiosyncratic style of theoretical framing, alongside a technical underpinning to support a therapeutic dyad between the two subjectivities. This is a metaphor that I will stick with throughout this chapter, to keep coming back to the human component of film as a personal meaning-making activity – for filmmakers behind the films as much as for the individuals enjoying them (and the relationships formed between them) – as much as they contain collective meanings for the societies that produce them at particular moments in time (Campbell, 2003).

Speaking of metaphor and in reference to Joseph Campbell, we see the relevance of different forms of psychoanalysis in bringing out the personal and social mythic metaphors embedded in film. (In fact, psychoanalysis itself, in its different forms and places can be seen as its own mythic metaphor.) For Campbell, 'there's no better medium in the world than film' (2003, p. 217) when it comes to the transmission of myth for contemporaneous audiences. Campbell argued not only that societies need myths that speak to them today (rather than just those we have inherited), but that individuals also need to live their own myths – and mythical qualities can be identified with through film. That myths should be contemporary is crucial, says Campbell, 'Mythology is an organisation of symbolic images and narratives metaphorical of the possibilities and fulfilment *in a given culture in a given time*' (p. 165, my emphasis). Further, and rather grandiosely it must be said, Campbell also states 'myth is the secret opening through which the inexhaustible energies of the cosmos pour into human cultural manifestation' (2008, p. 1). If such is the power of myth, and cinema is a way through which myth may be conveyed, we are talking about a very important medium in transmitting contemporary cultural myths. However, the capacity for film to convey myth is not a given, and many films in Campbell's (2003) opinion lack mytho-poetics and simply serve to 'put people into bed and take them out again' (p. 217). As I will be arguing here, the contemporary state of 'post-cinema' leaves film and its related media in a potential space that enables it to transmit myth for our times while at the same time the technology that aids this transmission serves to disrupt an individual's communion with their individual and cultural myths, to 'put them to bed' as it were, through distraction into brain-numbing activity.

For Freud, the application of psychoanalytic theory outside the clinic and on to culture appears to have been supported by his own interest in myth and literature, even if he did seem less at ease with its application to the more popular expressions of cultural production. According to Frosh (2010, p. 40),

> Freud was on the look out for ways in which psychoanalysis might draw on evidence from outside the consulting room in order to establish itself more firmly, as well as for opportunities to use psychoanalysis for wider cultural and scientific ends in the service of knowledge in general.

In this approach of Freud's we see the doubling of the psychoanalytic will to understand alongside that very nature of understanding that developed psychoanalysis itself. Just as he plundered his patients with an aim to build psychoanalytic knowledge, he applied this newfound knowledge right back into the clinical field. 'Freud believed', Frosh continues, 'that the psychological processes fuelling artistic creativity were identical to those reviewed by psychoanalysis in the clinic' (p. 43). Of course, psychoanalysis *not* being a science meant that the psychological process of one artistic creator was distinctive from the process driving the other: the same holds true for the individual enjoying the fruits of another's artistic endeavour in relation to media and film.

The experience of engaging with a film in order to commune with any of its mythic components is also highly personal and the effect that any film will have on an individual is a function of the way in which that individual is engaged in that filmic experience. As Hauke and Alister (2001, p. 2) note:

> Cinema offers both a means and a space to witness the psyche … films deliver a contemporary experience set apart of 'daily life' – collectively experienced with others in a dark place … cinema has the possibility of becoming an imaginal space – a *temenos* – and by engaging with films a version of active imagination is stimulated which can then engage the unconscious – potentially in as successful a fashion as our conscious attention of dream imagery and other fantasies.

The conditions that Hauke and Alister suggest are required in order for such successful engagement with the unconscious importantly include that they are set apart from everyday life, can be enjoyed communally, and that they can provide the imaginal space for a version of active imagination to act upon them. With these elements in play, the engagement with film becomes a deeply personal one. If for Campbell (2008) '[d]ream is the personalised myth, myth the depersonalised dream' (p. 14) then perhaps for us, the 'right kind of film', the one with mythic qualities, can also function as a personalised myth – particularly if Hauke and Alister's components are present. Immediately, however, we are drawn to the rather disturbing realisation that one of the main components that they highlight, that the film is enjoyed apart from everyday life and 'collectively experienced with others in a dark place' is less and less common in the way we engage in film these days. What, then, is the consequence of engaging with film when it is viewed piecemeal while streaming through the small screen of a mobile phone on a short bus journey? Is the viewer engaging with their personal myth in a wish to deepen their engagement with their unconscious, or are they distracting themselves from that very same engagement through a medium of cheap entertainment?

Where it happens and how it happens: the sacred and the banal

Until very recently, just like the experience of attending a psychoanalytic session, very little has changed about going to the cinema. In psychotherapy, generally one arrives in a consultation room, takes a seat or lies down, and speaks to his or her therapist: two people talking in a room – that is psychoanalysis. When one goes to the movie theatre, he or she purchases a ticket, maybe buys a tub of popcorn, and enters a giant dark room in the company of others to enjoy the experience. Admittedly, we can assume one's experience of film in the days of the silent pictures was somewhat different from after the arrival of sound: showing up to see *The Jazz Singer* (dir. Crosland, 1927) in 1927 would have been a phenomenally different experience from the exclusively silent films viewed before it; not to mention the experience of very early cinema enjoyed in carnival tents and nickelodeons (Singh, 2016). Same again with other innovations such as the development of colour and the increasing quality of sound and picture; later shifts to the cinema-going experience would include the arrival of 3D (gaining prominence in the 1950s but achieving technical sophistication much more recently) and IMAX, both tipping towards a virtual reality experience that we appear to be right on cusp of at the time of writing.

Outside the rather niche field of Cinematherapy where specific films or clips are used to provoke emotional experiences for clients in a therapeutic way, psychoanalysis has generally concerned itself with analysing the content of films as they are presented much more so than their method of delivery and consumption. This is likely to be because, until recently, so little has changed. Despite the notable shifts in cinema-going I outlined above, the experience of watching a digitally re-mastered film from generations ago, *The Wizard of Oz* (dir. Fleming, 1939), for example, could be experienced today not so differently from how it was in 1939. Though we have seen the development of more sophisticated immersive developments such as IMAX 3D and the capacity to render entire universes in three-dimensional CGI (e.g. James Cameron's *Avatar* (2009)), a quick re-acquaintance with Fritz Lang's *Metropolis* (1927) will soon set you straight on the capacity for our filmic forbears to create a wholly fictional immersive experience. While I do not mean to suggest that *Metropolis* in essence looks the same as *Avatar*, what I do mean is that all of the essential qualities are there. As I will be arguing below, by far the biggest difference in relation to cinema-going has more to do with the devices that either interrupt us while we are engaged with film in the cinema, or when we are not, those very same devices that may mediate our experience of film at home or elsewhere; this important qualitative distinction is discussed in detail in Part II in Singh's (2014a) *Feeling Film*. The very way in which we consume media today is probably the biggest single change since the videocassette recorder (VCR) found its way into the average family home in the 1980s.

If you cast your mind back to the days of VCRs and the video rental shop (should you be old enough to remember), you can get a sense of the paradigmatic shift that has occurred between then and now. While I might be idealising the past in a somewhat nostalgic way, I seem to remember that when the video-cassette slid into that oversized machine and the trademark image and music from Universal, MGM, or whatever studio production it was appeared on the screen, the domestic space in which the television magically flickered suddenly transformed into a cinema at home. Today the television is only one of many devices through which one might consume a film; our portable technologies enable each individual within a household to watch different films or television programmes in isolation, in different spaces at the same time, often with multiple screens in operation for each viewer (Google, 2012). The communal experience has been exchanged for an internal and private one, and the capacity to engage in any form of media, uninterrupted, seems positively anachronistic. For those media events that continue to be aired nationally to a public 'live to air' schedule (an 'event' programme that can be anything from a television premier of a much loved film to the latest instalment of *The Great British Bake Off)* the synchronised gasp of a packed house as the proverbial great white shark lurches at the protagonists has been exchanged for the snarky hash-tagged tweet shared with a nation of double screeners.

The generalised mode of consuming media outside the cinema involves constant disruption to the point that disruption becomes part of the experience rather than an impingement to it. The introduction of disruption and multi-tasking across screens is paradigmatically different from the more traditional experience of sitting through a programme with fully focused attention. The uninterrupted focused attention given to a film can induce a form of reverie, an activity that can be of great benefit in communing with unconscious aspects of the self. In psychoanalytic terms, reverie is an activity that is derived from an attuned mother's awareness of the internal state of her infant, 'a state of calm receptiveness to take in the infant's own feelings and give them meaning' (Hinshelwood, 1991, p. 420). This concept has been extrapolated from maternal experience with an aim to apply it to the way in which a psychoanalyst may do something similar with his or her patient. To extrapolate even further, this state of reverie can be seen as a necessary component of communion between an audience member and a film in order to really connect to the cultural and personal mythic patterns that Campbell was referring to above. Though this is a huge generalisation, one can broadly witness the lack or presence of a capacity to engage in reverie in relation to films viewed outside the cinema between the generations of what might be called digital natives (those born after about 1980) and digital immigrants (generation X and their seniors) (Palfrey and Gasser, 2008) – anecdotally, digital natives seem more comfortable multi-screening whereas immigrants prefer one at a time: each cohort feeling less comfortable with the habits of the other. It was from my own personal experience of sharing a much admired film with millennials that provoked me to blog about why people under thirty should watch a long film like *The Godfather* (dir. Coppola, 1972) without interruption (Balick, 2013a) as I noticed that particularly in relation to a long-form character dramas like this, multi-tasking audience members were missing out on the micro-cues one needs to be aware of to get a sense of where the characters' minds were and their developing alliances or conflicts: micro-cues which, more frequently than not, are non-verbal. In order to enjoy a film like *The Godfather* or its first sequel, one needs to employ a combination of reverie and close attention for a film that runs at two hours and fifty-five minutes. Today this is a feat akin to meditation.

While viewing films outside the cinema is particularly vulnerable to such disruption, the sacred space of the movie theatre too is slowly being subjected to impingements that rudely and frustratingly pull cinemagoers out of their attention and reverie. Because most cinemas go out of their way to remind us to turn off our phones before the show begins, we are fortunately less likely to be disrupted by other people's tiny glowing screens. However, the more subtle and pernicious form of interruption may simply be that silent and subtle vibration of your own phone in your back pocket because you chose to put it on silent mode instead of airplane – what in a general 'always on' sense is addressed by Turkle (2011). Just like the protected and sacred space of the psychoanalyst's consultation room is no longer safe from similar digital intrusions, nor is the cinematic experience. The nature of this silent interruption, which I refer to as 'virtual impingement' (Balick, 2012c), is one that only the afflicted cinemagoer would be aware of. Such an impingement has the capacity to rip one out of reverie and straight into anxiety introducing a variety of disruptive thoughts such as, 'Who is that?' and 'What do they want?' What, then, happens to this individual's communion with their cultural and individual myths as deployed on screen? Such a technologically provoked internal conversation with the self has the capacity to disrupt engagement with the film to the degree that it takes several minutes to return to it; this nature of continual disruption, or 'continuous partial attention' (Stone, 2012) is now a part of daily life and results in people multi-tasking as a default. Only the most disciplined and thoughtful individuals can avoid them by *preparing to watch a film* and turning their devices off completely. Going to the cinema with the mobile off might be the longest period many people go these days without interruption outside sleep.

Resonant with the cinema, the therapist's consultation room, for many, represents a sacred space or a safe zone where one is encouraged to allow their unconscious to present itself: a place where therapist and client alike can enter into reverie together. In recent years this sacred space has come under attack not by the profane, but rather by the banal (Balick, 2015). In the same manner that a silent vibrating phone in a back pocket can disrupt one's intensive immersion in a film, a psychotherapy session can equally be interrupted, silently cutting across the spirit of a moment in a way that only one of the parties may be consciously aware. Further, the sacred space of the consultation room can be foregone altogether for the convenience of a Skype session that occurs across most banal of mediators, the home computer or laptop: the very same place where emails are received, spreadsheets are constructed, bills are paid, and pornography is consumed. Similarly a 'serious film' can be now be consumed through the all-too-tiny screen of a mobile device in equally banal locations, such as a bus or aeroplane, where one is certain to be disrupted by external events or flashing notifications. Just as the ritual of going to see a therapist is rich in sensual detail – the climbing of the stairs, the quality of the air in the room, moving through the threshold of the doorway, and seating one's self on the chair or the couch – so too is the arrival at the cinema, the passing over the ticket, the smell of the popcorn, the chewed gum on the underside of the chair, and whether or not you stick around for the credits (and why). Interestingly, Netflix by default prevents one from enjoying the credits, consequently jolting the viewer out of finishing or 'coming down' from a film and suggesting a new one to watch straight away.

Both the consultation room and the cinema can be seen as sacred spaces that are directly vulnerable to banalisation. The mode of consumption of our media today is completely embedded in our technology rich environment which has important consequences of our psychological, emotional, and spiritual experience of making meaning from our engagement with film and other media. For the remainder of this chapter we shall try our best to understand, through the lens of psychoanalysis, the effect of viewing cinema in the myriad ways that today's technology enables. In 'Post-cinema affect' Shaviro notes that he wants to develop an account of,

> what it feels like to live in the early 21st century ... I am interested in the ways that recent film and video works are expressive: that is to say, in the ways that they give voice (or better, give sounds and images) to a kind of ambient, free-floating sensibility that permeates our society today, although it cannot be attributed to any subject in particular. By the term expressive, I mean both symptomatic and productive. (Shaviro, 2016)

Shaviro's perspective is resonant, even though in this particular case he is taking a content perspective on how film and video today may express the zeitgeist. As we have seen, however, this 'ambient, free-floating sensibility' is also clearly evident within the way that we engage in media today and not just what is represented upon it. Above, I have described our techno-media landscape and how it related to our experience of meaning making in relation to film. Next I will look into how this landscape invites and enables us to divert our attention away from ourselves into what could be called a distraction economy of contemporary media.

Displacement and the capacity (not) to be alone

Throughout this chapter I have been working with the underlying metaphor of intersubjective process as demonstrated by the psychotherapeutic dyad. There is no patient without a therapist and it is the same the other way around. In a true Hegelian dialectic each creates the other within the mutual dynamic – just like the relationship between a film and its audience. The relationship between film and psychoanalysis is similar. As put succinctly by Fuery, 'Psychoanalytic theory opens up the possibilities of reading cinema as a symptom: and cinema allows us to consider the cultural significance of psychoanalysis because it can be seen as a cultural symptom and a symptom of psychoanalytic theory' (2008, p. 230). For Fuery both psychoanalysis and cinema can be seen as a cultural symptom and such symptoms can be read and understood much like the hysterical symptoms of Freud's day. If we see cinema as 'a symptom of various cultural processes and issues' as Fuery does (p. 229) we can also learn a lot about our culture from the mode in which we engage in both psychoanalysis and cinema. Singh (2014b, p. 121), for example, draws us to the Channel 4 production of *Black Mirror* in which:

> Throughout all of the stories, the characters are somehow beholden to a particular technology, or are otherwise trapped in a dysfunctional relationship with it; and in amongst these more discernible science-fictional narratives, the themes of recognition and trust emerge as the human stories here – which, as I will argue, is a 'negative affordance' of this dysfunctional relationship, more often than not ending up with the various characters misrecognising the relationships they have with other people, and therefore feeling the bite of their alienated existence.

These themes have become more and more familiar to us in their representations in film and television as we attempt to process the speedy development of technology as a culture. Programmes like *Black Mirror* confront us not simply with fantasies about what *could* happen if technology continues to develop in ways that we are unable to control, but also holds up a mirror to our *contemporary* feelings of being out of control with our technologies as they are today. The rather obscure 2002 film *My Little Eye* (dir. Evans) does something similar by exploring the already dark consequences of reality television, whereas *The Blair Witch Project* (dirs Myrick and Sánchez, 1999) uses the function of the democratisation of video technologies into the hands of the masses as the conceit for the found footage structure of the horror. *Eye in the Sky* (dir. Hood, 2015), a film that explores the morality of drone warfare, beautifully and tragically communicates the feeling of contemporary displacement by carrying out its main drama at three geologically discrete locations across the globe. Though the main military action of the film is conducted far away in Kenya, the vast majority of those involved in directing this action via drones and their one actual man on the ground are doing so remotely from dark rooms in London and Nevada. Those directing the operation are making life and death decisions and doing so from comfort-cooled environments in the safety of their 'global north' countries from which they deliver deadly payloads in the global south via joysticks and interfaces that resemble videogame consoles. When the intense drama is complete, the screens conveying while the conflagration of violence and death in another part of the world are turned off: one protagonist emerges into the English rain, the other exits into the Nevada sun. The viewer is left reeling from a real sense of displacement in identification with the characters who have just been in two or three places at one time, all the while sharing the same virtual environment in which scores of other lives, far away, hang in the balance. Yes, this is a film about the worrying consequences of wars waged via remote controlled drones that serve to separate the major players from the actuality of their consequences for the real human beings on the ground but it's also a metaphor for the rest of us who live in a world in which technology aids and abets our daily sense of displacement.

In *The Psychodynamics of Social Networking: Connected-up Instantaneous Culture and the Self* (Balick, 2014b) I explore how social media alongside the mobile devices that deploy it, can serve as a surrogate for real complex and human interpersonal interaction in a way that ultimately diminishes relational experience. What is notable in relation to social media is the way in which it enables a psychological outsourcing of recognition and validation to online social networks in a way that potentially cripples an individual's ability to witness and recognise him- or herself on his or her own terms. Hence, one could say that there are a number of conditions in which 'quality' interpersonal relations can take place, and these might include variables such as a period of uninterrupted time within a shared physical space where complex interactions can be shared: these interactions are inclusive of verbal and non-verbal, conscious and unconscious. Similarly, in relation to film, as Hauke and Alister described above, there are some necessary conditions that enable what might be called an 'intentional' engagement with film. By intentional I mean to describe a purposeful engagement with film with the aim of psychological, intellectual, and/ or emotional understanding towards some degree of personal growth, cultural or social engagement, or as an aid to understanding the self or society through identification with narrative and characters. I hold this in distinction to using film as an escape from daily life or as a means to rest an over-stimulated mind. There is certainly room for both types of engagement, but perhaps we should be less passive in our consumption of film and be clearer about what we are seeking when we choose to watch film. I would argue that today's techno-media-rich environment mitigates against the intentional approach while encouraging us 'veg out' and simply consume all sorts of media without thinking. While the content of programmes like *Black Mirror* or a film like *Eye in the Sky* draw attention to our underlying discomfort with technological developments through the content of their productions, the nature of our difficult contemporary relationship to stillness, mindfulness, introspection, and quiet reverie surrounds us everyday through the challenging intrusion of our devices.

Psychoanalyst D. W. Winnicott (1986) focused much of his work on the early mother–infant dyad in order to illustrate how the quality of this early relational environment continues to influence or relationship with ourselves and others, long after we are infants. He refers to this quality as 'transitional phenomena' because it represents the transition we make from viewing others around us as objects to seeing them as fully human subjects. This transition occurs within an 'intermediate area of experience' (p. 266) which is duplicated not only in our continued relationship with others, that space between 'you' and 'me', but arguably, too, between an individual and a film 'properly watched'. This intermediate area, often called transitional space, offers the opportunity for creative engagement with that which is outside the self:

> The transitional phenomena represent the early stages of the use of illusion, without which there is no meaning for the human being in the idea of a relationship with an object that is perceived by another as external to that being.
>
> *(Winnicott, p. 266)*

Confusingly, in psychoanalysis, the term 'object' can be used to mean an object or a subject (as in another person). In contemporary psychoanalysis we are almost always referring to another subject and have come to term that other as such as a 'subject'. In other words, the transitional space offers an individual a way to communicate, engage, commune, and imagine with another.

Without the transitional space, others revert to mere two-dimensional objects and the experience is mostly solipsistic (or more accurately, narcissistic).

This short segue into Object Relations and Relational Theory is necessary in order to suggest the possibility that our social transitional spaces, as well as our cinematic ones, are diminishing. You see, Winnicott suggested that by creating a safe 'facilitating environment' in which the infant would grow, parents would enable their children to make those first steps through transitional space to become a subject in their own right, safely integrated within a world of other subjects. Additionally, they would develop a 'capacity to be alone' a form of emotional maturity which enables the individual to be alone but not lonely, because they have managed to incorporate and integrate the care of the other into the self because they have identified with their good enough parent (Winnicott, 1982). For Winnicott this capacity to be alone, if developed, would be retained for life; and if not, it could be built up and encouraged through a good analysis. I argue that both transitional space and the capacity to be alone are necessary for reverie. Engagement with film that enables the kind of communion with personal myth that Joseph Campbell describes requires reverie. Today's media and technology rich media environment militates against this.

To come back to the central metaphor, the interpersonal attention required to get the most out of a psychotherapy session involves the uninterrupted attention of both parties, who create the meaning of that session between them. As soon as that session is moved across to the banal environment of a screen, or should a piece of technology buzz or ring in one's back pocket, there is a diminution of quality.

Recent research into the quality of psychotherapeutic process over video conferencing (Balick, 2015) showed that while profound moments of meeting were reported by therapists working online, there were also a series of difficulties inherent in the work being carried out via a video conferencing platform. While the quality of the therapeutic relationship between therapist and client varied a great deal from high to low quality, nearly all therapists agreed that sessions mediated via a computer screen were not the 'functional equivalent' of a live 'co-present' session (Russell, 2015). Similarly if one wants to give cinema the important role of meaning making in the mythical variety outlined by Campbell and described by Hauke and Alister, above, a similar attention and 'quality' is required, and a similar ritual in arriving in a sacred space. Such is the diminution of the capacity to be alone today, that many of us revert to our devices *before* we register a sense of loneliness in much the same way we grab for food before knowing we are hungry. In the worst of both worlds, we may use media to avoid our inner worlds, while at the same time using technology to interrupt opportunities for communion with media when it can be used to enable us to grow.

How to watch a film in a post-cinema environment

Given the dangers that I have outlined above, it does not seem beyond the pale to offer some sort of suggested intervention here about how we might address these concerns in a post-cinematic environment. Though I would be reluctant to be prescriptive about how one *should* watch film and other media, I do suggest that in our post-cinema world we need to be more conscious and aware of the challenges that are implicit in our technology and media–rich environments. Our consumption of media continues to grow as our access to it becomes easier and easier. While people have always turned to the cinema as an escape and refuge from real life, fantasy has at the same time served as a source for personal identification and an opportunity to commune with our personal and collective unconscious. The opportunity for reverie and free-floating attention in relation to a film gives one the opportunity to integrate unconscious material into conscious material. Bettelheim, though referring to fairy tales and their importance to children's development, nonetheless highlights the importance of fantasy over rationality when it comes to understanding the conscious self in relation to the unconscious. He argues that a child does this,

> not through rational comprehension of the nature and content of his unconscious, but by becoming familiar with it through spinning out daydreams – ruminating, rearranging, and fantasizing about suitable story elements in response to unconscious pressures. By doing this the child fits unconscious content into conscious fantasies ... It is here that fairy tales have unequalled value, because they offer new dimensions to the child's imagination which would be impossible for him to discover as truly his own.
>
> *(1977, p. 7)*

Adults, no doubt, have similar needs. In today's media/technology/distraction rich world, we need more than ever the opportunity to commune with mythic representations in a space that affords the requisite conditions for the unconscious to explore and play with ideas, themes, and tropes that trigger the ways in which we make meaning of our worlds. However, not all media is created equally. Some might necessarily be engaged with for pleasant distraction, fun, a laugh, or as an opportunity to escape the mundane pressures of daily life, or, indeed, to make that long haul journey a little less onerous. What is important is that a conscious choice is made instead of simple passive consumption. We can ask ourselves, how might I choose to watch *this* film?

To return to the founding metaphor of this chapter, let's think of the old-fashioned therapy session. There is something profound and rather prosaic about the way in which an individual shows up for therapy. At the same time every week this individual makes his or her way to their therapist's consultation room where they will engage in a conversation about his or her internal world, ideally unimpeded by the distractions of the external world for fifty minutes. No technologies are employed other than the attention that each gives the other, in a time set aside for this purpose. Afterwards, this individual returns to the world, hopefully in his or her own time, before plugging into the onslaught of daily life. These fifty minutes, this analytic hour, is one for reflection – a fifty minutes that is opted into, it is chosen.

When engaging with any form of media, perhaps a similar choice could be made. Throughout I have been drawing attention to the notion that media can be an opportunity to engage with the self or to check out. Neither of these uses is essentially good or bad. However, if one is checking out when one might be better off engaging, and vice versa, he or she is potentially inviting a lack of grounding into their life. Perhaps now that we occupy an environment in which we often engage in media without thinking about it, we should pause and ask a question: 'What is the mode of my engagement here?' Simply because the possibility of losing one's self in diverting and stimulating media becomes available to us, should we take it up? Or should we instead, on this occasion, sit with ourselves and see what arises? To respond to the call of media stimulation simply because we can, implies a passive response to our techno-media environment. Perhaps our responses could be more conscious and active. Alternatively when we are about to make that choice to engage in a more profound experience of media, whether that be at the cinema or at home, perhaps we can pause for a moment and wonder what we may wish to get out of this opportunity. We can use this opportunity to consciously eradicate impingements in order to activate our capacity to be alone in relation to the projected image and allow our reverie to roam un-impinged: to enjoy that transitional space between the reality principle and the world of fantasy, and to see what emerges there. When the film is done, perhaps we can pause before we tweet, blog, or look up our burning questions on IMDB and allow that reverie to continue. Then, once we have made that choice, we can avail ourselves to all the wonderment available in our techno-media landscape and go wild. Share your thoughts, ask questions, contribute to fan-fiction, and use your active imagination to amplify your experience. In the end, the technologies available to us don't care what we do with them in relation to our experience of media, so it is up to us to engage with them in ways that feel rich and productive, rather than depleting and distracting.

References

Bainbridge, C. (2011) 'From "the Freud squad" to "the good Freud guide": a genealogy of media images of psychoanalysis and reflections on their role in the public imagination', *Free Associations: Psychoanalysis and Culture, Media, Groups, Politics*, 62, pp. 31–59.

Balick, A. (2012c) 'TMI in the transference LOL: psychoanalytic reflections on Google, social networking, and "virtual impingement"', *Psychoanalysis, Culture and Society*, 17(2), pp. 120–36.

Balick, A. (2014b) *The psychodynamics of social networking: connected-up instantaneous culture and the self.* London: Karnac.

Bettelheim, B. (1977) *The uses of enchantment: the meaning and importance of fairy tales.* New York: Vintage Books.

Bolter, J. D. and Grusin, R. (1999) *Remediation: understanding new media.* London and Cambridge, MA: MIT Press.

Campbell, J. (2003) *The hero's journey: Joseph Campbell on his life and work.* New York: New World Library.

Campbell, J. (2008) *The hero with a thousand faces.* Novato, CA: New World Library.

Denson, S. and Leyda, J. (2016) 'Perspectives on post-cinema: an introduction', in S. Denson and J. Leyda (eds), *Post-cinema: theorizing 21st-century film.* Online E-Book: Reframe Books. pp. 1–19.

Freud, S. (1917) 'Mourning and melancholia', SE 14: 243–258. London: Hogarth Press. 1957.

Frosh, S. (2010) *Psychoanalysis outside the clinic: interventions in psycho-social studies.* London: Palgrave.

Fuery, P. (2008) 'Psychoanalysis and cinema', in J. Donald and M. Renov (eds), *The Sage handbook of film studies.* London: Sage. pp. 226–43.

Hauke, C. (2000) *Jung and the postmodern.* London: Routledge.

Hauke, C. and Alister, I. (2001) 'Introduction', in C. Hauke and I. Alister (eds), *Jung & film: post-Jungian takes on the moving image.* Hove: Routledge. pp. 1–13.

Heath, S. (1981) *Questions of cinema.* London: Macmillan Press.

Hinshelwood, B. (1991) *A dictionary of Kleinian thought.* London: Free Association Books.

Hockley, L. (2011) 'Depth psychology and the cinematic experience', in C. Hauke and L. Hockley (eds), *Jung & film II: the return.* London and New York: Routledge. pp. 132–47.

Jones, E. (1957) *The life and works of Sigmund Freud: volume three, the last phase, 1919–1939.* New York: Basic Books.

Jones, R. (2007) *Jung, psychology, postmodernity.* Hove: Routledge.

Jung, C. G. (1995) *Modern man in search of a soul*, trans. W. Dell and C. Baynes. London: Routledge.

Ogden, T. H. (1994) 'The analytic third: working with intersubjective clinical facts', *International Journal of Psychoanalysis*, 75, pp. 3–19.

Palfrey, J. and Gasser, U. (2008) *Born digital: understanding the first generation of digital natives.* New York: Basic Books.

Russell, G. (2015) *Screen relations: the limits of computer mediated psychoanalysis and psychotherapy.* London: Karnac.

Shaviro, S. (2016) 'Post-cinematic affect', in S. Denson and J. Leyda (eds), *Post-cinema: theorizing 21st-century film.* Online E-Book: Reframe Books. pp. 129–44.

Singh, G. (2011) 'Cinephilia: or, looking for meaningfulness in encounters with cinema', in C. Hauke and L. Hockley (eds), *Jung & film II: the return.* London and New York: Routledge. pp. 163–84.

Singh, G. (2014a) *Feeling film: affect and authenticity in popular cinema.* London: Routledge.

Singh, G. (2014b) 'Recognition and the image of mastery as themes in *Black Mirror* (Channel 4, 2011–present): an eco-Jungian approach to "always-on" culture', *International Journal of Jungian Studies*, special issue on moving image, 6(2), pp. 120–32.

Singh, G. (2016) Personal communication.

Turkle, S. (2011) *Alone together: why we expect more from technology and less from each other.* New York: Basic Books.

Winnicott, D. W. (1982) 'The capacity to be alone', in J. Southerland (ed.), *The maturational processes and the facilitating environment: studies in the theory of emotional development.* London: Hogarth Press. pp. 29–36.

Winnicott, D. W. (1986) 'Transitional objects and transitional phenomena: a study of the first not-me possession', in P. Buckley (ed.), *Essential papers on object relations.* New York: New York University Press. pp. 254–71.

Online sources

Balick, A. (2011, October 23) *We need to talk about Kevin (with Melanie Klein)* [blog]. Available at: www.aaronbalick.com/blog/we-need-to-talk-about-kevin-with-melanie-klein/ [Accessed 14 June 2017].

Balick, A. (2012a, June 3) *Alien: a Kleinian (psycho) analysis* [blog]. Available at: www.aaronbalick.com/blog/alien-a-kleinian-psychoanalysis/ [Accessed 14 June 2017].

Balick, A. (2012b) *In Skyfall M stands for mother* [blog]. Available at: www.aaronbalick.com/blog/category/everything/film-and-tv-criticism/page/2/ [Accessed 14 June 2017].

Balick, A. (2013a, June 3) *Why Richard (meaning anyone under 30) should watch The Godfather: the value of investing in an epic film without interruption* [blog]. Available at: www.aaronbalick.com/blog/why-richard-meaning-anyone-under-30-should-watch-the-godfather-the-value-of-investing-in-an-epic-film-without-interruption/ [Accessed 14 June 2017].

Balick, A. (2013b, November 9) *Gravity: on letting go in order to live* [blog]. Available at: www.aaronbalick.com/blog/gravity-on-letting-go-in-order-to-live/ [Accessed 14 June 2017].

Balick, A. (2013c, October 7) *The Xanax doesn't work: Blue Jasmine and the psychology of relating* [blog]. Available at: www.aaronbalick.com/blog/category/everything/film-and-tv-criticism/ [Accessed 14 June 2017].

Balick, A. (2014a, February 16) *Enlightenment 2.0: her and technologically assisted transcendence* [blog]. Available at: www.aaronbalick.com/blog/category/everything/film-and-tv-criticism/ [Accessed 14 June 2017].

Balick, A. (2015, May 15) *Sacred, profane, or just banal? Research into online (Skype) psychotherapy* [blog]. Available at: www.aaronbalick.com/blog/?s=banal [Accessed 14 June 2017].

Google. (2012) 'The new multi-screen world: understanding cross-platform consumer behaviour' [online]. Available at: http://services.google.com/fh/files/misc/multiscreenworld_final.pdf [Accessed 20 September 2016].

Stone, L. (2012) 'Continuous partial attention' [online]. Available at: https://lindastone.net/qa/continuous-partial-attention/ [Accessed 26 August 2016].

Filmography

Alien. (1979) [film] Directed by Ridley Scott. USA.

Avatar. (2009) [film] Directed by James Cameron. USA.

Blair witch project, The. (1999) [film] Directed by Daniel Myrick and Edwardo Sánchez. USA.

Blue jasmine. (2013) [film] Directed by Woody Allen. USA.

Eye in the sky. (2015) [film] Directed by Gavin Hood. UK.

Godfather, The. (1972) [film] Directed by Francis Coppola. USA.

Gravity. (2013) [film] Directed by Alfonso Cuaròn. UK.

Great British bake off, The. (2010–17) [television series – factual], BBC Television. UK.

Her. (2013) [film] Directed by Spike Jonze. USA.

Jazz singer, The. (1927) [film] Directed by Alan Crosland. USA.

Metropolis. (1927) [film] Directed by Fritz Lang. Germany.

My little eye. (2002) [film] Directed by Mark Evans. UK.

Psycho. (1960) [film] Directed by Alfred Hitchcock. USA.

Secrets of a soul. (1926) [film] Directed by George Wilhelm Pabst. Germany.

Skyfall. (2012) [film] Directed by Sam Mendes. UK.

Spellbound. (1945) [film] Directed by Alfred Hitchcock. USA.

We need to talk about Kevin. (2011) [film] Directed by Lynne Ramsay. UK.

Wizard of Oz, The. (1939) [film] Directed by Victor Fleming and George Cukor. USA.

31

DIGITAL MEDIA
AS TEXTUAL THEORY

Audiovisual, pictorial and data analyses of *Alien* and *Aliens*

Andrew McWhirter

Introduction

'Media As Its Own Theory'
(Rombes, 2009, p. 59)

'The medium is the message'
(McLuhan, 1964)

'A film by itself is just that and it only becomes meaningful when watched'
(Hockley, 2014, p. 50)

'Experience the freedom of total control [Betamax ad 1980]'
(Rombes, 2009, p. 113)

This chapter considers new methods of film analysis in the digital media landscape and whether or not the phenomenological experience of cinema exhibition, long considered superior to other means of consuming movies, can be matched or even exceeded by the ways that creative film analyses are now produced and consumed readily on smaller and mobile screens. Given that these modes, audiovisual essays, picture essays and cinemetrics, foreground the producer or 'produser' the potentially augmented experience will reside mainly with those creating the media but it is also argued that the audiences, however small, consuming the content are privy to certain distilled and immediate knowledge otherwise implicit or intangible in the cinema experience. These digital media are considered through their respective textual analyses of the films *Alien* (dir. Ridley Scott, 1979) and *Aliens* (dir. James Cameron, 1986). These films have been chosen mainly as a cipher due to their familiarity and because they offer less of a necessity for the reader to view them prior to learning about these newer analytical methods; a cultural awareness of the texts is, at the very least, assumed. This, then, is a textual analysis of the ways in which the films themselves are tackled rather than a strict analysis of the content of the films. The frame of reference being used is that of integration between analytical psychology and phenomenology as well as the loss and strived-for regain of the film object. Here the ideas of Luke Hockley (2011, 2014), Vivian Sobchak (1992, 2004) and Jennifer Barker (2009) are all useful in positing the affect and embodiment visible in these forms of digital media.

Information crises

Digital film theory developments have emerged in a disruptive information age and the very notion of such a thing is itself contested. Even its conceptualisation is problematic given that digital space is not actually space but, to use Charles Sanders Peirce's taxonomy of objects and the sign, indexical. It is always pointing to something that cannot be conceptualised materially or tangentially. This is why, as click theory reminds us, we are continually trying to reaffirm ourselves, our bodies. Consider the preposterous Amazon button as the most recent example as we attempt to 'touch' the space in order to feel the contact of our bodies. Cyberspace is dataspace, the space between us and that which we cannot touch but can be touched by. Body, mind and data are coalescing now more than ever and this has led some to posit the idea of a Fourth Industrial Revolution whereby the 'boundaries between the physical-biological and digital worlds are being eliminated – fuelled by data' (Hasselbalch and Transberg, 2016).

This is not the only problem of intellectualising cyberspace because the very idea of intellect is itself fragmented and dispersed. Imagine a world where being an analyst of imagery, be it film and television studies or psychotherapy, your curtain is suddenly pulled back and your secrets revealed. Your theories lay bare and your ivory tower razed to the ground. Since Tim Berners-Lee granted the world the web for free, this has been the trajectory anyone with an internet connection could follow made easier now by the black mirrors carried in the pockets of 2.08 billion citizens (Statistica, 2016). Those are the facts but whether such information power results in the actuality to destabilise systems and ideologies or transcend class or poverty is another matter. It does however make some humanities scholars twitchy and consider that expertise and academia in visual culture is radically changed forever.

When all knowledge is apparently thrown into uncertainty in an era of Web 2.0 ideologies that purport to offer digital democracy and utopia, search becomes the default for, simultaneously, the most basic and most complex enquiries, and post-truth is mainstream, then it is little wonder that theory is pushed to its logical conclusion of being defined as simply not practice. 'Cutting edge' seems to be the constant descriptor to follow most theoretical ideas in film theory today, largely because there are not the same visible or dominant characteristics as in the past. While there was certainly overspill we could see the period of formalism, or auteur theory, or psychoanalysis, or postmodernism or audience studies. It is little coincidence that one over-arching theme rather than theory coincides with the growth of Jungian Film Studies which is that of the personal (cinephilia and presumption, for example). There is no single dominant theory or even small group of theories we could point to, such as the return of cinephilia or blossoming of affect theory for instance. What is increasingly recognised by scholars are the ways in which the digital world can re-invigorate the discipline of film studies (Grant, 2012; Heftberger, 2012).

The processes of analysing film texts that will be discussed here are part of a wider area termed the digital humanities, which tries to be at the intersection of the technological sciences and the human interface with those technologies. Audiovisual ways of researching and reporting, post-archives, infographics, metrics and other computer visualisations are all part of this period some have termed Digital Formalism (Heftberger, 2012). And clearly some of these practices are easily linked to the re-appraisal of terms like cinephilia (Hockley, 2014) or, in the words of Mulvey (2015, p. 160), 'New ways of consuming old movies on electronic and digital technologies should bring about a "reinvention" of textual analysis and a new wave of cinephilia.' That it has but not just for old movies.

But cinephilia has been foregrounded, just as fandom has, via the same emergence of a digitally networked society that has enabled community mapping where before there was the disparate and uncharted. What this means is that virtually any theoretical idea can stake a claim, and this is partly why this chapter takes up a simple notion expressed by Nicholas Rombes when he considers that digital media themselves can be taken as theory. The central tenet of Rombes' (2009, p. 7) *Cinema in the Digital Age* is that film theory is domesticated and digital media itself is the new radical theory. He claims critics and academics must come at texts from 'odd and unexpected angles' which can be taken to mean by using said media, filmic or otherwise. Movies are no longer mysterious. Media is the new theory. Anyone can make films. Hollywood blockbusters are the new avant-garde. Rombes is certainly provocative but that is what makes his ideas about film studies so compatible with the personal engagement with films advocated by Hockley and others. It is perhaps telling that in the five years between his publications *Cinema in the Digital Age* and *10/40/70* – the most famous picture essay method in film studies in recent years – Rombes' own language changed from describing his 2009 blog and processes of screen capture as 'digital poetics' (McWhirter, 2016, p. 177) to 'digital film theory' in the latter 2014 project. Digital film theory is nothing if not an unstable conceptualisation.

Rombes (2009, p. 59) considers theory to be 'banished' by technocratic university environs as students become customers and deconstruction is now 'culture's new lyricism'. Whilst polemical, what should be taken from his ideas is that the ability to analyse and study film is now entirely democratised from its initial path in the late 1970s and early 1980s with the advent of home video. Even if he seems to foreground the cinematic experience as best for embodied affect, he is prophetic (writing before smart phones, the social media explosion, Go-Pros and Google Glass) in recognising the dominance of mobile screens today for a variety of production and consumption habits. One central argument he makes with regards to mobile screens relates to the fundamental shift in viewing as interruptive. Indeed the deliberate style of his book, written in short burst chapters, knowing the reader is about to be 'interrupted' herself and will put it down at any minute, also formalises this notion.

Size doesn't matter, does it?

When we are considering newer forms of digital media as potentially as phenomenological and affecting and thus in large part theoretical ways then there are the obvious and inescapable associations drawn between experiencing film as a continuous and captive event in the cinema and film as criticism, analysis or further interest. In the past there would be no comparison but now that films themselves can be used as the objects of their own critiques to produce other films, as with audiovisual essays, then the distinction becomes less rigid. The ability to repeat view, manipulate and learn virtually everything about the production histories of films calls into question the nature of experience and which is better or in Jungian terms more personal or affecting. Tackling this possibility will involve considerations of the screen, the act of remembering and also the body. It is not my intention here to say that cinema is not popular or the perfect apparatus to reproduce what Hockley (2011, 2014) terms 'The third image' as the best place to facilitate an intensely personal experience between individual and screen via the space between. Cinema is as popular as it has ever been and in 2015 showed the highest Box Office in the UK since records began. This is alongside, or perhaps in spite of depending on your perspective, all the bells and whistles approaches of reinvented 3D, and more recently 4DX, experiences – which itself takes the phenomenological experience of the cinema in new directions, spraying water on the face of the audience as they view is just one sensory action among many of its other tricks. My argument relates to the ability to engage with film and its critique outside the cinema as equally experiential and personal. I consider that the screen remains the same and only the frame and environment changes because it is more often than not a mobile screen.

Before outlining the themes of the screen, memory and body with relevance to cinema and digital media as theory it is useful to outline an important post-Jungian conceptualisation of the third image by Hockley as well as the images that precede it. This is because it will be used and referred to in order to understand digital film theory methods below.

Images: one to three

The first image is collective and shared with meaning inscribed in it for all to see. It is perhaps in this way that if it does not fulfil this shared meaning then it fails as a work of genre. Indeed this is how much evaluation of arts and culture works (Carroll, 2009). So, if it is a comedy and it does not make us laugh or a love story and we feel little sentiment or a horror without feeling scared or perturbed. Whether it fulfils these cause and affect designs is the job of evaluation and judgment but the very idea that it should or should subvert them is the inscribed meaning we should all be able to see. Izod and Dovalis (2014) have added to the growing work on embodiment in film theory in their analysis of Terrence Malick's *Tree of Life* (2011) and although not talking about the third image they do talk of the 'audience dependency on easily generic markers' (p. 152) that can be considered a useful summation of the function of the first image.

The second image is more sophisticated in that it is a minority image. The image not always readily available to those who attend at the cinema (although it certainly may be to fans and cinephiles) as much as academic agents as interpreters of films. This line of thinking is akin to splitting the critical act into hierarchies as has been done previously with taxonomies and schools models which consider more and less sophisticated forms of cinematic engagement (McWhirter, 2016). The majority or populist view of the first image becomes the privileged view of the serious and intellectual critique that searches for deeper signifiers and signification. To some extent this is also what film journalists do but that is largely dependent on whether they are journalists who have to think about an audience and to what extent.

Hockley (2011, pp. 142–143) talks of the third image as largely relatable to transference and countertransference and in both therapy and the cinema looking is taken as a central act. In this way he is also making a clear distinction between psychoanalysis that has historically taken looking out of the equation with the therapist sitting behind the patient (Milton *et al.*, 2011, p. 7). His suggestion is that as viewers are looking into the screen and thus themselves they also experience a midway point between their bodies and the screen where they can experience a third image. Therefore this is a highly personal experience and what transpires as an intensive experience for one person could be entirely unrelated to the person sitting next to them who may be experiencing the first, second or indeed a third image of their own. It is this that links Hockley's idea to that of Jung's discussions of a third image as a symbol, complete with personal meaning or a new meaning creation not easily explained. This is the archetypal quality of the image whereby making the image any more conscious could turn symbol into sign and psychology to semiosis in denotative form (Hockley, 2011, p. 141). The third image in cinema for Hockley is not exactly the same idea but the transference and countertransference between screen and body and the space and the facilitating action of the film itself ensures that the body is felt and the third image experienced (ibid., p. 142).

If the third image is the one most connected with body for Hockley then this particular conceptualisation might lend itself to further investigation when looking at digital film theory methods that work outside the cinema space. However, it is also pertinent to note that these images, as Hockley himself recognises, cannot function in isolation and oscillate and overlap in order to generate the experience. So, if the first image is collective and the second subjective then the third is intersubjective because it involves both the individual perspective and the screen, availably looked at by others in the space. Although Hockley does not express it explicitly it is possible to see, from the first image to the third, a movement from what Jung termed directed thinking to fantasy thinking. The latter of which can be considered as pre-conscious (Samuels *et al.*, 2005) and is akin to coalescing in this space between viewer and screen that Hockley talks about as the conditions for the third image to emerge.

Screen

The rise of live and event cinema in recent years prompts not only a reappraisal of the cinematic experience but fuelled by the rise of digital media access to information about films might suggest that a deeper engagement – historically thought the preserve of the apparatus of cinema itself – is just as likely to come from mobile screens and new forms of creative criticism. Is there a potential fallacy of the frame and its influence when it comes to cinematic experience versus filmic experience on television or mobile devices? Audiovisual essays, picture essays that use screen grabs and cinemetrics that measure a film's data such as average shot length, are all processes that can be understood with reference to the three images. Video, stills and metrics can be discussed to greater or lesser extents in each. The content of the screen and thus the screen itself does not change, only the frame and environment does. Audiovisual essays can be encountered on a tablet, mobile or desktop as can screen grabs that can also be viewed in a book. Cinemetrics can be encountered on a tablet, mobile, desktop or an art installation or lecture screen. Then of course platforms can also contribute to a change in environment beyond the physical one in which the content is viewed and worked with (personal blog, YouTube, Vimeo, commercial or non-commercial website and so on). The argument here is one of a direct engagement with the screen so that these external or peripheral factors (a window in a room or an advert banner on a social media page) – at least in fleeting moments – are not a concern to the phenomenological experience of given moments of the film. Indeed it is in this fragmented – or interrupted way that Rombes discusses – that viewing on mobile devices and smaller screens is just as associated with creating potential third images as the cinematic experience. Hockley himself discusses the ways that patients often discuss films and snippets of films via interpretations of given scenes or sequences that actually have nothing to do with the narrative or collective first image intended by the filmmakers and experienced by the majority of the audience.

The popularity of viewing content on mobile devices shows that the human psyche can connect directly with any size screen and give it primary focus and attention regardless of that size. It is actually the very processes of consciousness itself that tell us this, i.e. we are never entirely conscious of everything and could never be, so therefore it is quite easy to be fully conscious of the one event we are undertaking if that is as simple as paying attention to a screen of any size. Rombes (2014, p. 2) makes reference to Robert Ray's 1985 work *A Certain Tendency of the Hollywood Cinema* when he claims that since the advent of television (and mobile screens now) the irony of the audience has increased and the mythic aura of movies has been eroded. Considering that we can have a phenomenological experience of film on any size of screen disputes this to some extent arguing that one can 'lose oneself' as much as in the movie theatre. There exists a fallacy over frame size in direct correlation to affect that hopefully can be supported by investigating the newer processes of digital media below.

Rombes (2009, pp. 65–66) reiterates the largely Lacanian influence of one being sutured into the screen in the cinema by claiming that the downsizing of screens is a fragment and cannot allow us to 'lose ourselves' and because 'Small mobile screens are not a medium for watching two-hour movies uninterrupted, and in fact interruption is now an important structural component of the narrative logical of many digital-era films.' His last point about interruption is a good one and accurate but what about falling into consciousness with the screen. It does not mean that the moments when viewers are looking into these screens that they are not equally affected by what they see, on a small screen on a long bus journey or on a flight for instance. The phenomenology of how our bodies react might be different when being in the light as opposed to the dark but if we consider film in this way then the experience on any screen can be taken to the level of viewing alone in comparison with others.

In his chapter 'Being in the cinema', Hockley (2014, pp. 31–50) intends to foreground the importance of the cinema experience in making the connection between the collective and the personal psychological reading of film. Yet his argument can be taken as so convincing of the part played by personal interpretations that if the viewer has such an intensive experience with the screen then one could ask why should the apparatus of the cinema have more of a profound affect than any other screen? Indeed he goes on to highlight that Roland Barthes said back in 1975, in *En sortant du cinéma*, that the cinema is actually composed of two experiences: of the physical location and the other of the viewing of the screen. Therefore we can easily be just as distracted by the heat, cold, sticky floor, chair kicking, mobile light, unfiltered laughter and so on of the cinema experience. We are actually seeing the form of distraction as a key formal aspect to the experience in cinema taken out of its historical place in a darkened room to include Secret Cinema and Open Air Cinema experiences, live re-scores, inflatable screens and directional audio opening up spaces thought previously to be incompatible with a viewing experience (Atkinson, 2015). I certainly do not dispute the work and traditional thought that has gone into considering the cinematic experience to be the most dominant and the most powerful in terms of sound, frame and inculcation into the film – this is why I only go to a very specific IMAX with the largest screen in Europe with multiple sound lasers pointed at my chest – but this cinematic experience is becoming far more diffuse with other smaller screens and home systems. Both related to technology and the quality of the image and sound, from 24 fps to UHD 4K. Watching a film on a couch on an iPad Pro or at the back of a local repertory theatre is, for me, a close call as to which experience is more significant in terms of delivering on each of those three types of images (or at least the second and third images).

If emotion is the chief cause of consciousness according to Jung (cited in Izod and Dovalis, 2014) then it cannot be shown definitely that a cinematic experience is more evocative of emotion or consciousness than a non-cinematic one. The act of producing a video essay or taking screen grabs or using metrics on any given film deepens the experience further than in the cinema as the discrete units of the text are given greater attention than could be possible there: from editing tracks to single frames to the entire data visualisation of any given film. We have to consider that those interested in film on any level might gain a deeper phenomenological experience and insight just by the closer processes and proximities of interpretations and contact with the images regardless of how discontinuous and interruptive this might be. Looking deeper into objects is equally looking deeper into the self and vice versa (Brooke, 1993, p. 173). This is in many ways the essence of phenomenology even (or especially) if the object is that of the body. In discussing analytical psychology's contribution to a phenomenological analytical psychology Brooke (1993, p. 174) notes that 'Existence is lived as a multiplicity of images, and it is within this relational matrix of images that we seek to understand ourselves and others, and out of which we seek to constitute ourselves as persons.' When we are considering that digital film theory democratises the field and its methods are used by anyone and this coincides with not a reduction of the popularity of cinema but a juxtaposition of smaller screens to compliment the experience to be had in the cinema. This works not only for the creators of such digital media methods but for the consumers and audiences viewing them because the film experience is distilled, concentrated and magnified.

Memory

One can imagine this era would be a nightmarish one for the late film critic Pauline Kael, who regularly spoke about only ever viewing films once. Equally so for some scholars such a world where everything can be accessed instantly and memory corrected is not only troubling but is actually damaging to the psyche. Frankel claims that:

> The inflationary excess of virtuality, in the name of being able to see everything at anytime and anywhere, enacts this disavowal of *lethe* [the river of forgetting and oblivion], of the nonsubjective dimension of being, which brings us right back to the question of narcissism, although now we are speaking of an existential narcissism, an anthropocentrism that is fueled [*sic*] by the magnifying power of technological memory.
>
> *(2013, p. 18)*

It is not in dispute here that forgetting is an important part of the wellbeing of the psyche – as has been known from ancient Greek culture and as psychologist Hermann Ebbinghaus discovered in the nineteenth century – after all it is actually the central philosophy of consciousness itself in crude and reductive form. What being able to interact with culture and make it malleable does is offer not only the possibility of narcissism but the probability of greater reflection in an era painfully immediate and forgetful as data streams flow by to recording every action and inaction faster than our latest status update, blissfully unaware of our wider contribution to capitalist structures and the paradoxical data pile that simultaneously can and cannot be read at the same time. Drawing on the work of Danny Kahneman and Amos Tversky, Michael Lewis's latest work *The Undoing Project* (2016) discusses how the mental short cuts of heuristics can cause mistakes, mental illusions and tricks of the eye. Combining the ideas of Ebbinghaus's forgetting curve and heuristics it is quite easy to suggest that the act of remembering the experience of cinema is equally one of mis-remembering and potential false images even if we are not under pressure to recall the experiences. Perhaps this calls into relief the second and third images when reflecting on the experience of the cinema event. The personal investment in parts of the narrative might then be said to be inaccurate in others ways beyond an individual reading that goes against the plot.

The act of remembering is not so much unnecessary with digital media but more like a reminder of the inescapability of testing memory. Therefore digital film theory is like a Möbius strip whereby remembering and evidence are entwined and forever run into one another. *Enantiodromia* (the running together of opposites) as a principle might force us to want material connections in a networked era where there are none and it also works here to remind us of warmer imaginations in an era of cold data. Breaking the film down into a variety of scenes or images and frames still does not offer the entire representation of the film as a whole. Even when we can see the film as a whole with cinemetrics we cannot see it in detail, only from above, but it is immediately searchable. If an embodiment theory and phenomenological model of cinema and affect are to be taken forward then it means that we are all going to remember films in a certain way but what happens when a re-engagement with the film takes place outside the cinema space? Such embodiment must be altered in some way on different screens and with audiovisual essays, screen grabs and data visualisations (as opposed to re-viewing on TV but the same principle applies) we are more evolved as we revisit the text. In this way Peirce's idea of unlimited semiosis (cited in Chandler, 2007, p. 31) as sign reading as progressive and intellectually evolving comes into play. The question then becomes, is this at the expense of losing the symbolic or the mythic or does it re-charge and re-energise these areas? At first glance it would appear that any attempt and detailed sign-reading and deep analysis like this would reduce the symbolic experience but actually what happens is that our embodiment reaches a numinous level as analysts (or viewers privy to the analysis) because we are in god-like control of the image in ways that we cannot be in the cinema; it is the idea of viewing a film and its content through its 'peak experiences' (Samuels *et al.*, 2005, p. 100) of the numen.

Body

What the work of Sobchack (1992, 2004) and Barker (2009) argues is that we arrive at meaning and experience in the cinema inescapably through our bodies and bodily experience. This phenomeno-logical model for cinema is clearly quite compatible with Jungian film theory. For Sobchack experience is only possible because of consciousness and our bodies (2004, p. 60). If Barker (2009, p. 136) is correct in her assertion that 'cinema is a technological metaphor for the body – that is, drawing its forms from the human body and expressing them back to us in cinematic form' then new processes of digital media and textual analysis are surgically experiential both for the creator and those consuming them via the precision of argument and analysis made compared to the suture applied by the nursemaid of the cinema. To use Barker's own terms, the textural analysis of the skin, musculature and viscera is in terms of its phenomenology more precise. The haptic, kinetic and rhythmic energies are far more relevant to practically critiquing and working with imagery than discussing them in the context of affect theory or film theory alone. Barker's idea, when applied to the cinema, allows us to consciously consider the manifestation of our bodies and their reactions to films, how they mimic the bodies or the action/tension on screen – even if this is to reinforce the notion of suspending our disbelief and knowing that, for example, a horror is not real but simultaneously questing the reason we would then jump, flinch or contort our faces. Some forms of digital media, using technology to express and critique media objects and texts, lend themselves to current film theory as well as methods of analytical psychology. For instance, in deploying the 10/40/70 technique (Rombes, 2014) – when a screen grab is taken from each of those time codes – to analyse film, one sees relations to the film's body (Sobchak, 1992; Barker, 2009), the third image (Hockley, 2011) and the Jungian amplification method of interpretation.

If Barker's argument is that we are not in the film but neither are we entirely outside it (2009, p. 12) then leaving the direct cinematic experience in the dark aside, we can argue that there is a conscious connection between mind, body and whatever moving imagery we are experiencing at any given time if we are viewing it, that is investing it with meaning and active in that meaning rather than imbibing it as Hockley (2014, p. 5) considers the word 'spectator' to connote. We can use the idea of the third image alongside the notion of an embodied connection with the screen to uncover the relative merits of newer forms of working with the screen through audiovisual essays, picture essays and cinemetrics. Consciously these newer processes cannot relate to those uninterested in anything beyond the first image. However, engagement with video essays is increasing (McWhirter, 2015, 2016). These works are not only being sought out by film fans and cinephiles but produced by them too. To a lesser extent cinemetrics can be said to do the same, allowing the same vested interests to create a data trail for a given film they may be interested in scrutinising. This means that it is no longer critics and academics alone who are the privileged few that deal with Hockley's idea of the second image but certainly it still pertains to the personalisation of that idea.

If Jung considered that body and mind are indivisible then Jungian film studies approaches are particularly suited to the recent turn to the affect in moving-image cultural studies. Hockley (2014) develops his earlier idea of the third image into his *Somatic Cinema* which aims to elevate these bridges which may be somewhat buried under the weight of earlier psychological influence in film theory from Freud and Lacan. This work makes visible the connections between the screen and the body, touch, presence and experience. What will be demonstrated below is that even though the films chosen have generic markers and the potential for second and third images it is also the processes through which they are considered – digital media as textual theory – that can offer not only additional meaning but a sharper focus and embodied experience on a par with the cinematic one. Izod and Dovalis (2014) discuss a personal communication on *The Tree of Life* (dir. Malik, 2011), in which a colleague remarks that it is a body film before it is a head film and this might well be true of the entire *Alien* franchise as well in places. However it is clear that *Alien* is far more of a body or embodiment film and if *Aliens* is a head film then it is one in which we do not have to use the contents of our head too much to understand the significantly increased action, dialogue and explication from the first film. If phenomenology attempts to acknowledge our subjective role in experiential moments of the creation of meaning and it does this via our interaction with external objects then what the digital media processes below try to do is to help regulate our attitude to any given film in question but in different ways. There is a breaking and re-assembling with audiovisual essays; a stillness with picture essays and a measurable data trail of emotion with cinemetrics. Each might be processes of what some consider a fourth industrial age where data and psyche entwine (Hasselbalch and Transberg, 2016). Given the discussion of screen, memory and body as a context it is now beneficial to consider each of the three chosen digital film theory methods for phenomenological potency via the two well-known cultural cinematic texts, *Alien* and *Aliens*.

Audiovisual essays: *Aliens*

If there is a 'pleasure in repetition' with cinema and a desire to return to the same film over and over again (Mulvey, 2015, p. 161) then there are undoubtedly multiple reasons for doing so. What a phenomenological perspective on the newer practice, or at least popularity, of audiovisual essays has us consider is that the repeated viewing is to uncover greater meaning or at least continually remember the meaning we have already uncovered. Audiovisual essays or more commonly known as video essays – short films about cinema or television (or other art forms too but clearly those who gave birth to editing will dominate the form) – not only offer the creator the chance to repeat view but they offer potential second and third images to the audience viewing them in a condensed and highly concentrated topical timeframe. While these essays have historical antecedents it is possible to consider their form as indicative to the restraints of YouTube's initial limitations of ten minute uploads (McWhirter, 2015) as most tend to be ten minutes or under or are split into series. Of course this is now changing and we are seeing longer visual essays as that restriction no longer exists. If we look at one of the most popular of the sites that curates these video essays on film and television, Fandor, we can see one titled 'Why Aliens is the mother of action movies' by Leigh Singer. Although it is impossible to say for sure, it is likely this essay comes from the film journalist Leigh Singer, an experienced writer from the UK with some filmmaking experience and having made around 20 video essays. His six-minute video essay uses masks within the frame, one for text and other for image examples, to argue that *Aliens* changed action movies by grappling with the challenge of depicting a female lead in a male-dominated genre via its exploration of the theme of motherhood.

The purpose here is not to pursue the mother archetype, although clearly *Alien* and *Aliens* are both texts which can be illuminated with reference to Jung's 'Psychological aspects of the mother archetype' (1954). Hockley (2014, p. 46) already points out that both films can be viewed with the framework of the mother complex and also the mythic devouring mother. Audiovisual essays – time spent editing, repeat viewing, reimagining the first imagine, via the second. The point is that Singer's work magnifies the key theme, the second image (because the first is a SF/action film about aliens), and offers the audience of the essay a more concentrated experience and the opportunity for a third image to emerge. There are multiple screens within the screen, the shots and scenes are remembered according to the theme as evidence and the body reacts to the images while reading the text. Here the imagery of the film is given far more primacy than in the cinematic experience. It is strange no greater time is given to *Alien* as it does fit with the motherhood theme. Clearly the second film has more evidence but the first draws on Jonah and the Whale and the iconography of the open legs of the alien craft. The voyeuristic opening sequence exploring the innards of the *Nostromo* is accompanied by comments like 'What's the story mother' and 'mother has woken us up'.

10/40/70: *Alien*

If, according to Jean-Luc Godard's film *Le Petit Soldat* (1963), cinema is truth 24 times a second, in reference to standard frame rates of the time, then we might consider close engagement and analysis with each one of those individual frames extremely experiential. Rombes developed the 10/40/70 rule in 2009 on a personal blog. It is a method of film analysis whereby the essayist stops the film at those eponymous time codes in order to inspire interpretation and analysis of the text. Following increasing interest in the technique Rombes published a book on it in 2014. To my mind it is clear that Rombes' technique is treating the film quite literally in the mould of phenomenological thinking by Sobchak and Barker to a degree giving new meaning to the phrase body of the text. Here the distinct body reveals parts of itself otherwise hidden to the analyst. We must also not forget the historical import placed upon the single frame in cinema history by the avant-garde tradition of using 'freeze frame' (Mulvey, 2015, p. 30). Mulvey (p. 161) also reminds us that it is because the cinematic experience is so ephemeral that audiences have had an ongoing relationship with the single image, from production stills to posters and pin-ups. As Rombes (2014) own use of the technique shows it can be intensely personal and the power of single images of not just the film but the actors and stars within them can function to represent those individuals and freeze them in time immemorial when the recollection of the actual subject's psyche has long faded in the cultural conscious. Does digital film criticism itself bridge this gap between personal and collective – by reducing the film images to those from 10/40/70 we concentrate on a single unit with less chance to be distracted, not fully conscious of all of the other frames, shots, scenes and sequences? Certainly the desire to keep the analysis linked as closely to the individual frames as possible is an intensive explication of the film's events for both the writer and the viewer/reader. The following images are from the 10/40/70 minutes of the *Alien* (1979) film.

To finalise the point of motherhood apparent in this film also the very first screengrab is of mother, the onboard computer system and other screen. Rombes (2011) does not pick up on this but instead focuses on the lived-in aesthetic future of the film and the ambient noise. He augments his analysis with clips explaining what he means by mother intercepting the aliens' broadcast and other footnotes to deleted scenes, excerpts from the script and even an intertextual reference from a Chanel N° 5 advert. The Nietzschean idealism and admiration of the alien by Ash, its indiscriminate violence as well as the pacing of the film are all topics spurred on by the frame depicting the acid burning through the hull. In the final frame he discusses the 'sheer terrorising beauty' of cinematographer Derek Vanlint, remarking on more production history from Sigourney Weaver who considers the cameraman to treat every shot like a 'little masterpiece, like a little Vermeer painting'. What we get from 10/40/70 is not only a reminder of the phenomenological experience of witnessing the moving images (at home or in the cinema) but a description of them and their places in contexts of other forms of culture and the production history of the film – even history and politics and information about the film's release and the close proximity of Jimmy Carterns 'Crisis of Confidence' high inflation speech.

The central phenomenological experience of considering the movie in this way is that 10/40/70 gives *Alien* a cinematic spine and the flesh and musculature, the nerves of analysis is added by the essayist. Mulvey (2006, p. 151) considers that it is when we freeze the frame that we can get to the 'unexpected, deferred meaning'. We can consider 10/40/70 with reference to Hockley's notion of the third image (2011, 2014) and the two image types that precede it. The smallest unit of cinema is the frame and it shares affinity with visual art. Indeed it is the number of these units taken together in blockbuster graphics and CGI that Rombes (2009, pp. 142–153) provocatively considers to be the new avant-garde. Hockley (2011, p. 138) reminds us of the 'diegetic conceit' of the Daguerrotype – a large format matte-esque painting that would draw audiences to view it. As they did directed and refracted and diffused light and colour would direct their attention to different parts of it or even the same details cast in new perspectives and this all played a part in the individual observers' own psychology too. In that way 10/40/70 is immediately images 1, 2 and 3. It invokes the direct image, an interpretation of the image via textual analysis and, perhaps, something in the viewer that must fill the space between body and frame: a memory, a feeling, the rest of the film heuristically remembered or otherwise. Elements of montage are at play here as well. Consider the historical weight of Sergei Eisenstein who was among the first to consider editing as dialectical, placing two (seemingly) unrelated shots together to create an idea or association in the viewer. Rather than working against memory or making memory somehow redundant it works with memory, certainly if we believe that when watching a text we take everything in consciously or otherwise.

Cinemetrics: *Alien* and *Aliens*

If the first two examples embody the idea of Jean Epstein (1946, cited in Mulvey 2015, p. 175) that cinema is fusion of the mobile (audio visual essays) and static (10/40/70) then the method of cinemetrics is the fusion. Certainly in one form of this data visualisation it is possible to see the whole of the film, the individual frames and the movement as one. Cinemetrics is literally the process of computising and coding or quantification of the film text in order to analyse it mathematically as well as visually. Film scholar and historian Yuri Tsivian founded www.cinemetrics.lv unearthing the irony of early apocryphal accounts of cinema critique and its literary adaptations mocked as '300 meters of poetry! – 3,000 feet of Shakespeare' and reminding us that feet and metres are exactly what separates such work from prose more generally. He also explains that counting frames, constructing diagrams and charts was the practice of a number of directors in the 1920s who wanted to visualise the rhythm of their films. His open-source website allows users to calculate the average shot length of any film but it does require time and patience on the part of the analyst. It is, though, a time-intensive form of digital labour free from capitalism. The software was created by statistician and computer scientist Gunars Civjans who sadly passed away in 2016. The enthused reader can learn more about the process by visiting the site or perhaps trying it out with a film of their choosing but here I want to concentrate on the experience of the audience or viewer of such a work more than on the user or analyst who would create the data.

There are three entries listed for *Alien* (1979) and one for *Aliens* (1986) and although they vary slightly due to human input into the software, they are all suggesting that the average shot length is around six seconds. For *Aliens* this is measured at 4.2. For consistency the comparison in Figures 31.2 and 31.3 is taken from the same user 'Stang' submitting the data for both films in the Salt database (named after Barry Salt writing about ASL in *Film Quarterly* (1974), although such measurements are traceable to 1920s cinema) is recorded at 5.76 and *Aliens* at 3.72 ASL along with direct, cinematographer and editor categories. Both are not telling us anything we

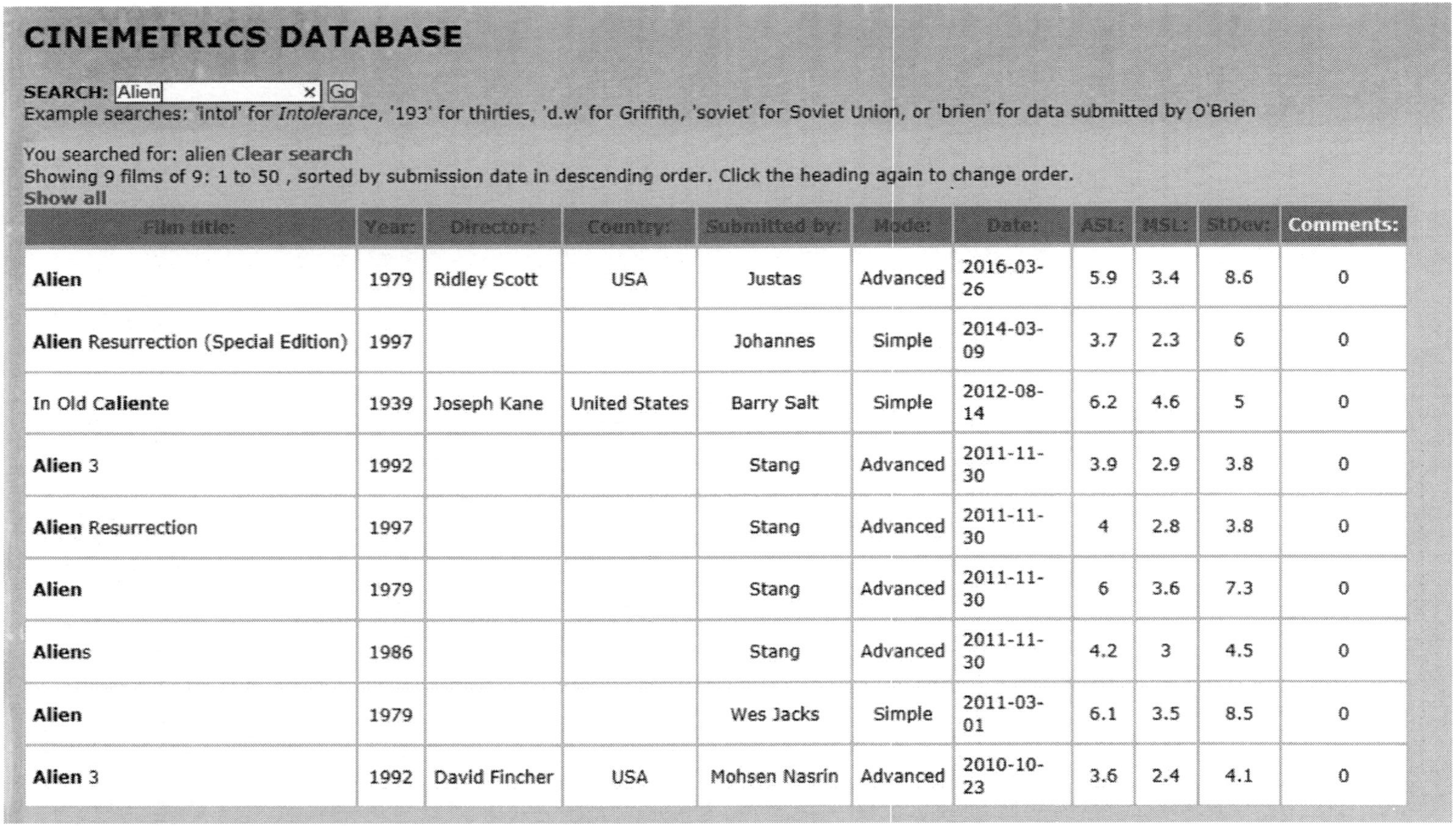

CINEMETRICS DATABASE

SEARCH: [Alien] [x] [Go]
Example searches: 'intol' for *Intolerance*, '193' for thirties, 'd.w' for Griffith, 'soviet' for Soviet Union, or 'brien' for data submitted by O'Brien

You searched for: alien Clear search
Showing 9 films of 9 : 1 to 50 , sorted by submission date in descending order. Click the heading again to change order.
Show all

Film title:	Year:	Director:	Country:	Submitted by:	Mode:	Date:	ASL:	MSL:	StDev:	Comments:
Alien	1979	Ridley Scott	USA	Justas	Advanced	2016-03-26	5.9	3.4	8.6	0
Alien Resurrection (Special Edition)	1997			Johannes	Simple	2014-03-09	3.7	2.3	6	0
In Old Caliente	1939	Joseph Kane	United States	Barry Salt	Simple	2012-08-14	6.2	4.6	5	0
Alien 3	1992			Stang	Advanced	2011-11-30	3.9	2.9	3.8	0
Alien Resurrection	1997			Stang	Advanced	2011-11-30	4	2.8	3.8	0
Alien	1979			Stang	Advanced	2011-11-30	6	3.6	7.3	0
Aliens	1986			Stang	Advanced	2011-11-30	4.2	3	4.5	0
Alien	1979			Wes Jacks	Simple	2011-03-01	6.1	3.5	8.5	0
Alien 3	1992	David Fincher	USA	Mohsen Nasrin	Advanced	2010-10-23	3.6	2.4	4.1	0

Figure 31.1 A cinemetric analysis of *Alien* (1979).

Source: www.cinemetrics.lv/movie.php?movie_ID=10039.

could not discern from watching the films or Stringer's assertion in his video essay that one is a SF/horror and the other is SF/action but the empirical data from cinemetrics here can be coded and used in other ways, for instance shot types or content within shots: Alien/landscape/vehicle/computer/SFX/no SFX etc. From the data encoded an interested viewer can calculate that there are 1097 in *Alien* and 2056 shots in *Aliens*.

There has been another more visualised form of cinemetrics by Frederic Brodbeck available at http://cinemetrics.fredericbrodbeck.de/. The difference here is that Brodbeck developed this as an undergraduate project and although he has released the source code it has not been given

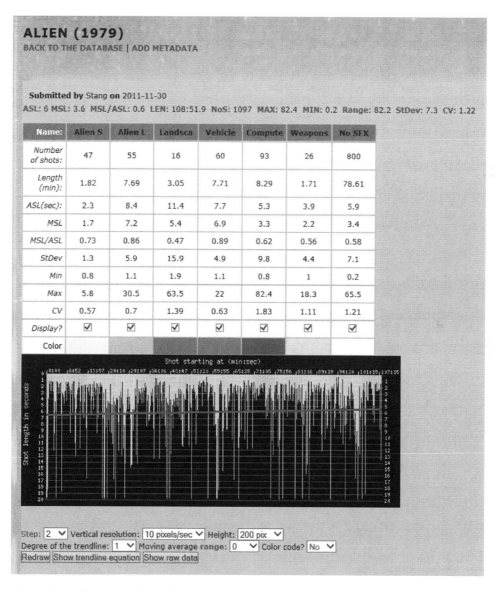

Figure 31.2 A cinemetric analysis of *Aliens* (1986).

Source: www.cinemetrics.lv/movie.php?movie_ID=10041.

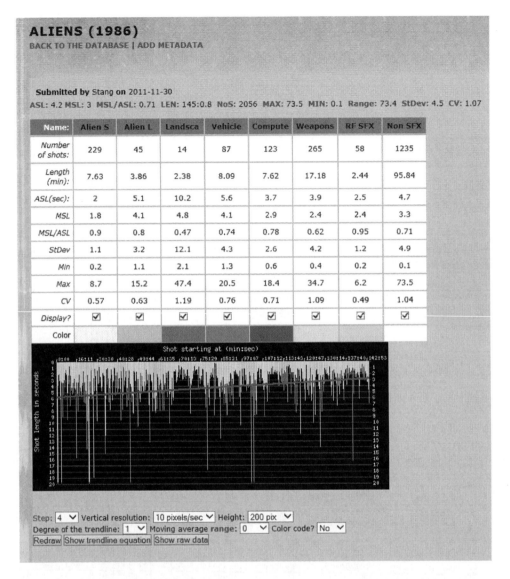

Figure 31.3 The cinemetrics database.

Source: www.cinemetrics.lv/database.php.

the same curation as Tsivian's site and so in order to replicate what he has done the analyst would need to be skilled at coding. Brodbeck is now a freelancer who works in design. His method is particularly more affective on the body, imputing colours on a five-point scale as well as quantifying movement in shots, and he himself cannot escape this phenomenological description when considering his cinemetrics process as extracting a 'fingerprint' from films. Clearly for any film fan with a more fleeting interest in movies his approach is more detailed and visually more appealing. Brodbeck's method lends itself to a phenomenological reading because it is telling the viewer exactly how they could (or perhaps should) be feeling at any given moment. For example, it can show how much movement or cutting is happening in a particular scene and infer that this might translate into excitement of some kind at the moment(s) of experience. What it cannot do is tell us where we might be having that experience with the screen and how that too would factor into any 'feeling'. For instance, this could be on our smartphone or with an audience. It is a literal representation similar to 10/40/70 that follows the arguments of Sobchak and then Barker that all genres are body genres.

The engagement with the film is one of bodily engagement and cinemetrics is one way of showing the quite literal version of what the aforementioned have referred to as the film's body in the past. It is a means of textual analysis that can feed back to its audience that 'this scene made the hairs on your arms stand up'. While the textural work of Barker might be useful in application, exploring haptic, kinetic and rhythmic engagement with cinema across skin, musculature and viscera, we still can't see the film's body in the same way that Brodbeck's cinemetrics is able to show us.

When you consider *Alien* or *Aliens* and the amount of movement within these films and you can see the colour hue and you are able to tell the average shot length it is certainly useful and in being able to cycle through the frames as easily as navigating the circle wheel with the cursor it inadvertently categorises some of those bodily descriptions Barker would be proud of: palpitation, grasp, stretch, smiling, swallow, ingest, contours, flesh, carnal, bleed, clench and so on. The sweat, pulsing, pods, explosions, glistening from inside 'mother' spined, vertebrate (as machine in the walls), leathery eggs, all allow recall from those personal or third image experiences, my own the childish humour in the retort to John Hurt's: 'there's movement. Seems to have moment, life, organic life' – 'no shit it just sucked your face!' Like 10/40/70, cinemetrics, while at the same time showing us movement, cannot recreate the experience of movement in each scene – at least yet. Brodbeck's is a project which has more to offer from further collaborations and developments. It is interesting, without consideration of Jung I'm sure, that he playfully also displays cinemetrics for topical 'archetypes' such as football, porn and Jacque Cousteau.

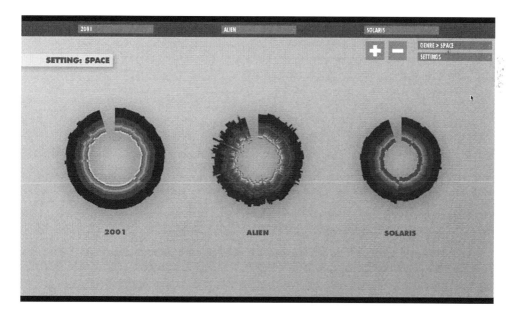

Figure 31.4 Space films analysed using Frederic Brodbeck's cinemetrics.

Source: http://cinemetrics.fredericbrodbeck.de/.

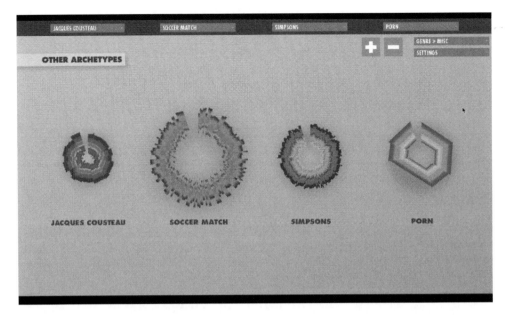

Figure 31.5 Frederic Brodbeck's cinemetric analyses of Jacques Cousteau, soccer, The Simpsons and porn.
Source: http://cinemetrics.fredericbrodbeck.de/.

Conclusion

While this chapter has focused on three specific types of digital media as textual film theory there are many more processes in the digital humanities that could be looked at and similarly analysed for their phenomenological merits in comparison to viewing films in the cinema, including interrupted screenings, post-archives and other means of creative criticism both in terms of poetics and exposition. There are also some not insurmountable buttresses such as viewing a narrative versus viewing a film or piece of criticism about narratives but it is hoped that the reader can see enough merit in the interactive processes involved with viewers and consumers of these methods, as well as those analysts who actually participate in the creation of them, as potential challenges to the idea that the best experience of a film has to come from sitting in the cinema. What seems to unite such disparate forays into new forms of critical engagement with the moving image is the idea of interactivity as experience. Digital environments lend themselves to a discussion of phenomenology almost as easily as they do to psychology broadly and in its various incarnations/disciplines. This is because it is rarely considered what we are doing with our bodies in physical space while our minds inhabit digital space. The central tenets of affect theory that we need to consider this when viewing a film becomes more pronounced when we consider films on smaller screens and alongside their digital discourses and textual analyses. If a phenomenological perspective of the cinema has drawn on Lacan or Jungian dialectics of mind and body then a phenomenological perspective of engagement with film on any type of screen can use Jungian ideas to help consider a trialectic of mind, body and computational data. Here all images are possible.

References

Barker, J. M. (2009) *The tactile eye*. Berkeley, CA: University of California Press.
Brooke, R. (1993) *Jung and phenomenology*. London: Routledge.

Carroll, N. (2009) *On criticism*. New York: Routledge.

Chandler, D. (2007) *Semiotics: the basics*, 2nd edn. London: Routledge.

Frankel, R. (2013) 'Digital melancholy', *Jung Journal: Culture and Psyche*, 7(4), pp. 9–20.

Hasselbalch, G. and Transberg, P. (2016) *Data ethics: the new competitive advantage*. Online: Publishare.

Hockley, L. (2011) 'The third image: depth psychology and the cinematic experience', in C. Hauke and L. Hockley (eds), *Jung & film II: the return*. Hove: Routledge. pp. 132–47.

Hockley, L. (2014) *Somatic cinema: the relationship between body and screen – a Jungian perspective*. Oxford: Routledge.

Izod J. and Dovalis, J. (2014) 'Ogni pensiero vola: the embodied psyche in Terrence Malick's The Tree of Life', *International Journal of Jungian Studies*, 6(2), pp. 151–8.

Jung, C. G. (1954) 'Psychological aspects of the mother archetype', in *The collected works of C. G. Jung*, Vol. 9.i, *The archetypes and the collective unconscious*, 2nd edn. London: Routledge & Kegan Paul, 1968.

Lewis, L. (2016) *The undoing project: a friendship that changed our minds*. London: Penguin.

McLuhan, M. (1994 [1964]) *Understanding media: the extensions of man*. Cambridge, MA: MIT Press.

McWhirter, A. (2015) 'Film criticism, film scholarship and the video essay', *Screen*, 53(3), pp. 369–77.

McWhirter, A. (2016) *Film criticism and digital cultures: journalism, social media and the democratisation of opinion*. London: I.B. Tauris.

Milton, J., Polmear, C. and Fabricius, J. (2011) *A short introduction to psychoanalysis*. London: Sage.

Mulvey, L. (2015 [2006]) *Death 24x a second: stillness and the moving image*. London: Reaktion Books.

Rombes, N. (2009) *Cinema in the digital age*. London: Wallflower Press.

Rombes, N. (2014) *10/40/70: constraint as liberation in the era of digital film theory*. Alresford, UK: Zero Books.

Salt, B. (1974) 'Statistical style analysis of motion pictures', *Film Quarterly*, 28(1), pp. 13–22.

Samuels, A., Shorter, B. and Plaut, F. (2005) *A critical dictionary of Jungian analysis*. London: Routledge.

Sobchak, V. (1992) *The address of the eye: a phenomenology of film experience*. Princeton, NJ: Princeton University Press.

Sobchack, V. (2004) *Carnal knowledge: embodiment and moving image culture*. Berkeley, CA: University of California Press.

Online sources

Atkinson, S. (2015) 'Secret, immersive cinema is likely to change the future of film', *Conversation*, 1 December [online]. Available at: https://theconversation.com/secret-immersive-cinema-is-likely-to-change-the-future-of-film-50034 [Accessed 14 December 2016].

Grant, C. (2012) 'Film and moving image studies: re-born digital? Some participant observations', *Frames Cinema Journal*, 1 [online]. Available at: http://framescinemajournal.com/article/re-born-digital/ [Accessed 4 December 2017].

Heftberger, A. (2012) 'Ask not what your web can do for you – ask what you can do for your web! Some speculations about film studies in the age of the digital Humanities', *Frames Cinema Journal*, 1 [online]. Available at: http://framescinemajournal.com/article/ask-not-what-your-web-can-do-for-you/ [Accessed 4 December 2017].

Rombes, N. (2011) '10/40/70 #34 *Alien*', *Rumpus*, 23 February [online]. Available at: http://therumpus.net/2011/02/104070-34-alien/ [Accessed 13 December 2016].

Singer, L. (2016) 'Why Aliens is the mother of action movies', *Fandor*, 30 August [online]. Available at: www.fandor.com/keyframe/watch-why-aliens-is-the-mother-of-action-movies [Accessed 13 December 2016].

Statistica (2016) 'Number of smartphone users worldwide from 2014 to 2019 (in millions)' [online]. Available at: www.statista.com/statistics/330695/number-of-smartphone-users-worldwide/ [Accessed 28 September 2016].

Filmography

Alien. (1979) [film] Directed by Ridley Scott. USA.

Aliens. (1986) [film] Directed by James Cameron. USA.

Petit soldat, Le. (1963) [film] Directed by Jean-Luc Godard. France.

Tree of life, The. (2011) [film] Directed by Terence Malik. USA.

32

A NETWORKED IMAGINATION

Myth-making in fan fiction's story and soul

Leigh Melander

Introduction: a fable

'Once upon a time, so long ago, nobody but the storytellers remember' (Jennings and Ponder, 2009) there was a funny crew of creatures who came upon the earth, who learned to walk upright and speak, and with their magic tongues, tell stories.

'A fable! A fable! Bring it! Bring it!' they cried to one another, and so they began' (ibid.). They sang stories that helped the world come into being, they wove tales about themselves and the wonder and awe of their intimate universe and their vast psyches. They made their stories and their stories made them.

After a time, some of those stories began to grow larger and land in memory with a sense of rightness, and became the stories of a people, the mythos – word – of the deepest and lightest truth together on the same tongue. And still people told each other stories.

And then, one day, something remarkable happened. Those people imagined a way to capture their stories so they would not be forgotten, and to write them on a bit of smashed tree or woven fiber so they would stand still, safe. And frozen.

And slowly, the people began to believe that their own stories were somehow smaller than the ones that had been written down. That the frozen stories were the ones that held magic. And that their own tongues could not shape the stories that mattered. Stories, people realized, had great power, and if your story was the one written on the paper, your power would reach as far as the words could tumble.

Great civilizations rose and fell on the power of their stories, driven by those who owned them, who controlled their magic. And then owners of stories began to learn new ways to capture them, on the hum of radio waves and the flicker of film. And the people began to forget that their tongues could make stories, and instead thought that stories could only be eaten, consumed, not made in their own mouths.

But, as is the way of things, one day that began to change again…

A mythic glance at fan fiction/but first a word on myth

As traditional stories begin in ambivalence, 'Once there was, once there was, and once there was not…' (Jennings and Ponder, 2009), they begin to hint at an understanding of the power of myth and how it holds both that which is, and that which is not. One of the ongoing beautiful tensions in the study of myth, and the use of myth as a tool to understand the human psyche, is the tug between the free-flowing, intuitive understanding of *mythos* and the desire for the concrete knowledge and construction of *Logos*. C. G. Jung was caught by this binary tension, preferring to characterize psychology as a science rather than an art, perceiving science from the rather terrifying chaos that creativity engendered in him (Wojtkowski, 2009, p. 27). In *The Spirit of Man, Art and Literature*, Jung writes:

> As long as we ourselves are caught in the process of creation, we neither see nor understand; indeed we ought not to understand, for nothing is more injurious to immediate experience than cognition. But for the purpose of cognitive understanding we must detach ourselves from the creative process and look at it from outside; only then does it become an image that expresses what we are bound to call 'meaning.' What was a mere phenomenon before becomes something that in association with other phenomena has meaning, that has a definite role to play, serves certain ends, and exerts meaningful effects. And when we have seen all this we get the feeling of having understood and explained something. In this way we meet the demands of science.
>
> *(1931: §121)*

Psychology both as a practice and as an academic field has been thought forward as a scientific discipline, valuing empirical constructs and scientific modes of inquiry and understanding. This draw toward science can freeze the story just as the fable above suggests, marking the story inherent in a scientific understanding as the story within the lexicon, elevated and no longer living.

Miller challenges such instincts toward binarism in the study of myth and psychology, pointing out that human predisposition to split ideas and experiences pits them against one another. He lists nineteen such splits, such as 'left brain against right, thinking against feeling, word against image, literal against metaphorical, analytic against synthetic, exclusion against inclusion, form against matter,' and interestingly, 'logos against eros' rather than against mythos – suggesting a split not in how thought is approached, either logically or mythically, but, instead, how life is approached via brain or heart. He states:

> In each case there is a privileging of the latter term against the former in a hierarchicalism that oddly claims to be against hierarchy, inscribing an oppositional thinking that prides itself on being inclusive and against dualisms, arguing a formalism in the name of stressing materiality. Nor is the matter only in the streets. It is also in the academy.
>
> *(2002)*

As Steven Shaviro suggests, the shifting landscape of a post-cinematic culture has 'given birth to radically new ways of manufacturing and articulating lived experience' (2010, p. 2). He suggests that there has been a shift in the way digital video is conceptualized and produced, noting 'where classical cinema was analogical and indexical, digital video is processual and combinatorial. Where analog cinema was about the duration of bodies and images, digital video is about the articulation and composition of forces' (p. 17).

The story-making in fan fiction pushes even further into the heart of this perceived binarism, challenging the idea that any story should be frozen, that its ownership rests in individual authors, that there is a hierarchy of how, what, why, and by whom the story is crafted. Instead fan fiction celebrates the confusing melting of such binary thinking, stepping into its own building of story, and in this moment, begins to become an exercise in myth-making, unfreezing the story.

Myth is a similarly challenging word in contemporary Western culture, particularly for those who have learned to see it as a lie, an object of contempt. 'Oh, that's just a myth,' people say, content that they have dismissed whatever 'that' was safely from their concerns with a flick of their fingers. But, that sense of myth being just a lie, is, itself, a lie.

Instead, myth sits in the paradox of being both/and. It is real and not real, true and untrue. It is metaphor – *meta*, carrying; *phor*, across – making meaning by moving from the literal to the abstract, the concrete to the intuited. Hellenistic Greeks spoke of myths as being stories that were simultaneously least and most true. Fourth century Greek writer Sallustius wrote in his catechism *On the Gods and the World*, 'Now these things never happened, but always are' (Murray, 2011). Its truth resides in how it resonates in our psyches, how it captures abstractions that bring flashes of insight that can be deeper than what we see in the tangible world in front of us.

As writer Jeannette Winterson (2006) said to Bill Moyers on his series on *Faith and Reason*, 'I look [at myths] to arrive at truth about the human condition, about myself, about how people live and die, about how they betray, about how they have sex, children, how they love their country, love others.' Myths sit as the big stories humming in the background that shape our sense of who we are and our understanding of the world around us. Often, in Western industrialized culture, we are only passingly aware of them, in a secular culture that tends to think of itself as beyond such things. Instead of robbing them of their power, this dismissal can actually tighten their grip; things ignored or repressed in the aegis of psyche have the tendency to overwhelm us.

Myths can perform a variety of purposes for communities and for individuals. Joseph Campbell (2013) has defined four overriding functions of myth: the first is about mysticism and wonder; the second, cosmological, bringing order to the universe and its constructs; the third is sociological, supporting certain cultural constructs and social order; and lastly, the one that is perhaps most relevant to an effort to open the mythopoesis of creating culture and story and community in a virtual way, is what Campbell calls a pedagogical function – essentially, giving us the tools via story how people might live a human lifetime under whatever circumstances emerge. While this might not be the expressed purpose of fan fiction, it rides under the surface of much creative work both professional and amateur.

It is in a shift from being the consumers of story into the resonating connection of ideas and narrative lines, identity and fantasy, memory and imagination that brings those who live in the imaginal world of fiction into developing tools to greet what shows up on the doorstep. In the making of story, within the particular shapes of community co-creation and ongoing arcs, fan fiction creators of all media become mythmakers.

Many of the chroniclers and assessors of fan fiction are both scholars and participants, wearing their dual identities carefully, aware that for all of the collectivity of the experience, it is problematic to forget that this is an experience that is also deeply intimate and personal. As such, for example, Anne Jamison (2013) warns scholars of picking up brushes with too broad a span as the academic community tries to pry open a swirling, shifting, liminal world, pointing out that the zeitgeist of fandom is as much about individuals as community. However, others reach to explore and understand 'the collective nature of fandom, its internal communications, and the relationship between fans that arises out of a joint interest in a particular text (Busse and Hellekson, 2006, p. 23), including the self-reflecting Henry Jenkins on his blog, *Confessions of an Aca-Fan*. In one of many explorations of this intimate relationship between the observer and celebrant, he invites scholars to wrestle with what this relationship means to their work and to the insights that they're trying to explore. In one of many conversations about the intersections of scholarship and fandom on Jenkins' site, Rhiannon Bury points out that even in defining oneself as an aca-fan, there is a risk of freezing the fluidity of the process, writing:

My reservation is in part a discontent with labels and their effects. As others have already remarked, they serve to homogenize the heterogenous, to constrain and erase difference and to draw boundaries that mark out who is an insider and who is an outsider.

(Jenkins, 2011)

This sense of the dance between insider and outsider, the individual and the collective, this co-created world that emerges and is always emerging, always process, the never-ending story, and its connection between people and ideas and real and not real and liminal and canonical and fantastical all sitting in servers that may archive well or may not, this world of fiction that feels almost as if it has its own life, that is made up of so many exquisitely human, intimate, micro-cosmic moments, and at the same time pulses with a broad archetypal energy – this long swirl of ideas is, in a word, mythic. This chapter, then, is an effort to lay back into those broad brush strokes, to ride their lines in the hopes of inviting a glance at an idea that feels deeply true, and worthy of fictionalizing in itself.

Coming to mythopoesis/enlivening psyche and soul

The story-maker invites his audience (and co-creators) into the mythic, into this unfrozen, ambivalent, liminal and deeply alive place, 'in a place, neither near nor far, and a time, neither now nor then …' (Jennings and Ponder, 2009). While it is possible to see reasonably easily the general mythic implications of the story-making and community interactions of the fan fiction universe in a participatory culture, the leap to this actually being a mythopoetic process – a myth-making – in itself is a bolder jump.

Obviously, stories being birthed from fiction are not, in the traditional explanation of myth as a sacred or religious story. That said, there are several ways in which fan fiction, both in its creation and in what it both evokes and invites in its participants both as community and as individuals, invites a deepening and understanding of psyche in several ways.

First, and foremost, fan fiction lives in, explores, creates, and builds itself and its community through story itself and through the making of that story. The act of building story, of stepping into metaphor itself by becoming an artist is, on some level, inherently mythic. Stepping further into constructed fantasy and or legendary worlds, not simply as consumers but as co-creators, invites an even deeper resonance with myth. James Hillman suggests, 'our life is less the resultants of pressures and forces than the enactment of mythical scenarios' (1976, p. 22). As such, our lives are built imaginally in story, all the time. We create meaning while both awake and dreaming by building story, starting with an image and crafting a narrative around it. Bachelard defines image used in this way as 'an *image conteuse*, an image that automatically produces a story. It asks that one imagine a before and an after' (1948, p. 130). This is the image of storytelling, and the image of myth. Working from the 'foundational mythology' of a fan fiction lexicon, fans create story fluidly from images imbedded in the original narrative, and they create these stories within a community that resonates with both their crafting and their telling.

The deep sense of community that emerges as collective story is being created invites an opening into community and connection in a way that serves soul. Derek Robinson states:

Having direct experiences, personal experiences, a sense of engagement is so much on many people's agendas currently; I think it is a quest for the spiritual. I think there is a convergence on what that sense of direct, non-conceptual, immediate experience

421

means, where art, mysticism, and spirituality all collide. There is a phenomenology with this that plays very interestingly in the 'nowness' of the Internet. You are there – you're eyeing it – it's some kind of shared moment.

(Melander, 2009, p. 180)

This is a virtual community, one that is in the storyteller's words, 'in a place, neither near nor far, and a time, neither now nor then.' This is a community not bounded by geography, time, socio-economic barriers, or even identity, as fan fiction creators build narratives around their own identities so richly that where 'real' people end and characters begin can become completely intertwined and amorphous. As an example from the film-driven gaming world, on PRX's *A Disturbance in the Force*, host Aaron Henkin unravels a remarkable story about layers of constructed identity that end up with a Star Wars gamer who thinks he is building a relationship with a woman playing the character his character partners with, is actually communicating with another man who has borrowed his girlfriend's real life story. Ultimately the girlfriend abandons her rather manipulative boyfriend and moves across country to move in with the gamer (Henkin, 2004).

A mythic sense of *communitas* emerges in such a liminal community, in Pierre Lévy's sense of *cosmopedia*. As Lévy states, 'the members of a thinking community search, inscribe, connect, consult, explore' and when the community finds questions it can't answer, those questions create 'tension within cosmopedic space, indicating regions where invention and innovation are required' (1999, p. 217). This *cosmopedia* shapes the stories and archetypes of the community itself, the narratives it creates about itself. How and why it functions are as crafted as the stories that it has gathered to imagine together.

Imagination and its dance back and forth between memory and creativity form the basis of myth, and what Hillman calls the poetic basis of mind (1989). This dance is superbly, deeply present in the storytelling and world-making in fan fiction. As Shaviro notes:

> Such a world cannot be represented, in any ordinary sense. There is no stable point of view from which we could apprehend it. Each perspective only leads us to another perspective, in an infinite regress of networked transformations – which is to say, in an infinite series of metamorphoses of capital.

(2010, p. 131)

Post-cinematic fan fiction and its spiraling world of co-creators and story is the 'voyage into the land of the infinite' that is imagination as characterized by Bachelard (1998, p. 23); a deeply mythic sense of imagination that invites the imaginer ever inward and outward simultaneously.

Play is inherent in this infinite imagination. This is a playful world, in many senses of the word, from literal gaming to play with ideas, with story, with co-creators. Play can both be full of lightness and also serious business. It forms the basis of culture, as posited by Johan Huizinga (1949) in *Homo Ludens*. Humans are creatures of play as much as of story, and within the community and play of creating fan fiction, the soul of play arises. Rules are made, and broken, players join the game of world-making and leave it, and build a sense of movement, of leeway, of possibility into the stories their creative work/play springs from.

This shared moment in community and the collective/collaborative/co-created work and play of fan fiction evokes a connection to Jung's ideas about the collective unconscious (1959), a shared experience of ancestral memory and archetypal images. This sense of the collective co-creating story echoes in Jenkins' sense of how we construct personal and connected story:

Convergence does not occur through media appliances, however sophisticated they may become. Convergence occurs within the brains of individual consumers and through their social interactions with others. Each of us constructs our own personal mythology from bits and fragments of information extracted from the media flow and transformed into resources through which we make sense of our everyday lives. Because there is more information on any given topic than anyone can store in their head, there is an added incentive for us to talk among ourselves about the media we consume. This conversation creates buzz that is increasingly valued by the media industry. Consumption has become a collective process – and that's what this book means by collective intelligence, a term coined by French cybertheorist Pierre Lévy. None of us can know everything; each of us knows something; and we can put the pieces together if we pool our resources and combine our skills.

(2008, p. 9)

Corbin's workings of Islamic philosophies on the imaginal realm of the *Mundus Imaginalis* – the realm of imagination – and their intersections with ideas on the *Anima Mundi* – the soul of the world – ultimately are the imaginal, soul-filled world of fan fiction. The drive in this world is to imagine beyond where we can know. He writes:

[We] are drawn to master what can be known about a world which always expands beyond our grasp. This is a very different pleasure than we associate with the closure found in most classically constructed narratives, where we expect to leave the theatre knowing everything that is required to make sense of a particular story.

(1972)

In the *Mundus Imaginalis*, the classically constructed narrative is only the beginning, not the ending. As he concludes *Post Cinematic Affect*, Shaviro works an existential fear that the current real world and its potential futures are perhaps innately dystopian, and that it is increasingly difficult to imagine any different future. He quotes Frederic Jameson, calling for 'a meditation on the impossible, on the unrealizable in its own right … a rattling of the bars and an intense spiritual concentration and preparation for another stage which has not yet arrived' (Jameson, 2005, pp. 232–233). The *Mundus Imaginalis* provides precisely that world in which to meditate on the impossible.

Story in *communitas*/crafting story together

The story-maker promises us that we will know more when we are done, beginning the tale with a command and a promise: '*Now we are about to begin and you must attend! And when we get to the end of the story, you will know more than you do now …*' (Andersen, 2013, p. 188).

'Perhaps nothing is more human than sharing stories, whether by fire or by "cloud" (so to speak)' (Jenkins et al., 2013 p. 2). For much of human history, stories were shared orally, growing and contracting with each telling, and sitting in a fairly comfortable place of shared origin and ownership. The period of written story is remarkably short in the span of human consciousness, with widespread reading emerging really only with the last few centuries.

With the advent of media culture over the last century, shifting story back away again from printed words on paper to radio, and then to film and television, storytelling has already begun to shift again. In what Shaviro (2011) has characterized as post-cinematic culture, the dominant aesthetic form of the twentieth century has already lost its position in the twenty-first. Digital storytelling through various media has invited a new orality and literacy (Ong, 1982), a different sense of ownership of story and intellectual property, and a new sense of a particular form of participatory culture. The public becomes not 'simply consumers of pre-constructed messages' but instead, 'people who are shaping, sharing, reframing, and remixing media content in ways which might not have been previously imagined' (Jenkins et al., 2013, p. 2).

While Jenkins et al. admonish against assumptions that participatory culture is simply a function of new digital technology, it certainly has played a central role in its development. Jamison (2010) echoes this thought and takes it a step further, recognizing that the technology is changing so quickly that it is difficult to imagine where it might be next headed. She writes:

> With implications we are in no way yet able to understand – because we are so fully in it, and 'it' is changing so fast – the digital world is transforming the relationship between speech and writing and, simultaneously, body and text.
>
> *(2010)*

Gere works the sense of disorientation that can come from such rapid changes, echoing some of Shaviro's thoughts about the frightening disconnections and possibilities that can happen in a post-modern, digital world:

> The concurrent development of science, media and capital under the aegis of digital technology produces a kind of fast-forward effect in which everything appears to take place at an accelerated rate and to produce dramatic change in a very short time. This excites both euphoria and terror, not least because of the shocking pace at which things happen. One has barely enough time to register one set of events and its possible consequences when another makes it irrelevant.
>
> *(2008, p. 14)*

Yet, in the face of this rapid change, and within the rapidly, exponentially expanding universes of fan fiction, it also sits comfortably behind the fan fiction creator. Jamison continues:

> Fanfiction is an old story. Literally, of course: fanfiction takes someone else's old story and, arguably, makes it new, or makes it over, or just simply makes more of it, because the fan writer loves the story so much they want it to keep going. But fanfiction is also an old story in that people have been doing this since – to borrow a phrase I absolutely disallow my students – the Dawn of Time. Reworking an existing story, telling tales of heroes already known to be heroic, was the model of authorship until very recently.
>
> *(2013, p. 17)*

So, then, story is being imagined and worked in new and old ways in fan fiction, blending the collective, seemingly 'authorless' processes that wove into oral, folk cultures with new technologies, leaping from individually author driven, in the case of written story, or an identified collective of artists and producers in film or television narratives into a complex dance of individual writers and media producers who move the story forward in dialogue with one another, with invited 'beta's' online readers and critics, and an open, often immediate response from the community invested in both the fan fiction's canon (which, incidentally, is referred to within the community as 'mythology' and as origin stories) and its fanon, the spiraling world that opens from the original canon.

In the Forward to Jamison's work *Fic*, writer Lev Grossman asserts:

Before the modern era of copyright and intellectual property, stories were things held in common, to be passed from hand to hand and narrator to narrator. There's a reason Virgil was never sued by the estate of Homer for borrowing Aeneas from the Iliad and spinning him off in the Aeneid. Fictional characters and worlds were shared resources.

(2013, p. xiv)

He continues, 'or all its radically new implications and subversions … fanfiction also represents the swinging back of the pendulum toward that older way of thinking' (Jamison, 2013, p. xiv).

Fan fiction creators, whether they are writing fiction that spins forward from books, films, or television series, or even as is the case in the marvelously self-reflected fiction-within-fiction story of Jamison's search for an elusive article, *The Theory of Narrative Causality* where she realizes that the original article is long gone, perhaps never having existed, but an entire narrative has grown up around it, and she, finds herself 'ficcing it – twisting it, taking it out of context' (2013, p. 7), are working together both formally and informally to create new story.

This move toward creating story that leaps from a fictionalized world, expanding that world and breaking the barriers between what is fiction and what exists in so-called 'real life' begins to resonate with the mythic. It does so in a variety of ways. For example, in its liminality, its sitting on the edge of thresholds of authorship, and its both/and quality of truth, whether relative to the narrative fiction it emerges from or its playfulness in bending truth in community and archiving contexts. Its sense of *communitas*, of the play between individual and collective is another 'tell,' whether that community connection is characterized as collaborative as advocated by Turk and Johnson (2012), as a sense of a group coming together to work toward a common purpose, or collective, which they intuit as a less connected experience. If, however, the idea of the collective begins to reverberate with Jung's thoughts (1959) on the collective unconscious, this connectivity begins to deepen even further into work of the soul.

Turk and Johnson envision this as an ecology as they examine vidding – the fan community's art of creating music videos that expand upon and recontextualize original films – leaving room for the exploration by both its scholars and practitioners,

> of the collaborative nature of vidding without erasing individual authorship; to inves-
> tigate the relationships not only between vids and media texts but also between vidders
> and their audiences; and to treat fan conversations both as responses to mass media and
> as sites for the generation and circulation of interpretive conventions that guide both
> the creation and reception of vids.
>
> *(2012)*

This collective begins to become its own liminal place, with ownership of ideas belonging to a complex weave of the individuals and collectives who originated the first stories, the individuals creating new fiction based on old, and the community.

Soul and imagination/memory, realness, and openings

The story-maker begins again, invoking fantastical sources and audiences, opening up the audience's sense of infinite possibility, 'Here's a story I learnt from an owl. I told it to a king. He gave me a purse of gold and this pin…' (Jennings and Ponder, 2009). Fan fiction participants can engage deeply in fantasy worlds, either imaginally on list serves and communal media and word-based storytelling, and via the articulation of online personas, or, even, at times in more active role-playing. For example, the *Great Game*, played by Sherlock Holmes fans that Jamison describes, which builds a whole alternate reality of a 'real' biographer writing about a 'real' detective.

> In the game, these chronicles are known as 'the Sacred Writings,' for which Sir Arthur Conan Doyle served as literary agent, and they are discussed exhaustively in these terms. The Great Game is itself a kind of participatory fiction – a roleplaying game (RPG) in which the fans play exaggerated versions of themselves, taking their obsession seriously and ironically at the same time.
>
> *(Jamison, 2013, p. 8)*

For all that, though, this is an exercise in story-making rather than creating anything that might be literally construed as a religious cosmology that demands any level of belief or faith in its inherent truth. However, as James Hillman writes, 'to mythic consciousness, the persons of the imagination are real' (Chalquist, 2009). Again, this is 'real' in a mythic sense, holding metaphorical realness more closely than literal realness.

If, then, a genre of creation becomes not simply a place to explore fictions, but to build identities (fictional, yes, but ones that spill over in metaphorical and imaginal ways into the literal and back again), it becomes a place where paradox brings its own clarity. It is in this paradox of truth/nontruth, of moving between memory and imagination, of creating imaginal worlds and the experience of this, remembering Campbell's pedagogical function of myth (2013), that fan fiction can first be seen as mythopoetic. The liminality of this digital, fictionalized world invites a non-dualistic understanding of soul in several ways.

It invites 'the *archai*, the deepest patterns of psychic functioning, the fundamental fantasies that animate all life' (Hillman, 1989, p. 36) as Thomas Moore describes Hillman's work in archetypal psychology. Moore suggests participants dive deeply into not only the fantasy of the work they are savoring and dreaming forward, but also the very apparent patterns and structures of the digital landscape in which they create that work and talk to one another about their work (ibid.).

Fan fiction and its sprawling, never-ending opening of infinite numbers of stories, both within a particular canon and combining canons and worlds (like, for example, the imaginal play that connects inter-genre mythologies such as the fan fiction that cast Harry Potter as a cowboy), evokes, in a rather literal way, Gaston Bachelard's (1998, p. 23) characterization of imagination as 'the voyage into the land of the infinite.' And it resonates with Corbin's (1989) thoughts on imaginal cognition as something spiritual that exists beyond the physical body.

Ultimately, imagination is an ongoing balance between *Mnemosyne*, the Greek archetype of memory and her daughters, the Muses, goddesses of creativity. Imagination works backwards and forwards simultaneously, its logic content in paradox, and the koan of not knowing what we know (Melander, 2004). Derek Robinson puts this breakdown of the linear narrative in an imaginal collective world, noting:

> We live, mostly, in a logical, linear, self-narrativizing, rationalizing, and objectivizing mode of cognition – this narrative that is, by turns, our guide and our pet. Sometimes we lead our little thought monkey, and sometimes it leads us. Most people are completely self-identified with it, even if many of them aren't even aware that it's there. It's so intimate, it's so much who we take ourselves to be.
>
> But, it breaks down when confronted with the a-logicality and alocality of a network. It gets shaken out of its self-absorption. Circular causality breaks the logical, rational, hierarchical, categorical mind. Not permanently, but long enough to stop and question 'the general in the head,' as Deleuze and Guattari put it. It challenges the

linearality of general's logic: X is true, so it follows that Y is true. In circular causality, X is also true because Y is true!

(Melander, 2009, p. 184)

As it invites soul into life, imagination is, truly 'essentially *open, evasive*. In the human psyche, it is the very experience of *opening* and *newness*' (Bachelard, 1998, p. 19). Just like the opening, evasiveness newness of the collective imagination and stories of fan fiction.

On play/bricolage and leeway

The story-maker plays with what is possible as the tale begins, 'In ancient times, when the magpie was a Cossack chief and the duck a policeman, the bear had a long stumpy tail, as splendid as Mistress Fox's…' (Jennings and Ponder, 2009), inviting the audience to play along in a world of flipping sense and nonsense. In his addendum to *Homo Ludens* about play in contemporary civilization, Huizinga (1949) asks a provocative question about whether current cultures develop playforms and live in a spirit of playfulness. He critiques much of what are characterized as organized games as being far more codified and rigid than they had originally been at their inception, and throughout much of history. Organized sports in the current era leap to mind at this criticism, from obsessive Little League parents and coaches who batter children from ball players into wannabe winners, to the billion dollar businesses of major sports franchises and all of the shadow and excesses they contain. There is little freedom in much of what is defined as play in this era, at least in American culture.

Fan fiction stands in stark contrast to this rigidity. As Grossman suggests, 'fan fiction isn't just an homage to the original – it's subversive and perverse and boundary-breaking' (Jamison, 2013, p. xii). Fan fiction breaks rules and barriers in all sorts of directions, including expectations about ownership, gender, storylines, memory, and possibility, and blurs the lines between fiction and reality. Its serious work of fantasy is innately about play. Jung states,

> The dynamic principle of fantasy is *play*, a characteristic also of the child, and as such it appears inconsistent with the principle of serious work. But without this playing with fantasy no creative work has ever yet come to birth. The debt we owe to the play of the imagination is incalculable.

(1921, §93)

Play is not simply gaming, not simply fun, not simply entertainment. It is about bricolage (Miller, 1996): the art of creating something with the materials at hand. And bricolage is the play of myth; Lévi-Strauss wrote:

> The characteristic feature of mythical thought is that it expresses itself by means of a heterogeneous repertoire. … It has nothing else at its disposal. Mythical thought is therefore a kind of intellectual 'bricolage. … The bricoleur uses the means at hand.'

(1966, p. 16)

Play is also about movement, and possibility. To borrow a story from Miller (1966) as he describes himself as a newly published young scholar, star-struck and nervous on awaiting approval from Hans-George Gadamer for his book, *Gods and Games*. In Miller's story, after waiting weeks for a reaction, Gadamer says gently but mercilessly, that the books was quite nice and it almost got the point. Crushed, Miller wondered where he'd gone wrong. Gadamer replies:

'English,' he explained, 'has a doublet for the idea: play, the verb, and game, the noun, are different words in English, whereas German says it with one and the same word, *ein Spiel spielen*, as does French, *jouer un jeu*.' So, he explained to me that I had wrongly thought that play has something to do with fun and games. 'Very American!' he said in a way that was not at all reassuring.

So what was the point of play? Gadamer asked me if I rode a bicycle. I said that I did. Then he asked me about the front wheel, the axle, and the nuts. He remarked that I probably knew that it was important not to tighten the nuts too tightly, else the wheel could not turn. 'It has to have some play!' he announced pedagogically and a little exultantly, I thought. And then he added, '...and not too much play, or the wheel will fall off.' 'You know,' he said, '*Spielraum*. Play room.'

(Miller, 1970)

It is this particular kind of playroom, this leeway, that breathes life into the soul of the work (and play!) of the fan fiction vidder or writer. This play is the essence of fan fiction, finding the power of the stories in between the canon, beyond the canon, and bringing it into an ongoing openness. Simultaneously, this is the play of soul. It is the movement that myth as metaphor opens, crossing from literal to nonliteral meaning. As Hillman (1976) suggests, soul is innately connected to our play of imaginal possibility in our psyches, pointing us toward a recognition of all realities ultimately as symbolic or metaphorical.

Collective unconscious/Jung's intuiting of an intuited world

The storyteller dreams of a world that conjures magic, and invites dreaming together, beginning his story, 'In olden times when wishing still helped ...' (Jennings and Ponder, 2009). It is that wishing together that creates the intuited, co-created digital world of post-cinematic fan fiction. While individual identities and voices are the fabric of fan fiction, its weave is one of community. It is a universe made up of the poly over the mono – polyvocal, polytextual, polyvalent, polymorphous, polysexual, to name a few – it is the inverse of monolithic belief systems. Even the canon, while generally respected (and occasionally revered) as origin stories, is not understood as a monotheism by most within the fan fiction community, but instead, as a single source in a collective world. It may be weighted more heavily than other sources, in terms of its legitimacy and meaning, but it is not the sole source of inspiration. Indeed, depending upon the fan fiction community, it may recede deeply into the background as an ancient mythology, with current pieces of fan fiction and the energies and new creative synapses they snap into being as the source of greatest inspiration.

Obviously, the fan fiction universe is not only connected but richly collaborative, as Turk and Johnson (2012) suggest, but the connections it both builds, and builds on, run even more deeply than self-aware collaboration between community members. These connections go subterranean, to unconscious levels. As potentially global story co-creation by multitudes of people, fan fiction resides not only in collaboration of conscious story-making, but in the deeper mythopoesis of the collective unconscious.

Jung (1959: §3) describes this as a group experience of the soul, suggesting that the 'personal unconscious rests upon a deeper layer, which does not derive from personal experience and is not a personal acquisition but is inborn.' He calls this deeper layer 'the collective unconscious ... this part of the unconscious is not individual but universal.' He argues that behind the individual psyche,

There exists a second psychic system of a collective, universal, and impersonal nature which is identical in all individuals. This collective unconscious does not develop individually but is inherited. It consists of pre-existent forms, the archetypes, which can only become conscious secondarily and which give definite form to certain psychic contents.

(1929, §369)

He continues elsewhere:

The existence of the collective unconscious means that individual consciousness is any-thing but a *tabula rasa* and is not immune to predetermining influences. On the contrary, it is in the highest degree influenced by inherited presuppositions, quite apart from the unavoidable influences exerted upon it by the environment. The collective unconscious comprises in itself the psychic life of our ancestors right back to the earliest beginnings. It is the matrix of all conscious psychic occurrences, and hence it exerts an influence that compromises the freedom of consciousness in the highest degree, since it is continually striving to lead all conscious processes back into the old paths.

(1963, p. 112)

Just as creativity and imagination seep up from the unconscious for each individual, cooking down and re-imagining memories and mixing them with thoughts in the process of creating something new, the same process for the collective is bound to occur. People seize on tropes and storylines that create resonance in them, that feel both new and revolutionary but also somehow familiar.

This familiarity is, of course, the domain of archetypes. Jung describes these as 'primordial images' belonging 'to the basic stock of the unconscious psyche and cannot be explained as personal acquisitions. Together they make up that psychic stratum which has been called the collective unconscious' (1929: §229). The characters and story arcs of fan fiction are intimately entwined with archetypes. At their worst, they may flatten to stereotypes, but at their most articulated, they begin to do what Jung continues on to describe as the process of the collective unconscious:

The primordial image, or archetype is a figure – be it a daemon, a human being, or a process – that constantly recurs in the course of history and appears wherever creative fantasy is freely expressed. Essentially, therefore, it is a mythological figure. When we examine these images more closely, we find that they give form to countless typical experiences of our ancestors. They are, so to speak, the psychic residua of innumerable experiences of the same type. They present a picture of psychic life in the average, divided up and projected into the manifold figures of the mythological pantheon. But the mythological figures are themselves products of creative fantasy and still have to be translated into conceptual language…. In each of these images there is a little piece of human psychology and human fate, a remnant of the joys and sorrows that have been repeated countless times in our ancestral history.

(1931: §127)

Suddenly, what feels like 'mere' fantasy and fiction begins to pulse with a genuine sense of the mythic. In the interchange between collective memories and common archetypal images and the individual, the myths that fan fiction community members live within begin to take form.

Jung (1963, p. 171) asks the question, 'what is your myth – the myth in which you live?' He asks this against the background of 'the contents that press up from the unconscious' (p. 326).

Essentially, he is suggesting that the individual's own mythic process springs in large part from the unconscious, both individual and ultimately collective. It is how people begin to individuate, to understand their own individual identity against the backdrop of the collective, a healing effect as these two sometimes divergent pressures begin to transform into a unified sense of Self.

While the creation of fan fiction media is not, at least generally, a prescribed therapy, for many participants, this creation of fiction can offer psychological healing. It allows people myriad opportunities to explore and define their own identities in ways that are predominately fairly safe, and while the fan fiction community is, like any community, not immune from conflict, there are fairly constant, fairly effective efforts to maintain a generative energy for those who arrive.

Certainly, creativity and art as therapy are a valid tradition in the psychological community and, true to form, the fan fiction community tends toward a co-created sense of group therapy of peers rather than seeking official, exterior guidance. Story is the work of psyche, and crafting it can be deeply therapeutic. James Hillman writes:

> Inasmuch as a goal is a guiding fiction showing a way, it is a healing fiction. 'To be healed' is that goal that takes one into therapy, and we are healed of that goal when we recognize it as a fiction. Now the goal as fiction has become a psychic reality, become a psychic reality itself, so that indeed the way did become the goal. This deliteralized method of healing, so ironic, slippery, paradoxical, that seems to fulfill and defeat our striving at the same time (as if the two senses of 'want' suddenly conjoin), bespeaks the mercurial consciousness of Hermes, Guide of Souls, Guide of Ways.
>
> *(1983, p.105)*

Hermetic story … what better metaphor might emerge for fan fiction? Quicksilver, clever, and carrying consummate trickster energy, he carries that paradoxical, ironic, slippery magic of fiction with him lightly, casting its energy off with a flick of his winged sandals. And in the words of Lewis Hyde (1998), trickster makes this world.

*Mundus imaginalis/anima mundi/*the soul of the imaginal world

The story-maker reaches back to begin the story in a world that hasn't yet hardened into a frozen version of itself: 'Long, long ago when stones were soft…' (Jennings and Ponder, 2009) Fan fictions reside in nested imaginal worlds, rather like Ukrainian dolls that pop open to reveal another, with the original source stories as the smallest doll in the center, and the interlocking, at times loosely aligned videos and writings that emerge from them, whether film, television, written word, or some combination, as is increasingly the case, of the two, each a larger doll. Harry Potter lives on print and on film and now in multiple fan fiction galaxies; the same is true for Sherlock Holmes, the elaborate characters and worlds of Tolkien, and even Jane Austen's characters. Other stories began first in television and then expanded into film and print and fan fiction, sometimes even simultaneously. *Star Trek*, one of the great fan galaxies, has spawned both its own multiple worlds and mythologies in multiple media.

All of these canons have birthed sprawling interconnected worlds and galaxies online (sometimes intersecting in the most unexpected ways), and many have enormous investments by multiple people creating both within the original canon and within the fanon to articulating cohesive, coherent language, place, culture, religious traditions, and anything else you might think of to bring an imaginal world to life.

Some even spill over into imaginary versions of the so-called real world. Again, as Anne Jamison was on the hunt for an intriguing sounding article she had seen referenced, she found herself in a constructed reality that echoed what the theme of the (very possibly) imaginary article. She writes (2013),

> but 'The Theory of Narrative Causality' … goes all Roland Barthes, and the readers take over. The story morphs into a multiplayer internet RPG. It continues outside itself, as successful stories and characters have always done – but with a difference. However similar to past forms of collective storytelling, this is something new.

Worlds exist within worlds, worlds exist outside worlds, and worlds exist alongside worlds, and are all, on some level or another, imaginal. And they are all living on that most ephemeral of imaginal worlds, the internet. Rose (2011, p. 2) echoes this idea:

> The Internet is a chameleon. It is the first medium that can act like all media – it can be text, or audio, or video, or all of the above. It is nonlinear, thanks to the World Wide Web and the revolutionary convention of hyperlinking. It is inherently participatory – not just interactive, in the sense that it responds to your commands, but an instigator constantly encouraging you to comment, to contribute, to join in. And it is immersive – meaning that you can use it to drill down as deeply as you like about anything you care to.

In 1972, Henri Corbin offered a short treatise exploring an idea from within Islamic philosophy, an idea of a imaginal place that existed outside normal experience. He writes:

> We realize immediately that we are no longer confined to the dilemma of thought and extension, to the schema of a cosmology and a gnoseology restricted to the empirical world and the world of abstract intellect. Between them there is a world that is both intermediary and intermediate, described by our authors as the *alam al-mithal*, the world of the image, the *mundus imaginalis*: a world that is ontologically as real as the world of the senses and that of the intellect. This world requires its own faculty of perception, namely, imaginative power, a faculty with a cognitive function, a noetic value which is as real as that of sense perception or intellectual intuition.
>
> *(1972, p. 5)*

His thoughts on the *mundus imaginalis* were innately religious/sacred, and he warned against confusing 'it with the imagination identified by so-called modern man with "fantasy," and which, according to him, is nothing but an outpour of "imaginings".'

That warning aside, the image of the *mundus imaginalis* is a richly relevant one to fan fiction. While the place he speaks of is not literal, it is real – holding the both/and of most and least real/true of mythological thinking – and this corresponds quite literally ontologically to his world. Beyond that, though, the dance between the realness of the communal imaginal world that is created by the inhabitants of fan fiction and the meaning that emerges for them through their myth-making can be as powerful and real as what he is defining. While the fiction being created may simply be fantasy (though even that might be an over-simplification), the realness of the world that is being by the community itself is undeniable.

In any case, it is a powerful metaphor for fan fiction and its community, and one that the community seems to intuit as they play with the boundaries of what is real and what is not. It also invites an exploration of a connection into ideas about *anima mundi*, the soul of the world, and how that intersects with imagination and psyche.

> Let us imagine the anima mundi neither above the world encircling it as a divine and remote emanation of spirit, a world of powers, archetypes, and principles transcendent to things, nor within the material world as its unifying panpsychic life principle. Rather let us imagine the anima mundi as that particular soul spark, that seminal image, which offers itself through each thing in its visible form.
>
> *(Hillman, 1982, p. 77)*

In this moment, the animating force in the world becomes the interiority of each creature, idea, or each image that comes fully into itself. This is *a mundus imaginalis*, then, that emerges through the very essence of the pieces that make the whole. It is a world ensouled by itself. It breathes life into itself, through its own perception, echoing the Greek word, *aisthesis*, 'which means at root a breathing in or taking in of the world, the gasp, "aha," the "uh" of the breath in wonder, shock, amazement, an aesthetic response to the image (*eidolon*) presented' (ibid., p. 107).

This is a world that self creates, breathing itself in. This is fan fiction.

Conclusion/a never-ending story?

The story-maker creates a fiction in order to find truth: 'Just tell it, straight up, let the listener decide what's at the heart of it...' (Jennings and Ponder, 2009). Any endings like in its beginnings, as the new story sits within the old and what might be at the heart of it both changes and stays the same. As 'older media forms don't necessarily disappear; instead, they are repurposed' (Shaviro, 2011) and they seem to sit remarkably comfortably.

As Shaviro wrestles with the psycho-social implications of post-cinematic culture, he examines the paradoxical world of the movie, *Gamers*, and how its characters reach to make the game 'real.' Shaviro describes the desire to blur the lines between game and life, between fantasy and reality:

> Everyone in the world, it seems, is addicted to MMORPGs (massively multiplayer online role-playing games). But these games are themselves viscerally 'real,' in a way that is not (or not yet) the case today. The basic science-fictional extrapolation of the movie is to envision a form of gaming in which players control the actions, not of virtual figures on a screen, but of real, physical, flesh-and-blood bodies: human 'actors' or avatars.
>
> *(2010, p. 94)*

In this story set up, the filmmakers mythologize the literalizing of the fiction, of the game. Paradoxically, the dystopia emerges when the game becomes 'real,' even though that may be a deep wish of the gamers – or the role players, or creators of fan fiction. It is easy to yearn for the mythos to become sharp-edged and tangible. However, what is play in a game, what is truth in a fiction, often becomes something much darker when it leaks out into real life.

In the post-cinematic world, 'digital technologies, together with neoliberal economic relations, have given birth to radically new ways of manufacturing and articulating lived experience' (ibid., p. 2). The ways to consume, make, and disseminate both stories and games have had an impact on how people make their lives the ways they tell their stories of that making. Shaviro critiques the move from consumer to 'autonomous economic units' (p. 3) as culture steps into what he describes as neoliberal capitalism. However and importantly in that move he misses the opening that digital technologies really can bring: a post-entrepreneurial approach to the nature of creativity, where the dance between fiction and reality, community and individuality, ownership and gifting, is messy and beloved for that messiness. In another moment, he intuits that opening into possibility and creativity, stating that digital 'technologies correspond to, or help to instantiate, new forms of spatiotemporal construction' (p. 94). If the spatiotemporal construction in co-created digital media can be bent like the space–time continuum in a *Star Trek* film, the mythic nature of that move can take the creator right back into making mythic worlds.

It could be that the gifts that these technologies bring are ultimately in the fictionalizing of the lived experience Shaviro describes, for it allows the infinite to reside in the smallest of intersections, for the stories, the makers, and even the characters themselves. It could be that the Promethean use of technology that invites its users – and its characters – to make their own fire. At the very least, they can discover that 'technology … is not necessarily the enemy of the heart; technology is not inherently soulless' (Hillman, quoted in Goleman, 1985).

Perhaps to move the spiral forward (for there is no circle to be completed here) the mythic technological tools and layers of fan fiction might wish that fans might fiction mythology itself – Hermes would certainly approve – and spin out the intersections of stories that they tell and the stories that tell them. Perhaps that has already happened.

The story-maker concludes this chapter of the tale by looking backwards to look forwards imagining a story that ended '…a great while ago, when the world was full of wonders…' (Jennings and Ponder, 2009). The biggest wonder is of a world that stories itself into being. For then, truly, all things are possible. That is the soul of fan fiction.

References

Andersen, H. C. (2013) *Fairy tales from Hans Christian Andersen: illustrated by Thomas, Charles and W. Heath Robinson*, Kindle edn. Read Books Ltd.

Bachelard, G. (1948) *La terre et les rêveries du repos*. Paris: Librairie José Corti.

Bachelard, G. (1998) *On poetic imagination and reverie*, trans. C. Gaudin. Dallas, TX: Spring Publications.

Busse, K. and Hellekson, K. (2006) 'Work in progress', in K. Hellekson and K. Busse (eds), *Fan fiction and fan communities in the age of the internet*. Jefferson, NC: McFarland. pp. 5–32.

Corbin, H. (1989) *Spiritual body and celestial earth: from Mazdean Iran to Shi'ite Iran*, 5th edn. Princeton, NJ: Princeton University Press.

Gere, C. (2008) *Digital culture*. London: Reaktion Books Ltd.

Hillman, J. (1976) *Revisioning psychology*. New York: Harper & Row.

Hillman, J. (1982) *The thought of the heart and the soul of the world*. Woodstock, CT: Spring Publications Inc.

Hillman, J. (1983) *Healing fiction*. Woodstock: Spring Publications Inc.

Hillman, J. (1989) *A blue fire: selected writings by James Hillman*, ed. T. Moore. New York: Harper Collins.

Huizinga, J. (1949) *Homo ludens: a study of the play element in culture*. London: Routledge & Kegan Paul.

Hyde, L. (1998) *Trickster makes this world: mischief, myth, and art*. New York: Farrar, Straus & Giroux.

Jameson, F. (2005) *Archaeologies of the future: the desire called utopia and other science fictions*. New York: Verso.

Jamison, A. (2013) *Fic: why fanfiction is taking over the world*, Kindle edn. BenBella Books, Inc.

Jenkins, H. (2008) *Convergence culture: where old and new media collide*. New York: New York University Press.

Jenkins, H., Ford, S. and Green, J. (2013) *Spreadable media: creating value and meaning in a networked culture (postmillennial pop)*, Kindle edn. New York: New York University Press.

Jung, C. G. (1921) 'The problem of types in the history of classical and medieval thought', in *The collected works of C. G. Jung*, Vol. 6, *Psychological types*, 3rd edn. London: Routledge, 1971.

Jung, C. G. (1929) 'The significance of constitution and heredity in psychology', in *The collected works of C. G. Jung*, Vol 8, *The structure and dynamics of the psyche*, 2nd edn. Princeton, NJ: Princeton University Press, 1969.

Jung, C. G. (1931) 'On the relation of analytical psychology to poetry', in *The collected works of C. G. Jung*, Vol. 15, *The spirit in man, art, and literature*. London: Routledge, 1966.

Jung, C. G. (1959) 'Four archetypes: mother/rebirth/spirit/trickster', in *The collected works of C. G. Jung*, Vol. 9i, *The archetypes and the collective unconscious*, 2nd edn. Princeton, NJ: Princeton University Press, 1968.

Jung, C. G. (1963) *Memories, dreams and reflections*. New York: Random House Inc.

Jung, C. G. (2011) *Modern man in search of a soul*, Kindle edn. Christopher Prince.

Lévi-Strauss, C. (1966) *The savage mind*. London: Weidenfeld & Nicolson.

Lévy, P. (1999) *Collective intelligence: mankind's emerging world in cyberspace*. New York: Basic Books.

Melander, L. (2009) 'Paradox neverending: psyche and the soul of the web: a conversation with Derek Robinson', *Spring 80: Technology, Cyberspace and Psyche*, 80.

Miller, D. (2013) *Gods and games: towards a theory of play*. New York: Colophon Books.

Murray, G. (2011) *Five stages of Greek religion*, Kindle edn. ReadaClassic.com.

Ong, W. J. (1982) *Orality and literacy: the technologizing of the word*. London: Methuen.

Rose, F. (2011) *The art of immersion: how the digital generation is remaking Hollywood, Madison Avenue, and the way we tell stories*. New York: W.W. Norton & Company.

Shaviro, S. (2010) *Post cinematic affect*. Ropley: Zero Books.

Online sources

Campbell, J. (2013) 'The four functions of mythology', Lecture I.2.3 *Confrontation of east and west in religion*, added by Joseph Campbell Foundation [video online]. Available at: www.youtube.com/watch?v=lpRsq9EPbb4 [Accessed 10 August 2016].

Chalquist, C. (2009) 'In the words of James Hillman, psyche's hermetic highwayman', *Terrapsychology* [online]. Available at: www.terrapsych.com/hillman.html [Accessed 30 September 2016].

Corbin. H. (1972) 'Mundus imaginalis or the imaginary and the imaginal', *Bahia Studies Webserver*, trans. R. Horine [Online]. Available at: www.bahaistudies.net/asma/mundus_imaginalis.pdf [Accessed 30 August 2016].

Goleman, D. (1985) 'In spirit of Jung, analyst creates therapy nearer art than science', *New York Times*, 2 July [online]. Available at: www.nytimes.com/1985/07/02/science/in-spirit-of-jung-analyst-creates-therapy-nearer-art-than-science.html?pagewanted=all [Accessed 11 December 2017].

Henkin, A. (2004) 'A disturbance in the force', PRX [online]. Available at: https://beta.prx.org/stories/2090 [Accessed 12 September 2016].

Jamison, A. (2010) 'Text embodied', *TANK Magazine/Art Attack Issue*, 6(4). Available at: http://tank-magazine.com/issue-64/features/anne-jamison [Accessed 1 September 2016].

Jenkins, H. (2007) 'Transmedia storytelling 101', *Confessions of an aca-fan* [online]. Available at: http://henryjenkins.org/2007/03/transmedia_storytelling_101.html [Accessed 30 November 2016].

Jenkins, H. (2011) 'Aca-fandom and beyond: Rhianon Bury and Matt Yockey (Part One)', *Confessions of an aca-fan* [online]. Available at: http://henryjenkins.org/2011/09/aca-fandom_and_beyond_rhianon.html [Accessed 30 November 2016].

Jennings, T. and Ponder, L. (2009) 'Folktale openings from storytell', *Ageless tales and music* [online]. Available at: www.folktale.net/openers.html [Accessed 2 August 2016].

Melander, L. (2004) 'Defining logic, defying logic: reflections of the logic of imagination' [online]. Available at: www.leighmelander.com/ImaginalLogic.pdf [Accessed 1 June 2016].

Miller, D. (1996) 'Bricoleur in the tennis court: pedagogy in postmodern context' [online]. Available at: http://dlmiller.mysite.syr.edu [Accessed 5 May 2000].

Miller, D. (2002) '*Légende-Image*: the word/image problem' [online]. Available at: http://dlmiller.mysite.syr.edu/LegendeImage.htm [Accessed 12 November 2016].

Shaviro, S. (2011) 'What is the post-cinematic?' *The Pinocchio theory*, 11 August [online]. Available at: www.shaviro.com/Blog/?p=992 [Accessed 1 September 2016].

Turk, T. and Johnson, J. (2012) 'Toward an ecology of vidding', In 'Fan/Remix Video', ed. F. Coppa and J. Levin Russo, special issue, *Transformative Works and Cultures*, 9. Available at: journal.transformative-works.org/index.php/twc/article/view/326/294 [Accessed 18 January 2018].

Winterson, J. (2006) 'Perspectives on myths and sacred texts', *Bill Moyers on Faith and Reason*, 7 July, Segment 5 [online]. Available at: www.pbs.org/moyers/faithandreason/perspectives1.html [Accessed 20 September 2016].

Wojtkowski, S. (2009) 'Jung's art complex', Archive for Research in Archetypal Symbolism [online]. Available at: https://aras.org/sites/default/files/docs/00028Wojtkowski.pdf [Accessed 30 November 2016].

Filmography

Gamers. (2006) [fiction film] Directed by Matt Vancil. Slideshow Production, USA.

33

THE UNLIVED LIVES OF CINEMA

Post-cinematic doubling, imitation and supplementarity

Kelli Fuery

Introduction

To what extent has the transition from the cinematic to the post-cinematic shaped cinema culture and our understanding of what 'cinema' can be? One of the key changes post-cinematic media have incurred within the twenty-first century is the recognition of doublings within the technologies themselves as well as our interactions with them. As Shane Denson and Julia Leyda write, 'post-cinematic media are in conversation with and are engaged in actively re-shaping our inherited cultural forms, our established forms of subjectivity, and our embodied sensibilities' (2016, p. 2), where we can understand 're-shaping' to be an acknowledgement of mimesis, duplication and relational distance between visual media objects (film, television, video games) and the context they interact and are engaged with.

The post-cinematic transcends its apparatus, moving beyond screens and spectators, to fuller, more conscious engagement of body-knowledge, the aesthetic experience of post-cinematic encounters, and the affective properties of the reflective surfaces and psychic spaces inhabited by post-cinematic subjects. Vivian Sobchack (2016) has written on the integration and oscillation between perceptive and expressive technologies, where the lived body experience has not simply altered to a post-cinematic landscape but has (at least) doubled, via the virtual, projected body within it. Shane Denson (2016) has written on the 'discorrelation' of images, noting the deviation from cinematographic and perceptual norms within twenty-first century moving image culture, but retaining the doubling of contemporary embodied experience through the potential reflexive responses that result from such 'affective discorrelation'. Steven Shaviro's *Post-Cinematic Affect* (2010) identifies different qualities of links between form and affective experience of 'post' media platforms, concerning post-cinematic affect and post-continuity aesthetics, providing 'an account of *what it feels like* to live in the early twenty-first century' (2010, p. 2). In each case the attention given to the transition from cinema to post-cinematic media is directed to all the things cinema could not do, has not done or now does differently, particularly in terms of realizing and generating affect and feeling within spectator (or user) subjectivity. Time, as an example of such 'links', has certainly taken on a 'reshaping' when we consider access to cinema, television or moving image culture generally. No longer are audiences bound to specific days of the week and time slots to watch favourite television shows, limits – geographic or otherwise – are not what they once were, especially in terms of seeing the latest film, playing the newest game or becoming a participant within a global specular community.

Embedded within the theorizing of post-cinema and its media landscapes then, is the strong implication, if not production, of the processes that involve doubling and the double as an affective resonance. Such reshaping calls attention to the growing awareness of how our interactions have changed since the dominance of cinema in the twentieth century, to being able to speak about what our interactions with visual media do in order to make us feel. It asks that we attend to post-cinema effects as much as we think about their stories. Nicholas Royle writes:

> [The double is] strangely disorienting to think about. It is uncanny because it involves a strangeness contaminated with sameness, difference as repetition. It is one thing *and* something else. The double is matter of life and death. On the one hand, it seems to illustrate or promise immortality: you can be repeated, replicated, duplicated. The life of an individual is no longer precariously confined to a single body. One the other hand, it is the very disordering of identity. The individual is no longer individual. There is a dividing of the one, division within the self. Seeing your double you are obliged to suppose that your own identity is dissolving or has come to an end.
>
> *(2014, p. 123)*

Royle is referring to Sigmund Freud's conceptualization and use of the double, as an exemplar of the uncanny within the individual, but there is room to see how the same ideas of duplicity and repetition work within a post-Jungian film studies context, particularly when we view the double as an archetypal activity rather than individual uncanniness. Here, through the framework of the double, are the spectral frustrations of the twentieth century cinema parent to its twenty-first century post-cinematic media children, echoing Jung's claim that the child must bear the vexing unconscious expectations of the parents' unlived life:

> The more 'impressive' the parents are, and the less they accept their own problems (mostly on the excuse of 'sparing the children'), the longer the children will have to suffer from the unlived life of their parents and the more they will be forced into fulfilling all the things the parents have repressed and kept unconscious.
>
> *(1926/46: §154)*

In Royle's definition of the double, we see the implicit presence of Jung's child archetype through the references of repetition, replication and duplicity. I use Jung's child archetype here in its capacity and implication that moves beyond the principal, literal embodiment of parent and child, engaging more with its feeling-value and motif aspect, 'mythological components, which because of their typical nature, we can call them "motifs," "primordial images," types or – as I have named them – *archetypes*' (1940: §260). The aim of this chapter is to consider the transition that has transpired between cinema and post-cinema within this post-Jungian context of the child archetype, as it provides a framework to reflect on many qualities of the double that exist in the interrelationships between cinema and post-cinematic media.

Shaviro's qualification of the post-cinematic reads as a genealogy of media platforms, with film as parent: 'Why "post-cinematic"? Film gave way to television as a "cultural dominant" a long time ago, in the mid-twentieth century; and television in turn has given way in recent years to computer – and network-based, and digitally generated, "new media"' (2010, p. 1). I read Shaviro's use of the term 'cultural dominant' to refer to the wide accessibility and sharing of media, particularly mobile media, as becoming the more dominant platform in media ecology and culture rather than as a reference to any ideological dominance in visual culture. Such 'cultural dominance' read in this way echoes the scholarship of Henry Jenkins (2006), Graham

Meikle and Sherman Young (2012) and Stephen Keane (2007) on the convergence of contemporary media ecology. Further, I follow Shaviro's lineage and precedent, using examples from cinema and television to explore how the 'difference in repetition' is emblematic of the 'post' of post-cinematic media, invoking the sensibility and affect of Jung's child archetype through evoking qualities of the double. Charlie Kauffman and Duke Johnson's stop-motion feature, *Anomalisa* (2015) and Nic Pizzolatto's *True Detective* (S1) (2014), are used as examples of post-cinematic media to exemplify doubling as an archetypal process.

Archetype, as used here, follows the Jungian treatise that any archetype has no definite or specific form. Rather the individual comes to know and think the archetype indirectly and internally, 'the archetype does not proceed from physical facts, but describes how the psyche experiences the physical fact' (Jung, 1940: §262). We can never know the archetype in its pure form, only through projections of unconscious processes that effect emotions and meaning specific to the correlating archetype. In 'Cinephilia: or, looking for meaningfulness in encounters with cinema' (2011), Greg Singh distinguishes between different conceptualizations of the archetype, noting specifically Umberto Eco's semiotic treatment of archetypes as intertextual structures within cinema. Singh compares Eco and Jung's consideration of archetypes, noting how both emphasize the aspect of repetition. The 'recycling' of cultural and textual symbols in other texts is argued to function similarly to Luke Hockley's 'third image' (2011), where the image seen on screen is also met by the viewer's own emotional and affective experience:

> The symbol is not just what the image represents, nor is it solely the personal associations that someone may bring to the image; it has a third meaning, the exact nature and function of which is not available to consciousness and which is archetypal in quality.
>
> *(p. 141)*

Cinema, as a commanding myth-sustaining, fairytale-presenting and fantasy-reflecting medium facilitates inherited and collective myths, which assist the structuring presence of archetypes, whose expression is present only in the sense that an archetype is a co-creation between personal and collective unconscious materials on the one hand, and cultural symbols on the other, in the encounter with cultural artefacts (such as cinema and post-cinematic media).

The scholarship on the child in cinema is rich and rewarding. For example Vicky Lebeau's *Childhood and Cinema* (2008) clearly outlines the polysemy and function of the image of the child in cinema. Lebeau moves beyond the literal child figure, discussing the function of the ideology of the child and the landscape of cinema, 'the image of the child on screen is an object to *think* with, an idea through which to encounter the institution of cinema' (p. 13). Karen Lury's *The Child in Film: Tears, Fears and Fairytales* (2010) treats the representation and use of the child within film as a disruptive mechanism, particularly with regard to time. Debbie Olson and Andrew Schaill's *Lost and Othered Children in Contemporary Cinema* (2013) discusses how analysis of the many representations of children in cinema can offer comment on our collective investment of childhood. Emma Wilson's *Cinema's Missing Children* (2003) questions the repetition of abused and abandoned children in cinematic narratives as motifs that engender spectator reflexivity. Pamela Robertson Wojcik's *Fantasies of Neglect: Imagining the Urban Child in American Film and Fiction* (2016) discusses the consequences of competing ideologies that have been constructed between children and urban space. Terrie Waddell has written on Jungian aspects of childhood and collective loss in her piece on Australia's lost children in the films of Baz Luhrmann (2014). These works demonstrate that the child motif is a recurrent and ongoing cultural concern within post-cinema. Each title does not simply discuss the representation of children, but makes very plain that analyses of childhood and its cartography within the media landscape has something greater to say about the overall situation of society, its fears, its anxieties and its collective unconscious life.

The Jungian child archetype offers an interpretive structure between the cinematic parent and its post-cinematic media children, looking beyond the literal representation of the 'double' to its function. Imitation and supplementarity – terms that I have discussed elsewhere (Fuery, 2009) – are the factors of repetition and duality through which this chapter considers the purpose of doubling within the cinema to post-cinematic media relationship.

On the double

The double, first given specific psychoanalytic attention in Otto Rank's study (1914) and a formative element in Freud's theory of the 'Uncanny' (1919), has become a widely applied concept that is referred to within film studies scholarship to highlight 'dramatic conflict' and star performance (Barnett, 2007, p. 86), of fantasy and threat, 'as an element of and in cinema' (Andrade, 2008, p. 3) and elsewhere to articulate the reflexive quality of feeling within cinema between viewer and what is viewed (Singh, 2014). Here I focus on the functionality of doubling, rather than any literal presentation of pairs or doublings. I am interested in the double as a repetitive and processual experience that occurs between the media that is viewed as transformative and indicative of the post-cinematic landscape. The double, as duality and binary, is consistently referred to throughout Jung's collected works, so much so that beyond the examination of specific doubles themselves (the shadow aspect, introvert/extrovert, *anima/animus*, collective/individual; conscious/unconscious) we might question the function of doubling as it works within a 'post' context – post-Jungian, post-cinematic. The notion of 'post' follows Andrew Samuels' (2004) context of being a connection to, but critical distance from, the subject under discussion – Jung's ideas and the newness of post-cinematic media respectively. Doubling is read through two typologies of relational distance – imitation and supplementarity – linking the different aspects of Jung's child archetype, which he lists as:

1   The Archetype as a Link with the Past
2   The Function of the Archetype
3   The Futurity of the Archetype
4   Unity and Plurality of the Child Motif
5   Child God and Child Hero.

It is through the formal analysis of imitation and supplementarity, and the meta-analysis of the characteristics of the Jungian child archetype that the relational distance and association between cinema and post-cinematic media is interpreted through the metaphor of parent to child. Each typology not only represents a specific distance from twentieth century media but articulates an aspect of the child archetype. As such I acknowledge (a) the link of post-cinematic media to its cinematic past, (b) consider its current twenty-first century affective function and futurity and (c) address the unity and plurality, which showcases what post-cinematic media do differently as well as illustrating the doubling that occurs consistently within media progression and innovation. An analysis of *Anomalisa* (dirs Duke Johnson and Charlie Kaufman, 2015) reveals the relational distance of imitation within cinematic techniques, including it in the domain of cinema but preserving its difference from it through the doubling of formal post-cinema techniques that occur specifically within stop-motion animation – imitation representing the closest relational distance to cinematic form. The second element of doubling outlined here is supplementarity, drawing on Jacques Derrida's theory of the supplement as both a thing and as a process which 'adds only to replace. It intervenes or insinuates itself *in-the-place-of*' (Derrida, 1976, p. 145). It intercedes between twentieth century television and cinema, interjecting cinematic aesthetics within twenty-first century televisual modes. Derrida's examination of the supplement is that, unlike Rousseau, the supplement is not lesser than, or added to, a more important and originary presence. Rather it is something unique within itself, no lesser than, and certainly not lacking, than the 'center' or origin. This is precisely why Derrida speaks of the origin being the supplement of another supplement. In cinema and its post-cinema contexts, this means that post-cinema is not the supplement to the origin of cinema, and should not be read within the confines of history (be it technique, form or even narrative). The argument here is that Jung's child motif provides us with a critical frame to better understand how 'post' operates within these contexts.

As such, Jung's idea of the child archetype is a theoretical keystone, enabling us to better understand relational contexts of cinema and its 'posts'. Just as the child is seen as the parents' supplement until he/she asserts a life lived independent of these origins, post-cinema media can be read as something emerging from, but independent to, their cinematic roots. In other words, post-cinema media read as a Jungian child motif, devise a multitude of possibilities and alternatives. Perhaps with some irony, these unlived lives of cinema/parent are revealed most apparently in those moments/forms/technics that evoke self-reflexivity. The 'child' becomes something other than the parents' supplement when those texts evoke an aspect of cinema. ('Childhood' as an ideological category, as much as it is an embodied sensory experience, is politicized here. The concept of 'child' invoking the agitational qualities involved with authority in time and of order, as much as it relates to the specificities of literal parent–child relations: see Andrew Samuels' (1993) socio-political reading of the father–child relationship.) The specific cinematic techniques found in animation and television of the twenty-first century are more than simply references to cinematic origins; they are the moments precisely when supplementarity is challenged, self-reflexivity acknowledged, and new forms and techniques are developed. This is the creative force of the supplement as child archetype – when post-cinema media begin to live the unlived life and become something more. These are the emerging forms of post-cinematic media that can be found in self-reflexivity, creations of hybridity (between parent–child/origin–supplement), and the development of completely new textualities.

The television series, *True Detective* (S1), is used to define the supplement as both an emblematic aspect of doubling and factor of the child archetype, foregrounding the efficacy of 'adding only to replace' within post-cinematic media. Post-cinematic television exists entirely as supplement deconstructing both television of twentieth century and televisual affect in the twenty-first. Derrida's theory of supplementarity does not simply rest on the activity of adding to replace; rather the supplement functions on the relationship of presence and absence, where the supplement adds, contributes and furthers – which is why there are always further and future supplements to be created, more 'children' to be made. The television of today's post-cinematic media will be supplemented in the future. The supplementarity of post-cinematic television shows that there is replication that occurs within twenty-first century post-cinematic media, which works as supplement to and of cinema that both unifies past genre conventions as well as pluralizes the current media landscape. Let us look more closely at Jung's framework of the child archetype in order to contextualize the relationship of the double to the concepts of imitation and supplementarity.

The child archetype

Jung first establishes the child archetype as a link with the past; suggesting doubling is a continual process throughout life (Jung, 1940: §271). In so doing the archetype articulates the function of nostalgia or return, both characterizations of imitation seen as a dominant narrative that occurs within post-cinematic media. The archetype of the child moves beyond the literal representation of a child – where the 'child motif' (whilst inclusive of representations of childhood and children) is not limited or bound to them. Where we might see representations of children, and there are *a lot* within feature animations, they are more symbolic of Jung's child archetype being an acknowledgment of unconscious patterns of behaviour, repetition of collective attentions that highlight the resonance between a past to a future in order to contextualize lived experience. If, as Jung states, 'the archetype is an element of our psychic structure and thus a vital and necessary component in our psychic economy' (1940: §271) then it is not the specific representation of children, doubles or doubling that is of value but, more broadly, how processes that incur and imply hidden doubling (through forms and practices of imitation and supplementarity) that are most useful. He writes of the child motif (and we can begin now to consider 'child' through narratives and developments of emergent and inceptive digital and electronic media born from previous cinema technologies and histories) as linking to forgotten experiences within a collective rather than individual context. For post-cinematic media, we can take this association of the child archetype to refer to not just new media practices or forms but, equally, to the sense of the future suggested in all new technological development, regardless of its actual specific electronic or digital configurations. In this sense, the 'new' or the 'post' is the linking back of the child archetype that facilitates a return (as a mnemonic act) and an alternative life to media and cinema past. Post-cinematic media implicitly aim to address as well as ameliorate the frustrations or limits of past-cinema experience, perceptually, haptically or visually, yet at the same time are often stuck within the generic formations of its visual platforms.

An example is found in Denson's discussion of the digital lens flare, which he argues is diegetically excessive and yet reflexive of the filmmaking process, 'the lens flare draws attention to itself and highlights the images' artificiality by emulating (and indeed foregrounding the emulation of) the material presence of a (non-diegetic) camera' (Denson, 2016). Lisa Purse's work on lens flare, cityscapes and digital cinema in *Digital Imaging in Popular Cinema*, discusses how

> digital imaging interventions allow the sequence to produce the illusion of photographic indexicality, the idea that the scene we are witnessing has to have happened in the real word in front of the camera because it has been imprinted by the action of light onto a strip of celluloid.
>
> *(2013, p. 2)*

Here the lens flare not only draws attention to itself, it is an aesthetic of post-cinema that expresses Jung's child motif as a 'linking back to the past' of cinematic realism and the spectator's relationship to the materiality of film. Denson states that such simulation of lens flare is a paradox, a technique that both establishes reality while at the same time exposing the artifice of realist filmmaking tendencies. Though Denson's focus rests on the phenomenological implications of the lens flare and perceptibility within CGI and digital filmmaking, his work registers what the function of the lens flare does beyond its literal virtual presence. It is a synecdoche for the historical transition between cinema and post-cinema filmmaking, its imitation (or mimetic capacity) articulating 'a transformation of mediation itself in the post-cinematic era' (Denson, 2016). Let us look more closely at examples of post-cinema (specifically stop-motion animation and television) which illuminates their existence as relational distances to cinema within the context of Jung's child archetype and the frames of imitation and supplementarity.

Animation: the relational distance of imitation

Qualities of the child motif are invested in origins creating an historical determinism. To repeat and replicate visual form, even if to deviate from it, places the novelty in 'post'-cinema at the forefront of the spectator's mind, maintaining the association with the originary media. We see this in *Anomalisa*, which examines internal crises and loneliness through the character Michael Stone (David Thewlis) – a motivational speaker on customer service who experiences a lack of authentic connection with others. Michael stays in the hotel Fregoli – a reference to the disorder that sees others as sharing the same intention towards one's ruination, and the isolation that results from it – and has an affair with Lisa (Jennifer Jason Leigh), who has come to hear Michael speak. There is irony in Michael's isolation, formally conveyed through voices all sounding the same, who everyone else has come to hear speak.

One scene in particular illustrates the post-cinematic imitation quality present throughout *Anomalisa*, where Michael is running away from the Hotel Manager, back to Lisa who is waiting in his hotel room. Michael is unravelling emotionally. He has just heard the Hotel Manager tell him that he loves him, that everyone in the hotel loves him, and as Michael looks over the office, characters all at their desks, his fear of isolation and loneliness increases in a sea of homogeneous anonymity. All the puppets look and sound the same. At the height of his panicked escape from the hotel's basement, Michael's bottom jaw falls off his face. Until this point, there has been no self-reference of any kind about his puppet body, either within the film's story or through its style. Even though Michael is a puppet, he doesn't ever refer to it or show that he is aware of his non-human figure. Michael appears entirely pre-occupied with the difficulty of human emotion. It is worth noting Freud's discussion of the automaton in the essay of the 'Uncanny' as it established key psychoanalytic treatments of the function of the double and its relationship to the non-human. See also the work of Paul Bowman (2011) who analyses animation through the political philosophy of Jacques Rancière; and Alan Cholodenko (2009) whose work is a complex application and reworking of Derrida's hauntology to the practice of animation. But, to return to the film, who does Michael's face fall off *for*? This is another example of Denson's affective self-reflexivity as discorrelation, the 'phenomenological disconnect between viewing subjects and the object-images they view'. Denson's view is that the purpose of such discorrelation is to engender responsibility for the affects we create and experience within the realm of post-cinema. In more Jungian words, to be able to link the past to the present and the future through the media we engage with. Another consequence of linking such periods of time is the recognition of repeated visual forms, repetition in this sense working as mimicry or imitation – not dissimilar from the notion of remediation (Bolter and Grusin, 1999) where a residue of old media is presented through new media forms, and there is a doubling of both recognition and reflexivity in the space between viewer and viewed.

Imitation is defined as 'the action or practice of imitating or copying' (*OED* online). For psychology, the mental activity of imitation is argued to be the foundation of subjectivity. Lee Grieveson writes 'Imitation of others was at the base of the subject and hence the subject was socially formed, given a broad definition of "the social" as the effect of others' (2008, p. 7). Grieveson via Gabriel Tarde argues that imitation, in association with suggestion, was the basis for social formation, 'mimesis stood at the center of subject and social formation' (p. 7). Imitation, or mimetic behaviour, is a core feature of Jung's child archetype, taking into consideration the importance of linking back to the past, its purpose is most definitely directed to the creation of subjectivity within the social environment and the development of the ego in relation to authority. When we read imitation working as a 'doubling process' through Jung's archetype, imitation adopts the connotation of linking past to present and the quality of invention embedded within what is imitated, as well as a controlling of the innovation. The motif of the child undeniably reflects this myth, as the child imitates the parent through physical resemblance (also via the unconscious expression of affect through facial expressions) or through likeness in personality (if we accept that personality is part invention as well as imitation). If we can claim the function of imitation is the intent to embed subjectivity within a social and collective context, then it is formed of two parts that can be related to post-cinematic media: through maturation and innovation of form and of content.

Anomalisa exemplifies imitation as a typology of relational distance within post-cinematic media replicating specific cinematic language in a more reflexive way than its traditional stop-motion counterparts. Historically, stop-motion animation can be traced to *The Humpty Dumpty Circus* (dir. Blackton, 1908) (Figure 33.1), where inanimate circus animals and circus performers were brought to life. Blackton's short lacked narrative, yet it established the cinematic language and subsequent social authority of illusion through visual semiotic practice that has become specific to animation, and which has been imitated ever since. The idea of toys (or inanimate objects) coming to life has persisted as a narrative within animated features, starting with Émile Cohl's *Fantasmagorie* (1908) to Disney's *Pinocchio* (dir. Ferguson, 1940), Pixar's *Toy Story* (dir. Lasseter, 1996), *Wall-E* (dir. Stanton, 2008), *Frankenweenie* (dir. Burton, 2012) that we can find truth in Tarde's claim 'Invention and imitation are … the elementary social acts' (1962, p. 144) and that '*even the desire to invent*, has the same origin … this desire completes and is part of the logical need for unification' (p. 150). (Unification here referring to the relationship between cinematic histories and practices.)

Figure 33.1 Film still from what is said to be the first short-length stop-motion animation film made, *The Humpty Dumpty Circus* (Blackton, 1898). This film has been lost due to lack of preservation.

Source: http://lostmedia.wikia.com/wiki/The_Humpty_Dumpty_Circus_(Lost_Stop_Motion_Film).

Post-cinematic animation has not radically departed from form when compared to traditional 2D cel-animation, or 3D computer animation. The same concerns of synchronicity in sound to pacing within editing are still present, as are the frame-by-frame character placings and compositions of claymation and stop-motion animation. *Anomalisa* has adapted stop-motion animation as a style normally used for children's film (Nick Park's *Wallace and Gromit* shorts (1989–1996) and his features, *Chicken Run* (2000), *The Curse of the Were-Rabbit* (2005)) and used it to convey adult themes. In addition to lens flares, *Anomalisa* is indicative of post-cinematic media through its imitation of cinematography and lighting. Tracking shots follow Michael down hotel corridors, long shots engender awkward affect when Michael meets the Hotel Manager in the basement, and extreme close ups mimic intimacy when Michael gives Lisa oral sex. (The sex scene between Michael and Lisa is particularly imitative of cinematic storytelling.) The lighting effects a particularly grey hue – a doubling of the film's oppressive atmosphere and murkiness to Michael's own depressive feelings and selfish intentions regarding Lisa. She is an object to distract Michael from his loneliness, a usefulness foreshadowed in Bella, Michael's ex-girlfriend.

Sound synchronicity is used creatively in *Anomalisa*, where voices, from Michael's point-of-view, duplicate each other, save the interruption of Lisa's voice. From the start, every voice is heard both by Michael and by the audience as the same, indicating Michael has lost interest in the life that surrounds him. The homogeneity of voices between the other characters in the film (until Michael meets Lisa) further mirrors the mechanics of the puppets themselves. Voice is one of the most recognizably distinctive parts of a person, where variations in tonality convey expression of emotion and feeling. The sound of voice is one of cinema's most under discussed affective technologies (except for Michel Chion (1994, 2016)). The homogenization of voices within *Anomalisa* is used to effect 'mimesis – again understood as connected to representations as mediated events – was thus posited as central to subject formation'. Grieveson also writes that 'the mind and self [are to be considered as] a consequence of interaction and imitative response with, and to, others' (2008, p. 9). For as long as Lisa relieves Michael's loneliness, she has a different voice, or rather her voice fractures her own duplicity and carries her 'difference' for Michael. At breakfast, the morning after their affair, her voice transitions back into sounding like every other character. Jung writes that 'Child' means something evolving towards independence' (1940: §287) and in this classification we can argue that the innovation embedded within the imitation of post-cinematic animation is an apt example of emergent media moving towards independence, seen here through the use of sound and voice to unify and pluralize visual meaning.

Whereas 'post' may be seen to represent a departure from what has historically gone before, it can only ever serve as a linguistic reminder of what it is currently a derivative of. This postness, as emblematic of the child archetype of cinema,

> represents not only something that existed in the distant past but also something that exists *now*, that is to say; it ['post'] is not just a vestige but a system functioning in the present whose *purpose is to compensate or correct.*
>
> *(1940: §276, italics added)*

'Post' as a qualifier of twenty-first century media then, invokes supplementarity – a purpose that 'is to compensate *and* correct'. The typologies of doubling discussed as imitation and supplementarity are relational affects specific to post-cinematic media. Cinema and post-cinematic media are connected through their disconnections as supplements, specifically in the desire to resolve the tensions that arise from the duplicity of subjectivity that cinema presents and post-cinema makes participatory and specular. Here, it is the link to the past, from cinema to post-cinema that is seen as reflective of Jung's archetype of the child, where post-cinema has had to respond not just to the unlived life of cinema, but must also include in its adaptation and development, show the capacity to be seen to be doing things differently, as well as doing them more reflexively within moving image culture.

True Detective: the relational distance of supplementarity

Supplementarity, as a concept as well as a process, rotates on the notion and experience of distance, that is how things relate to each other by becoming meaningful through their association. These relational distances mark how the supplement is at once attached to and disconnected from the origin – in this case cinema. 'Distance' because what we witness is the forming of unlived lives moving away; 'relational' because we also witness reminders and remnants embedded in these supplements. This is why they are supplements rather than replacements or completely distinct innovations. This is the supplement read within the context of post-Jungian film studies – the hierarchy challenged is that of cinema to post-cinema (as parent–child) as well as the deconstructive discorrelation to it. I argue that post-cinematic media can be read through the idea of supplementarity in its capacity to simultaneously add and replace previous media, which is evocative of Jung's concept of the child archetype. It is to 'dream the myth onwards and give it a modern dress' (1940: §271). A narrow reading of the supplement would be to see post-cinematic media only ever in a secondary capacity by adding to what is already present, rather than contribute and further the media landscape through replacing and developing.

Television in the twenty-first century adds to the television already present, but as a post-cinematic supplement it enriches through its capacity to include substitutionary media practices. If the televisual parent is evident in television's traditional format of studio-sets, fixed cameras, low production values, adherence to genre narrative, episodic and serialized structure and con-sistent actors (to name a few qualities) then the post-cinema televisual 'child' as demonstrated in *True Detective* offers a televisual hybridity. *True Detective* is an HBO crime television series that follows the relationship of Louisiana State Police homicide detectives Rust Cohle (Matthew McConaughey) and Marty Hart (Woody Harrelson) and their investigation of the murder of Dora Lange. Cohle and Hart discover that Lange's murder leads to a series of unsolved murders and, more metaphorically, uncover the hidden underbelly of Louisiana's rural religious society. Despite this seemingly simple synopsis, *True Detective* does not follow traditional televisual formats, even though it clearly falls within the genre of detective-noir. Against the background of serial killers, toxic religious culture and manipulative social institutions, *True Detective* explores the difficulty between people, of secrets held and the impact of time and history on people and their bodies. Its nonlinear narrative, whilst reminiscent of voiceover in the noir genre, is a sup-plement of it. Past and present co-exist within the same episode where we see the vagaries of age between both Cohle and Hart's bodies jarring the generic structure of traditional 'whodun-nits'. Their relationship is foregrounded much more than the murder investigation, indeed it is the focus of the present-day inquiry for which they are interviewed. The supplement attributes that are found in *True Detective* and other similar shows (such as *Game of Thrones*, *House of Cards*), include on-location setting, drone camera shots, CGI, using the film-noir genre as backdrop to the drama of Cohle's and Hart's relationship (finding out 'whodunnit' is secondary to seeing Cohle and Hart's relationship develop). These supplementary additions and replacements are what recognizes and adheres to its post-cinema platform, but only so far as to offer alternatives. Not all television programmes will use film actors (like McConaughey), or use CGI, but the supplement of television in the twenty-first century is not engaged within the same modalities as it once was. These features of *True Detective* are examples of post-cinematic media that exemplify Derrida's logic of supplementarity and Jung's futurity of the child.

If we claim that *True Detective* is a televisual example of a supplement to twentieth century media (cinema, as well as television), then its 'additive' qualities would exist to support the distinction and differences between visual platforms and aesthetics. That is, *True Detective* should look and feel like a different style of television. It should remind us, as we watch it, that it is significantly different from other television programmes and remains different from cinema. In this capacity it *adds* to the mode of television, *substitutes* (replaces) previous television styles, appears excessive to cinema yet also fulfils the absence of cinema. To reconfigure a key line from Jung, *True Detective* 'anticipates future developments, even though at first sight it may seem like a retrospective configuration' (1940: §278).

True Detective's self-reflexively refers back to many of cinema's techniques and generic styles (notably film noir and, even preceding cinema, the Gothic tradition), yet this 'retrospective configuration' is very much a future development precisely because it is a hybridity. In this we witness the dissolution of the parent–child bond so that post-cinematic media become their own forms. Jung is particularly consistent in these terms of past and future. His recurring theme of the past's intervention in the future, via the child motif, shapes how he theorizes key aspects of the unconscious. This leads him to state, for example, 'The child motif represents the preconscious, childhood aspect of the collective psyche' (1940: §273). *True Detective*, as the exemplar here, can be seen as a textual and thematic rendition of this relationship. Not only do Cohle and Hart have to bury themselves into a truly Jungian collective unconscious, filled with images and storylines reminiscent of *animus* and *anima*, mandalas constructed from twigs and an altogether more primitive psychical world, but they must also act in terms of the collective unconscious. In their search for Dora Lange's killer they discover hidden worlds of abused and molested children, exploitation of power and authority structures (the police, the church), all of which suggest a neglectful attention on the corruption that occurs within humanity. The 'children' they set out to avenge are the literal, missing children, as well as that of the world losing its innocence. So much of *True Detective* is based around recounting the past, speaking of unlived lives, and attempting to make sense of the present through the events of the past. In this sense this text operates both thematically and formally as the child archetype. Perhaps this is why it is so effective as a supplement of post-cinematic media.

What Derrida's theory of supplementarity offers for a discussion of post-cinematic media within the context of post-Jungian film studies, is the acknowledgment of the production of meaning through innovation; that is cinema became supplemented because of the drive to futurity (Jung's third characteristic of the child archetype). Cinema had developed technology to give mobility and expression to its visual language, connecting form to narrative storytelling. Movement and time within cinematography was what made cinema cinematic. Animation, particularly vector-based and 3D, doesn't *have* to follow cinematographic practice, but it does, and in doing so returns a loving gaze to its cinematic parent. The integration and imitation of cinematographic styles (particularly when formal aesthetics are used to create similar visual meaning – noted through the use of lighting and lens flares discussed above) is an acknowledgment of its connection and relational distance to cinema. Cinema's 'supplements' (television, video games, YouTube) possess the same qualities that typified cinema itself. The imitation we have seen in animation is a further example of supplementarity through its mirroring of cinematic storytelling aesthetics. In order for cinema to continue to be technologically relevant and reflective of the current era, its specific and particular cinematic qualities had to typify post-cinematic media (as supplement). Television as supplement that adds and replaces, particularly the television of twenty-first century post-cinematic media, advances beyond the old dichotomy between cinema and television. Television as supplement in moving image culture, by incorporating its own quality of replication, moves more consistently to replace its forms, its genres, its narrative structures, in continuous supplementarity. In this sense, we witness at least a duality of supplements: television as cinema supplement and television producing its own supplementarity (including other media, such as video games).

The simultaneity of adding and replacing indicative of supplementarity reflects another quality of Jung's child archetype. 'One of the essential features of the child motif is its futurity. The child is potential future' (1940: §278). In this idea is a core attribute of Derrida's theory of the supplement – it exposes an absence within a previous presence. Children are often described as 'filling a hole' or 'completing a family' – their entire corporeality fulfilling an existential absence. However, in the futurity of the child, the 'child paves the way for a future change of personality' (ibid.: §278), and we must expect that in the revolution of television of twenty-first post-cinematic media, that the logic of supplementary will expose diversity and difference within what the supplement becomes as another supplement.

Reviews of the programme can be read in terms of this supplementarity: in the UK's *Guardian* newspaper, Gwilym Mumford wrote 'there's little in this first hour of *True Detective* that would lead you to confuse it with *Silent Witness*, *CSI*, or even one of the more inventive forensic thrillers such as Hannibal'; blogger Brian Tallerico, for Roger Ebert, wrote

> [*True Detective*] is dense, complex, rewarding storytelling, heightened by a sense of location from its writer and director that is mesmerizing and a character-driven storytelling aesthetic that brings to mind great films like David Fincher's 'Zodiac' and Bong Joon-ho's 'Memories of Murder.'
>
> *(2014)*

This demonstrates that the likeness of *True Detective* was seen as more indicative of a cinematic sensibility rather than its televisual identity. Tim Goodman, reviewer for Los Angeles's *Hollywood Reporter*, identified that it was the experimentation of 'tone, pace, structure and visual impact … that made astute viewers keenly aware that originality was kicking at the corners of their television sets'.

Renatus in novam infantiam

The significance of Jung's child archetype, as an interpretive structure, is that it identifies the processes and functionality of doubling within post-cinematic media through the techniques of imitation and supplementarity. For Jung, the 'child' – '*renatus in novam infantiam*' 'is thus both beginning and end, an initial and a terminal creature' (1940: §299), and I have used it here to signal that the developments of post-cinema in the twenty-first century are just beginning. The child archetype offers a frame for rethinking the interrelationships and affect of post-cinematic media, their use and users within the twenty-first century. The usefulness of a Jungian approach is found in the foregrounding of such ideas on doubling, imitation and supplementarity, anticipating the kinds of issues that any unruly child produces.

References

Andrade, P. (2008) 'Cinema's doubles, their meaning and literary intertexts', *Comparative Literature and Culture*, 10(4).

Barnett, V. (2007) 'Dualling for Judy: the concept of the double in the films of Kim Novak', *Film History*, 19(1), pp. 86–101.

Bolter, J. D. and Grusin, R. (1999) *Remediation: understanding new media*. Cambridge: MIT Press.

Bowman, P. and Stamp, R. (2011) *Reading Rancière: critical dissensus*. New York: Bloomsbury Academic Press.

Chion, M. (1994) *Audio-vision: sound on screen*, trans. C. Gorbman. New York: Columbia University Press.

Chion, M. (2016) *Sound: an acoulogical treatise*, trans. J. A. Steintrager. Durham, NC: Duke University Press.

Cholodenko, A. (2009) 'Animation (theory) as the poematic: a reply to the cognitivists', *Animation Studies*, 4.

Denson, S. (2016) 'Crazy cameras, discorrelated images, and the post-perceptual mediation of post-cinematic affect', in S. Denson and J. Leyda (eds), *Post-cinema: theorizing 21st-century film*. Falmer, UK: REFRAME Books. pp. 193–233.

Denson, S. and Leyda, J. (eds) (2016) *Post-cinema: theorizing 21st-century film*. Falmer, UK: REFRAME Books.

Derrida, J. (1976) *Of grammatology*, trans. G. Chakravorty Spivak. Baltimore, MD and London: Johns Hopkins University Press.

Freud, S. (2001 [1919]) 'The "uncanny"', in *The Standard Edition of the Complete Psychological Works of Sigmund Freud, Volume XVII (1917–1919): an infantile neurosis and other works*. London: Vintage Press.

Fuery, K. (2009) *New media: culture and image*. Basingstoke: Palgrave Macmillan.

Grieveson, L. (2008) 'Cinema studies and the conduct of conduct', in L. Grieveson and H. Wasson (eds), *Inventing film studies*. Durham, NC: Duke University Press. pp. 3–37.

Hockley, L. (2011) 'The third image: depth psychology and the cinematic experience', in C. Hauke and L. Hockley (eds), *Jung & film II: the return*. London and New York: Routledge. pp. 132–47.

Jenkins, H. (2006) *Convergence culture: where old and new media collide*. New York: New York University Press.

Jung, C. G. (1926/46) 'Analytical psychology and education: three lectures', in *The collected works of C. G. Jung*, Vol. 17, *The development of the personality*, 2nd edn. London: Routledge, 1964.

Jung, C. G. (1940) 'The psychology of the child archetype', in *The collected works of C. G. Jung*, Vol. 9i, *The archetypes and the collective unconscious*, 2nd edn. London: Routledge, 1959.

Keane, S. (2007) *CineTech: film, convergence and new media*. Basingstoke: Palgrave Macmillan.

Lebeau, V. (2008) *Childhood and cinema*. London: Reaktion Books.

Lury, K. (2010) *The child in film: tears, fears and fairytales*. London: I.B. Tauris.

Meikle, G. and Young, S. (2012) *Media convergence: networked digital media in everyday life*. Basingstoke: Palgrave Macmillan.

Olson, D. and Schaill, A. (2013) *Lost and othered children in contemporary cinema*. Plymouth, UK: Lexington Books.

Purse, L. (2013) *Digital imaging in popular cinema*. Edinburgh: Edinburgh University Press.

Rank, O. (1971 [1914]) *The double: a psychoanalytic study*, trans. H. Tucker. Chapel Hill, NC: University of North Carolina Press.

Royle, N. (2014) 'Freud's double', in L. Marcus and A. Mukherjee (eds), *A concise companion to psychoanalysis, literature, and culture*. Chichester: John Wiley & Sons. pp. 122–36.

Samuels, A. (1993) *The political psyche*. London: Routledge.

Samuels, A. (2004) 'Foreword', in J. S. Baumlin, T. French Bauqlin and G. H. Jensen (eds), *Post-Jungian criticism: theory and practice*. Albany, NY: State University of New York Press. pp. vii–xv.

Shaviro, S. (2010) *Post-cinematic affect*. Ropley: Zero Books.

Singh, G. (2011) 'Cinephilia: or, looking for meaningfulness in encounters with cinema', in C. Hauke and L. Hockley (eds), *Jung & film II: the return*. London and New York: Routledge. pp. 163–84.

Singh, G. (2014) *Feeling film: affect and authenticity in popular cinema*. London: Routledge.

Sobchack, V. (2016) 'The scene of the screen: envisioning photographic, cinematic, and electronic "presence"', in S. Denson and J. Leyda (eds), *Post-cinema: theorizing 21st-century film*. Falmer, UK: REFRAME Books. pp. 88–129.

Tarde, G. (1962) *The laws of imitation*, trans. E. C. Parsons, introduction by F. Giddings. Gloucester, MA: Peter Smith.

Waddell, T. (2014) 'Australia's lost children at play: the films of Baz Luhrmann', *International Journal of Jungian Studies*, 6(2), pp. 96–107.

Wilson, E. (2003) *Cinema's missing children*. New York: Wallflower Press.

Wojcik, R. P. (2016) *Fantasies of neglect: imagining the urban child in American and film fiction*. New Brunswick, NJ: Rutgers University Press.

Online sources

Goodman, T. (2014) 'True detective: TV review' [online]. Available at: www.hollywoodreporter.com/review/hbos-true-detective-starring-matthew-668182 [Accessed 13 July 2016].

Mumford, G. (2014) 'True Detective recap: season one, episode one – the long, bright dark' [online]. Available at: www.theguardian.com/tv-and-radio/tvandradioblog/2014/feb/27/true-detective-season-one-episode-one-long-bright-dark [Accessed 13 July 2016].

OED Online (2016) Oxford University Press. Available at: www.oed.com.libproxy.chapman.edu/view/Entry/91777?redirectedFrom=imitation [Accessed 1 September 2016].

Tallerico, B. (2014) 'A-list actors on the small screen: from "True detective" to "The spoils of Babylon" to "House of lies"' [online]. Available at: www.rogerebert.com/balder-and-dash/a-list-actors-on-the-small-screen [Accessed 13 July 2016].

Filmography

Anomalisa. (2015) [film] Directed by Duke Johnson and Charlie Kaufman. USA.

Chicken run. (2000) [film] Directed by Peter Lord and Nick Park. UK.

Curse of the were-rabbit, The. (2005) [film] Directed by Steve Box and Nick Park. UK.

Fantasmagorie a.k.a., *A Fantasy*. (1908) [film] Directed by Emile Cohl. France.

Frankenweenie. (2012) [film] Directed by Tim Burton. USA.

Game of thrones. (2012–) [television series] THQ. USA.

House of cards. (2013–2017) [television series] Media Rights Capital. USA.

Humpty Dumpty circus, The (1908) [film short] Directed by Stuart Blackton and Albert E. Smith. USA.

Pinocchio. (1940) [film] Directed by Norman Fergusson *et al*. USA.

Toy story. (1996) [film] Directed by John Burton. USA.

True detective. (2014) [television series] Written by Nic Pizzolatto. Season 1, HBO. USA.

Wallace and Gromit. (1989–1996) [films] Directed by Nick Park *et al*. UK.

Wall-E. (2008) [film] Directed by Andrew Stanton. USA.

TITLE INDEX

Page numbers in *italics* denote figures.

SUBJECT INDEX

Page numbers in *italics* denote figures.
Page spans may indicate repeated mentions rather than continuous discussion.

454

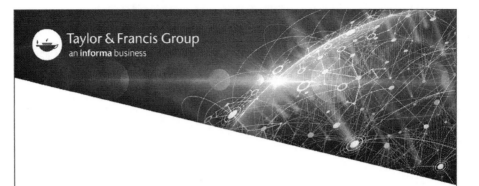

Made in the USA
Monee, IL
10 July 2021